NEW PERSPECTIVES ON
Microsoft® Excel® 2013

INTRODUCTORY

NEW PERSPECTIVES ON
Microsoft® Excel® 2013

INTRODUCTORY

June Jamrich Parsons
Dan Oja
Roy Ageloff
Patrick Carey

Carol A. DesJardins
St. Clair County Community College

CENGAGE
Learning·

Australia · Brazil · Japan · Korea · Mexico · Singapore · Spain · United Kingdom · United States

New Perspectives on Microsoft Excel 2013, Introductory

Director of Development: Marah Bellegarde

Product Director: Donna Gridley

Associate Product Manager: Amanda Lyons

Product Development Manager: Leigh Hefferon

Senior Product Manager: Kathy Finnegan

Product Manager: Julia Leroux-Lindsey

Content Developer: Robin M. Romer

Product Assistant: Melissa Stehler

Brand Manager: Elinor Gregory

Market Development Managers: Kristie Clark, Gretchen Swann

Senior Content Project Manager: Jennifer Goguen McGrail

Composition: GEX Publishing Services

Art Director: GEX Publishing Services

Text Designer: Althea Chen

Cover Art: © ksyutoken/Shutterstock

Copyeditor: Suzanne Huizenga

Proofreader: Lisa Weidenfeld

Indexer: Alexandra Nickerson

Library of Congress Control Number: 2013941751
ISBN-13: 978-1-285-16936-1
ISBN-10: 1-285-16936-0

Cengage Learning
200 First Stamford Place, 4th Floor
Stamford, CT 06902
USA

Cengage Learning is a leading provider of customized learning solutions with office locations around the globe, including Singapore, the United Kingdom, Australia, Mexico, Brazil, and Japan. Locate your local office at: **www.cengage.com/global**

Cengage Learning products are represented in Canada by Nelson Education, Ltd.

For your course and learning solutions, visit **www.cengage.com**

Purchase any of our products at your local college store or at our preferred online store **www.cengagebrain.com**

ProSkills Icons © 2014 Cengage Learning.

Printed in the United States of America
2 3 4 5 6 7 19 18 17 16 15 14 13

Preface

The New Perspectives Series' critical-thinking, problem-solving approach is the ideal way to prepare students to transcend point-and-click skills and take advantage of all that Microsoft Office 2013 has to offer.

In developing the New Perspectives Series, our goal was to create books that give students the software concepts and practical skills they need to succeed beyond the classroom. We've updated our proven case-based pedagogy with more practical content to make learning skills more meaningful to students.

With the New Perspectives Series, students understand *why* they are learning *what* they are learning, and are fully prepared to apply their skills to real-life situations.

About This Book

> "This text presents students with scenarios that reflect real-world Excel problems they must analyze and solve. I recommend my students keep this text to use as a reference when they attempt to solve similar problems in the future."
>
> — Peggy Foreman
> Texas State University

This book provides thorough coverage of Microsoft Excel 2013, and includes the following:

- Detailed, hands-on instruction of Microsoft Excel 2013, including creating and formatting a workbook; working with formulas and functions; creating charts, tables, and PivotTables; managing multiple workbooks; and developing an Excel application
- Coverage of important spreadsheet concepts, including order of precedence in formulas, function syntax, absolute and relative cell references, what-if analysis, and data validation
- Exploration of features new to Excel 2013, including Flash Fill, the Quick Analysis tool, and the recommended charts tool

New for this edition!

- Each tutorial has been updated with new case scenarios throughout, which provide a rich and realistic context for students to apply the concepts and skills presented.
- A new Troubleshoot type of Case Problem, in which certain steps of the exercise require students to identify and correct errors—which are intentionally placed in the files students work with—promotes problem solving and critical thinking.
- The new "Managing Your Files" tutorial at the beginning of the book provides students with a solid foundation in organizing their files and folders.

System Requirements

This book assumes a typical installation of Microsoft Excel 2013 and Microsoft Windows 8 Professional. (You can also complete the material in this text using another version of Windows 8 or using Windows 7. You may see only minor differences in how some windows look.) The browser used for any steps that require a browser is Internet Explorer 10.

www.cengage.com/series/newperspectives

The New Perspectives Approach

Context

Each tutorial begins with a problem presented in a "real-world" case that is meaningful to students. The case sets the scene to help students understand what they will do in the tutorial.

Hands-on Approach

Each tutorial is divided into manageable sessions that combine reading and hands-on, step-by-step work. Colorful screenshots help guide students through the steps. **Trouble?** tips anticipate common mistakes or problems to help students stay on track and continue with the tutorial.

VISUAL OVERVIEW

Visual Overviews

Each session begins with a Visual Overview, a two-page spread that includes colorful, enlarged screenshots with numerous callouts and key term definitions, giving students a comprehensive preview of the topics covered in the session, as well as a handy study guide.

PROSKILLS

ProSkills Boxes and Exercises

ProSkills boxes provide guidance for how to use the software in real-world, professional situations, and related ProSkills exercises integrate the technology skills students learn with one or more of the following soft skills: decision making, problem solving, teamwork, verbal communication, and written communication.

KEY STEP

Key Steps

Important steps are highlighted in yellow with attached margin notes to help students pay close attention to completing the steps correctly and avoid time-consuming rework.

INSIGHT

InSight Boxes

InSight boxes offer expert advice and best practices to help students achieve a deeper understanding of the concepts behind the software features and skills.

TIP

Margin Tips

Margin Tips provide helpful hints and shortcuts for more efficient use of the software. The Tips appear in the margin at key points throughout each tutorial, giving students extra information when and where they need it.

REVIEW

APPLY

Assessment

Retention is a key component to learning. At the end of each session, a series of Quick Check questions helps students test their understanding of the material before moving on. Engaging end-of-tutorial Review Assignments and Case Problems have always been a hallmark feature of the New Perspectives Series. Colorful bars and headings identify the type of exercise, making it easy to understand both the goal and level of challenge a particular assignment holds.

REFERENCE

TASK REFERENCE

GLOSSARY/INDEX

Reference

Within each tutorial, Reference boxes appear before a set of steps to provide a succinct summary and preview of how to perform a task. In addition, a complete Task Reference at the back of the book provides quick access to information on how to carry out common tasks. Finally, each book includes a combination Glossary/Index to promote easy reference of material.

Our Complete System of Instruction

Coverage To Meet Your Needs

Whether you're looking for just a small amount of coverage or enough to fill a semester-long class, we can provide you with a textbook that meets your needs.

- Brief books typically cover the essential skills in just 2 to 4 tutorials.
- Introductory books build and expand on those skills and contain an average of 5 to 8 tutorials.
- Comprehensive books are great for a full-semester class, and contain 9 to 12+ tutorials.

So if the book you're holding does not provide the right amount of coverage for you, there's probably another offering available. Go to our Web site or contact your Cengage Learning sales representative to find out what else we offer.

CourseCasts – Learning on the Go. Always available…always relevant.

Want to keep up with the latest technology trends relevant to you? Visit http://coursecasts.course.com to find a library of weekly updated podcasts, CourseCasts, and download them to your mp3 player.

Ken Baldauf, host of CourseCasts, is a faculty member of the Florida State University Computer Science Department where he is responsible for teaching technology classes to thousands of FSU students each year. Ken is an expert in the latest technology trends; he gathers and sorts through the most pertinent news and information for CourseCasts so your students can spend their time enjoying technology, rather than trying to figure it out. Open or close your lecture with a discussion based on the latest CourseCast.

Visit us at http://coursecasts.course.com to learn on the go!

Instructor Resources

We offer more than just a book. We have all the tools you need to enhance your lectures, check students' work, and generate exams in a new, easier-to-use and completely revised package. This book's Instructor's Manual, ExamView testbank, PowerPoint presentations, data files, solution files, figure files, and a sample syllabus are all available on a single CD-ROM or for downloading at http://www.cengage.com.

SAM: Skills Assessment Manager

Get your students workplace-ready with SAM, the premier proficiency-based assessment and training solution for Microsoft Office! SAM's active, hands-on environment helps students master computer skills and concepts that are essential to academic and career success.

Skill-based assessments, interactive trainings, business-centric projects, and comprehensive remediation engage students in mastering the latest Microsoft Office programs on their own, allowing instructors to spend class time teaching. SAM's efficient course setup and robust grading features provide faculty with consistency across sections. Fully interactive MindTap Readers integrate market-leading Cengage Learning content with SAM, creating a comprehensive online student learning environment.

Acknowledgments

We would like to thank the many people whose invaluable contributions made this book possible. First, sincere thanks go to our reviewers: Will Demeré, Michigan State University; Peggy Foreman, Texas State University; Martha Huggins, Pitt Community College; Steve Luzier, Fortis Institute; and Paul Smith, Brown Mackie College. At Cengage Learning we would like to thank Donna Gridley, Executive Editor for the New Perspectives Series; Leigh Hefferon, Product Development Manager; Amanda Lyons, Associate Acquisitions Editor; Julia Leroux-Lindsey, Product Manager; Melissa Stehler, Editorial Assistant; Jennifer Goguen McGrail, Senior Content Project Manager; Chris Scriver, Manuscript Quality Assurance (MQA) Project Leader; and John Freitas, Serge Palladino, Susan Pedicini, Danielle Shaw, Ashlee Welz Smith, and Susan Whalen, MQA Testers. Special thanks to Robin Romer, Developmental Editor, for her exceptional efforts in improving this text; and to Kathy Finnegan, Senior Product Manager, for keeping us on task and focused.

– June Jamrich Parsons
– Dan Oja
– Roy Ageloff
– Patrick Carey
– Carol A. DesJardins

BRIEF CONTENTS

TABLE OF CONTENTS

OBJECTIVES

- Explore the differences between Windows 7 and Windows 8
- Plan the organization of files and folders
- Use File Explorer to view and manage libraries, folders, and files
- Open and save files
- Create folders
- Copy and move files and folders
- Compress and extract files

Managing Your Files

Organizing Files and Folders with Windows 8

Case | *Savvy Traveler*

After spending a summer traveling in Italy, Matt Marino started Savvy Traveler, a travel company that organizes small tours in Europe. To market his company, Matt created flyers, brochures, webpages, and other materials that describe the tours he offers. Matt uses the Savvy Traveler office computer to locate and store photos, illustrations, and text documents he can include in his marketing materials. He recently hired you to help manage the office. To keep Matt connected to the office while traveling, he just purchased a new laptop computer running Windows 8. He is familiar with Windows 7, so he needs an overview explaining how Windows 8 is different. Matt asks you to train him on using Windows 8 to organize his files and folders. Although he has only a few files, he knows it's a good idea to set up a logical organization now so he can find his work later as he stores more files and folders on the computer.

In this tutorial, you'll explore the differences between Windows 7 and Windows 8, especially those related to file management tools. You'll also work with Matt to devise a plan for managing his files. You'll learn how Windows 8 organizes files and folders, and then create files and folders yourself and organize them on Matt's computer. You'll also use techniques to display the information you need in folder windows, and explore options for working with compressed files.

STARTING DATA FILES

FM → Tutorial	Review	Case1	Case2
Artists.rtf	Banner.png	Fall Classes.rtf	Budget1.xlsx
Chianti.jpg	Colosseum.jpg	Instructors.txt	Budget2.xlsx
Florence.jpg	Lectures.xlsx	Kings Canyon.jpg	Report1.xlsx
List.rtf	Rome.jpg	Mojave.jpg	Report2.xlsx
Logo.png	Rome.rtf	Redwoods.jpg	Report3.xlsx
Market.jpg	Schedule.rtf	Spring Classes.rtf	Report4.xlsx
Marketing.txt	Tours.rtf	Summer Classes.rtf	Tips1.rtf
Tour Rates.rtf		Winter Classes.rtf	Tips1 – Copy.rtf
Tuscany.rtf		Workshops.rtf	Tips2.rtf
		Yosemite.jpg	Tips2 – Copy.rtf

Visual Overview:

You use the Change your view button to change the size of the icons in the window.

In Windows 7, you use **Windows Explorer** to navigate the contents of your computer.

Use the arrow buttons in the Address bar to navigate to other locations on your computer.

The **file path** is a notation that indicates a file's location on your computer.

Use the Search box to search for files in the current folder.

The Windows Explorer **toolbar** provides buttons for completing tasks.

Windows Explorer includes a **navigation pane**, which displays icons and links to resources and locations on your computer.

By default, Windows Explorer includes the **Details pane** at the bottom of the window, which displays the properties of the selected object.

Windows provides **libraries** so you can organize files by category—documents, music, pictures, and video.

A thumbnail image previews the file contents for certain types of files.

The zipped folder icon indicates a **compressed folder**, which stores files so they take up less disk space.

Windows 7

Comparing Windows 7 & Windows 8

The **View tab** on the ribbon contains options for specifying how the information displays in File Explorer.

The **Quick Access toolbar** contains buttons for viewing properties and creating a folder.

Windows provides **libraries** so you can organize files by category—documents, music, pictures, and videos.

Use the arrow buttons in the Address bar to navigate to other locations on your computer.

The **file path** in the Address bar shows a file's location on your computer.

In Windows 8, you use **File Explorer** to navigate the contents of your computer.

File Explorer includes a ribbon with tools organized on tabs for working with files and folders.

A thumbnail image previews the file contents for certain types of files.

A **filename** is the name you give to a file when you save it to identify the file's contents.

A **file icon** indicates the file type.

Clicking the Computer icon in the navigation pane shows the drives on your computer.

Data Files for this tutorial are stored on a removable disk on this computer.

You can use the Large icons view button on the status bar or in the Layout group on the View tab to switch to Large icons view.

File Explorer includes a **navigation pane**, which displays icons and links to resources and locations on your computer.

Windows 8

Exploring the Differences Between Windows 7 and Windows 8

Windows 8, the most recent version of the Microsoft operating system, is significantly different from Windows 7, the previous version. The major difference is that Windows 8 is designed for touchscreen computers such as tablets and laptops with touch-activated displays, though it runs on computers with more traditional pointing devices such as a mouse or a trackpad. This design change affects many of the fundamental Windows features you use to work on a computer. Figure 1 compares how to perform typical tasks in Windows 7 and Windows 8.

Figure 1 Comparing Windows 7 and Windows 8

Task	Windows 7 Method	Windows 8 Method
Start applications (sometimes called apps)	**Start menu** Open the Start menu by clicking the Start button.	**Start screen** The Start screen appears when you start Windows.
Access applications, documents, settings, and other resources	**Start menu** Use the Start menu, All Programs list, and Search box.	**Charms bar** The Charms bar appears when you point to the upper-right or lower-right corner of the screen, and displays buttons, called charms, for interacting with Windows 8 and accessing applications.
Select objects and commands	**Icons** Icons are small and detailed, designed for interaction with mechanical pointing devices.	**Icons and tiles** Icons and tiles are large and simplified, designed for interaction with your fingertips.
Open and work in applications	**Desktop** Applications all use a single desktop interface featuring windows and dialog boxes.	**Windows 8 and desktop** Applications use one of two interfaces: the Windows 8 interface (featuring tiles and a full-screen layout) or the desktop.
Display content out of view	**Vertical scrolling** Applications allow more vertical scrolling than horizontal scrolling.	**Horizontal scrolling** The Start screen and applications allow more horizontal scrolling than vertical scrolling to take advantage of wide-screen monitors.
Store files	**Physical storage devices** Windows primarily provides access to disks physically connected to the computer.	**Cloud storage locations** A Microsoft user account provides access to information stored online.
Enter text	**Physical keyboard** Type on the keyboard attached to the computer.	**On-screen keyboard** If your computer does not have a physical keyboard, type using the on-screen keyboard.

© 2014 Cengage Learning

Although Windows 7 introduced a few gestures for touchscreen users, Windows 8 expands the use of gestures and interactions. In Windows 8, you can use touch gestures to do nearly everything you can do with a pointing device. Figure 2 lists common Windows 8 interactions and their touch and mouse equivalents.

| Figure 2 | Windows 8 touch and mouse interactions |

Interaction	Touch Gesture	Mouse Action
Display a ScreenTip, text that identifies the name or purpose of the button	Touch and hold (or press) an object such as a button.	Point to an object such as a button.
Display an Apps bar, which displays options related to the current task and access to the Apps screen	Swipe from the top or bottom of the screen toward the center.	Right-click the bottom edge of the screen.
Display the Charms bar	Swipe from the right edge of the screen toward the center.	Point to the upper-right or lower-right corner of the screen.
Display thumbnails of open apps (the Switch List)	Swipe from the left edge of the screen toward the center.	Point to the upper-left corner of the screen, and then drag the pointer down.
Drag an object	Press and then drag.	Click, hold, and then drag.
Scroll the Start screen	Swipe from the right edge of the screen to the left.	Click the scroll arrows, or drag the scroll bar.
Select an object or perform an action such as starting an app	Tap the object.	Click the object.
Zoom	Pinch two fingers to zoom out or move the fingers apart to zoom in.	Click the Zoom button.

© 2014 Cengage Learning

Despite the substantial differences between how you interact with Windows 7 and Windows 8, the steps you follow to perform work in either operating system are the same. In a typical computer session, you start an application and open a **file**, often referred to as a document, which is a collection of data that has a name and is stored on a computer. You view, add, or change the file contents, and then save and close the file. You can complete all of these steps using Windows 7 or Windows 8. Because most of your work involves files, you need to understand how to save and organize files so you can easily find and open them when necessary.

Organizing Files and Folders

Knowing how to save, locate, and organize computer files makes you more productive when you are working with a computer. After you create a file, you can open it, edit its contents, print the file, and save it again—usually using the same application you used to create the file. You organize files by storing them in folders. A **folder** is a container for files. You need to organize files and folders so that you can find them easily and work efficiently.

A file cabinet is a common metaphor for computer file organization. As shown in Figure 3, a computer is like a file cabinet that has two or more drawers—each drawer is a storage device, or **disk**. Each disk contains folders that hold files. To make it easy to retrieve files, you arrange them logically into folders. For example, one folder might contain financial data, another might contain your creative work, and another could contain information you're gathering for an upcoming vacation.

| Figure 3 | Computer as a file cabinet |

disks contain folders

folders contain files

each drawer is a storage device, or disk

© 2014 Cengage Learning

A computer can store folders and files on different types of disks, ranging from removable media—such as **USB drives** (also called USB flash drives) and digital video discs (DVDs)—to **hard disks**, or fixed disks, which are permanently housed in a computer. Hard disks are the most popular type of computer storage because they provide an economical way to store many gigabytes of data. (A **gigabyte**, or **GB**, is about 1 billion bytes, with each byte roughly equivalent to a character of data.)

To have your computer access a removable disk, you must insert the disk into a **drive**, which is a device that can retrieve and sometimes record data on a disk. A computer's hard disk is already contained in a drive inside the computer, so you don't need to insert it each time you use the computer.

A computer distinguishes one drive from another by assigning each a drive letter. The hard disk is assigned to drive C. The remaining drives can have any other letters, but are usually assigned in the order that the drives were installed on the computer—so your USB drive might be drive D or drive F.

Understanding How to Organize Files and Folders

Windows stores thousands of files in many folders on the hard disk of your computer. These are system files that Windows needs to display the Start screen and desktop, use drives, and perform other operating system tasks. To keep the system stable and to find files quickly, Windows organizes the folders and files in a hierarchy, or **file system**. At the top of the hierarchy, Windows stores folders and important files that it needs when you turn on the computer. This location is called the **root directory** and is usually drive C (the hard disk). As Figure 4 shows, the root directory contains all the other folders and files on the computer. The figure also shows that folders can contain other folders. An effectively organized computer contains a few folders in the root directory, and those folders contain other folders, also called **subfolders**.

| Figure 4 | Organizing folders and files on a hard disk |

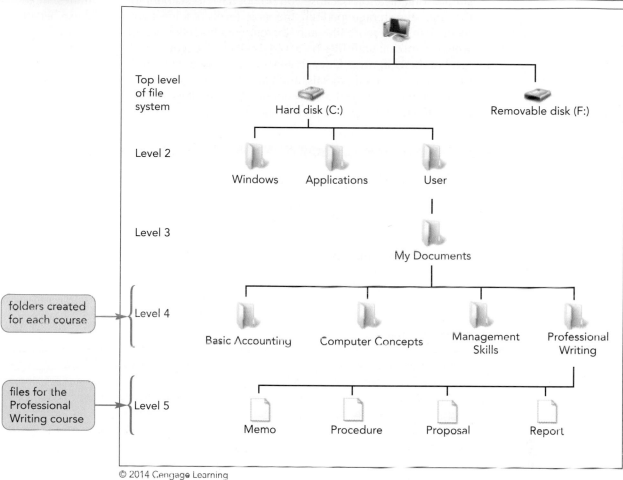

© 2014 Cengage Learning

The root directory is the top level of the hard disk and is for system files and folders only. You should not store your own work in the root directory because your files could interfere with Windows or an application. (If you are working in a computer lab, you might not be allowed to access the root directory.)

Do not delete or move any files or folders from the root directory of the hard disk; doing so could disrupt the system so that you can't start or run the computer. In fact, you should not reorganize or change any folder that contains installed software because Windows 8 expects to find the files for specific applications within certain folders. In Figure 4, folders containing software are stored at Level 2 of the file system. If you reorganize or change these folders, Windows 8 can't locate and start the applications stored in those folders. Likewise, you should not make changes to the folder (usually named Windows) that contains the Windows 8 operating system.

Level 2 of the file system also includes a folder for your user account, such as the User folder. This folder contains all of your system settings, preferences, and other user account information. It also contains subfolders, such as the My Documents folder, for your personal files. The folders in Level 3 of the file system are designed to contain subfolders for your personal files. You can create as many subfolders at Level 4 of the file system as you need to store other folders and files and keep them organized.

Figure 4 shows how you could organize your files on a hard disk if you were taking a full semester of business classes. To duplicate this organization, you would open the main folder for your documents, such as My Documents, create four folders— one each for the Basic Accounting, Computer Concepts, Management Skills, and Professional Writing courses—and then store the writing assignments you complete in the Professional Writing folder.

If you store your files on removable media, such as a USB drive, you can use a simpler organization because you do not have to account for system files. In general, the larger the storage medium, the more levels of folders you should use because large media can store more files and, therefore, need better organization. For example, if you were organizing your files on a 12 GB USB drive, you could create folders in the top level of the USB drive for each general category of documents you store—one each for Courses, Creative, Financials, and Vacation. The Courses folder could then include one folder for each course (Basic Accounting, Computer Concepts, Management Skills, and Professional Writing), and each of those folders could contain the appropriate files.

PROSKILLS

Decision Making: Determining Where to Store Files

When you create and save files on your computer's hard disk, you should store them in subfolders. The top level of the hard disk is off-limits for your files because they could interfere with system files. If you are working on your own computer, store your files within the My Documents folder in the Documents library, which is where many applications save your files by default. When you use a computer on the job, your employer might assign a main folder to you for storing your work. In either case, if you simply store all your files in one folder, you will soon have trouble finding the files you want. Instead, you should create subfolders within a main folder to separate files in a way that makes sense for you.

Even if you store most of your files on removable media, such as USB drives, you still need to organize those files into folders and subfolders. Before you start creating folders, whether on a hard disk or removable disk, you need to plan the organization you will use. Following your plan increases your efficiency because you don't have to pause and decide which folder to use when you save your files. A file organization plan also makes you more productive in your computer work—the next time you need a particular file, you'll know where to find it.

Exploring Files and Folders

As shown in the Visual Overview, you use File Explorer in Windows 8 to explore the files and folders on your computer. File Explorer displays the contents of your computer by using icons to represent drives, folders, and files. When you open File Explorer, it shows the contents of the Windows built-in libraries by default. Windows provides these libraries so you can organize files by category—documents, music, pictures, and video. A library can display these categories of files together, no matter where the files are actually stored. For example, you might keep some music files in a folder named Albums on your hard disk. You might also keep music files in a Songs folder on a USB drive. Although the Albums and Songs folders are physically stored in different locations, you can set up the Music library to display both folders in the same File Explorer window. You can then search and arrange the files as a single collection to quickly find the music you want to open and play. In this way, you use libraries to organize your files into categories so you can easily locate and work with files.

The File Explorer window is divided into two sections, called panes. The left pane is the navigation pane, which contains icons and links to locations on your computer. The right pane displays the contents of the location selected in the navigation pane. If the navigation pane showed all the contents on your computer at once, it could be a very long list. Instead, you open drives and folders only when you want to see what they contain. For example, to display the hierarchy of the folders and other locations on your computer, you select the Computer icon in the navigation pane, and then select the icon for a drive, such as Local Disk (C:) or Removable Disk (F:). You can then open and explore folders on that drive.

If a folder contains undisplayed subfolders, an expand icon appears to the left of the folder icon. (The same is true for drives.) To view the folders contained in an object, you click the expand icon. A collapse icon then appears next to the folder icon; click the collapse icon to hide the folder's subfolders. To view the files contained in a folder, you click the folder icon, and the files appear in the right pane. See Figure 5.

Figure 5   **Viewing files in File Explorer**

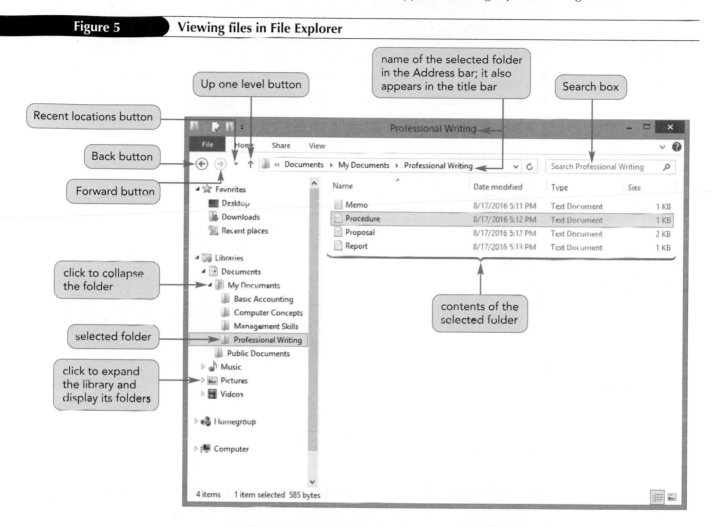

Using the navigation pane helps you explore your computer and orients you to your current location. As you move, copy, delete, and perform other tasks with the files and folders in the right pane of File Explorer, you can refer to the navigation pane to see how your changes affect the overall organization of the selected location.

In addition to using the navigation pane, you can explore your computer in File Explorer using the following navigation techniques:

- Opening drives and folders in the right pane—To view the contents of a drive or folder, double-click the drive or folder icon in the right pane of File Explorer.
- Using the Address bar—You can use the Address bar to navigate to a different folder. The Address bar displays the file path for your current folder. (Recall that a file path shows the location of a folder or file.) Click a folder name such as My Documents in the Address bar to navigate to that folder, or click an arrow button to navigate to a different location in the folder's hierarchy.
- Clicking the Back, Forward, Recent locations, and Up to buttons—Use the Back, Forward, and Recent locations buttons to navigate to other folders you have already opened. Use the Up to button to navigate up to the folder containing the current folder.
- Using the Search box—To find a file or folder stored in the current folder or its subfolders, type a word or phrase in the Search box. The search begins as soon as you

start typing. Windows finds files based on text in the filename, text within the file, and other properties of the file.

You'll practice using some of these navigation techniques later in the tutorial. Right now, you'll show Matt how to open File Explorer. Your computer should be turned on and displaying the Start screen.

To open File Explorer:

▸ **1.** On the Start screen, click the **Desktop** tile to display the desktop.

▸ **2.** On the taskbar, click the **File Explorer** button 📁. The File Explorer window opens, displaying the contents of the default libraries.

▸ **3.** In the Libraries section of the navigation pane, click the **expand** icon ▷ next to the Documents icon. The folders in the Documents library appear in the navigation pane; see Figure 6. The contents of your computer will differ.

| Figure 6 | Viewing the contents of the Documents library |

- four tabs on the File Explorer ribbon
- Documents library is expanded to display its folders
- My Documents and Public Documents folders are included in the Documents library by default
- four default libraries provided with Windows 8

Trouble? If your window displays icons in a size or arrangement different from the one shown in the figure, you can still explore files and folders. The same is true for all the figures in this tutorial.

▸ **4.** In the navigation pane, click the **My Documents** folder to display its contents in the right pane.

TIP

When you are working in the navigation pane, you only need to click a folder to open it; you do not need to double-click it.

As Figure 6 shows, the File Explorer window includes a ribbon, which is collapsed by default so it displays only tab names, such as File, Home, Share, and View. The Visual Overview shows the expanded ribbon, which displays the options for the selected tab. You'll work with the ribbon and learn how to expand it later in the tutorial.

Navigating to Your Data Files

To navigate to the files you want, it helps to know the file path because the file path tells you exactly where the file is stored in the hierarchy of drives and folders on your computer. For example, Matt has a file named "Logo," which contains an image of the company's logo. If Matt stored the Logo file in a folder named "Marketing" and saved that folder in a folder named "Savvy Traveler" on drive F (a USB drive) on his computer, the Address bar would show the following file path for the Logo file:

Computer ▸ Removable Disk (F:) ▸ Savvy Traveler ▸ Marketing ▸ Logo.png

This path has five parts, with each part separated by an arrow button:

- Computer—The main container for the file, such as "Computer" or "Network"
- Removable Disk (F:)—The drive name, including the drive letter followed by a colon, which indicates a drive rather than a folder
- Savvy Traveler—The top-level folder on drive F
- Marketing—A subfolder in the Savvy Traveler folder
- Logo.png—The name of the file

Although File Explorer uses arrow buttons to separate locations in a file path, printed documents use backslashes (\ ). For example, if you read an instruction to open the Logo file in the Savvy Traveler\Marketing folder on your USB drive, you know you must navigate to the USB drive attached to your computer, open the Savvy Traveler folder, and then open the Marketing folder to find the Logo file.

File Explorer displays the file path in the Address bar so you can keep track of your current location as you navigate between drives and folders. You can use File Explorer to navigate to the Data Files you need for this tutorial. Before you perform the following steps, you should know where you stored your Data Files, such as on a USB drive. The following steps assume that drive is Removable Disk (F:), a USB drive. If necessary, substitute the appropriate drive on your system when you perform the steps.

To navigate to your Data Files:

1. Make sure your computer can access your Data Files for this tutorial. For example, if you are using a USB drive, insert the drive into the USB port.

   Trouble? If you don't have the starting Data Files, you need to get them before you can proceed. Your instructor will either give you the Data Files or ask you to obtain them from a specified location (such as a network drive). If you have any questions about the Data Files, see your instructor or technical support person for assistance.

2. In the navigation pane of File Explorer, click the **expand** icon ▷ next to the Computer icon to display the drives on your computer, if necessary.

3. Click the **expand** icon ▷ next to the drive containing your Data Files, such as Removable Disk (F:). A list of the folders on that drive appears below the drive name.

4. If the list of folders does not include the FM folder, continue clicking the **expand** icon ▷ to navigate to the folder that contains the FM folder.

5. Click the **expand** icon ▷ next to the FM folder to expand the folder, and then click the **FM** folder so that its contents appear in the navigation pane and in the right pane of the folder window. The FM folder contains the Case1, Case2, Review, and Tutorial folders, as shown in Figure 7. The other folders on your computer might vary.

Figure 7   Navigating to the FM folder

file path displayed in the Address bar

contents of the FM folder; your Date modified information might differ

selected FM folder is expanded in the navigation pane

the name of the selected folder appears in the File Explorer title bar

your Data Files might be stored on a different drive

Tutorial folder

6. In the navigation pane, click the **Tutorial** folder. The files it contains appear in the right pane.

You can change the appearance of the File Explorer window to suit your preferences. You'll do so next so you can see more details about folders and files.

Changing the View

TIP

The default view for any folder in the Pictures library is Large icons view, which provides a thumbnail image of the file contents.

File Explorer provides eight ways to view the contents of a folder: Extra large icons, Large icons, Medium icons, Small icons, List, Details, Tiles, and Content. For example, the files in the Tutorial folder are currently displayed in Details view, which is the default view for all folders except those stored in the Pictures library. Details view displays a small icon to identify each file's type and lists file details in columns, such as the date the file was last modified, the file type, and the size of the file. Although only Details view lists the file details, you can see these details in any other view by pointing to a file to display a ScreenTip.

To change the view of File Explorer to any of the eight views, you use the View tab on the ribbon. To switch to Details view or Large icons view, you can use the view buttons on the status bar.

REFERENCE

Changing the View in File Explorer

- Click a view button on the status bar.

or

- Click the View tab on the ribbon.
- In the Layout group, click the view option; or click the More button, if necessary, and then click a view option.

You'll show Matt how to change the view of the Tutorial folder in the File Explorer window.

To change the view of the Tutorial folder in File Explorer:

1. On the ribbon, click the **View** tab.

2. In the Layout group, click **Medium icons**. The files appear in Medium icons view in File Explorer. See Figure 8.

Files in the Tutorial folder in Medium icons view

View tab on the ribbon

Expand the Ribbon button

icons are displayed in Medium icons view

thumbnail image previews the file contents for certain file types

file icon identifies the file type; your icons might be different

Tutorial folder is selected in the navigation pane

Details view button

9 items

Photos courtesy of Lisa Ruffolo

Because the icons used to identify types of files depend on the applications installed on your computer, the file icons that appear in your window might be different.

TIP

When you change the view, it only changes the view for the currently selected folder.

3. On the status bar, click the **Large icons view** button ▣. The window shows the files with large icons and no file details.

When you clicked the View tab in the previous steps, the ribbon expanded so you could select an option and then collapsed after you clicked the Medium icons option. You can keep the ribbon expanded in the File Explorer window so you can easily access all of its options. You'll show Matt how to expand the ribbon and then use the View tab to switch to Details view.

To expand the ribbon in File Explorer:

1. Click the **Expand the Ribbon** button ⌄ to expand the ribbon. The Expand the Ribbon button changes to the Minimize the Ribbon button, which you could click if you wanted to collapse the ribbon.

2. On the View tab, in the Layout group, click **Details**. The window shows the files with small icons and lists the file details.

No matter which view you use, you can sort the file list by the name of the files or another detail, such as size, type, or date. When you **sort** files, you list them in ascending order (A to Z, 0 to 9, or earliest to latest date) or descending order (Z to A, 9 to 0, or latest to earliest date) by a file detail. If you're viewing music files, you can sort by details such as contributing artists or album title; and if you're viewing picture files, you can sort by details such as date taken or size. Sorting can help you find a particular file in a long file listing. For example, suppose you want to work on a document that you know you edited on June 4, 2016, but you can't remember the name of the file. You can sort the file list by date modified to find the file you want.

When you are working in Details view in File Explorer, you sort by clicking a column heading that appears at the top of the file list. In other views, you use the View tab on the ribbon to sort. In the Current view group, click the Sort by button, and then click a file detail.

TIP

To sort by a file detail that does not appear as a column heading, right-click any column heading and then select a file detail.

To sort the file list by date modified:

1. At the top of the file list, click the **Date modified** column heading button. The down arrow that appears above the label of the Date modified button indicates that the files are sorted in descending (newest to oldest) order by the date the file was modified. At the top of the list is the List file, which was modified on June 18, 2016.

   Trouble? If your folder window does not contain a Date modified column, right-click any column heading, click Date modified on the shortcut menu, and then repeat Step 1.

2. Click the **Date modified** column heading button again. The up arrow on the Date modified button indicates that the sort order is reversed, with the files listed in ascending (oldest to newest) order.

3. Click the **Name** column heading button to sort the files in alphabetical order by name. The Artists file is now listed first.

Now that Matt is comfortable working in File Explorer, you're ready to show him how to manage his files and folders.

Managing Files and Folders

As discussed earlier, you manage your personal files and folders by storing them according to a logical organization so that they are easy to find later. You can organize files as you create, edit, and save them, or you can do so later by creating folders, if necessary, and then moving and copying files into the folders.

To create a file-organization plan for Matt's files, you can review Figure 8 and look for files that logically belong together. In the Tutorial folder, Chianti, Florence, Logo, and Market are all graphics files that Matt uses for marketing and sales. He created the Artists and Tuscany files to describe Italian tours. The Marketing and Tour Rates files relate to business finances. Matt thinks the List file contains a task list for completing a project, but he isn't sure of its contents. He does recall creating the file using WordPad.

If the List file does contain a project task list, you can organize the files by creating four folders—one for graphics, one for tours, another for the financial files, and a fourth folder for projects. When you create a folder, you give it a name, preferably one that describes its contents. A folder name can have up to 255 characters, and any character is allowed, except / \ : * ? " < > and |. Considering these conventions, you could create four folders to contain Matt's files, as follows:

- Marketing Graphics folder—Chianti, Florence, Logo, and Market files
- Tours folder—Artists and Tuscany files
- Financial folder—Marketing and Tour Rates files
- Projects folder—List file

Before you start creating folders according to this plan, you need to verify the contents of the List file. You can do so by opening the file.

Opening a File

TIP

To select the default application for opening a file, right-click the file in File Explorer, point to Open with, and then click Choose default application. Click an application in the list that opens, and then click OK.

You can open a file from a running application or from File Explorer. To open a file in a running application, you select the application's Open command to access the Open dialog box, which you use to navigate to the file you want, select the file, and then open it. In the Open dialog box, you use the same tools that are available in File Explorer to navigate to the file you want to open. If the application you want to use is not running, you can open a file by double-clicking it in the right pane of File Explorer. The file usually opens in the application that you used to create or edit it.

Occasionally, File Explorer will open the file in an application other than the one you want to use to work with the file. For example, double-clicking a digital picture file usually opens the picture in a picture viewer application. If you want to edit the picture, you must open the file in a graphics editing application. When you need to specify an application to open a file, you can right-click the file, point to Open with on the shortcut menu, and then click the name of the application that you want to use.

Matt says that he might want to edit the List file to add another task. You'll show him how to use File Explorer to open the file in WordPad, which he used to create the file, and then edit it.

To open and edit the List file:

▶ 1. In the right pane of File Explorer, right-click the **List** file, and then point to **Open with** on the shortcut menu to display a list of applications that can open the file. See Figure 9.

   Trouble? If a list does not appear when you point to Open with on the shortcut menu, click Open with to display a window asking how you want to open this file.

Figure 9   **Shortcut menu for opening a file**

List is the selected file

Open with command

applications on this computer that can open the List file

▶ 2. Click **WordPad** to open the List file in WordPad. The file contains a task list for the marketing project, which includes three items.

Trouble? If you had to click Open with instead of pointing to it, in the window that asks how you want to open this file, click Keep using WordPad.

▶ 3. Press the **Ctrl+End** keys to move the insertion point to the end of the document, press the **Enter** key if necessary to start a new line, and then type **4. Review the Tours in Italy webpage.**

Now that you've added text to the List file, you need to save it to preserve the changes you made.

Saving a File

As you are creating or editing a file, you should save it frequently so you don't lose your work. When you save a file, you need to decide what name to use for the file and where to store it. Most applications provide a default location for saving a file, which makes it easy to find the file again later. However, you can select a different location depending on where you want to store the file.

Besides a storage location, every file must have a filename, which provides important information about the file, including its contents and purpose. A filename such as Italian Tours.docx has the following three parts:

- Main part of the filename—When you save a file, you need to provide only the main part of the filename, such as "Italian Tours."
- Dot—The dot (.) separates the main part of the filename from the extension.
- Extension—The **extension** includes the three or four characters that follow the dot in the filename and identify the file's type.

Similar to folder names, the main part of a filename can have up to 255 characters. This gives you plenty of room to name your file accurately enough so that you'll recognize the contents of the file just by looking at the filename. You can use spaces and certain punctuation symbols in your filenames. However, filenames cannot contain the symbols / \ : * ? " < > or | because these characters have special meanings in Windows 8.

Windows and other software add the dot and the extension to a filename, though File Explorer does not display them by default. Instead, File Explorer shows the file icon associated with the extension or a thumbnail for some types of files, such as graphics. For example, in a file named Italian Tours.docx, the docx extension identifies the file as one created in Microsoft Word, a word-processing application. File Explorer displays this file using a Microsoft Word icon and the main part of its filename. For a file named Italian Tours.png, the png extension identifies the file as one created in a graphics application such as Paint. In Details view or List view, File Explorer displays this file using a Paint icon and the main part of its filename. In other views, File Explorer does not use an icon, but displays the file contents in a thumbnail. File Explorer treats the Italian Tours.docx and Italian Tours.png files differently because their extensions distinguish them as different types of files, even though the main parts of their filenames are identical.

When you save a new file, you use the Save As dialog box to provide a filename and select a location for the file. You can create a folder for the new file at the same time you save the file. When you edit a file you saved previously, you can use the application's Save command to save your changes to the file, keeping the same name and location. If you want to save the edited file with a different name or in a different location, however, you need to use the Save As dialog box to specify the new name or location.

As with the Open dialog box, you specify the file location in the Save As dialog box using the same navigation techniques and tools that are available in File Explorer. You might need to click the Browse Folders button to expand the Save As dialog box so it displays these tools. In addition, the Save As dialog box always includes a File name box where you specify a filename.

INSIGHT

Saving Files on SkyDrive

Some Windows 8 applications, such as Microsoft Office, include SkyDrive as a location for saving and opening files. **SkyDrive** is a Microsoft service that provides up to 7 GB of online storage space for your files at no charge. You can purchase additional space if you need it. For example, if you create a document in Microsoft Word, your SkyDrive appears as a location for saving the document. (Your SkyDrive appears with your username, such as Matt's SkyDrive.) If you have a Microsoft account, you can select a folder on your SkyDrive to save the document online. (If you don't have a Microsoft account, you can sign up for one by visiting the SkyDrive website.) Because the file is stored online, it takes up no storage space on your computer and is available from any computer with an Internet connection. You access the document by opening it in Word or by visiting the SkyDrive website, and then signing in to your Microsoft account. To share the document with other people, you can send them a link to the document via email. They can use the link to access the document even if they do not have a Microsoft account.

One reason that Matt had trouble remembering the contents of the List file is that "List" is not a descriptive name. A better name for this file is Task List. You will save this document in the Tutorial subfolder of the FM folder provided with your Data Files. You will also use the Save As dialog box to specify a new name for the file as you save it.

To save the List file with a new name:

1. On the ribbon in the WordPad window, click the **File** tab to display commands for working with files.

2. Click **Save as** to open the Save As dialog box, as shown in Figure 10. The Tutorial folder is selected as the storage location for this file because you opened the file from this folder.

| Figure 10 | Saving a file using the Save As dialog box |

use the navigation pane or the Address bar to navigate to a different location for saving the file

the Save As dialog box displays the original location of the file as the default storage location

type the name for the file in the File name box

Save as type box

clicking the Hide Folders button collapses the dialog box

Trouble? If the navigation pane does not appear in the Save As dialog box, click the Browse Folders button. The Browse Folders button toggles to become the Hide Folders button.

TIP

To change the file type, click the Save as type box, and then click a file type such as Text Document.

3. With the current filename selected in the File name box, type **Task List**. The Save as type box shows that WordPad will save this file as a Rich Text Format (RTF) file, which is the default file type for WordPad files.

   Trouble? If the current filename is not selected in the File name box, drag to select the text in the File name box and then type Task List.

4. Click the **Save** button. The Save As dialog box closes, WordPad saves the Task List file in the Tutorial folder, and the new filename appears in the WordPad title bar.

5. On the title bar, click the **Close** button ✕ to close WordPad.

Now you're ready to start creating the folders you need to organize Matt's files.

Creating Folders

You originally proposed creating four new folders for Matt's files: Marketing Graphics, Tours, Financial, and Projects. Matt asks you to create these folders now. After that, you'll move his files to the appropriate folders. You create folders in File Explorer using one of three methods: using the New folder button in the New group on the Home tab; using the New folder button on the Quick Access Toolbar; or right-clicking to display a shortcut menu that includes the New command.

INSIGHT

Guidelines for Creating Folders

Consider the following guidelines as you create folders:

- Keep folder names short yet descriptive of the folder's contents. Long folder names can be more difficult to display in their entirety in folder windows, so use names that are short but clear. Choose names that will be meaningful later, such as project names or course numbers.
- Create subfolders to organize files. If a file list in File Explorer is so long that you must scroll the window, you should probably organize those files into subfolders.
- Develop standards for naming folders. Use a consistent naming scheme that is clear to you, such as one that uses a project name as the name of the main folder, and includes step numbers in each subfolder name (for example, 1-Outline, 2 First Draft, 3-Final Draft, and so on).

In the following steps, you will create the four folders for Matt in your Tutorial folder. Because it is easier to work with files using large file icons, you'll switch to Large icons view first.

To create the folders:

1. On the status bar in the File Explorer window, click the **Large icons view** button ⊞ to switch to Large icons view.

2. Click the **Home** tab to display the Home tab on the ribbon.

3. In the New group, click the **New folder** button. A folder icon with the label "New folder" appears in the right pane of the File Explorer window. See Figure 11.

Figure 11   Creating a new folder in the Tutorial folder

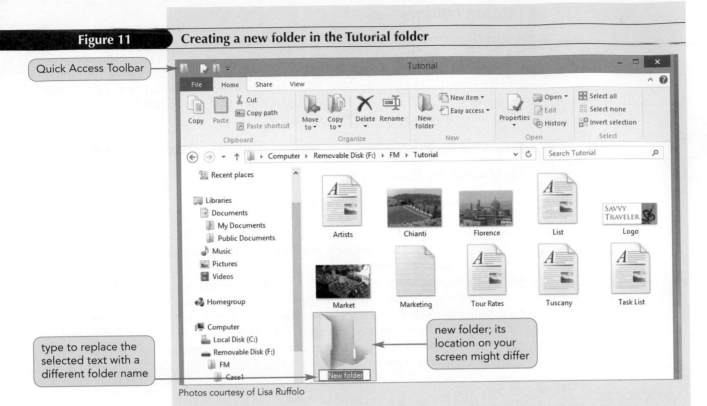

Quick Access Toolbar

type to replace the selected text with a different folder name

new folder; its location on your screen might differ

Photos courtesy of Lisa Ruffolo

> **Trouble?** If the "New folder" name is not selected, right-click the new folder, click Rename on the shortcut menu, and then continue with Step 4.
>
> Windows uses "New folder" as a placeholder, and selects the text so that you can replace it immediately by typing a new name. You do not need to press the Backspace or Delete key to delete the text.

4. Type **Marketing Graphics** as the folder name, and then press the **Enter** key. The new folder is named Marketing Graphics and is the selected item in the right pane. To create a second folder, you can use a shortcut menu.

5. In the right pane, right-click a blank area, point to **New** on the shortcut menu, and then click **Folder**. A folder icon appears in the right pane with the "New folder" text selected.

6. Type **Tours** as the name of the new folder, and then press the **Enter** key. To create the third folder, you can use the Quick Access Toolbar.

7. On the Quick Access Toolbar, click the **New folder** button ▯, type **Financial**, and then press the **Enter** key to create and name the folder.

8. Create a new folder in the Tutorial folder named **Projects**.

After creating four folders, you're ready to organize Matt's files by moving them into the appropriate folders.

Moving and Copying Files and Folders

You can either move or copy a file from its current location to a new location. **Moving** a file removes it from its current location and places it in a new location that you specify. **Copying** a file places a duplicate version of the file in a new location that you specify, while leaving the original file intact in its current location. You can also move and copy folders. When you do, you move or copy all the files contained in the folder. (You'll practice copying folders in a Case Problem at the end of this tutorial.)

In File Explorer, you can move and copy files by using the Move to or Copy to buttons in the Organize group on the Home tab; using the Copy and Cut commands on a file's shortcut menu; or using keyboard shortcuts. When you copy or move files using these methods, you are using the **Clipboard**, a temporary storage area for files and information that you copy or move from one location to place in another.

You can also move files by dragging the files in the File Explorer window. You will now organize Matt's files by moving them to the appropriate folders you have created. You'll start by moving the Marketing file to the Financial folder by dragging the file.

To move the Marketing file by dragging it:

1. In File Explorer, point to the **Marketing** file in the right pane, and then press and hold the mouse button.

2. While still pressing the mouse button, drag the **Marketing** file to the **Financial** folder. See Figure 12.

Figure 12   Dragging a file to move it to a folder

3. When the Move to Financial ScreenTip appears, release the mouse button. The Marketing file is removed from the main Tutorial folder and stored in the Financial subfolder.

   Trouble? If you released the mouse button before the Move to Financial ScreenTip appeared, press the Ctrl+Z keys to undo the move, and then repeat Steps 1–3.

   Trouble? If you moved the Market file instead of the Marketing file, press the Ctrl+Z keys to undo the move, and then repeat Steps 1–3.

4. In the right pane, double-click the **Financial** folder to verify that it contains the Marketing file.

TIP

If you drag a file or folder to a location on a different drive, the file is copied, not moved, to preserve the file in its original location.

Trouble? If the Marketing file does not appear in the Financial folder, you probably moved it to a different folder. Press the Ctrl+Z keys to undo the move, and then repeat Steps 1–3.

5. Click the **Back** button ⊖ on the Address bar to return to the Tutorial folder.

You'll move the remaining files into the folders using the Clipboard.

To move files using the Clipboard:

1. Right-click the **Artists** file, and then click **Cut** on the shortcut menu. Although the file icon still appears selected in the right pane of File Explorer, Windows removes the Artists file from the Tutorial folder and stores it on the Clipboard.

2. In the right pane, right-click the **Tours** folder, and then click **Paste** on the shortcut menu. Windows pastes the Artists file from the Clipboard to the Tours folder. The Artists file icon no longer appears in the File Explorer window, which is currently displaying the contents of the Tutorial folder.

3. In the navigation pane, click the **expand** icon ▷ next to the Tutorial folder, if necessary, to display its contents, and then click the **Tours** folder to view its contents in the right pane. The Tours folder now contains the Artists file. See Figure 13.

| Figure 13 | Artists file in its new location |

Artists file is now stored in the Tours folder

selected folder

Next, you'll use the Clipboard again to move the Tuscany file from the Tutorial folder to the Tours folder. But this time, you'll access the Clipboard using the ribbon.

▶ **4.** On the Address bar, point to the **Up to** button ⬆ to display its ScreenTip (Up to "Tutorial"), click the **Up to** button ⬆ to return to the Tutorial folder, and then click the **Tuscany** file to select it.

▶ **5.** On the Home tab, in the Clipboard group, click the **Cut** button to remove the Tuscany file from the Tutorial folder and temporarily store it on the Clipboard.

▶ **6.** In the Address bar, click the **arrow** button ▶ to the right of "Tutorial" to display a list of subfolders in the Tutorial folder, and then click **Tours** to display the contents of the Tours folder in File Explorer.

▶ **7.** In the Clipboard group, click the **Paste** button to paste the Tuscany file in the Tours folder. The Tours folder now contains the Artists and Tuscany files.

Finally, you'll move the Task List file from the Tutorial folder to the Projects folder using the Move to button in the Organize group on the Home tab. This button and the Copy to button are ideal when you want to move or copy files without leaving the current folder. When you select a file and then click the Move to or Copy to button, a list of locations appears, including all of the Windows libraries and one or more folders you open frequently. You can click a location in the list to move the selected file to that library or folder. You can also select the Choose location option to open the Move Items or Copy Items dialog box, and then select a location for the file, which you'll do in the following steps.

To move the Task List file using the Move to button:

▶ **1.** In the Address bar, click **Tutorial** to return to the Tutorial folder, and then click the **Task List** file to select it.

▶ **2.** On the Home tab, in the Organize group, click the **Move to** button to display a list of locations to which you can move the selected file. The Projects folder is not included on this list because you haven't opened it yet.

▶ **3.** Click **Choose location** to open the Move Items dialog box. See Figure 14.

| Figure 14 | Move Items dialog box |

locations on your computer; yours might differ

▶ **4.** If necessary, scroll the list of locations, and then click the **expand** icon ▷ next to the drive containing your Data Files, such as Removable Disk (F:).

▶ **5.** Navigate to the FM ▶ Tutorial folder, and then click the **Projects** folder to select it.

▶ **6.** Click the **Move** button to close the dialog box and move the Task List file to the Projects folder.

▶ **7.** Open the Projects folder to confirm that it contains the Task List file.

One way to save steps when moving or copying multiple files or folders is to select all the files and folders you want to move or copy, and then work with them as a group. You can use several techniques to select multiple files or folders at the same time, which are described in Figure 15.

| Figure 15 | Selecting multiple files or folders |

Items to Select in the Right Pane of File Explorer	Method
Files or folders listed together	Click the first item, press and hold the Shift key, click the last item, and then release the Shift key.
	or
	Drag the pointer to create a selection box around all the items you want to include.
Files or folders not listed together	Press and hold the Ctrl key, click each item you want to select, and then release the Ctrl key.
All files and folders	On the Home tab, in the Select group, click the Select all button.

Items to Deselect in the Right Pane of File Explorer	Method
Single file or folder in a selected group	Press and hold the Ctrl key, click each item you want to remove from the selection, and then release the Ctrl key.
All selected files and folders	Click a blank area of the File Explorer window.

© 2014 Cengage Learning

Next, you'll copy the four graphics files from the Tutorial folder to the Marketing Graphics folder using the Clipboard. To do this efficiently, you will select multiple files at once.

To copy multiple files at once using the Clipboard:

▶ **1.** Display the contents of the Tutorial folder in File Explorer.

▶ **2.** Click the **Chianti** file, press and hold the **Shift** key, click the **Market** file, and then release the **Shift** key.

▶ **3.** Press and hold the **Ctrl** key, click the **List** file to deselect it, and then release the **Ctrl** key. Four files—Chianti, Florence, Logo, and Market—are selected in the Tutorial folder window.

▶ **4.** Right-click a selected file, and then click **Copy** on the shortcut menu. Windows copies the selected files to the Clipboard.

▶ **5.** Right-click the **Marketing Graphics** folder, and then click **Paste** on the shortcut menu.

▶ **6.** Open the **Marketing Graphics** folder to verify it contains the four files you copied, and then return to the Tutorial folder.

7. Right-click the **Tour Rates** file, and then click **Copy** on the shortcut menu.

8. In the right pane, double-click the **Financial** folder to open it, right-click a blank area of the right pane, and then click **Paste** on the shortcut menu.

INSIGHT

Duplicating Your Folder Organization

If you work on two computers, such as one computer at an office or school and another computer at home, you can duplicate the folders you use on both computers to simplify the process of transferring files from one computer to another. For example, if you have four folders in your My Documents folder on your work computer, create these same four folders on a USB drive and in the My Documents folder of your home computer. If you change a file on the hard disk of your home computer, you can copy the most recent version of the file to the corresponding folder on your USB drive so the file is available when you are at work. You also then have a **backup**, or duplicate copy, of important files. Having a backup of your files is invaluable if your computer has a fatal error.

All the files that originally appeared in the Tutorial folder are now stored in appropriate subfolders. You can streamline the organization of the Tutorial folder by deleting the duplicate files you no longer need.

Deleting Files and Folders

TIP

In most cases, a file deleted from a USB drive does not go into the Recycle Bin. Instead, it is deleted when Windows 8 removes its icon, and the file cannot be recovered.

You should periodically delete files and folders you no longer need so that your main folders and disks don't get cluttered. In File Explorer, you delete a file or folder by deleting its icon. When you delete a file from a hard disk, Windows 8 removes the file from the folder but stores the file contents in the Recycle Bin. The Recycle Bin is an area on your hard disk that holds deleted files until you remove them permanently. When you delete a folder from the hard disk, the folder and all of its files are stored in the Recycle Bin. If you change your mind and want to retrieve a deleted file or folder, you can double-click the Recycle Bin on the desktop, right-click the file or folder you want to retrieve, and then click Restore. However, after you empty the Recycle Bin, you can no longer recover the files it contained.

Because you copied the Chianti, Florence, Logo, Market, and Tour Rates files to the subfolders in the Tutorial folder, you can safely delete the original files. You can also delete the List file because you no longer need it. You can delete a file or folder using various methods, including using a shortcut menu or selecting one or more files and then pressing the Delete key.

To delete files in the Tutorial folder:

1. Display the Tutorial folder in the File Explorer window.

2. In the right pane, click **Chianti**, press and hold the **Shift** key, click **Tour Rates**, and then release the **Shift** key. All files in the Tutorial folder are now selected. None of the subfolders should be selected.

Make sure you have copied the selected files to the Marketing Graphics and Financial folders before completing this step.

3. Right-click the selected files, and then click **Delete** on the shortcut menu. A message box appears, asking if you're sure you want to permanently delete these files.

4. Click the **Yes** button to confirm that you want to delete the files.

Renaming Files

After creating and naming a file or folder, you might realize that a different name would be more meaningful or descriptive. You can easily rename a file or folder by using the Rename command on the file's shortcut menu.

Now that you've organized Matt's files into folders, he reviews your work and notes that the Artists file was originally created to store text specifically about Florentine painters and sculptors. You can rename that file to give it a more descriptive filename.

To rename the Artists file:

▶ **1.** In the right pane of the File Explorer window, double-click the **Tours** folder to display its contents.

▶ **2.** Right-click the **Artists** file, and then click **Rename** on the shortcut menu. The filename is highlighted and a box appears around it.

▶ **3.** Type **Florentine Artists**, and then press the **Enter** key. The file now appears with the new name.

Trouble? If you make a mistake while typing and you haven't pressed the Enter key yet, press the Backspace key until you delete the mistake and then complete Step 3. If you've already pressed the Enter key, repeat Steps 2 and 3 to rename the file again.

Trouble? If your computer is set to display filename extensions, a message might appear asking if you are sure you want to change the filename extension. Click the No button, and then repeat Steps 2 and 3.

TIP

To rename a file, you can also click the file, pause, click it again to select the filename, and then type to enter a new filename.

Working with Compressed Files

You compress a file or a folder of files so it occupies less space on the disk. It can be useful to compress files before transferring them from one location to another, such as from your hard disk to a removable disk or vice versa, or from one computer to another via email. You can then transfer the files more quickly. Also, if you or your email contacts can send and receive files only up to a certain size, compressing large files might make them small enough to send and receive. Compare two folders—a folder named Photos that contains files totaling about 8.6 MB, and a compressed folder containing the same files but requiring only 6.5 MB of disk space. In this case, the compressed files use about 25 percent less disk space than the uncompressed files.

You can compress one or more files in File Explorer using the Zip button, which is located in the Send group on the Share tab of the ribbon. Windows stores the compressed files in a special type of folder called an **archive**, or a compressed folder. File Explorer uses an icon of a folder with a zipper to represent a compressed folder. To compress additional files or folders, you drag them into the compressed folder. You can open a file directly from a compressed folder, although you cannot modify the file. To edit and save a compressed file, you must extract it first. When you **extract** a file, you create an uncompressed copy of the file in a folder you specify. The original file remains in the compressed folder.

Matt suggests that you compress the files and folders in the Tutorial folder so that you can more quickly transfer them to another location.

TIP

Another way to compress files is to select the files, right-click the selection, point to Send to on the shortcut menu, and then click Compressed (zipped) folder.

To compress the folders and files in the Tutorial folder:

1. In File Explorer, navigate to the Tutorial folder, and then select all the folders in the Tutorial folder.

2. Click the **Share** tab on the ribbon.

3. In the Send group, click the **Zip** button. After a few moments, a new compressed folder appears in the Tutorial window with the filename selected. By default, File Explorer uses the name of the first selected item as the name of the compressed folder. You'll replace the name with a more descriptive one.

4. Type **Savvy Traveler**, and then press the **Enter** key to rename the compressed folder. See Figure 16.

Figure 16   Compressing files and folders

5. Double-click the **Savvy Traveler** compressed folder to open it, open the **Tours** folder, and then note the size of the compressed Tuscany file, which is 1,815 KB.

6. Navigate back to the Tutorial folder.

You can move and copy the files and folders from an opened compressed folder to other locations, although you cannot rename the files. More often, you extract all of the files from the compressed folder to a new location that you specify, preserving the files in their original folders as appropriate.

To extract the compressed files:

1. Click the **Savvy Traveler** compressed folder to select it, and then click the **Compressed Folder Tools Extract** tab on the ribbon.

2. In the Extract all group, click the **Extract all** button. The Extract Compressed (Zipped) Folders Wizard starts and opens the Select a Destination and Extract Files dialog box.

3. Press the **End** key to deselect the path in the box and move the insertion point to the end of the path, press the **Backspace** key as many times as necessary to delete the Savvy Traveler text, and then type **Backups**. The final three parts of the path in the box should be \FM\Tutorial\Backups. See Figure 17.

Figure 17   Extracting files from a compressed folder

your path might differ, but should end with FM\Tutorial\Backups

check box should be selected

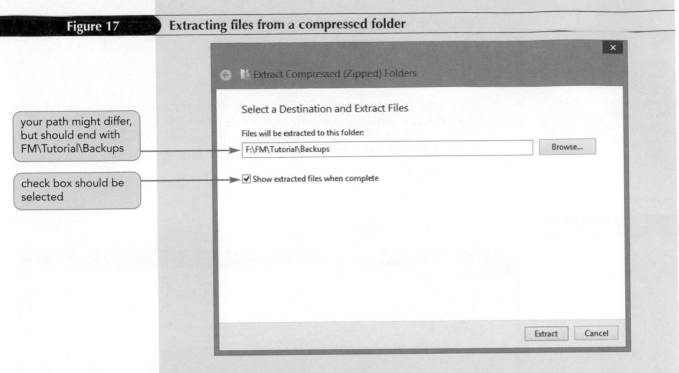

4. Make sure the Show extracted files when complete check box is checked, and then click the **Extract** button. Windows extracts the files and then opens the Backups folder, showing the Financial, Marketing Graphics, Projects, and Tours folders.

5. Open each folder to make sure it contains the files you worked with in this tutorial. When you open the Tours folder, note the uncompressed size of the Tuscany file, which is about four times as large as its compressed version.

6. Close all open windows.

In this tutorial, you examined the purpose of organizing files and folders, and you planned and created an organization for a set of related files and folders. You also explored your computer using File Explorer and learned how to navigate to your Data Files using the navigation pane. You used File Explorer to manage files and folders by opening and saving files; creating folders; and selecting, moving, and copying files. You also renamed and deleted files according to your organization plan. Finally, you compressed and extracted files.

REVIEW

Quick Check

1. You organize files by storing them in _____.
2. What is the purpose of the Address bar in File Explorer?
3. A filename _____ identifies the file's type and indicates the application that created the file.
4. Explain how to use File Explorer to navigate to a file in the following location: E: ▸ Courses ▸ Computer Basics ▸ Operating Systems.txt.
5. One way to move files and folders is to use the _____, a temporary storage area for files and information that you copied or moved from one place and plan to use somewhere else.
6. What happens if you click the first file in a folder window, press the Shift key, click the last file, and then release the Shift key?
7. When you delete a file from a hard disk, Windows removes the file from the folder but stores the file contents in the _____ .
8. Describe how to compress a file or folder.
9. What are the benefits of compressing files and folders?

PRACTICE

Review Assignments

Data Files needed for the Review Assignments: **Banner.png, Colosseum.jpg, Lectures.xlsx, Rome.jpg, Rome.rtf, Schedule.rtf, Tours.rtf**

Matt has saved a few files from his old computer to a removable disk. He gives you these files in a single, unorganized folder, and asks you to organize them logically into subfolders. To do this, you will need to devise a plan for managing the files, and then create the subfolders you need. Next, you will rename, copy, move, and delete files, and then perform other management tasks to make it easy for Matt to work with these files and folders. Complete the following steps:

1. Use File Explorer to navigate to and open the FM ▶ Review folder provided with your Data Files. Examine the seven files in this folder and consider the best way to organize the files.
2. Open the **Rome** text file in WordPad, and then add the following tip to the end of the document: **Dine on the Italian schedule, with the main meal in the middle of the day.**
3. Save the document as **Rome Dining Tips** in the Review folder. Close the WordPad window.
4. In the Review folder, create three folders: **Business**, **Destinations**, and **Supplements**.
5. To organize the files into the correct folders, complete the following steps:
   - Move the Banner and Schedule files from the Review folder to the Business folder.
   - Move the Colosseum and Rome JPEG image files and the Rome Dining Tips and Tours text files to the Destinations folder.
   - Copy the Lectures file to the Supplements folder.
6. Copy the Tours file in the Destinations folder to the Business folder.
7. Rename the Schedule file in the Business folder as **2016 Schedule**. Rename the Lectures file in the Supplements folder as **On-site Lectures**.
8. Delete the Lectures file and the Rome text file from the Review folder.
9. Create a compressed (zipped) folder in the Review folder named **Rome** that contains all the files and folders in the Review folder.
10. Extract the contents of the Rome compressed folder to a new folder named **Rome Backups** in the Review folder. (*Hint:* The file path will end with \FM\Review\Rome Backups.)
11. Close the File Explorer window.

Case Problem 1

See the Starting Data Files section at the beginning of this tutorial for the list of Data Files needed for this Case Problem.

Bay Shore Arts Center   Casey Sullivan started the Bay Shore Arts Center in Monterey, California, to provide workshops and courses on art and photography. Attracting students from the San Francisco and San José areas, Casey's business has grown and she now holds classes five days a week. She recently started a course on fine art landscape photography, which has quickly become her most popular offering. Casey hired you to help her design new classes and manage other parts of her growing business, including maintaining electronic business files and communications. Your first task is to organize the files on her new Windows 8 computer. Complete the following steps:

1. Open File Explorer. In the FM ▶ Case1 folder provided with your Data Files, create three folders: **Classes**, **Landscapes**, and **Management**.
2. Move the Fall Classes, Spring Classes, Summer Classes, and Winter Classes files from the Case1 folder to the Classes folder.
3. Rename the four files in the Classes folder by deleting the word "Classes" from each filename.
4. Move the four JPEG image files from the Case1 folder to the Landscapes folder.
5. Copy the remaining two files to the Management folder.
6. Copy the Workshops file to the Classes folder.
7. Delete the Instructors and Workshops files from the Case1 folder.
8. Make a copy of the Landscapes folder in the Case1 folder. The name of the duplicate folder appears as Landscapes – Copy. Rename the Landscapes – Copy folder as **California Photos**.
9. Copy the Workshops file from the Classes folder to the California Photos folder. Rename this file **California Workshops**.
10. Compress the graphics files in the California Photos folder in a new compressed folder named **Photos**.
11. Move the compressed Photos folder to the Case1 folder.
12. Close File Explorer.

TROUBLESHOOT

Case Problem 2

See the Starting Data Files section at the beginning of this tutorial for the list of Data Files needed for this Case Problem.

Charlotte Area Business Incubator   Antoine Jackson is the director of the Charlotte Area Business Incubator, a service run by the University of North Carolina in Charlotte to consult with new and struggling small businesses. You work as an intern at the business incubator and spend part of your time organizing client files. Since Antoine started using Windows 8, he has been having trouble finding files on his computer. He sometimes creates duplicates of files and then doesn't know which copy is the most current. Complete the following steps:

1. Navigate to the FM ▸ Case2 folder provided with your Data Files, and then examine the files in this folder. Based on the filenames and file types, begin to create an organization plan for the files.

⚙ **Troubleshoot** 2. Open the Tips1 and the Tips1 – Copy files and consider the problem these files could cause. Close the files and then fix the problem, renaming one or more files as necessary to reflect the contents.

⚙ **Troubleshoot** 3. Open the Tips2 and the Tips2 – Copy files and compare their contents. Change the filenames to clarify the purpose and contents of the files.

4. Complete the organization plan for Antoine's files. In the FM ▸ Case2 folder, create the subfolders you need according to your plan.

5. Move the files in the Case2 folder to the subfolders you created. When you finish, the Case2 folder should contain at least two subfolders containing files.

6. Rename the spreadsheet files in each subfolder according to the following descriptions.
   - Budget1: **Website budget**
   - Budget2: **Marketing budget**
   - Report1: **Travel expense report**
   - Report2: **Project expense report**
   - Report3: **Balance sheet**
   - Report4: **Event budget**

⚙ **Troubleshoot** 7. Make sure all files have descriptive names that accurately reflect their contents.

⚙ **Troubleshoot** 8. Based on the work you did in Steps 6 and 7, move files as necessary to improve the file organization.

9. Close File Explorer.

OBJECTIVES

Session 1.1
- Open and close a workbook
- Navigate through a workbook and worksheet
- Select cells and ranges
- Plan and create a workbook
- Insert, rename, and move worksheets
- Enter text, dates, and numbers
- Undo and redo actions
- Resize columns and rows

Session 1.2
- Enter formulas and the SUM and COUNT functions
- Copy and paste formulas
- Move or copy cells and ranges
- Insert and delete rows, columns, and ranges
- Create patterned text with Flash Fill
- Add cell borders and change font size
- Change worksheet views
- Prepare a workbook for printing
- Save a workbook with a new filename

Getting Started with Excel

Creating a Customer Order Report

Case | *Sparrow & Pond*

Sally Hughes is part owner of Sparrow & Pond, a small bookstore in Hudson, New Hampshire. Among her many tasks is to purchase new books from publishers. She also purchases rare and first edition books from online auctions as well as local library, estate, and garage sales.

Sally needs to quickly track sales data, compile customer profiles, and generate financial reports. She can perform all of these tasks with **Microsoft Excel 2013** (or **Excel**), an application used to enter, analyze, and present quantitative data. Sally asks you to use Excel to record a recent book order from a regular Sparrow & Pond customer.

EXCEL

STARTING DATA FILES

Excel1 → Tutorial
SP Finances.xlsx

Review
(none)

Case1
Pacific.xlsx

Case2
Tropical.xlsx

Case3
Physics.xlsx

Case4
Turf.xlsx

Session 1.1 Visual Overview:

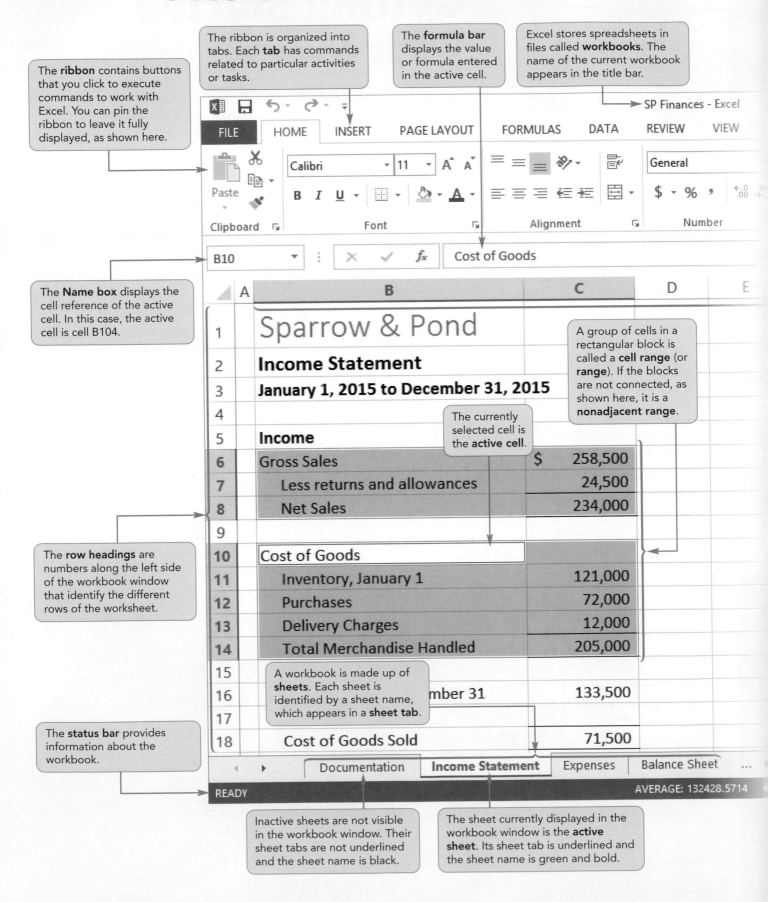

The **ribbon** contains buttons that you click to execute commands to work with Excel. You can pin the ribbon to leave it fully displayed, as shown here.

The ribbon is organized into tabs. Each **tab** has commands related to particular activities or tasks.

The **formula bar** displays the value or formula entered in the active cell.

Excel stores spreadsheets in files called **workbooks**. The name of the current workbook appears in the title bar.

SP Finances - Excel

The **Name box** displays the cell reference of the active cell. In this case, the active cell is cell B104.

A group of cells in a rectangular block is called a **cell range** (or **range**). If the blocks are not connected, as shown here, it is a **nonadjacent range**.

The currently selected cell is the **active cell**.

The **row headings** are numbers along the left side of the workbook window that identify the different rows of the worksheet.

A workbook is made up of **sheets**. Each sheet is identified by a sheet name, which appears in a **sheet tab**.

The **status bar** provides information about the workbook.

Sparrow & Pond

Income Statement

January 1, 2015 to December 31, 2015

Income		
Gross Sales	$	258,500
Less returns and allowances		24,500
Net Sales		234,000
Cost of Goods		
Inventory, January 1		121,000
Purchases		72,000
Delivery Charges		12,000
Total Merchandise Handled		205,000
	mber 31	133,500
Cost of Goods Sold		71,500

Documentation | **Income Statement** | Expenses | Balance Sheet

READY

AVERAGE: 132428.5714

Inactive sheets are not visible in the workbook window. Their sheet tabs are not underlined and the sheet name is black.

The sheet currently displayed in the workbook window is the **active sheet**. Its sheet tab is underlined and the sheet name is green and bold.

The Excel Window

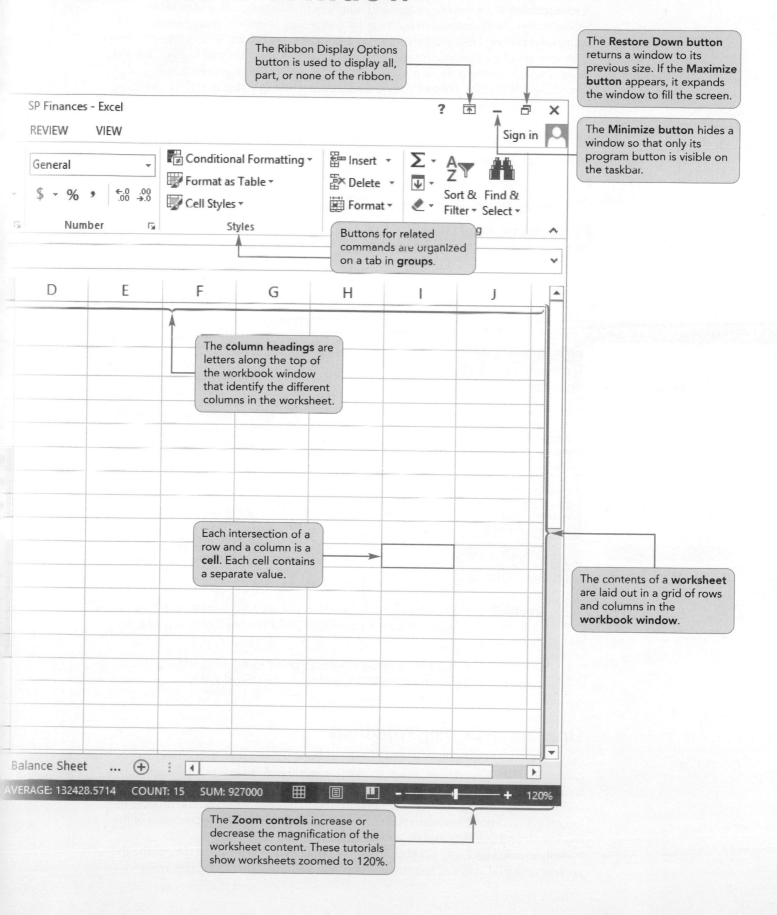

The **Ribbon Display Options** button is used to display all, part, or none of the ribbon.

The **Restore Down button** returns a window to its previous size. If the **Maximize button** appears, it expands the window to fill the screen.

The **Minimize button** hides a window so that only its program button is visible on the taskbar.

Buttons for related commands are organized on a tab in **groups**.

The **column headings** are letters along the top of the workbook window that identify the different columns in the worksheet.

Each intersection of a row and a column is a **cell**. Each cell contains a separate value.

The contents of a **worksheet** are laid out in a grid of rows and columns in the **workbook window**.

The **Zoom controls** increase or decrease the magnification of the worksheet content. These tutorials show worksheets zoomed to 120%.

SP Finances - Excel

REVIEW   VIEW

Sign in

General

$ - % , ←.0 .00
          .00 →.0

Number

Conditional Formatting ▼
Format as Table ▼
Cell Styles ▼

Styles

Insert ▼
Delete ▼
Format ▼

Σ ▼
↓ ▼

Sort & Find &
Filter ▼ Select ▼

D   E   F   G   H   I   J

Balance Sheet   ...   ⊕

AVERAGE: 132428.5714   COUNT: 15   SUM: 927000   120%

Introducing Excel and Spreadsheets

A **spreadsheet** is a grouping of text and numbers in a rectangular grid or table. Spreadsheets are often used in business for budgeting, inventory management, and financial reporting because they unite text, numbers, and charts within one document. They can also be employed for personal use for planning a personal budget, tracking expenses, or creating a list of personal items. The advantage of an electronic spreadsheet is that the content can be easily edited and updated to reflect changing financial conditions.

To start Excel:

▶ **1.** Display the Windows Start screen, if necessary.

   Using Windows 7? To complete Step 1, click the Start button on the taskbar.

▶ **2.** Click the **Excel 2013** tile. Excel starts and displays the Recent screen in Backstage view. **Backstage view** provides access to various screens with commands that allow you to manage files and Excel options. On the left is a list of recently opened workbooks. On the right are options for creating new workbooks. See Figure 1-1.

Figure 1-1   **Recent screen in Backstage view**

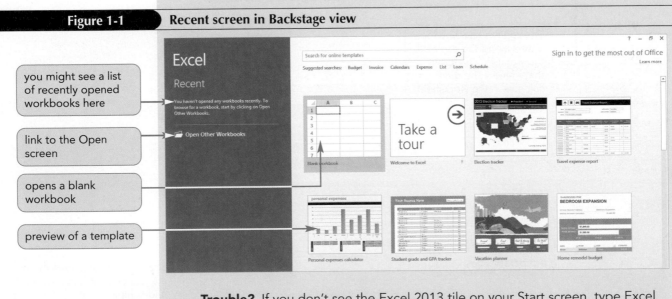

you might see a list of recently opened workbooks here

link to the Open screen

opens a blank workbook

preview of a template

Trouble? If you don't see the Excel 2013 tile on your Start screen, type Excel to display the Apps screen with the Excel 2013 tile highlighted, and then click the tile.

Using Windows 7? To complete Step 2, point to All Programs on the Start menu, click Microsoft Office 2013, and then click Excel 2013.

Opening an Existing Workbook

Excel documents are called workbooks. From the Recent screen in Backstage view, you can open a blank workbook, open an existing workbook, or create a new workbook based on a template. A **template** is a preformatted workbook with many design features and some content already filled in. Templates can speed up the process of creating a workbook because much of the work in designing the appearance of the workbook and entering its data and formulas is already done for you.

Sally created an Excel workbook that contains several worksheets describing the current financial status of Sparrow & Pond. You will open that workbook now.

To open Sally's workbook:

1. In the navigation bar on the Recent screen, click the **Open Other Workbooks** link. The Open screen is displayed and provides access to different locations where you might store files. The Recent Workbooks list shows the workbooks that were most recently opened on your computer.

2. Click **Computer**. The list of recently opened workbooks is replaced with a list of recently accessed folders on your computer and a Browse button.

   Trouble? If you are storing your files on your SkyDrive, click SkyDrive, and then log in if necessary.

3. Click the **Browse** button. The Open dialog box appears.

4. Navigate to the **Excel1 ▸ Tutorial** folder included with your Data Files.

   Trouble? If you don't have the starting Data Files, you need to get them before you can proceed. Your instructor will either give you the Data Files or ask you to obtain them from a specified location (such as a network drive). If you have any questions about the Data Files, see your instructor or technical support person for assistance.

5. Click **SP Finances** in the file list to select it.

6. Click the **Open** button. The SP Finances workbook opens in Excel.

   Trouble? If you don't see the full ribbon as shown in the Session 1.1 Visual Overview, the ribbon may be partially or fully hidden. To pin the ribbon so that the tabs and groups are fully displayed and remain visible, click the Ribbon Display Options button 📌, and then click Show Tabs and Commands.

7. If the Excel window doesn't fill the screen, click the **Maximize** button ☐ in the upper-right corner of the title bar. See Figure 1-2.

Figure 1-2   SP Finances workbook

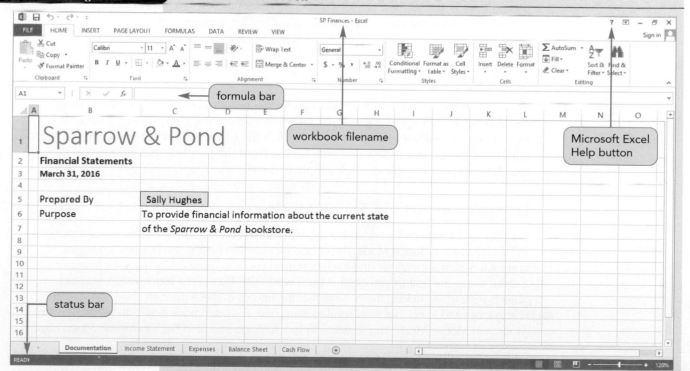

Using Keyboard Shortcuts to Work Faster

Keyboard shortcuts can help you work faster and more efficiently because you can keep your hands on the keyboard. A **keyboard shortcut** is a key or combination of keys that you press to access a feature or perform a command. Excel provides keyboard shortcuts for many commonly used commands. For example, Ctrl+S is the keyboard shortcut for the Save command, which means you hold down the Ctrl key while you press the S key to save the workbook. (Note that the plus sign is not pressed; it is used to indicate that an additional key is pressed.) When available, a keyboard shortcut is listed next to the command's name in a ScreenTip. A **ScreenTip** is a box with descriptive text about a command that appears when you point to a button on the ribbon. Figure 1-3 lists some of the keyboard shortcuts commonly used in Excel. The tutorials in this text show the corresponding keyboard shortcuts for accomplishing an action when available.

Figure 1-3   **Excel keyboard shortcuts**

Press	To	Press	To
Alt	Display the Key Tips for the commands and tools on the ribbon	Ctrl+V	Paste content that was cut or copied
Ctrl+A	Select all objects in a range	Ctrl+W	Close the current workbook
Ctrl+C	Copy the selected object(s)	Ctrl+X	Cut the selected object(s)
Ctrl+G	Go to a location in the workbook	Ctrl+Y	Repeat the last command
Ctrl+N	Open a new blank workbook	Ctrl+Z	Undo the last command
Ctrl+O	Open a saved workbook file	F1	Display the Excel Help window
Ctrl+P	Print the current workbook	F5	Go to a location in the workbook
Ctrl+S	Save the current workbook	F12	Save the current workbook with a new name or to a new location

© 2014 Cengage Learning

You can also use the keyboard to quickly select commands on the ribbon. First, you press the Alt key to display the **Key Tips**, which are labels that appear over each tab and command on the ribbon. Then, you press the key or keys indicated to access the corresponding tab, command, or button while your hands remain on the keyboard.

Getting Help

If you are unsure about the function of an Excel command or you want information about how to accomplish a particular task, you can use the Help system. To access Excel Help, you either press the F1 key or click the Microsoft Excel Help button in the title bar of the Excel window or dialog boxes. From the Excel Help window, you can search for a specific topic or click a topic in a category.

Using Excel 2013 in Touch Mode

In Office 2013, you can work with a mouse or, if you have a touchscreen, you can work in Touch Mode. In **Touch Mode**, the ribbon increases in height, the buttons are bigger, and more space appears around each button so you can more easily use your finger or a stylus to tap the button you need. As you work with Excel on a touchscreen, you tap objects instead of clicking them. Note that the figures in these tutorials show the screen with Mouse Mode on, but it's helpful to learn how to switch back and forth between Touch Mode and Mouse Mode. You'll switch to Touch Mode and then back to Mouse Mode now.

Note: The following steps assume that you are using a mouse. If you are instead using a touch device, please read these steps but don't complete them, so that you remain working in Touch Mode.

To switch between Touch Mode and Mouse Mode:

1. On the Quick Access Toolbar, click the **Customize Quick Access Toolbar** button ☰. A menu opens listing buttons you can add to the Quick Access Toolbar as well as other options for customizing the toolbar.

   Trouble? If the Touch/Mouse Mode command on the menu has a checkmark next to it, press the Esc key to close the menu, and then skip Step 2.

2. Click **Touch/Mouse Mode**. The Quick Access Toolbar now contains the Touch/Mouse Mode button 👆, which you can use to switch between Mouse Mode, the default display, and Touch Mode.

3. On the Quick Access Toolbar, click the **Touch/Mouse Mode** button 👆. A menu opens listing Mouse and Touch, and the icon next to Mouse is shaded to indicate it is selected.

   Trouble? If the icon next to Touch is shaded, press the Esc key to close the menu and skip Step 4.

4. Click **Touch**. The display switches to Touch Mode with more space between the commands and buttons on the ribbon. See Figure 1-4.

Figure 1-4	Ribbon displayed in Touch Mode

Touch/Mouse Mode button

buttons are larger with more space around them

Now you'll return to Mouse Mode.

Trouble? If you are working with a touchscreen and want to use Touch Mode, skip Steps 5 and 6.

5. On the Quick Access Toolbar, click the **Touch/Mouse Mode** button 👆, and then click **Mouse**. The ribbon returns to the Mouse Mode display shown in Figure 1-2.

6. On the Quick Access Toolbar, click the **Customize Quick Access Toolbar** button ☰, and then click **Touch/Mouse Mode** to deselect it. The Touch/Mouse Mode button is removed from the Quick Access Toolbar.

Exploring a Workbook

Workbooks are organized into separate pages called sheets. Excel supports two types of sheets: worksheets and chart sheets. A worksheet contains a grid of rows and columns into which you can enter text, numbers, dates, and formulas, and display charts. A **chart sheet** contains a chart that provides a visual representation of worksheet data. The contents of a workbook are shown in the workbook window.

Changing the Active Sheet

The sheets in a workbook are identified in the sheet tabs at the bottom of the workbook window. The SP Finances workbook includes five sheets labeled Documentation, Income Statement, Expenses, Balance Sheet, and Cash Flow. The sheet currently displayed in the workbook window is the active sheet, which in this case is the Documentation sheet. To make a different sheet active and visible, you click its sheet tab. You can tell which sheet is active because its name appears in bold green.

If a workbook includes so many sheets that not all of the sheet tabs can be displayed at the same time in the workbook window, you can use the sheet tab scrolling buttons to scroll through the list of tabs. Scrolling the sheet tabs does not change the active sheet; it only changes which sheet tabs are visible.

You will view the different sheets in the SP Finances workbook.

To change the active sheet:

▶ 1. Click the **Income Statement** sheet tab. The Income Statement worksheet becomes the active sheet, and its name is in bold green type. See Figure 1-5.

| Figure 1-5 | Income Statement worksheet |

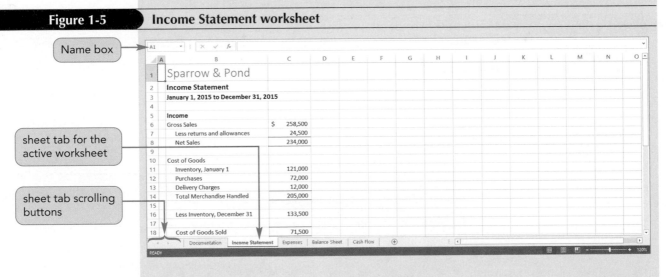

▶ 2. Click the **Expenses** sheet tab to make it the active sheet. The Expenses sheet is an example of a chart sheet containing only an Excel chart. See Figure 1-6.

| Figure 1-6 | Expenses chart sheet |

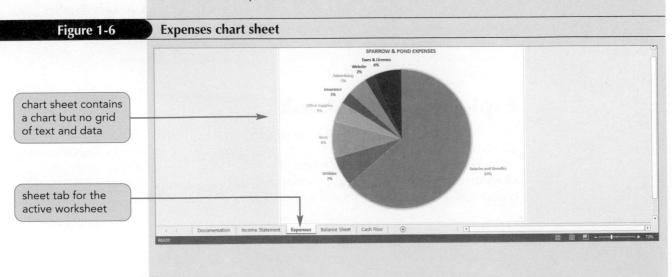

TIP

You can move to the previous or next sheet in the workbook by pressing the Ctrl+PgUp or Ctrl+PgDn keys.

3. Click the **Balance Sheet** sheet tab to make it the active sheet. Note that this sheet contains a chart embedded into the grid of data values. A worksheet can contain data values, charts, pictures, and other design elements.

4. Click the **Cash Flow** sheet tab. The worksheet with information about the company's cash flow is now active.

5. Click the **Income Statement** sheet tab to make the Income Statement worksheet the active sheet.

Navigating Within a Worksheet

The worksheet is organized into individual cells. Each cell is identified by a **cell reference**, which is based on the cell's column and row location. For example, in Figure 1-5, the company name, Sparrow & Pond, is in cell B1, which is the intersection of column B and row 1. The column letter always appears before the row number in any cell reference. The cell that is currently selected in the worksheet is referred to as the active cell. The active cell is highlighted with a thick green border, its cell reference appears in the Name box, and the corresponding column and row headings are highlighted. The active cell in Figure 1-5 is cell A1.

Row numbers range from 1 to 1,048,576, and column labels are letters in alphabetical order. The first 26 column headings range from A to Z. After Z, the next column headings are labeled AA, AB, AC, and so forth. Excel allows a maximum of 16,384 columns in a worksheet (the last column has the heading XFD). This means that you can create large worksheets whose content extends well beyond what is visible in the workbook window.

To move different parts of the worksheet into view, you can use the horizontal and vertical scroll bars located at the bottom and right edges of the workbook window, respectively. A scroll bar has arrow buttons that you can click to shift the worksheet one column or row in the specified direction, and a scroll box that you can drag to shift the worksheet in the direction you drag.

You will scroll the active worksheet so you can review the rest of the Sparrow & Pond income statement.

To scroll through the Income Statement worksheet:

1. On the vertical scroll bar, click the down arrow button ▼ to scroll down the Income Statement worksheet until you see cell C36, which displays the company's net income value of $4,600.

2. On the horizontal scroll bar, click the right arrow button ▶ three times. The worksheet scrolls three columns to the right, moving columns A through C out of view.

3. On the horizontal scroll bar, drag the scroll box to the left until you see column A.

4. On the vertical scroll bar, drag the scroll box up until you see the top of the worksheet and cell A1.

Scrolling the worksheet does not change the location of the active cell. Although the active cell might shift out of view, you can always see the location of the active cell in the Name box. To make a different cell active, you can either click a new cell or use the keyboard to move between cells, as described in Figure 1-7.

Figure 1-7 Excel navigation keys

Press	To move the active cell
↑ ↓ ← →	Up, down, left, or right one cell
Home	To column A of the current row
Ctrl+Home	To cell A1
Ctrl+End	To the last cell in the worksheet that contains data
Enter	Down one row or to the start of the next row of data
Shift+Enter	Up one row
Tab	One column to the right
Shift+Tab	One column to the left
PgUp, PgDn	Up or down one screen
Ctrl+PgUp, Ctrl+PgDn	To the previous or next sheet in the workbook

© 2014 Cengage Learning

You will use both your mouse and your keyboard to change the location of the active cell in the Income Statement worksheet.

To change the active cell:

1. Move your pointer over cell **B5**, and then click the mouse button. The active cell moves from cell A1 to cell B5. A green border appears around cell B5, the column heading for column B and the row heading for row 5 are both highlighted, and the cell reference in the Name box changes from A1 to B5.

2. Press the → key. The active cell moves one cell to the right to cell C5.

3. Press the **PgDn** key. The active cell moves down one full screen.

4. Press the **PgUp** key. The active cell moves up one full screen, returning to cell C5.

5. Press the **Ctrl+Home** keys. The active cell returns to the first cell in the worksheet, cell A1.

The mouse and keyboard provide quick ways to navigate the active worksheet. For larger worksheets that span several screens, you can move directly to a specific cell using the Go To command or by typing a cell reference in the Name box. You will try both of these methods.

To use the Go To dialog box and the Name box:

1. On the HOME tab, in the Editing group, click the **Find & Select** button, and then click **Go To** on the menu that opens (or press the **F5** key). The Go To dialog box opens.

2. Type **C36** in the Reference box. See Figure 1-8.

Figure 1-8   Go To dialog box

cell reference of the cell you want to make active

3. Click the **OK** button. Cell C36 becomes the active cell, displaying $4,600, which is Sparrow & Pond's net income for the year. Because cell C36 is the active cell, its cell reference appears in the Name box.

4. Click in the Name box, type **A1**, and then press the **Enter** key. Cell A1 is again the active cell.

Selecting a Cell Range

Many tasks in Excel require you to work with a group of cells. You can use your mouse or keyboard to select those cells. A group of cells in a rectangular block is called a cell range (or simply a range). Each range is identified with a **range reference** that includes the cell reference of the upper-left cell of the rectangular block and the cell reference of the lower-right cell separated by a colon. For example, the range reference A1:G5 refers to all of the cells in the rectangular block from cell A1 through cell G5.

As with individual cells, you can select cell ranges using your mouse, the keyboard, or commands. You will select a range in the Income Statement worksheet.

To select a cell range:

TIP

You can also select a range by clicking the upper-left cell of the range, holding down the Shift key as you click the lower-right cell in the range, and then releasing the Shift key.

1. Click cell **B5** to select it, and without releasing the mouse button, drag down to cell **C8**.

2. Release the mouse button. The range B5:C8 is selected. See Figure 1-9. The selected cells are highlighted and surrounded by a green border. The first cell you selected in the range, cell B5, is the active cell in the worksheet. The active cell in a selected range is white. The Quick Analysis button appears, providing options for working with the range; you will use this button in another tutorial.

Figure 1-9 **Range B5:C8 selected**

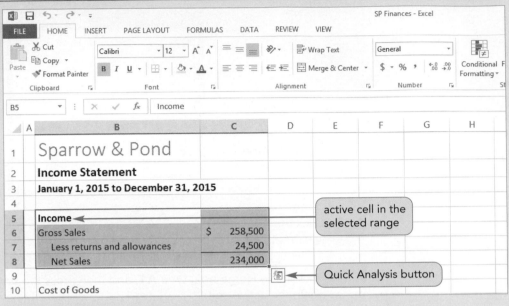

3. Click cell **A1** to deselect the range.

A nonadjacent range is a collection of separate ranges. The range reference for a nonadjacent range includes the range reference to each range separated by a semicolon. For example, the range reference A1:G5;A10:G15 includes two ranges—the first range is the rectangular block of cells from cell A1 to cell G5, and the second range is the rectangular block of cells from cell A10 to cell G15.

You will select a nonadjacent range in the Income Statement worksheet.

To select a nonadjacent range in the Income Statement worksheet:

1. Click cell **B5**, hold down the **Shift** key as you click cell **C8**, and then release the **Shift** key to select the range B5:C8.

2. Hold down the **Ctrl** key as you select the range **B10:C14**, and then release the **Ctrl** key. The two separate blocks of cells in the nonadjacent range B5:C8;B10:C14 are selected. See Figure 1-10.

Figure 1-10   Nonadjacent range B5:C8;B10:C14 selected

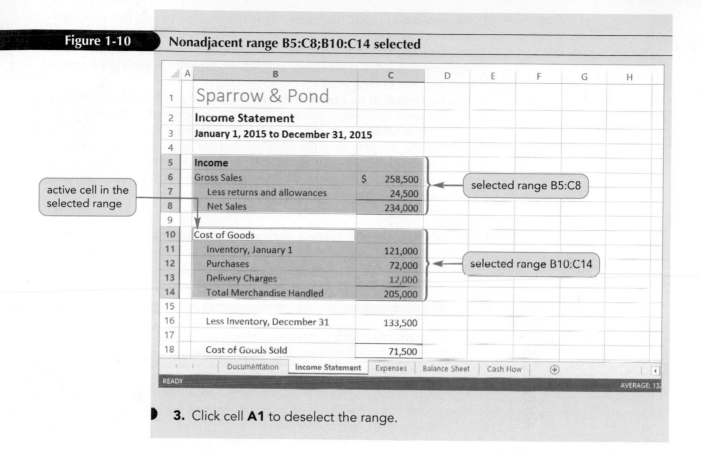

3. Click cell **A1** to deselect the range.

Closing a Workbook

When you close a workbook, a dialog box might open, asking whether you want to save the workbook. If you have made changes that you want to keep, you should save the workbook. You have finished reviewing the SP Finances workbook, so you will close it. You will not save the workbook because you want the original version to remain unchanged.

To close the SP Finances workbook:

1. On the ribbon, click the **FILE** tab to display Backstage view, and then click **Close** in the navigation bar (or press the **Ctrl+W** keys).

2. If a dialog box opens asking whether you want to save your changes to the workbook, click the **Don't Save** button. The workbook closes without saving any changes. Excel remains opens, ready for you to create or open another workbook.

Planning a Workbook

Before you begin creating a new workbook, you should develop a plan. You can do this by using a **planning analysis sheet**, which includes the following questions that help you think about the workbook's purpose and how to achieve your desired results:

1. **What problems do I want to solve?** The answer identifies the goal or purpose of the workbook. For example, Sally needs an easy way to record customer orders and analyze details from these orders.

2. **What data do I need?** The answer identifies the type of data that you need to collect and enter into the workbook. For example, Sally needs customer contact information, an order ID number, the date the order shipped, the shipping method, a list of books ordered, the quantity of each book ordered, and the price of each book.

3. **What calculations do I need to enter?** The answer identifies the formulas you need to apply to the data you have collected and entered. For example, Sally needs to calculate the charge for each book ordered, the number of books ordered, the shipping cost, the sales tax, and the total cost of the order.

4. **What form should my solution take?** The answer describes the appearance of the workbook content and how it should be presented to others. For example, Sally wants the information stored in a single worksheet that is easy to read and prints clearly.

Based on Sally's plan, you will create a workbook containing the details of a recent customer order. Sally will use this workbook as a model for future workbooks detailing other customer orders.

PROSKILLS

Written Communication: Creating Effective Workbooks

Workbooks convey information in written form. As with any type of writing, the final product creates an impression and provides an indicator of your interest, knowledge, and attention to detail. To create the best impression, all workbooks—especially those you intend to share with others such as coworkers and clients—should be well planned, well organized, and well written.

A well-designed workbook should clearly identify its overall goal and present information in an organized format. The data it includes—both the entered values and the calculated values—should be accurate. The process of developing an effective workbook includes the following steps:

- Determine the workbook's purpose, content, and organization before you start.
- Create a list of the sheets used in the workbook, noting each sheet's purpose.
- Insert a documentation sheet that describes the workbook's purpose and organization. Include the name of the workbook author, the date the workbook was created, and any additional information that will help others to track the workbook to its source.
- Enter all of the data in the workbook. Add labels to indicate what the values represent and, if possible, where they originated so others can view the source of your data.
- Enter formulas for calculated items rather than entering the calculated values into the workbook. For more complicated calculations, provide documentation explaining them.
- Test the workbook with a variety of values; edit the data and formulas to correct errors.
- Save the workbook and create a backup copy when the project is completed. Print the workbook's contents if you need to provide a hard-copy version to others or for your files.
- Maintain a history of your workbook as it goes through different versions, so that you and others can quickly see how the workbook has changed during revisions.

By including clearly written documentation, explanatory text, a logical organization, and accurate data and formulas, you will create effective workbooks that others can use easily.

Creating a New Workbook

You create new workbooks from the New screen in Backstage view. Similar to the Recent screen that opened when you started Excel, the New screen include templates for a variety of workbook types. You can see a preview of what the different workbooks will look like. You will create a new workbook from the Blank workbook template, in which you can add all of the content and design Sally wants for the Sparrow & Pond customer order worksheet.

To start a new, blank workbook:

1. On the ribbon, click the **FILE** tab to display Backstage view.

TIP

You can also create a new, blank workbook by pressing the Ctrl+N keys.

2. Click **New** in the navigation bar to display the New screen, which includes access to templates for a variety of workbooks.

3. Click the **Blank workbook** tile. A blank workbook opens. See Figure 1-11.

Figure 1-11   Blank workbook

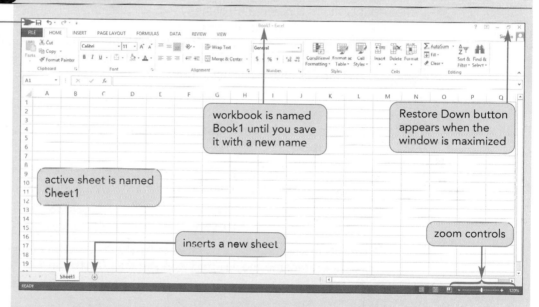

Save button on the Quick Access Toolbar

workbook is named Book1 until you save it with a new name

Restore Down button appears when the window is maximized

active sheet is named Sheet1

inserts a new sheet

zoom controls

In these tutorials, the workbook window is zoomed to 120% for better readability. If you want to zoom your workbook window to match the figures, complete Step 4. If you prefer to work in the default zoom of 100% or at another zoom level, read but do not complete Step 4; you might see more or less of the worksheet on your screen, but this will not affect your work in the tutorials.

4. If you want your workbook window zoomed to 120% to match the figures, click the **Zoom In** button ➕ on the status bar twice to increase the zoom level to 120%. The 120% magnification increases the size of each cell, but reduces the number of worksheet cells visible in the workbook window.

The name of the active workbook, Book1, appears in the title bar. If you open multiple blank workbooks, they are named Book1, Book2, Book3, and so forth until you save them with a more descriptive name.

Renaming and Inserting Worksheets

Blank workbooks open with a single blank sheet named Sheet1. You can give sheets more descriptive and meaningful names. This is a good practice so that you and others can easily tell what a sheet contains. Sheet names cannot exceed 31 characters, but they can contain blank spaces and include upper- and lowercase letters.

Because Sheet1 is not a very descriptive name, Sally wants you to rename the worksheet as Customer Order.

To rename the Sheet1 worksheet:

▶ **1.** Double-click the **Sheet1** tab. The Sheet1 label in the tab is selected.

▶ **2.** Type **Customer Order** as the new name, and then press the **Enter** key. The width of the sheet tab expands to fit the longer sheet name.

Many workbooks include multiple sheets so that data can be organized in logical groups. A common business practice is to include a worksheet named Documentation that contains a description of the workbook, the name of the person who prepared the workbook, and the date it was created.

You will create two new worksheets. You will rename one worksheet as Documentation and you will rename the other worksheet as Customer Contact to record the customer's contact information.

To insert and name the Documentation and Customer Contact worksheets:

▶ **1.** To the right of the Customer Order sheet tab, click the **New sheet** button ⊕. A new sheet named Sheet2 is inserted to the right of the Customer Order sheet.

▶ **2.** Double-click the **Sheet2** sheet tab, type **Documentation** as the new name, and then press the **Enter** key. The second worksheet is renamed.

▶ **3.** To the right of the Documentation sheet, click the **New sheet** button ⊕, and then rename the inserted worksheet as **Customer Contact**.

Moving Worksheets

A good practice is to place the most important sheets at the beginning of the workbook (the leftmost sheet tabs) and less important sheets at the end (the rightmost sheet tabs). To change the placement of sheets in a workbook, you drag them by their sheet tabs to the new location.

Sally wants you to move the Documentation worksheet to the front of the workbook, so that it appears before the Customer Order sheet.

To move the Documentation worksheet:

▶ **1.** Point to the **Documentation** sheet tab.

TIP

To copy a sheet, hold down the Ctrl key as you drag and drop its sheet tab.

▶ **2.** Press and hold the mouse button. The pointer changes to ⬚, and a small arrow appears in the upper-left corner of the tab.

▶ **3.** Drag to the left until the small arrow appears in the upper-left corner of the Customer Order sheet tab, and then release the mouse button. The Documentation worksheet is now the first sheet in the workbook.

Deleting Worksheets

In some workbooks, you will want to delete an existing sheet. The easiest way to delete a sheet is by using a **shortcut menu**, which is a list of commands related to a selection that opens when you click the right mouse button. Sally asks you to include the customer's contact information on the Customer Order worksheet so all of the information is on one sheet.

To delete the Customer Contact worksheet from the workbook:

▶ **1.** Right-click the **Customer Contact** sheet tab. A shortcut menu opens.

▶ **2.** Click **Delete**. The Customer Contact worksheet is removed from the workbook.

Saving a Workbook

As you modify a workbook, you should save it regularly—every 10 minutes or so is a good practice. The first time you save a workbook, the Save As dialog box opens so you can name the file and choose where to save it. You can save the workbook on your computer or network, or to your account on SkyDrive.

To save your workbook for the first time:

▶ **1.** On the Quick Access Toolbar, click the **Save** button 🔲 (or press the **Ctrl+S** keys). The Save As screen in Backstage view opens.

▶ **2.** Click **Computer** in the Places list, and then click the **Browse** button. The Save As dialog box opens.

   Trouble? If your instructor wants you to save your files to your SkyDrive account, click SkyDrive, and then log in to your account, if necessary.

▶ **3.** Navigate to the location specified by your instructor.

▶ **4.** In the File name box, select **Book1** (the suggested name) if it is not already selected, and then type **SP Customer Order**.

▶ **5.** Verify that **Excel Workbook** appears in the Save as type box.

▶ **6.** Click the **Save** button. The workbook is saved, the dialog box closes, and the workbook window reappears with the new filename in the title bar.

As you modify the workbook, you will need to resave the file. Because you already saved the workbook with a filename, the next time you save, the Save command saves the changes you made to the workbook without opening the Save As dialog box.

Entering Text, Dates, and Numbers

Workbook content is entered into worksheet cells. Those cells can contain text, numbers, or dates and times. **Text data** is any combination of letters, numbers, and symbols. Text data is often referred to as a **text string** because it contains a series, or string, of text characters. **Numeric data** is any number that can be used in a mathematical calculation. **Date** and **time data** are commonly recognized formats for date and time values. For example, Excel interprets the cell entry April 15, 2016 as a date and not as text. New data is placed into the active cell of the current worksheet. As you enter data, the entry appears in both the active cell and the formula bar. By default, text is left-aligned in cells, and numbers, dates, and times are right-aligned.

Entering Text

Text is often used in worksheets to label other data and to identify areas of a sheet. Sally wants you to enter some of the information from the planning analysis sheet into the Documentation sheet.

To enter the text for the Documentation sheet:

1. Press the **Ctrl+Home** keys to make sure cell A1 is the active cell on the Documentation sheet.

2. Type **Sparrow and Pond** in cell A1. As you type, the text appears in cell A1 and in the formula bar.

3. Press the **Enter** key twice. The text is entered into cell A1 and the active cell moves down two rows to cell A3.

4. Type **Author** in cell A3, and then press the **Tab** key. The text is entered and the active cell moves one column to the right to cell B3.

5. Type your name in cell B3, and then press the **Enter** key. The text is entered and the active cell moves one cell down and to the left to cell A4.

6. Type **Date** in cell A4, and then press the **Tab** key. The text is entered and the active cell moves one column to the right to cell B4, where you would enter the date you created the worksheet. For now, you will leave the cell for the date blank.

7. Click cell **A5** to make it the active cell, type **Purpose** in the cell, and then press the **Tab** key. The active cell moves one column to the right to cell B5.

8. Type **To record customer book orders**. in cell B5, and then press the **Enter** key. Figure 1-12 shows the text entered in the Documentation sheet.

Figure 1-12	Documentation sheet

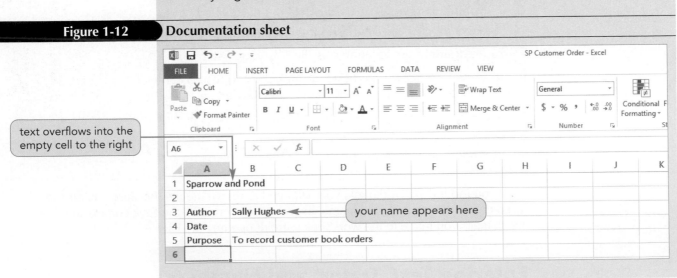

The text you entered in cell A1 is so long that it appears to overflow into cell B1. The same is true for the text you entered in cells B3 and B5. Any text you enter in a cell that doesn't fit within that cell will cover the adjacent cells to the right as long as they are empty. If the adjacent cells contain data, only the text that fits into the cell is displayed. The rest of the text entry is hidden from view. The text itself is not affected. The complete text is still entered in the cell; it is just not displayed. (You will learn how to display all text in a cell in the next session.)

Undoing and Redoing an Action

As you enter data in a workbook, you might need to undo a previous action. Excel maintains a list of the actions you performed in the workbook during the current session, so you can undo most of your actions. You can use the Undo button on the Quick Access Toolbar or press the Ctrl+Z keys to reverse your most recent actions one at a time. If you want to undo more than one action, you can click the Undo button arrow and then select the earliest action you want to undo—all of the actions after the earliest action you selected are also undone.

You will undo the most recent change you made to the Documentation sheet—the text you entered into cell B5. Then you will enter more descriptive and accurate description of the worksheet's purpose.

To undo the text entry in cell B5:

▶ 1. On the Quick Access Toolbar, click the **Undo** button 🔄 (or press the **Ctrl+Z** keys). The last action is reversed, removing the text you entered in cell B5.

▶ 2. In cell B5, type **To record book orders from a Sparrow & Pond customer.** and then press the **Enter** key.

If you want to restore actions you have undone, you can redo them. To redo one action at a time, you can click the Redo button 🔁 on the Quick Access Toolbar or press the Ctrl+Y keys. To redo multiple actions at once, you can click the Redo button arrow and then click the earliest action you want to redo. After you undo or redo an action, Excel continues the action list starting from any new changes you make to the workbook.

Editing Cell Content

As you work, you might find mistakes you need to correct or entries that you want to change. If you want to replace all of the content in a cell, you simply select the cell and then type the new entry to overwrite the previous entry. However, if you need to replace only part of a cell's content, you can work in **Edit mode**. To switch to Edit mode, you double-click the cell. A blinking insertion point indicates where the new content you type will be inserted. In the cell or formula bar, the pointer changes to an I-beam, which you can use to select text in the cell. Anything you type replaces the selected content.

You need to edit the text in cell A1 to Sparrow & Pond. You will switch to Edit mode to correct the text.

To edit the text in cell A1:

▶ 1. Double-click cell **A1** to select the cell and switch to Edit mode. A blinking insertion point appears within the text of cell A1. The status bar displays EDIT instead of READY to indicate that the cell is in Edit mode.

▶ 2. Press the arrow keys to move the insertion point directly to the right of the word "and" in the company name.

▶ 3. Press the **Backspace** key three times to delete the word "and."

▶ 4. Type **&** to enter the new text, and then press the **Enter** key. The cell text changes to Sparrow & Pond. See Figure 1-13.

| Figure 1-13 | Revised Documentation sheet |

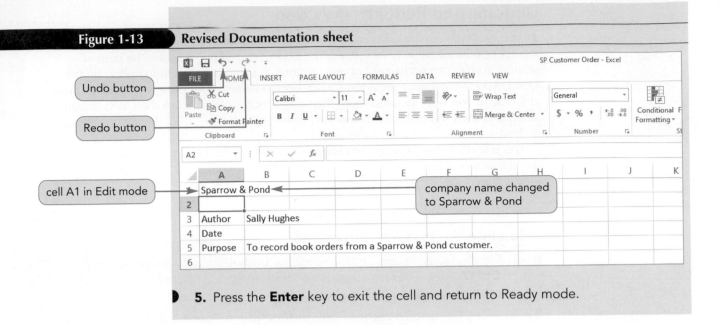

5. Press the **Enter** key to exit the cell and return to Ready mode.

Understanding AutoComplete

As you type text in the active cell, Excel tries to anticipate the remaining characters by displaying text that begins with the same letters as a previous entry in the same column. This feature, known as **AutoComplete**, helps make entering repetitive text easier. To accept the suggested text, press the Tab or Enter key. To override the suggested text, continue to type the text you want to enter in the cell. AutoComplete does not work with dates or numbers, or when a blank cell is between the previous entry and the text you are typing.

Next, you will enter the contact information for Tobias Gregson, a customer who recently placed an order with Sparrow & Pond. You will enter the contact information on the Customer Order worksheet.

To enter Tobias Gregson's contact information:

1. Click the **Customer Order** sheet tab to make it the active sheet.

2. In cell A1, type **Customer Order** as the worksheet title, and then press the **Enter** key twice. The worksheet title is entered in cell A1, and the active cell is cell A3.

3. Type **Ship To** in cell A3, and then press the **Enter** key. The label is entered in the cell, and the active cell is now cell A4.

4. In the range A4:A10, enter the following labels, pressing the **Enter** key after each entry and ignoring any AutoComplete suggestions: **First Name**, **Last Name**, **Address**, **City**, **State**, **Postal Code**, and **Phone**.

5. Click cell **B4** to make that cell the active cell.

6. In the range B4:B10, enter the following contact information, pressing the **Enter** key after each entry and ignoring any AutoComplete suggestions: **Tobias, Gregson, 412 Apple Grove St., Nashua, NH, 03061,** and **(603) 555-4128**. See Figure 1-14.

Figure 1-14   **Text entered in the Customer Order worksheet**

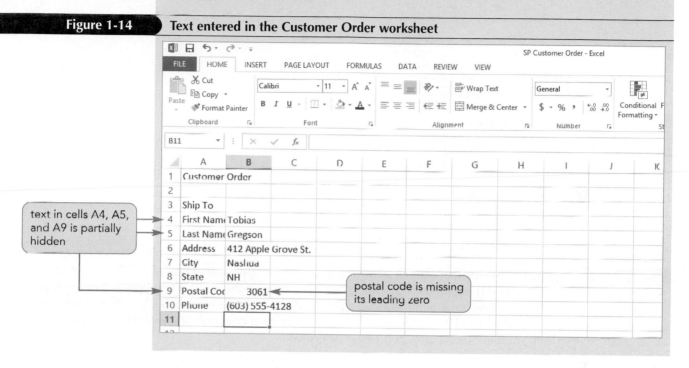

Displaying Numbers as Text

When you type numbers in the active cell, Excel treats the entry as a number and ignores any leading zero. For example, in cell B9, the first digit of the postal code 03061 is missing; Excel displays 3061 because the numbers 3061 and 03061 have the same value. To specify that a number entry should be considered text and all digits should be displayed, you include an apostrophe (') before the numbers.

You will make this change in cell B9 so that Excel treats the postal code as text and displays all of the digits you type.

To enter the postal code as text:

1. Click cell **B9** to select it. Notice that the postal code is right-aligned in the cell, unlike the other text entries, which are left-aligned—another indication that the entry is being treated as a number.

2. Type **'03061** in cell B9, and then press the **Enter** key. The text 03061 appears in cell B9 and is left-aligned in the cell, matching all of the other text entries. See Figure 1-15.

Figure 1-15   **Number displayed as text**

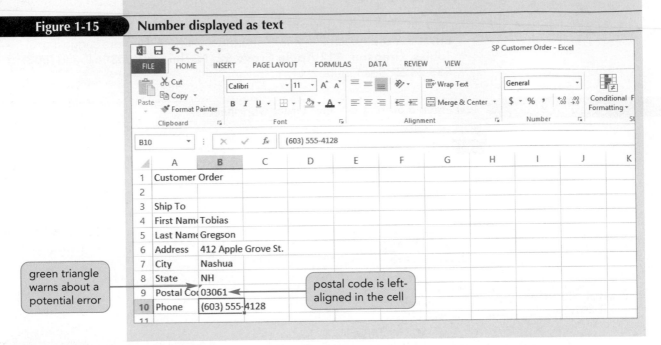

green triangle warns about a potential error

postal code is left-aligned in the cell

TIP

To remove a green triangle, click the cell, click the yellow caution icon that appears to the left of the cell, and then click Ignore Error.

Notice that a green triangle appears in the upper-left corner of cell B9. Excel uses green triangles to flag potential errors in cells. In this case, it is simply a warning that you entered a number as a text string. Because this is intentional, you do not have to edit the cell to fix the "error." Green triangles appear only in the workbook window and not in any printouts of the worksheet.

Entering Dates

You can enter dates in any of the standard date formats. For example, all of the following entries are recognized by Excel as the same date:

- 4/6/2016
- 4/6/16
- 4-6-2016
- April 6, 2016
- 6-Apr-16

Even though you enter a date as text, Excel stores the date as a number equal to the number of days between the specified date and January 0, 1900. Times are also entered as text and stored as fractions of a 24-hour day. For example, the date and time April 4, 2016 @ 6:00 PM is stored by Excel as 42,464.75. Dates and times are stored as numbers so that Excel can easily perform date and time calculations, such as determining the elapsed time between one date and another.

Based on the default date format your computer uses, Excel might alter the format of a date after you type it. For example, if you enter the date 4/6/16 into the active cell, Excel might display the date with the four-digit year value, 4/6/2016; if you enter the text April 6, 2016, Excel might convert the date format to 6-Apr-16. Changing the date or time format does not affect the underlying date or time value.

International Date Formats

As business transactions become more international in scope, you may need to adopt international standards for expressing dates, times, and currency values in your workbooks. For example, a worksheet cell might contain 06/05/16. This format could represent any of the following dates: the 5th of June, 2016; the 6th of May, 2016; and the 16th of May, 2006.

The date depends on which country the workbook has been designed for. You can avoid this problem by entering the full date, as in June 5, 2016. However, this might not work with documents written in foreign languages, such as Japanese, that use different character symbols.

To solve this problem, many international businesses adopt ISO (International Organization for Standardization) dates in the format yyyy-mm-dd, where yyyy is the four-digit year value, mm is the two-digit month value, and dd is the two-digit day value. So, a date such as June 5, 2016 is entered as 2016/06/05. If you choose to use this international date format, make sure that people using your workbook understand this format so they do not misinterpret the dates. You can include information about the date format in the Documentation sheet.

For the SP Customer Order workbook, you will enter dates in the format mm/dd/yyyy, where mm is the 2-digit month number, dd is the 2-digit day number, and yyyy is the 4-digit year number.

To enter the current date into the Documentation sheet:

1. Click the **Documentation** sheet tab to make the Documentation sheet the active worksheet.

2. Click cell **B4** to make it active, type the current date in the mm/dd/yyyy format, and then press the **Enter** key. The date is entered in the cell.

   Trouble? Depending on your system configuration, Excel might change the date to the date format dd-mmm-yy. This difference will not affect your work.

3. Make the **Customer Order** worksheet the active sheet.

The next part of the Customer Order worksheet will list the books the customer purchased from Sparrow & Pond. As shown in Figure 1-16, the list includes identifying information about each book, its price, and the quantity ordered.

Figure 1-16   **Book order from Tobias Gregson**

ISBN	CATEGORY	BINDING	TITLE	AUTHOR(S)	PRICE	QTY
0-374-25385-4	Used	Hardcover	Samurai William: The Englishman Who Opened Japan	Milton, Giles	$5.95	2
4-889-96213-1	New	Softcover	Floral Origami Globes	Fuse, Tomoko	$24.95	3
0-500-27062-7	New	Hardcover	Tao Magic: The Secret Language of Diagrams and Calligraphy	Legeza, Laszlo	$8.95	1
0-785-82169-4	Used	Hardcover	The Holy Grail	Morgan, Giles	$3.75	1
0-854-56516-7	New	Softcover	Murder on the Links	Christie, Agatha	$7.50	2

© 2014 Cengage Learning

You will enter the first five columns of the book order into the worksheet.

To enter the first part of the book order:

1. In the Customer Order worksheet, click cell **A12** to make it the active cell, type **ISBN** as the column label, and then press the **Tab** key to move to cell B12.

2. In the range B12:E12, type the following labels, pressing the **Tab** key to move to the next cell: **CATEGORY**, **BINDING**, **TITLE**, and **AUTHOR(S)**.

3. Press the **Enter** key to go to the next row of the worksheet, making cell A13 the active cell.

4. In the range A13:E17, enter the ISBN, category, binding, title, and author text for the five books listed in Figure 1-16, pressing the **Tab** key to move from one cell to the next, and pressing the **Enter** key to move to a new row. See Figure 1-17. The text in some cells will be partially hidden; you will fix that problem shortly.

Figure 1-17   **Tobias Gregson's partial book order**

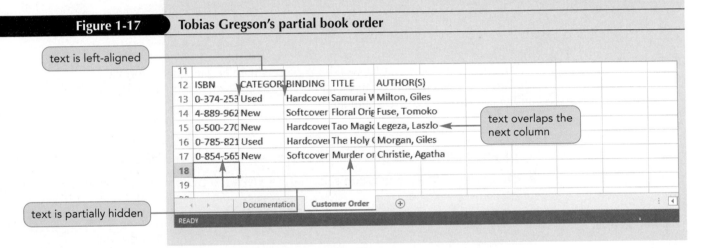

Entering Numbers

In Excel, numbers can be integers such as 378, decimals such as 1.95, or negatives such as −5.2. In the case of currency and percentages, you can include the currency symbol and percent sign when you enter the value. Excel treats a currency value such as $87.25 as the number 87.25, and a percentage such as 95% as the decimal 0.95. Much like dates, currency and percentages are formatted in a convenient way for you to read, but only the number is stored within the cell. This makes it easier to perform calculations with currency and percentage values.

You will complete the information for Tobias Gregson's order by entering the price for each title and the quantity of each title he ordered.

To enter the price and quantity of books ordered:

1. In the range F12:G12, enter **PRICE** and **QTY** as the labels.

2. In cell F13, enter **$5.95** as the price of the first book. The book price is stored as a number but displayed with the $ symbol.

3. In cell G13, enter **2** as the quantity of books ordered.

4. In the range F14:G17, enter the remaining prices and quantities shown in Figure 1-16. See Figure 1-18.

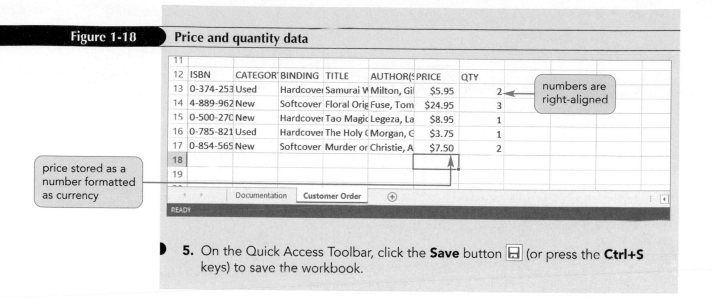

Figure 1-18   **Price and quantity data**

	ISBN	CATEGOR'	BINDING	TITLE	AUTHOR(S	PRICE	QTY	
11								
12	ISBN	CATEGOR'	BINDING	TITLE	AUTHOR(S	PRICE	QTY	
13	0-374-253	Used	Hardcover	Samurai W	Milton, Gil	$5.95	2	numbers are right-aligned
14	4-889-962	New	Softcover	Floral Orig	Fuse, Tom	$24.95	3	
15	0-500-270	New	Hardcover	Tao Magic	Legeza, La	$8.95	1	
16	0-785-821	Used	Hardcover	The Holy (	Morgan, G	$3.75	1	
17	0-854-565	New	Softcover	Murder or	Christie, A	$7.50	2	
18								
19								

price stored as a number formatted as currency

Documentation | Customer Order | (+)

READY

5. On the Quick Access Toolbar, click the **Save** button 🖫 (or press the **Ctrl+S** keys) to save the workbook.

Resizing Columns and Rows

Much of the information in the Customer Order worksheet is difficult to read because of the hidden text. You can make the cell content easier to read by changing the size of the columns and rows in the worksheet.

Changing Column Widths

Column widths are expressed as the number of characters the column can contain. The default column width is 8.43 standard-sized characters. In general, this means that you can type eight characters in a cell; any additional text is hidden or overlaps the adjacent cell. Column widths are also expressed in terms of pixels. A **pixel** is a single point on a computer monitor or printout. A column width of 8.43 characters is equivalent to 64 pixels.

Setting Column Widths

On a computer monitor, pixel size is based on screen resolution. As a result, cell contents that look fine on one screen might appear very different when viewed on a screen with a different resolution. If you work on multiple computers or share your workbooks with others, you should set column widths based on the maximum number of characters you want displayed in the cells rather than pixel size. This ensures that everyone sees the cell contents the way you intended.

You will increase the width of column A so that the contact information labels in cells A4 and A5 and the ISBN numbers in the range A13:A17 are completely displayed.

To increase the width of column A:

1. Move the pointer over the right border of the column A heading until the pointer changes to ╂.

2. Click and drag to the right until the width of the column heading reaches **15** characters, but do not release the mouse button. The ScreenTip that appears as you resize the column shows the new column width in characters and in pixels.

3. Release the mouse button. The width of column A expands to 15 characters, and all of the text within that column is visible within the cells. See Figure 1-19.

| Figure 1-19 | Width of column A increased |

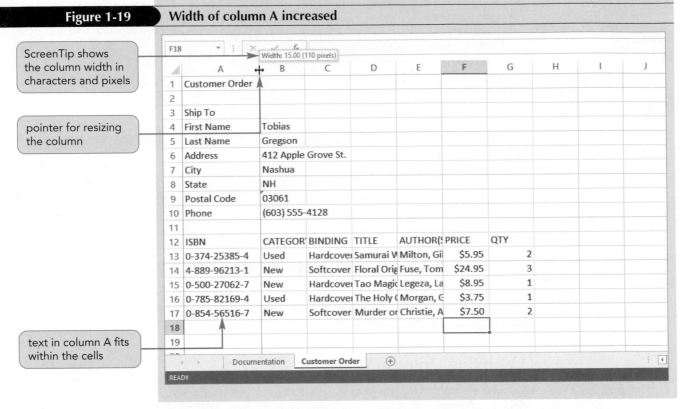

ScreenTip shows the column width in characters and pixels

pointer for resizing the column

text in column A fits within the cells

You will increase the widths of columns B and C to 18 characters so that their complete entries are visible. Rather than resizing each column separately, you can select both columns and adjust their widths at the same time.

To increase the widths of columns B and C:

1. Click the **column B** heading. The entire column is selected.

2. Hold down the **Ctrl** key, click the **column C** heading, and then release the **Ctrl** key. Both columns B and C are selected.

3. Move the pointer to the right border of the column C heading until the pointer changes to ✛.

4. Drag to the right until the column width changes to **18** characters, and then release the mouse button. Both column widths increase to 18 characters and display all of the entered text.

TIP

To select multiple columns, you can also click and drag the pointer over multiple column headings.

The book titles in column D are partially hidden. You will increase the width of this column to 30 characters. Rather than using your mouse, you can set the column width using the Format command on the HOME tab. The Format command gives you precise control over setting column widths and row heights.

To set the width of column D with the Format command:

1. Click the **column D** heading. The entire column is selected.

2. On the HOME tab, in the Cells group, click the **Format** button, and then click **Column Width**. The Column Width dialog box opens.

3. Type **30** in the Column width box to specify the new column width.

4. Click the **OK** button. The width of column D changes to 30 characters.

5. Change the width of column E to **15** characters.

6. Click cell **A1**. The revised column widths are shown in Figure 1-20.

Figure 1-20 Resized columns

TIP

If the row or column is blank, autofitting restores its default height or width.

Even with the width of column D increased, some of the book titles still don't fit within the allotted space. Instead of manually changing the column width to display all of the text, you can autofit the column. **AutoFit** changes the column width or row height to display the longest or tallest entry within the column or row. You autofit a column or a row by double-clicking the right border of the column heading or the bottom border of the row heading.

To autofit the contents of column D:

1. Move the pointer over the right border of column D until the pointer changes to ✛.

2. Double-click the right border of the column D heading. The width of column D increases to about 54 characters so that the longest book title is completely visible.

Wrapping Text Within a Cell

Sometimes, resizing a column width to display all of the text entered in the cells makes the worksheet more difficult to read. This is the case with column D in the Customer Order worksheet. Another way to display long text entries is to wrap text to a new line when it extends beyond the column width. When text wraps within a cell, the row height increases so that all of the text within the cell is displayed.

You will resize column D, and then wrap the text entries in the column.

To wrap text in column D:

1. Resize the width of column D to **30** characters.

2. Select the range **D13:D17**. These cells include the titles that extend beyond the new cell width.

3. On the HOME tab, in the Alignment group, click the **Wrap Text** button. The Wrap Text button is toggled on, and text in the selected cells that exceeds the column width wraps to a new line.

4. Click cell **A12** to make it the active cell. See Figure 1-21.

Figure 1-21 **Text wrapped within cells**

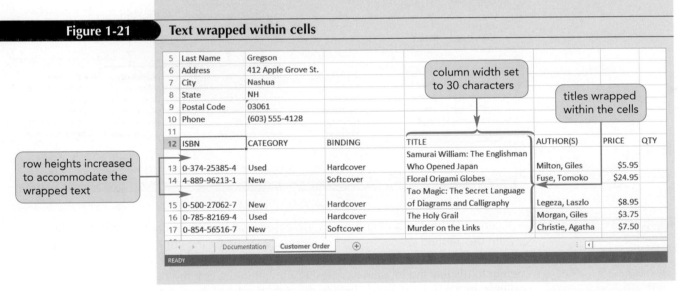

If you want to create a new line within a cell, press the Alt+Enter keys to move the insertion point to the next line within the cell. Whatever you type next will appear on the new line in the cell.

Changing Row Heights

The height of a row is measured in points or pixels. A **point** is approximately 1/72 of an inch. The default row height is 15 points or 20 pixels. Row heights are set in the same way as column widths. You can drag the bottom border of the row heading to a new row height, specify a row height using the Format command, or autofit the row's height to match its content.

Sanjit wants you add more space above the labels in the book list by resizing row 12.

To increase the height of row 12:

1. Move the pointer over the bottom border of the row 12 heading until the pointer changes to ✛.

TIP

You can also set the row height by clicking the Format button in the Cells group on the HOME tab and then using the Row Height command.

2. Drag the bottom border down until the height of the row is equal to **30** points (or **40** pixels), and then release the mouse button. The height of row 12 is set to 30 points.

3. Press the **Ctrl+S** keys to save the workbook.

You have entered most of the data for Tobias Gregson's order at Sparrow & Pond. In the next session, you will calculate the total charge for the order and print the worksheet.

Session 1.1 Quick Check

REVIEW

1. What are the two types of sheets used in a workbook?
2. What is the cell reference for the cell located in the fourth column and third row of a worksheet?
3. What is the range reference for the block of cells B10 through C15?
4. What is the reference for the nonadjacent block of cells B10 through C15 and cells B20 through D25?
5. What keyboard shortcut changes the active cell to cell A1?
6. What is text data?
7. Cell A4 contains *May 3, 2016*; why doesn't Excel consider this entry a text string?
8. How do you resize a column or row?

Session 1.2 Visual Overview:

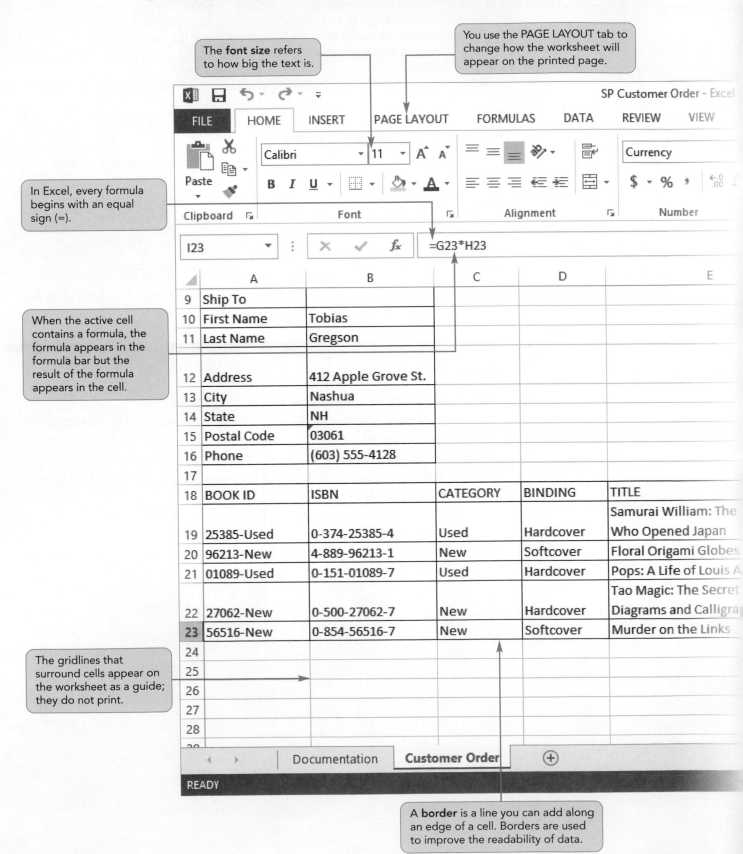

The **font size** refers to how big the text is.

You use the PAGE LAYOUT tab to change how the worksheet will appear on the printed page.

In Excel, every formula begins with an equal sign (=).

When the active cell contains a formula, the formula appears in the formula bar but the result of the formula appears in the cell.

The gridlines that surround cells appear on the worksheet as a guide; they do not print.

A **border** is a line you can add along an edge of a cell. Borders are used to improve the readability of data.

SP Customer Order - Excel

Formula bar: =G23*H23

	A	B	C	D	E
9	Ship To				
10	First Name	Tobias			
11	Last Name	Gregson			
12	Address	412 Apple Grove St.			
13	City	Nashua			
14	State	NH			
15	Postal Code	03061			
16	Phone	(603) 555-4128			
17					
18	BOOK ID	ISBN	CATEGORY	BINDING	TITLE
19	25385-Used	0-374-25385-4	Used	Hardcover	Samurai William: The Who Opened Japan
20	96213-New	4-889-96213-1	New	Softcover	Floral Origami Globes
21	01089-Used	0-151-01089-7	Used	Hardcover	Pops: A Life of Louis A
22	27062-New	0-500-27062-7	New	Hardcover	Tao Magic: The Secret Diagrams and Calligra
23	56516-New	0-854-56516-7	New	Softcover	Murder on the Links
24					
25					
26					
27					
28					

Documentation   **Customer Order**   ⊕

READY

Formulas and Functions

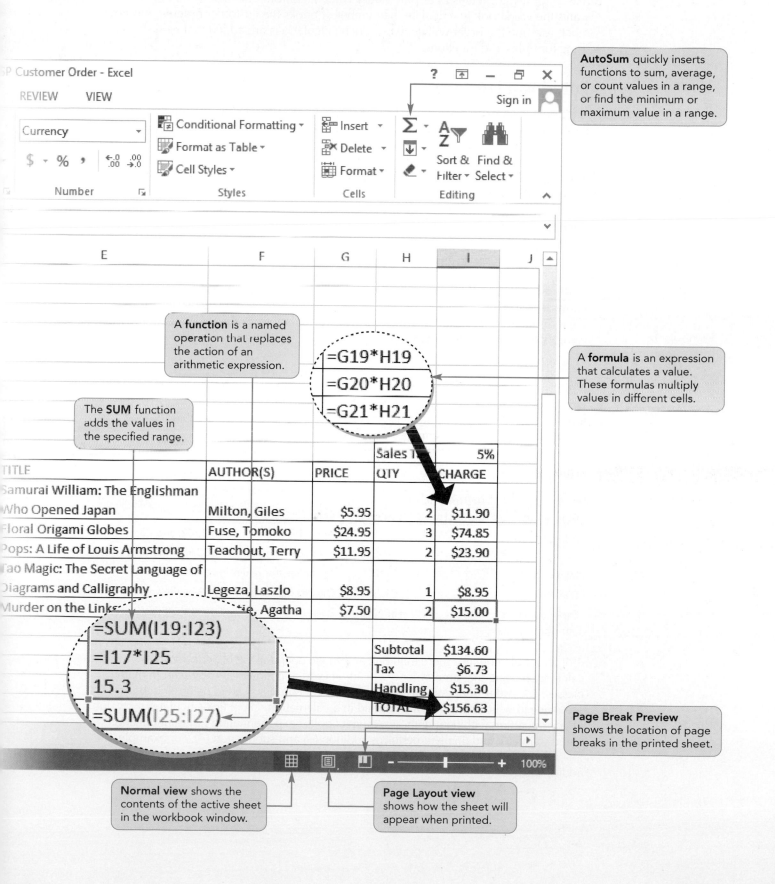

AutoSum quickly inserts functions to sum, average, or count values in a range, or find the minimum or maximum value in a range.

A **function** is a named operation that replaces the action of an arithmetic expression.

A **formula** is an expression that calculates a value. These formulas multiply values in different cells.

The **SUM** function adds the values in the specified range.

=G19*H19
=G20*H20
=G21*H21

TITLE	AUTHOR(S)	PRICE	QTY	CHARGE
			Sales Tax	5%
Samurai William: The Englishman Who Opened Japan	Milton, Giles	$5.95	2	$11.90
Floral Origami Globes	Fuse, Tomoko	$24.95	3	$74.85
Pops: A Life of Louis Armstrong	Teachout, Terry	$11.95	2	$23.90
Tao Magic: The Secret Language of Diagrams and Calligraphy	Legeza, Laszlo	$8.95	1	$8.95
Murder on the Links	tie, Agatha	$7.50	2	$15.00
			Subtotal	$134.60
			Tax	$6.73
			Handling	$15.30
			TOTAL	$156.63

=SUM(I19:I23)
=I17*I25
15.3
=SUM(I25:I27)

Page Break Preview shows the location of page breaks in the printed sheet.

Normal view shows the contents of the active sheet in the workbook window.

Page Layout view shows how the sheet will appear when printed.

Adding Formulas to a Worksheet

So far you have entered text, numbers, and dates in the worksheet. However, the main reason for using Excel is to display values calculated from data. For example, Sally wants the workbook to calculate the number of books the customer ordered and how much revenue the order will generate. Such calculations are added to a worksheet using formulas and functions.

Entering a Formula

A formula is an expression that returns a value. In most cases, this is a number—though it could also be text or a date. In Excel, every formula begins with an equal sign (=) followed by an expression describing the operation that returns the value. If you don't begin the formula with the equal sign, Excel assumes that you are entering text and will not treat the cell contents as a formula.

A formula is written using **operators** that combine different values, resulting in a single value that is then displayed in the cell. The most common operators are **arithmetic operators** that perform addition, subtraction, multiplication, division, and exponentiation. For example, the following formula adds 5 and 7, returning a value of 12:

=5+7

Most Excel formulas contain references to cells rather than specific values. This allows you to change the values used in the calculation without having to modify the formula itself. For example, the following formula returns the result of adding the values stored in cells A1 and B2:

=A1+B2

If the value 5 is stored in cell A1 and the value 7 is stored in cell B2, this formula would also return a value of 12. If you later changed the value in cell A1 to 10, the formula would return a value of 17. Figure 1-22 describes the different arithmetic operators and provides examples of formulas.

Figure 1-22 Arithmetic operators

Operation	Arithmetic Operator	Example	Description
Addition	+	=B1+B2+B3	Adds the values in cells B1, B2, and B3
Subtraction	–	=C9–B2	Subtracts the value in cell B2 from the value in cell C9
Multiplication	*	=C9*B9	Multiplies the values in cells C9 and B9
Division	/	=C9/B9	Divides the value in cell C9 by the value in cell B9
Exponentiation	^	=B5^3	Raises the value of cell B5 to the third power

© 2014 Cengage Learning

If a formula contains more than one arithmetic operator, Excel performs the calculation using the same order of operations you might have already seen in math classes. The **order of operations** is a set of predefined rules used to determine the sequence in which operators are applied in a calculation. Excel first calculates the value of any operation within parentheses, then it applies exponentiation (^), multiplication (*), and division (/), and finally it performs addition (+) and subtraction (–). For example, the following formula returns the value 23 because multiplying 4 by 5 takes precedence over adding 3:

=3+4*5

If a formula contains two or more operators with the same level of priority, the operators are applied in order from left to right. In the following formula, Excel first multiplies 4 by 10 and then divides that result by 8 to return the value 5:

=4*10/8

When parentheses are used, the value inside them is calculated first. In the following formula, Excel calculates (3+4) first, and then multiplies that result by 5 to return the value 35:

=(3+4)*5

Figure 1-23 shows how slight changes in a formula affect the order of operations and the result of the formula.

| Figure 1-23 | Order of operations applied to Excel formulas |

Formula	Application of the Order of Operations	Result
=50+10*5	10*5 calculated first and then 50 is added	100
=(50+10)*5	(50+10) calculated first and then 60 is multiplied by 5	300
=50/10–5	50/10 calculated first and then 5 is subtracted	0
=50/(10–5)	(10–5) calculated first and then 50 is divided by that value	10
=50/10*5	Two operators at same precedence level, so the calculation is done left to right in the expression	25
=50/(10*5)	(10*5) is calculated first and then 50 is divided by that value	1

© 2014 Cengage Learning

Sally wants the Customer Order worksheet to include the total amount charged for each book. The charge is equal to the number of books ordered multiplied by the book's price. You already entered this information in columns F and G. Now you will enter a formula to calculate the charge for books ordered in column H.

To enter the formula to calculate the charge for the first book order:

▸ 1. Make cell **H12** the active cell, type **CHARGE** as the column label, and then press the **Enter** key. The label text is entered in cell H12, and cell H13 is now the active cell.

▸ 2. Type **=F13*G13** (the price of the book multiplied by the quantity of books ordered). As you type the formula, a list of Excel function names appears in a ScreenTip, which provides a quick method for entering functions. The list will close when you complete the formula. You will learn more about Excel functions shortly. Also, as you type each cell reference, Excel color codes the cell reference with the cell. See Figure 1-24.

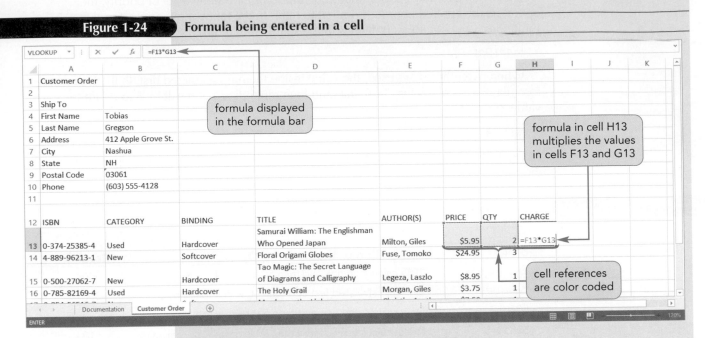

Figure 1-24 Formula being entered in a cell

3. Press the **Enter** key. The formula is entered in cell H13, which displays the value $11.90. The result is displayed as currency because cell F13, which is referenced in the formula, contains a currency value.

4. Click cell **H13** to make it the active cell. The cell displays the result of the formula, and the formula bar displays the formula you entered.

For the first book, you entered the formula by typing each cell reference in the expression. You can also insert a cell reference by clicking the cell as you type the formula. This technique reduces the possibility of error caused by typing an incorrect cell reference. You will use this method to enter the formula to calculate the charge for the second book.

To enter the cell references in the formula using the mouse:

1. Click cell **H14** to make it the active cell.

2. Type **=**. The equal sign indicates that you are entering a formula. Any cell you click from now on inserts the cell reference of the selected cell into the formula until you complete the formula by pressing the Enter or Tab key.

3. Click cell **F14**. The cell reference is inserted into the formula in the formula bar. At this point, any cell you click changes the cell reference used in the formula. The cell reference isn't locked until you type an operator.

4. Type ***** to enter the multiplication operator. The cell reference for cell F14 is locked in the formula, and the next cell you click will be inserted after the operator.

5. Click cell **G14** to enter its cell reference in the formula. The formula is complete.

6. Press the **Enter** key. Cell H14 displays the value $74.85, which is the total charge for the second book.

Be sure to type = as the first part of the entry; otherwise, Excel will not interpret the entry as a formula.

Copying and Pasting Formulas

Sometimes you will need to repeat the same formula throughout a worksheet. Rather than retyping the formula, you can copy a formula from one cell and paste it into another cell. When you copy a formula, Excel places the formula into the **Clipboard**, which is a temporary storage location for text and graphics. When you paste, Excel takes the formula from the Clipboard and inserts it into the selected cell or range. Excel adjusts the cell references in the formula to reflect the formula's new location in the worksheet. This occurs because you usually want to copy the actions of a formula rather than the specific value the formula generates. In this case, the formula's action is to multiply the price of the book by the quantity. By copying and pasting the formula, you can quickly repeat that action for every book listed in the worksheet.

You will copy the formula you entered in cell H14 to the range H15:H17 to calculate the charges on the remaining three books in Tobias Gregson's order. By copying and pasting the formula, you will save time and avoid potential mistakes from retyping the formula.

To copy and paste the formula:

1. Click cell **H14** to select the cell that contains the formula you want to copy.

2. On the HOME tab, in the Clipboard group, click the **Copy** button (or press the **Ctrl+C** keys). Excel copies the formula to the Clipboard.

3. Select the range **H15:H17**. You want to paste the formula into these cells.

4. In the Clipboard group, click the **Paste** button (or press the **Ctrl+V** keys). Excel pastes the formula into the selected cells, adjusting each formula so that the total charges calculated for the books are based on the corresponding values within each row. A button appears below the selected range, providing options for pasting formulas and values. See Figure 1-25.

Figure 1-25   Copied and pasted formula

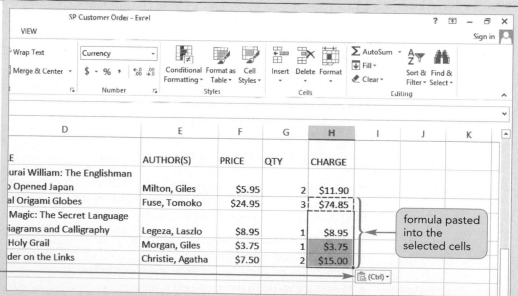

5. Click cell **H15** and verify that the formula =F15*G15 appears in the formula bar. The formula was updated to reflect the cell references in the corresponding row.

6. Click the other cells in column H and verify that the corresponding formulas are entered in those cells.

Simplifying Formulas with Functions

In addition to cell references and operators, formulas can also contain functions. A function is a named operation that replaces the arithmetic expression in a formula. Functions are used to simplify long or complex formulas. For example, to add the values from cells A1 through A10, you could enter the following long formula:

   =A1+A2+A3+A4+A5+A6+A7+A8+A9+A10

Or, you could use the SUM function to calculate the sum of those cell values by entering the following formula:

   =SUM(A1:A10)

In both instances, Excel adds the values in cells A1 through A10, but the SUM function is faster and simpler to enter and less prone to a typing error. You should always use a function, if one is available, in place of a long, complex formula. Excel supports more than 300 different functions from the fields of finance, business, science, and engineering. Excel provides functions that work with numbers, text, and dates.

Introducing Function Syntax

Every function follows a set of rules, or **syntax**, which specifies how the function should be written. The general syntax of all Excel functions is

   FUNCTION (argument1, argument2, …)

where *FUNCTION* is the function name, and *argument1, argument2*, and so forth are values used by that function. For example, the SUM function shown above uses a single argument, A1:A10, which is the range reference of the cells whose values will be added. Some functions do not require any arguments and are entered as *FUNCTION*(). Functions without arguments still require the opening and closing parentheses, but do not include a value within the parentheses.

Entering Functions with AutoSum

A fast and convenient way to enter commonly used functions is with AutoSum. The AutoSum button includes options to insert the SUM, AVERAGE, COUNT, MIN, and MAX functions to generate the following:

- Sum of the values in the specified range
- Average value in the specified range
- Total count of numeric values in the specified range
- Minimum value in the specified range
- Maximum value in the specified range

After you select one of the AutoSum options, Excel determines the most appropriate range from the available data and enters it as the function's argument. You should always verify that the range included in the AutoSum function matches the range that you want to use.

You will use AutoSum to enter the SUM function to add the total charges for Tobias Gregson's order.

To use AutoSum to enter the SUM function:

1. Click cell **G18** to make it the active cell, type **Subtotal** as the label, and then press the **Tab** key to make cell H18 the active cell.

2. On the HOME tab, in the Editing group, click the **AutoSum button arrow**. The button's menu opens and displays five common summary functions: Sum, Average, Count Numbers, Max (for maximum), and Min (for minimum).

3. Click **Sum** to enter the SUM function. The formula =SUM(H13:H17) is entered in cell H18. The cells involved in calculating the sum are selected and highlighted on the worksheet so you can quickly confirm that Excel selected the most appropriate range from the available data. A ScreenTip appears below the formula describing the function's syntax. See Figure 1-26.

| Figure 1-26 | SUM function being entered with the AutoSum button |

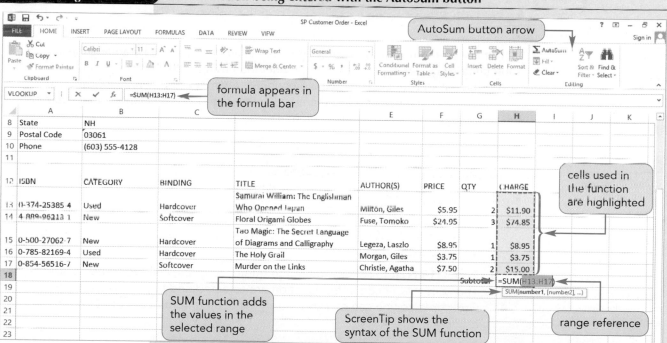

4. Press the **Enter** key to accept the formula. The subtotal of the book charges returned by the SUM function is $114.45.

AutoSum makes entering a commonly used formula such as the SUM function fast and easy. However, AutoSum can determine the appropriate range reference to include only when the function is adjacent to the cells containing the values you want to summarize. If you need to use a function elsewhere in the worksheet, you will have to select the range reference to include or type the function yourself.

Each sale made by Sparrow & Pond is subject to a 5 percent sales tax and a $15.30 handling fee. You will add these to the Customer Order worksheet so you can calculate the total charge for the order.

To add the sales tax and handling fee to the worksheet:

▶ 1. Click cell **G11**, type **Sales Tax** as the label, and then press the **Tab** key to make cell H11 the active cell.

▶ 2. In cell H11, type **5%** as the sales tax rate, and then press the **Enter** key. The sales tax rate is entered in the cell, and can be used in other calculations. The value is displayed with the % symbol, but is stored as the equivalent decimal value 0.05.

▶ 3. Click cell **G19** to make it the active cell, type **Tax** as the label, and then press the **Tab** key to make cell H19 the active cell.

▶ 4. Type **=H11*H18** as the formula to calculate the sales tax on the book order, and then press the **Enter** key. The formula multiples the sales tax value in cell H11 by the order subtotal value in cell H18. The value $5.72 is displayed in cell H19, which is 5 percent of the book order subtotal of $114.45.

▶ 5. In cell G20, type **Handling** as the label, and then press the **Tab** key to make cell H20 the active cell. You will enter the handling fee in this cell.

▶ 6. Type **$15.30** as the handling fee, and then press the **Enter** key.

The last part of the customer order is to calculate the total cost by adding the subtotal, the tax, and the handling fee. Rather than using AutoSum, you will type the SUM function so you can enter the correct range reference for the function. You can type the range reference or select the range in the worksheet. Remember, that you must type parentheses around the range reference.

To calculate the total order cost:

▶ 1. In cell G21, type **TOTAL** as the label, and then press the **Tab** key.

▶ 2. Type =**SUM(** in cell H21 to enter the function name and the opening parenthesis. As you begin to type the function, a ScreenTip lists the names of all functions that start with S.

▶ 3. Type **H18:H20** to specify the range reference of the cells you want to add. The cells referenced in the function are selected and highlighted on the worksheet so you can quickly confirm that you entered the correct range reference.

Make sure the cell reference in the function matches the range you want to calculate.

4. Type **)** to complete the function, and then press the **Enter** key. The value of the SUM function appears in cell H21, indicating that the total charge for the order is $135.47. See Figure 1-27.

Figure 1-27   **Total charge for the customer order**

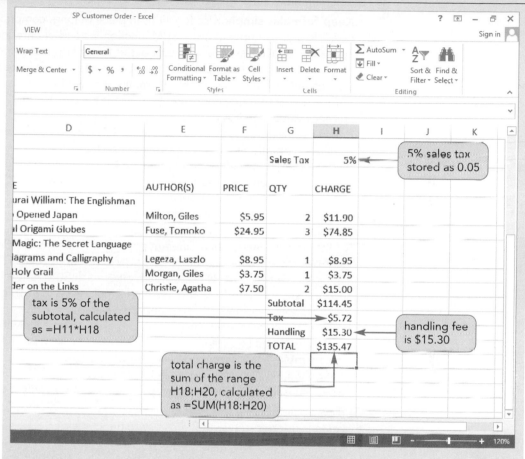

The SUM function makes it simple to quickly add the values in a group of cells.

Problem Solving: Writing Effective Formulas

You can use formulas to quickly perform calculations and solve problems. First, identify the problem you need to solve. Then, gather the data needed to solve the problem. Finally, create accurate and effective formulas that use the data to answer or resolve the problem. Follow these guidelines:

- **Keep formulas simple.** Use functions in place of long, complex formulas whenever possible. For example, use the SUM function instead of entering a formula that adds individual cells, which makes it easier to confirm that the formula is making an accurate calculation as it provides answers needed to evaluate the problem.
- **Do not hide data values within formulas.** The worksheet displays formula results, not the actual formula. For example, to calculate a 5 percent interest rate on a currency value in cell A5, you could enter the formula =0.05*A5. However, this doesn't show how the value is calculated. A better approach places the value 0.05 in a cell accompanied by a descriptive label and uses the cell reference in the formula. If you place 0.05 in cell A6, the formula =A6*A5 would calculate the interest value. Other people can then easily see the interest rate as well as the resulting interest, ensuring that the formula is solving the right problem.
- **Break up formulas to show intermediate results.** When a worksheet contains complex computations, other people can more easily comprehend how the formula results are calculated when different parts of the formula are distinguished. For example, the formula =SUM(A1:A10)/SUM(B1:B10) calculates the ratio of two sums, but hides the two sum values. Instead, enter each SUM function in a separate cell, such as cells A11 and B11, and use the formula =A11/B11 to calculate the ratio. Other people can see both sums and the value of their ratio in the worksheet and better understand the final result, which makes it more likely that the best problem resolution will be selected.
- **Test formulas with simple values.** Use values you can calculate in your head to confirm that your formula works as intended. For example, using 1s or 10s as the input values lets you easily figure out the answer and verify the formula.

Finding a solution to a problem requires accurate data and analysis. With workbooks, this means using formulas that are easy to understand, clearly show the data being used in the calculations, and demonstrate how the results are calculated. Only then can you be confident that you are choosing the best problem resolution.

Modifying a Worksheet

As you develop a worksheet, you might need to modify its content and structure to create a more logical organization. Some ways you can modify a worksheet include moving cells and ranges, inserting rows and columns, deleting rows and columns, and inserting and deleting cells.

Moving and Copying a Cell or Range

One way to move a cell or range is to select it, position the pointer over the bottom border of the selection, drag the selection to a new location, and then release the mouse button. This technique is called **drag and drop** because you are dragging the range and dropping it in a new location. If the drop location is not visible, drag the selection to the edge of the workbook window to scroll the worksheet, and then drop the selection.

You can also use the drag-and-drop technique to copy cells by pressing the Ctrl key as you drag the selected range to its new location. A copy of the original range is placed in the new location without removing the original range from the worksheet.

Moving or Copying a Cell or Range

- Select the cell or range you want to move or copy.
- Move the pointer over the border of the selection until the pointer changes shape.
- To move the range, click the border and drag the selection to a new location (or to copy the range, hold down the Ctrl key and drag the selection to a new location).

or

- Select the cell or range you want to move or copy.
- On the HOME tab, in the Clipboard group, click the Cut or Copy button (or right-click the selection, and then click Cut or Copy on the shortcut menu, or press the Ctrl+X or Ctrl+C keys).
- Select the cell or the upper-left cell of the range where you want to paste the content.
- In the Clipboard group, click the Paste button (or right-click the selection and then click Paste on the shortcut menu, or press the Ctrl+V keys).

Sally wants the subtotal, tax, handling, and total values in the range G18:H21 moved down one row to the range G19:H22 to provide more space from the book orders. You will use the drag-and-drop method to move the range.

To drag and drop the range G18:H21:

1. Select the range **G18:H21**. These are the cells you want to move.

2. Move the pointer over the bottom border of the selected range so that the pointer changes to ⇱.

3. Press and hold the mouse button to change the pointer to ⇱, and then drag the selection down one row. Do not release the mouse button. A ScreenTip appears, indicating that the new range of the selected cells will be G19:H22. A darker border also appears around the new range. See Figure 1-28.

Figure 1-28   **Range G18:H21 being moved to range G19:H22**

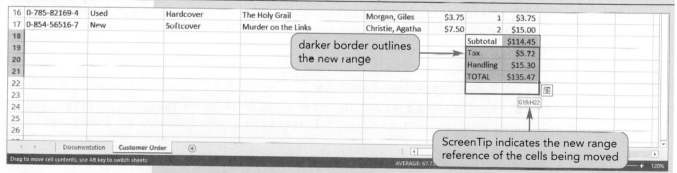

4. Make sure the ScreenTip displays the range **G19:H22**, and then release the mouse button. The selected cells move to their new location.

Some people find dragging and dropping a difficult and awkward way to move a selection, particularly if the selected range is large or needs to move a long distance in the worksheet. In those situations, it is often more efficient to cut or copy and paste the cell contents. Cutting moves the selected content, whereas copying duplicates the selected content. Pasting places the selected content in the new location.

Sally wants the worksheet to include a summary of the customer order starting in row 3. You will cut the customer contact information and the book listing from range A3:A22 and paste it into range A9:H23, freeing up space for the order information.

To cut and paste the customer contact information and book listing:

▶ **1.** Click cell **A3** to select it.

▶ **2.** Press the **Ctrl+Shift+End** keys to extend the selection to the last cell in the lower-right corner of the worksheet (cell H22).

▶ **3.** On the HOME tab, in the Clipboard group, click the **Cut** button (or press the **Ctrl+X** keys). The range is surrounded by a moving border, indicating that it has been cut.

▶ **4.** Click cell **A9** to select it. This is the upper-left corner of the range where you want to paste the range that you cut.

▶ **5.** In the Clipboard group, click the **Paste** button (or press the **Ctrl+V** keys). The range A3:H22 is pasted into the range A9:H28. All of the formulas in the moved range were automatically updated to reflect their new locations.

Using the COUNT Function

Sometimes you will want to know how many unique items are included in a range, such as the number of different books in the customer order. To calculate that value, you use the COUNT function, which has the syntax

```
=COUNT(range)
```

where *range* is the range of cells containing numeric values to be counted. Note that any cell in the range containing a non-numeric value is not counted in the final tally.

You will include the count of the number of different books for the order in the summary information. The summary will also display the order ID (a unique number assigned by Sparrow & Pond to the order), the shipping date, and the type of delivery (overnight, two-day, or standard) in the freed-up space at the top of the worksheet. In addition, Sally wants the total charge for the order to be displayed with the order summary so she does not have to scroll to the bottom of the worksheet to find that value.

To add the order summary:

▶ **1.** Click cell **A3**, type **Order ID** as the label, press the **Tab** key, type **14123** in cell B3, and then press the **Enter** key. The order ID is entered, and cell A4 is the active cell.

▶ **2.** Type **Shipping Date** as the label in cell A4, press the **Tab** key, type **4/3/2016** in cell B4, and then press the **Enter** key. The shipping date is entered, and cell A5 is the active cell.

▶ **3.** Type **Delivery** as the label in cell A5, press the **Tab** key, type **Overnight** in cell B5, and then press the **Enter** key. The delivery type is entered, and cell A6 is the active cell.

▶ **4.** Type **Items Ordered** as the label in cell A6, and then press the **Tab** key. Cell B6 is the active cell. You will enter the COUNT function to determine the number of different books ordered.

▶ **5.** In cell B6, type **=COUNT(** to begin the function.

6. With the insertion point still blinking in cell B6, select the range **G19:G23**. The range reference is entered as the argument for the COUNT function.

7. Type **)** to complete the function, and then press the **Enter** key. Cell B6 displays the value 5, indicating that five items were ordered by Tobias Gregson. Cell A7 is the active cell.

8. Type **Total Charge** as the label in cell A7, and then press the **Tab** key to make cell B7 the active cell.

9. Type **=** to start the formula, and then click cell **H28** to enter its cell reference in the formula in cell B7. The formula =H28 tells Excel to display the contents of cell H28 in the current cell.

10. Press the **Enter** key to complete the formula. See Figure 1-29.

| Figure 1-29 | Customer order summary |

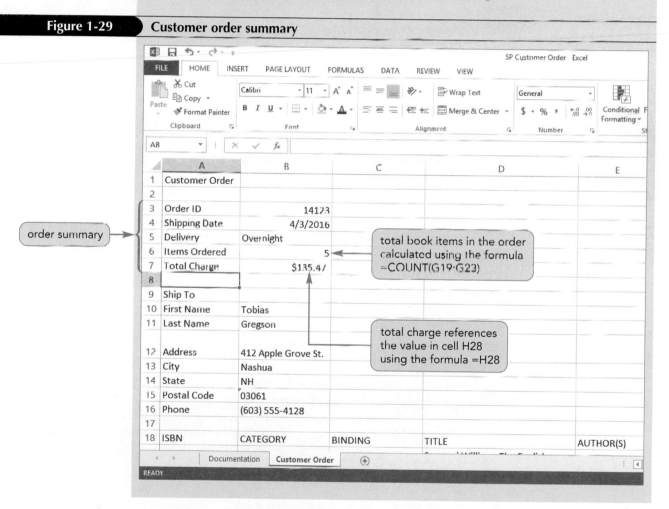

Inserting a Column or Row

You can insert a new column or row anywhere within a worksheet. When you insert a new column, the existing columns are shifted to the right and the new column has the same width as the column directly to its left. When you insert a new row, the existing rows are shifted down and the new row has the same height as the row above it. Because inserting a new row or column moves the location of the other cells in the worksheet, any cell references in a formula or function are updated to reflect the new layout.

REFERENCE

Inserting or Deleting a Column or Row

To insert a column or row:
- Select the column(s) or row(s) where you want to insert the new column(s) or row(s). Excel will insert the same number of columns or rows as you select to the *left* of the selected columns or *above* the selected rows.
- On the HOME tab, in the Cells group, click the Insert button (or right-click a column or row heading or selected column and row headings, and then click Insert on the shortcut menu; or press the Ctrl+Shift+= keys).

To delete a column or row:
- Select the column(s) or row(s) you want to delete.
- On the HOME tab, in the Cells group, click the Delete button (or right-click a column or row heading or selected column and row headings, and then click Delete on the shortcut menu; or press the Ctrl+− keys).

Tobias Gregson's order is missing an item. You need to insert a row directly below *Floral Origami Globes* in which to enter the additional book.

To insert a new row for the missing book order:

1. Click the **row 21** heading to select the entire row.

TIP

You can insert multiple columns or rows by selecting that number of column or row headings, and then clicking the Insert button or pressing the Ctrl+Shift+= keys.

2. On the HOME tab, in the Cells group, click the **Insert** button (or press the **Ctrl+Shift+=** keys). A new row is inserted below row 20 and becomes the new row 21.

3. Enter **0-151-01089-7** in cell A21, enter **Used** in cell B21, enter **Hardcover** in cell C21, enter **Pops: A Life of Louis Armstrong** in cell D21, enter **Teachout, Terry** in cell E21, enter **$11.95** in cell F21, and then enter **2** in cell G21.

4. Click cell **H20** to select the cell with the formula for calculating the book charge, and then press the **Ctrl+C** keys to copy the formula in that cell.

5. Click cell **H21** to select the cell where you want to insert the formula, and then press the **Ctrl+V** keys to paste the formula into the cell.

6. Click cell **H26**. The formula in this cell is now =SUM(H19:H24); the range reference was updated to reflect the inserted row. Also, the tax amount increased to $6.92 based on the new subtotal value of $138.35, and the total charge increased to $160.57 because of the added book order. See Figure 1-30. Also, the result of the COUNT function in cell B6 increased to 6 to reflect the item added to the book order.

Figure 1-30   New row inserted

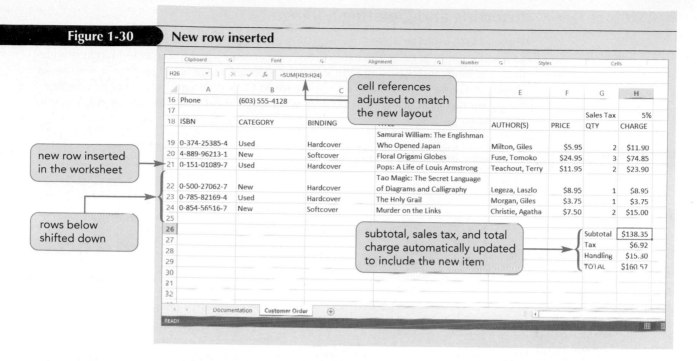

new row inserted in the worksheet

rows below shifted down

cell references adjusted to match the new layout

subtotal, sales tax, and total charge automatically updated to include the new item

Deleting a Row or Column

You can delete rows or columns from a worksheet. **Deleting** removes the data from the row or column as well as the row or column itself. The rows below the deleted row shift up to fill the vacated space. Likewise, the columns to the right of the deleted column shift left to fill the vacated space. Also, all cell references in the worksheet are adjusted to reflect the change. You click the Delete button in the Cells group on the HOME tab to delete selected rows or columns.

Deleting a column or row is not the same as clearing a column or row. **Clearing** removes the data from the selected row or column but leaves the blank row or column in the worksheet. You press the Delete key to clear the contents of the selected row or column, which leaves the worksheet structure unchanged.

Tobias Gregson did not order *The Holy Grail* by Giles Morgan, so that book needs to be removed from the order. You will delete the row containing that book.

To delete the *The Holy Grail* row from the book order:

1. Click the **row 23** heading to select the entire row.

2. On the HOME tab, in the Cells group, click the **Delete** button (or press the **Ctrl+−** keys). Row 23 is deleted, and the rows below it shift up to fill the space.

All of the cell references in the worksheet are again updated automatically to reflect the impact of deleting row 23. The subtotal value in cell H25 now returns a value of $134.60 based on the sum of the cells in the range H19:H23. The sales tax amount in cell H26 decreases to $6.73. The total cost of the order decreases to $156.63. Also, the result of the COUNT function in cell B6 decreases to 5 to reflect the item deleted from the book order. As you can see, one of the great advantages of using Excel is that it modifies the formulas to reflect the additions and deletions you make to the worksheet.

Inserting and Deleting a Range

You can also insert or delete ranges within a worksheet. When you use the Insert button to insert a range of cells, the existing cells shift down when the selected range is wider than it is long, and they shift right when the selected range is longer than it is wide, as shown in Figure 1-31. When you use the Insert Cells command, you specify whether the existing cells shift right or down, or whether to insert an entire row or column into the new range.

Figure 1-31	Cells being inserted in a worksheet

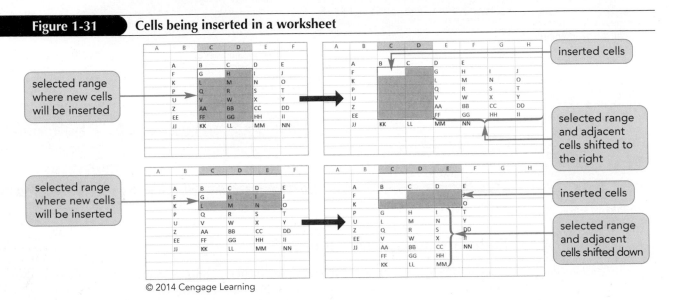

© 2014 Cengage Learning

The process works in reverse when you delete a range. As with deleting a row or column, the cells adjacent to the deleted range either move up or left to fill in the space vacated by the deleted cells. The Delete Cells command lets you specify whether you want to shift the adjacent cells left or up, or whether you want to delete the entire column or row.

When you insert or delete a range, cells that shift to a new location adopt the width of the columns they move into. As a result, you might need to resize columns and rows in the worksheet.

REFERENCE

Inserting or Deleting a Range

- Select a range that matches the range you want to insert or delete.
- On the HOME tab, in the Cells group, click the Insert button or the Delete button.

or

- Select the range that matches the range you want to insert or delete.
- On the HOME tab, in the Cells group, click the Insert button arrow and then click Insert Cells, or click the Delete button arrow and then click Delete Cells (or right-click the selected range, and then click Insert or Delete on the shortcut menu).
- Click the option button for the direction to shift the cells, columns, or rows.
- Click the OK button.

Sally wants you to insert cells in the book list that will contain the Sparrow & Pond book ID for each book. You will insert these new cells into the range A17:A28, shifting the adjacent cells to the right.

To insert a range in the book list:

1. Select the range **A17:A28**. You want to insert cells in this range.

2. On the HOME tab, in the Cells group, click the **Insert button arrow**. A menu of insert options appears.

3. Click **Insert Cells**. The Insert dialog box opens.

4. Verify that the **Shift cells right** option button is selected.

5. Click the **OK** button. New cells are inserted into the selected range, and the adjacent cells move to the right. The cell contents do not fit well in the columns and rows they shifted into, so you will resize the columns and rows.

6. Resize columns C and D to **12** characters, resize column E to **30** characters, and then resize column F to **15** characters. The text is easier to read in the resized columns.

7. Select the row **19** through row **23** headings.

8. In the Cells group, click the **Format** button, and then click **AutoFit Row Height**. The selected rows autofit to their contents.

9. Click cell **A18**, type **BOOK ID** as the label, and then press the **Enter** key. See Figure 1-32.

TIP

You can also autofit by double-clicking the bottom border of row 23.

| Figure 1-32 | Range added to the worksheet |

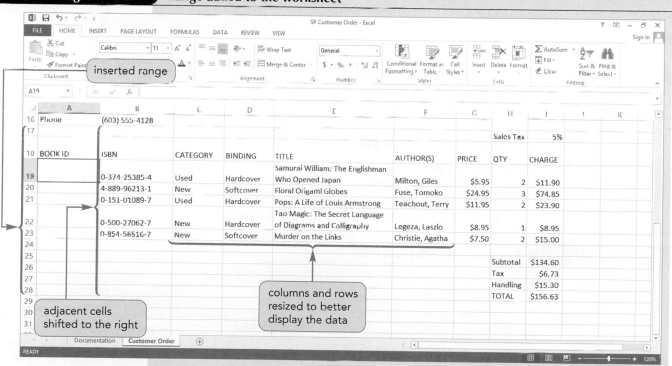

Why did you insert cells in the range A17:A28 even though the book ID values will be entered only in the range A18:A23? You did this to retain the layout of the page design. Selecting the additional rows ensures that the sales tax and summary values still line up with the QTY and CHARGE columns. Whenever you insert a new range, be sure to consider its impact on the layout of the entire worksheet.

Hiding and Unhiding Rows, Columns, and Worksheets

Workbooks can become long and complicated, filled with formulas and data that are important for performing calculations but are of little interest to readers. In those situations, you can simplify these workbooks for readers by **hiding** rows, columns, and even worksheets. Although the contents of hidden cells cannot be seen, the data in those cells is still available for use in formulas and functions throughout the workbook.

Hiding a row or column essentially decreases that row height or column width to 0 pixels. To a hide a row or column, select the row or column heading, click the Format button in the Cells group on the HOME tab, point to Hide & Unhide on the menu that appears, and then click Hide Rows or Hide Columns. The border of the row or column heading is doubled to mark the location of hidden rows or columns.

A worksheet often is hidden when the entire worksheet contains data that is not of interest to the reader and is better summarized elsewhere in the document. To hide a worksheet, make that worksheet active, click the Format button in the Cells group on the HOME tab, point to Hide & Unhide, and then click Hide Sheet.

Unhiding redisplays the hidden content in the workbook. To unhide a row or column, click in a cell below the hidden row or to the right of the hidden column, click the Format button, point to Hide & Unhide, and then click Unhide Rows or Unhide Columns. To unhide a worksheet, click the Format button, point to Hide & Unhide, and then click Unhide Sheet. The Unhide dialog box opens. Click the sheet you want to unhide, and then click the OK button. The hidden content is redisplayed in the workbook.

Although hiding data can make a worksheet and workbook easier to read, be sure never to hide information that is important to the reader.

Sally wants you to add one more piece of data to the worksheet—a book ID that is used by Sparrow & Pond to identify each book in stock. You will use Flash Fill to create the book IDs.

Using Flash Fill

Flash Fill enters text based on patterns it finds in the data. As shown in Figure 1-33, Flash Fill generates customer names from the first and last names stored in the adjacent columns in the worksheet. To enter the rest of the names, you press the Enter key; to continue typing the names yourself, you press the Esc key.

Figure 1-33   **Entering text with Flash Fill**

	A	B	C	D	E
1	First	M.I.	Last	Full Name	
2	Tobias	A.	Gregson	Tobias Gregson	
3	Maria	R.	Sanchez	Maria Sanchez	
4	Andrew	T.	Lewis	Andrew Lewis	
5	Brett	K.	Carls	Brett Carls	
6	Carmen	A.	Hzu	Carmen Hzu	
7	Karen	M.	Schultz	Karen Schultz	
8	Howard	P.	Gary	Howard Gary	
9	Natalia	N.	Shapiro	Natalia Shapiro	
10	Paul	O.	Douglas	Paul Douglas	
11					

you enter the full name twice to begin the pattern

Flash Fill generates the remaining full names based on the pattern in the first two cells

Flash Fill works best when the pattern is clearly recognized from the values in the data. Be sure to enter the data pattern in the column or row right next to the related data. The data used to generate the pattern must be in a rectangular grid and cannot have blank columns or rows. Also, Flash Fill enters text, not formulas. If you edit or replace an entry originally used by Flash Fill, the content generated by Flash Fill will not be updated.

The Sparrow & Pond book ID combines five digits of the book's ISBN and its category (used or new). For example, *Floral Origami Globes* has the ISBN 4-889-96213-1 and is new, so its book ID is 96213-New. The book IDs follow a consistent and logical pattern. Rather than typing every book ID, you will use Flash Fill to enter the book IDs into the worksheet.

To enter the book IDs using Flash Fill:

1. Make sure that cell **A19** is the active cell.

2. Type **25385-Used** as the ID for the first book in the list, and then press the **Enter** key.

3. Type **9** in cell A20. As soon as you start typing, Flash Fill generates the remaining entries in the column based on the pattern you entered. See Figure 1-34.

Book IDs generated by Flash Fill

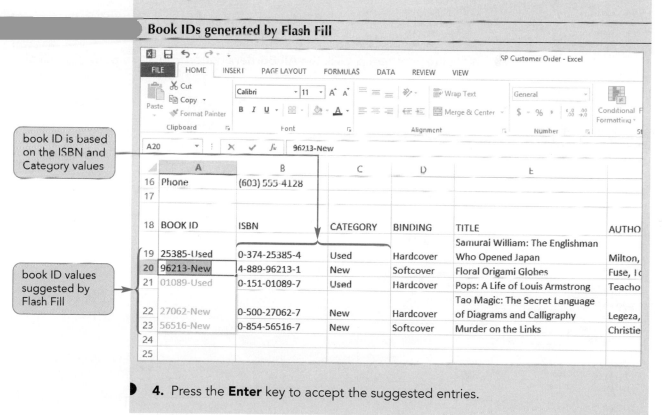

4. Press the **Enter** key to accept the suggested entries.

Formatting a Worksheet

Formatting changes a workbook's appearance to make the content of a worksheet easier to read. Two common formatting changes are adding borders to cells and changing the font size of text.

Adding Cell Borders

Sometimes you want to include lines along the edges of cells to enhance the readability of rows and columns of data. You can do this by adding borders to the left, top, right, or bottom edge of a cell or range. You can also specify the thickness of and the number of lines in the border. This is especially helpful when a worksheet is printed because the gridlines that surround the cells are not printed by default; they appear on the worksheet only as a guide.

Sally wants add borders around the cells that contain content in the Customer Order worksheet to make the content easier to read.

To add borders around the worksheet cells:

1. Select the range **A3:B7**. You will add borders around all of the cells in the selected range.

2. On the HOME tab, in the Font group, click the **Borders button arrow** , and then click **All Borders**. Borders are added around each cell in the range. The Borders button changes to reflect the last selected border option, which in this case is All Borders. The name of the selected border option appears in the button's ScreenTip.

3. Select the nonadjacent range **A9:B16;H17:I17**. You will add borders around each cell in the selected range.

4. In the Font group, click the **All Borders** button to add borders to all of the cells in the selected range.

5. Click cell **A17** to deselect the cells. See Figure 1-35.

| Figure 1-35 | Borders added to selected cells |

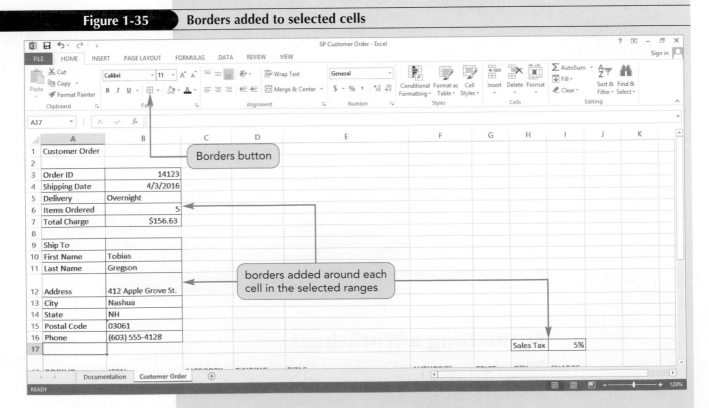

6. Select the nonadjacent range **A18:I23;H25:I28**, and then click the **All Borders** button to add borders to all of the cells in the selected range.

Changing the Font Size

Changing the size of text in a sheet provides a way to identify different parts of a worksheet, such as distinguishing a title or section heading from data. The size of the text is referred to as the font size and is measured in points. The default font size for worksheets is 11 points, but it can be made larger or smaller as needed. You can resize text in selected cells using the Font Size button in the Font group on the HOME tab. You can also use the Increase Font Size and Decrease Font Size buttons to resize cell content to the next higher or lower standard font size.

Sally wants you to increase the size of the worksheet title to 26 points to make it stand out more.

To change the font size of the worksheet title:

1. Click cell **A1** to select it. The worksheet title is in this cell.

2. On the HOME tab, in the Font group, click the **Font Size button arrow** to display a list of font sizes, and then click **28**. The worksheet title changes to 28 points. See Figure 1-36.

Figure 1-36   Font size of cell content increased

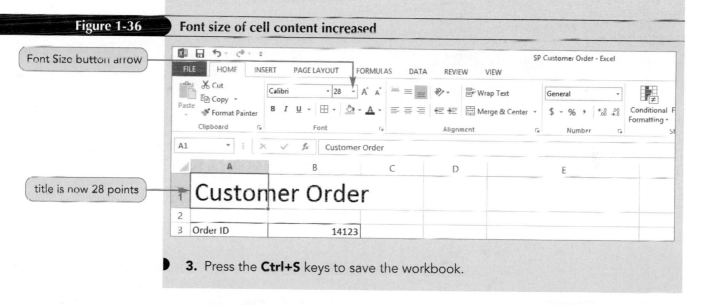

3. Press the **Ctrl+S** keys to save the workbook.

Printing a Workbook

Now that you have finished the workbook, Sally wants you to print a copy of the book order. Before you print a workbook, you should preview it to ensure that it will print correctly.

Changing Worksheet Views

You can view a worksheet in three ways. Normal view, which you have been using throughout this tutorial, shows the contents of the worksheet. Page Layout view shows how the worksheet will appear when printed. Page Break Preview displays the location of the different page breaks within the worksheet. This is useful when a worksheet will span several printed pages and you need to control what content appears on each page.

Sally wants you to see how the Customer Order worksheet will appear on printed pages. You will do this by switching between views.

To switch the Customer Order worksheet to different views:

1. Click the **Page Layout** button 🔲 on the status bar. The page layout of the worksheet appears in the workbook window.

2. Drag the **Zoom slider** to reduce the zoom level to 50%. The reduced magnification makes it clear that the worksheet will spread over two pages when printed. See Figure 1-37.

Figure 1-37 | Worksheet in Page Layout view

worksheet will span two printed pages

TIP

You can relocate a page break by dragging the dotted blue border in the Page Break Preview window.

3. Click the **Page Break Preview** button 🔲 on the status bar. The view switches to Page Break Preview, which shows only those parts of the current worksheet that will print. A dotted blue border separates one page from another.

4. Zoom the worksheet to **70%** so that you can more easily read the contents of the worksheet. See Figure 1-38.

Figure 1-38   **Worksheet in Page Break Preview**

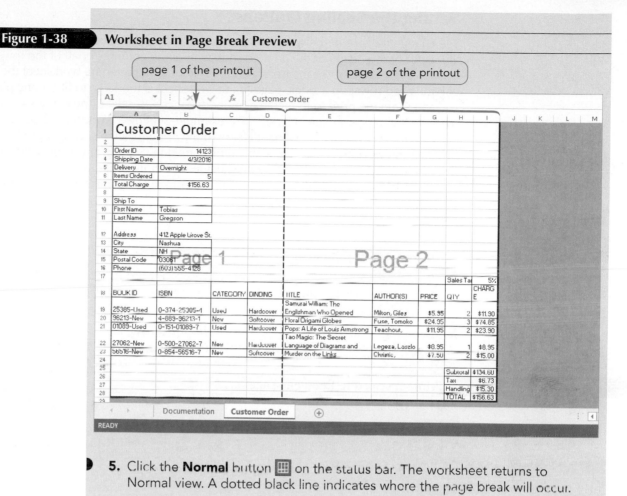

5. Click the **Normal** button on the status bar. The worksheet returns to Normal view. A dotted black line indicates where the page break will occur.

Changing the Page Orientation

Page orientation specifies in which direction content is printed on the page. In **portrait orientation**, the page is taller than it is wide. In **landscape orientation**, the page is wider than it is tall. By default, Excel displays pages in portrait orientation. Changing the page orientation affects only the active sheet.

As you saw in Page Layout view and Page Break Preview, the Customer Order worksheet will print on two pages—columns A through D will print on the first page, and columns E through I will print on the second page, although the columns that print on each page may differ slightly depending on the printer. Sally wants the entire worksheet to print on a single page, so you'll change the page orientation from portrait to landscape.

To change the page orientation of the Customer Order worksheet:

1. On the ribbon, click the **PAGE LAYOUT** tab. The tab includes options for changing how the worksheet is arranged.

2. In the Page Setup group, click the **Orientation** button, and then click **Landscape**. The worksheet switches to landscape orientation.

3. Click the **Page Layout** button on the status bar to switch to Page Layout view. The worksheet will still print on two pages.

Setting the Scaling Options

You change the size of the worksheet on the printed page by **scaling** it. You can scale the width or the height of the printout so that all of the columns or all of the rows fit on a single page. You can also scale the printout to fit the entire worksheet (both columns and rows) on a single page. If the worksheet is too large to fit on one page, you can scale the print to fit on the number of pages you select. You can also scale the worksheet to a percentage of its size. For example, scaling a worksheet to 50% reduces the size of the sheet by half when it is sent to the printer. When scaling a printout, make sure that the worksheet is still readable after shrinking. Scaling affects only the active worksheet, so you can scale each worksheet to best fit its contents.

Sally asks you to scale the printout so that all of the Customer Order worksheet fits on one page in landscape orientation.

To scale the printout of the Customer Order worksheet:

1. On the PAGE LAYOUT tab, in the Scale to Fit group, click the **Width arrow**, and then click **1 page** on the menu that appears. All of the columns in the worksheet now fit on one page.

2. In the Scale to Fit group, click the **Height arrow**, and then click **1 page**. All of the rows in the worksheet now fit on one page. See Figure 1-39.

Figure 1-39	Printout scaled to fit on one page

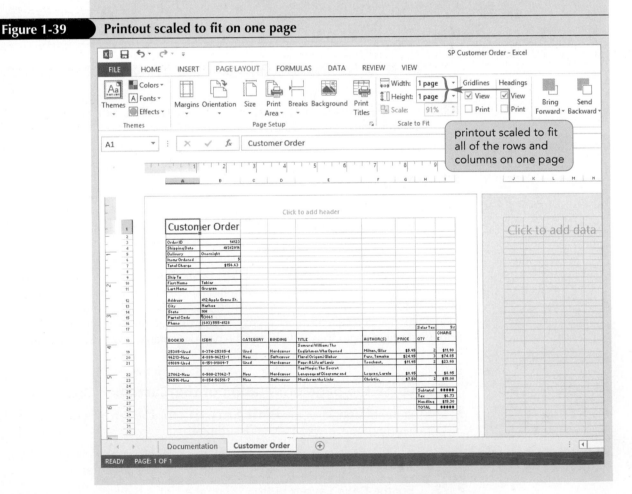

Setting the Print Options

TIP

To print the gridlines or the column and row headings, click the corresponding Print check box in the Sheet Options group on the PAGE LAYOUT tab.

You can print the contents of a workbook by using the Print screen in Backstage view. The Print screen provides options for choosing where to print, what to print, and how to print. For example, you can specify the number of copies to print, which printer to use, and what to print. You can choose to print only the selected cells, only the active sheets, or all of the worksheets in the workbook that contain data. The printout will include only the data in the worksheet. The other elements in the worksheet, such as the row and column headings and the gridlines around the worksheet cells, will not print by default. The preview shows you exactly how the printed pages will look with the current settings. You should always preview before printing to ensure that the printout looks exactly as you intended and avoid unnecessary reprinting.

Sally asks you to preview and print the Sparrow & Pond workbook now.

Note: Check with your instructor first to make sure you should complete the steps for printing the workbook.

To preview and print the workbook:

1. On the ribbon, click the **FILE** tab to display Backstage view.

2. Click **Print** in the navigation bar. The Print screen appears with the print options and a preview of the Customer Order worksheet printout. See Figure 1-40.

Figure 1-40   **Print screen in Backstage view**

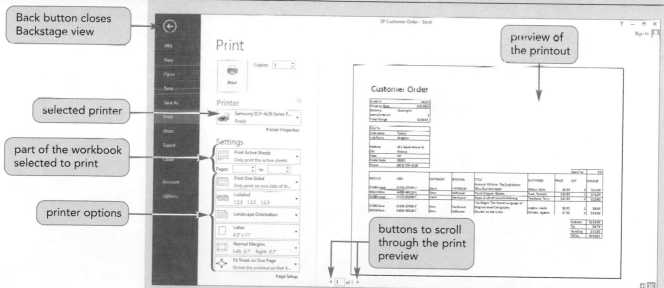

Back button closes Backstage view

preview of the printout

selected printer

part of the workbook selected to print

printer options

buttons to scroll through the print preview

3. Click the **Printer** button, and then click the printer to which you want to print, if it is not already selected. By default, Excel will print only the active sheet.

4. In the Settings options, click the top button, and then click **Print Entire Workbook** to print all of the sheets in the workbook—in this case, both the Documentation and the Customer Order worksheets. The preview shows the first sheet in the workbook—the Documentation worksheet. Note that this sheet is still in the default portrait orientation.

5. Below the preview, click the **Next Page** button ▶ to view the Customer Order worksheet. As you can see, the Customer Order worksheet will print on a single page in landscape orientation.

6. If you are instructed to print, click the **Print** button to send the contents of the workbook to the specified printer. If you are not instructed to print, click the **Back** button ⬅ in the navigation bar to exit Backstage view.

Viewing Worksheet Formulas

Most of the time, you will be interested in only the final results of a worksheet, not the formulas used to calculate those results. However, in some cases, you might want to view the formulas used to develop the workbook. This is particularly useful when you encounter unexpected results and you want to examine the underlying formulas, or you want to discuss your formulas with a colleague. You can display the formulas instead of the resulting values in cells.

If you print the worksheet while the formulas are displayed, the printout shows the formulas instead of the values. To make the printout easier to read, you should print the worksheet gridlines as well as the row and column headings so that cell references in the formulas are easy to find in the printed version of the worksheet.

You will look at the Customer Order worksheet with the formulas displayed.

To display the formulas in cells in the Customer Order worksheet:

1. Make sure the Customer Order worksheet is in Page Layout view.

TIP

You can also display formulas in a worksheet by clicking the Show Formulas button in the Formula Auditing group on the FORMULAS tab.

2. Press the **Ctrl+`** keys (the grave accent symbol ` is usually located above the Tab key). The worksheet changes to display all of the formulas instead of the resulting values. Notice that the columns widen to display all of the formula text in the cells.

3. Look at the entry in cell B4. The underlying numeric value of the shipping date (42463) is displayed instead of the formatted date value (4/3/2016). See Figure 1-41.

Figure 1-41 | Worksheet with formulas displayed

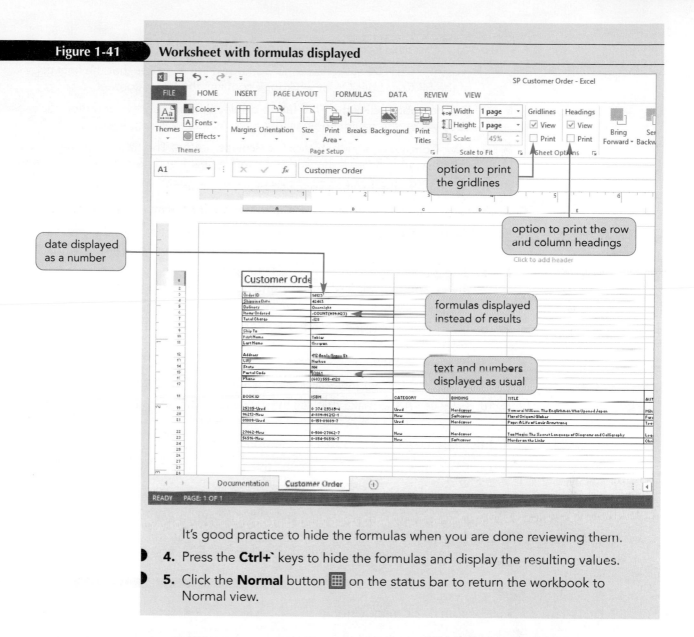

It's good practice to hide the formulas when you are done reviewing them.

▶ **4.** Press the **Ctrl+`** keys to hide the formulas and display the resulting values.

▶ **5.** Click the **Normal** button ⊞ on the status bar to return the workbook to Normal view.

Saving a Workbook with a New Filename

Whenever you click the Save button on the Quick Access Toolbar or press the Ctrl+S keys, the workbook file is updated to reflect the latest content. If you want to save a copy of the workbook with a new filename or to a different location, you need to use the Save As command. When you save a workbook with a new filename or to a different location, the previous version of the workbook remains stored as well.

You have completed the SP Customer Order workbook. Sally wants to use the workbook as a model for other customer order reports. You will save the workbook with a new filename to avoid overwriting the Tobias Gregson book order. Then you'll clear the information related to Tobias Gregson, leaving the formulas intact. This new, revised workbook will then be ready for a new customer order.

To save the workbook with a new filename:

▶ **1.** Press the **Ctrl+S** keys to save the workbook. This ensures that the final copy of the SP Customer Order workbook contains the latest content.

▶ **2.** On the ribbon, click the **FILE** tab to display Backstage view, and then click **Save As** on the navigation bar. The Save As screen is displayed.

▶ **3.** Click **Computer**, and then click the **Browse** button. The Save As dialog box opens so you can save the workbook with a new filename or to a new location.

▶ **4.** Navigate to the location specified by your instructor.

▶ **5.** In the File name box, type **SP Customer Order Form** as the new filename.

▶ **6.** Click the **Save** button. The workbook is saved with the new filename and is open in Excel.

▶ **7.** Select the range **B3:B5**, right-click the selected range to open the shortcut menu, and then click **Clear Contents** to clear the contents of the order ID, shipping date, and delivery type cells.

▶ **8.** Select the nonadjacent range **B10:B16;A19:H23**, and then press the **Delete** key to clear the contact information for Tobias Gregson and the list of books he ordered from those cells.

▶ **9.** Select cell **I27**, and then clear the handling fee.

▶ **10.** Click cell **A3** to make that cell the active cell. The next time someone opens this workbook, cell A3 will still be the active cell.

▶ **11.** Press the **Ctrl+S** keys to save the workbook.

▶ **12.** Click the **Close** button ⊠ on the title bar (or press the **Ctrl+W** keys). The workbook closes, and the Excel program closes.

> **TIP**
>
> Save the workbook with the new name *before* making your changes to avoid inadvertently saving your edits to the wrong file.

Sally is pleased with the workbook you created. With the calculations already in place in the new workbook, she will be able to quickly enter new customer orders and see the calculated book charges without having to recreate the worksheet.

REVIEW

Session 1.2 Quick Check

1. What formula would you enter to add the values in cells B4, B5, and B6? What function would you enter to achieve the same result?

2. What formula would you enter to count the number of numeric values in the range B2:B100?

3. What formula would you enter to find the maximum value of the cells in the range B2:B100?

4. If you insert cells into the range C1:D10 shifting the cells to the right, what is the new location of the data that was previously in cell E5?

5. Cell E11 contains the formula =SUM(E1:E10). How does this formula change if a new row is inserted above row 5?

6. Describe four ways of viewing the content of a workbook in Excel.

7. How are page breaks indicated in Page Break Preview?

8. How do you display the formulas used in a worksheet instead of the formula results?

SAM Projects

Put your skills into practice with SAM Projects! SAM Projects for this tutorial can be found online. If you have a SAM account, go to www.cengage.com/sam2013 to download the most recent Project Instructions and Start Files.

Review Assignments

There are no Data Files needed for the Review Assignments.

Sally wants you to create a workbook to record the recent book purchases made by Sparrow & Pond. The workbook should list the recent acquisitions from private sellers, libraries, and other vendors; include a description of each book; and calculate the total number of books acquired and the total amount spent by Sparrow & Pond. Complete the following:

1. Create a new, blank workbook, and then save the workbook as **Book List** in the location specified by your instructor.
2. Rename the Sheet1 worksheet as **Documentation**, and then enter the data shown in Figure 1-42 in the specified cells.

Figure 1-42   Documentation sheet data

Cell	Data
A1	Sparrow & Pond
A3	Author
A4	Date
A5	Purpose
B3	*your name*
B4	*current date*
B5	To record book acquisitions by Sparrow & Pond

© 2014 Cengage Learning

3. Set the font size of the title text in cell A1 to 26 points.
4. Add a new worksheet after the Documentation sheet, and then rename the sheet as **Books**.
5. In cell A1, enter the text **Book Acquisitions**. Set the font size of this text to 26 points.
6. In cell A2, enter the text **DATE** as the label. In cell B2, enter the date **4/3/2016**.
7. In the range A4:G9, enter the data shown in Figure 1-43.

Figure 1-43	Book list

ISBN	STATUS	BINDING	TITLE	AUTHOR	CONDITION	PRICE
0-670-02103-2	New	Softcover	Rocket Men: The Epic Story of the First Men on the Moon	Nelson, Craig	Excellent	$12.95
0-195-09076-4	Used	Hardcover	Buildings of Colorado	Noel, Thomas J.	Good	$22.50
0-375-70365-9	New	Softcover	American Visions: The Epic History of Art in America	Hughes, Robert	Excellent	$22.50
1-564-77848-7	New	Softcover	Simple Comforts: 12 Cozy Lap Quilts	Diehl, Kim	Very Good	$9.25
1-851-70006-4	Used	Hardcover	Beautiful Stories About Children	Dickens, Charles	Good	$33.50

© 2014 Cengage Learning

8. Insert cells into the range A4:A9, shifting the other cells to the right.

9. Enter the label **BOOK ID** in cell A4, type **02103-New** in cell A5, and then type **09076-Used** in cell A6.

10. Use Flash Fill to fill in the remaining book IDs.

11. Set the width of columns A through D to 15 characters each. Set the width of column E to 30 characters. Set the width of column F to 20 characters. Set the width of column G to 15 characters.

12. Set the book titles in the range E4:E9 to wrap to a new line.

13. Autofit the heights of rows 4 through 9.

14. Move the book list in the range A4:H9 to the range A8:H13.

15. In cell G15, enter the text **TOTAL**. In cell H15, enter a function to add the prices in the range H9:H13.

16. In cell A4, enter the text **TOTAL BOOKS**. In cell B4, enter a function to count the number of numeric values in the range H9:H13.

17. In cell A5, enter the text **TOTAL PRICE**. In cell B5, display the value from cell H15.

18. In cell A6, enter the text **AVERAGE PRICE**. In cell B6, enter a formula to calculate the total price paid for the books (listed in cell B5) divided by the number of books purchased (listed in cell B4).

19. Add borders around each cell in the nonadjacent range A4:B6;A8:H13;G15:H15.

20. For the Books worksheet, change the page orientation to landscape and scale the worksheet to print on a single page for both the width and the height. If you are instructed to print, print the entire workbook.

21. Display the formulas in the Books worksheet, and set the gridlines and row/column headings to print. If you are instructed to print, print the entire worksheet.

22. Save and close the workbook.

Case Problem 1

Data File needed for this Case Problem: Pacific.xlsx

American Wheel Tours   Kevin Bennett is a tours manager at American Wheel Tours, a bicycle touring company located in Philadelphia, Pennsylvania, that specializes in one- and two-week supported tours in destinations across the United States. Kevin wants you to create a workbook that details the itinerary of the company's Pacific Coast tour. The workbook will list the tour itinerary shown in Figure 1-44 and calculate the total number of riding days, total mileage, and average mileage per ride.

Figure 1-44   Pacific Tour itinerary

DATE	START	FINISH	CAMPSITE	MILES	DESCRIPTION
10-Oct-16	Eugene	Eugene	Richardson Park		Orientation day. Meet at Richardson Park, located at the Fern Ridge Reservoir.
11-Oct-16	Eugene	Florence	Honeyman State Park	66	Cycle over Low Pass to Honeyman State Park.
12-Oct-16	Florence	Charleston	Sunset Bay State Park	56	Cycle through Oregon Dunes National Recreation Area to Sunset Bay State Park.
13-Oct-16	Charleston	Port Orford	Humbug Mountain State Park	60	Cycle around Bullards Beach State Park and camp at Humbug Mountain State Park.
14-Oct-16	Port Orford	Brookings	Harris Beach State Park	52	Cycle past the mouth of the Rogue River to Harris Beach State Park.
15-Oct-16	Brookings	Crescent City	Jedediah State Park	48	Pass into California and camp at Jedediah State Park.
16-Oct-16	Crescent City	Eureka	Eureka Fairgrounds	72	A long day through Del Norte Coast Redwoods State Park to Eureka.

© 2014 Cengage Learning

Complete the following:

1. Open the **Pacific** workbook located in the Excel1 ▸ Case1 folder included with your Data Files, and then save the workbook as **Pacific Coast** in the location specified by your instructor.
2. In the Documentation worksheet, enter your name in cell B3 and the date in cell B4.
3. Add a new sheet to the end of the workbook and rename it as **Itinerary**.
4. In cell A1, enter the text **Pacific Coast Tour** and set the font size to 28 points.
5. In the range A3:A8, enter the following labels: **Start Date**, **End Date**, **Total Days**, **Riding Days**, **Total Miles**, and **Miles per Day**.
6. Enter the date **October 10, 2016** in cell B3, and then enter the date **October 16, 2016** in cell B4.
7. In the range D3:D8, enter the labels **Type**, **Surface**, **Difficulty**, **Tour Leader**, **Cost**, and **Deposit**.
8. In the range E3:E8, enter **Van Supported**, **Paved**, **Intermediate**, **Kevin Bennett**, **$1,250**, and **$350**.
9. In the range A11:F18, enter the data shown in Figure 1-44, including the column labels. Leave the mileage value for October 10th blank.
10. In cell B5, enter a formula to calculate the total number of days in the tour by subtracting the starting date (cell B3) from the ending date (cell B4) and adding 1.

11. In cell B6, enter a function to count the total number of riding days based on the numbers in the range E12:E18.

12. In cell B7, enter a function to add the total number of miles in the range E12:E18.

13. In cell B8, enter a formula to calculate the average miles per day by dividing the total miles by the number of riding days.

14. Insert cells in the range A11:A18, shifting the cells to the right. In cell A11, enter **DAY**. In the range A12:A18, enter the numbers 1 through 7 to number each day of the tour.

15. Set the column widths so that column A is 12 characters, columns B through E are 14 characters each, column F is 6 characters, and column G is 50 characters.

16. Wrap text in the range A11:G18 as needed so that any hidden entries are displayed on multiple lines within the cell.

17. Autofit the height of rows 11 through 18.

18. Add borders around the ranges A3:B8, D3:E8, and A11:G18.

19. Format the Itinerary worksheet so that it prints on a single page in landscape orientation. If you are instructed to print, print the entire workbook.

20. Display the formulas in the Itinerary worksheet, and set the gridlines and column/row headings to print. If you are instructed to print, print the worksheet.

21. Return the Itinerary worksheet to Normal view, hide the formulas, set the gridlines and column/ row headings so that they won't print, and then save the workbook.

22. Save the workbook as **Pacific Coast Revised** in the location specified by your instructor.

23. Determine what the total mileage and average mileage per day of the tour would be if Kevin adds a 10-mile warm-up ride on October 10th but decreases the length of the October 15th ride to 41 miles. Save the workbook.

Case Problem 2

APPLY

Data File needed for this Case Problem: Tropical.xlsx

Tropical Foods   Tropical Foods is a health food grocery store located in Keizer, Oregon. Monica Li is working on the store's annual financial report. One part of the financial report will be the company's balance sheet for the previous two years. Monica already entered the labels for the balance sheet. You will enter the numeric data and formulas to perform the financial calculations. Complete the following:

1. Open the **Tropical** workbook located in the Excel1 ▸ Case2 folder included with your Data Files, and then save the workbook as **Tropical Foods Balance Sheet** in the location specified by your instructor.

2. In cells B3 and B4 of the Documentation sheet, enter your name and the date. In cell A1, increase the font size of the title to 28 points.

3. Go to the Balance Sheet worksheet. Increase the font size of the title in cell A1 to 28 points, and then increase the font size of the subtitle in cell A2 to 20 points.

4. In the corresponding cells of columns C and D, enter the numbers shown in Figure 1-45 for the company's assets and liabilities.

Figure 1-45   **Tropical Foods assets and liabilities**

		2015	2014
Assets	Cash	$645,785	$627,858
	Accounts Receivable	431,982	405,811
	Inventories	417,615	395,648
	Prepaid Expenses	2,152	4,151
	Other Assets	31,252	26,298
	Fixed Assets @ Cost	1,800,000	1,750,000
	Accumulated Depreciation	82,164	$77,939
Liabilities	Accounts Payable	$241,191	$193,644
	Accrued Expenses	31,115	32,151
	Current Portion of Debt	120,000	100,000
	Income Taxes Payable	144,135	126,524
	Long-Term Debt	815,000	850,000
	Capital Stock	1,560,000	1,525,000
	Retain Earnings	335,181	304,508

5. Set the width of column A to 12 characters, column B to 28 characters, columns C and D to 14 characters each, column E to 2 characters, and column F to 10 characters.

6. In cells C8 and D8, enter formulas to calculate the current assets value for 2014 and 2015, which is equal to the sum of the cash, accounts receivable, inventories, and prepaid expenses values.

7. In cells C14 and D14, enter formulas to calculate the net fixed assets value for 2014 and 2015, which is equal to the difference between the fixed assets value and the accumulated depreciation value.

8. In cells C16 and D16, enter formulas to calculate the total assets value for 2014 and 2015, which is equal to the sum of the current assets, other assets, and net fixed assets value.

9. In cells C23 and D23, enter formulas to calculate the sum of the accounts payable, accrued expenses, current portion of debt, and income taxes payable values for 2014 and 2015.

10. In cells C29 and D29, enter formulas to calculate the shareholders' equity value for 2014 and 2015, which is equal to the sum of the capital stock and retained earnings.

11. In cells C31 and D31, enter formulas to calculate the total liabilities & equity value for 2014 and 2015, which is equal to the sum of the current liabilities, long-term debt, and shareholders' equity.

12. In a balance sheet, the total assets should equal the total liabilities & equity. Compare the values in cells C16 and C31, and then compare the values in cells D16 and D31 to confirm that this is the case for the Tropical Foods balance sheet in 2014 and 2015. If the account doesn't balance, check your worksheet for errors in either values or formulas.

13. In cell F4, enter a formula to calculate the percentage change in cash from 2014 to 2015, which is equal to (C4–D4)/D4.

14. Copy the formula in cell F4 and paste it in the nonadjacent range F5:F8;F10;F12:F14;F16; F19:F23;F25;F27;F29;F31 to show the percentage change in all values of the balance sheet.

15. Add borders around the cells in columns B, C, D, and F of the balance sheet, excluding the cells in rows 9, 11, 15, 17, 18, 24, 26, and 30.

16. Set the page layout of the Balance Sheet worksheet to portrait orientation and scaled to print on a single page. If you are instructed to print, print the entire workbook.

17. Display the formulas in the Balance Sheet worksheet, and then set the gridlines and row/column headings to print. If you are instructed to print, print the worksheet.

18. Display the Balance Sheet worksheet in Normal view, hide the formulas, set the gridlines and column/row headings so that they won't print, and then save the workbook.

Case Problem 3

CHALLENGE

Data File needed for this Case Problem: Physics.xlsx

Gladstone Country Day School   Beatrix Melendez teaches Introduction to Physics at Gladstone Country Day School in Gladstone, Missouri. She wants to record students' quiz scores, and then calculate each student's total and average scores. She also wants to calculate the class average, high score, and low score for each quiz in her records. Beatrix has entered scores from 10 quizzes for 20 students in a worksheet. You will summarize these grades by student and by quiz using the functions listed in Figure 1-46.

Figure 1-46   **Excel summary functions**

Function	Description
=AVERAGE *(range)*	Calculates the average of the values from the specified *range*
=MEDIAN *(range)*	Calculates the median or midpoint of the values from the specified *range*
=MIN *(range)*	Calculates the minimum of the values from the specified *range*
=MAX *(range)*	Calculates the maximum of the values from the specified *range*

© 2014 Cengage Learning

Complete the following:

1. Open the **Physics** workbook located in the Excel1 ▶ Case3 folder included with your Data Files, and then save the workbook as **Physics Grading Sheet** in the location specified by your instructor.

2. In the Documentation sheet, enter your name in cell B3 and the date in cell B4. Increase the font size of the title in cell A1 to 28 points.

3. Go to the Grades worksheet. Increase the font size of cell A1 to 28 points, and then increase the font size of cell A2 to 22 points.

✦ **Explore** 4. In cell M5, enter a formula to calculate the median or midpoint of the quiz scores for Debra Alt. In cell N5, enter a formula to calculate the average of Debra Alt's quiz scores.

5. Copy the formulas in the range M5:N5 to the range M6:N24 to summarize the scores for the remaining students.

✦ **Explore** 6. In cell B26, enter a formula to calculate the minimum class score from the first quiz. In cell B27, enter a formula to calculate the median class score.

✦ **Explore** 7. In cell B28, use the MAX function to calculate the high score from the first quiz.

8. In cell B30, enter a formula to calculate the average score from the first quiz.

9. Copy the formulas in the range B26:B30 to the range C26:K30 to calculate the summary statistics for the rest of the quizzes.

10. Insert 10 new rows above row 4, shifting the student grade table and summary from the range A4:N30 to the range A14:N40. You will enter a summary of all of the students from all of the quizzes at the top of the worksheet.

11. In cell A4, enter the text **Class Size**. In cell B4, enter a formula to calculate the count of scores from the range N15:N34.

12. In the range A6:A9, enter the labels **Overall Scores**, **Lowest Average**, **Median Average**, and **Highest Average**. In cell A11, enter **Class Average**.

13. Using the average scores in the range N15:N34, enter formulas to calculate the overall lowest average score in cell B7, the median of the class averages in cell B8, the overall highest average in cell B9, and the average overall class score in cell B11.

14. Add cell borders around the ranges A4:B4, A7:B9, A11:B11, A14:K34, M14:N34, A36:K38, and A40:K40.

15. Set the page layout of the Grades worksheet to landscape orientation and scaled to print on a single page. If you are instructed to print, print the entire workbook.

16. Display the formulas in the Grades worksheet. Set the gridlines and the row/column headings to print. If you are instructed to print, print the worksheet.

17. Display the Grades worksheet in Normal view, hide the formulas, set the gridlines and column/row headings so that they won't print, and then save the workbook.

18. Determine the effect of raising each student's score on the first quiz by 10 points to curve the results. Report what impact this has on the overall class average from all 10 quizzes.

19. Save the workbook as **Physics Grading Sheet Revised**. If you are instructed to print, print the Grades worksheet.

Case Problem 4

Data File needed for this Case Problem: Turf.xlsx

Turf Toughs   Tim Gables is the owner and operator of Turf Toughs, a lawn and tree removal service located in Chicopee, Massachusetts. He created a workbook to record and analyze the service calls made by his company. So far, the workbook calculates the cost of each service call, the total charges for all of the calls, and the total number of billable hours. Unfortunately, the workbook contains several errors. You will fix these errors and then complete the workbook. Complete the following:

1. Open the **Turf** workbook located in the Excel1 ▸ Case4 folder included with your Data Files, and then save the workbook as **Turf Toughs Service Calls** in the location specified by your instructor.

2. In the Documentation sheet, enter your name in cell B3 and the date in cell B4.

3. Go to the Service Log worksheet. The log lists the contact information and the service calls for each customer.

   Tim wants you to insert a column of IDs for each customer. The customer ID is in the form *last-phone*, where *last* is the customer's last name and *phone* is the last four digits of the customer's phone number.

4. Insert cells in the range A4:A34, shifting the other cells to the right. Type **Cust ID** in cell A4, and then enter **Morris-4380** as the customer ID for Michael Morris. Use Flash Fill to fill in the remaining customer IDs in the column.

5. Add borders around the cells in the range A4:A32.

⚙ **Troubleshoot** 6. There is a problem with the all of the customer zip codes. Each zip code should begin with zero. Make the necessary changes to fix this problem.

7. Resize the columns of the worksheet so that all of the column labels in the service calls list are displayed entirely.

⚙ **Troubleshoot** 8. The formula in cell L5 is not correctly calculating the number of hours for each service call. Fix the formula so that it multiplies the difference between the starting and ending time by 24.

TROUBLESHOOT

9. Copy the formula you created for cell L5 to the range L6:L32, replacing the previous calculated values.

10. Calculate the service charge for each service call so that it equals the base fee added to the hourly rate times the number of hours worked.

⚙ **Troubleshoot** 11. Cell N34 contains a formula to calculate the total service charges for all customer visits. Is it calculating the value correctly? If not, edit the formula to fix any errors you find.

12. Above row 4, insert six new rows, shifting the range A4:N34 down to the range A10:N40.

13. In the range A4:A8, enter the labels **From**, **To**, **Total Service Calls**, **Billable Hours**, and **Total Charges**.

14. In cell B4, calculate the starting date of the service calls by entering a formula that finds the minimum value of the dates in the Date column.

15. In cell B5, calculate the ending date of the service calls by entering a formula that finds the maximum value of the dates in the Date column.

16. In cell B6, enter a formula that counts the total number of service calls using the values in the Date column.

17. In cell B7, enter a formula that calculates the sum of hours from the Hours column.

18. In cell B8, enter a formula that references the value of cell N40.

19. Add borders around each cell in the range A4:B8.

20. Set the page layout of the Service Log worksheet so that it prints on a single page in landscape orientation. If you are instructed to print, print the entire workbook.

21. Display the formulas in the Service Log worksheet, scale the worksheet to fit on a single page, and then set the gridlines and row/column headings to print. If you are instructed to print, print the Service Log worksheet.

22. Return the Service Log worksheet to Normal view, hide the formulas, set the gridlines and column/row headings so that they won't print, and then save the workbook.

Formatting Workbook Text and Data

Designing a Sales Report

EXCEL

OBJECTIVES

Session 2.1
- Change fonts, font style, and font color
- Add fill colors and a background image
- Create formulas to calculate sales data
- Apply Currency and Accounting formats and the Percent style
- Format dates and times
- Align, indent, and rotate cell contents
- Merge a group of cells

Session 2.2
- Use the AVERAGE function
- Apply cell styles
- Copy and paste formats with the Format Painter
- Find and replace text and formatting
- Change workbook themes
- Highlight cells with conditional formats
- Format a worksheet for printing
- Set the print area, insert page breaks, add print titles, create headers and footers, and set margins

Case | *Big Red Wraps*

Sanjit Chandra is a sales manager for Big Red Wraps, a growing restaurant chain that specializes in preparing made-to-order sandwich wraps, seasonal soups, and fresh salads. The first Big Red Wraps opened in Madison, Wisconsin, and has since expanded to 20 restaurants across six states. Four of these restaurants were opened this year. Each spring, the company has a sales conference where the restaurant managers meet to discuss sales concerns and review marketing plans for the upcoming year. Sanjit created a workbook that summarizes the sales data for the previous year and is part of a sales report that will be given to all conference attendees. He wants you to calculate some summary statistics and format the workbook.

STARTING DATA FILES

Excel2 → Tutorial
Background.jpg
Sales.xlsx

Review
Background2.png
Menu.xlsx

Case1
Salon.xlsx

Case2
Waist.xlsx

Access3 → Wind.xlsx

Case4
Office.xlsx

Session 2.1 Visual Overview:

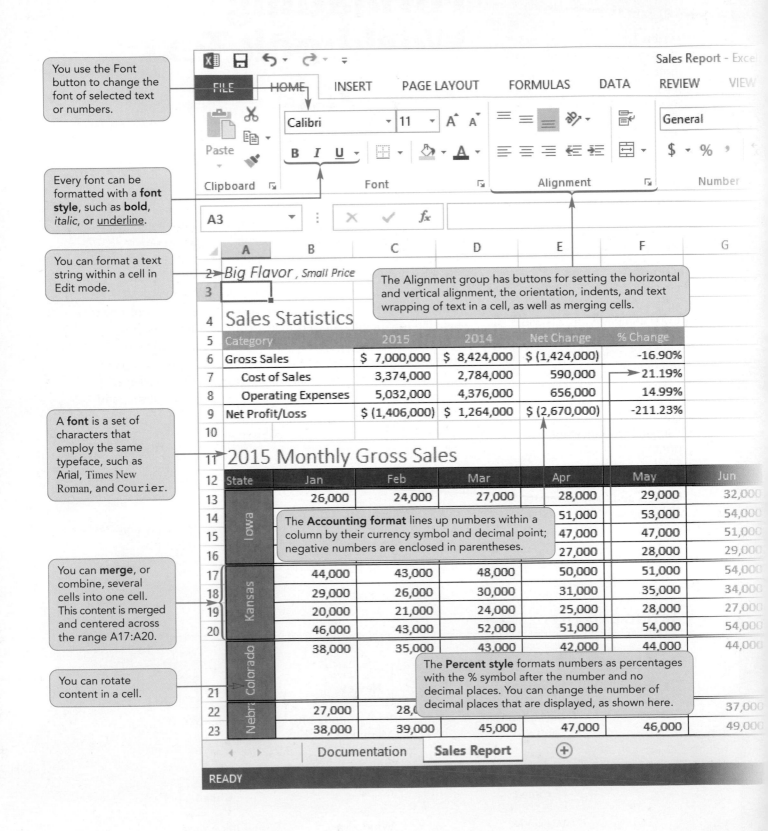

You use the Font button to change the font of selected text or numbers.

Every font can be formatted with a **font style**, such as **bold**, *italic*, or <u>underline</u>.

You can format a text string within a cell in Edit mode.

A **font** is a set of characters that employ the same typeface, such as Arial, Times New Roman, and Courier.

You can **merge**, or combine, several cells into one cell. This content is merged and centered across the range A17:A20.

You can rotate content in a cell.

The Alignment group has buttons for setting the horizontal and vertical alignment, the orientation, indents, and text wrapping of text in a cell, as well as merging cells.

The **Accounting format** lines up numbers within a column by their currency symbol and decimal point; negative numbers are enclosed in parentheses.

The **Percent style** formats numbers as percentages with the % symbol after the number and no decimal places. You can change the number of decimal places that are displayed, as shown here.

Sales Report - Excel

FILE   HOME   INSERT   PAGE LAYOUT   FORMULAS   DATA   REVIEW   VIEW

Calibri   11   A A   General

B I U $ % ,

Clipboard   Font   Alignment   Number

A3

Big Flavor, Small Price

Sales Statistics

Category	2015	2014	Net Change	% Change
Gross Sales	$ 7,000,000	$ 8,424,000	$ (1,424,000)	-16.90%
Cost of Sales	3,374,000	2,784,000	590,000	21.19%
Operating Expenses	5,032,000	4,376,000	656,000	14.99%
Net Profit/Loss	$ (1,406,000)	$ 1,264,000	$ (2,670,000)	-211.23%

2015 Monthly Gross Sales

State	Jan	Feb	Mar	Apr	May	Jun
Iowa	26,000	24,000	27,000	28,000	29,000	32,000
				51,000	53,000	54,000
				47,000	47,000	51,000
				27,000	28,000	29,000
Kansas	44,000	43,000	48,000	50,000	51,000	54,000
	29,000	26,000	30,000	31,000	35,000	34,000
	20,000	21,000	24,000	25,000	28,000	27,000
	46,000	43,000	52,000	51,000	54,000	54,000
Colorado	38,000	35,000	43,000	42,000	44,000	44,000
Nebr	27,000	28,0				37,000
	38,000	39,000	45,000	47,000	46,000	49,000

Documentation   **Sales Report**   +

READY

Worksheet with Formatting

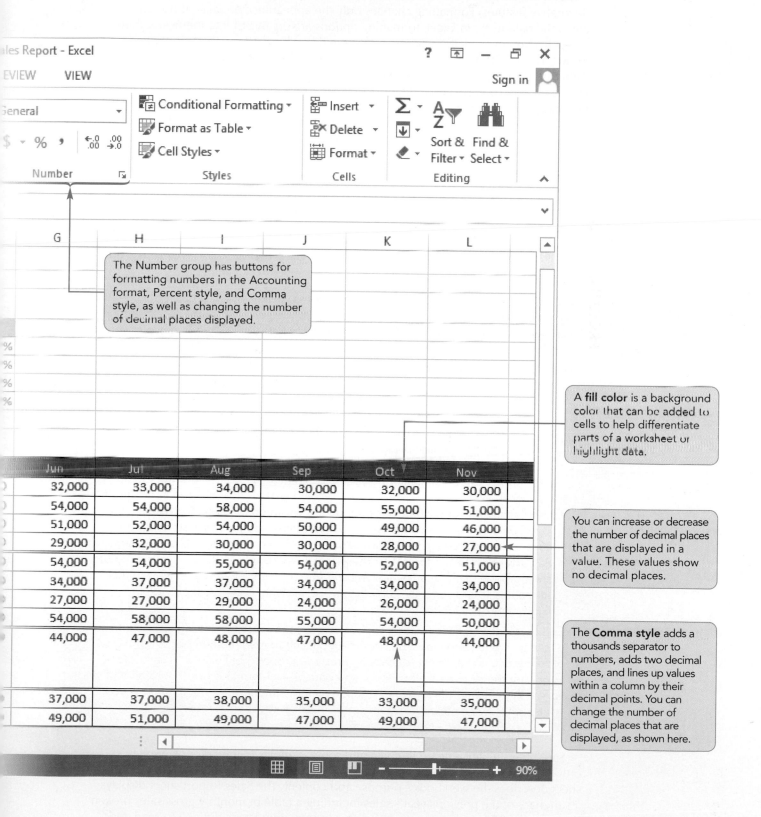

The Number group has buttons for formatting numbers in the Accounting format, Percent style, and Comma style, as well as changing the number of decimal places displayed.

A **fill color** is a background color that can be added to cells to help differentiate parts of a worksheet or highlight data.

You can increase or decrease the number of decimal places that are displayed in a value. These values show no decimal places.

The **Comma style** adds a thousands separator to numbers, adds two decimal places, and lines up values within a column by their decimal points. You can change the number of decimal places that are displayed, as shown here.

Jun	Jul	Aug	Sep	Oct	Nov	
32,000	33,000	34,000	30,000	32,000	30,000	
54,000	54,000	58,000	54,000	55,000	51,000	
51,000	52,000	54,000	50,000	49,000	46,000	
29,000	32,000	30,000	30,000	28,000	27,000	
54,000	54,000	55,000	54,000	52,000	51,000	
34,000	37,000	37,000	34,000	34,000	34,000	
27,000	27,000	29,000	24,000	26,000	24,000	
54,000	58,000	58,000	55,000	54,000	50,000	
44,000	47,000	48,000	47,000	48,000	44,000	
37,000	37,000	38,000	35,000	33,000	35,000	
49,000	51,000	49,000	47,000	49,000	47,000	

90%

Formatting Cell Text

You can add formatting to a workbook by choosing its fonts, styles, colors, and decorative features. Formatting changes only the appearance of data—it does not affect the data itself. In Excel, formatting options are organized into themes. A **theme** is a collection of formatting for text, colors, and graphical effects that are applied throughout a workbook to create a specific look and feel. Each theme has a name. Although the Office theme is the default theme, you can apply other themes or create your own. You can also add formatting to a workbook using fonts and colors that are not part of the current theme.

As you format a workbook, galleries and Live Preview show how a workbook would be affected by a formatting selection. A **gallery** is a menu or grid that shows a visual representation of the options available for the selected button. As you point to options in a gallery, **Live Preview** shows the results of clicking each option. By pointing to different options, you can quickly see different results before selecting the format you want.

PROSKILLS

Written Communication: Formatting Workbooks for Readability and Appeal

Designing a workbook requires the same care as designing any written document or report. A well-formatted workbook is easy to read and establishes a sense of professionalism with readers. Do the following to improve the appearance of your workbooks:

- **Clearly identify each worksheet's purpose.** Include column or row titles and a descriptive sheet name.
- **Include only one or two topics on each worksheet.** Don't crowd individual worksheets with too much information. Place extra topics on separate sheets. Readers should be able to interpret each worksheet with a minimal amount of horizontal and vertical scrolling.
- **Place worksheets with the most important information first in the workbook.** Position worksheets summarizing your findings near the front of the workbook. Position worksheets with detailed and involved analysis near the end as an appendix.
- **Use consistent formatting throughout the workbook.** If negative values appear in red on one worksheet, format them in the same way on all sheets. Also, be consistent in the use of thousands separators, decimal places, and percentages.
- **Pay attention to the format of the printed workbook.** Make sure your printouts are legible with informative headers and footers. Check that the content of the printout is scaled correctly to the page size, and that page breaks divide the information into logical sections.

Excel provides many formatting tools. However, too much formatting can be intrusive, overwhelm data, and make the document difficult to read. Remember that the goal of formatting is not simply to make a "pretty workbook," but also to accentuate important trends and relationships in the data. A well-formatted workbook should seamlessly convey your data to the reader. If the reader is thinking about how your workbook looks, it means he or she is not thinking about your data.

Sanjit has already entered the data and some formulas in a workbook, which is only a rough draft of what he wants to submit to the company. The Documentation sheet describes the workbook's purpose and content. The Sales Report sheet displays a summary of the previous year's sales including a table of monthly gross sales broken down by the 20 franchise stores. In its current form, the data is difficult to read and interpret. Sanjit wants you to format the contents of the workbook to improve its readability and visual appeal.

To open the workbook:

  1. Open the **Sales** workbook located in the Excel2 ▸ Tutorial folder included with your Data Files, and then save the workbook as **Sales Report** in the location specified by your instructor.

  2. In the Documentation sheet, enter your name in cell B4 and the date in cell B5.

Applying Fonts and Font Styles

Excel organizes fonts into theme and non-theme fonts. A **theme font** is associated with a particular theme and used for headings and body text in the workbook. These fonts change automatically when you change the theme applied to the workbook. Text formatted with a **non-theme font** retains its appearance no matter what theme is used with the workbook.

Fonts appear in different character styles. **Serif fonts**, such as Times New Roman, have extra strokes at the end of each character that aid in reading passages of text. **Sans serif fonts**, such as Arial, do not include these extra strokes. Other fonts are purely decorative, such as a font used for specialized logos. Every font can be further formatted with a font style such as *italic*, **bold**, or ***bold italic***; with <u>underline</u>; and with special effects such as ~~strikethrough~~ and color. You can also increase or decrease the font size.

REFERENCE

Formatting Cell Content

- To change the font, select the cell or range. On the HOME tab, in the Font group, click the Font arrow, and then click a font.
- To change the font size, select the cell or range. On the HOME tab, in the Font group, click the Font Size arrow, and then click a font size.
- To change a font style, select the cell or range. On the HOME tab, in the Font group, click the Bold, Italic, or Underline button.
- To change a font color, select the cell or range. On the HOME tab, in the Font group, click the Font Color button arrow, and then click a color.
- To format a text selection, double-click the cell to enter Edit mode, and then select the text to format. Change the font, size, style, or color, and then press the Enter key.

Sanjit wants the company name at the top of each worksheet to appear in large, bold letters using the default heading font from the Office theme. He wants the slogan "Big Flavor, Small Price" displayed below the company name to appear in the heading font, but in smaller, italicized letters.

To format the company name and slogan in the Documentation sheet:

  1. In the Documentation sheet, select cell **A1** to make it the active cell. The cell with the company name is selected.

  2. On the HOME tab, in the Font group, click the **Font button arrow** to display a gallery of fonts available on your computer. Each name is displayed in its corresponding font. When you point to a font in the gallery, Live Preview shows how the text in the selected cell will look with that font. The first two fonts are the theme fonts for headings and body text—Calibri Light and Calibri.

3. Point to **Algerian** (or another font) in the All Fonts list. Live Preview shows the effect of the Algerian font on the text in cell A1. See Figure 2-1.

Figure 2-1   **Font gallery**

fonts in the Office theme

Live Preview of the Algerian font

all available fonts

pointer on the Algerian font

4. Point to three other fonts in the Font gallery to see the Live Preview showing how cell A1 could look with those fonts.

5. Click **Calibri Light** in the Theme Fonts list. The company name in cell A1 changes to the Calibri Light font, the default headings font in the current theme.

6. In the Font group, click the **Font Size button arrow** to display a list of font sizes, and then click **26**. The company name changes to 26 points.

7. In the Font group, click the **Bold** button B (or press the **Ctrl+B** keys). The company name is set in bold.

8. Select cell **A2** to make it active. The cell with the slogan text is selected.

9. In the Font group, click the **Font Size button arrow**, and then click **10**. The slogan text changes to 10 points.

10. In the Font group, click the **Italic** button I (or press the **Ctrl+I** keys). The slogan in cell A2 is italicized.

11. Select the range **A4:A6**, and then press the **Ctrl+B** keys to change the font to bold.

12. Select cell **A7** to deselect the range. The column labels are set in bold. See Figure 2-2.

Figure 2-2   Formatted cell text

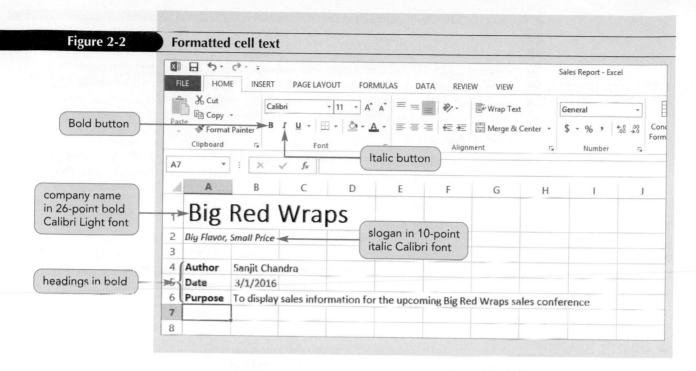

Applying a Font Color

Color can transform a plain workbook filled with numbers and text into a powerful presentation that captures the user's attention and adds visual emphasis to the points you want to make. By default, Excel displays text in a black font color.

Like fonts, colors are organized into theme and non-theme colors. **Theme colors** are the 12 colors that belong to the workbook's theme. Four colors are designated for text and backgrounds, six colors are used for accents and highlights, and two colors are used for hyperlinks (followed and not followed links). These 12 colors are designed to work well together and to remain readable in all combinations. Each theme color has five variations, or accents, in which a different tint or shading is applied to the theme color.

Ten **standard colors**—dark red, red, orange, yellow, light green, green, light blue, blue, dark blue, and purple—are always available regardless of the workbook's theme. You can open an extended palette of 134 standard colors. You can also create a custom color by specifying a mixture of red, blue, and green color values, making available 16.7 million custom colors—more colors than the human eye can distinguish. Some dialog boxes have an automatic color option that uses your Windows default text and background colors, usually black text on a white background.

INSIGHT

Creating Custom Colors

Custom colors let you add subtle and striking colors to a formatted workbook. To create custom colors, you use the **RGB Color model** in which each color is expressed with varying intensities of red, green, and blue. RGB color values are often represented as a set of numbers in the format

(*red*, *green*, *blue*)

where *red* is an intensity value assigned to red light, *green* is an intensity value assigned to green light, and *blue* is an intensity value assigned to blue light. The intensities are measured on a scale of 0 to 255—0 indicates no intensity (or the absence of the color) and 255 indicates the highest intensity. So, the RGB color value (255, 255, 0) represents a mixture of high-intensity red (255) and high-intensity green (255) with the absence of blue (0), which creates the color yellow.

To create colors in Excel using the RGB model, click the More Colors option located in a color menu or dialog box to open the Colors dialog box. In the Colors dialog box, click the Custom tab, and then enter the red, green, and blue intensity values. A preview box shows the resulting RGB color.

Sanjit wants the labels in the Documentation sheet to stand out, so you will change the Big Red Wraps company name and slogan to red.

To change the company name and slogan font color:

1. Select the range **A1:A2**. The company name and slogan are selected.

2. On the HOME tab, in the Font group, click the **Font Color button arrow** to display the gallery of theme and standard colors. (The two colors for hyperlinked text are not shown.)

3. Point to the **Red** color (the second color) in the Standard Colors section. The color name appears in a ScreenTip and you see a Live Preview of the text with the red font color. See Figure 2-3.

Figure 2-3   **Font color gallery**

4. Click the **Red** color. The company name and slogan change to red.

Formatting Text Selections

In Edit mode, you can select and format selections of text within a cell. When the Big Red Wraps slogan is used in marketing materials, "Big Flavor" is set slightly larger than "Small Price." Sanjit wants you to recreate this effect in the workbook by increasing the font size of "Big Flavor" while leaving the rest of the text unchanged. You will use Edit mode to apply a different format to part of the cell text.

To format part of the company slogan:

1. Double-click cell **A2** to select the cell and enter Edit mode (or click cell **A2** and press the **F2** key). The status bar shows EDIT to indicate that you are working with the cell in Edit mode. The pointer changes to the I-beam pointer.

2. Drag the pointer over the phrase **Big Flavor** to select it. The Mini toolbar appears above the selected text with buttons to change the font, size, style, and color of the selected text in the cell. See Figure 2-4.

Figure 2-4	Mini toolbar in Edit mode

Mini toolbar includes common formatting options

3. On the Mini toolbar, click the **Font Size button arrow**, and then click **14**. The font size of the selected text increases to 14 points.

4. Select cell **A7** to deselect cell A2. See Figure 2-5.

Figure 2-5	Formatted text selection

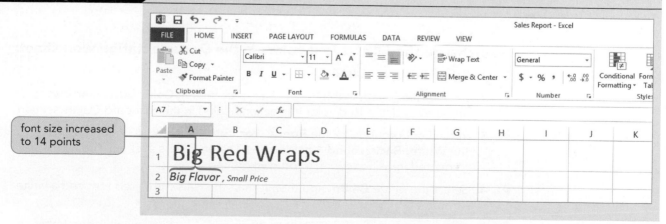

font size increased to 14 points

Working with Fill Colors and Backgrounds

Another way to distinguish sections of a worksheet is by formatting the cell background. You can fill the cell background with color or an image. Sanjit wants you to add fill colors and background images to the Documentation worksheet.

INSIGHT

Using Color to Enhance a Workbook

When used wisely, color can enhance any workbook. However, when used improperly, color can distract the user, making the workbook more difficult to read. As you format a workbook, keep in mind the following tips:

- Use colors from the same theme to maintain a consistent look and feel across the worksheets. If the built-in themes do not fit your needs, you can create a custom theme.
- Use colors to differentiate types of cell content and to direct users where to enter data. For example, format a worksheet so that formula results appear in cells without a fill color and users enter data in cells with a light gray fill color.
- Avoid color combinations that are difficult to read.
- Print the workbook on both color and black-and-white printers to ensure that the printed copy is readable in both versions.
- Understand your printer's limitations and features. Colors that look good on your monitor might not look as good when printed.
- Be sensitive to your audience. About 8 percent of all men and 0.5 percent of all women have some type of color blindness and might not be able to see the text when certain color combinations are used. Red-green color blindness is the most common, so avoid using red text on a green background or green text on a red background.

Changing a Fill Color

TIP

You can also change a sheet tab's color. Right-click a sheet tab, point to Tab Color on the shortcut menu, and then click a color.

By default, worksheet cells do not include any background color. But background colors, also known as fill colors, can be helpful for distinguishing different parts of a worksheet or adding visual interest. You add fill colors to selected cells in the worksheet from the Fill Color gallery, which has the same options as the Font Color gallery.

Sanjit wants the labels and text in the Documentation sheet to stand out. You will format the labels in a white font on a red background, and then you'll format the author's name, current date, and purpose of the worksheet in a red font on a white background.

To change the fill and font colors in the Documentation worksheet:

1. Select the range **A4:A6**.

2. On the HOME tab, in the Font group, click the **Fill Color button arrow** 🖌 ▾, and then click the **Red** color (the second color) in the Standard Colors section.

3. In the Font group, click the **Font Color button arrow** 🇦 ▾, and then click the **White, Background 1** color in the Theme Colors section. The labels are formatted in white text on a red background.

4. Select the range **B4:B6**, and then format the cells with a red font and a white background.

5. Increase the width of column B to **30** characters, and then wrap the text in the selected range.

6. Select the range **A4:B6**, and then add all borders around each of the selected cells.

7. Click cell **A7** to deselect the range. See Figure 2-6.

| Figure 2-6 | Font and fill colors in the Documentation sheet |

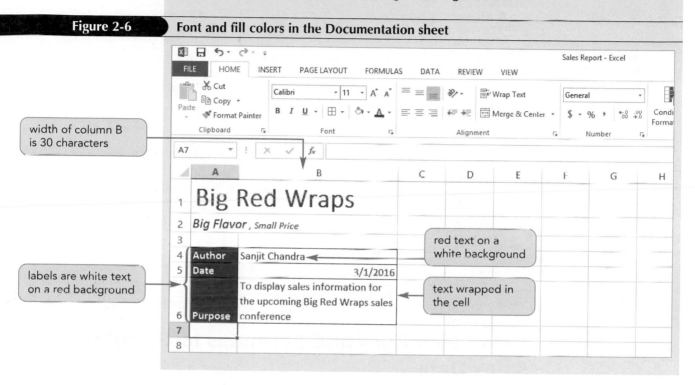

width of column B is 30 characters

labels are white text on a red background

red text on a white background

text wrapped in the cell

Adding a Background Image

A background image can provide a textured appearance, like that of granite, wood, or fibered paper, to a worksheet. The image is repeated until it fills the entire sheet. The background image does not affect any cell's format or content. Fill colors added to cells appear on top of the image, covering that portion of the image. Background images are visible only on the screen; they do not print.

Sanjit has provided an image that he wants you to use as the background of the Documentation sheet.

To add a background image to the Documentation sheet:

1. On the ribbon, click the **PAGE LAYOUT** tab to display the page layout options.

2. In the Page Setup group, click the **Background** button. The Insert Pictures dialog box opens with options to select a picture from a file, select Office.com Clip Art, or perform a Bing Image Search.

3. Click the **Browse** button next to the From a file label. The Sheet Background dialog box opens.

4. Navigate to the **Excel2 ▸ Tutorial** folder included with your Data Files, click the **Background** JPEG image file, and then click the **Insert** button. The image is added to the background of the Documentation sheet, and the Background button changes to the Delete Background button, which you can use to remove the background image. See Figure 2-7.

Figure 2-7   **Background image in the Documentation sheet**

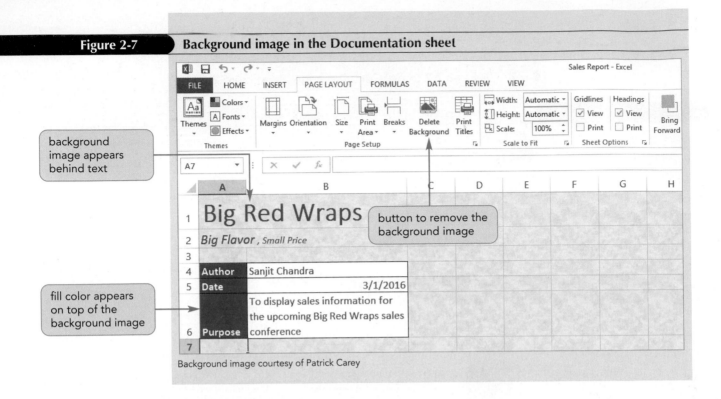

background image appears behind text

button to remove the background image

fill color appears on top of the background image

Background image courtesy of Patrick Carey

Using Functions and Formulas to Calculate Sales Data

In the Sales Report worksheet, you will format the gross sales from each of the store's 20 restaurants and the summary statistics for those stores. The Sales Report worksheet is divided into two areas. The table at the bottom of the worksheet displays gross sales for the past year for each month by restaurant. The section at the top of the worksheet summarizes the sales data for the past two years. Sanjit collected the following sales data:

- **Gross Sales**—the total amount of sales at all of the restaurants
- **Cost of Sales**—the cost of producing the store's menu items
- **Operating Expenses**—the cost of running the stores including the employment and insurance costs
- **Net Profit/Loss**—the difference between the income from the gross sales and the total cost of sales and operating expenses
- **Units Sold**—the total number of menu items sold by the company during the year
- **Customers Served**—the total number of customers served by the company during the year

Sanjit wants you to calculate these sales statistics for the entire company and per store so he can track how well the stores are performing. First, you will calculate the total gross sales for Big Red Wraps and the company's overall net profit and loss.

To calculate the company's sales and profit/loss:

▶ **1.** Click the **Sales Report** sheet tab to make the Sales Report worksheet active.

2. Click cell **C6**, type the formula **=SUM(C27:N46)** to calculate the total gross sales from all stores in the previous year, and then press the **Enter** key. Cell C6 displays 9514000, which means that Big Red Wraps' total gross sales for the previous year were more than $9.5 million.

TIP

To enter content in a cell, you select the cell, type the specified content, and then press the Enter key.

3. In cell **C9**, enter the formula **=C6–(C7+C8)** to calculate the current year's net profit/loss, which is equal to the difference between the gross sales and the sum of the cost of sales and operating expenses. Cell C9 displays 1108000, which means that the company's net profit for 2015 was more than $1.1 million.

4. Copy the formula in cell **C9**, and then paste it into cell **D9** to calculate the net profit/loss for 2014. Cell D9 displays 1264000, which means that the company's net profit for that year was more than $1.26 million.

Next, Sanjit asks you to summarize the sales statistics for each store. Sanjit wants the same per-store statistics calculated for the 2015 and 2014 sales data. Per-store sales statistics are calculated by dividing the overall statistics by the number of stores. In this case, you will divide the overall statistics by the value in cell C23, which contains the total number of stores in the Big Red Wraps chain. After you enter the 2015 formulas, you can copy and paste them to calculate the 2014 results.

To calculate the per-store statistics:

1. In cell **C16**, enter the formula **=C6/C23** to calculate the gross sales per store in 2015. The formula returns 475700, which means that the annual gross sales amount for a Big Red Wraps store in 2015 was more than $475,000.

2. In cell **C17**, enter the formula **=C7/C23** to calculate the cost of sales per store in 2015. The formula returns the value 168700, which means that the cost of sales for a Big Red Wraps store in 2015 was typically $168,700.

3. In cell **C18**, enter the formula **=C8/C23** to calculate the operating expenses per store in 2015. The formula returns the value 251600, which means that operating expenses of a typical store in 2015 were $251,600.

4. In cell **C19**, enter the formula **=C9/C23** to calculate the net profit/loss per store in 2015. The formula returns the value 55400, indicating that the net profit/loss of a typical store in 2015 was $55,400.

5. In cell **C21**, enter the formula **=C11/C23** to calculate the units sold per store in 2015. The formula returns the value 67200, indicating that a typical store sold 67,200 units during 2015.

6. In cell **C22**, enter the formula **=C12/C23** to calculate the customers served per store in 2015. The formula returns the value 7770, indicating that a typical store served 7,770 customers during that year.

7. Copy the formulas in the range **C16:C22** and paste them into the range **D16:D22**. The cell references in the formulas change to calculate the sales data for the year 2014.

8. Select cell **B24** to deselect the range. See Figure 2-8.

Figure 2-8   **Sales statistics for the entire company and per store**

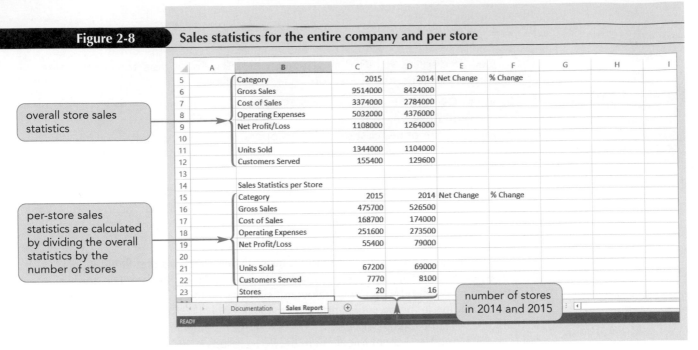

overall store sales statistics

per-store sales statistics are calculated by dividing the overall statistics by the number of stores

number of stores in 2014 and 2015

Sanjit also wants to explore how the company's sales and expenses have changed from 2014 to 2015. To do this, you will calculate the net change in sales from 2014 to 2015 as well as the percent change. The percent change is calculated using the following formula:

$$percent\ change = \frac{2015\ value - 2014\ value}{2014\ value}$$

You will calculate the net and percent changes for all of the sales statistics.

To calculate the net and percent changes for 2015 and 2014:

1. In cell **E6**, enter the formula **=C6–D6** to calculate the difference between the 2015 and 2014 gross sales. The formula returns 1090000, indicating that gross sales increased by $1.09 million between 2014 and 2015.

2. In cell **F6**, enter the formula **=(C6–D6)/D6** to calculate the percent change in gross sales from 2014 to 2015. The formula returns 0.129392213, indicating a nearly 13% increase in gross sales from 2014 to 2015.

   Next, you'll copy and paste the formulas in cells E6 and F6 to the rest of the sales data to calculate the net change and percent change from 2014 to 2015.

3. Select the range **E6:F6**, and then copy the selected range. The two formulas are copied to the Clipboard.

4. Select the nonadjacent range **E7:F9;E11:F12;E16:F19;E21:F23**, and then paste the formulas from the Clipboard into the selected range. The net and percent changes are calculated for the remaining sales data.

5. Click cell **B24** to deselect the range, and then scroll the worksheet up to display row 5. See Figure 2-9.

Be sure to include the parentheses as shown to calculate the percent change correctly.

Figure 2-9 | Net and percent changes calculated

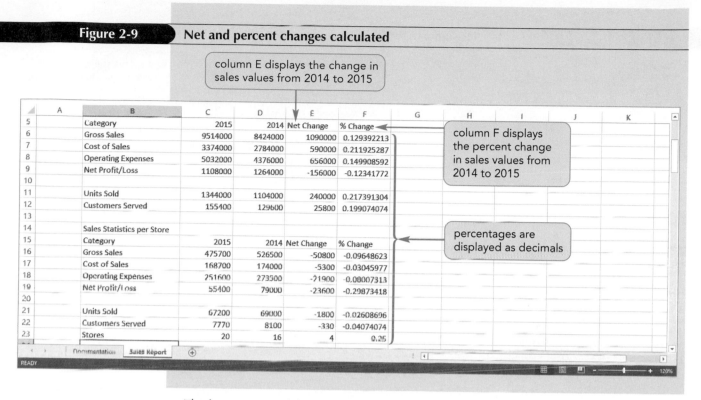

The bottom part of the worksheet contains the sales for each restaurant from 2015. You will use the SUM function to calculate the total gross sales for each restaurant during the entire year, the total monthly sales of all 20 restaurants, and the total gross sales of all restaurants and months.

To calculate different subtotals of the gross sales:

1. Select cell **O26**, type **TOTAL** as the label, and then press the **Enter** key. Cell O27 is now the active cell.

2. On the HOME tab, in the Editing group, click the **AutoSum** button, and then press the **Enter** key to accept the suggested range reference and enter the formula =SUM(C27:N27) in cell O27. The cell displays 355000, indicating gross sales in 2015 for the 411 Elm Drive restaurant were $355,000.

3. Copy the formula in cell **O27**, and then paste that formula into the range **O28:O46** to calculate the total sales for each of the remaining 19 restaurants in the Big Red Wraps chain.

4. Select cell **B47**, type **TOTAL** as the label, and then press the **Tab** key. Cell C47 is now the active cell.

5. Select the range **C47:O47** so that you can calculate the total monthly sales for all of the stores.

6. On the HOME tab, in the Editing group, click the **AutoSum** button, and then press the **Enter** key to calculate the total sales for each month as well as the total sales for all months. For example, cell C47 displays 680000, indicating that monthly sales for January 2015 for all stores were $680,000.

7. Select cell **O48** to deselect the range. See Figure 2-10.

Figure 2-10 — **Gross sales summarized by store and month**

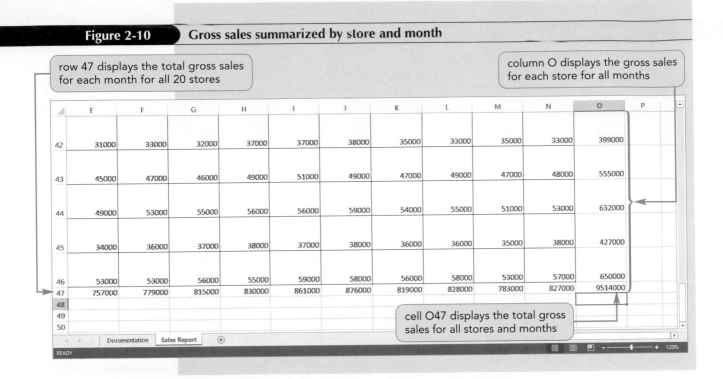

row 47 displays the total gross sales for each month for all 20 stores

column O displays the gross sales for each store for all months

cell O47 displays the total gross sales for all stores and months

	E	F	G	H	I	J	K	L	M	N	O	P
42	31000	33000	32000	37000	37000	38000	35000	33000	35000	33000	399000	
43	45000	47000	46000	49000	51000	49000	47000	49000	47000	48000	555000	
44	49000	53000	55000	56000	56000	59000	54000	55000	51000	53000	632000	
45	34000	36000	37000	38000	37000	38000	36000	36000	35000	38000	427000	
46	53000	53000	56000	55000	59000	58000	56000	58000	53000	57000	650000	
47	757000	779000	815000	830000	861000	876000	819000	828000	783000	827000	9514000	
48												
49												
50												

Documentation   Sales Report   (+)

READY   120%

Formatting Numbers

The goal in formatting any workbook is to make the content easier to interpret. For numbers, this can mean adding a comma to separate thousands, setting the number of decimal places, and using percentage and currency symbols to make numbers easier to read and understand. Sanjit asks you to format the numbers in the Sales Report worksheet to improve their readability.

Applying Number Formats

You can use a number format to display values in a way that makes them easier to read and understand. Changing the number format of the displayed value does not affect the stored value. Numbers are originally formatted in the **General format**, which, for the most part, displays numbers exactly as they are typed. If the number is calculated from a formula or function, the cell displays as many digits after the decimal point as will fit in the cell with the last digit rounded. Calculated values too large to fit into the cell are displayed in scientific notation.

The General format is fine for small numbers, but some values require additional formatting to make the numbers easier to interpret. For example, you might want to:

- Change the number of digits displayed to the right of the decimal point
- Add commas to separate thousands in large numbers
- Apply currency symbols to numbers to identify the monetary unit being used
- Display percentages using the % symbol

Excel supports two monetary formats: currency and accounting. Both formats add a thousands separator to the currency values and display two digits to the right of the decimal point. However, the **Currency format** places a currency symbol directly to the left of the first digit of the currency value and displays negative numbers with a negative sign. The **Accounting format** fixes a currency symbol at the left edge of the column, and displays negative numbers within parentheses and zero values with a dash. It also slightly indents the values from the right edge of the cell to allow room for parentheses around negative values. Figure 2-11 compares the two formats.

Figure 2-11   **Currency and Accounting number formats**

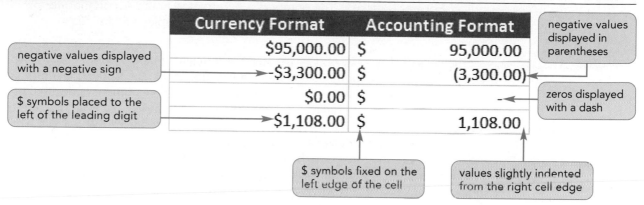

negative values displayed with a negative sign

$ symbols placed to the left of the leading digit

Currency Format	Accounting Format
$95,000.00	$ 95,000.00
-$3,300.00	$ (3,300.00)
$0.00	$ -
$1,108.00	$ 1,108.00

negative values displayed in parentheses

zeros displayed with a dash

$ symbols fixed on the left edge of the cell

values slightly indented from the right cell edge

PROSKILLS

Written Communication: Formatting Monetary Values

Spreadsheets commonly include monetary values. To make these values simpler to read and comprehend, keep in mind the following guidelines when formatting the currency data in a worksheet:

- **Format for your audience.** For general financial reports, round values to the nearest hundred, thousand, or million. Investors are generally more interested in the big picture than in exact values. However, for accounting reports, accuracy is important and often legally required. So, for those reports, be sure to display the exact monetary value.
- **Use thousands separators.** Large strings of numbers can be challenging to read. For monetary values, use a thousands separator to make the amounts easier to comprehend.
- **Apply the Accounting format to columns of monetary values.** The Accounting format makes columns of numbers easier to read than the Currency format. Use the Currency format for individual cells that are not part of long columns of numbers.
- **Use only two currency symbols in a column of monetary values.** Standard accounting format displays one currency symbol with the first monetary value in the column, and optionally displays a second currency symbol with the last value in that column. Use the Accounting format to fix the currency symbols, lining them up within the column.

Following these standard accounting principles will make your financial data easier to read both on the screen and in printouts.

Sanjit wants you to format the gross sales amounts in the Accounting format so that they are easier to read.

To format the gross sales in the Accounting format:

1. Select the range **C6:E6** with the gross sales.

TIP

To select other currency symbols, click the Accounting Number Format button arrow, and then click a currency symbol.

2. On the HOME tab, in the Number group, click the **Accounting Number Format** button $. The numbers are formatted in the Accounting format. You cannot see the format because the cells display ##########.

The cells display ########## because the formatted number doesn't fit into the column. One reason for this is that monetary values, by default, show both dollars and cents in the cell. However, you can increase or decrease the number of decimal places displayed in a cell. The displayed value might then be rounded. For example, the stored value 11.7 will appear in the cell as 12 if no decimal places are displayed to the right of the decimal point. Changing the number of decimal places displayed in a cell does not change the value stored in the cell.

Because Sanjit and the other conference attendees are interested only in whole dollar amounts, he wants you to hide the cents values of the gross sales by decreasing the number of decimal places to zero.

To decrease the number of decimal places displayed in the gross sales:

1. Make sure the range **C6:E6** is selected.

2. On the HOME tab, in the Number group, click the **Decrease Decimal** button twice. The cents are hidden for gross sales.

3. Select cell **C4** to deselect the range. See Figure 2-12.

Figure 2-12   **Formatted gross sales values**

The Comma style is identical to the Accounting format except that it does not fix a currency symbol to the left of the number. The advantage of using the Comma style and the Accounting format together is that the numbers will be aligned in the column.

Sanjit asks you to apply the Comma style to the remaining sales statistics.

To apply the Comma style to the sales statistics:

1. Select the nonadjacent range **C7:E9;C11:E12** containing the sales figures for all stores in 2014 and 2015.

2. On the HOME tab, in the Number group, click the **Comma Style** button 🔢. In some instances, the number is now too large to be displayed in the cell.

3. In the Number group, click the **Decrease Decimal** button 🔢 twice to remove two decimal places. Digits to the right of the decimal point are hidden for all of the selected cells.

4. Select cell **C13** to deselect the range. See Figure 2-13.

Figure 2-13	Formatted sales values

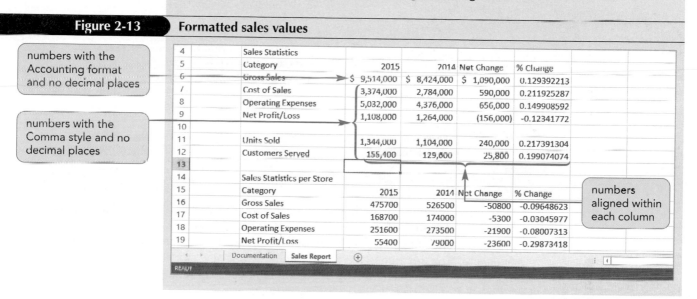

numbers with the Accounting format and no decimal places

numbers with the Comma style and no decimal places

numbers aligned within each column

4	Sales Statistics				
5	Category	2015	2014	Net Change	% Change
6	Gross Sales	$ 9,514,000	$ 8,424,000	$ 1,090,000	0.129392213
7	Cost of Sales	3,374,000	2,784,000	590,000	0.211925287
8	Operating Expenses	5,032,000	4,376,000	656,000	0.149908592
9	Net Profit/Loss	1,108,000	1,264,000	(156,000)	-0.12341772
10					
11	Units Sold	1,344,000	1,104,000	240,000	0.217391304
12	Customers Served	155,100	129,600	25,800	0.199074074
13					
14	Sales Statistics per Store				
15	Category	2015	2014	Net Change	% Change
16	Gross Sales	475700	526500	-50800	-0.09648623
17	Cost of Sales	168700	174000	-5300	-0.03045977
18	Operating Expenses	251600	273500	-21900	-0.08007313
19	Net Profit/Loss	55400	79000	-23600	-0.29873418

Documentation   **Sales Report**   ⊕

READY

The Percent style formats numbers as percentages. When you format values as percentages, the % symbol appears after the number and no digits appear to the right of the decimal point. You can always change how many decimal places are displayed in the cell if that is important to show with your data.

Sanjit wants you to format the percent change from the 2014 to 2015 sales statistics with a percent symbol to make the percent values easier to read.

To format percentages:

1. Select the nonadjacent range **F6:F9;F11:F12** containing the percent change values.

2. On the HOME tab, in the Number group, click the **Percent Style** button % (or press the **Ctrl+Shift+%** keys). The values are displayed as percentages.

3. In the Number group, click the **Increase Decimal** button 🔢 twice. The displayed number includes two decimal places.

4. Select cell **F13** to deselect the range. See Figure 2-14.

Figure 2-14 Formatted percent changes

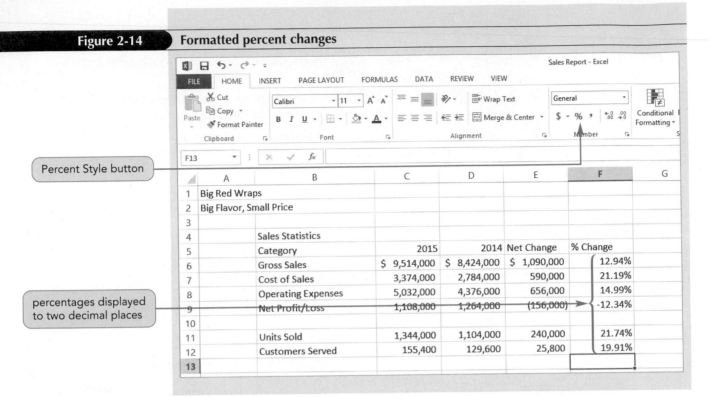

With the data reformatted, the worksheet clearly shows that Big Red Wraps' gross sales increased from 2014 to 2015 by almost 13 percent. However, both the cost of sales and the operating expenses increased by about 21.2 percent and 15 percent, respectively, probably due to the cost of building four new stores. As a result, the company's net profit decreased by $156,000 or about 12.3 percent.

Formatting Dates and Times

Because Excel stores dates and times as numbers and not as text, you can apply different formats without affecting the date and time value. The abbreviated format, *mm/dd/yyyy*, entered in the Documentation sheet is referred to as the **Short Date format**. You can also apply a **Long Date format** that displays the day of the week and the full month name in addition to the day of the month and the year. Other built-in formats include formats for displaying time values in 12- or 24-hour time format.

You will change the date in the Documentation sheet to the Long Date format.

To format the date in the Long Date format:

1. Go to the **Documentation** sheet, and then select cell **B5**.

2. On the ribbon, make sure the HOME tab is displayed.

3. In the Number group, click the **Number Format button arrow** to display a list of number formats, and then click **Long Date**. The date is displayed with the weekday name, month name, day, and year. Notice that the date in the formula bar did not change because you changed only the display format, not the date value.

Formatting Worksheet Cells

You can format the appearance of individual cells by modifying the alignment of text within the cell, indenting cell text, or adding borders of different styles and colors.

Aligning Cell Content

By default, text is aligned with the left and bottom borders of a cell, and numbers are aligned with the right and bottom borders. You might want to change the alignment to make the text and numbers more readable or visually appealing. In general, you should center column titles, left-align other text, and right-align numbers to keep their decimal places lined up within a column. Figure 2-15 describes the buttons you use to set these alignment options, which are located in the Alignment group on the HOME tab.

Figure 2-15   **Alignment buttons**

Button	Name	Description
	Top Align	Aligns the cell content with the cell's top edge
	Middle Align	Vertically centers the cell content within the cell
	Bottom Align	Aligns the cell content with the cell's bottom edge
	Align Left	Aligns the cell content with the cell's left edge
	Center	Horizontally centers the cell content within the cell
	Align Right	Aligns the cell content with the cell's right edge
	Decrease Indent	Decreases the size of the indentation used in the cell
	Increase Indent	Increases the size of the indentation used in the cell
	Orientation	Rotates the cell content to any angle within the cell
	Wrap Text	Forces the cell text to wrap within the cell borders
	Merge & Center	Merges the selected cells into a single cell

© 2014 Cengage Learning

The date in the Documentation sheet is right-aligned in the cell because Excel treats dates and times as numbers. Sanjit wants you to left-align the date and center the column titles in the Sales Report worksheet.

To left-align the date and center the column titles:

1. In the Documentation sheet, make sure cell **B5** is still selected.

2. On the HOME tab, in the Alignment group, click the **Align Left** button. The date shifts to the left edge of the cell.

3. Make the **Sales Report** worksheet the active worksheet.

4. Select the range **C5:F5**. The column titles are selected.

5. In the Alignment group, click the **Center** button. The column titles are centered in the cells.

Indenting Cell Content

Sometimes you want a cell's content moved a few spaces from the cell's left edge. This is particularly useful to create subsections in a worksheet or to set off some entries from others. You can increase the indent to shift the contents of a cell away from the left edge of the cell, or you can decrease the indent to shift a cell's contents closer to the left edge of the cell.

Sanjit wants the Cost of Sales and Operating Expenses labels in the sales statistics table offset from the other labels because they represent expenses to the company. You will increase the indent for the expense categories.

To indent the expense categories:

▶ 1. Select the range **B7:B8** containing the expense categories.

▶ 2. On the HOME tab, in the Alignment group, click the **Increase Indent** button ⬚ twice to indent each label two spaces in its cell.

Adding Cell Borders

Common accounting practices provide guidelines on when to add borders to cells. In general, a single black border appears above a subtotal, a single bottom border is added below a calculated number, and a double black bottom border appears below the total.

Sanjit wants you to follow these common accounting practices in the Sales Report worksheet. You will add borders below the column titles and below the gross sales values. You will add a top border to the net profit/loss values. Finally, you will add a top and bottom border to the Units Sold and Customers Served rows.

To add borders to the sales statistics data:

▶ 1. Select the range **B5:F5** containing the table headings.

▶ 2. On the HOME tab, in the Font group, click the **All Borders button arrow** ⬚ ▾, and then click **Bottom Border**. A border is added below the column titles.

▶ 3. Select the range **B6:F6** containing the gross sales amounts.

▶ 4. In the Font group, click the **Bottom Border** button ⬚ to add a border below the selected gross sales amounts.

▶ 5. Select the range **B9:F9**, click the **Bottom Border button arrow** ⬚ ▾, and then click **Top Border** to add a border above the net profit/loss amounts.

The Units Sold and Customers Served rows do not contain monetary values as the other rows do. You will distinguish these rows by adding a top and bottom border.

▶ 6. Select the range **B11:F12**, click the **Top Border button arrow** ⬚ ▾, and then click **Top and Bottom** to add a border above the number of units sold and below the number of customers served.

▶ 7. Select cell **B3** to deselect the range. See Figure 2-16.

Figure 2-16   Worksheet with formatted cells

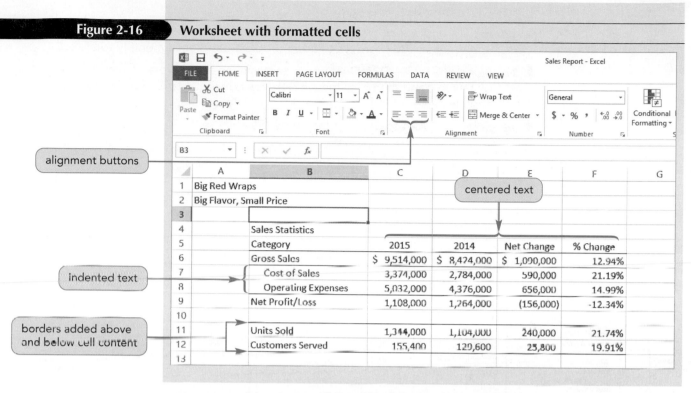

You can apply multiple formats to the same cell to create the look that best fits the data. For example, one cell might be formatted with a number format, alignments, borders, indents, fonts, font sizes, and so on. The monthly sales data needs to be formatted with number styles, alignment, indents, and borders. You'll add these formats now.

To format the monthly sales table:

1. Click the **Name** box to select the cell reference, type **C27:O47**, and then press the **Enter** key to quickly select the range C27:O47 containing the monthly gross sales for each restaurant.

2. On the HOME tab, in the Number group, click the **Comma Style** button ⟨⟩ to add a thousands separator to the values.

3. In the Number group, click the **Decrease Decimal** button to hide the cents from the sales results.

4. In the Alignment group, click the **Top Align** button to align the sales numbers with the top of each cell.

5. Select the range **C26:O26** containing the labels for the month abbreviations and the TOTAL column.

6. In the Alignment group, click the **Center** button to center the column labels.

7. Select the range **B27:B46** containing the store addresses.

8. Reduce the font size of the store addresses to **9** points.

9. In the Alignment group, click the **Increase Indent** button to indent the store addresses.

10. In the Alignment group, click the **Top Align** button to align the addresses at the top of each cell.

11. Select the range **B47:O47** containing the monthly totals.

12. In the Font group, click the **Top and Bottom Borders button arrow** 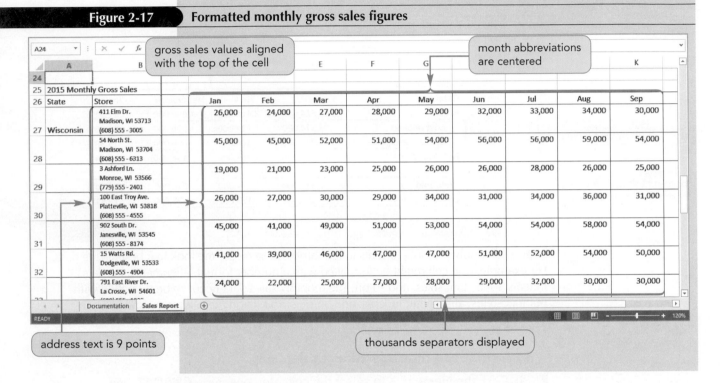 , and then click **All Borders** to add borders around each monthly totals cell.

13. Select the range **O26:O46**, which contains the annual totals for each restaurant, and then click the **All Borders** button to add borders around each restaurant total.

14. Select cell **A24** to deselect the range. See Figure 2-17.

Figure 2-17 **Formatted monthly gross sales figures**

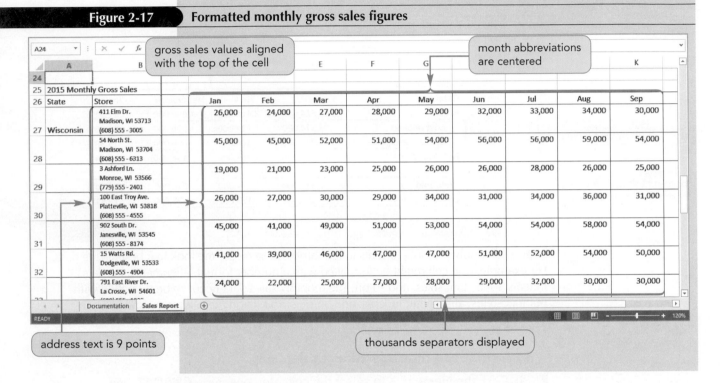

gross sales values aligned with the top of the cell

month abbreviations are centered

State	Store		Jan	Feb	Mar	Apr	May	Jun	Jul	Aug	Sep
	411 Elm Dr. Madison, WI 53713 (608) 555-3005		26,000	24,000	27,000	28,000	29,000	32,000	33,000	34,000	30,000
Wisconsin	54 North St. Madison, WI 53704 (608) 555-6313		45,000	45,000	52,000	51,000	54,000	56,000	56,000	59,000	54,000
	3 Ashford Ln. Monroe, WI 53566 (779) 555-2401		19,000	21,000	23,000	25,000	26,000	26,000	28,000	26,000	25,000
	100 East Troy Ave. Platteville, WI 53818 (608) 555-4555		26,000	27,000	30,000	29,000	34,000	31,000	34,000	36,000	31,000
	902 South Dr. Janesville, WI 53545 (608) 555-8174		45,000	41,000	49,000	51,000	53,000	54,000	54,000	58,000	54,000
	15 Watts Rd. Dodgeville, WI 53533 (608) 555-4904		41,000	39,000	46,000	47,000	47,000	51,000	52,000	54,000	50,000
	791 East River Dr. La Crosse, WI 54601		24,000	22,000	25,000	27,000	28,000	29,000	32,000	30,000	30,000

25 2015 Monthly Gross Sales

address text is 9 points

thousands separators displayed

Merging Cells

You can merge, or combine, several cells into one cell. A merged cell contains two or more cells with a single cell reference. When you merge cells, only the content from the upper-left cell in the range is retained. The cell reference for the merged cell is the upper-left cell reference. So, if you merge cells A1 and A2, the merged cell reference is cell A1. After you merge cells, you can align the content within the merged cell. The Merge & Center button in the Alignment group on the HOME tab includes the following options:

- **Merge & Center**—merges the range into one cell and horizontally centers the content
- **Merge Across**—merges each row in the selected range across the columns in the range
- **Merge Cells**—merges the range into a single cell, but does not horizontally center the cell content
- **Unmerge Cells**—reverses a merge, returning the merged cell to a range of individual cells

The first column of the monthly sales data lists the states in which Big Red Wraps has stores. You will merge the cells for each state name.

To merge the state name cells:

1. Select the range **A27:A33** containing the cells for the Wisconsin stores. You will merge these seven cells into a single cell.

2. On the HOME tab, in the Alignment group, click the **Merge & Center** button. The range A27:A33 merges into one cell with the cell reference A27, and the text is centered and bottom-aligned within the cell.

3. Select the range **A34:A36**, and then click the **Merge & Center** button in the Alignment group to merge and center the Minnesota cells.

4. Select the range **A37:A40**, and then click the **Merge & Center** button to merge and center the Iowa cells.

5. Select cell **A41**, and then center it horizontally to align the Colorado text with the text in the other state cells.

6. Merge and center the range **A42:A43** containing the Nebraska cells.

7. Merge and center the range **A44:A46** containing the Kansas cells. See Figure 2-18. The merged cells make it easier to distinguish restaurants in each state.

Figure 2-18   Merged cells

	A	B	C	D	E	F	G
40	Iowa	414 Main St. Des Moines, IA 50311 (515) 555 - 3134	46,000	43,000	52,000	51,000	54
41	Colorado	112 Reservoir Ln. Greeley, CO 80631 (970) 555 - 2138	38,000	35,000	43,000	42,000	44
42		5155 Pocane Dr. Grand Island, NE 68801 (402) 555 - 7734	27,000	28,000	31,000	33,000	32
43	Nebraska	42 East River Rd. Omaha, NE 68111 (402) 555 - 9148	38,000	39,000	45,000	47,000	46
44		975 Business Dr. Manhattan, KS 66502 (785) 555 - 0444	46,000	45,000	49,000	53,000	55
45		47 Valley View Ln. Topeka, KS 66604 (785) 555 - 6106	31,000	31,000	34,000	36,000	37
46	Kansas	87210 Causeway Dr. Salina, KS 67401 (785) 555 - 8103	47,000	45,000	53,000	53,000	56
47		TOTAL	600,000	639,000	757,000	779,000	815
48							

merged cell A42 contains the range A42:A43

merged cell A44 contains the range A44:A46

Documentation   **Sales Report**   (+)

READY

Rotating Cell Contents

Text and numbers are displayed horizontally within cells. However, you can rotate cell text to any angle to save space or to provide visual interest to a worksheet. The state names at the bottom of the merged cells would look better and take up less room if they were rotated vertically within their cells. Sanjit asks you to rotate the state names.

To rotate the state names:

1. Select the merged cell **A27**.

2. On the HOME tab, in the Alignment group, click the **Orientation** button to display a list of rotation options, and then click **Rotate Text Up**. The state name rotates 90 degrees counterclockwise.

3. In the Alignment group, click the **Middle Align** button 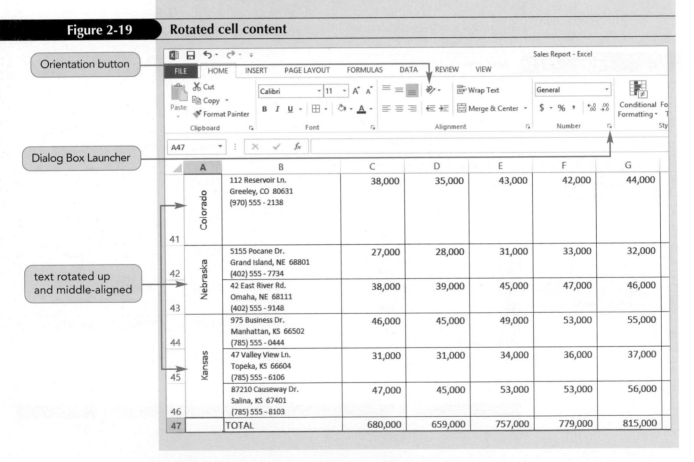 to vertically center the rotated text in the merged cell.

4. Select the merged cell range **A34:A44**, and then repeat Steps 2 and 3 to rotate and vertically center the rest of the state names in their cells.

5. Select cell **A41** to deselect the range, and then increase the height of row 41 (the Colorado row) to **75** points (**100** pixels) so that the entire state name appears in the cell.

6. Reduce the width of column A to **7** characters because the rotated state names take up less space.

7. Select cell **A47**. See Figure 2-19.

| Figure 2-19 | Rotated cell content |

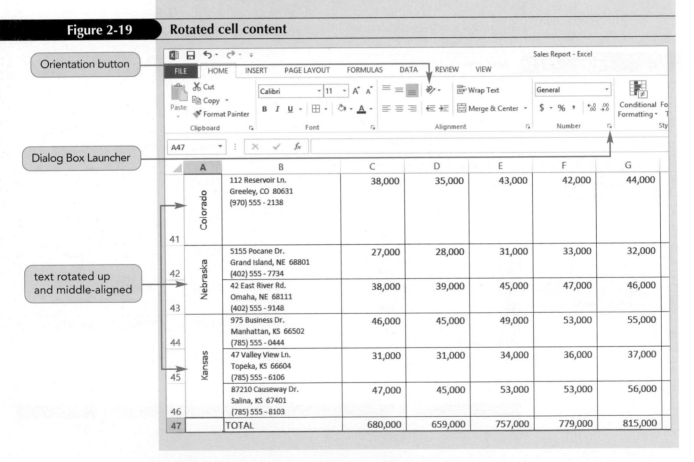

Exploring the Format Cells Dialog Box

The buttons on the HOME tab provide quick access to the most commonly used formatting choices. For more options, you can use the Format Cells dialog box. You can apply the formats in this dialog box to the selected worksheet cells. The Format Cells dialog box has six tabs, each focusing on a different set of formatting options, as described below:

• **Number**—provides options for formatting the appearance of numbers, including dates and numbers treated as text such as telephone or Social Security numbers
• **Alignment**—provides options for how data is aligned within a cell
• **Font**—provides options for selecting font types, sizes, styles, and other formatting attributes such as underlining and font colors

- **Border**—provides options for adding and removing cell borders as well as selecting a line style and color
- **Fill**—provides options for creating and applying background colors and patterns to cells
- **Protection**—provides options for locking or hiding cells to prevent other users from modifying their contents

Although you have applied many of these formats from the HOME tab, the Format Cells dialog box presents them in a different way and provides more choices. You will use the Font and Fill tabs to format the column titles with a white font on a red background.

To use the Format Cells dialog box to format the column labels:

1. Select the range **A26:O26** containing the column labels for the table.

2. On the HOME tab, in the Number group, click the **Dialog Box Launcher** located to the right of the group name (refer to Figure 2-19). The Format Cells dialog box opens with the Number tab displayed.

3. Click the **Font** tab to display the font formatting options.

4. Click the **Color** box to display the color palette, and then click the **White, Background 1** theme color. The font is set to white. See Figure 2-20.

Figure 2-20   Font tab in the Format Cells dialog box

5. Click the **Fill** tab to display background options.

6. In the Background Color palette, click the **red** standard color (the second color in the last row). The background is set to red, as you can see in the Sample box.

7. Click the **OK** button. The dialog box closes, and the font and fill options you selected are applied to the column titles.

You will also use the Format Cells dialog box to change the appearance of the row titles. You'll format them to be displayed in a larger white font on a gray background.

To format the row labels:

1. Select the range **A27:A46** containing the rotated state names.

2. Right-click the selected range, and then click **Format Cells** on the shortcut menu. The Format Cells dialog box opens with the last tab used displayed—in this case, the Fill tab.

3. In the Background Color palette, click the **gray** theme color (the first color in the seventh column). Its preview is shown in the Sample box.

4. Click the **Font** tab to display the font formatting options.

5. Click the **Color** box, and then click the **White, Background 1** theme color to set the font color to white.

6. Scroll down the **Size** box, and then click **16** to set the font size to 16 points.

7. Click the **OK** button. The dialog box closes, and the font and fill formats are applied to the state names.

The Border tab in the Format Cells dialog box provides options for changing the border style and color as well as placing the border anywhere around a cell or cells in a selected range. Sanjit wants you to format the borders in the monthly sales data so that the sales result from each state is surrounded by a double border.

To add a double border to the state results:

1. Select the range **A27:O33** containing the monthly sales totals for the Wisconsin restaurants.

2. Open the Format Cells dialog box, and then click the **Border** tab to display the border options.

3. In the Style box, click the **double line** in the lower-right corner of the box.

4. In the Presets section, click the **Outline** option. The double border appears around the outside of the selected cells in the Border preview. See Figure 2-21.

Figure 2-21   **Border tab in the Format Cells dialog box**

> **5.** Click the **OK** button. The selected border is applied to the Wisconsin monthly sales.

> **6.** Repeat Steps 2 through 5 to apply double borders to the ranges **A34:O36**, **A37:O40**, **A41:O41**, **A42:O43**, and **A44:O46**.

> **7.** Select cell **A48** to deselect the range. See Figure 2-22.

Figure 2-22   Worksheet with font, fill, and border formatting

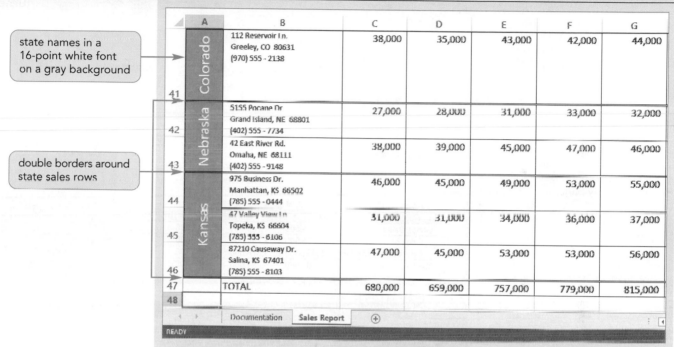

state names in a 16-point white font on a gray background

double borders around state sales rows

	A	B	C	D	E	F	G
	Colorado	112 Reservoir Ln. Greeley, CO 80631 (970) 555 - 2138	38,000	35,000	43,000	42,000	44,000
41							
42	Nebraska	5155 Pocane Dr Grand Island, NE 68801 (402) 555 - 7734	27,000	28,000	31,000	33,000	32,000
43		42 East River Rd. Omaha, NE 68111 (402) 555 - 9148	38,000	39,000	45,000	47,000	46,000
44	Kansas	975 Business Dr. Manhattan, KS 66502 (785) 555 - 0444	46,000	45,000	49,000	53,000	55,000
45		47 Valley View Ln Topeka, KS 66604 (785) 555 - 6106	31,000	31,000	34,000	36,000	37,000
46		87210 Causeway Dr. Salina, KS 67401 (785) 555 - 8103	47,000	45,000	53,000	53,000	56,000
47		TOTAL	680,000	659,000	757,000	779,000	815,000
48							

Documentation   **Sales Report**   (+)

READY

> **8.** Save the Sales Report worksheet.

You have completed much of the formatting that Sanjit wants in the Sales Report worksheet for the Big Red Wraps sales conference. In the next session, you will explore other formatting options.

Session 2.1 Quick Check

REVIEW

1. What is the difference between a serif font and a sans serif font?
2. What is the difference between a theme color and a standard color?
3. A cell containing a number displays #######. Why does this occur and what can you do to fix it?
4. What is the General format?
5. Describe the differences between Currency format and Accounting format.
6. The range A1:C5 is merged into a single cell. What is its cell reference?
7. How do you format text so that it is set vertically within the cell?
8. Where can you access all the formatting options for worksheet cells?

Session 2.2 Visual Overview:

The PAGE LAYOUT tab has options for setting how the worksheet will print.

The **Format Painter** copies and pastes formatting from one cell or range to another without duplicating any data.

Print titles are rows and columns that are included on every page of the printout. In this case, the text in rows 1 and 2 will print on every page.

A **manual page break** is one you set to indicate where a new page of the printout should start and is identified by a solid blue line.

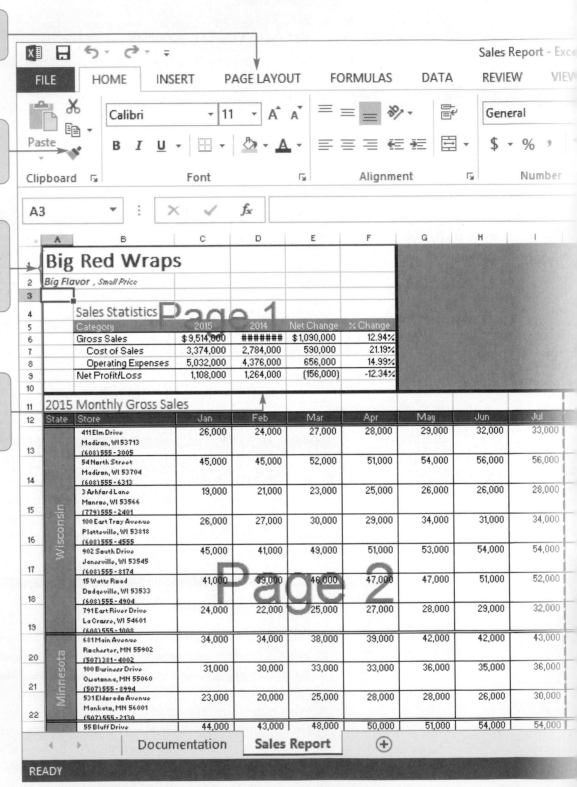

	State	Store	Jan	Feb	Mar	Apr	May	Jun	Jul
13	Wisconsin	411 Elm Drive Madison, WI 53713 (608) 555-3005	26,000	24,000	27,000	28,000	29,000	32,000	33,000
14		54 North Street Madison, WI 53704 (608) 555-6313	45,000	45,000	52,000	51,000	54,000	56,000	56,000
15		3 Ashford Lane Monroe, WI 53566 (779) 555-2401	19,000	21,000	23,000	25,000	26,000	26,000	28,000
16		100 East Troy Avenue Platteville, WI 53818 (608) 555-4555	26,000	27,000	30,000	29,000	34,000	31,000	34,000
17		902 South Drive Janesville, WI 53545 (608) 555-8174	45,000	41,000	49,000	51,000	53,000	54,000	54,000
18		15 Watts Road Dodgeville, WI 53533 (608) 555-4904	41,000	39,000	46,000	47,000	47,000	51,000	52,000
19		791 East River Drive La Crosse, WI 54601 (608) 555-1008	24,000	22,000	25,000	27,000	28,000	29,000	32,000
20	Minnesota	681 Main Avenue Rochester, MN 55902 (507) 381-4002	34,000	34,000	38,000	39,000	42,000	42,000	43,000
21		100 Business Drive Owatonna, MN 55060 (507) 555-8994	31,000	30,000	33,000	33,000	36,000	35,000	36,000
22		531 Eldorado Avenue Mankato, MN 56001 (507) 555-2130	23,000	20,000	25,000	28,000	28,000	26,000	30,000
		55 Bluff Drive	44,000	43,000	48,000	50,000	51,000	54,000	54,000

Sales Statistics **Page 1**

Category	2015	2014	Net Change	% Change
Gross Sales	$9,514,000	########	$1,090,000	12.94%
Cost of Sales	3,374,000	2,784,000	590,000	21.19%
Operating Expenses	5,032,000	4,376,000	656,000	14.99%
Net Profit/Loss	1,108,000	1,264,000	(156,000)	-12.34%

Big Red Wraps

Big Flavor , Small Price

2015 Monthly Gross Sales

Page 2

Documentation | **Sales Report** | ⊕

READY

Worksheet Formatted for Printing

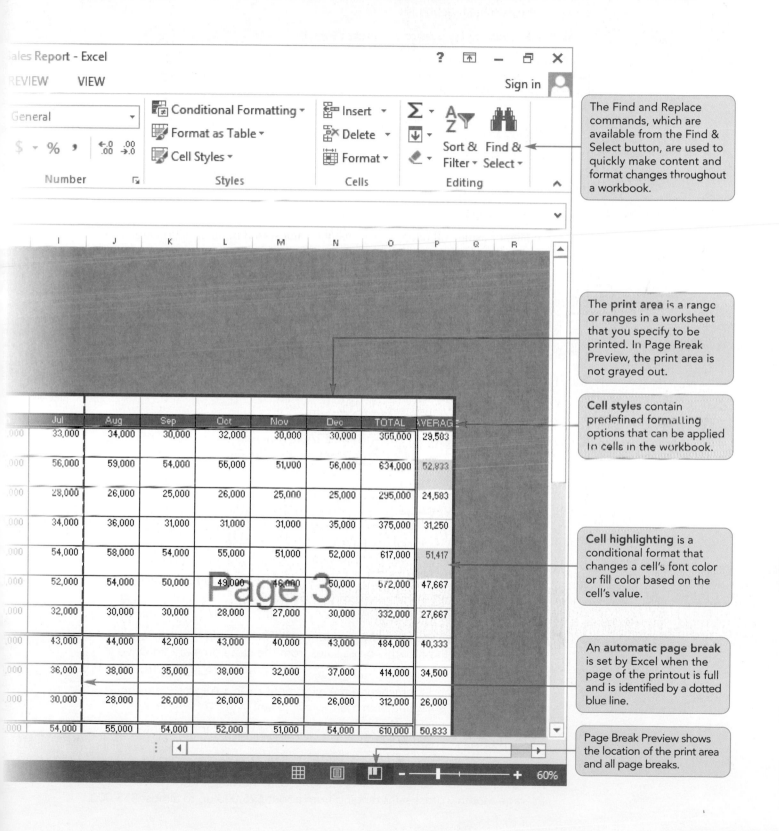

The Find and Replace commands, which are available from the Find & Select button, are used to quickly make content and format changes throughout a workbook.

The **print area** is a range or ranges in a worksheet that you specify to be printed. In Page Break Preview, the print area is not grayed out.

Cell styles contain predefined formatting options that can be applied to cells in the workbook.

Cell highlighting is a conditional format that changes a cell's font color or fill color based on the cell's value.

An **automatic page break** is set by Excel when the page of the printout is full and is identified by a dotted blue line.

Page Break Preview shows the location of the print area and all page breaks.

Using the Average Function

The **AVERAGE function** calculates the average value from a collection of numbers. The syntax of the Average function is

```
AVERAGE (number1, number2, number3, …)
```

where *number1*, *number2*, *number3*, and so forth are either numbers or cell references to the cells or a range where the numbers are stored. For example, the following formula uses the AVERAGE function to calculate the average of 1, 2, 5, and 8, returning the value 4:

```
=AVERAGE(1, 2, 5, 8)
```

However, functions usually reference values entered in a worksheet. So, if the range A1:A4 contains the values 1, 2, 5, and 8, the following formula also returns the value 4:

```
=AVERAGE(A1:A4)
```

The advantage of using cell references is that the values used in the function are visible and can be easily edited.

Sanjit wants to show the average monthly sales for each of the 20 Big Red Wraps stores in addition to the total sales for each store. You will use the AVERAGE function to calculate these values.

To calculate the average monthly sales for each store:

▶ **1.** If you took a break after the previous session, make sure the Sales Report workbook is open and the Sales Report worksheet is active.

▶ **2.** In cell **P26**, enter the text **AVERAGE** as the label.

▶ **3.** Select cell **P27**. You will enter the AVERAGE function in this cell to calculate the average monthly sales for the store on 411 Elm Drive in Madison, Wisconsin.

▶ **4.** On the HOME tab, in the Editing group, click the **AutoSum button arrow**, and then click **AVERAGE**. The formula =AVERAGE(C27:O27) appears in the cell. The range reference that was included in the function is incorrect. It includes cell O27, which contains the total gross sales for all months. You need to correct the range reference.

▶ **5.** Select **O27** in the function's argument, and then click cell **N27** to replace the cell reference. The range reference now correctly includes only the gross sales for each month.

▶ **6.** Press the **Enter** key to complete the formula. The formula results show 29,583, which is the monthly gross sales from the store on 411 Elm Drive in Madison, Wisconsin.

▶ **7.** Select cell **P27**, and then change the alignment to **Top Align** so that the calculated value is aligned with the top of the cell.

▶ **8.** Copy the formula in cell **P27**, and then paste the copied formula into the range **P28:P47**.

▶ **9.** Select cell **P48** to deselect the range. As shown in Figure 2-23, the average monthly sales from all of the stores are $792,833. Individual stores have average monthly gross sales ranging from about $25,000 up to almost $55,000.

Figure 2-23   AVERAGE function results

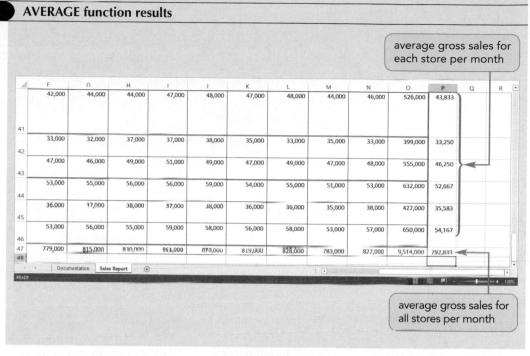

average gross sales for each store per month

average gross sales for all stores per month

With the last formulas added to the worksheet, Sanjit wants you to continue formatting the workbook.

Applying Cell Styles

A workbook often contains several cells that store the same type of data. For example, each worksheet might have a cell displaying the sheet title, or a range of financial data might have several cells containing totals and averages. It is good design practice to apply the same format to worksheet cells that contain the same type of data.

One way to ensure that similar data is displayed consistently is with styles. A **style** is a collection of formatting options that include a specified font, font size, font styles, font color, fill color, and borders. The Cell Styles gallery includes a variety of built-in styles that you can use to format titles and headings, different types of data such as totals or calculations, and cells that you want to emphasize. For example, you can use the Heading 1 style to display sheet titles in a bold, blue-gray, 15-point Calibri font with no fill color and a blue bottom border. You can then apply the Heading 1 style to all titles in the workbook. If you later revise the style, the appearance of any cell formatted with that style is updated automatically. This saves you the time and effort of reformatting each cell individually.

You already used built-in styles when you formatted data in the Sales Report worksheet with the Accounting, Comma, and Percent styles. You can also create your own cell styles by clicking New Cell Style at the bottom of the Cell Styles gallery.

Sanjit wants you to add more color and visual interest to the Sales Report worksheet. You'll use some of the styles in the Cell Styles gallery to do this.

To apply cell styles to the Sales Report worksheet:

▶ **1.** Select cell **B4** containing the text "Sales Statistics."

▶ **2.** On the HOME tab, in the Styles group, click the **Cell Styles** button. The Cell Styles gallery opens.

▶ **3.** Point to the **Heading 1** style in the Titles and Headings section. Live Preview shows cell B4 in a 15-point, bold font with a solid blue bottom border. See Figure 2-24.

Figure 2-24   **Cell Styles gallery**

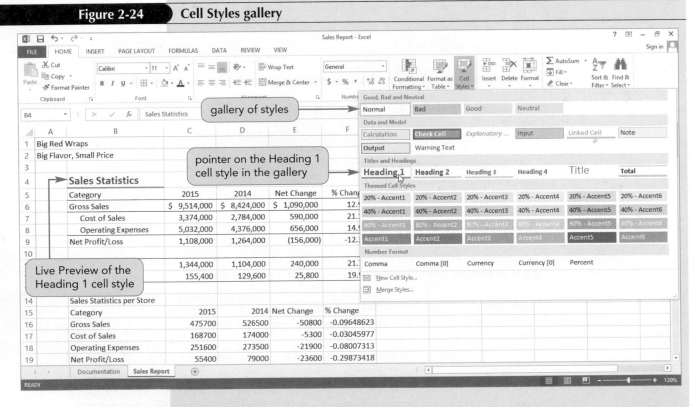

▶ **4.** Move the pointer over different styles in the Cell Styles gallery to see cell B4 with a Live Preview of each style.

▶ **5.** Click the **Title** style. The Title style is applied to cell B4.

▶ **6.** Select the range **B5:F5** containing the column labels for the Sales Statistics data.

▶ **7.** In the Styles group, click the **Cell Styles** button, and then click the **Accent3** style in the Themed Cell Styles section of the Cell Styles gallery.

▶ **8.** Select cell **A25** containing the text "2015 Monthly Gross Sales," and then apply the **Title** cell style to the cell.

▶ **9.** Select cell **A3**. See Figure 2-25.

Figure 2-25   **Cell styles applied to the worksheet**

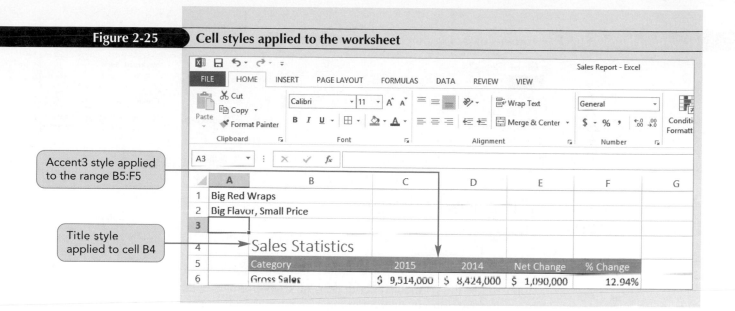

Accent3 style applied to the range B5:F5

Title style applied to cell B4

Copying and Pasting Formats

Large workbooks often use the same formatting on similar data throughout the workbook, sometimes in widely scattered cells. Rather than repeating the same steps to format these cells, you can copy the format of one cell or range and paste it to another.

Copying Formats with the Format Painter

The Format Painter provides a fast and efficient way of copying and pasting formats, ensuring that a workbook has a consistent look and feel. The Format Painter does not copy formatting applied to selected text within a cell, and it does not copy data.

Sanjit wants the Sales Report worksheet to use the same formats you applied to the Big Red Wraps company name and slogan in the Documentation sheet. You will use the Format Painter to copy and paste the formats.

To use the Format Painter to copy and paste a format:

1. Go to the **Documentation** worksheet, and then select the range **A1:A2**.

2. On the HOME tab, in the Clipboard group, click the **Format Painter** button. The formats from the selected cells are copied to the Clipboard, and a flashing border appears around the selected range and the pointer changes to ⊕🖌.

3. Return to the **Sales Report** worksheet, and then click cell **A1**. The formatting from the Documentation worksheet is removed from the Clipboard and applied to the range A1:A2. Notice that the larger font size you applied to the text "Big Flavor" was not included in the pasted formats.

4. Double-click cell **A2** to enter Edit mode, select **Big Flavor**, and then increase the font size to **14** points. The format for the slogan now matches the slogan on the Documentation sheet.

5. Select cell **A3** to exit Edit mode. See Figure 2-26.

TIP

To paste the same format multiple times, double-click the Format Painter button to leave the Format Painter on until you click the button again or press the Esc key.

Figure 2-26 Formats pasted in the Sales Report worksheet

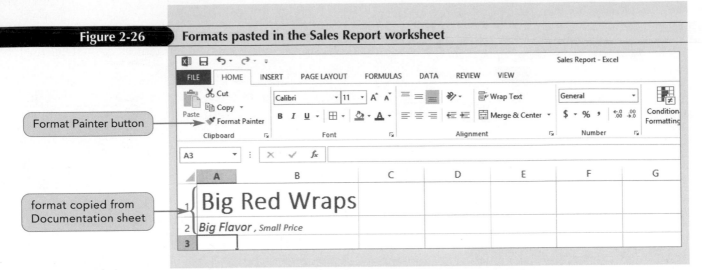

Format Painter button

format copied from Documentation sheet

You can use the Format Painter to copy all of the formats within a selected range and then apply those formats to another range that has the same size and shape by clicking the upper-left cell of the range. Sanjit wants you to copy all of the formats you applied to the Sales Statistics data to the sales statistics per store.

To copy and paste multiple formats:

1. Select the range **B4:F12** in the Sales Report worksheet.

2. On the HOME tab, in the Clipboard group, click the **Format Painter** button.

3. Click cell **B14**. All of the number formats, cell borders, fonts, and fill colors are pasted into the range B14:F22.

4. Select the range **C23:E23**.

5. On the HOME tab, in the Number group, click the **Comma Style** button 🔳, and then click the **Decrease Decimal** button 🔳 twice to remove the decimal places to the right of the decimal point. The numbers are vertically aligned in their columns.

6. Select cell **F23**.

7. In the Number group, click the **Percent Style** button 🔳 to change the number to a percentage, and then click the **Increase Decimal** button 🔳 twice to display two decimal places in the percentage.

8. Click cell **B24**. See Figure 2-27.

TIP

If the range in which you paste the formats is bigger than the range you copied, Format Painter will repeat the copied formats to fill the pasted range.

Figure 2-27   **Formats pasted from a range**

	A	B	C	D	E	F	G	H
6		Gross Sales	$ 9,514,000	$ 8,424,000	$ 1,090,000	12.94%		
7		Cost of Sales	3,374,000	2,784,000	590,000	21.19%		
8		Operating Expenses	5,032,000	4,376,000	656,000	14.99%		
9		Net Profit/Loss	1,100,000	1,264,000	(156,000)	-12.34%		
10								
11		Units Sold	1,344,000	1,104,000	240,000	21.74%		
12		Customers Served	155,400	129,600	25,800	19.91%		
13								
14		Sales Statistics per Store						
15		Category	2015	2014	Net Change	% Change		
16		Gross Sales	$ 475,700	$ 526,500	$ (50,800)	-9.65%		
17		Cost of Sales	168,700	174,000	(5,300)	-3.05%		
18		Operating Expenses	251,600	273,500	(21,900)	-8.01%		
19		Net Profit/Loss	55,400	79,000	(23,600)	-29.87%		
20								
21		Units Sold	67,200	69,000	(1,800)	-2.61%		
22		Customers Served	7,770	8,100	(330)	-4.07%		
23		Stores	20	16	4	25.00%		
24								

copied formats (pointing to rows 6–12, column F)

pasted formats (pointing to rows 16–22)

Documentation   Sales Report   (+)

READY

Copying Formats with the Paste Options Button

Another way to copy and paste formats is with the Paste Options button [⊞ (Ctrl) ▾], which provides options for pasting only values, only formats, or some combination of values and formats. Each time you paste, the Paste Options button appears in the lower-right corner of the pasted cell or range. You click the Paste Options button to open a list of pasting options, shown in Figure 2-28, such as pasting only the values or only the formatting. You can also click the Transpose button to paste the column data into a row, or to paste the row data into a column.

Figure 2-28   **Paste Options button**

options to paste formulas and borders with or without formatting

Transpose button

options to paste values with or without formatting

options to paste hypertext links, pictures, and formats only

button appears in the lower-left corner of the pasted range

Copying Formats with Paste Special

The Paste Special command provides another way to control what you paste from the Clipboard. To use Paste Special, select and copy a range, select the range where you want to paste the Clipboard contents, click the Paste button arrow in the Clipboard group on the HOME tab, and then click Paste Special to open the dialog box shown in Figure 2-29.

Figure 2-29   Paste Special dialog box

specifies what to paste

applies the specified arithmetic operation to the copied value

avoids pasting into empty cells

pastes column data into a row or row data into a column

From the Paste Special dialog box, you can control exactly how to paste the copied range.

Finding and Replacing Text and Formats

The Find and Replace commands let you make content and design changes to a worksheet or the entire workbook quickly. The Find command searches through the current worksheet or workbook for the content or formatting you want to locate, and the Replace command then substitutes it with the new content or formatting you specify.

Sanjit wants you to replace all the street title abbreviations (such as Ave.) in the Sales Report with their full names (such as Avenue). You will use Find and Replace to make these changes.

To find and replace the street title abbreviations:

1. On the HOME tab, in the Editing group, click the **Find & Select** button, and then click **Replace** (or press the **Ctrl+H** keys). The Find and Replace dialog box opens.

2. Type **Ave.** in the Find what box.

3. Press the **Tab** key to move the insertion point to the Replace with box, and then type **Avenue**. See Figure 2-30.

Figure 2-30   Find and Replace dialog box

You can choose to find each occurrence of the search text one at a time and decide whether to replace it. You can choose to highlight all occurrences of the search text in the worksheet. Or, you can choose to replace all occurrences at once without reviewing them. In this case, you want to replace every occurrence of the search text with the replacement text.

4. Click the **Replace All** button to replace all occurrences of the search text without reviewing them. A dialog box opens, reporting that three replacements were made in the worksheet.

5. Click the **OK** button to return to the Find and Replace dialog box.

   Next, you will replace the other street title abbreviations.

6. Repeat Steps 2 through 5 to replace all occurrences of each of the following: **St.** with **Street**, **Ln.** with **Lane**, **Dr.** with **Drive**, and **Rd.** with **Road**.

7. Click the **Close** button to close the Find and Replace dialog box.

8. Scroll through the Sales Report worksheet to verify that all street title abbreviations were replaced with their full names.

The Find and Replace dialog box can also be used to replace one format with another or to replace both text and a format simultaneously. Sanjit wants you to replace all occurrences of the white text in the Sales Report worksheet with light yellow text. You'll use the Find and Replace dialog box to make this formatting change.

To replace white text with yellow text:

1. On the HOME tab, in the Editing group, click the **Find & Select** button, and then click **Replace** (or press the **Ctrl+H** keys). The Find and Replace dialog box opens.

2. Click the **Options** button to expand the dialog box.

3. Click the **Format** button in the Find what row to open the Find Format dialog box, which is similar to the Format Cells dialog box you used earlier to format a range.

4. Click the **Font** tab to make it active, click the **Color** box, and then click the **White, Background 1** theme color.

5. Click the **OK** button to close the dialog box and return to the Find and Replace dialog box.

6. Click the **Format** button in the Replace with row to open the Replace Format dialog box.

▶ **7.** Click the **Color** box, and then click the **Yellow** standard color.

▶ **8.** Click the **OK** button to close the dialog box and return to the Find and Replace dialog box. See Figure 2-31.

Figure 2-31 **Expanded Find and Replace dialog box**

▶ **9.** Verify that the Within box lists **Sheet** to limit the search to the current worksheet.

▶ **10.** Click the **Replace All** button to replace all occurrences of white text in the Sales Report worksheet with yellow text. A dialog box appears, reporting that 32 replacements were made.

▶ **11.** Click the **OK** button to return to the Find and Replace dialog box.

It is a good idea to clear the find and replace formats after you are done so that they won't affect any future searches and replacements. You'll remove the formats from the Find and Replace dialog box.

▶ **12.** Click the **Format button arrow** in the Find what row, and then click **Clear Find Format**. The search format is removed.

▶ **13.** Click the **Format button arrow** in the Replace with row, and then click **Clear Replace Format**. The replacement format is removed.

▶ **14.** Click the **Close** button to return to the worksheet. Notice that every cell in the worksheet that had white text now has yellow text.

Working with Themes

Recall that a theme is a coordinated selection of fonts, colors, and graphical effects that are applied throughout a workbook to create a specific look and feel. When you switch to a different theme, the theme-related fonts, colors, and effects change throughout the workbook to reflect the new theme. The appearance of non-theme fonts, colors, and effects remains unchanged no matter which theme is applied to the workbook.

Most of the formatting you have applied to the Sales Report workbook is based on the Office theme. Sanjit wants you to change the theme to see how it affects the workbook's appearance.

To change the workbook's theme:

1. Click the **PAGE LAYOUT** tab on the ribbon.

2. In the Themes group, click the **Themes** button. The Themes gallery opens. Office—the current theme—is the default.

3. Point to the **Organic** theme in the Themes gallery. Live Preview shows how the appearance of the Sales Report worksheet will change if you select the Organic theme. See Figure 2-32.

Figure 2-32 Live Preview of the Organic theme

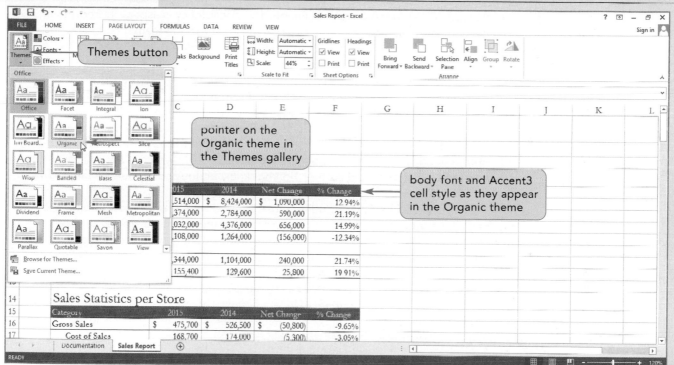

4. Point to several other themes in the Themes gallery to see how the worksheet appearance would change.

5. Click the **Wisp** theme to apply that theme to the workbook.

Changing the theme made a significant difference in the worksheet's appearance. The most obvious changes to the worksheet are the fill colors and the fonts. Only formatting options directly tied to a theme change when you select a different theme. Any formatting options you selected that were not theme-based remain unaffected by the change. For example, the yellow standard color you just applied to the different column labels is still yellow, even with the Wisp theme applied, because yellow is not a theme color. For the same reason, the red fill color used in the column labels of the monthly sales table remains unchanged under the new theme.

Sanjit informs you that Big Red Wraps requires all documents to be formatted with the Office theme. You will reapply the Office theme to the workbook.

To reapply the Office theme to the workbook:

1. On the PAGE LAYOUT tab, in the Themes group, click the **Themes** button, and then click the **Office** theme from the gallery of themes.

The workbook now complies with the company's standard formatting.

INSIGHT

Sharing Styles and Themes

Using a consistent look and feel for all the files you create in Microsoft Office is a simple way to project a professional image. This consistency is especially important when a team is collaborating on a set of documents. When all team members work from a common set of style and design themes, readers will not be distracted by inconsistent or clashing formatting.

To quickly copy the styles from one workbook to another, open the workbook with the styles you want to copy, and then open the workbook in which you want to copy those styles. On the HOME tab, in the Styles group, click the Cell Styles button, and then click Merge Styles. The Merge Styles dialog box opens, listing the currently open workbooks. Select the workbook with the styles you want to copy, and then click the OK button to copy those styles into the current workbook. If you modify any styles, you must copy the styles to the other workbook; Excel does not update styles between workbooks.

Because other Office files, including those created with Word or PowerPoint, use the same file format for themes, you can create one theme to use with all of your Office files. To save a theme, click the Themes button in the Themes group on the PAGE LAYOUT tab, and then click Save Current Theme. The Save Current Theme dialog box opens. Select a save location (in a default Theme folder on your computer or another folder), type a descriptive name in the File name box, and then click the Save button. If you saved the theme file in a default Theme folder, the theme appears in the Themes gallery, and any changes made to the theme are reflected in any Office file that uses that theme.

Highlighting Cells with Conditional Formats

Conditional formats are often used to help analyze data. A **conditional format** applies formatting to a cell when its value meets a specified condition. For example, a conditional format can be used to format negative numbers in red and positive numbers in black. Conditional formats are dynamic, which means that the formatting can change when the cell's value changes. Each conditional format has a set of rules that define how the formatting should be applied and under what conditions the format will be changed.

REFERENCE

Highlighting Cells with a Conditional Format

- Select the range in which you want to highlight cells.
- On the HOME tab, in the Styles group, click the Conditional Formatting button, point to Highlight Cells Rules or Top/Bottom Rules, and then click the appropriate rule.
- Select the appropriate options in the dialog box.
- Click the OK button.

Excel has four conditional formats—data bars, highlighting, color scales, and icon sets. In this tutorial, you will apply cell highlighting, which changes the cell's font color or fill color based on the cell's value, as described in Figure 2-33. You can enter a value or a cell reference if you want to compare other cells with the value in a certain cell.

Figure 2-33   **Highlight Cells rules**

Rule	Highlights Cell Values
Greater Than	Greater than a specified number
Less Than	Less than a specified number
Between	Between two specified numbers
Equal To	Equal to a specified number
Text that Contains	That contain specified text
A Date Occurring	That contain a specified date
Duplicate Values	That contain duplicate or unique values

© 2014 Cengage Learning

Highlighting Cells Based on Their Values

Sanjit wants to highlight important trends and sales values in the Sales Report worksheet. He wants you to use a conditional format to display sales statistics that showed a negative net or percent change in a red font so that they stand out. You will do this by creating a rule to format the cells in ranges E6:F12 and E16:F22 with numbers that are less than 0.

To highlight negative numbers in red:

1. Select the nonadjacent range **E6:F12;E16:F22** in the Sales Report worksheet.

2. On the ribbon, click the **HOME** tab.

3. In the Styles group, click the **Conditional Formatting** button, and then point to **Highlight Cells Rules** to display a menu of the available rules.

4. Click **Less Than**. The Less Than dialog box opens so you can select the value and formatting to highlight negative values.

5. Type **0** (a zero) in the Format cells that are LESS THAN box, click the **with** arrow, and then click **Red Text**. Live Preview shows that the rule formats any cells in the selected range that have a negative value in a red font. See Figure 2-34.

Figure 2-34   **Live Preview of the Less Than conditional format**

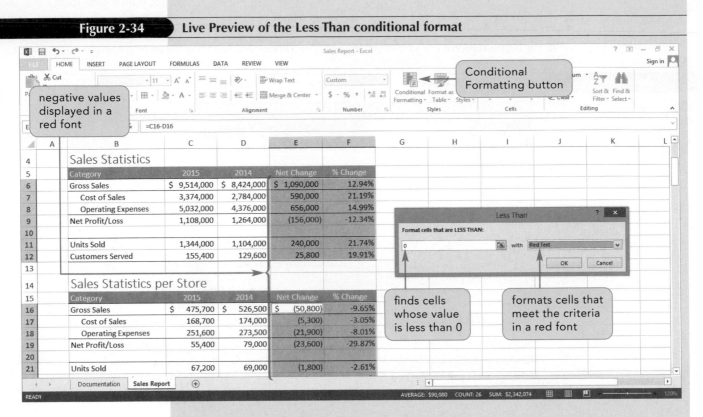

6. Click the **OK** button to apply the highlighting rule. You will verify that this format is conditional.

7. In cell D8, enter **4,576,000** to change the Operating Expenses value. The now positive values in cells E9 and F9 are formatted in a black font.

8. Press the **Ctrl+Z** keys to return the value in cell D8 to 4,376,000. The values in cells E9 and F9 are again negative and in a red font.

The highlighted values show at a glance that Big Red Wraps' gross sales, units sold, and customers served increased from 2014 to 2015, while the company's net profit declined during the same period. The average gross sales per store also declined in 2015. Big Red Wraps opened four new stores in 2015, and Sanjit will argue that the cost of this expansion and low sales from the new stores caused this apparent decline.

Highlighting Cells with a Top/Bottom Rule

Another way of applying conditional formats is with the Quick Analysis tool. The **Quick Analysis tool**, which appears whenever you select a range of cells, provides access to the most common tools for data analysis and formatting. The FORMATTING category includes buttons for the Greater Than and Top 10% conditional formatting rules. You can highlight cells based on their values in comparison to other cells. For example, you can highlight cells with the 10 highest or lowest values in a selected range, or you can highlight the cells with above-average values in a range.

Sanjit wants you to highlight the five stores in the Big Red Wraps chain that had the highest gross sales in the last fiscal year. You will use a Top/Bottom rule to do this.

To use a Top/Bottom Rule to highlight the stores with the highest gross sales:

1. Select the range **P27:P46** containing the average monthly gross sales for each of the 20 Big Red Wraps stores. The Quick Analysis button appears in the lower-right corner of the selected range.

2. Click the **Quick Analysis** button [image], and then point to **Top 10%**. Live Preview colors the cells in the top 10 percent with red font and a red fill. See Figure 2-35.

Figure 2-35   **Quick Analysis tool**

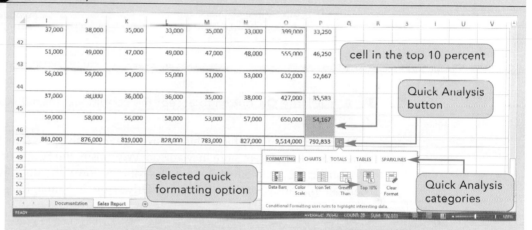

Sanjit wants to see the top five items rather than the cells with values in the top 10 percent, so you won't apply this conditional formatting.

3. Press the **Esc** key to close the Quick Analysis tool. The range P27:P46 remains selected.

4. On the HOME tab, in the Styles group, click the **Conditional Formatting** button, and then point to **Top/Bottom Rules** to display a menu of available rules.

5. Click **Top 10 Items** to open the Top 10 Items dialog box.

6. Click the down arrow on the spin box five times to change the value from 10 to 5. This specifies that the top five values in the selected range will be formatted.

7. Click the **with** arrow, and then click **Green Fill with Dark Green Text** to specify the formatting to apply to the five cells with the top values. Live Preview highlights the top five stores in terms of gross sales. See Figure 2-36.

Figure 2-36   **Live Preview of the top five selling stores**

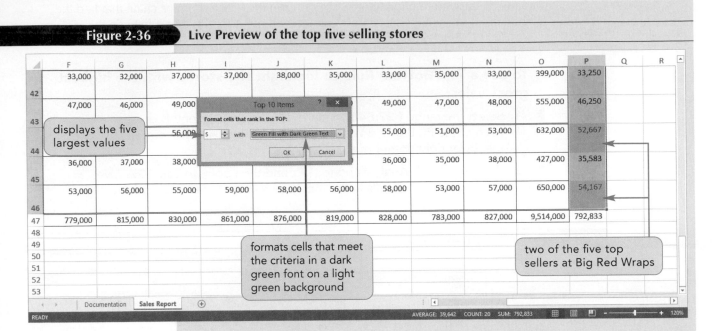

8. Click the **OK** button to accept the conditional formatting.

The Top/Bottom rule highlights the average monthly gross sales for the five top-selling stores: the North Street store in Madison, Wisconsin; the South Drive store in Janesville, Wisconsin; the Main Street store in Des Moines, Iowa; the Business Drive store in Manhattan, Kansas; and the Causeway Drive store in Salina, Kansas.

Clearing a Conditional Format

You can remove a conditional format at any time without affecting the underlying data by selecting the range containing the conditional format, clicking the Conditional Formatting button, and then clicking the Clear Rules button. A menu opens, providing options to clear the conditional formatting rules from the selected cells or the entire worksheet. You can also click the Quick Analysis button that appears in the lower-right corner of the selected range, and then click the Clear Format button in the FORMATTING category.

Creating a Conditional Formatting Legend

When you use conditional formatting to highlight cells in a worksheet, the purpose of the formatting is not always immediately apparent. To ensure that everyone knows why certain cells are highlighted, you should include a **legend**, which is a key that identifies each color and its meaning.

You will add a legend to the Sales Report worksheet to document the Top 5 highlighting rule you just created.

To create a conditional formatting legend:

1. Select cell **P49**, type **light green**, and then press the **Enter** key. You will use a highlight rule to fill this cell with a dark green font on a light green fill.

2. Select cell **P49** to make it the active cell.

3. On the HOME tab, in the Styles group, click the **Conditional Formatting** button, point to **Highlight Cells Rules**, and then click **Text that Contains**. The Text That Contains dialog box opens.

4. Verify that **light green** appears in the Format cells that contain the text box. The box shows the text entered in the selected cell.

5. Click the **with** arrow, and then click **Green Fill with Dark Green Text** to format cell P49 with the same format used for the top five gross sales.

6. Click the **OK** button. Cell P49 remains selected.

7. In the Alignment group, click the **Center** button to center the text in the cell.

8. In cell **O49**, enter **Top 5 Stores** to identify the format's purpose, and then select cell **O49**.

9. In the Styles group, click the **Cell Styles** button, and then click the **Explanatory Text** style (the third style in the first row of the Data and Model section). The cell style is applied to the selected cell.

10. Click cell **O51**. The legend is complete, as shown in Figure 2-37.

Figure 2-37 Conditional formatting legend

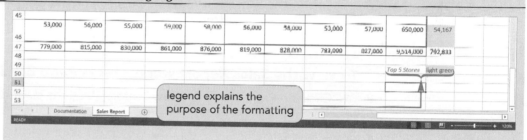

The conditional formatting makes the top-selling stores stand out.

Written Communication: Using Conditional Formatting Effectively

Conditional formatting is an excellent way to highlight important trends and data values to clients and colleagues. However, be sure to use it judiciously. Overusing conditional formatting might obscure the very data you want to emphasize. Keep in mind the following tips as you make decisions about what to highlight and how it should be highlighted:

- **Document the conditional formats you use.** If a bold, green font means that a sales number is in the top 10 percent of all sales, include that information in a legend in the worksheet.
- **Don't clutter data with too much highlighting.** Limit highlighting rules to one or two per data set. Highlights are designed to draw attention to points of interest. If you use too many, you will end up highlighting everything—and, therefore, nothing.
- **Use color sparingly in worksheets with highlights.** It is difficult to tell a highlight color from a regular fill color, especially when fill colors are used in every cell.
- **Consider alternatives to conditional formats.** If you want to highlight the top 10 sales regions, it might be more effective to simply sort the data with the best-selling regions at the top of the list.

Remember that the goal of highlighting is to provide a strong visual clue to important data or results. Careful use of conditional formatting helps readers to focus on the important points you want to make rather than distracting them with secondary issues and facts.

Formatting a Worksheet for Printing

You should format any worksheets you plan to print so that they are easy to read and understand. You can do this using the print settings, which enable you to set the page orientation, the print area, page breaks, print titles, and headers and footers. Print settings can be applied to an entire workbook or to individual sheets. Because other people will likely see your printed worksheets, you should format the printed output as carefully as you format the electronic version. Sanjit wants you to format the Sales Report worksheet so he can distribute the printed version at the upcoming sales conference.

Using Page Break Preview

Page Break Preview shows only those parts of the active sheet that will print and how the content will be split across pages. A dotted blue border indicates a page break, which separates one page from another. As you format the worksheet for printing, you can use this view to control what content appears on each page.

Sanjit wants to know how the Sales Report worksheet would print in portrait orientation and how many pages would be required. You will look at the worksheet in Page Break Preview to find these answers.

To view the Sales Report worksheet in Page Break Preview:

▶ **1.** Click the **Page Break Preview** button 🔲 on the status bar. The worksheet switches to Page Break Preview.

▶ **2.** Change the zoom level of the worksheet to **30%** so you can view the entire contents of this large worksheet. See Figure 2-38.

| Figure 2-38 | Sales Report worksheet in Page Break Preview |

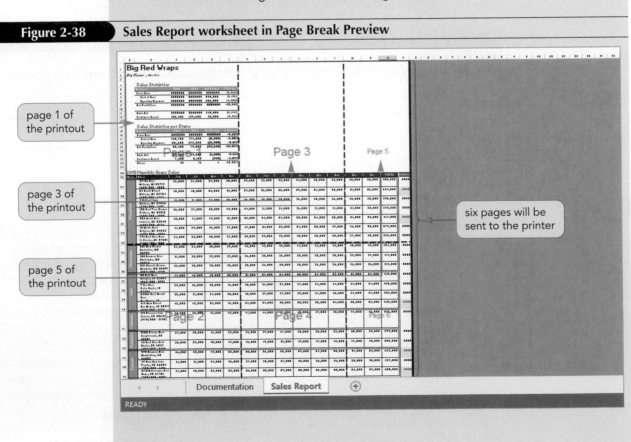

page 1 of the printout

page 3 of the printout

page 5 of the printout

six pages will be sent to the printer

Trouble? If you see a different page layout or the worksheet is split onto a different number of pages, don't worry. Each printer is different, so the layout and pages might differ from what is shown in Figure 2-38.

Page Break Preview shows that a printout of the Sales Report worksheet requires six pages in portrait orientation, and that pages 3 and 5 would be mostly blank. Note that each printer is different, so your Page Break Preview might show a different number of pages. With this layout, each page would be difficult to interpret because the data is separated from the descriptive labels. Sanjit wants you to fix the layout so that the contents are easier to read and understand.

Defining the Print Area

By default, all cells in a worksheet containing text, formulas, or values are printed. If you want to print only part of a worksheet, you can set a print area, which is the region of the worksheet that is sent to the printer. Each worksheet has its own print area. Although you can set the print area in any view, Page Break Preview shades the areas of the worksheet that are not included in the print area, making it simple to confirm what will print.

Sanjit doesn't want the empty cells in the range G1:O24 to print, so you will set the print area to eliminate those cells.

To set the print area of the Sales Report worksheet:

1. Change the zoom level of the worksheet to **80%** to make it easier to select cells and ranges.

2. Select the nonadjacent range **A1:F24;A25:P49** containing the cells with content.

3. On the ribbon, click the **PAGE LAYOUT** tab.

4. In the Page Setup group, click the **Print Area** button, and then click **Set Print Area**. The print area changes to cover only the nonadjacent range A1:F24;A25:P49. The rest of the worksheet content is shaded to indicate that it will not be part of the printout.

5. Select cell **A1** to deselect the range.

6. Change the zoom level to **50%** so you can view more of the worksheet. See Figure 2-39.

Figure 2-39 **Print area set for the Sales Report worksheet**

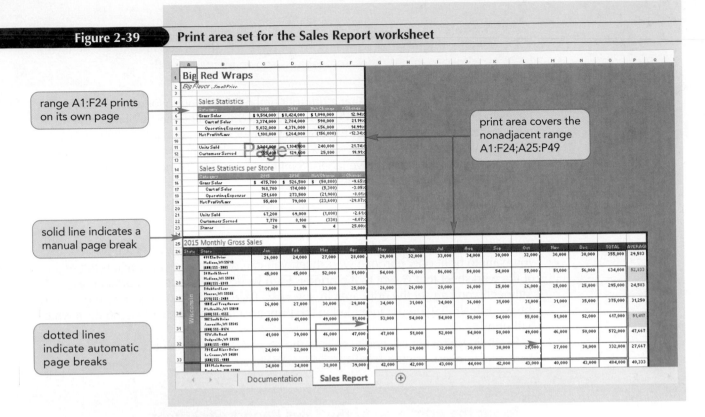

range A1:F24 prints on its own page

print area covers the nonadjacent range A1:F24;A25:P49

solid line indicates a manual page break

dotted lines indicate automatic page breaks

Inserting Page Breaks

Often, the contents of a worksheet will not fit onto a single printed page. When this happens, Excel prints as much of the content that fits on a single page without resizing, and then inserts automatic page breaks to continue printing the remaining worksheet content on successive pages. The resulting printouts might split worksheet content in awkward places, such as within a table of data.

To split the printout into logical segments, you can insert manual page breaks. Page Break Preview identifies manual page breaks with a solid blue line and automatic page breaks with a dotted blue line. When you specify a print area for a nonadjacent range, as you did for the Sales Report worksheet, you also insert manual page breaks around the adjacent ranges. So a manual page break already appears in the print area you defined (see Figure 2-39). You can remove a page break in Page Break Preview by dragging it out of the print area.

REFERENCE

Inserting and Removing Page Breaks

To insert a page break:
- Click the first cell below the row where you want to insert a page break, click a column heading, or click a row heading.
- On the PAGE LAYOUT tab, in the Page Setup group, click the Breaks button, and then click Insert Page Break.

To remove a page break:
- Select any cell below or to the right of the page break you want to remove.
- On the PAGE LAYOUT tab, in the Page Setup group, click the Breaks button, and then click Remove Page Break.

or
- In Page Break Preview, drag the page break line out of the print area.

The Sales Report worksheet has automatic page breaks along columns F and L. You will remove these automatic page breaks from the Sales Report worksheet.

To remove the automatic page breaks and insert manual page breaks:

▶ **1.** Point to the dotted blue page break directly to the right of column L until the pointer changes to ↔.

▶ **2.** Drag the page break to the right and out of the print area. The page break is removed from the worksheet.

▶ **3.** Point to the page break located in cell F31 until the pointer changes to ↔, and then drag the page break to the right and out of the print area.

   On the PAGE LAYOUT tab, in the Scale to Fit section, notice that the Scale box shows 43%. After removing the two page breaks from the Sales Report printout, Excel scaled the printout from 100% of its actual size to 43% to fit the printout onto two pages.

▶ **4.** Click the **column I** heading to select the entire column. You will add a manual page break between columns H and I to split the monthly gross sales data onto two pages so the printout will be larger and easier to read.

▶ **5.** On the PAGE LAYOUT tab, in the Page Setup group, click the **Breaks** button, and then click **Insert Page Break**. A manual page break is added between columns H and I, forcing the monthly gross sales onto a new page after the June data.

▶ **6.** Select cell **A1** to deselect the column. The printout of the Sales Report worksheet is now limited to three pages. However, the gross sales data in the range A25:O49 is split across pages. See Figure 2-40.

Figure 2-40   Manual page break added to the print area

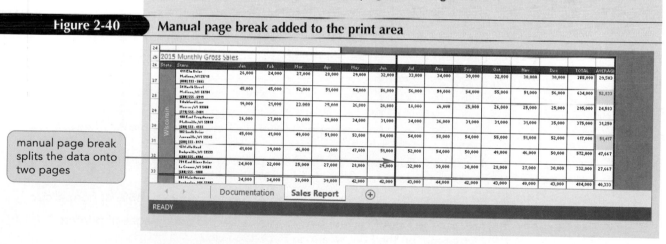

manual page break splits the data onto two pages

Adding Print Titles

It is a good practice to include descriptive information such as the company name, logo, and worksheet title on each page of a printout in case a page becomes separated from the other pages. You can repeat information, such as the company name, by specifying which rows or columns in the worksheet act as print titles. If a worksheet contains a large table, you can print the table's column headings and row headings on every page of the printout by designating those columns and rows as print titles.

In the Sales Report worksheet, the company name and slogan currently appear on the first page of the printout, but do not appear on subsequent pages. Also, the descriptive row labels for the monthly sales table in column A do not appear on the third page of the printout. You will add print titles to fix these issues.

To set the print titles:

TIP

You can also open the Page Setup dialog box by clicking the Dialog Box Launcher in the Page Setup group on the PAGE LAYOUT tab.

1. On the PAGE LAYOUT tab, in the Page Setup group, click the **Print Titles** button. The Page Setup dialog box opens with the Sheet tab displayed.

2. In the Print titles section, click the **Rows to repeat at top** box, move the pointer over the worksheet, and then select the range **A1:A2**. A flashing border appears around the first two rows of the worksheet to indicate that the contents of the first two rows will be repeated on each page of the printout. The row reference $1:$2 appears in the Rows to repeat at top box.

3. Click the **Columns to repeat at left** box, and then select columns A and B from the worksheet. The column reference $A:$B appears in the Columns to repeat at left box. See Figure 2-41.

Figure 2-41   **Sheet tab in the Page Setup dialog box**

4. Click the **Page** tab in the Page Setup dialog box. You will rescale the worksheet so that it doesn't appear too small in the printout.

5. In the Scaling section, change the Adjust to amount to **65%** of normal size.

6. Click the **Print Preview** button to preview the three pages of printed material on the Print screen in Backstage view.

7. Verify that each of the three pages has the Big Red Wraps title and slogan at the top of the page, and that the state and store names appear in the leftmost columns of pages 2 and 3. See Figure 2-42.

Figure 2-42   Print titles on page 3 of the Sales Report worksheet

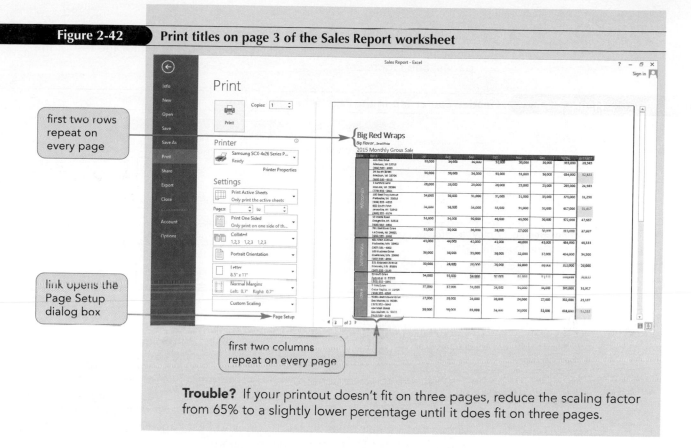

first two rows repeat on every page

link opens the Page Setup dialog box

first two columns repeat on every page

Trouble? If your printout doesn't fit on three pages, reduce the scaling factor from 65% to a slightly lower percentage until it does fit on three pages.

Creating Headers and Footers

You can also use headers and footers to repeat information on each printed page. A **header** appears at the top of each printed page; a **footer** appears at the bottom of each printed page. Headers and footers contain helpful and descriptive text that is usually not found within the worksheet, such as the workbook's author, the current date, or the workbook's filename. If the printout spans multiple pages, you can display the page number and the total number of pages in the printout to help ensure you and others have all the pages.

Each header and footer has three sections—a left section, a center section, and a right section. Within each section, you type the text you want to appear, or you insert elements such as the worksheet name or the current date and time. These header and footer elements are dynamic; if you rename the worksheet, for example, the name is automatically updated in the header or footer. Also, you can create one set of headers and footers for even and odd pages, and you can create another set for the first page in the printout.

Sanjit wants the printout to display the workbook's filename in the header's left section, and the current date in the header's right section. He wants the center footer to display the page number and the total number of pages in the printout, and the right footer to display your name as the workbook's author.

To create the header and footer:

1. Click the **Page Setup** link near the bottom of the Print screen to open the Page Setup dialog box.

2. Click the **Header/Footer** tab to display the header and footer options.

3. Click the **Different first page** check box to select it. This lets you create one set of headers and footers for the first page, and one set for the rest of the pages. See Figure 2-43.

Figure 2-43   **Header/Footer tab in the Page Setup dialog box**

when selected, displays a different header and footer for even- and odd-numbered pages

displays a different header or footer for the first page

---

4. Click the **Custom Header** button to open the Header dialog box. The dialog box contains two tabs—Header and First Page Header—because you selected the Different first page option.

5. On the Header tab, type **Filename:** in the Left section box, press the **spacebar**, and then click the **Insert File Name** button. The code &[File], which displays the filename of the current workbook, is added to the left section of the header.

6. Press the **Tab** key twice to move to the right section of the header, and then click the **Insert Current Date** button. The code &[Date] is added to the right section of the header. See Figure 2-44.

Figure 2-44   **Header dialog box**

inserts the current date

inserts the workbook's filename

code to print the workbook's filename

code to print the current date

---

7. Click the **OK** button to return to the Header/Footer tab in the Page Setup dialog box. You did not define a header for the first page of the printout, so no header information will be added to that page.

Now you will format the page footer for all pages of the printout.

8. Click the **Custom Footer** button to open the Footer dialog box, which is similar to the Header dialog box.

9. Click the **Center section** box, type **Page**, press the **spacebar**, and then click the **Insert Page Number** button ⊡. The code &[Page], which inserts the current page number, appears after the label "Page."

10. Press the **spacebar**, type **of**, press the **spacebar**, and then click the **Insert Number of Pages** button ⊡. The code &[Pages], which inserts the total number of pages in the printout, is added to the Center section box. See Figure 2-45.

Figure 2-45   **Footer dialog box**

click to set footer options for the first page

inserts the total number of pages

inserts the page number

prints the current page number out of the total page count

---

11. Click the **First Page Footer** tab so you can create the footer for the first page of the printout.

12. Click the **Right section** box, type **Prepared by:**, press the **spacebar**, and then type your name.

13. Click the **OK** button to return to the Page Setup dialog box.

Setting the Page Margins

A **margin** is the space between the page content and the edges of the page. By default, Excel sets the page margins to 0.7 inch on the left and right sides, and 0.75 inch on the top and bottom; and it allows for 0.3-inch margins around the header and footer. You can reduce or increase these margins as needed by selecting predefined margin sizes or setting your own.

Sanjit's reports need a wider margin along the left side of the page to accommodate the binding. He asks you to increase the left margin for the printout from 0.7 inch to 1 inch.

TIP

To select preset margins, click the Margins button in the Page Setup group on the PAGE LAYOUT tab.

To set the left margin:

1. Click the **Margins** tab in the Page Setup dialog box to display options for changing the page margins.

2. Double-click the **Left** box to select the setting, and then type **1** to increase the size of the left margin. See Figure 2-46.

Figure 2-46   **Margins tab in the Page Setup dialog box**

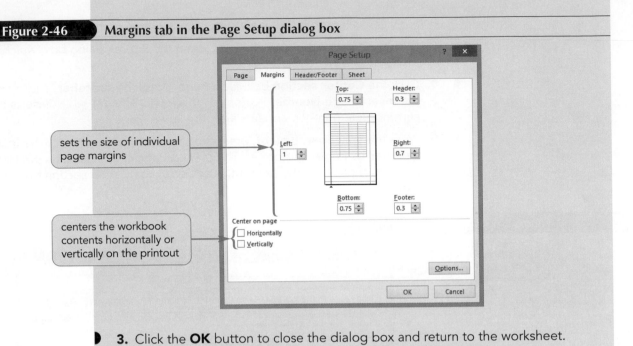

sets the size of individual page margins

centers the workbook contents horizontally or vertically on the printout

▶ **3.** Click the **OK** button to close the dialog box and return to the worksheet.

Sanjit is happy with the appearance of the worksheet and the layout of the printout. You'll save the workbook, and then print the Documentation and Sales Report sheets.

To save and print the workbook:

▶ **1.** Return the Sales Report worksheet to **Normal** view, and then save the workbook.

▶ **2.** Display the Print screen in Backstage view, and then change the first Settings box to **Print Entire Workbook**. Both the Sales Report worksheet and the Documentation sheet appear in the preview. As you can see, the printout will include a header with the filename and date on every page except the first page, and a footer with your name on the first page and the page number along with the total number of pages on subsequent pages.

▶ **3.** If you are instructed to print, print the entire workbook, and then close it.

REVIEW

Session 2.2 Quick Check

1. Describe two methods of applying the same format to different ranges.
2. Red is a standard color. What happens to red text when you change the workbook's theme?
3. What is a conditional format?
4. How would you highlight the top five values in the range A1:C20?
5. How do you insert a manual page break in a worksheet?
6. What is a print area?
7. What are print titles?
8. Describe how to add the workbook filename to the center section of the footer on every page of the printout.

ASSESS

SAM Projects

Put your skills into practice with SAM Projects! SAM Projects for this tutorial can be found online. If you have a SAM account, go to www.cengage.com/sam2013 to download the most recent Project Instructions and Start Files.

PRACTICE

Review Assignments

Data Files needed for the Review Assignments: Menu.xlsx, Background2.png

Sanjit has a worksheet that details the sales of individual items from the Big Red Wraps menu. He asks you to format the sales figures and design a layout for the printed sheet as you did for the Sales Report workbook. Complete the following:

1. Open the **Menu** workbook located in the Excel2 ▸ Review folder included with your Data Files, and then save the workbook as **Menu Sales** in the location specified by your instructor.

2. In the Documentation sheet, enter your name in cell B4 and the date in cell B5.

3. Make the following formatting changes to the Documentation sheet:

   a. Set the background image to the **Background2.png** file located in the Excel2 ▸ Review folder.

   b. Format the text in cell A1 in red 26-point bold Calibri Light.

   c. Format the text in cell A2 to red 10-point italic Calibri Light. Change the text string "Big Flavor" to 14 points.

   d. Apply the Accent2 cell style to the range A4:A6.

   e. Change the font color of range B4:B6 to red and change its fill color to white.

   f. Format the date in the Long Date format and left-align the cell contents.

4. Use the Format Painter to copy the formatting in the range A1:A2 in the Documentation sheet and paste it to the same range in the Menu Sales worksheet. (*Hint*: You must increase the size of the text "Big Flavor" manually.)

5. Apply the Title cell style to the titles in cells B4, B12, and A20.

6. Make the following changes to the Units Sold table in the range B5:F10:

   a. In cell C6, calculate the total number of wraps sold by the company (found in the range C22:N31). In cell C7, calculate the total number of soups. In cell C8, calculate the total number of sides. In cell C9, calculate the total number of salads.

   b. In cell C10, calculate the sum of the range C6:C9. Copy the formula to cell D10.

   c. In the range E6:E10, calculate the difference between the 2015 and 2014 values. In the range F6:F10, calculate the percent change from 2014 to 2015.

   d. Apply the Accent2 cell style to the headings in the range B5:F5. Center the headings in the range C5:F5.

   e. Apply the Comma style to the values in the range C6:E10. Do not display any numbers to the right of the decimal point.

   f. Apply the Percent style to the values in the range F6:F10 and show two decimal places.

   g. Add a top border to the values in the range B10:F10.

7. Make the following changes to the range B13:F18:

   a. In cells C18 and D18, calculate the totals of the 2014 and 2015 sales. In the range E14:F18, calculate the change in sales and the percent change.

   b. Copy the format from the range B5:F10 and paste it into the range B13:F18.

   c. Change the format for the values in the ranges C14:E14 and C18:E18 to Accounting format with no decimal places.

8. Make the following changes to the Units Sold per Month table in the range A21:O46:

   a. In the range O22:O45, calculate the total units sold for each menu item. In the range C46:O46, calculate the total items sold per month and overall.

   b. Format the headings in the range A21:O21 with the Accent2 cell style. Center the headings in the range C21:O21.

   c. Format the units sold values in the range C22:O46 with the Comma style and no decimal places.

   d. Change the fill color of the subtotals in the range O22:O45 and C46:N46 to White, Background 1, Darker 15% (the first color in the third row of the theme colors).

   e. Merge each of the menu categories in the range A22:A45 into single cells. Rotate the text of the cells up. Increase the font size to 18 points and middle-align the cell contents.

   f. Format cell A22 with the "Wraps" label in a white font on a Gray-25%, Background 2, Darker 50% fill. Format cell A32 with the "Soups" label in a white font on Blue, Accent 1, Darker 25% fill. Format of cell A37 with the "Sides" label in a white font on a Gold, Accent 4, Darker 25% fill. Format cell A42 with the "Salads" label in a white font on a Green, Accent 6, Darker 25% fill.

   g. Add a thick box border around each category of menu item in the ranges A22:O31, A32:O36, A37:O41, and A42:O45.

9. Create a conditional format for the subtotals in the range O22:O45 highlighting the top five selling items with a yellow fill and dark yellow text.

10. Create a legend for the conditional format. Enter the text **Top 5 Sellers** in cell O48. Add a thick box border around the cell, and then use a conditional format that displays this text in dark yellow text on a yellow fill.

11. Set the following print formats for the Menu Sales worksheet:

    a. Set the print area to the nonadjacent range A1:F19;A20:O48.

    b. Remove any automatic page breaks in the large Units Sold table. Insert a manual page break to separate the June and July sales figures. The printout of the Menu Sales worksheet should fit on three pages.

    c. Scale the printout to 70 percent of normal size.

    d. Define the print titles to repeat the first three rows at the top of the sheet, and the first two columns at the left of the sheet.

    e. Increase the left margin of the printout from 0.7 inch to 1 inch.

    f. Create headers and footers for the printout with a different header for the first page.

    g. For the first page header, print **Prepared by** *your name* in the right section. For every other page, print **Filename:** *file* in the left section and *date* in the right section, where *file* is the name of the workbook file and *date* is the current date. (*Hint*: Use the buttons in the Header dialog box to insert the filename and date.)

    h. For every footer, print **Page** *page* **of** *pages* in the center section, where *page* is the page number and *pages* is the total number of pages in the printout.

12. If you are instructed to print, print the entire workbook in portrait orientation. Verify that the company name and slogan appear on every page of the Menu Sales worksheet printout, and that the menu category and menu item name appear on both pages with the Units Sold table.

13. Save and close the workbook.

Case Problem 1

APPLY

Data File needed for this Case Problem: Salon.xlsx

Special Highlights Hair Salon   Sarah Jones is developing a business plan for a new hair salon, Special Highlights Hair Salon, located in Hatton, North Dakota. As part of the business plan, she needs a projected income statement for the company. You will help her develop and format the income statement. Complete the following:

1. Open the **Salon** workbook located in the Excel2 ▸ Case1 folder included with your Data Files, and then save the workbook as **Salon Income Statement** in the location specified by your instructor.

2. In the Documentation sheet, enter your name in cell B3 and the date in cell B4.

3. Apply the following formatting to the Documentation sheet:
   a. Format cell A1 using the Title cell style.
   b. Format the range A3:A5 using the Accent6 cell style.
   c. In cell B4, format the date value using the long date format, and left-align the cell contents.
   d. In cell B5, format the text string "Special Highlights Hair Salon" in italic.

4. In the Income Statement worksheet, format cell A1 using the Title cell style.

5. Calculate the following items in the Income Statement worksheet:
   a. In cell C7, calculate the Gross Profit, which is equal to the Gross Sales minus the Cost of Sales.
   b. In cell C21, calculate the Total Operating Expenses, which is equal to the sum of the operating expenses.
   c. In cell C22, calculate the Total Operating Profit/Loss, which is equal to the Gross Profit minus the Total Operating Expenses.
   d. In cell C23, calculate the projected Income Taxes, which is equal to 35 percent of the Total Operating Profit/Loss.
   e. In cell C24, calculate the Net Profit/Loss, which is equal to the Total Operating Profit/Loss minus the projected Income Taxes.

6. Set the following formats to the Income Statement worksheet:
   a. Format cells A3 and A26 using the Heading 2 cell style.
   b. Format cells A4 and A9 and the range A27:A38 in bold.
   c. Format cells B5, C7, B10, C21, and C24 using the Accounting format with no decimal places.
   d. Format cells B6, B11:B19, C22, and C23 using the Comma style with no decimal places.
   e. Indent the text in the ranges A5:A6 and A10:A19 two spaces. Indent the text in cell A7 and the range A21:A24 four spaces.
   f. Add a bottom border to cells B6, C7, C21, C22, and C23. Add a double bottom border to cell C24.

7. Merge cells A26:E26 and then left-align the merged cell's contents.

8. Merge the contents of the range B27:E27. Left-align the merged cell's contents and wrap the text within the cell. Increase the height of row 27 to display the entire contents of the cell.

9. Top-align and left-align the range A27:B38.

10. Copy the format from the range A27:B27 to the range A28:B38. Merge columns B through E in each row, left-align the text, and resize the row heights to display the complete contents of the cells.

11. Italicize the text string "National Salon News" in cells B27 and B28.

12. Set the following printing formats to the Income Statement worksheet:

   a. Insert a manual page break directly above row 26 so that the Income Statement prints on two pages.

   b. Set rows 1 and 2 as a print title to print on both pages.

   c. Change the page margins to 1 inch on every side.

   d. On the first page of the printout, print **Prepared by *your name*** in the left section of the header, where *your name* is your name. Print the ***current date*** in the right section of the header. Do not display header text on any other page.

   e. For every page, add a footer that prints the workbook ***filename*** in the left section, **Page *page*** in the center section, and the ***worksheet name*** in the right section.

13. If you are instructed to print, print the entire contents of the workbook in portrait orientation.

14. Save and close the workbook.

Case Problem 2

Data File needed for this Case Problem: Waist.xlsx

Waist Trainers   Alexandra Roulez is a dietician at Waist Trainers, a company in Fort Smith, Arkansas, that specializes in personal improvement, particularly in areas of health and fitness. Alexandra wants to create a meal-planning workbook for her clients who want to lose weight and improve their health. One goal of meal planning is to decrease the percentage of fat in the diet. Alexandra thinks it would be helpful to highlight foods that have a high percentage of fat as well as list their total fat calories. She already created a workbook that contains a few sample food items and lists the number of calories and grams of fat in each item. She wants you to format this workbook. Complete the following:

1. Open the **Waist** workbook located in the Excel2 ▸ Case2 folder included with your Data Files, and then save the workbook as **Waist Trainers Nutrition Table** in the location specified by your instructor.

2. In the Documentation sheet, enter your name in cell B3 and the date in cell B4.

3. Set the following formatting to the Documentation sheet:

   a. In cell A1, apply the Title cell style, increase the font size to 24 points, and then change the font color to a medium orange.

   b. Apply the Accent2 cell style to the range A3:A5.

   c. Wrap the text within the range B3:B5, and then left- and top-align the text in the cells.

   d. Change the format of the date in cell B4 to the long date format.

   e. Add borders around all of the cells in the range A3:B5.

4. Copy the cell format for cell A1 in the Documentation sheet to cell A1 in the Meal Planner worksheet.

5. In cell F4, enter the text **Calories from Fat**. In cell G4, enter the text **Fat Percentage**.

6. In the range F5:F54, calculate the calories from fat for each food item, which is equal to the Grams of Fat multiplied by 9. In the range G5:G54, calculate the fat percentage of each food item, which is equal to the Calories from Fat divided by the Calories.

7. Format cell A3 using the Heading 4 cell style.

8. Format the range A4:G4 using the Accent2 cell style.

9. Format the range D5:F54 with the Comma style and display one decimal place.

10. Format the range G5:G54 with the Percent style and display two decimal places.

11. Merge the cells in the range A5:A8, rotate the text up, and then center-align the cell content both horizontally and vertically. Change the fill color to medium gold, increase the font size to 14 points, and then change the font color to white.

12. Place a thick box border around the beef food items in the range A5:G8.

13. Repeat Steps 11 and 12 for the other six food categories.

14. For good health, the FDA recommends that the fat percentage in a person's diet should not exceed 30 percent of the total calories per day. Create a Conditional Formatting rule for the fat percentages to highlight those food items that exceed the FDA recommendation in dark red text on a light red fill.

15. In cell G2, enter the text **High Fat Food**. Center the text in the cell. Change the format of the cell to dark red text on a light red fill. Add a thick black border around the cell.

16. Set the following print formats for the Meal Planner worksheet:

    a. Change the page orientation to landscape.

    b. Scale the printout so that the width of the worksheet fits on a single page.

    c. If necessary, create manual page breaks directly above row 25 and above row 44. The worksheet should print on three separate pages.

    d. Repeat the first four rows of the worksheet on every printed page.

    e. For every page, add a footer that prints **Prepared by** *your name* in the left section, **Page** *page* in the center section, and the *worksheet name* in the right section.

17. If you are instructed to print, print the entire contents of the workbook.

18. Save and close the workbook.

CHALLENGE

Case Problem 3

Data File needed for this Case Problem: Wind.xlsx

Winds of Change   Odette Ferris is a researcher at Winds of Change, a privately run wind farm providing supplemental power for communities near Topeka, Kansas. One of Odette's jobs is to record wind speeds from different sectors of the wind farm. She has entered the wind speed data into a workbook as a table with wind speed measures laid out in a grid. Because the numbers are difficult to read and interpret, she wants you to color code the wind speed values using conditional formatting. Complete the following:

1. Open the **Wind** workbook located in the Excel2 ► Case3 folder included with your Data Files, and then save the workbook as **Wind Speed Grid** in the location specified by your instructor.

2. In the Documentation sheet, enter your name in cell B3 and the date in cell B4.

3. In the Wind Speed Grid worksheet, merge the range A1:V1, and then apply the Heading 1 cell style to the merged cell and set the font size to 20 points.

4. Format the range B3:V3 as white text on a black background. Copy this formatting to the grid coordinates in the range A4:A64.

✛ **Explore** 5. Create a conditional format that highlights cells in the range B4:V64 whose value equals 18 with fill color equal to (99, 37, 35). (*Hint:* In the Equal To dialog box, select Custom Format in the with box to open the Format Cells dialog box. On the Fill tab, in the Background Color section, click the More Colors button, and then click the Custom tab to enter the RGB color value.)

✛ **Explore** 6. Repeat Step 5 to continue creating conditional formats that set highlight colors for the wind speed values in the range B4:V64 using the wind speeds and color values shown in Figure 2-47.

Figure 2-47   **Wind speed color values**

Wind Speed	RGB Color Value
16 m/s	(150, 54, 52)
14 m/s	(218, 150, 148)
12 m/s	(230, 184, 183)
10 m/s	(242, 220, 219)
8 m/s	(242, 242, 242)
6 m/s	(255, 255, 255)
4 m/s	(197, 217, 241)
2 m/s	(141, 180, 226)
0 m/s	(83, 141, 213)

© 2014 Cengage Learning

7. Reduce the font size of the values in the range B4:V64 to 1 point.

⊕ **Explore** 8. Enclose each cell in the range B4:V64 in a light gray border. (*Hint*: Use the Border tab in the Format Cells dialog box.)

9. Use the Format Painter to copy the formats from the range B4:V64 and apply them to the range X3:X12. Increase the font size of the cells in that range to 11 points.

10. Merge the range Y3:Y12, center the contents of the merged cell horizontally and vertically, and then rotate the text down. Format the text in a bold 18-point font.

11. Set the following print formats to the Wind Speed Grid worksheet:

   a Change the page orientation to landscape.

   b. Set the print area to the range A1:Y64.

   c. Scale the worksheet so that the width and the height of the sheet fit on a single page.

   d. Add a header to the printed page with your name in the left section of the header and the worksheet name in the right section of the header.

12. Save and close the workbook.

Case Problem 4

Data File needed for this Case Problem: Office.xlsx

Office Cart   Robert Trenton is a shipping manager at Office Cart, an online office supply store located in Muncie, Indiana. He wants to use an Excel workbook to track shipping orders. Robert asks you to create and format a worksheet that he can use to enter information for packing slips. Complete the following:

1. Open the **Office** workbook located in the Excel2 ▸ Case4 folder included with your Data Files, and then save the workbook as **Office Cart Packing Slip** in the location specified by your instructor.

2. In the Documentation sheet, enter your name in cell B3 and the date in cell B4.

3. Set the following formats in the Documentation sheet:

   a. Merge cells A1 and B1, and then left-align the contents of the merged cell. Change the font to 28-point white Calibri Light on a dark green background.

   b. Change the font of the range A3:A5 to 14-point white Calibri Light on a dark green background.

   c. Change the format of the date value in cell B4 to the Long Date style, and then left-align the date in the cell.

   d. Italicize the text "Office Cart" in cell B5.

   e. Add a border around each cell in the range A3:B5.

4. Insert a new worksheet at the end of the workbook and name it **Packing Slip**.

5. In the Packing Slip worksheet, select all of the cells in the worksheet. (*Hint*: Click the Select All button at the intersection of the row and column headings, or press the Ctrl+A keys.) Change the font to 10-point dark green Calibri.

6. Add a thick box border around the range A1:D40.

7. For the range A1:D3, change the format to a white Calibri Light font on a dark green background.

8. Set the width of column A to 15 characters. Set the width of column B to 20 characters. Set the width of column C to 30 characters. Set the width of column D to 20 characters.

9. Merge the range A1:B3. Merge the range C1:D3, and then right- and top-align the merged cell. Set the row height of row 1 to 36 points and the heights of rows 2 and 3 to 15 points.

10. In cell A1, enter the following three lines of text, pressing the Alt+Enter keys to start a new line within the cell:
    Office Cart
    14 Trenke Lane
    Muncie, IN 47303
    Format the first line in a 26-point bold font.

11. In cell C1, enter **Packing Slip**, and then format the text in a 26-point bold font using the Headings font of the current theme.

12. In the range A5:A7, enter the following three lines of text in a bold font, and then right-align the text and indent the text one character:
    Order Date
    Order Number
    Purchase Order

13. Format cell B5 in the Long Date format and left-align the cell contents. Insert border lines around each of the cells in the range B5:B7.

14. In the range C5:C7, enter the following three lines of text, and then use the Format Painter to copy the formats from the range A5:B7 to the range C5:D7:
    Date
    Sales Rep
    Account Num

15. In cell B9, enter **Ship To**. In cell D9, enter **Bill To**. Format the text in both cells in bold.

16. In cell A10, enter **Address**, format the text in bold, right-align the text, and then indent it one character.

17. Merge the cells in the range B10:B15, left- and top-align the cell contents, insert a border around the merged cell, and then wrap the text within this cell.

18. In cell C10, enter **Address**. Copy the format from the range A10:B15 to the range C10:D15.

19. Enter the following data in the indicated cells in the worksheet:
    cell A17: **Item**
    cell B17: **Product No.**
    cell C17: **Description**
    cell D17: **Order Quantity**

20. Format the range A17:D17 in bold white Calibri on a dark green background.

21. Format the range A18:D18 with a bottom border and a light green background. Format the range A19:D19 with a bottom border and a white background. Copy the format in the range A18:D19 to the range A20:D27.

22. Apply a Top and Double Bottom Border to the range A28:D28. Merge the contents of the range A28:C28. Enter **Total** in cell A28, bold the text, and right-align the cell contents.

23. In cell D28, enter a formula to calculate the sum of the values in the range D18:D27. Bold the text.

24. In cell A30, enter **Comments** and then bold the text.

25. Merge the range A31:D39, left- and top-align the cell contents, and then add a thick box border around the merged cell.

26. In cell D40, enter **Thank you for your business!** in italic 16-point Calibri, and then right-align the cell contents.

27. Make sure the worksheet is set to portrait orientation, and then add a footer that displays your name in the left section, the filename in the center section, and the current date in the right section. Scale the printout so that it fits onto a single page.

28. Enter the packing slip data shown in Figure 2-48. Save and close the workbook.

Figure 2-48   **Office Cart packing slip form**

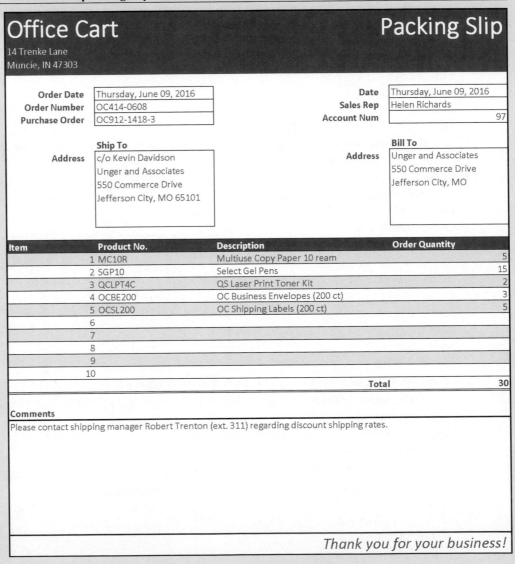

Office Cart	Packing Slip

14 Trenke Lane
Muncie, IN 47303

Order Date	Thursday, June 09, 2016	Date	Thursday, June 09, 2016
Order Number	OC414-0608	Sales Rep	Helen Richards
Purchase Order	OC912-1418-3	Account Num	97

Ship To

Address	c/o Kevin Davidson
	Unger and Associates
	550 Commerce Drive
	Jefferson City, MO 65101

Bill To

Address	Unger and Associates
	550 Commerce Drive
	Jefferson City, MO

Item	Product No.	Description	Order Quantity
1	MC10R	Multiuse Copy Paper 10 ream	5
2	SGP10	Select Gel Pens	15
3	QCLPT4C	QS Laser Print Toner Kit	2
4	OCBE200	OC Business Envelopes (200 ct)	3
5	OCSL200	OC Shipping Labels (200 ct)	5
6			
7			
8			
9			
10			
		Total	30

Comments

Please contact shipping manager Robert Trenton (ext. 311) regarding discount shipping rates.

Thank you for your business!

OBJECTIVES

Session 3.1
- Make a workbook user-friendly
- Translate an equation into an Excel formula
- Understand function syntax
- Enter formulas and functions with the Quick Analysis tool
- Enter functions with the Insert Function dialog box
- Interpret error values
- Change cell references between relative and absolute

Session 3.2
- Use the AutoFill tool to enter formulas and data and complete a series
- Display the current date with the TODAY function
- Find the next weekday with the WORKDAY function
- Use the COUNT and COUNTA functions to tally cells
- Use an IF function to return a value based on a condition
- Perform an exact match lookup with the VLOOKUP function
- Perform what-if analysis using trial and error and Goal Seek

Calculating Data with Formulas and Functions

Creating a Fitness Tracker

Case | *Fit Fathers Inc.*

Ken Dorsett is a certified fitness professional and founder of Fit Fathers Inc., which is a fitness program he developed to help fathers stay fit and active. From its beginnings in Blue Springs, Missouri, where Ken led daily workouts with three other dads, his program has grown to an enrollment of 318 fathers in five different cities in the northwest corner of the state.

Ken wants to help his members evaluate their fitness goals and track their workouts. He has been working on an Excel workbook that can assess each participant's fitness level and track his workout progress. Ken has developed the basic structure of the workbook, but still needs to enter the formulas to calculate the different statistics and data that are important for his clients. He asks you to enter the appropriate formulas to complete the workbook. To do this, you will use a variety of formulas and functions.

STARTING DATA FILES

Excel3 → Tutorial
Fitness.xlsx

Review
Mothers.xlsx

Case1
Hernandez.xlsx

Case2
Econ.xlsx

Case3
Homes.xlsx

Case4
Quality.xlsx

Session 3.1 Visual Overview:

Functions are organized by category in the Function Library group. Select a function to open the Function Arguments dialog box.

The Insert Function button opens the Insert Function dialog box from which you can select a function.

The SUM function adds the values in the range.

The AVERAGE function calculates the average value of the range.

The **MEDIAN function** determines the middle value in the range.

The **MAX function** displays the maximum value in the range.

The **MIN function** displays the minimum value in the range.

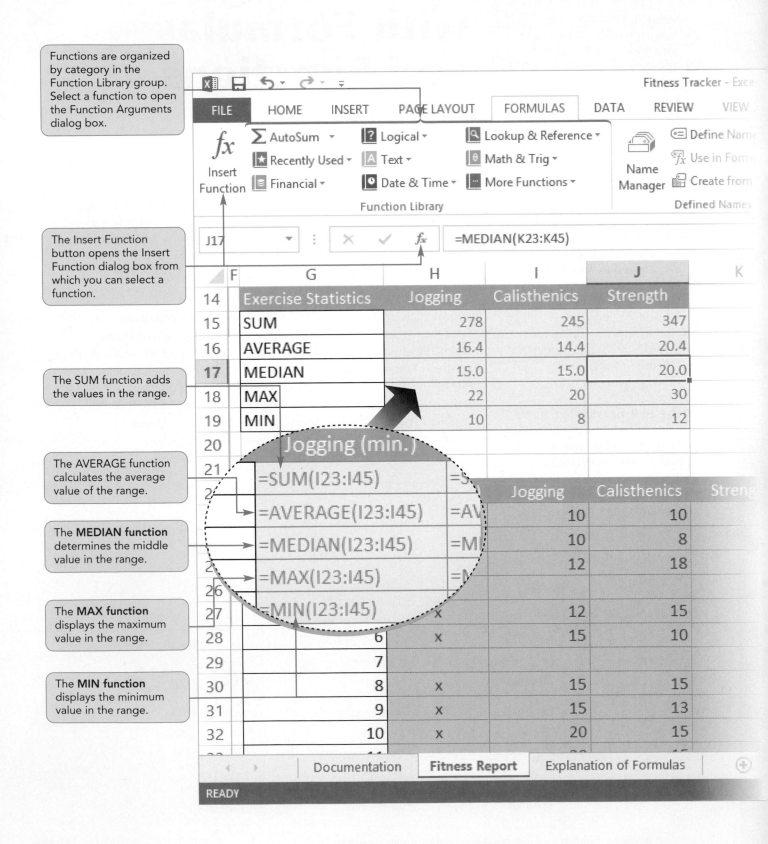

Fitness Tracker - Exce

FILE   HOME   INSERT   PAGE LAYOUT   FORMULAS   DATA   REVIEW   VIEW

fx
Insert Function

Σ AutoSum ▾   ? Logical ▾   Lookup & Reference ▾
Recently Used ▾   A Text ▾   θ Math & Trig ▾
Financial ▾   Date & Time ▾   More Functions ▾

Function Library

Name Manager

Define Name
Use in Form
Create from

Defined Names

J17   =MEDIAN(K23:K45)

	F	G	H	I	J	K
14		Exercise Statistics	Jogging	Calisthenics	Strength	
15		SUM	278	245	347	
16		AVERAGE	16.4	14.4	20.4	
17		MEDIAN	15.0	15.0	20.0	
18		MAX	22	20	30	
19		MIN	10	8	12	

Jogging (min.)

=SUM(I23:I45)   =S
=AVERAGE(I23:I45) =AV
=MEDIAN(I23:I45)   =MI
=MAX(I23:I45)   =M
=MIN(I23:I45)   x

	Jogging	Calisthenics	Streng
	10	10	
	10	8	
	12	18	
27	12	15	
28	6	x	15	10
29	7			
30	8	x	15	15
31	9	x	15	13
32	10	x	20	15

Documentation   **Fitness Report**   Explanation of Formulas

READY

Functions and Cell References

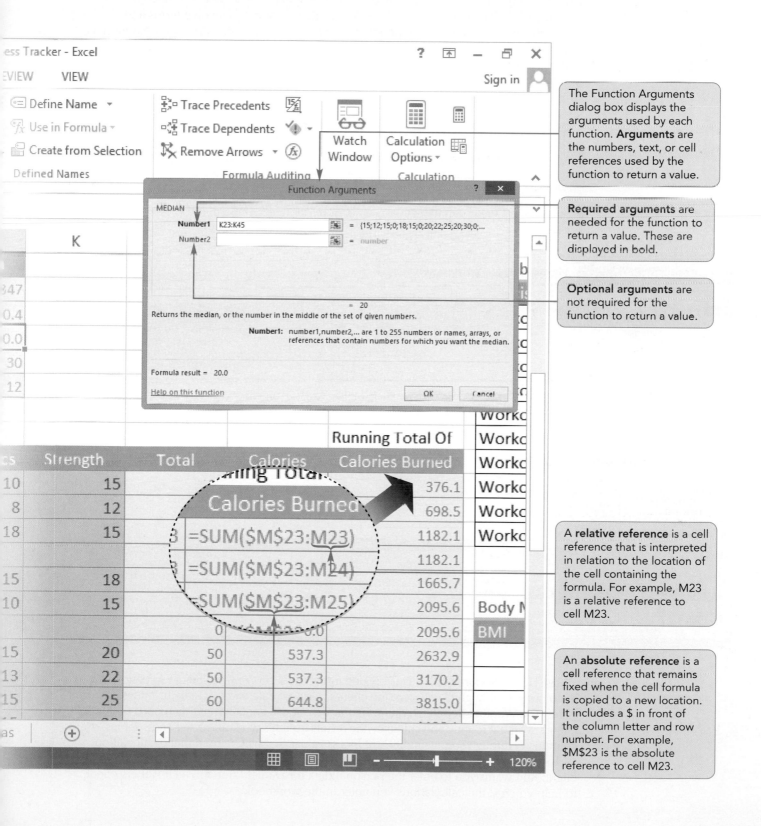

The Function Arguments dialog box displays the arguments used by each function. **Arguments** are the numbers, text, or cell references used by the function to return a value.

Required arguments are needed for the function to return a value. These are displayed in bold.

Optional arguments are not required for the function to return a value.

A **relative reference** is a cell reference that is interpreted in relation to the location of the cell containing the formula. For example, M23 is a relative reference to cell M23.

An **absolute reference** is a cell reference that remains fixed when the cell formula is copied to a new location. It includes a $ in front of the column letter and row number. For example, $M$23 is the absolute reference to cell M23.

Making Workbooks User-Friendly

Every workbook should be accessible to its intended users. When a workbook is user-friendly, anyone who needs to enter data in the workbook or interpret its results can understand the workbook's contents, including any jargon or unusual terms, what is being calculated, and how the equations make those calculations.

Many of the fitness calculations needed for Ken's workbook involve terms and equations that are unfamiliar to people not in the fitness industry. Because both trainers and clients will access this workbook, these terms and equations need to be explained. Ken has already included information about the fitness equations in the workbook. You will open the workbook, and examine its layout and structure.

To open and review the Fitness workbook:

1. Open the **Fitness** workbook located in the Excel3 ▶ Tutorial folder included with your Data Files, and then save the workbook as **Fitness Tracker** in the location specified by your instructor.

2. In the Documentation sheet, enter your name in cell B3 and the date in cell B4.

3. Go to the **Fitness Report** worksheet. See Figure 3-1.

Figure 3-1	Fitness Tracker workbook

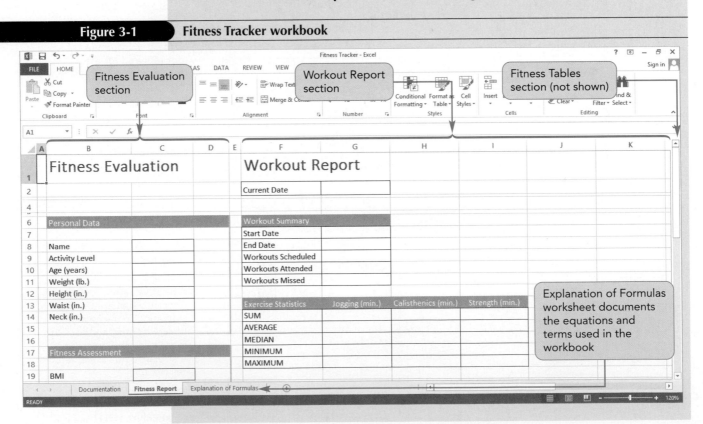

The Fitness Report worksheet is divided into three sections. The Fitness Evaluation in columns B through D will store the client's personal data and calculate his fitness status. The Workout Report in columns F through M will contain monthly reports on the client's workout routine and calculate the results from his workouts. The Fitness Tables in columns O through P contain different fitness values that will be used in the calculations.

The Fitness Evaluation contains a section for personal information on a Fit Fathers client. Ken wants you to enter the personal data for Daniel Pridham, a Fit Fathers client, to help you test the calculations you enter in the workbook.

To enter Daniel's personal data:

▶ **1.** In cell **C8**, enter **Daniel Pridham** as the client's name.

▶ **2.** In cell **C9**, enter **Sedentary** to describe Daniel's activity level.

▶ **3.** In the range **C10:C14**, enter **45** for his age, **193** for his weight in pounds, **70** for his height in inches, **37** for his waist size in inches, and **15.5** for his neck size in inches.

Documenting Formulas

Documenting the contents of a workbook helps to avoid errors and confusion. This type of information can make a workbook easier for other people to understand. For workbooks that include many calculations, as the Fitness Tracker workbook does, it is helpful to explain the formulas and terms used in the calculations. Such documentation also can serve as a check that the equations are accurate. Another way to document formulas and terms is to include notes of explanation within the worksheet where the equations are used.

Ken has included explanations of different fitness terms and equations in the Explanation of Formulas worksheet, and explanatory notes in cells B26 and F46 of the Fitness Report worksheet. Before proceeding, he wants you to review the documentation in these worksheets.

To review the documentation in the Fitness Tracker workbook:

▶ **1.** Click the **Explanation of Formulas** sheet tab to make it the active sheet.

▶ **2.** Read the sheet contents, reviewing the descriptions of common fitness terms and formulas. As you continue developing the Fitness Tracker workbook, you'll learn about these terms and formulas in more detail.

▶ **3.** Click the **Fitness Report** sheet tab to return to the Fitness Report worksheet.

▶ **4.** Read the explanatory notes in cells B26 and F46.

Using Constants in Formulas

The first fitness equation Ken wants you to enter is BMI, or body mass index, which estimates the amount of human body fat. The BMI equation is based on the individual's body weight divided by the square of his or her height. The specific formula is

$$BMI = \frac{703w}{h^2}$$

where w is the body weight in pounds and h is the height in inches. BMI values from 18.5 to 24.9 are considered normal; anything higher is considered overweight.

One common skill you need when creating a workbook is to translate an equation like the BMI equation into an Excel formula. Some equations use constants. A **constant** is a value in a formula that doesn't change. In the BMI equation, 703 is a constant because that value never changes when calculating the body mass index.

Deciding Where to Place a Constant

Should a constant be entered directly into the formula or placed in a separate worksheet cell and referenced in the formula? The answer depends on the constant being used, the purpose of the workbook, and the intended audience. Placing constants in separate cells that you reference in the formulas can help users better understand the worksheet because no values are hidden within the formulas. Also, when a constant is entered in a cell, you can add explanatory text next to each constant to document how it is being used in the formula. On the other hand, you don't want a user to inadvertently change the value of a constant and throw off all the formula results. You will need to evaluate how important it is for other people to immediately see the constant, and whether the constant requires any explanation for other people to understand the formula. For example, Ken wants you to include the 703 constant in the BMI formula rather than in a separate cell because he doesn't feel that clients need to see this constant to understand BMI.

To convert the BMI equation into a formula, you need to replace *w* and *h* in the equation with Daniel's actual weight and height. Because Daniel's weight is stored in cell C11 and his height is stored in cell C12, you replace the *w* in the formula with the C11 cell reference, and replace the *h* in the formula with the C12 cell reference. The resulting Excel formula is:

```
=703*C11/C12^2
```

Note that the exponent operator ^ is used to square the height value in the denominator of the fraction. Recall that exponentiation raises a value to a power; in this case, the value in cell C12 is raised to the second power, or squared. Following the order of operations, Excel will first square the height value, then multiply the weight value by 703, and finally divide that product by the squared height. You will enter the BMI formula in the Fitness Report worksheet now.

To enter the BMI formula in the Fitness Report worksheet:

1. In cell **C19**, enter the formula **=703*C11/C12^2**. The formula multiplies the weight in cell C11 by the constant 703, and then divides the resulting value by the square of the height in cell C12. The calculated BMI value that is displayed in cell C19 is 27.68959184.

   Trouble? If your BMI formula results differ from 27.68959184, you probably entered the formula incorrectly. Edit your formula as needed so that the numbers and cell references match those shown in the formula in Step 1.

2. Select cell **C19**, and then reduce the number of displayed decimals to one. Cell C19 displays 27.7 as the formula results.

The next fitness equation, which calculates the individual's resting basal metabolic rate (BMR), includes four constants. The resting BMR estimates the number of calories a person expends daily (not counting any actual activity). For men, the BMR is calculated with the equation

$$BMR = 6.23w + 12.7h - 6.76a + 66$$

where *w* is the weight in pounds, *h* is the height in inches, and *a* is the age in years. BMR is calculated by multiplying the weight, height, and age by different constants, and then adding the results to another constant. Heavier and taller people require more daily calories to sustain them. As people age, their metabolism slows, resulting in a lower BMR. Daniel's weight, height, and age are stored in cells C11, C12, and C10, respectively, so the BMR equation translates to the following Excel formula:

```
=6.23*C11+12.7*C12-6.76*C10+66
```

You will enter this formula in the Fitness Report worksheet to calculate Daniel's BMR.

To enter the BMR formula in the Fitness Report worksheet:

1. In cell **C21**, enter the formula **=6.23*C11+12.7*C12–6.76*C10+66**. Cell C21 displays 1853.19, indicating that Daniel burns about 1853 calories per day before performing any activity.

   Trouble? If your BMR formula results differ from 1853.19, you might have entered the formula incorrectly. Edit the formula as needed so that the numbers and cell references match those shown in the formula in Step 1.

2. Select cell **C21**, and then reduce the number of decimals displayed in the cell to zero. The number of calories per day displayed in cell C21 is 1853.

The 1853 calories per day amount assumes no physical activity. However, even the most sedentary person moves a little bit during the day, which increases the BMR value. The table in the range O7:P12 in the Fitness Report worksheet lists the constant multipliers for different activity levels. For example, the BMR of a sedentary man like Daniel is multiplied by 1.2 (shown in cell P8) to account for daily movements. If Daniel were to increase his activities to a moderate level, the multiplier would increase to 1.55 (as shown in cell P10).

You will enter the formula to calculate Daniel's active BMR based on his sedentary lifestyle. Ken wants you to use the constant value stored in the table rather entering it into the formula because he anticipates that Daniel will increase his activity level under the direction of Fit Fathers, and it is easier to update the amount in a cell rather than editing a formula.

To calculate Daniel's active BMR:

1. In cell **C22**, enter the formula **=C21*P8** to multiply Daniel's resting BMR by the sedentary activity level. Based on this calculation, Daniel's active BMR is 2223.828 calories per day.

2. Select cell **C22**, and then decrease the number of decimal places displayed in the cell to zero. The displayed value changes to 2224. See Figure 3-2.

Figure 3-2   **BMI and BMR calculated values**

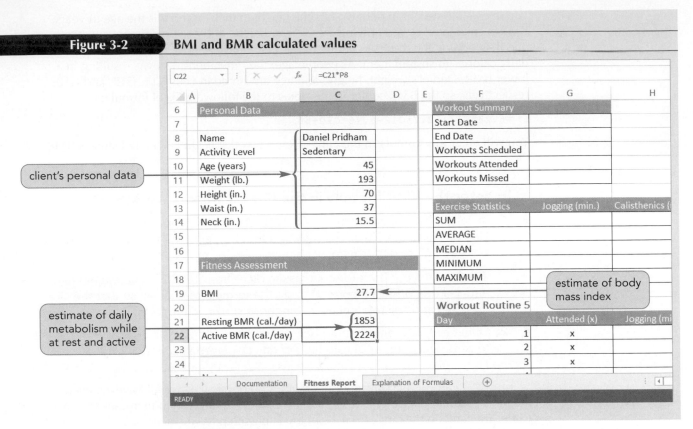

client's personal data

estimate of body mass index

estimate of daily metabolism while at rest and active

The active BMR shows that Daniel needs about 2224 calories per day to maintain his current weight.

Identifying Notes, Input Values, and Calculated Values

When worksheets involve notes and many calculations, it is useful to distinguish input values that are used in formulas from calculated values that are returned by formulas. Formatting that clearly differentiates input values from calculated values helps others more easily understand the worksheet. Such formatting also helps prevent anyone from entering a value in a cell that contains a formula.

You can use cell styles to identify cells as containing explanatory text, input values, and calculated values. When you use cell styles or other formatting to identify a cell's purpose, you should include a legend in the worksheet describing the purpose of the formatting.

Ken wants to be sure that whenever he and his staff members update a client's workbook, they can easily see where to enter numbers. You will apply cell styles to distinguish between notes, input cells, and formula cells.

To apply cell styles to differentiate cells with notes, input values, and calculated values:

▶ 1. Select the merged cell **B26**.

▶ 2. On the HOME tab, in the Styles group, click the **Cell Styles** button to open the Cell Styles gallery.

▶ 3. Click the **Explanatory Text** cell style located in the Data and Model group. Cell B26 is formatted with the Explanatory Text cell style.

▶ 4. Format cell **F46** with the **Explanatory Text** cell style.

5. Format the range **C8:C14** with the **Input** cell style. These cells contain the personal information about Daniel that you entered earlier.

6. Format the nonadjacent range **C19;C21:C22** containing the calculated BMI and BMR values with the **Calculation** cell style.

7. Format the range **G22:J44** with the **Input** cell style. These cells store information about Daniel's workout routine, which Ken enters after each workout.

   Next, you'll create a legend to identify which cells are input cells and which cells are calculated cells.

8. In cell **C2**, enter **Input Values** as the label, format the cell with the **Explanatory Text** cell style, and then right-align the text in the cell.

9. In cell **C4**, enter **Calculated Values** as the label, and then use the Format Painter to copy the formatting in cell C2 and paste it to cell C4.

10. Format cell **D2** with the **Input** cell style, and then format cell **D4** with the **Calculation** cell style.

11. Select cell **C19**. See Figure 3-3.

Figure 3-3	Input and calculated values formatted with cell styles

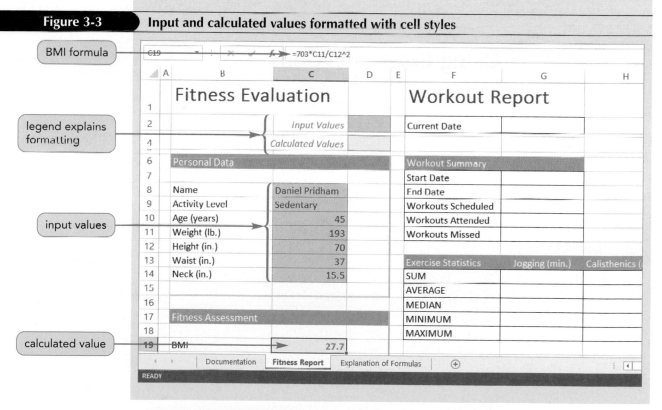

The built-in cell styles are a quick way of marking different types of values in your worksheet. If the formats do not match what you want for your workbook, you can create your own cell styles. However you design your worksheet, your purpose is to make the values easy to interpret.

Written Communication: Displaying Significant Digits

Excel stores numbers with up to 15 digits and displays as many digits as will fit into the cell. So even the result of a simple formula such as =10/3 will display 3.33333333333333 if the cell is wide enough.

A number with 15 digits is difficult to read, and calculations rarely need that level of accuracy. Many scientific disciplines, such as chemistry or physics, have rules for specifying exactly how many digits should be displayed with any calculation. These digits are called **significant digits** because they indicate the accuracy of the measured and calculated values. For example, an input value of 19.32 has four significant digits.

The rules are based on several factors and vary from one discipline to another. Generally, a calculated value should display no more digits than are found in any of the input values. For example, because the input value 19.32 has four significant digits, any calculated value based on that input should have no more than four significant digits. Showing more digits would be misleading because it implies a level of accuracy beyond that which was actually measured.

Because Excel displays calculated values with as many digits as can fit into a cell, you need to know the standards for your profession and change the display of your calculated values accordingly.

Using Excel Functions

Functions provide a quick way to calculate summary data such as the total, average, and median values in a collection of values. Ken recorded the amount of time Daniel spent at each workout doing brisk jogging, calisthenics, and strength exercise. Ken wants you to analyze the results from Daniel's workout routine. You will use Excel functions to summarize these results.

Excel supports an extensive library of functions, organized into the 12 categories shown in Figure 3-4. You can use Excel functions to perform statistical analysis, work with financial data, retrieve information from databases, and generate text strings, among many other tasks.

Figure 3-4   Excel function categories

Category	Description
Cube	Retrieve data from multidimensional databases involving online analytical processing (OLAP)
Database	Retrieve and analyze data stored in databases
Date & Time	Analyze or create date and time values and time intervals
Engineering	Analyze engineering problems
Financial	Analyze information for business and finance
Information	Return information about the format, location, or contents of worksheet cells
Logical	Return logical (true-false) values
Lookup & Reference	Look up and return data matching a set of specified conditions from a range
Math & Trig	Perform math and trigonometry calculations
Statistical	Provide statistical analyses of data sets
Text	Return text values or evaluate text
Web	Provide information on web-based connections

The Excel Help system provides information on all of the Excel functions.

Exploring Function Syntax

Before you use functions, you should understand the function syntax. Recall that the syntax of an Excel function follows the general pattern

$$FUNCTION(argument1,argument2,...)$$

where *FUNCTION* is the name of the function, and *argument1*, *argument2*, and so forth are arguments used by the function. An argument can be any type of value including text, numbers, cell references, or even other formulas or functions. Not all functions require arguments.

TIP

Optional arguments are always placed last in the argument list.

Some arguments are optional. You can include an optional argument in the function or omit it from the function. Some optional arguments have default values associated with them, so that if you omit the optional argument, Excel will use the default value. These tutorials show optional arguments within square brackets along with the argument's default value (if any), as

$$FUNCTION(argument1[, argument2=value2,...])$$

where *argument1* is a required argument, *argument2* is optional, and *value2* is the default value for *argument2*. As you work with specific functions, you will learn which arguments are required and which are optional as well as any default values associated with optional arguments.

Figure 3-5 describes some of the more common Math, Trig, and Statistical functions and provides the syntax of those functions.

Figure 3-5	Common Math, Trig, and Statistical functions

Function	Category	Description
AVERAGE(number1[, number2, number3, ...])	Statistical	Calculates the average of a collection of numbers, where *number1*, *number2*, and so forth are numbers or cell references; only *number1* is required
COUNT(value1[, value2, value3, ...])	Statistical	Counts how many cells in a range contain numbers, where *value1*, *value2*, and so forth are text, numbers, or cell references; only *value1* is required
COUNTA(value1[, value2, value3, ...])	Statistical	Counts how many cells are not empty in ranges *value1*, *value2*, and so forth, or how many numbers are listed within *value1*, *value2*, etc.
INT(number)	Math & Trig	Displays the integer portion of *number*
MAX(number1[, number2, number3, ...])	Statistical	Calculates the maximum value of a collection of numbers, where *number1*, *number2*, and so forth are either numbers or cell references
MEDIAN(number1[, number2, number3, ...])	Statistical	Calculates the median, or middle, value of a collection of numbers, where *number1*, *number2*, and so forth are either numbers or cell references
MIN(number1[, number2, number3, ...])	Statistical	Calculates the minimum value of a collection of numbers, where *number1*, *number2*, and so forth are either numbers or cell references
RAND()	Math & Trig	Returns a random number between 0 and 1
ROUND(number, num_digits)	Math & Trig	Rounds *number* to the number of digits specified by *num_digits*
SUM(number1[, number2, number3, ...])	Math & Trig	Adds a collection of numbers, where *number1*, *number2*, and so forth are either numbers or cell references

For example, the ROUND function rounds a number to a specified number of decimal places and has the syntax

`ROUND(number, num_digits)`

where *number* is the number to be rounded and *num_digits* is the number of decimal places to which you want to round the *number* argument. The following function rounds 2.718282 to two decimal places, resulting in 2.72:

`ROUND(2.718282, 2)`

However, you usually reference data values stored in worksheet cells rather than entering the numbers directly in the function. For example, the following function rounds the number in cell A10 to three decimal places:

`ROUND(A10, 3)`

Both arguments in the ROUND function are required. An example of a function that uses optional arguments is the AVERAGE function, which can calculate averages from several ranges or entered values. For example, the function

`AVERAGE(A1:A10)`

averages the values in the range A1:A10, while the function

`AVERAGE(A1:A10, C5:C10, E10)`

includes two optional arguments and averages the values from the cells in range A1:A10, range C5:C10, and cell E10.

Functions can be included as part of larger formulas. The following formula calculates the average of the values in the range A1:A100, and then squares that result using the ^ operator:

`=AVERAGE(A1:A100)^2`

Functions can also be placed inside another function, or **nested**. If a formula contains several functions, Excel starts with the innermost function and then moves outward. For example, the following formula first calculates the average of the values in the range A1:A100 using the AVERAGE function, and then rounds that value to two decimal places:

`=ROUND(AVERAGE(A1:A100),2)`

One challenge of nesting functions is to make sure that you include all of the parentheses. You can check this by counting the number of opening parentheses and making sure that number matches the number of closing parentheses. Excel also displays each level of nested parentheses in different colors to make it easier for you to match the opening and closing parentheses in the formula. If the number of parentheses doesn't match, Excel will not accept the formula and will provide a suggestion for how to rewrite the formula so the number of opening and closing parentheses does match.

There are several ways to enter a function. You have already entered a function by typing directly in a cell and using the AutoSum button. Another way to enter a function is with the Quick Analysis tool.

Entering Functions with the Quick Analysis Tool

The Quick Analysis tool, which you have already used to apply conditional formats that highlight specific data values, can also be used to generate columns and rows of summary statistics that can be used for analyzing data.

Columns F through M in the Fitness Report worksheet will contain the workout report. The range H22:J44 records the number of minutes Daniel spent at each workout jogging, doing calisthenics, and doing strength training. Ken needs to know the total minutes Daniel spent at each exercise to evaluate Daniel's workout effort during the past month. The most efficient way to calculate these totals is with the SUM function. You will use the Quick Analysis tool to enter the SUM function to calculate the total minutes spent at each exercise.

To calculate the total minutes spent on each exercise:

1. Select the range **H22:J44** containing the minutes spent on each exercise during each workout. The Quick Analysis button appears in the lower-right corner of the selected range.

2. Click the **Quick Analysis** button (or press the **Ctrl+Q** keys) to display the Quick Analysis tool.

3. Click the **TOTALS** category to display Quick Analysis tools for calculating totals.

4. Point to the **Sum** button. Live Preview shows the results of Sum. See Figure 3-6.

Figure 3-6   Quick Analysis tool to calculate totals

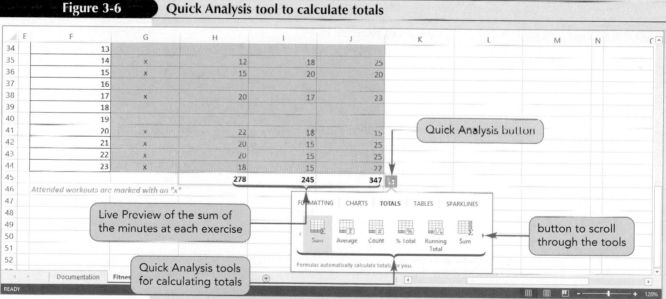

5. Click **Sum** to enter the SUM function for each cell in the selected range. The results show that Daniel spent 278 minutes jogging, 245 minutes doing calisthenics, and 347 minutes doing strength exercises during the previous month's workouts.

   The Quick Analysis tool automatically inserts the formulas containing the SUM function at the bottom of the table. Ken wants you to move this information near the top of the worksheet where it can be viewed first.

6. Select the range **H45:J45**, and then cut the selected range.

7. Select cell **G14**, and then paste the formulas with the SUM functions. The totals now appear in the range G14:I14.

The Quick Analysis tool can also be used to quickly calculate averages. An average provides an estimate of the most typical value from a data sample. Ken wants to know the average number of minutes that Daniel spent on each exercise during his sessions.

To calculate the average minutes spent per exercise:

▶ **1.** Select the range **H22:J44**, and then click the **Quick Analysis** button that appears in the lower-right corner of the selected range (or press the **Ctrl+Q** keys).

▶ **2.** Click the **TOTALS** category, and then click **Average** to enter the AVERAGE function in the range H45:J45 and calculate the average minutes per exercise type.

▶ **3.** Cut the formulas from the range **H45:J45**, and then paste them into the range **G15:I15**.

   Excel displays the averages to eight decimal places, which implies a far greater accuracy in measuring the exercise time than could be recorded.

▶ **4.** In the range **G15:I15**, decrease the number of decimal places displayed to one. On average, Daniel spent about 16.4 minutes per session jogging, 14.4 minutes on calisthenics, and 20.4 minutes on strength exercises. See Figure 3-7.

| Figure 3-7 | Sums and averages of exercise times |

The Quick Analysis tool can be used to summarize values across rows as well as down columns. Ken wants to calculate how long Daniel worked out each day. You will use the Quick Analysis tool to calculate the total exercise minutes per workout.

To calculate the total workout times per session:

▶ **1.** In cell **K21**, enter **Total Minutes** as the heading.

▶ **2.** Select the range **H22:J44**, and then open the Quick Analysis tool.

▶ **3.** Click the **TOTALS** category, and then click the right scroll button to scroll to the right through the list of calculations.

▶ **4.** Click the **Sum** button for the column of summary statistics. SUM functions are entered in the range K22:K44, calculating the sum of the workout minutes per session.

   The Quick Analysis tool applies its own style to the formulas it generates. Instead of the bold text, you want the formulas to be formatted with the Calculation style.

▶ **5.** Format the range **K22:K44** with the **Calculation** cell style.

6. In cell **J13**, enter **Total Minutes** as the heading.

7. Copy the formulas in the range **I14:I15**, and then paste them into the range **J14:J15** to calculate the sum and average of the total exercise minutes from all of the workouts. As shown in Figure 3-8, Daniel worked out for 870 minutes during the month with an average of 37.8 minutes per workout.

Figure 3-8 Total exercise time per workout

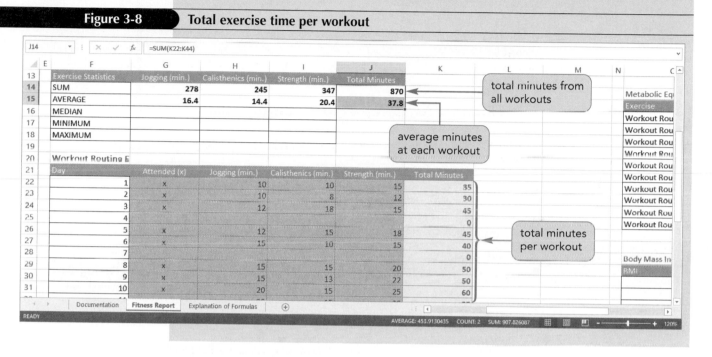

Entering Functions with the Insert Function Dialog Box

Functions are organized in the Function Library group on the FORMULAS tab. In the Function Library, you can select a function from a function category. You can also open the Insert Function dialog box to search for a particular function based on a description you enter. When you select a function, the Function Arguments dialog box opens, listing all of the arguments associated with that function. Required arguments are in bold type; optional arguments are in normal type.

Ken wants his report to include the median exercise times for the three exercise categories. The **median** provides the middle value from a data sample. You can use the MEDIAN function to determine the middle value in a range of numbers. The Quick Analysis tool doesn't include median, so you will use the Insert Function and Function Arguments dialog boxes to help you correctly insert the MEDIAN function.

To calculate the median exercise time:

1. Select cell **G16**. This is the cell in which you will enter the MEDIAN function.

2. Click the **Insert Function** button f_x to the left of the formula bar to open the Insert Function dialog box. From the Insert Function dialog box, you can describe the function you want to search for.

3. In the Search for a function box, type **middle value**, and then click the **Go** button. Functions for finding a middle value appear in the Select a function box. The second entry in the list, MEDIAN, is the one you want to use. See Figure 3-9.

Figure 3-9 Insert Function dialog box

description of the function you want to find

functions that match your search description

description of the selected function

4. In the Select a function box, click **MEDIAN** to select it, and then click the **OK** button. The Function Arguments dialog box opens with the arguments for the MEDIAN function.

5. With the insertion point in the Number1 box, click the **Collapse Dialog Box** button to shrink the dialog box so you can see more of the worksheet.

6. In the worksheet, select the range **H22:H44**. These cells contain the times Daniel spent jogging.

7. In the Function Arguments dialog box, click the **Expand Dialog Box** button to redisplay the entire dialog box. The dialog box now shows a preview of the MEDIAN function and the value it will return to the formula. See Figure 3-10.

Figure 3-10 Function Arguments dialog box

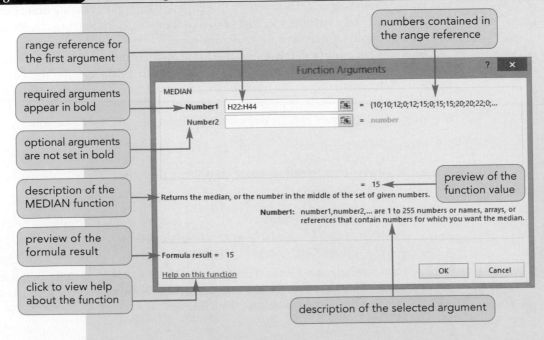

range reference for the first argument

required arguments appear in bold

optional arguments are not set in bold

description of the MEDIAN function

preview of the formula result

click to view help about the function

numbers contained in the range reference

preview of the function value

description of the selected argument

8. Click the **OK** button. The formula =MEDIAN(H22:H44) is entered in cell G16, which displays 15 (the median exercise time for jogging).

9. Copy cell **G16**, and then paste the copied formula into the range **H16:J16** to calculate the median exercise times for calisthenics, strength training, and all exercises. See Figure 3-11.

Figure 3-11   **Median exercise times**

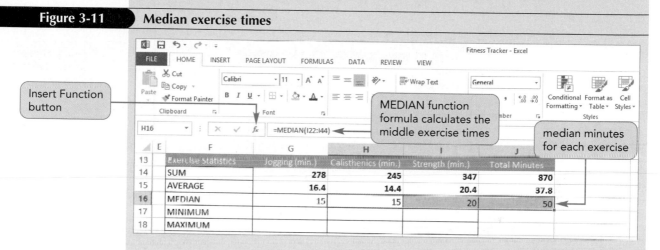

Daniel spent a median time of 15 minutes on calisthenics and 20 minutes on strength training. The median total exercise time was 50 minutes, which is quite a bit higher than the average total exercise time of 37.8 minutes. Why this difference? One reason is that averages are greatly influenced by extremely low or high values. Because Daniel missed several workouts, his exercise time for those days was 0, bringing down the overall average. A median, or middle value, is not as affected by these extreme values, which is why some statisticians advocate medians over averages for analyzing data with widely spaced values.

Ken also wants to know the minimum and maximum minutes Daniel spent exercising during the month. You can access functions by scrolling through the Function Library. You will use this method to enter the functions to calculate the minimum and maximum exercise times.

To calculate the minimum and maximum minutes of exercise:

1. Select cell **G17**, which is where you will calculate the minimum exercise time.

2. On the ribbon, click the **FORMULAS** tab to display the function categories in the Function Library.

3. Click the **More Functions** button to display the rest of the function categories. Calculations involving maximums and minimums are included with the Statistical functions.

4. Click **Statistical** to display the statistical functions, and then scroll down and point to **MIN**. A ScreenTip appears, displaying the MIN function syntax and a description of the function. See Figure 3-12.

Figure 3-12 **MIN function in the Function Library**

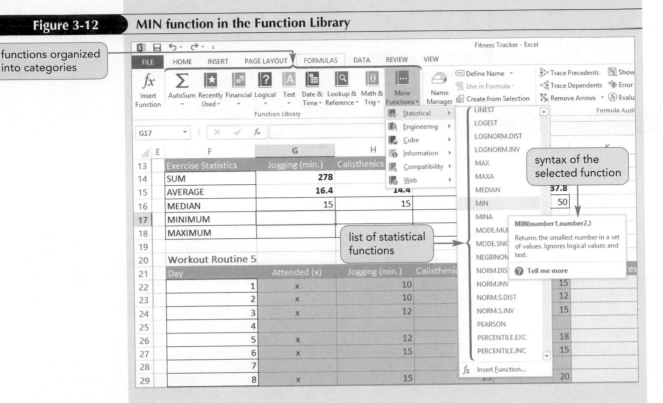

5. Click **MIN** to open the Function Arguments dialog box.

6. With the insertion point in the Number1 box, select the range **H22:H44** in the worksheet. These cells store the amount of time Daniel spent jogging.

7. Click the **OK** button. The dialog box closes, and the formula =MIN(H22:H44) is entered in cell G17, which displays 10, the minimum minutes that Daniel spent jogging during the month.

8. Select cell **G18**, click the **More Functions** button in the Function Library group, click **Statistical**, and then scroll down and click **MAX**. The Function Arguments dialog box opens.

9. With the insertion point in the Number1 box, select the range **H22:H44** in the worksheet, and then click the **OK** button. The formula =MAX(H22:H44) is entered in cell G18, which displays 22, the maximum minutes that Daniel spent jogging.

10. Copy the range **G17:G18**, and then paste the formulas in the range **H17:J18** to calculate the minimum and maximum times for the other exercises and overall.

11. Format the range **G14:J18** with the **Calculation** cell style, and then select cell **F19**. See Figure 3-13.

Figure 3-13   Summary statistics of the exercise times

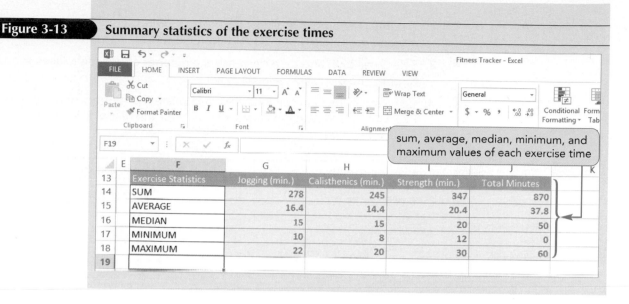

Referencing Function Results in a Formula

The amount of calories burned during exercise is a function of intensity and time. The more intense the exercise or the longer it lasts, the more calories burned. Ken uses the fitness equation

$$\text{Calories} = \frac{METS \times w \times t}{125.7143}$$

to calculate how many calories will be used during exercise, where *METS* is a metabolic factor that measures the intensity of the exercise, *w* is the individual's weight in pounds, *t* is the exercise time in minutes, and 125.7143 is a constant that converts the quantity into calories. Ken listed the METS values for the different workout routines he created in the range O15:P25 of the Fitness Report worksheet. For example, the METS for Workout Routine 5 is 7.0 and the METS for Workout Routine 10 is 16.0. Using the METS information and the weight and exercise times, you can calculate the total calories burned during each workout.

The fitness equation that calculates calories burned during the first workout translates into the formula

```
=P20*C11*K22/125.7143
```

where P20 references the cell with the METS for Workout Routine 5, C11 references the cell that stores Daniel's weight, and K22 references the cell that calculates the total exercise time of the first workout.

You will enter this formula in cell L22, and then copy it to the remaining cells in the column to calculate the calories burned during each workout.

To calculate the calories burned during Daniel's first workout:

1. In cell **L21**, enter **Calories Burned** as the label.

2. In cell **L22**, enter the formula **=P20*C11*K22/125.7143** to calculate the calories Daniel burned at his first workout. Cell P20 stores the METS value, cell C11 contains Daniel's weight, and cell K22 is the total exercise time for Workout Routine 5 on the first day of the month. Cell L22 displays 376.1306391, which is the number of calories burned at the first workout.

Trouble? If your value differs from 376.1306391, edit your formula as needed so it exactly matches the formula shown in Step 2.

3. Select cell **L22**, and then decrease the number of decimal places shown to one. The displayed value is 376.1.

4. Copy the formula in cell **L22**, and then paste the formula to the range **L23:L44** to calculate the calories burned for the rest of the workouts. See Figure 3-14.

Figure 3-14   **Formulas incorrectly calculating the calories burned per workout**

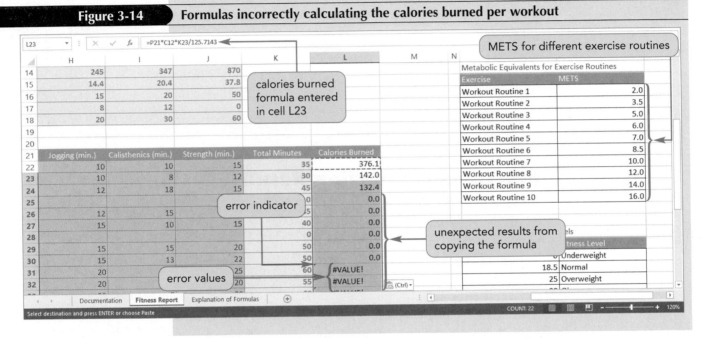

The first few values seem somewhat reasonable, but then several workouts show no calories burned. These are followed by cells displaying #VALUE! rather than a number. Obviously something went wrong when you copied and pasted the formula.

Interpreting Error Values

The #VALUE! that appears in some of the cells in the Fitness Report worksheet is an error value. An **error value** indicates that some part of a formula is preventing Excel from returning a calculated value. An error value begins with a pound sign (#) followed by an error name that indicates the type of error. Figure 3-15 describes common error values that you might see instead of the results from formulas and functions. For example, the error value #VALUE! indicates that the wrong type of value is used in a function or formula. You will need to examine the formulas in the cells with error values to determine exactly what went wrong.

Figure 3-15	**Excel error values**

Error Value	Description
#DIV/0!	The formula or function contains a number divided by 0.
#NAME?	Excel doesn't recognize text in the formula or function, such as when the function name is misspelled.
#N/A	A value is not available to a function or formula, which can occur when a workbook is initially set up prior to entering actual data values.
#NULL!	A formula or function requires two cell ranges to intersect, but they don't.
#NUM!	Invalid numbers are used in a formula or function, such as text entered in a function that requires a number.
#REF!	A cell reference used in a formula or function is no longer valid, which can occur when the cell used by the function was deleted from the worksheet.
#VALUE!	The wrong type of argument is used in a function or formula. This can occur when you reference a text value for an argument that should be strictly numeric.

© 2014 Cengage Learning

The error value messages are not particularly descriptive or helpful. To help you locate the error, an error indicator appears in the upper-left corner of the cell with the error value. When you point to the error indicator, a ScreenTip appears with more information about the source of the error.

INSIGHT

Deciding When to Correct an Error Value

An error value does not mean that you must correct the cell's formula or function. Some error values appear simply because you have not yet entered any data into the workbook. For example, if you use the AVERAGE function to find the average value of an empty column, the #DIV/0! error value appears because the formula cannot calculate the average of a collection of empty cells. However, as soon as you begin entering data, the #DIV/0! message will disappear.

Ken wants you to figure out why the #VALUE error value appears in some of the cells where you copied the calories burned formula. To figure this out, you will examine the formula in cell L31, which is the first cell that displays the error value instead of the expected number results.

To view the formula in cell L31 that results in an error value:

1. Double-click cell **L31**, which displays the #VALUE! error value. In Edit mode, the cell references used in the formula are color coded to match the corresponding cells, making it easier to see which cells are used in the formula.

2. Observe that cell L31 contains the formula =P29*C20*K31/125.7143.

   3. Look at the first cell reference in the formula. The first cell reference is to cell P29 containing the text "Fitness Level" instead of cell P20 containing the METS value for Workout Routine 5. The formula is attempting to multiply the text in cell P29, but multiplication can be done only with numbers. This is the problem causing the #VALUE! error value.

   4. Look at the second cell reference in the formula. The second cell reference is to cell C20, an empty cell, rather than to cell C11 containing Daniel's weight.

   5. Look at the third cell reference in the formula. The third cell reference is to cell K31, which contains the total exercise times for the tenth workout—the correct cell reference.

Exploring Cell References

Most workbooks include data entered in cells that are then referenced in formulas to perform calculations on that data. The formulas can be simple, such as the formulas you entered to add the total minutes of each workout, or they can be more complex, such as the formulas you entered to calculate the calories burned during each workout. Each of these formulas includes one or more cell references.

Understanding Relative References

When a formula includes a cell reference, Excel interprets that cell reference as being located relative to the position of the current cell. For example, Excel interprets the following formula entered in cell A1 to mean "add the value of the cell one column to the right of this cell to the value of the cell one column to the right and one row below this cell":

   =B1+B2

This relative interpretation is retained when the formula is copied to a new location. So, if the formula in cell A1 is copied to cell A3 (two rows down in the worksheet), the relative references in the formula also shift two rows down, resulting in the following formula:

   =B3+B4

   Figure 3-16 shows another example of how relative references change when a formula is copied to new cell locations. In this figure, the formula =A4 entered in cell D7 displays 10, which is the number entered in cell A4. When pasted to a new location, each of the pasted formulas contains a reference to a cell that is three rows up and three rows to the left of the current cell's location.

Figure 3-16   **Formulas using relative references**

formula references a cell three rows up and three columns to the left of the active cell

when copied to new cells, each formula still references a cell three rows up and three columns to the left

values returned by each formula

© 2014 Cengage Learning

This explains what happened with the relative references you used to calculate calories burned for each workout. When you entered the following formula in cell L22, cell C11 correctly references the client's weight and the other cells correctly reference the METS for Workout Routine 5 and the total exercise time:

=P20*C11*K22/125.7143

When you copied the formula down to cell L31, all of the cell references contained in that formula also shifted down nine rows, resulting in the following formula, which accurately references the total exercise time for the corresponding workout but no longer references Daniel's weight or the METS for Workout Routine 5—both of which are necessary for the calculation:

=P29*C20*K31/125.7143

What you need is a cell reference that remains fixed when the formula is copied to a new location.

Understanding Absolute References

A fixed reference—one that always references the same cell no matter where it is moved—is called an absolute reference. In Excel, absolute references include a $ (dollar sign) before each column and row designation. For example, B8 is a relative reference to cell B8, and $B$8 is an absolute reference to that cell. When you copy a formula that contains an absolute reference to a new location, that cell reference does not change.

Figure 3-17 shows an example of how copying a formula with an absolute reference results in the same cell reference being pasted in different cells regardless of their position compared to the location of the original copied cell. In this example, the formula =$A$4 will always reference cell A4 no matter where the formula is copied to, because the cell is referenced with the absolute reference $A$4.

Figure 3-17   **Formulas using absolute references**

formula absolutely references the cell located in column A and row 4

when copied to new cells, the reference remains fixed on cell A4

values returned by each formula

© 2014 Cengage Learning

Understanding Mixed References

A formula can also include cell references that are mixed. A **mixed reference** contains both relative and absolute references. For example, a mixed reference for cell A2 can be either $A2 or A$2. In the mixed reference $A2, the reference to column A is absolute and the reference to row 2 is relative. In the mixed reference A$2, the column reference is relative and the row reference is absolute. A mixed reference "locks" one part of the cell reference while the other part can change. When you copy and paste a cell with a mixed reference to a new location, the absolute portion of the cell reference remains fixed and the relative portion shifts along with the new location of the pasted cell.

Figure 3-18 shows an example of using mixed references to complete a multiplication table. The first cell in the table, cell B3, contains the formula =$A3*B$2, which multiplies the first column entry (A3) by the first row entry (B2), returning 1. When this formula is copied to another cell, the absolute portions of the cell references remain unchanged and the relative portions of the references change. For example, if the formula is copied to cell E6, the first mixed cell reference changes to $A6 because the column reference is absolute and the row reference is relative, and the second cell reference changes to E$2 because the row reference is absolute and the column reference is relative. The result is that cell E6 contains the formula =$A6*E$2 and returns 16. Other cells in the multiplication table are similarly modified so that each entry returns the multiplication of the intersection of the row and column headings.

Figure 3-18   **Formulas using mixed references**

mixed cell reference that fixes the column reference for the first term and the row reference for the second term

	A	B	C	D	E	F	G
1		Multiplication Table					
2		1	2	3	4	5	
3	1	=$A3*B$2					
4	2						
5	3						
6	4						
7	5						
8							

when copied to the B3:B7 range, the fixed references remain unchanged and the relative references are shifted

	A	B	C	D	E	F	G
1		Multiplication Table					
2		1	2	3	4	5	
3	1	=$A3*B$2	=$A3*C$2	=$A3*D$2	=$A3*E$2	=$A3*F$2	
4	2	=$A4*B$2	=$A4*C$2	=$A4*D$2	=$A4*E$2	=$A4*F$2	
5	3	=$A5*B$2	=$A5*C$2	=$A5*D$2	=$A5*E$2	=$A5*F$2	
6	4	=$A6*B$2	=$A6*C$2	=$A6*D$2	=$A6*E$2	=$A6*F$2	
7	5	=$A7*B$2	=$A7*C$2	=$A7*D$2	=$A7*E$2	=$A7*F$2	
8							

values returned by each formula

	A	B	C	D	E	F	G
1		Multiplication Table					
2		1	2	3	4	5	
3	1	1	2	3	4	5	
4	2	2	4	6	8	10	
5	3	3	6	9	12	15	
6	4	4	8	12	16	20	
7	5	5	10	15	20	25	
8							

Changing Cell References in a Formula

You can quickly switch a cell reference from relative to absolute or mixed. Rather than retyping the formula, you can select the cell reference in Edit mode and then press the F4 key. As you press the F4 key, Excel cycles through the different reference types—starting with the relative reference, followed by the absolute reference, then to a mixed reference with the row absolute, and finally to a mixed reference with the column absolute.

Ken wants you to fix the problem with the cell references in the calories burned formulas. You need to revise the formula to use absolute references to Daniel's weight and the METS value that will not change when the formula is copied to new locations. You will leave the relative reference to the total exercise time so that the copied formulas will retrieve the exercise times from the corresponding workouts. The revised formula in cell L22 uses an absolute reference to the METS values in $P$20 and an absolute reference to Daniel's weight in $C$11, as follows:

```
=$P$20*$C$11*K22/125.7143
```

You will edit the calories burned formula in cell L22, and then paste it to the rest of the workouts.

To revise the calories burned formulas to use absolute references:

1. Double-click cell **L22** to select it and enter Edit mode.

2. Click immediately to the left of cell reference **P20** in the formula to move the insertion point before the letter P, type **$** to change the column reference to absolute, press the → key to move the insertion point between the letter P and 20, and then type **$** to change the row reference to absolute. The complete absolute reference is now $P$20.

3. Double-click the cell reference **C11** in the formula to select it, and then press the **F4** key to change it to the absolute reference $C$11. The formula is now =$P$20*$C$11*K22/125.7143.

4. Press the **Enter** key to complete the edit. The 376.1 calories burned displayed in the cell is unchanged because the relative references were accurate in this first formula.

5. Copy cell **L22** and paste it into the range **L23:L44**. The worksheet shows 322.4 calories burned for the second workout and 483.6 calories burned for the third workout. The next row in the list shows 0 calories burned because Daniel did not work out that day. As you can see, the remaining formulas now correctly calculate the calories burned at each workout.

6. Format the range **L22:L44** with the **Calculation** cell style. See Figure 3-19.

> Select only the cell reference you want to change before you press the F4 key.

| Figure 3-19 | Formulas with absolute and relative references |

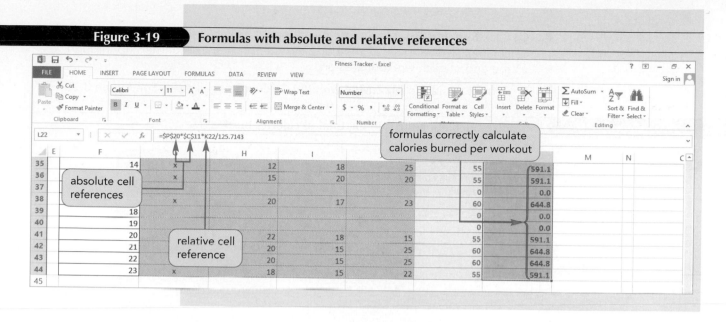

Planning Which Cell Reference to Use in a Formula

You can include the correct type of cell reference in a formula as you create the formula. This requires a little more thought up front, as you consider how each cell in a formula needs to be referenced before you create the formula. Ken wants you to create a running total of the calories burned during each workout. You can use the SUM function with a combination of absolute and relative cell references to add the values in a range. The formula to calculate the total in the first cell is:

    =SUM($L$22:L22)

In this formula, the starting cell of the range is fixed at cell L22, but the ending cell of the range is relative. When you copy this formula down the column, the starting cell remains absolutely referenced to cell L22, but the ending cell changes to include the current row. For example, when the formula is pasted three rows down, the formula changes to add the numbers in cells L22, L23, L24, and L25, as follows:

    =SUM($L$22:L25)

Continuing in this way, the last cell will contain the sum of all of the calories burned totals using the following formula:

    =SUM($L$22:L44)

Instead of entering the formulas yourself, you can use the Quick Analysis tool to calculate the total calories burned up through the end of each workout session.

To calculate the running total of calories burned:

1. In cell **M21**, enter **Calories Subtotal** as the label.

2. Select the range **L22:L44** containing the calories burned during each workout, and then click the **Quick Analysis** button 📧 (or press the **Ctrl+Q** keys).

3. Click the **TOTALS** category, and then scroll right to the end of the TOTALS tools.

4. Click **Running Total** (the last entry in the list, which is the Running Total of a column). The range M22:M44 displays the total calories burned up through the end of each workout session.

5. Format the range **M22:M44** with the **Calculation** cell style. See Figure 3-20.

Figure 3-20   **Formulas calculating the running total of calories burned**

Daniel burned 698.5 calories during the first two workouts and more than 1180 calories after the first three workouts. The formula used to calculate the running totals for the column includes both absolute and relative references. You will review the formulas in column M to see the formulas calculating the running totals.

To view the formulas for the running totals:

1. Select cell **M22**, and then review the formula, which is =SUM($L$22:L22). Notice the absolute and relative references to cell L22.

2. Select cell **M23**, and then review the formula, which is =SUM($L$22:L23). Notice that the absolute reference to cell L22 remains unchanged, but the relative reference is now cell L23, expanding the range being added with the SUM function.

3. Select each cell in column M and review its formula, noticing that the absolute reference $L$22 always appears as the top cell of the range but the relative reference for the last cell of the range changes.

4. Save the workbook.

You can see that the running total is calculated with the SUM function using a combination of absolute and relative cell references. The top of the range used in the SUM function is locked at cell L22, but the bottom of the range is relative, expanding in size as the formula was copied down column M. Entered this way, with absolute and relative cell references, the SUM function calculates partial sums, providing the total calories burned up through the end of each workout session.

INSIGHT

Understanding When to Use Relative, Absolute, and Mixed References

Part of effective workbook design is knowing when to use relative, absolute, and mixed references. Use relative references when you want to apply the same formula with input cells that share a common layout or pattern. Relative references are commonly used when copying a formula that calculates summary statistics across columns or rows of data values. Use absolute references when you want your copied formulas to always refer to the same cell. This usually occurs when a cell contains a constant value, such as a tax rate, that will be referenced in formulas throughout the worksheet. Mixed references are seldom used other than when creating tables of calculated values such as a multiplication table in which the values of the formula or function can be found at the intersection of the rows and columns of the table.

So far, you have entered the fitness formulas and summary statistics in the Fitness Tracker workbook. In the next session, you will explore date and time functions, and then look up values to use in formulas and functions.

REVIEW

Session 3.1 Quick Check

1. What is an optional argument? What does Excel do if you do not include an optional argument?
2. Write the function to return the middle value from the values in the range X1:X10.
3. Write the function to round the value in cell A5 to the fourth decimal place.
4. The range of a set of values is defined as the maximum value minus the minimum value. Write the formula to calculate the range of values in the range Y1:Y10.
5. If cell A11 contains the formula =SUME(A1:A10), what error value will appear in the cell?
6. You need to reference cell Q57 in a formula. What is its relative reference? What is its absolute reference? What are the two mixed references?
7. If cell R10 contains the formula =R1+R2, which is then copied to cell S20, what formula is entered in cell S20?
8. If cell V10 contains the formula = AVERAGE($U1:$U5), which is then copied to cell W20, what formula is entered in cell W20?

Session 3.2 Visual Overview:

A **lookup table** stores the data you want to retrieve in categories. This is a vertical lookup table that organizes the categories in the first column of the table.

Compare values are the categories located in the first column of the lookup table and are used for matching to a lookup value specified by the user.

Return values are the data values you want to retrieve from the lookup table and are located in the second and subsequent columns.

A **lookup value** is the category you want to find in a lookup table.

The **VLOOKUP function** returns values from a vertical lookup table by specifying the lookup value to match to a compare value, the location of the lookup table, and the column in the table that contains the return values.

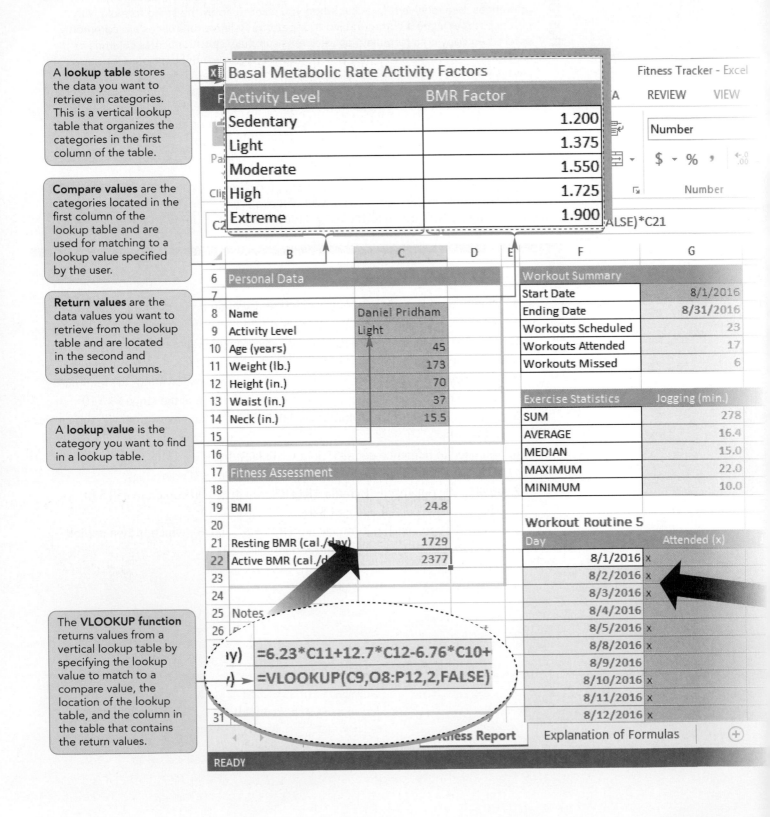

Basal Metabolic Rate Activity Factors

Activity Level	BMR Factor
Sedentary	1.200
Light	1.375
Moderate	1.550
High	1.725
Extreme	1.900

Fitness Tracker - Excel

REVIEW   VIEW

Number

$ ▾ % ,

Number

C2 ... ALSE)*C21

	B	C	D	E	F	G
6	Personal Data				Workout Summary	
7					Start Date	8/1/2016
8	Name	Daniel Pridham			Ending Date	8/31/2016
9	Activity Level	Light			Workouts Scheduled	23
10	Age (years)	45			Workouts Attended	17
11	Weight (lb.)	173			Workouts Missed	6
12	Height (in.)	70				
13	Waist (in.)	37			Exercise Statistics	Jogging (min.)
14	Neck (in.)	15.5			SUM	278
15					AVERAGE	16.4
16					MEDIAN	15.0
17	Fitness Assessment				MAXIMUM	22.0
18					MINIMUM	10.0
19	BMI	24.8				
20					Workout Routine 5	
21	Resting BMR (cal./day)	1729			Day	Attended (x)
22	Active BMR (cal./d	2377			8/1/2016	x
23					8/2/2016	x
24					8/3/2016	x
25	Notes				8/4/2016	
26					8/5/2016	x
	ay)	=6.23*C11+12.7*C12-6.76*C10+			8/8/2016	x
					8/9/2016	
	r)	=VLOOKUP(C9,O8:P12,2,FALSE)			8/10/2016	x
					8/11/2016	x
31					8/12/2016	x

ness Report   Explanation of Formulas   ⊕

READY

Logical and Lookup Functions

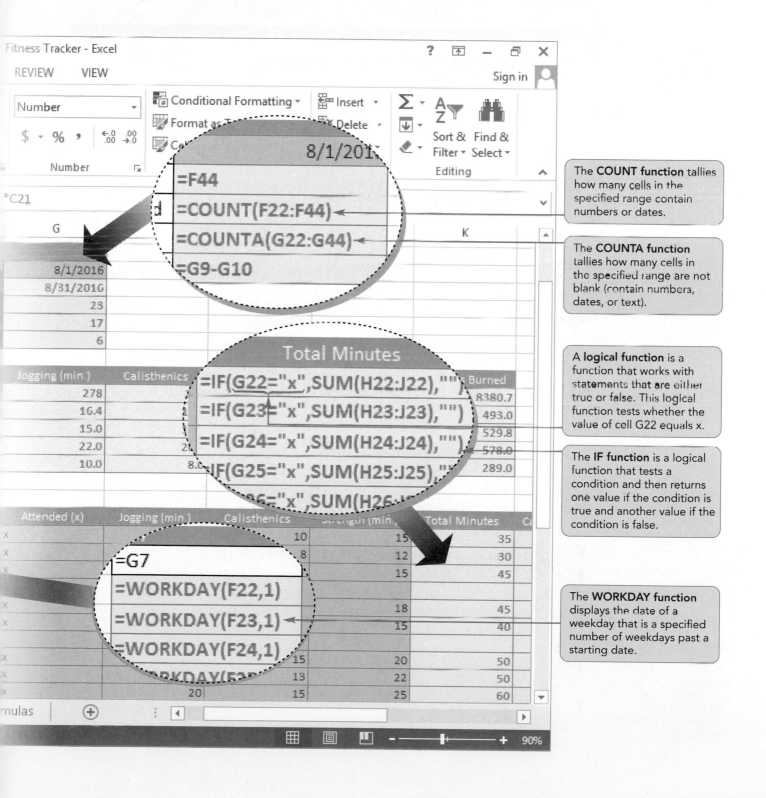

The **COUNT function** tallies how many cells in the specified range contain numbers or dates.

The **COUNTA function** tallies how many cells in the specified range are not blank (contain numbers, dates, or text).

A **logical function** is a function that works with statements that are either true or false. This logical function tests whether the value of cell G22 equals x.

The **IF function** is a logical function that tests a condition and then returns one value if the condition is true and another value if the condition is false.

The **WORKDAY function** displays the date of a weekday that is a specified number of weekdays past a starting date.

AutoFilling Formulas and Data

AutoFill provides a quick way to enter content and formatting in cells based on existing entries in adjacent cells. Ken wants you to include summary statistics for calories burned across all of the scheduled workouts. To add these statistics, you'll use the AutoFill tool.

REFERENCE

Copying Formulas and Formats with AutoFill

- Select the cell or range that contains the formula or formulas you want to copy.
- Drag the fill handle in the direction you want to copy the formula(s), and then release the mouse button.
- To copy only the formats or only the formulas, click the Auto Fill Options button and select the appropriate option.

or

- Select the cell or range that contains the formula or formulas you want to copy.
- On the HOME tab, in the Editing group, click the Fill button.
- Select a fill direction and fill type.

or

- On the HOME tab, in the Editing group, click Series.
- Enter the desired fill series options, and then click the OK button.

Using the Fill Handle

After you select a range, a **fill handle** appears in the lower-right corner of the selection. When you drag the fill handle over an adjacent cell or range, AutoFill copies the content and formats from the original cell or range into the adjacent cell or range. This process is often more efficient than the two-step process of copying and pasting.

Ken wants you to calculate the same summary statistics for the calories burned during the workouts as you did for the total minutes of each workout. Because the total minutes formulas use relative references, you can use the fill handle to copy these for the calories burned statistics.

To copy the calories burned summary statistics and formatting with the fill handle:

1. In cell **K13**, enter **Calories Burned** as the label.

2. Select the range **J14:J18**, which contains the cells with formulas for calculating the sum, average, median, minimum, and maximum total minutes. A fill handle appears in the lower-right corner of the selected range, directly above and to the left of the Quick Analysis button.

3. Point to the **fill handle**. The pointer changes to ✚.

4. Click and drag the fill handle over the range **K14:K18**. A solid outline appears around the selected range as you move the pointer.

5. Release the mouse button. The selected range is filled in with the formulas and formatting from the range J14:J18, and the Auto Fill Options button appears in the lower-right corner of the selected cells. See Figure 3-21.

TIP

You can also fill a series to the right by selecting both the cells to copy and the cells to be filled in, and then pressing the Ctrl+R keys.

Figure 3-21   **Formulas and formatting copied with AutoFill**

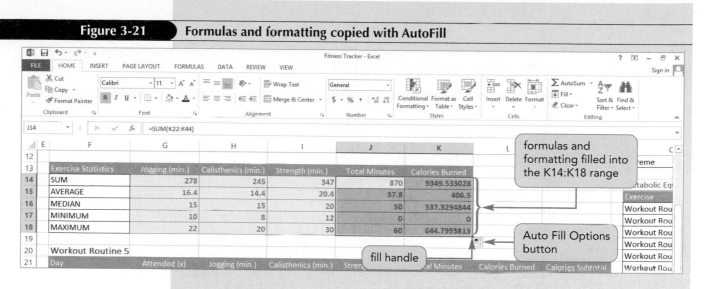

6. Format the range **K14:K18** to display one decimal place.

Based on the summary statistics, Ken can see that Daniel burned 9349.5 calories during the month, burned an average of 406.5 calories per session, burned a median of 537.3 calories per session, and burned a minimum of 0.0 calories and a maximum of 644.8 calories per session during the month.

Using the Auto Fill Options Button

By default, AutoFill copies both the content and the formatting of the original range to the selected range. However, sometimes you might want to copy only the content or only the formatting. The Auto Fill Options button that appears after you release the mouse button lets you specify what is copied. As shown in Figure 3-22, clicking this button provides a menu of AutoFill options. The Copy Cells option, which is the default, copies both the content and the formatting. The Fill Formatting Only option copies the formatting into the selected cells but not any content. The Fill Without Formatting option copies the content but not the formatting.

Figure 3-22   **Auto Fill Options button**

Because you want to copy the content and the formatting of the summary statistics, you don't need to use the Auto Fill Options button.

Filling a Series

AutoFill can also be used to create a series of numbers, dates, or text based on a pattern. To create a series of numbers, you enter the initial values in the series in a selected range and then use AutoFill to complete the series.

Figure 3-23 shows how AutoFill can be used to insert the numbers from 1 to 10 in a selected range. You enter the first few numbers in the range A2:A4 to establish the pattern you want AutoFill to use—consecutive positive numbers in this example. Then, you select the range and drag its fill handle over the cells where you want the pattern continued—in this case, the range A5:A11—and Excel fills in the rest of the series.

Figure 3-23 AutoFill extends a numeric sequence

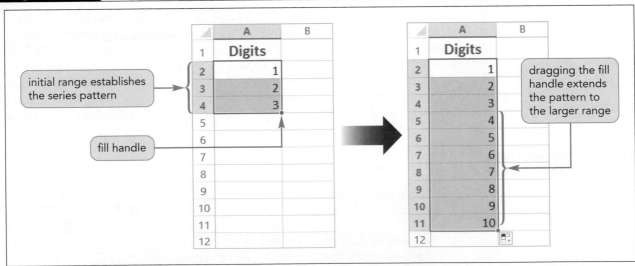

© 2014 Cengage Learning

AutoFill can extend a wide variety of series, including dates and times and patterned text. Figure 3-24 shows some examples of series that AutoFill can generate. In each case, you must provide enough information for AutoFill to identify the pattern. AutoFill can recognize some patterns from only a single entry—such as Jan or January, to create a series of month abbreviations or names, or Mon or Monday, to create a series of the days of the week. A text pattern that includes text and a number such as Region 1, Region 2, and so on can also be automatically extended using AutoFill. You can start the series at any point, such as Weds, June, or Region 10, and AutoFill will complete the next days, months, or text.

Figure 3-24   **AutoFill extends numbers, dates and times, and patterned text**

Type	Initial Pattern	Extended Series
Numbers	1, 2, 3	4, 5, 6, ..
	2, 4, 6	8, 10, 12, ...
Dates and Times	Jan	Feb, Mar, Apr, ...
	January	February, March, April, ...
	15-Jan, 15-Feb	15-Mar, 15-Apr, 15-May, ...
	12/30/2016	12/31/2016, 1/1/2017, 1/2/2017, ...
	12/31/2016, 1/31/2017	2/29/2017, 3/31/2017, 4/30/2017, ...
	Mon	Tue, Wed, Thu, ...
	Monday	Tuesday, Wednesday, Thursday, ...
	11:00AM	12:00PM, 1:00PM, 2:00PM, ...
Patterned Text	1st period	2nd period, 3rd period, 4th period, ...
	Region 1	Region 2, Region 3, Region 4, ...
	Quarter 3	Quarter 4, Quarter 1, Quarter 2, ...
	Qtr3	Qtr4, Qtr1, Qtr2, ...

© 2014 Cengage Learning

Ken wants you to fill in the dates of the workouts, replacing the numbers in the range F22:F44. You will use AutoFill to insert the calendar dates starting with 8/1/2016.

To use AutoFill to enter the calendar dates:

1. In cell **F22**, enter **8/1/2016**. This is the first date you want to use for the series.

2. Select cell **F22** to select the cell with the first date in the series.

3. Drag the fill handle over the range **F23:F44**.

4. Release the mouse button. AutoFill enters the calendar dates ending with 8/23/2016 in cell F44.

TIP

You can also fill a series down by selecting both the cells to copy and the cells to be filled in, and then pressing the Ctrl+D keys.

For more complex AutoFill patterns, you can use the Series dialog box to specify a linear or growth series for numbers; a date series for dates that increase by day, weekday, month, or year; or an AutoFill series for patterned text. With numbers, you can also specify the step value (how much each number increases over the previous entry) and a stop value (the endpoint for the entire series).

Ken notices that the workout dates are wrong in the Fitness Report worksheet. Fit Fathers meets only Monday through Friday. He asks you to change the fill pattern to include only weekdays. You will use the Series dialog box to set the fill pattern for the rest of the weekdays in the month.

To fill the dates of weekdays in August:

1. Make sure the range **F22:F44** is selected. Cell F22 contains the first value for the series that will be entered in the range F23:F44.

2. On the HOME tab, in the Editing group, click the **Fill** button, and then click **Series**. The Series dialog box opens.

3. In the Type section, make sure that the **Date** option button is selected.

4. In the Date unit section, click the **Weekday** option button so that the series includes only dates for Mondays through Fridays. See Figure 3-25.

Figure 3-25	Series dialog box

fills the series columns

specifies date as the type of series

specifies weekdays as the date unit

5. Click the **OK** button. The dates of weekdays in August are filled into the selected range ending with 8/31/2016. See Figure 3-26.

Figure 3-26	Weekday values filled in

only weekdays are entered in the selected range

	E	F	G	H	I	J	
20		Workout Routine 5					
21		Day	Attended (x)	Jogging (min.)	Calisthenics (min.)	Strength (min.)	Tota
22		8/1/2016	x	10	10	15	
23		8/2/2016	x	10	8	12	
24		8/3/2016	x	12	18	15	
25		8/4/2016					
26		8/5/2016	x	12	15	18	
27		8/8/2016	x	15	10	15	
28		8/9/2016					
29		8/10/2016	x	15	15	20	
30		8/11/2016	x	15	13	22	
31		8/12/2016	x	20	15	25	
32		8/15/2016	x	20	15	20	
33		8/16/2016	x	22	8	30	
34		8/17/2016					
35		8/18/2016	x	12	18	25	
36		8/19/2016	x	15	20	20	
37		8/22/2016					
38		8/23/2016	x	20	17	23	

Documentation   **Fitness Report**   Explanation of Formulas   ⊕

READY   AVERAGE: 8

Working with Date Functions

Excel has several functions that work with dates and times. **Date functions** insert or calculate dates and times. They are particularly useful in business workbooks that involve production schedules and calendar applications. Figure 3-27 describes some of the commonly used Date functions.

Figure 3-27	Date functions

Function	Description
DATE(*year, month, day*)	Creates a date value for the date represented by the *year*, *month*, and *day* arguments
DAY(*date*)	Extracts the day of the month from *date*
MONTH(*date*)	Extracts the month number from *date* where 1=January, 2=February, and so forth
YEAR(*date*)	Extracts the year number from *date*
NETWORKDAYS(*start, end*[, *holidays*])	Calculates the number of whole working days between *start* and *end*; to exclude holidays, add the optional *holidays* argument containing a list of holiday dates to skip
WEEKDAY(*date*[, *return_type*])	Calculates the weekday from *date*, where 1=Sunday, 2=Monday, and so forth; to choose a different numbering scheme, set *return_type* to 1 (1=Sunday, 2=Monday, ...), 2 (1=Monday, 2=Tuesday, ...), or 3 (0=Monday, 1=Tuesday, ...)
WORKDAY(*start, days*[, *holidays*])	Returns the workday after *days* workdays have passed since the *start* date; to exclude holidays, add the optional *holidays* argument containing a list of holiday dates to skip
NOW( )	Returns the current date and time
TODAY( )	Returns the current date

© 2014 Cengage Learning

Displaying the Current Date with the TODAY function

Many workbooks include the current date. You can use the **TODAY function** to display the current date in a worksheet. The TODAY function has the following syntax:

    =TODAY( )

Note that although the TODAY function doesn't have any arguments, you still must include the parentheses for the function to work. The date displayed by the TODAY function is updated automatically whenever you reopen the workbook or enter a new calculation.

Ken wants the Fitness Report worksheet to show the current date each time it is used or printed. You will use the TODAY function to display the current date in cell G2.

To display the current date with the TODAY function:

1. Select cell **G2**.

2. On the FORMULAS tab, in the Function Library group, click the **Date & Time** button to display the date and time functions.

3. Click **TODAY**. The Function Arguments dialog box opens and indicates that the TODAY function requires no arguments.

4. Click the **OK** button. The formula =TODAY() is entered in cell G2.

5. Verify that the current date is displayed in the cell.

6. Format the cell using the **Calculation** style.

Finding the Next Weekday with the WORKDAY function

Instead of using AutoFill to enter a series of dates in a range, you can use the WORKDAY function to fill in the remaining weekdays based on the start date you specify. The WORKDAY function displays the date of the weekday a specific number of weekdays past a starting date. The syntax of the WORKDAY function is

```
=WORKDAY(start, days[, holiday])
```

> **TIP**
>
> You can enter the dates to skip into worksheet cells, and then reference that range in the *holiday* argument of the WORKDAY function.

where *start* is a start date, *days* is the number of weekdays after *start*, and *holiday* is an optional list of dates to skip. If you do not include anything for the optional *holiday* argument, the WORKDAY function does not skip any days. For example, if cell A1 contains the date 11/4/2016, a Friday, the following formula displays the date 11/9/2016, a Wednesday that is three working days after 11/4/2016:

```
=WORKDAY(A1, 3)
```

Ken wants to automate the process of inserting the exercise dates. You will use the WORKDAY function to do this.

To insert the exercise dates using the WORKDAY function:

1. In cell **G7**, enter **8/1/2016** to specify the date the workouts will begin, and then format the cell using the **Input** cell style.

2. In cell **G8**, enter the formula **=F44** to display the date of the last scheduled workout, which is 8/31/2016 in this instance, and then format the cell using the **Calculation** cell style.

3. In cell **F22**, enter the formula **=G7** to replace the date with a reference to the start date you specified in cell G7. The cell still displays 8/1/2016.

4. Select cell **F23**, if necessary, and then click the **Insert Function** button f_x next to the formula bar. The Insert Function dialog box opens.

5. Type **working days** in the Search for a function box, and then click the **Go** button to find all of the functions related to working days.

6. In the Select a function box, click **WORKDAY** to select the function, and then click the **OK** button. The WORKDAY Function Arguments dialog box opens.

7. In the Start_date box, type the cell reference **F22** to specify that cell F22 contains the start date you want to use.

8. In the Days box, type **1** to specify the number of workdays after the date in cell F22 that you want the formula results to show. See Figure 3-28.

Figure 3-28   Function Arguments dialog box for the WORKDAY function

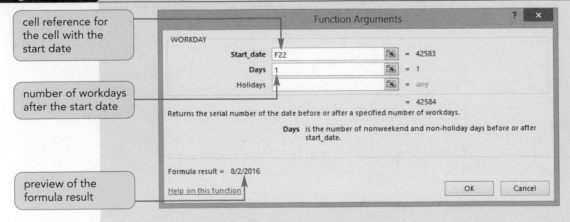

cell reference for the cell with the start date

number of workdays after the start date

preview of the formula result

TIP

To select a working day prior to the start date, enter a negative number rather than a positive number.

9. Click the **OK** button. Cell F23 contains the formula =WORKDAY(F22, 1) and displays the date 8/2/2016, which is the next workday after 8/1/2016.

   You want to use the same formula to calculate the rest of the workout dates. You can use AutoFill to quickly repeat the formula.

10. Select cell **F23**, and then drag the fill handle down over the range **F23:F44** to copy the formula and enter the rest of the workdays in the month.

    Because the copied formulas use relative references, each cell displays a date that is one workday after the date in the previous cell. The dates should not be different from the dates you entered previously using AutoFill.

11. Format the range **F22:F44** with the **Calculation** cell style to show that these dates are calculated by a formula rather than entered manually.

    You will test that the formulas in the range F22:F44 are working correctly by entering a different start date.

12. In cell **G7**, enter **9/1/2016** as the new start date.

13. Review the dates in the range F22:F44, verifying that the workout dates start with 9/2/2016 in cell F23, continue with 9/5/2016 in cell F24, and end with 10/3/2016 in cell F44.

    Trouble? If the workout dates do not end with 10/3/2016, compare the formula in cell F23 to the formula shown in Step 9, make any edits needed, and then repeat Step 10.

14. In cell **G7**, enter **8/1/2016** to return to the original start date.

INSIGHT

Selecting the Days in the Work Week

Different countries, regions, and even businesses might have different rules for what constitutes a workday. If you need to create a schedule that doesn't follow the standard U.S. business days (Monday through Friday), you can use the WORKDAY.INTL function to specify the days to use as the work week. The syntax of the WORKDAY.INTL function is:

```
=WORKDAY.INTL(start, days[, weekend=1, holidays])
```

The only difference between the syntax of the WORKDAY.INTL function and the syntax of the WORKDAY function is the optional *weekend* argument, which specifies the days of the week considered to be weekend or nonworking days. If you omit the *weekend* argument, weekends are considered to occur only on Saturday and Sunday. If you include the *weekend* argument, you enter one of the following numbers to specify the two days or the one day to consider as the weekend:

Weekend	Two-Day Weekend	Weekend	One-Day Weekend
1	Saturday, Sunday	11	Sunday
2	Sunday, Monday	12	Monday
3	Monday, Tuesday	13	Tuesday
...		...	
7	Friday, Saturday	17	Saturday

For example, a business that is open every day except Sunday would use a *weekend* value of 11 to indicate that only Sunday is considered a nonworking day, and a business that is closed on Monday and Tuesday would use a *weekend* value of 3 to specify a work week of Wednesday through Sunday. For other working week schedules, you can enter text to specify which days are workdays. See Excel Help for more information.

Counting Cells

Excel has two functions for counting cells—the COUNT function and the COUNTA function. The COUNT function tallies how many cells in a range contain numbers or dates (because they are stored as numeric values). The COUNT function does not count blank cells or cells that contain text. Its syntax is

COUNT(*value1*[, *value2*, *value3*, ...])

where *value1* is the first item or cell reference containing the numbers you want to count. The remaining *value* arguments are used primarily when you want to count numbers and dates in nonadjacent ranges. For example, the following function counts how many cells in the range A1:A10, the range C1:C5, and cell E5 contain numbers or dates:

COUNT(A1:A10, C1:C5, E5)

If you want to know how many cells contain entries—whether those entries are numbers, dates, or text—you use the COUNTA function, which tallies the nonblank cells in a range. The following is the syntax of the COUNTA function, which has the same arguments as the COUNT function:

COUNTA(*value1*[, *value2*, *value3*, ...])

Ken wants the Workout Summary to show the total number of scheduled workouts for the month, the number of attended workouts, and the number of missed workouts. You will use the COUNT function to count the total number of workout dates in the Workout Routine 5 table. Then, you will use the COUNTA function to count the number of workouts actually attended. Each attended workout is marked by an "x" in column G of the Workout Routine 5 table; missing workouts are left blank. Finally, you will enter a formula to calculate the missed workouts.

To count the scheduled, attended, and missed workouts:

1. In cell **G9**, enter the formula **=COUNT(F22:F44)**. Cell G9 displays 23, indicating that Ken scheduled 23 workouts for the month.

2. In cell **G10**, enter the formula **=COUNTA(G22:G44)**. Cell G10 displays 17, indicating that Daniel attended 17 of the 23 scheduled workouts.

3. In cell **G11**, enter the formula **=G9–G10** to calculate the difference between the number of scheduled workouts and the number of attended workouts. Cell G11 displays 6, which is the number of missed workouts.

4. Format the range **G9:G11** with the **Calculation** cell style.

5. Select cell **G10**. See Figure 3-29.

Figure 3-29   **Completed Workout Summary**

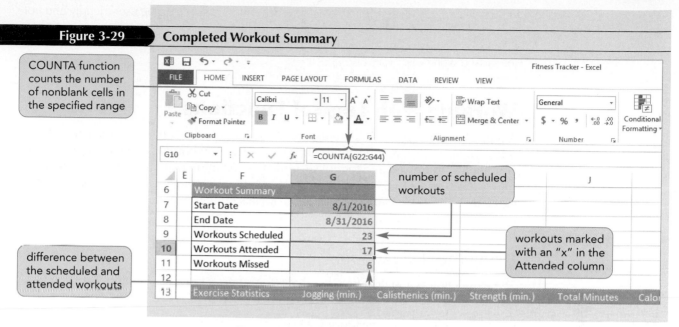

It is important to understand the difference between the COUNT and COUNTA functions. For example, if you had used the COUNT function in cell G10 to tally the number of attended workouts, the result would have been 0 because the range G22:G44 contains no entries with numbers.

Like the COUNT function, many of Excel's statistical functions ignore cells that are blank or contain text. This can create unexpected results with calculated values if you are not careful. Figure 3-30 shows how some of the common summary statistics change when blank cells are used in place of zeroes.

Figure 3-30   **Calculations involving blank cells and zeroes**

Some of the fitness statistics for total exercise minutes and calories burned include the six workouts that Daniel missed. For example, the minimum exercise minutes and calories burned are both listed as 0 because the calculated values show up as 0 in the worksheet when the workout session was missed. Ken wants the summary statistics based on only the workouts actually attended. One way to exclude missed workouts is to delete the zeroes, leaving blank cells. However, Ken wants the worksheet to be user-friendly and not require anyone to double-check and edit entries for missed workouts. Instead of editing the worksheet, you can use a logical function to automatically replace zeroes with blanks for missed workouts.

Working with Logical Functions

A logical function returns a different value depending on whether the given condition is true or false, such as whether or not a scheduled workout was attended. In Excel, the condition is expressed as a formula. Consider a condition that includes the expression A5=3. If cell A5 is equal to 3, this expression and condition are true; if cell A5 is not equal to 3, this expression and condition are false. The IF function is one of the many logical functions you can use in Excel.

Using the IF Function

The IF function is a logical function that returns one value if a condition is true, and returns a different value if that condition is false. The syntax of the IF function is

    IF(logical_test, value_if_true, value_if_false)

where logical_test is a condition that is either true or false, value_if_true is the value returned by the function if the condition is true, and value_if_false is the value returned if the condition is false. The value can be a number, text, a date, or a cell reference. For example, the following formula tests whether the value in cell A1 is equal to the value in cell B1:

    =IF(A1=B1, 100, 50)

If the value in cell A1 equals the value in cell B1, the formula result is 100; otherwise, the formula result is 50.

In many cases, however, you will not use values directly in the IF function. The following formula uses cell references, returning the value of cell C1 if A1 equals B1; otherwise, it returns the value of cell C2:

    =IF(A1=B1, C1, C2)

The = symbol in these formulas is a comparison operator. A **comparison operator** is a symbol that indicates the relationship between two values. Figure 3-31 describes the comparison operators that can be used within a logical function.

Figure 3-31 **Comparison operators**

Operator	Expression	Description
=	A1 = B1	Tests whether the value in cell A1 is equal to the value in cell B1
>	A1 > B1	Tests whether the value in cell A1 is greater than the value in cell B1
<	A1 < B1	Tests whether the value in cell A1 is less than the value in cell B1
>=	A1 >= B1	Tests whether the value in cell A1 is greater than or equal to the value in cell B1
<=	A1 <= B1	Tests whether the value in cell A1 is less than or equal to the value in cell B1
<>	A1 <> B1	Tests whether the value in cell A1 is not equal to the value in cell B1

© 2014 Cengage Learning

The IF function also works with text. For example, the following formula tests whether the value of cell A1 is equal to "yes":

```
=IF(A1="yes", "done", "restart")
```

If true (the value of cell A1 is equal to "yes"), the formula returns the text "done"; otherwise, it returns the text "restart". Notice that the text in the function is enclosed in quotation marks.

In addition, you can nest other functions inside an IF statement. The following formula first tests whether cell A5 is equal to the maximum of values within the range A1:A100:

```
=IF(A5=MAX(A1:A100), "Maximum", "")
```

If it is, the formula returns the text "Maximum"; otherwise, it returns no text.

In the Fitness Report worksheet, you need to rewrite the formulas that calculate the total minutes and total calories from each workout as IF functions that test whether Daniel actually attended the workout. Because every attended workout is marked with an "x" in column G, you can test whether the cell entry in column G is an "x". For example, the following formula in cell K22 is currently being used to calculate the total minutes from the first workout:

```
=SUM(H22:J22)
```

This formula can be revised to the following IF function, which first determines if cell G22 contains an "x" (indicating that the workout was attended), and then uses the SUM function to calculate the total minutes if there is an "x":

```
=IF(G22="x", SUM(H22:J22), "")
```

Otherwise, the formula displays nothing, leaving the cell blank.

You will use relative references in the revised formula so that you can copy it for the other workouts and total columns. You will create the formula with the IF function for the total minutes column now.

> **TIP**
>
> For the formula result to show no text, include opening and closing quotation marks with nothing between them.

To use an IF function to calculate total minutes for attended workouts:

1. Select cell **K22**, and then press the **Delete** key to clear the original formula from the cell.

2. Click the **Insert Function** button f_x next to the formula bar to open the Insert Function dialog box.

3. Type **if function** in the Search for a function box, and then press the **Enter** key. Functions that match your description appear in the Select a function box.

4. Click **IF** in the Select a function box, and then click the **OK** button to open the Function Arguments dialog box.

5. In the Logical_test box, type **G22="x"** as the expression that tests whether cell G22 is equal to x.

6. Press the **Tab** key to move the insertion point to the Value_if_true box, and then type **SUM(H22:J22)**. If cell G22 does contain an x (the logical test is true), the sum of the values in the range H22:J22 will be displayed in cell K22.

7. Press the **Tab** key to move the insertion point to the Value_if_false box, and then type **""** (opening and closing quotation marks). If cell G22 does not contain an x (the logical test is false), the cell will be left blank. See Figure 3-32.

Figure 3-32   **Function Arguments dialog box for the IF function**

statement to evaluate as true or false

displays nothing if the statement is false

preview of the formula result

calculates the sum if the statement is true

8. Click the **OK** button. The formula =IF(G22="x", SUM(H22:J22), "") is entered into cell K22. The cell displays 35, which is the number of minutes Daniel spent exercising at that workout session.

   You will copy the formula with the IF function to calculate the total minutes for the rest of the workouts.

9. Select cell **K22**, and then drag the fill handle down over the range **K22:K44** to copy the IF formula to the remaining cells in the column. The total number of minutes for each workout is recalculated so that the missed workouts in cells K25, K28, K34, K37, K39, and K40 are now left blank.

10. Select cell **K22**. The #VALUE! error value appears in columns L and M for each of the missed workouts because the current formulas cannot calculate calories burned when no total minutes are provided. See Figure 3-33.

Figure 3-33   **IF function excludes the total minutes for missed workouts**

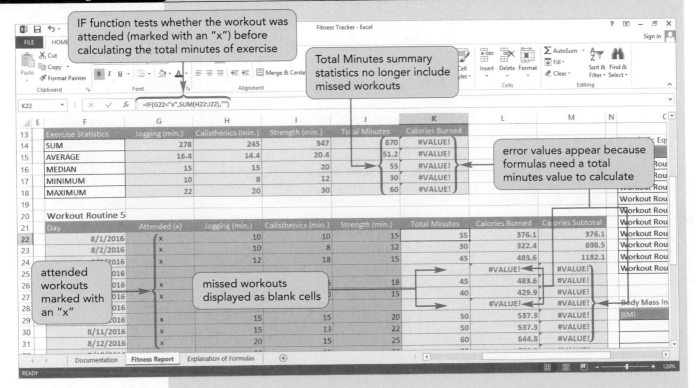

IF function tests whether the workout was attended (marked with an "x") before calculating the total minutes of exercise

Total Minutes summary statistics no longer include missed workouts

error values appear because formulas need a total minutes value to calculate

attended workouts marked with an "x"

missed workouts displayed as blank cells

Next, you will update the calories burned formulas so that they don't display the #VALUE! error value when a workout is missed. This requires another IF statement similar to the one you used to calculate total minutes. As with the total minutes calculation, any missed workout will display a blank cell for the calories burned in place of a 0. Rather than reentering the complete formula for calories burned, you can edit the existing formula, inserting the IF function.

To change the calories burned formulas to IF functions:

1. Double-click cell **L22** to enter Edit mode.

2. Press the **Home** key to move the insertion point to the beginning of the formula, and then press the → key to move the insertion point one space to the right, directly after = (the equal sign). You will begin the IF function after the equal sign.

3. Type **IF(G22="x",** to insert the function name and the expression for the logical test.

4. Press the **Ctrl+End** keys to move the insertion point to the end of the formula.

5. Type **, "")** to enter the value if false and complete the IF function. The complete formula is now =IF(G22="x", $P$20^$C$11*K22/125.7143, "").

6. Press the **Enter** key to exit Edit mode and make cell L23 active. Cell L22 still displays 376.1 because Ken did not miss the first workout.

   You will use AutoFill to copy the IF function to the rest of the cells in the Calories Burned column.

7. Select cell **L22**, and then drag the fill handle down over the range **L22:L44**. As shown in Figure 3-34, the missed workouts now display blank cells instead of zeroes, and the attended workouts show the same calculated values as earlier.

Make sure your formula matches the one shown here.

Figure 3-34   **IF function excludes the calories burned for missed workouts**

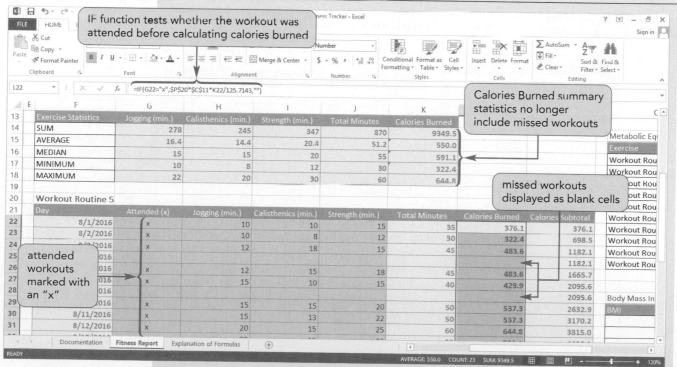

By excluding the missed workouts, Daniel's average exercise time increased from 37.8 minutes to 51.2 minutes, and the average calories burned increased to 550 calories. These averages more closely match the median values because zeroes were removed from the calculations. The minimum values for Total Minutes and Calories Burned now also reflect only attended workouts, changing from 0 (when they were based on a missed workout) to 30 minutes and 322.4 calories, respectively. These measures reflect the true results of the workouts Daniel attended.

Using a Lookup Function

Lookup functions find values in tables of data and insert them in another location in the worksheet such as cells or in formulas. For example, consider the active BMR calculated in cell C22, which adjusts the calculation of Daniel's metabolic rate to account for his activity level. The more active Daniel is, the more calories he can consume without gaining weight. The multiplying factors for each activity level (Sedentary, Light, Moderate, High, or Extreme) are stored in a table in the range O8:P12; you used the value in cell P8 to adjust Daniel's BMR value for his sedentary lifestyle. Instead of including a direct reference to one of the multiplying factors in the table, you can use a function to have Excel choose the multiplying factor that corresponds to the specified activity level.

The table that stores the data you want to retrieve is called a lookup table. A lookup table organizes numbers or text into categories. This particular lookup table organizes the BMR factors by activity levels, as shown in Figure 3-35. Every activity level category in the first column of the lookup table has a corresponding BMR factor in the second column of the table. This table is a vertical lookup table because the categories are arranged vertically. The entries in the first column of a vertical lookup table are referred to as the compare values because they are compared to the category you want to find (called the lookup value). When a match is found, the corresponding value in one of the subsequent columns is returned. For example, to find the return value for the Moderate lookup value, you look down the first column of the lookup table until you find the Moderate entry. Then, you move to the second column to locate the corresponding return value, which is 1.550, in this case.

Figure 3-35   **Finding an exact match from a vertical lookup table**

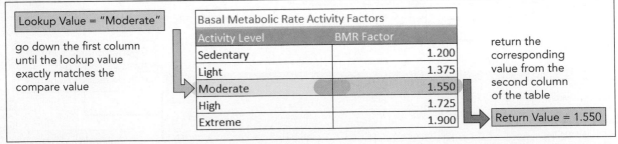

© 2014 Cengage Learning

Lookup tables can be constructed for exact match or approximate match lookups. An **exact match lookup** is when the lookup value must match one of the compare values in the first column of the lookup table. The table in Figure 3-35 is an exact match lookup because the activity level must match one of the compare values in the table or a value is not returned. An **approximate match lookup** occurs when the lookup value falls within a range of numbers in the first column of the lookup table. You will work with exact match lookups in this tutorial.

Finding an Exact Match with the VLOOKUP Function

To retrieve the return value from a vertical lookup table, you use the VLOOKUP function. The syntax of the VLOOKUP function is

```
VLOOKUP(lookup_value, table_array, col_index_num[, range_lookup=TRUE])
```

where `lookup_value` is the compare value to find in the first column of the lookup table, `table_array` is the range reference to the lookup table, and `col_index_num` is the number of the column in the lookup table that contains the return value. Keep in mind that `col_index_num` refers to the number of the column within the lookup table, not the worksheet column. For example, `col_index_num` 2 refers to the second column of the table, `col_index_num` 3 refers to the third column of the table, and so forth. Finally, `range_lookup` is an optional argument that specifies whether the compare values are an exact match or a range of values (for an approximate match). For an exact match, you set the `range_lookup` value to FALSE. For approximate match lookups, you set the `range_lookup` value to TRUE or you can omit it because its default value is TRUE.

For example, the following formula performs an exact match lookup to find the BMR factor for an Extreme activity level based on the values from the lookup table in the range O8:P12 (shown earlier in Figure 3-35):

```
=VLOOKUP("Extreme", O8:P12, 2, FALSE)
```

TIP

If the VLOOKUP function cannot find the lookup value, the #N/A error value is displayed in the cell.

The `col_index_num` is 2 because the BMR factors are in the second column of the table. The `range_lookup` is FALSE because this is an exact match. The function looks through the compare values in the first column of the table to locate the "Extreme" entry. When the exact entry is found, the function returns the corresponding value in the second column of the table, which in this case is 1.900.

Daniel's activity level in cell C9 is entered as Sedentary, which has a BMR factor of 1.2. The following active BMR formula you entered earlier calculated that Daniel can consume about 2224 calories per day and maintain his current weight:

```
=P8*C21
```

In this formula, P8 references the Sedentary BMR value in cell P8 and C21 references Daniel's base or resting metabolic rate. To have Excel look up the BMR value, you need to replace the P8 cell reference with a VLOOKUP function, as follows:

```
=VLOOKUP(C9, O8:P12, 2, FALSE)*C21
```

In this formula, C9 contains Daniel's activity level (Sedentary), O8:P12 references the lookup table, 2 specifies the table column to find the BMR factors, and FALSE indicates that this is an exact match lookup. You will enter this formula into the worksheet now.

To use the VLOOKUP function to calculate Daniel's active BMR:

1. Select cell **C22**, and then press the **Delete** key to clear the formula currently in the cell.

2. On the ribbon, click the **FORMULAS** tab. Because VLOOKUP has several arguments to manage, you will enter the function using the Function Arguments dialog box.

3. In the Function Library group, click **Lookup & Reference** to display a list of functions, and then click **VLOOKUP**. The Function Arguments dialog box opens.

4. With the insertion point in the Lookup_value box, click cell **C9** in the worksheet to enter that cell reference as the location containing the value to look up in the first column of the lookup table.

5. Press the **Tab** key to move the insertion point into the Table_array box, and then select the range **O8:P12**, which contains the vertical lookup table in the worksheet.

6. Press the **Tab** key to move the insertion point to the Col_index_num box, and then type **2** to return a value from the second column of the lookup table.

7. Press the **Tab** key to move the insertion point to the Range_lookup box, and then type **FALSE** to specify an exact match lookup. The dialog box shows the resulting value of the function with these arguments, which in this case is 1.2. See Figure 3-36.

Figure 3-36   **Function Arguments dialog box for the VLOOKUP function**

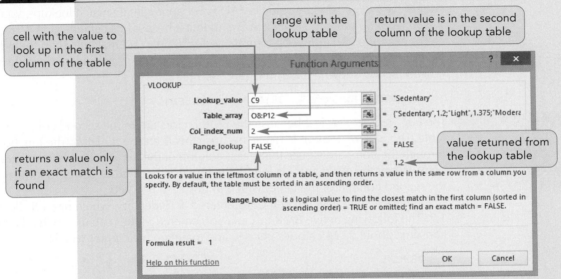

cell with the value to look up in the first column of the table

range with the lookup table

return value is in the second column of the lookup table

returns a value only if an exact match is found

value returned from the lookup table

8. Click the **OK** button to close the dialog box.

9. Double-click cell **C22** to enter Edit mode, press the **Ctrl+End** keys to move the insertion point to the end of the formula, type ***C21** to complete the formula, and then press the **Enter** key. The completed formula in cell C22 is =VLOOKUP(C9,O8:P12,2,FALSE)*C21, resulting in an active BMR of 2224 calories per day for a Sedentary activity level.

You will change the activity level to ensure that the formula works correctly.

10. In cell **C9**, enter **Moderate** to change the activity level from Sedentary. The active BMR value changes to 2872 because the VLOOKUP function returns a 1.55 BMR factor from the lookup table.

Ken decides that Light is a more accurate description of Daniel's activity level.

11. In cell **C9**, enter **Light** as the activity level. At that activity level, the active BMR changes to 2548. With a Light activity level, Daniel can consume about 2548 calories per day and maintain his current weight.

12. Select cell **C22** to view the formula. See Figure 3-37.

TIP

Exact matches are not case sensitive, so the lookup values Light, light, and LIGHT are considered to be the same.

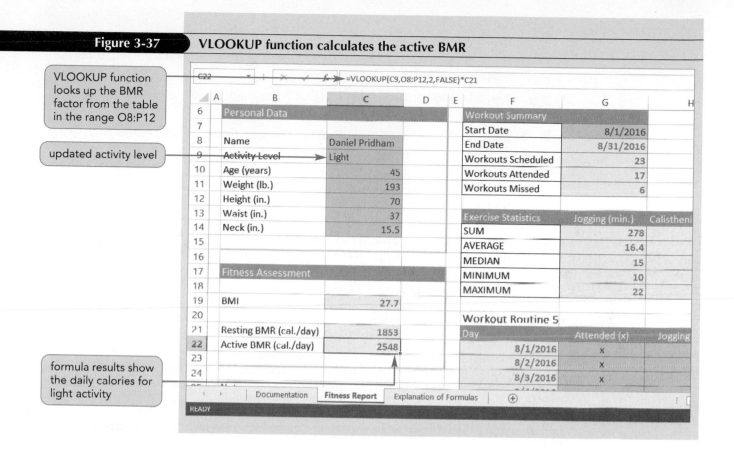

Figure 3-37   VLOOKUP function calculates the active BMR

VLOOKUP function looks up the BMR factor from the table in the range O8:P12

updated activity level

formula results show the daily calories for light activity

Performing What-If Analysis

A **what-if analysis** lets you explore the impact that changing input values has on the calculated values in the workbook. For example, Ken could perform a what-if analysis to determine how many pounds Daniel needs to lose to reach a more healthy weight. Current fitness standards suggest that a body mass index between 18.5 and 24.9 is considered to be within the "normal" classification. Daniel's body mass index is 27.7, which is rated as overweight. So Ken wants to know how many pounds Daniel needs to lose to reduce his body mass index to 24.9.

Using Trial and Error

One way to perform a what-if analysis is by changing one or more of the input values to see how they affect the calculated results. This **trial-and-error method** requires some guesswork as you estimate which values to change and by how much. In this case, Ken wants you to find out the weight at which Daniel would reach a BMI of 24.9. You'll start by checking the resulting body mass index if Daniel were to lose 10 pounds, reducing his weight to 183 pounds.

To perform a what-if analysis by trial and error:

1. In cell **C11**, change the weight from 193 pounds to **183** pounds. Daniel's body mass index decreases from 27.7 to 26.3, as shown in cell C19. At this weight, he is still considered overweight.

> **2.** In cell **C11**, enter **163** pounds. At this weight, Daniel's BMI shown in cell C19 is 23.4. So losing 30 pounds is more than enough to classify Daniel's body weight as normal.
>
> Ken wants to know if Daniel can lose fewer than 30 pounds to reach that classification.
>
> **3.** In cell **C11**, enter **168** pounds. At this weight, Daniel's BMI value is 24.1, which is still within the normal classification, but not exactly equal to 24.9.

If you want to find the exact weight that will result in a body mass index of 24.9, you would have to continue trying different weight values as you close in on the correct weight. This is why the method is called "trial and error." For some calculations, trial and error can be a very time-consuming way to locate the exact input value. A more direct approach to this problem is to use Goal Seek.

Using Goal Seek

Goal Seek automates the trial-and-error process by allowing you to specify a value for a calculated item, which Excel uses to determine the input value needed to reach that goal. In this case, because Ken wants to know how Daniel can reach a body mass index of exactly 24.9 (the upper level of the normal classification), the question that Goal Seek answers is: "What weight value is required to reach that goal?" Goal Seek starts by setting the calculated value and works backward to determine the correct input value.

REFERENCE

Performing What-If Analysis and Goal Seek

To perform a what-if analysis by trial and error:
- Change the value of a worksheet cell (the input cell).
- Observe its impact on one or more calculated cells (the result cells).
- Repeat until the desired results are achieved.

To perform a what-if analysis using Goal Seek:
- On the DATA tab, in the Data Tools group, click the What-If Analysis button, and then click Goal Seek.
- Select the result cell in the Set cell box, and then specify its value (goal) in the To value box.
- In the By changing cell box, specify the input cell.
- Click the OK button. The value of the input cell changes to set the value of the result cell.

You will use Goal Seek to find the weight that will result in Daniel's BMI reaching exactly 24.9.

To use Goal Seek to find a weight resulting in a 24.9 BMI:

> **1.** On the ribbon, click the **DATA** tab.
>
> **2.** In the Data Tools group, click the **What-If Analysis** button, and then click **Goal Seek**. The Goal Seek dialog box opens.
>
> **3.** Make sure the value in the Set cell box is selected, and then click cell **C19** in the Fitness Report worksheet. The absolute cell reference $C$19 appears in the Set cell box. The set cell is the calculated value you want Goal Seek to change to meet your goal.

4. Press the **Tab** key to move the insertion point to the To value box, and then type **24.9**. This indicates that you want Goal Seek to set this value to 24.9 (the highest body mass index in the normal classification).

5. Press the **Tab** key to move the insertion point to the By changing cell box. There are often various input values you can change to meet a goal. In this case, you want to change the weight value in cell C11.

6. Click cell **C11**. The absolute reference $C$11 appears in the By changing cell box. See Figure 3-38.

Figure 3-38	Goal Seek dialog box

7. Click the **OK** button. The Goal Seek dialog box closes, and the Goal Seek Status dialog box opens, indicating that Goal Seek found a solution.

8. Click the **OK** button. A weight value of about 173 pounds is displayed in cell C11. Daniel would need to lose roughly 20 pounds, reducing his weight to 173 pounds to reach a weight within the normal classification for BMI. See Figure 3-39.

Figure 3-39	Target weight determined by Goal Seek

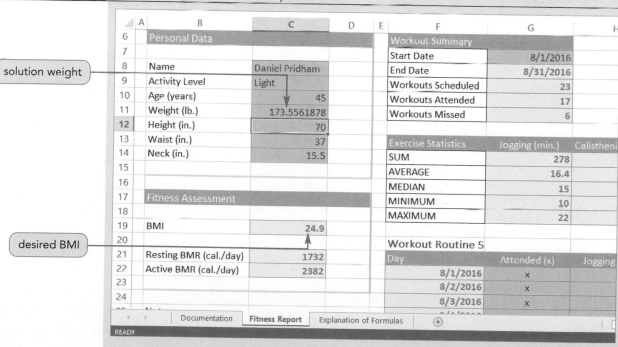

9. Save and close the workbook.

Ken appreciates all of the work you have done in developing the Fitness Tracker workbook. He will use this workbook as a model for all of his other clients at Fit Fathers.

REVIEW

Session 3.2 Quick Check

1. The first three values in a selected series are 3, 6, and 9. What are the next three values that will be inserted by AutoFill?
2. Write a formula to display the current date.
3. Write a formula to find the date four workdays after the date value stored in cell B10. There are no holidays.
4. Explain the difference between the COUNT function and the COUNTA function.
5. If cell Q3 is greater than cell Q4, you want to display the text "OK"; otherwise, display the text "RETRY". Write the formula that accomplishes this.
6. Jan is entering hundreds of temperature values into an Excel worksheet for a climate research project, and she wants to save time on data entry by leaving freezing point values as blanks rather than typing zeroes. Will this cause complications if she later tries to calculate an average temperature from her data values? Explain why or why not.
7. Provide the formula to perform an exact match lookup with the lookup value from cell G5 using a lookup table located in the range A1:F50. Return the value from the third column of the table.
8. What is the difference between a what-if analysis by trial and error and by Goal Seek?

ASSESS

PRACTICE

SAM Projects

Put your skills into practice with SAM Projects! SAM Projects for this tutorial can be found online. If you have a SAM account, go to www.cengage.com/sam2013 to download the most recent Project Instructions and Start Files.

Review Assignments

Data File needed for the Review Assignments: Mothers.xlsx

Ken and his wife, Sally, are expanding the business, changing its name to Fit Fathers and Mothers Inc., and adding fitness classes for mothers with a special emphasis on pregnant women. The fitness equations for women are different from those for men. Ken and Sally want you to create a workbook similar to the one you created for fathers, but focused on the fitness needs of women. Sally also wants you to calculate the total fat burned in the course of completing the workout schedule. She has already designed much of the workbook's contents, but she needs you to add the formulas and functions. Complete the following:

1. Open the **Mothers** workbook located in the Excel3 ► Review folder included with your Data Files, and then save the workbook as **Mothers Fitness** in the location specified by your instructor.

2. In the Documentation sheet, enter your name and the date.

3. Go to the Fitness Analysis worksheet. In the range C8:C15, enter the personal data for **Dorothy Young**. Her activity level is **Moderate**, she is **38** years old, **152** pounds, **64** inches tall, with a **33**-inch waist, **35**-inch hips, and a **14**-inch neck.

4. In cell C20, enter a formula to calculate Dorothy's body mass index based on the equation

   $BMI = 703w/h^2$

   where w is the weight in pounds and h is the height in inches. Display the formula results with one decimal place.

5. In cell C22, enter a formula to calculate the resting metabolism rate for women based on the equation

   $BMR - 4.338w + 4.698h - 4.68a + 655$

   where w is the weight in pounds, h is the height in inches, and a is the age in years. Display the formula results with no decimal places.

6. In cell C23, enter a formula using the VLOOKUP function to calculate the active BMR based on the equation

   Active BMR = $Activity\ Factor \times BMR$

   where $Activity\ Factor$ is an exact match lookup for the value in the range O8:Q12 that corresponds to the activity level entered in cell C9, and BMR is the value in cell C22. Display the formula results with no decimal places.

7. In cell K22, enter a formula using an IF function to calculate the total minutes for the first workout that displays a blank cell if Dorothy did not attend a workout that day.

8. Use AuotFill to copy the formula you entered in cell K22 to the range K23:K44 to calculate the total minutes for each workout.

9. In cell L22, enter a formula to calculate the calories burned at the first workout based on the equation

   $$Calories = \frac{METS \times w \times t}{125.7143}$$

   where $METS$ is the metabolic factor for the exercise, w is the client's weight, and t is the exercise time. Use the METS value located in cell P19, the weight value located in cell C11, and the time value located in the corresponding cell in column K. Be sure to use an absolute reference for both weight and METS.

10. Edit the formula you entered in cell L22 to be included as part of an IF function that returns a blank cell if Dorothy did not attend the workout that day. Display the formula results with one decimal place.

11. Use AutoFill to copy the formula you entered in cell L22 to the range L23:L44 to calculate the calories burned at each workout.

12. In the range M22:M44, use the Quick Analysis tool to calculate a column running total of the calories burned in the range L22:L44. Display the formula results with two decimal places.

13. Complete the exercise statistics in the range G14:K18 by entering formulas calculating the sum, average, median, maximum, and minimum values of the exercise times, and calories burned values from the workout log. Display the averages and the calories burned statistics with one decimal place.

14. In cell G2, use a function to display the current date whenever the workbook is opened.

15. In cell F22, enter a formula to reference the start date entered in cell G7.

16. In the range F23:F44, use a function to increase the value of the date in the previous row by 1 workday. Format the formula results with the Short Date format.

17. In cell G8, enter a formula to display the ending date entered in cell F44.

18. In cell G9, enter a formula to count the number of days included in the range F22:F44.

19. In cell G10, enter a formula to count the number of attended workouts as indicated in the range G22:G44.

20. In cell G11, enter a formula to calculate the difference between the number of scheduled workouts and the number of attended workouts. Save the workbook.

21. Use Goal Seek to determine the weight Dorothy must attain to reach a body mass index of 22.

22. Save the revised workbook as **Mothers Fitness Goal**, and then close the workbook.

Case Problem 1

Data File needed for this Case Problem: Hernandez.xlsx

Hernandez Family   Juan and Olivia Hernandez are a recently married couple in Fort Wayne, Indiana. Juan is currently in graduate school and Olivia is the manager at a local bakery. They want to use Excel to help manage their family budget, but they need help setting up the formulas and functions to project their monthly expenses and help them meet their financial goals. Complete the following:

1. Open the **Hernandez** workbook located in the Excel3 ► Case1 folder included with your Data Files, and then save the workbook as **Hernandez Budget** in the location specified by your instructor.

2. In the Documentation sheet, enter your name and the date.

3. Go to the Budget worksheet. In cell B7, calculate the couple's total monthly income.

4. In row 23, use AutoFill to replace the numbers 1 through 12 with the month abbreviations **Jan** through **Dec**.

5. In rows 24 and 25, enter the couple's monthly income by referencing the monthly income estimates in cells B5 and B6. Use an absolute cell reference.

6. In row 26, calculate the couple's monthly income.

7. In row 37, enter formulas to calculate the total estimated expenses for each month.

8. In row 38, calculate each month's net cash flow, which is equal to the total income minus the total expenses.

9. In row 39, calculate the running total of the net cash flow so that Olivia and Juan can see how their net cash flow changes as the year progresses.

10. In the range B10:B19, calculate the average monthly expenses by category based on the values previously entered in rows 27 through 36.

11. In cell B20, calculate the total average monthly expenses.

12. The couple currently has $7,350 in their savings account. Each month the couple will either take money out of their savings account or deposit money. In row 41, calculate the end-of-month balance in their savings account by adding the value in cell E5 to the running total values of the net cash flow in row 39. Use an absolute cell reference for cell E5.

13. In cell E6, enter a formula to display the value of the savings balance at the end of December.

14. Juan and Olivia would like to have $15,000 in their savings account by the end of the year. Olivia is planning to ask for a raise at her job. Use Goal Seek to determine the value of cell B6 that will achieve a final savings balance of $15,000.

15. Save and close the workbook.

Case Problem 2

Data File needed for this Case Problem: Econ.xlsx

Introduction to Economics 102   Alice Keyes teaches Introduction to Economics 102 at Mountain View Business School in Huntington, West Virginia. She wants to use Excel to track the grades from her class. Alice has already entered the homework, quiz, and final exam scores for all of her students in a workbook, and she has asked you to set up the formulas and functions for her.

You will calculate each student's final average based on his or her homework score, quiz scores, and final exam. Homework counts for 20 percent of the student's final grade. The first two quizzes count for 10 percent each. The second two quizzes count for 15 percent each. The final exam counts for 30 percent of the final grade.

You will also calculate each student's rank in the class. The rank will display which student placed first in terms of his or her overall score, which student placed second, and so forth. Ranks are calculated using the function

```
RANK(number, ref, [order=0])
```

where *number* is the value to be ranked, *ref* is a reference to the cell range containing the values against which the ranking is done, and *order* is an optional argument that specifies whether to rank in descending order or ascending order. The default *order* value is 0 to rank the values in descending order.

Finally, you will create formulas that will look up information on a particular student based on that student's ID so Alice doesn't have to scroll through the complete class roster to find a particular student. Complete the following:

1. Open the **Econ** workbook located in the Excel3 ► Case2 folder included with your Data Files, and then save the workbook as **Econ Grades** in the location specified by your instructor.

2. In the Documentation sheet, enter your name and the date.

3. Go to the Grade Book worksheet. In cell B5, count the number of student IDs in the range A22:A57.

✦ **Explore** 4. Cells C15 through H15 contain the weights assigned to each assignment, quiz, or exam. In cell J22, calculate the weighted average of the first student's scores by entering a formula that multiplies each score by its corresponding weight and adds the resulting products.

5. Edit the formula in cell J22, changing the references to the weights in cells C15 through H15 from relative references to absolute references.

6. Use AutoFill to copy the formula from cell J22 into the range J23:J57.

✦ **Explore** 7. In cell K22, use the RANK function to calculate how the first student compares to the other students in the class. Use the weighted average from cell J22 for the *number* argument and the range of weighted averages in the cell range $J$22:$J$57 for the *ref* argument. You do not need to specify a value for the *order* argument.

8. Use AutoFill to copy the formula you entered in cell K22 into the range K23:K57.

9. In the range C16:H18, calculate the class average, minimum, and maximum for each of the six grading components (homework, quizzes, and final exam).

10. In cell B8, enter the student ID **14858**.

⊕ **Explore**   11. Using the VLOOKUP function with an exact match and the student data table in the range A22:K57, retrieve the first name, last name, weighted average, and class rank for student 14858 in the range B9:B12. Use an absolute reference to the lookup table. Note that the first name is found in the third column of the student data table, the last name is found in the second column, the weighted average is found in the tenth column, and the class rank is found in the eleventh column.

12. Brenda Dunford missed the final exam and will be taking a make-up exam. She wants to know what score she would need on the final exam to achieve an overall weighted average of 90. Use Goal Seek to calculate what final exam score Brenda needs to result in a weighted average of 90.

13. Save and close the workbook.

Case Problem 3

CHALLENGE

Data File needed for this Case Problem: Homes.xlsx

Homes of Dreams   Larry Helt is a carpenter and a woodcrafter in Coventry, Rhode Island, who loves to design and build custom dollhouses. He started his business, Homes of Dreams, a few years ago and it has expanded into a very profitable sideline to his ongoing carpentry work. Larry wants to create a shipping form that will calculate the cost for the purchased items, including taxes, shipping, and handling. Larry already designed the worksheet, which includes a table of shipping rates, shipping surcharges, and items sold by Homes of Dreams. He asks you to complete the worksheet. Complete the following:

1. Open the **Homes** workbook located in the Excel3 ► Case3 folder included with your Data Files, and then save the workbook as **Homes of Dreams** in the location specified by your instructor.

2. In the Documentation sheet, enter your name and the date.

3. Go to the Order Form worksheet.

4. In cell B21, enter the Item ID **DH007**.

5. In cell C21, enter the VLOOKUP function with an exact match to return the name of the item referenced in cell B21. Reference the lookup table in the range M4:O50 using an absolute cell reference. Return the value from the second column of the table.

6. In cell E21, enter the VLOOKUP function with an exact match to return the price of the item referenced in cell B21. Use an absolute reference to the lookup table in the range M4:O50. Return the value from the third column of the table.

7. In cell F21, enter **1** as the quantity of the item ordered.

8. In cell G21, calculate the price of the item multiplied by the quantity ordered.

⊕ **Explore**   9. Revise your formulas in cells C21, E21, and G21, nesting them within an IF formula. For each cell, test whether the value of cell B21 is not equal to "" (a blank). If it is not, return the value of the VLOOKUP function in cells C21 and E21 and the calculated value in cell G21. Otherwise, those cells should return a blank ("") value.

10. Use AutoFill to copy the formulas in cells C21, E21, and G21 through row 30 in the order items table.

11. In row 22, enter **BD002** as the Item ID and **3** as the quantity of items ordered. Verify that the formulas you created automatically enter the name, price, and charge for the item.

12. In rows 23 through 25, enter **1** order for item **BH003**, **1** order for item **DR002**, and **1** order for item **KR009**.

13. In cell G32, calculate the sum of the item charges from all possible orders.

14. In cell G33, calculate the sales tax on the order, which is equal to the subtotal multiplied by the tax rate (entered in cell J9).

15. In cell C15, enter a function to insert the current date whenever the workbook is opened.

16. In cell C16, enter **3 Day** as the type of delivery for this order.

17. In cell C17, calculate the number of working days it will take to ship the order by inserting a VLOOKUP function using an exact match lookup. Use the delivery type in cell C16 as the lookup value, and use the shipping data in the range I4:K7 as the lookup table. Return the value from the third column of the table.

⊕ **Explore** 18. In cell C18, estimate the date of delivery. Use cell C15 as the start date and cell C17 as the number of working days after the start date.

⊕ **Explore** 19. The shipping and handling fee is based on the delivery method (Standard, 3 Day, 2 Day, or Overnight). In cell G34, calculate the shipping and handling fee for the order using an exact match lookup with the data in the range I4:J7. Use the delivery method specified in cell C16 to find the corresponding shipping and handling fee in the Delivery table.

20. In cell G36, calculate the sum of the merchandise subtotal, sales tax, and shipping and handling fee.

21. Save the workbook, and then delete the item IDs and quantities from the order table.

22. Save the workbook as **Homes of Dreams 2**, calculate the cost of ordering 1 of item BD001 using overnight delivery, and then save the workbook.

23. Save the workbook as **Homes of Dreams 3**, and then delete the item IDs and quantities from the order table. Calculate the cost of ordering 1 of item KR001, 2 of item BI1004, and 1 of item DR001 using standard delivery. Save and close the workbook.

Case Problem 4

TROUBLESHOOT

Data File needed for this Case Problem: Quality.xlsx

Karleton Manufacturing   Carmen Garza is a quality control manager at Karleton Manufacturing, a manufacturing plant located in Trotwood, Ohio. One project that Carmen oversees is the manufacture of tin cans for a major food company. The can widths must be consistent. To compensate for the fact that metal working tools tend to wear down during the day, the pressure behind the tools is increased as the blades become worn. Quality control technicians monitor the process to check that it remains "in control" creating cans whose widths are neither too narrow nor too wide. Carmen has recorded the widths of four cans from 39 batches in an Excel workbook that she wants to use to determine whether the process is "in control." One standard for determining whether a process is "in control" is whether the average value from a process batch falls within the lower and upper control limits. The workbook itself is in need of quality control as some of the formulas are not calculating correctly. You will fix these and then enter the remainder of the formulas needed in the worksheet. Complete the following:

1. Open the **Quality** workbook located in the Excel3 ▸ Case4 folder included with your Data Files, and then save the workbook as **Quality Control Analysis** in the location specified by your instructor.

2. In the Documentation sheet, enter your name and the date.

3. In the Quality Control worksheet, use AutoFill with the value in cell A7 and fill the series of batch numbers from B-1 to B-39 into the range A7:A45.

⚙ **Troubleshoot** 4. In the Quality Control worksheet, cells M3 and M4 display the #NAME? error value instead of the averages. Make the necessary changes to correct the formulas.

⚙ **Troubleshoot** 5. The formulas in the range H7:H45 are supposed to calculate the range of values (maximum minus minimum) within each batch. However, the formula results display 6.2 for every batch. Make the necessary changes in the formulas to fix the problem.

⚙ **Troubleshoot** 6. The formulas in the range I7:I45 are supposed to calculate the average width of the four cans tested in each batch. Unfortunately, the formulas' results don't equal the average widths. Make the necessary changes in the formulas to fix the problem.

7. In cell J7, calculate the lower control limit for the first batch based on the equation

$LCL = XBAR - A2 \times RBAR$

where LCL is the lower and upper control limits, $XBAR$ is the average value from all batches, $RBAR$ is the average range from all batches, and $A2$ is a correction factor that depends on the sample size of the batch. In this case, use the $XBAR$ value from cell M3 and the $RBAR$ value from cell M4. Determine the $A2$ value using an exact match lookup with the sample size in cell G7 as the reference value, and the second column from the table in the range O7:P30 as the return value.

8. AutoFill the lower control limit formula from cell J7 into the rest of the LCL column in the Control Limits table. Check to make sure your formulas were properly copied and that they still reference the correct cells.

9. In cell K7, calculate the upper control limit for the first batch based on the equation

$$UCL=XBAR+A2 \times RBAR$$

where *UCL* is the upper control limit. Copy your formula into the rest of the UCL column in the Control Limits table.

10. In cell L7, indicate whether the B-1 batch process is "in control low" by testing whether the batch's average is less than its LCL value. If it is, display "NO"; otherwise, display a blank cell.

11. In cell M7, indicate whether the B-1 batch process is "in control high" by testing whether the batch's average is greater than its UCL value. If it is, display "NO"; otherwise, display a blank cell.

12. Fill the in control low and in control high formulas for the rest of the batches.

13. Add conditional formatting to the range L7:M45 so that cells displaying "NO" are formatted in dark red text on a light red background.

⚙ **Troubleshoot** 14. The computer program that recorded the width values entered a missing width value as a 0 instead of leaving the cells blank. This affects the calculations about sample size and which batches are in control. Fix this in the data set and any formulas so that the worksheet accurately indicates which batches are not in control on the low side or not in control on the high side.

15. Save and close the workbook.

Analyzing and Charting Financial Data

Presenting Data for a Business Plan

EXCEL

Case | *Levitt Winery*

Bob and Carol Levitt want to establish a new winery in Northern Michigan near the town of Traverse City. After many years of working as a winemaker for other wineries, Bob is eager to strike out on his own. Carol will handle the business and finances side of the business, building on her experience managing other companies.

To establish Levitt Winery, Bob and Carol need to borrow money to supplement their personal funds. Bob and Carol are in the process of applying for a business loan. They plan to use this money to help cover the startup costs for their winery. As part of the business loan application, Bob and Carol need to develop a 10-year business plan. They have analyzed the market and made reasonable projections for future production, expenses, and revenue. This information is compiled in an Excel workbook.

Because they are providing a lot of detailed information, Bob and Carol want to include charts in their Excel workbook to make this information easy to read and interpret. Before you create the financial charts that Bob and Carol need for their workbook, you will complete the contents of this worksheet by calculating the cost of the business loan they will need to get started.

STARTING DATA FILES

Excel4 → Tutorial
Draft.png
Levitt.xlsx

Review
Market.xlsx
Watermark.png

Case1
Bertrand.xlsx

Case2
PetroChart.xlsx

Case3
Confidential.png
Frame.xlsx

Case4
Mortgage.xlsx

Session 4.1 Visual Overview:

A **chart**, or **graph**, is a visual representation of a set of data values. Charts show trends or relationships that may not be readily apparent from numbers alone.

An **embedded chart** is an object in a worksheet.

The **chart area** contains the chart and all of the other chart elements.

A **data label** is text associated with an individual data marker, such as the percentage value next to a pie slice.

Each chart has a **data source**, which is the range that contains the data displayed in the chart. The data source for the pie chart is the range B29:C34.

The **category values** are the groups or categories that the data series values belong to. These category values show the different wines produced.

A **data series** contains the actual values that are plotted or displayed on the chart. This data series shows the total cases that will be produced for each wine.

The **vertical axis**, or **value axis**, displays the values from the data series.

Chart Elements

The **CHART TOOLS** contextual tabs appear on the ribbon when a chart is selected.

Chart elements are individual parts of the chart, such as the title or the legend.

The **Format pane** provides a collection of commands to format chart elements. The options change based on the selected chart element.

The **chart title** is a descriptive label or name for the chart.

A **data marker** displays an individual value from a data series. These data markers are columns.

A **legend** identifies which data markers are associated with each data series.

The **horizontal axis**, or **category axis**, displays the category values from each data series.

Introduction to Financial Functions

Excel provides a wide range of financial functions related to loans and investments. One of these is the **PMT function**, which can be used to calculate the payment schedule required to completely repay a mortgage or other type of loan. Figure 4-1 describes the PMT function and some of the other financial functions often used to develop budgets and financial projections.

Figure 4-1 Financial functions for loans and investments

Function	Description
FV(rate, nper, pmt [,pv=0] [,type=0])	Calculates the future value of an investment, where *rate* is the interest rate per period, *nper* is the total number of periods, *pmt* is the payment in each period, *pv* is the present value of the investment, and *type* indicates whether payments should be made at the end of the period (0) or the beginning of the period (1)
PMT(rate, nper, pv [,fv=0] [,type=0])	Calculates the payments required each period on a loan or an investment, where *fv* is the future value of the investment
IPMT(rate, per, nper, pv [,fv=0] [,type=0])	Calculates the amount of a loan payment devoted to paying the loan interest, where *per* is the number of the payment period
PPMT(rate, per, nper, pv [,fv=0] [,type=0])	Calculates the amount of a loan payment devoted to paying off the principal of a loan
PV(rate, nper, pmt [,fv=0] [,type=0])	Calculates the present value of a loan or an investment based on periodic, constant payments
NPER(rate, pmt, pv [,fv=0] [,type=0])	Calculates the number of periods required to pay off a loan or an investment
RATE(nper, pmt, pv [,fv=0] [,type=0])	Calculates the interest rate of a loan or an investment based on periodic, constant payments

© 2014 Cengage Learning

Before you can use the PMT function, you need to understand some of the concepts and definitions associated with loans. The cost of a loan to the borrower is largely based on three factors—the principal, the interest, and the time required to repay the loan. **Principal** is the amount of money being loaned. **Interest** is the amount added to the principal by the lender. You can think of interest as a kind of "user fee" because the borrower is paying for the right to use the lender's money for an interval of time. Generally, interest is expressed at an annual percentage rate, or APR. For example, an 8 percent APR means that the annual interest rate on the loan is 8 percent of the amount owed to the lender.

An annual interest rate is divided by the number of payments per year (often monthly or quarterly). So, if the 8 percent annual interest rate is paid monthly, the resulting monthly interest rate is 1/12 of 8 percent, which is about 0.67 percent per month. If payments are made quarterly, then the interest rate per quarter would be 1/4 of 8 percent, which is 2 percent per quarter.

The third factor in calculating the cost of a loan is the time required to repay the loan, which is specified as the number of payment periods. The number of payment periods is based on the length of the loan multiplied by the number of payments per year. For example, a 10-year loan that is paid monthly has 120 payment periods (that is, 10 years × 12 months per year). If that same 10-year loan is paid quarterly, it has 40 payment periods (that is, 10 years × 4 quarters per year).

Using the PMT Function

To calculate the costs associated with a loan, such as the one that Bob and Carol need to start their winery, you must have the following information:

- The annual interest rate
- The number of payment periods per year
- The length of the loan in terms of the total number of payment periods
- The amount being borrowed
- When loan payments are due

The PMT function uses this information to calculate the payment required in each period to pay back the loan. The syntax of the PMT function is

```
PMT(rate, nper, pv [, fv=0] [, type=0])
```

where $rate$ is the interest rate for each payment period, $nper$ is the total number of payment periods required to repay the loan, and pv is the present value of the loan or the amount that needs to be borrowed. The PMT function has two optional arguments—fv and $type$. The fv argument is the future value of the loan. Because the intent with most loans is to repay them completely, the future value is equal to 0 by default. The $type$ argument specifies when the interest is charged on the loan, either at the end of the payment period ($type=0$), which is the default, or at the beginning of the payment period ($type=1$).

For example, you can use the PMT function to calculate the monthly payments required to repay a car loan of $10,000 over a 5-year period at an annual interest rate of 9 percent. The $rate$ or interest rate per period argument is equal to 9 percent divided by 12 monthly payments, which is 0.75 percent per month. The $nper$ or total number of payments argument is equal to 12×5 (12 monthly payments over 5 years), which is 60. The pv or present value of the loan is 10,000. In this case, because the loan will be repaid completely and payments will be made at the end of the month, you can accept the default values for the fv and $type$ arguments. The resulting PMT function

```
PMT(0.09/12, 5*12, 10000)
```

returns the value −207.58, or a monthly loan payment of $207.58. The PMT function results in a negative value because that value represents an expense to the borrower. Essentially, the loan is money you subtract from your funds to repay the loan.

Rather than entering the argument values directly in the PMT function, you should include the loan terms in worksheet cells that are referenced in the function. This makes it clear what values are being used in the loan calculation. It also makes it easier to perform a what-if analysis exploring other loan options.

Bob and Carol want to borrow $310,000 for their winery at an 8 percent annual interest rate. They plan to repay the loan in 10 years with monthly payments. You will enter these loan terms in the Overview worksheet.

To enter the loan information in the Overview worksheet:

1. Open the **Levitt** workbook located in the Excel4 ▸ Tutorial folder included with your Data Files, and then save the workbook as **Levitt Winery**.

2. In the Documentation sheet, enter your name in cell B4 and the date in cell B5.

3. Go to the **Overview** worksheet. The Overview worksheet provides a summary of Bob and Carol's business plan, including their loan request and business forecasts.

4. In cell **C5**, enter **310,000** as the loan amount.

5. In cell **C6**, enter **8%** as the annual interest rate.

6. In cell **C7**, enter **12** as the number of payments per year. Twelve payments indicate monthly payments.

7. In cell **C8**, enter the formula **=C6/C7** to calculate the interest rate per period. In this case, the 8 percent interest rate is divided by 12 payments per year, calculating the monthly interest rate of 0.67 percent.

8. In cell **C9**, enter **10** as the number of years in the loan.

9. In cell **C10**, enter **=C7*C9** to multiply the number of payments per year by the number of years in the loan, calculating the total number of payments on the loan, which is 120.

The Overview worksheet includes all the data you need to calculate the monthly payment required to repay the $310,000 loan in 10 years at an 8 percent annual interest rate paid monthly. Next, you will use the PMT function to calculate the monthly payment needed to repay the loan.

To use the PMT function to calculate Bob and Carol's monthly payment:

1. Select cell **C12** to make it the active cell. You will enter the PMT function in this cell.

2. On the ribbon, click the **FORMULAS** tab to display the function library.

3. In the Function Library group, click the **Financial** button, and then scroll down and click **PMT** in the list of financial functions. The Function Arguments dialog box opens.

4. With the insertion point in the Rate box, click cell **C8** in the worksheet to enter the reference to the cell with the interest rate per month.

5. Click in the **Nper** box, and then click cell **C10** in the worksheet to enter the reference to the cell with the total number of monthly payments required to repay the loan.

6. Click in the **Pv** box, and then click cell **C5** in the worksheet to enter the reference to the cell with the present value of the loan. See Figure 4-2.

Figure 4-2   **Function Arguments dialog box for the PMT function**

7. Click the **OK** button. The monthly payment amount ($3,761.16) appears in cell C12. The number is displayed in parentheses to indicate a negative amount, specifying the amount to be paid.

8. In cell **C13**, enter the formula **=C7*C12** to multiply the number of payments per year by the monthly payment amount, calculating the total payments for the entire year. The annual payments would be ($45,133.87), shown as a negative number to indicate money being paid out.

9. Select cell **C12**. See Figure 4-3.

Figure 4-3   **Monthly and annual costs of the business loan**

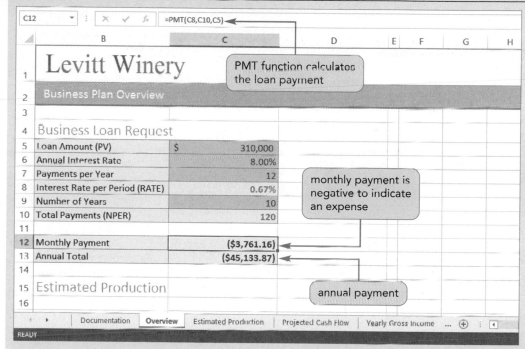

Carol wants to see the financial impact of taking out a smaller loan.

10. In cell **C5**, change the loan amount to **250,000**. With a loan of that size, the monthly payment drops to $3,033 and the annual total decreases to $36,398.

Although the lower loan amount will save money, Bob feels that the winery cannot get off the ground with less than a $310,000 loan.

11. In cell **C5**, return the loan amount to **310,000**.

Based on your analysis, the Levitts would spend about $45,000 a year repaying the $310,000 business loan. Carol and Bob want this information included in the Projected Cash Flow worksheet, which estimates Levitt Winery's annual revenue, expenses, and cash flow for the first 10 years. You will enter that amount as an expense for each year, completing the projected cash flow calculations.

To enter the loan repayment amount in the Projected Cash Flow worksheet:

▶ **1.** Go to the **Projected Cash Flow** worksheet and review the estimated annual revenue, expenses, and cash flow for the next decade.

▶ **2.** In cell **C17**, enter **45,000** as the projected yearly amount of the loan repayment. Because the projected cash flow is a rough estimate of the projected income and expenses, it is not necessary to include the exact dollar-and-cents cost of the loan.

▶ **3.** Copy the annual loan payment in cell **C17** into the range **D17:L17** to enter the projected annual loan payment in each year of the cash flow projections. See Figure 4-4.

Figure 4-4   **Completed Projected Cash Flow worksheet**

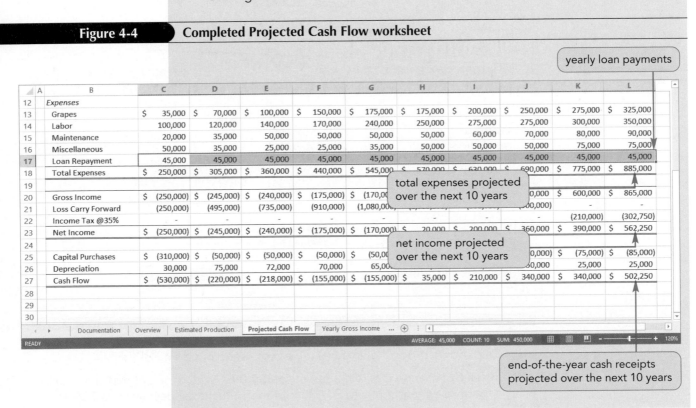

After including the projected annual loan payments, the Projected Cash Flow worksheet shows that the winery's projected net income at the end of the tenth year would be about $560,000, assuming all of the other projections are accurate. Based on these figures, the winery should have about $500,000 in cash at that time as well.

Using Functions to Manage Personal Finances

Excel has many financial functions to manage personal finances. The following list can help you determine which function to use for the most common personal finance calculations:

- To determine how much an investment will be worth after a series of monthly payments at some future time, use the FV (future value) function.
- To determine how much you have to spend each month to repay a loan or mortgage within a set period of time, use the PMT (payment) function.
- To determine how much of your monthly loan payment is used to pay the interest, use the IPMT (interest payment) function.
- To determine how much of your monthly loan payment is used for repaying the principal, use the PPMT (principal payment) function.
- To determine the largest loan or mortgage you can afford given a set monthly payment, use the PV (present value) function.
- To determine how long it will take to pay off a loan with constant monthly payments, use the NPER (number of periods) function.

For most loan and investment calculations, you need to enter the annual interest rate divided by the number of times the interest is compounded during the year. If interest is compounded monthly, divide the annual interest rate by 12; if interest is compounded quarterly, divide the annual rate by 4. You must also convert the length of the loan or investment to the number of payments per year. If you will make payments monthly, multiply the number of years of the loan or investment by 12.

Now that you have completed the cash flow projections for the winery, you can begin displaying this information in charts.

Creating a Chart

Charts show trends or relationships in data that are easier to see than by looking at the actual numbers. Creating a chart is a several-step process that involves selecting the data to display in the chart, choosing the chart type, moving the chart to a specific location in the workbook, sizing the chart so that it matches the layout of the worksheet, and formatting the chart's appearance. When creating a chart, remember that your goal is to convey important information that would be more difficult to interpret from columns of data in a worksheet.

Creating a Chart

- Select the range containing the data you want to chart.
- On the INSERT tab, in the Charts group, click the Recommended Chart button or a chart type button, and then click the chart you want to create (or click the Quick Analysis button, click the CHARTS category, and then click the chart you want to create).
- On the CHART TOOLS DESIGN tab, in the Location group, click the Move Chart button, select whether to embed the chart in a worksheet or place it in a chart sheet, and then click the OK button.

Selecting a Chart's Data Source

The data displayed in a chart comes from the chart's data source. A data source includes one or more data series and a series of category values. A data series contains the actual values that are plotted on the chart, whereas the category values provide descriptive labels for each data series or data value. Category values are usually located in the first column or first row of the data source. The data series are usually placed in subsequent columns or rows. However, you can select category and data values from anywhere within a workbook.

Bob and Carol want a chart to display information about the winery's estimated production in 10 years. The data source for this chart is located in the range B28:C34 of the Overview worksheet. You will select this range now as the data source for the chart.

To select the data source for a chart showing the projected production:

1. Go to the **Overview** worksheet. The production projections are included in this worksheet.

2. Select the range **B28:C34** containing the production estimates as the data source for the chart. See Figure 4-5.

| Figure 4-5 | Selected chart data source |

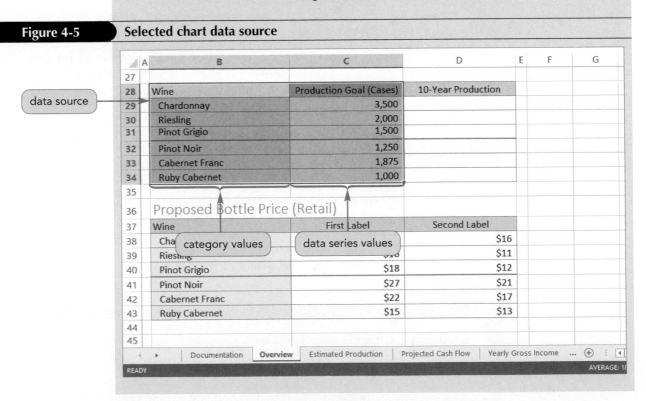

This data source includes two columns. The category values are located in the first column, and the one and only data series is located in the second column. When the selected range is taller than it is wide, Excel assumes that the category values and data series are laid out in columns. Conversely, a data source that is wider than it is tall is assumed to have the category values and data series laid out in rows. Note that the first row in this selected data source contains labels that identify the category values (Wine) and the data series (Production Goal).

Now that you've selected the data source for the chart, you want to consider the type of chart to create.

Exploring Chart Types and Subtypes

Excel provides 53 types of charts organized into the 10 categories described in Figure 4-6. Each category includes variations of the same chart type, which are called **chart subtypes**. You can also design your own custom chart types to meet the specific needs of your reports and projects.

Figure 4-6   Excel chart types

Chart Type	Description
Column	Compares values from different categories. Values are indicated by the height of the columns.
Line	Compares values from different categories. Values are indicated by the height of the lines. Often used to show trends and changes over time.
Pie	Compares relative values of different categories to the whole. Values are indicated by the areas of the pie slices.
Bar	Compares values from different categories. Values are indicated by the length of the bars.
Area	Compares values from different categories. Similar to the line chart except that areas under the lines contain a fill color.
X Y (Scatter)	Shows the patterns or relationship between two or more sets of values. Often used in scientific studies and statistical analyses.
Stock	Displays stock market data, including the high, low, opening, and closing prices of a stock.
Surface	Compares three sets of values in a three-dimensional chart.
Radar	Compares a collection of values from several different data sets.
Combo	Combines two or more chart types to make the data easy to visualize, especially when the data is widely varied.

© 2014 Cengage Learning

For example, Figure 4-7 presents the same labor cost data displayed as a line chart, a bar chart, and column charts. The column charts are shown with both a 2-D subtype that has two-dimensional or flat columns and a 3-D subtype that gives the illusion of three-dimensional columns. The various charts and chart subtypes are better suited for different data. You should choose the one that makes the data easiest to interpret.

Figure 4-7   **Chart types and subtypes**

Line chart

Bar chart

2-D Column chart

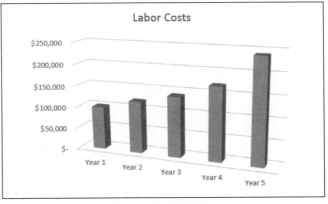

3-D Column chart

The first chart you will create is a pie chart. A **pie chart** is a chart in the shape of a circle divided into slices like a pie. Each slice represents a single value from a data series. Larger data values are represented with bigger pie slices. The relative sizes of the slices let you visually compare the data values and see how much each contributes to the whole. Pie charts are most effective with six or fewer slices, and when each slice is large enough to view easily.

Inserting a Pie Chart with the Quick Analysis Tool

After you select an adjacent range to use as a chart's data source, the Quick Analysis tool appears. It includes a category for creating charts. The CHART category lists recommended chart types, which are the charts that are most appropriate for the data source you selected.

For the wine production data, a pie chart provides the best way to compare the production levels for the six wines Levitt Winery plans to produce. You will use the Quick Analysis tool to create a pie chart of the projected wine production data that you selected.

To create a pie chart with the Quick Analysis tool:

1. Make sure the range **B28:C34** is selected.

2. Click the **Quick Analysis** button 📧 in the lower-right corner of the selected range (or press the **Ctrl+Q** keys) to open the Quick Analysis tool.

3. Click the **CHARTS** category. The chart types you will most likely want to use with the selected data source are listed. See Figure 4-8.

Figure 4-8   CHARTS category of the Quick Analysis tool

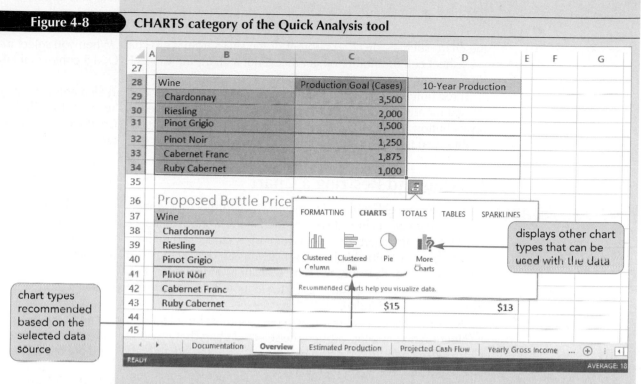

chart types recommended based on the selected data source

displays other chart types that can be used with the data

Recommended Charts help you visualize data.

4. Click **Pie**. A pie chart appears in the Overview worksheet. Each slice is a different size based on its value in the data series. The biggest slice represents the 3500 cases of Chardonnay that the Levitts estimate they will produce. The smallest slice of the pie represents 1000 cases of Ruby Cabernet. See Figure 4-9.

Figure 4-9   Pie chart in the Overview worksheet

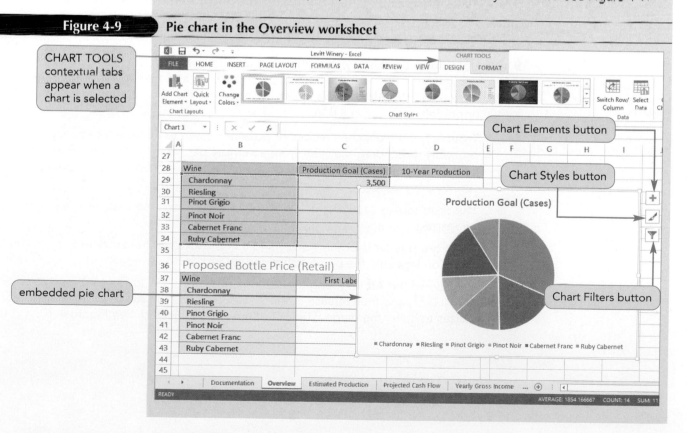

CHART TOOLS contextual tabs appear when a chart is selected

Chart Elements button

Chart Styles button

Chart Filters button

embedded pie chart

When you create or select a chart, two CHART TOOLS contextual tabs appear on the ribbon. The DESIGN tab provides commands to specify the chart's overall design. The FORMAT tab supplies the tools needed to format the graphic shapes found in the chart, such as the chart's border or the slices from a pie chart. When you select a worksheet cell or another object that is not a chart, the CHART TOOLS contextual tabs disappear until you reselect the chart.

Three buttons appear to the right of the selected chart. The Chart Elements button ⊞ is used for adding, removing, or changing elements displayed in the chart. The Chart Styles button ✎ sets the style and color scheme of the chart. The Chart Filters button ▼ enables you to edit the data points and names displayed on the chart.

Moving and Resizing a Chart

TIP

You can print an embedded chart with the rest of the worksheet, or you can select the embedded chart and print only the chart without the rest of the worksheet.

Excel charts are either placed in their own chart sheets or embedded in a worksheet. When you create a chart, it is embedded in the worksheet that contains the data source. For example, the chart shown in Figure 4-9 is embedded in the Overview worksheet. The advantage of an embedded chart is that you can display the chart alongside its data source and any text that describes the chart's meaning and purpose. Because an embedded chart covers worksheet cells, you might have to move or resize the chart so that important information is not hidden.

Before you can move or resize a chart, it must be selected. When a chart is selected, a **selection box** appears around the selected chart that is used to move or resize the chart. **Sizing handles** appear along the edges of the selection box and are used to change the chart's width and height.

Bob and Carol want the wine production chart to appear above its data source in the Overview worksheet. You will move and resize the chart to fit this location.

To move and resize the wine production pie chart:

1. Move the pointer over an empty area of the selected chart until the pointer changes to 🔁 and "Chart Area" appears in a ScreenTip.

Be sure to drag the chart from an empty part of the chart area so the entire chart moves, not just chart elements within the chart.

2. Hold down the **Alt** key, drag the chart up and to the left until its upper-left corner snaps to the upper-left corner of cell B16, and then release the mouse button and the **Alt** key. The upper-left corner of the chart is aligned with the upper-left corner of cell B16.

   Trouble? If the pie chart resizes or does not move to the new location, you probably didn't drag the chart from an empty part of the chart area. Press the Ctrl+Z keys to undo your last action, and then repeat Steps 1 and 2, being sure to drag the pie chart from the chart area.

   The chart moves to a new location, but it still covers some data and needs to be resized.

3. Move the pointer over the sizing handle in the lower-right corner of the selection box until the pointer changes to ⤢.

4. Hold down the **Alt** key, drag the sizing handle up to the lower-right corner of cell D27, and then release the mouse button and the **Alt** key. The chart resizes to cover the range B16:D27 and remains selected. See Figure 4-10.

Figure 4-10   **Moved and resized chart**

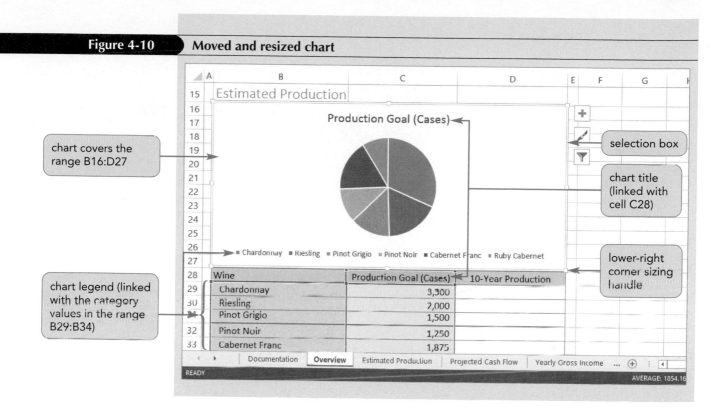

chart covers the range B16:D27

selection box

chart title (linked with cell C28)

chart legend (linked with the category values in the range B29:B34)

lower-right corner sizing handle

Working with Chart Elements

Every chart contains elements that can be formatted, added to the chart, or removed from the chart. For example, a pie chart has three elements—the chart title, the chart legend identifying each pie slice, and data labels that can be displayed next to each slice providing the data value or percentage associated with that slice. The Chart Elements button that appears next to a selected chart lists the elements associated with that chart. You can use this button to add, remove, and format individual elements. When you add or remove a chart element, the other elements resize to fit in the space. Live Preview shows how changing an element will affect the chart's appearance.

Carol doesn't want the pie chart to include a title because the text in cell B15 and the data in the range B28:D34 sufficiently explain the chart's purpose. However, she does want to display the data values next to the pie slices. You will remove the chart title element and add the data labels element.

TIP

To add and remove chart elements, you can also use the Add Chart Element button in the Chart Layouts group on the CHART TOOLS DESIGN tab.

To remove the pie chart title and add data labels to the slices:

1. Click the **pie chart** to select it. The selection box appears around the chart.

2. To the right of the selected chart, click the **Chart Elements** button +. A menu of chart elements that are available for the pie chart opens. As the checkmarks indicate, only the chart title and the chart legend are displayed in the pie chart.

3. Click the **Chart Title** check box to deselect it. The chart title is removed from the pie chart and the chart elements resize to fill the space.

4. Point to the **Data Labels** check box. Live Preview shows how the chart will look when the data labels showing the production goal for each wine are added to the pie slices.

5. Click the **Data Labels** check box to select it. The data labels are added to the chart. See Figure 4-11.

Figure 4-11 **Chart elements**

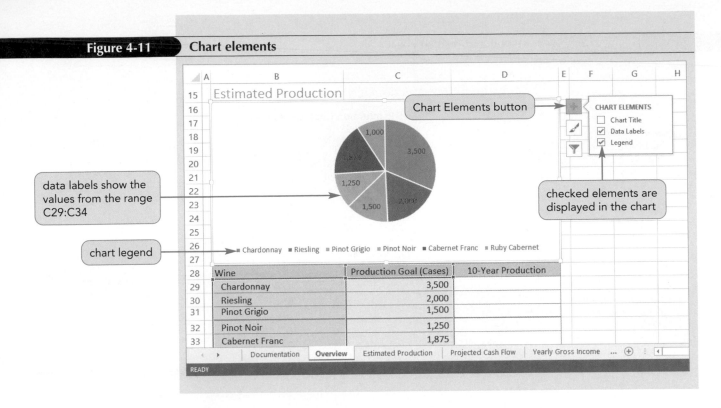

Choosing a Chart Style

When you create a chart, the chart is formatted with a style. Recall that a style is a collection of formats that are saved with a name and can then be applied at one time. In the pie chart you just created, the format of the chart title, the location of the legend, and the colors of the pie slices are all part of the default pie chart style. You can quickly change the appearance of a chart by selecting a different style from the Chart Styles gallery. Live Preview shows how a chart style will affect the chart.

Carol wants the pie slices to have a raised, three-dimensional look. You will explore different chart styles to find a style that best fulfills her request.

TIP

You can also select a chart style from the Chart Styles gallery in the Chart Styles group on the CHART TOOLS DESIGN tab.

To choose a different chart style for the wine production pie chart:

1. Click the **Chart Styles** button next to the selected pie chart. The Chart Styles gallery opens.

2. Point to different styles in the gallery. Live Preview shows the impact of each chart style on the pie chart's appearance.

3. Scroll to the bottom of the gallery, and then click the **Style 12** chart style. The chart style is applied to the pie chart. See Figure 4-12.

Figure 4-12   **Chart Styles gallery**

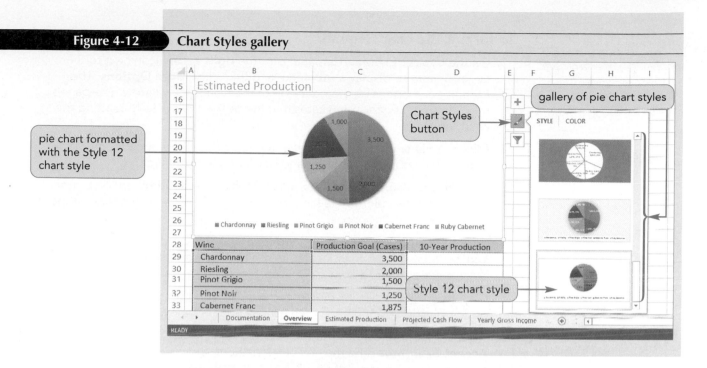

Formatting the Pie Chart Legend

You can fine-tune a chart style by formatting individual chart elements. From the Chart Elements button, you can open a submenu for each element that includes formatting options, such as the element's location within the chart. You can also open a Format pane, which has more options for formatting the selected chart element.

The default location for the pie chart legend is alongside the chart's bottom edge. Carol thinks the chart would look better if the legend were aligned with the right edge of the chart.

To reposition the pie chart legend:

1. Click the **Chart Elements** button [+] next to the selected pie chart.

2. Point to **Legend** in the CHART ELEMENTS menu to display a right arrow icon, and then click the **right arrow** icon [▶]. A submenu opens with formatting options available for the selected chart element. For a chart legend, the submenu offers placement options.

3. Point to **Left** to see a Live Preview of that formatting. The legend is aligned along the left side of the chart area, and the pie moves to the right to occupy the remaining space.

4. Click **Right** to place the legend along the right side of the chart area. The pie shifts to the left to make room for the legend.

The Chart Elements button also provides access to the Format pane, which has more design options. Carol wants you to add a drop shadow to the legend similar to the pie chart's drop shadow, change the fill color to a light gold, and add a light gray border. You'll use the Format pane to make these changes.

TIP

You can also open the Format pane by double-clicking any chart element.

To format the chart legend:

1. On the CHART ELEMENTS menu, click the **right arrow** icon next to the Legend entry to display a submenu, and then click **More Options**. The Format pane opens on the right side of the workbook window. The pane's title, "Format Legend," indicates that the options relate to formatting the chart legend.

2. Click the **Fill & Line** button near the top of the Format pane to display options for setting the fill color and border style of the legend.

3. Click **FILL** to display fill options, and then click the **Solid fill** option button to apply a solid fill color to the legend. Color and Transparency options appear below the fill color options.

4. Click the **Fill Color** button , and then click the **Gold, Accent 4, Lighter 60%** theme color located in the third row and eighth column of the color palette to add a light gold fill color to the legend.

5. Click **BORDER** to display the border options, and then click the **Solid line** option button. Additional border options appear below the border options.

6. Click the **Outline color** button , and then click the **Gray - 50%, Accent 3, Lighter 80%** theme color located in the second row and seventh column of the color palette to add a light gray border around the legend.

7. At the top of the Format Legend pane, click the **Effects** button to display options for special visual effects.

8. Click **Shadow** to display the shadow options, and then next to the Presets label, click the **Shadow** button to display a gallery of shadow effects.

9. Click the **Offset Diagonal Button Right** button in the first row and first column to apply the drop shadow effect to the legend. See Figure 4-13.

Figure 4-13   **Formatted chart legend**

Formatting Pie Chart Data Labels

You can modify the content and appearance of data labels, selecting what the labels contain as well as where the labels are positioned. By default, data labels are placed where they will keep the chart nicely proportioned, but you can specify a different location. For pie chart labels, you can move the labels to the center of the pie slices or place them outside of the slices. Another option is to set the labels as data callouts, with each label placed within a text bubble and connected to the slice with a callout line. Likewise, you can change the text and number styles used in the data labels as well. These options are all available in the Format pane. You can also drag and drop individual data labels, placing them anywhere within the chart. When a data label is placed far from its pie slice, a **leader line** is added to connect the data label to its pie slice.

The pie chart data labels display the production goal values for the different wines, but this information also appears on the worksheet directly below the chart. The Levitts want to include data labels that add new information to the chart—in this case, the percentage that each wine varietal adds to the whole. You will make this change.

TIP

You can also format chart elements using the formatting buttons on the HOME tab or on the CHART TOOLS FORMAT tab.

To display percentages in the wine production pie chart:

1. At the top of the Format pane, click the **Legend Options** arrow to display a menu of chart elements, and then click **Series "Production Goal (Cases)" Data Labels** to display the formatting options for data labels. The title of the Format pane changes to "Format Data Labels" and includes formatting options for data labels. Selection boxes appear around every data label in the pie chart.

2. Click the **Label Options** button ▥ near the top of the pane to display the options for the label contents and position. Data labels can contain series names, category names, values, and percentages.

3. Click the **Percentage** check box to display the percentage associated with each data label in the pie chart next to its value.

4. Click the **Value** check box to deselect it, removing the data series values from the data labels. The pie chart shows that Chardonnay accounts for 31.5 percent of the estimated wine production.

5. Click the **Outside End** option button to move the labels outside of the pie slices. The labels are easier to read in this location.

   The percentages are displayed with no decimal places, but Carol wants them to show one decimal place to provide a bit more accuracy in the chart.

6. Scroll down the Format pane, and then click **NUMBER** to show the formatting options for numbers.

7. Scroll down the Format pane, click the **Category** box to display the number formats, and then click **Percentage**. The percentages in the data labels include two decimal places.

8. In the Decimal places box, replace the value 2 with **1**, and then press the **Enter** key. The percentages display one decimal place. See Figure 4-14.

Figure 4-14 **Formatted data labels**

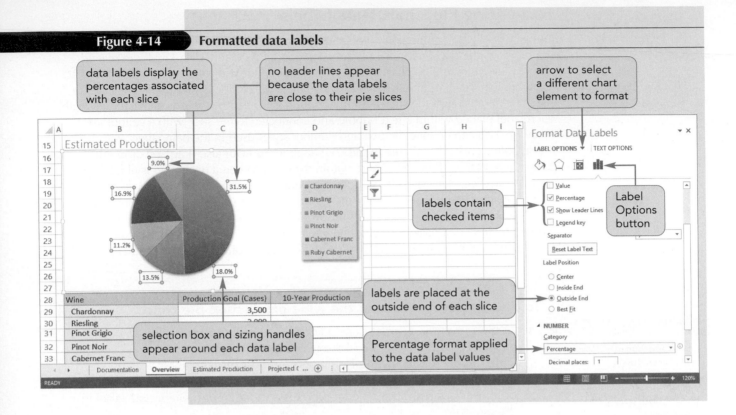

Setting the Pie Slice Colors

A pie slice is an example of a data marker that represents a single data value from a data series. You can format the appearance of individual data markers to make them stand out from the others. Pie slice colors should be as distinct as possible to avoid confusion. Depending on the printer quality or the monitor resolution, it might be difficult to distinguish between similarly colored slices. If data labels are displayed within the slice, you also need enough contrast between the slice color and the data label color to make the text readable.

The Levitts are concerned that the blue color of the Cabernet Franc slice will appear too dark when printed, and they want you to change it to a light shade of green.

To change the color of the Cabernet Franc pie slice:

1. Click any pie slice to select all of the slices in the pie chart.

2. Click the **Cabernet Franc** slice, which is the darker blue slice that represents 16.9 percent of the pie. Only that slice is selected, as you can see from the handles that appear at each corner of the slice.

3. Click the **HOME** tab, click the **Fill Color button arrow** in the Font group, and then click the **Green, Accent 6, Lighter 40%** theme color in the fourth row and last column of the gallery. The Cabernet Franc pie slice changes to a light green and the chart legend automatically updates to reflect that change.

You can also change the colors of all the pie slices by clicking the Chart Styles button next to the selected chart, clicking the COLOR heading, and then selecting a color scheme.

Exploding a Pie Chart

Pie slices do not need to be fixed within the pie. An **exploded pie chart** moves one slice away from the others as if someone were taking the piece away from the pie. Exploded pie charts are useful for emphasizing one category above all of the others. For example, to emphasize the fact that Levitt Winery will be producing more Chardonnay than any other wine, you could explode that single slice, moving it away from the other slices.

To explode a pie slice, first click the pie to select all of the slices, and then click the single slide you want to move. Make sure that a selection box appears around only that slice. Drag the slice away from the pie to offset it from the others. You can explode multiple slices by selecting each slice in turn and dragging them away. To explode all of the slices, select the entire pie and drag the pointer away from the pie's center. Each slice will be exploded and separated from the others. Although you can explode more than one slice, the resulting pie chart is rarely effective as a visual aid to the reader.

Formatting the Chart Area

The chart's background, which is called the chart area, can also be formatted using fill colors, border styles, and special effects such as drop shadows and blurred edges. The chart area fill color used in the pie chart is white, which blends in with the worksheet background. Carol wants you to change the fill color to a light gold to match the worksheet's color scheme, and to make the chart stand out better.

To change the chart area of the pie chart to light gold:

1. Click a blank area within the chart, not containing either a pie slice or the chart legend. The chart area is selected, which you can verify because the Format pane title changes to "Format Chart Area."

2. On the HOME tab, in the Font group, click the **Fill Color button arrow** , and then click the **Gold, Accent 4, Lighter 80%** theme color in the second row and eighth column. The chart area fill color is now light gold. See Figure 4-15.

Figure 4-15   Chart area fill color

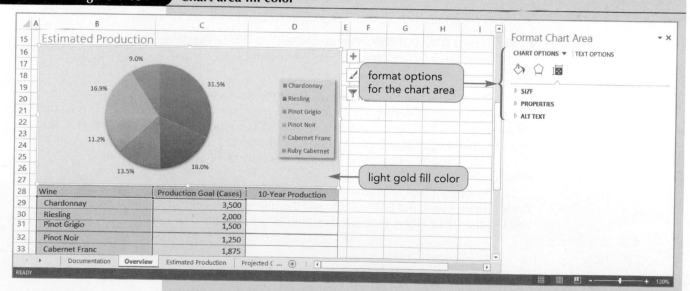

You are done formatting the pie chart, so you will close the Format pane to keep the window uncluttered.

3. Click the **Close** button ☒ on the title bar of the Format pane. The pane closes, leaving more space for viewing the worksheet contents.

Performing What-If Analyses with Charts

A chart is linked to its data source. For the wine production pie chart, the chart title is linked to the text of cell C28, the size of the pie slices is based on the production goals in the range C29:C34, and the category names are linked to the category values in the range B29:B34. Any changes to these cells affect the chart's content and appearance. This makes charts a powerful tool for data exploration and what-if analysis. Excel uses **chart animation** to slow down the effect of changing data source values, making it easier to see how changing one value affects the chart.

Bob and Carol want to see how the pie chart would change if they were to alter some of their production goals. You will edit the data source to see how the changes affect the chart.

To apply a what-if analysis to the pie chart:

1. In cell **C29**, enter **5500** to increase the production goal for Chardonnay by 2000 cases. The pie slice associated with Chardonnay becomes larger, slowly changing from 31.5 percent to 41.9 percent because of the chart animation. The size of the remaining slices and their percentages are reduced to compensate.

2. In cell **C29**, restore the value to **3,500**. The pie slices return to their initial sizes and the percentages return to their initial values.

3. In cell **C30**, change the production goal for Riesling from 2,000 to **4,000**. The orange slice representing Riesling is now the largest slice in the pie, comprising 30.5 percent of the projected production.

4. In cell **C30**, restore the value to **2,000**.

   Bob points out that the legend entry "Riesling" should be changed to "White Riesling" to distinguish it from other Riesling varietals.

5. In cells **B30** and **B39**, change the text to **White Riesling**. The chart legend automatically updates to show the revised wine name.

Another type of what-if analysis is to limit the data to a subset of the original values in a process called **filtering**. For example, the pie chart shows the estimated production for all six varietals of wine that Levitt Winery will produce. Sometimes, however, Carol and Bob might want to see information on only the red wines or only the white wines. Rather than creating a new chart that includes only those wines, you can filter an existing chart.

Levitt Winery plans to produce three white wines—Chardonnay, White Riesling, and Pinot Grigio. Carol and Bob want to see the different percentages of white wine. You will use the Chart Filters button to limit the pie chart to those three wines.

To filter the pie chart to show only white wines:

▶ **1.** Click the pie chart to select it.

▶ **2.** Click the **Chart Filters** button ▼ next to the chart to open a menu listing the categories in the chart. In this case, the categories are the different types of wines.

▶ **3.** Click the **Pinot Noir**, **Cabernet Franc**, and **Ruby Cabernet** check boxes to deselect them, leaving only the Chardonnay, White Riesling, and Pinot Grigio check boxes selected.

▶ **4.** At the bottom of the Chart Filters menu, click the **Apply** button. Excel filters the chart, showing only the white wines. After filtering the data, the chart shows that 50 percent of the white wines produced will be Chardonnay. See Figure 4-16.

Figure 4-16   **Filtered pie chart**

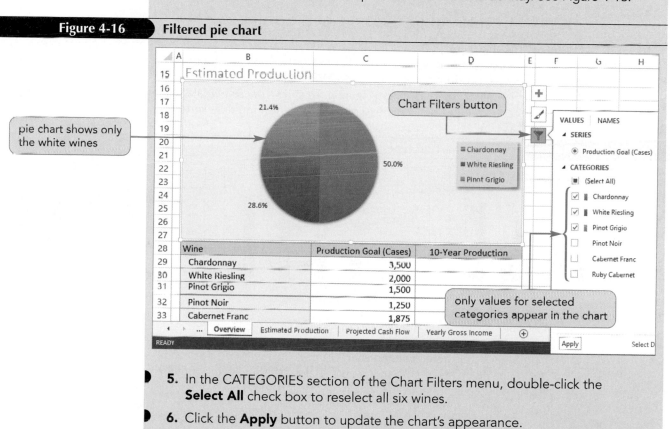

▶ **5.** In the CATEGORIES section of the Chart Filters menu, double-click the **Select All** check box to reselect all six wines.

▶ **6.** Click the **Apply** button to update the chart's appearance.

▶ **7.** Press the **Esc** key to close the menu, leaving the chart selected.

The pie chart that displays the winery's projected level of production for different wines is complete. Next, you'll use column charts to examine the winery's financial projections for the next 10 years.

Creating a Column Chart

A **column chart** displays data values as columns with the height of each column based on the data value. A column chart turned on its side is called a **bar chart**, with the length of the bar determined by the data value. It is better to use column and bar charts than pie charts when the number of categories is large or the data values are close in value. For example, Figure 4-17 displays the same data as a pie chart and a column chart. As you can see, it's difficult to determine which pie slice is biggest and by how much. It is much simpler to see the differences in a column or bar chart.

Figure 4-17   **Data displayed as a pie chart and a column chart**

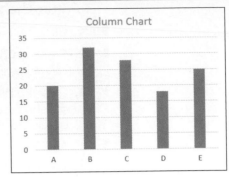

Comparing Column Chart Subtypes

Unlike pie charts, which can show only one data series, column and bar charts can display multiple data series. For example, you can plot three data series (such as the wine production of Chardonnay, White Riesling, and Cabernet Franc) against one category (such as Years). Figure 4-18 shows the same data charted on the three column chart subtypes available to display data from multiple series.

Figure 4-18   **Column chart subtypes**

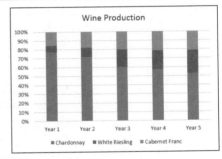

| Clustered Column | Stacked Column | 100% Stacked Column |

The **clustered column chart** displays the data series in separate columns side-by-side so that you can compare the relative heights of the columns in the three series. The clustered column chart in Figure 4-18 compares the number of cases of each wine produced in Year 1 through Year 5. Note that the winery produces mostly Chardonnay with the other varietals increasing in volume in the later years.

The **stacked column chart** places the data series values within combined columns showing how much is contributed by each series. The stacked column chart in Figure 4-18 gives information on the total number of wine cases produced each year, and how each year's production is split among the three wine varietals.

Finally, the **100% stacked column chart** makes the same comparison as the stacked column chart except that the stacked sections are expressed as percentages. As you can see from the 100% stacked column chart in Figure 4-18, Chardonnay accounts for about 75 percent of the wine produced in Year 1, and that percentage steadily declines to about 50 percent in Year 5 as more cases of White Riesling and Cabernet Franc are produced.

The chart subtype you use depends on what you want to highlight with your data.

Creating a Clustered Column Chart

The process for creating a column chart is the same as for creating a pie chart. First, you select the data source. Then, you select the type of chart you want to create. After the chart is embedded in the worksheet, you can move and resize the chart as well as change the chart's design, layout, and format.

Bob and Carol want to show the projected revenue and expenses for each of the next 10 years. Because this requires comparing the data series values, you will create a clustered column chart.

To create a column chart for the revenue and expenses data:

1. Go to the **Projected Cash Flow** worksheet.

2. Select the nonadjacent range **B4:L4;B10:L10;B18:L18** containing the Year categories in row 4, the Total Revenue data series in row 10, and the Total Expenses data series in row 18. Because you selected a nonadjacent range, the Quick Analysis tool is not available.

3. On the ribbon, click the **INSERT** tab. The Charts group contains buttons for inserting different types of charts.

TIP

You can also open the Insert Chart dialog box to see the chart types recommended for the selected data source.

4. In the Charts group, click the **Recommended Charts** button. The Insert Chart dialog box opens with the Recommended Charts tab displayed. The charts show how the selected data would appear in that chart type. See Figure 4-19.

Figure 4-19   **Clustered column chart being created**

5. Make sure the **Clustered Column** chart is selected, and then click the **OK** button. The clustered column chart is embedded in the Projected Cash Flow worksheet.

6. Click the **Chart Styles** button 🖊 next to the selected column chart.

7. In the STYLE gallery, scroll down and click the **Style 14** chart style to format the columns with drop shadows.

8. Click the **Chart Styles** button 🖊 to close the STYLE gallery.

Changing a Chart Type

After creating a chart, you can easily switch the chart to a different chart type without having to recreate the chart from scratch. For example, if the data in a column chart would be more effective presented as a line chart, you can change its chart type rather than creating a new chart. Clicking the Change Chart Type button in the Type group on the CHART TOOLS DESIGN tab opens a dialog box similar to the Insert Chart dialog box, from which you can select a new chart type.

Moving a Chart to a Different Worksheet

You can move a chart from one worksheet to another, or you can place the chart in its own chart sheet. In a chart sheet, the chart is enlarged to fill the entire workspace. The Move Chart dialog box provides options for moving charts between worksheets and chart sheets. You can also cut and paste a chart between workbooks.

Bob and Carol want all of the charts to be displayed in the Overview worksheet. You will move the clustered column chart to the Overview worksheet, and then resize it.

To move the clustered column chart to the Overview worksheet:

1. Make sure the clustered column chart is selected.

2. On the CHART TOOLS DESIGN tab, in the Location group, click the **Move Chart** button. The Move Chart dialog box opens.

3. Click the **Object in** arrow to display a list of the worksheets in the active workbook, and then click **Overview**.

4. Click the **OK** button. The embedded chart moves from the Projected Cash Flow worksheet to the Overview worksheet, and remains selected.

5. Hold down the **Alt** key as you drag the chart so that its upper-left corner is aligned with the upper-left corner of cell F16, and then release the mouse button and the **Alt** key to snap the upper-left corner of the chart to the worksheet.

6. Hold down the **Alt** key as you drag the lower-right sizing handle of the clustered column chart to the lower-right corner of cell **M29**, and then release the mouse button and the **Alt** key. The chart now covers the range F16:M29.

> **TIP**
>
> To set an exact chart size, enter the height and width values in the Size group on the CHART TOOLS FORMAT tab.

The revenue and expenses chart shows that the winery will produce little revenue during its first few years as it establishes itself and its customer base. It is only during Year 6 that the revenue will outpace the expenses. After that, Bob and Carol hope that the winery's revenue will increase rapidly while expenses grow at a more moderate pace.

Changing and Formatting a Chart Title

When a chart has a single data series, the name of the data series is used for the chart title. When a chart has more than one data series, the "Chart Title" placeholder appears as the temporary title of the chart. You can then replace the placeholder text with a more descriptive title.

The clustered column chart includes the Chart Title placeholder. Bob and Carol want you to replace this with a more descriptive title.

To change the title of the column chart:

1. At the top of the column chart, click **Chart Title** to select the placeholder text.

2. Type **Projected Revenue and Expenses** as the new title, and then press the **Enter** key. The new title is entered into the chart, and the chart title element remains selected.

3. Click the **HOME** tab, and then use the buttons in the Font group to remove the bold from the chart title, change the font to **Calibri Light**, and change the font color to the **Blue, Accent 1** theme color. See Figure 4-20.

Figure 4-20   Column chart

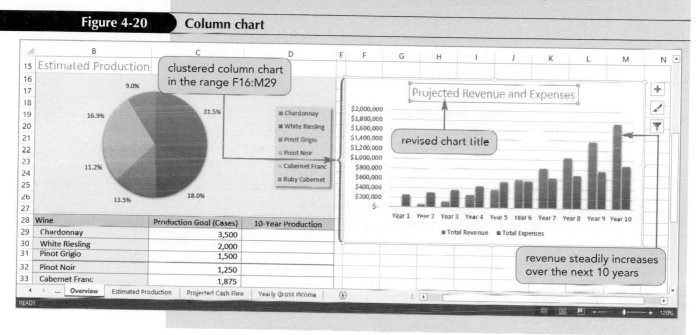

Creating a Stacked Column Chart

The next chart that the Levitts want added to the Overview worksheet is a chart that projects the expenses incurred by the winery over the next 10 years broken down by category. Because this chart looks at how different parts of the whole vary across time, it would be better to display that information in a stacked column chart. You will create this chart based on the data located in the Projected Cash Flow worksheet.

To create a stacked column chart:

1. Go to the **Projected Cash Flow** worksheet, and then select the nonadjacent range **B4:L4;B13:L17** containing the year categories and five data series for different types of expenses.

2. Click the **INSERT** tab, and then click the **Insert Column Chart** button in the Charts group. A list of column chart subtypes appears.

3. Click the **Stacked Column** icon (the second icon in the 2-D Column section). The stacked column chart is embedded in the Projected Cash Flow worksheet.

4. With the chart still selected, click the **Chart Styles** button ✎, and then apply the **Style 11** chart style located at the bottom of the style gallery.

You'll place this stacked column chart on the Overview worksheet.

5. On the CHART TOOLS DESIGN tab, in the Location group, click the **Move Chart** button to open the Move Chart dialog box.

6. Click the **Object in** arrow, and then click the **Overview** worksheet.

7. Click the **OK** button. The stacked column chart is moved to the Overview worksheet.

As with the clustered column chart, you'll move and resize the stacked column chart and add a descriptive chart title.

To edit the stacked column chart:

TIP

To retain the chart's proportions as you resize it, hold down the Shift key as you drag the sizing handle.

1. Move and resize the stacked column chart so that it covers the range **F31:M43** in the Overview worksheet. Use the Alt key to help you align the chart's location and size with the underlying worksheet grid.

2. Select the chart title, type **Breakdown of Business Expenses** as the new title, and then press the **Enter** key.

3. With the chart title still selected, change the font style to **non-bold**; **Blue, Accent 1**; **Calibri Light** font to match the clustered column chart. See Figure 4-21.

Figure 4-21 **Stacked column chart**

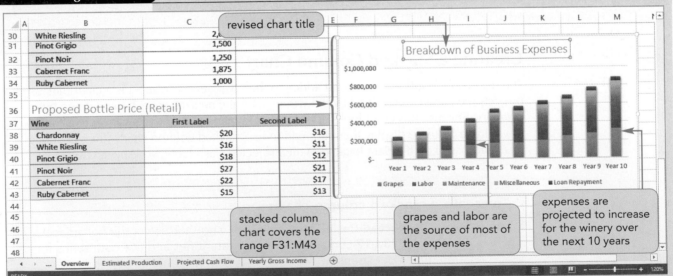

4. Save the workbook.

The chart clearly shows that the winery's main expenses over the next 10 years will come from the purchase of grapes and labor costs. General maintenance, miscellaneous, and the business loan repayment constitute a smaller portion of the company's projected expenses. The overall yearly expense of running the winery is expected to increase from about $250,000 in Year 1 to almost $900,000 by Year 10.

PROSKILLS

Written Communication: Communicating Effectively with Charts

Studies show that people more easily interpret information when it is presented as a graphic rather than in a table. As a result, charts can help communicate the real story underlying the facts and figures you present to colleagues and clients. A well-designed chart can illuminate the bigger picture that might be hidden by viewing only the numbers. However, poorly designed charts can mislead readers and make it more difficult to interpret data.

To create effective and useful charts, keep in mind the following tips as you design charts:

- **Keep it simple.** Do not clutter a chart with too many graphical elements. Focus attention on the data rather than on decorative elements that do not inform.
- **Focus on the message.** Design the chart to highlight the points you want to convey to readers.
- **Limit the number of data series.** Most charts should display no more than four or five data series. Pie charts should have no more than six slices.
- **Choose colors carefully.** Display different data series in contrasting colors to make it easier to distinguish one series from another. Modify the default colors as needed to make them distinct on the screen and in the printed copy.
- **Limit your chart to a few text styles.** Use a maximum of two or three different text styles in the same chart. Having too many text styles in one chart can distract attention from the data.

The goal of written communication is always to inform the reader in the simplest, most accurate, and most direct way possible. When creating worksheets and charts, everything in the workbook should be directed toward that end.

So far, you have determined monthly payments by using the PMT function, and created and formatted a pie chart and two column charts. In the next session, you'll continue your work on the winery's business plan by creating line charts, combination charts, sparklines, and data bars.

REVIEW

Session 4.1 Quick Check

1. You want to take out a loan for $130,000. The annual interest on the loan is 5 percent with payments due monthly. You plan to repay the loan in 15 years. Write the formula to calculate the monthly payment required to completely repay the loan under those conditions.
2. What function do you use to determine how many payment periods are required to repay a loan?
3. What three chart elements are included in a pie chart?
4. A data series contains values grouped into 10 categories. Would this data be better displayed as a pie chart or a column chart? Explain why.
5. A research firm wants to create a chart that displays the total population growth of a county over a 10-year period broken down by five ethnicities. Which chart type best displays this information? Explain why.
6. If the research firm wants to display the changing ethnic profile of the county over time as a percentage of the county population, which chart type should it use? Explain why.
7. If the research firm is interested in comparing the numeric sizes of different ethnic groups over time, which chart should it use? Explain why.
8. If the research firm wants to display the ethnic profile of the county only for the current year, which chart should it use? Explain why.
9. How does chart animation help you perform a what-if analysis?

Session 4.2 Visual Overview:

The SPARKLINE TOOLS DESIGN contextual tab provides commands to format sparklines.

A **sparkline** is a chart that is displayed within a cell. You can create line, column, and win/loss sparklines.

Line sparklines can contain data markers to identify the high and low points, negative points, first and last points, and all points.

These column sparklines have been ungrouped and formatted individually.

A **data bar** is a conditional format that adds a horizontal bar to the background of a cell proportional in length to the cell's value.

Wine	Production Goal (Cases)	10-Year Production
Chardonnay	3,500	
White Riesling	2,000	
Pinot Grigio	1,500	
Pinot Noir	1,250	
Cabernet Franc	1,875	
Ruby Cabernet	1,000	

Wine	First Label	Second Label
Chardonnay	$20	$16
White Riesling	$16	$11
Pinot Grigio	$18	$12
Pinot Noir	$27	$21
Cabernet Franc	$22	$17
Ruby Cabernet	$15	$13

Levitt Winery - Excel

FILE   HOME   INSERT   PAGE LAYOUT   FORMULAS   DATA   REVIEW   VIEW

Edit Data   Line   Column   Win/Loss

High Point   First Point
Low Point   Last Point
Negative Points   Markers

Sparkline   Type   Show

D29

Documentation   Overview   Estimated Production   Projected Ca ...

READY

Charts, Sparklines, and Data Bars

Sparklines can be grouped or ungrouped. **Grouped sparklines** share a common format. **Ungrouped sparklines** can be formatted individually.

The **plot area** is the part of the chart that contains the graphical representation of the data series.

A **combination chart** combines two or more Excel chart types into a single graph. This chart combines a column chart and a line chart.

An **axis title** is descriptive text that appears next to an axis.

Data callouts are data labels that appear as callout bubbles pointing to data markers.

A **line chart** displays data values using a connected line rather than columns or bars.

Gridlines extend the values of the major or minor tick marks across the plot area.

Creating a Line Chart

Line charts are typically used when the data consists of values drawn from categories that follow a sequential order at evenly spaced intervals, such as historical data that is recorded monthly, quarterly, or yearly. Like column charts, a line chart can be used with one or more data series. When multiple data series are included, the data values are plotted on different lines with varying line colors.

Bob and Carol want to use a line chart to show the winery's potential cash flow over the next decade. Cash flow measures the amount of cash flowing into and out of a business annually; it is one measure of a business's financial health and ability to make its payments. Because the cash flow values are the only data series, only one line will appear on the chart. You will create the line chart now.

To create the projected cash flow line chart:

When charting table values, do not include the summary totals because they will be treated as another category.

1. If you took a break at the end of the previous session, make sure the Levitt Winery workbook is open.

2. Go to the **Projected Cash Flow** worksheet, and then select the nonadjacent range **B4:L4;B27:L27** containing the Year categories from row 4 and the Cash Flow data series from row 27.

3. Click the **INSERT** tab, and then click the **Recommended Charts** button in the Charts group. The Insert Chart dialog box opens, showing different ways to chart the selected data.

4. Click the second chart listed (the Line chart), and then click the **OK** button. The line chart of the year-end cash flow values is embedded in the Projected Cash Flow worksheet.

5. Format the line chart with the **Style 15** chart style to give the line a raised 3-D appearance.

6. Move the chart to the **Overview** worksheet.

7. Move and resize the line chart in the Overview worksheet so that it covers the range **B45:D58**.

8. Format the chart title with the same **non-bold**; **Blue, Accent 1**; **Calibri Light** font you applied to the two column charts. See Figure 4-22.

Figure 4-22 — Line chart of the projected cash flow

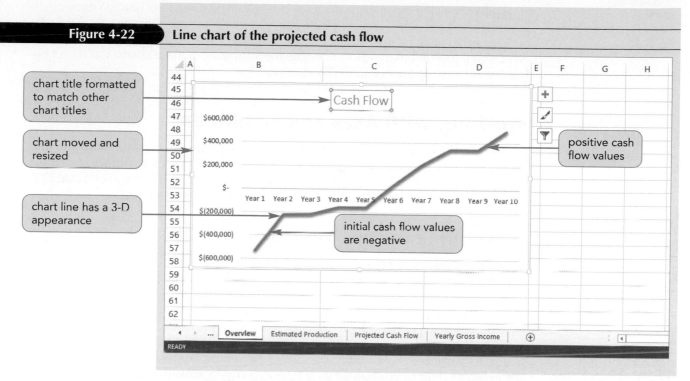

chart title formatted to match other chart titles

chart moved and resized

chart line has a 3-D appearance

positive cash flow values

initial cash flow values are negative

The line chart shows that Levitt Winery will have a negative cash flow in its early years and that the annual cash flow will increase throughout the decade, showing a positive cash flow starting in its sixth year.

Line Charts and Scatter Charts

INSIGHT

Line charts can sometimes be confused with XY (Scatter) charts; but they are very different chart types. A line chart is more like a column chart that uses lines instead of columns. In a line chart, the data series are plotted against category values. These categories are assumed to have some sequential order. If the categories represent dates or times, they must be evenly spaced in time. For example, the Cash Flow line chart plotted the cash flow values against categories that ranged sequentially from Year 1 to Year 10.

A scatter chart has no category values. Instead, one series of data values is plotted against another. For example, if you were analyzing the relationship between height and weight among high school students, you would use a scatter chart because both weight and height are data values. On the other hand, if you charted height measures against weight categories (Underweight, Normal, Overweight), a line chart would be more appropriate.

Scatter charts are more often used in statistical analysis and scientific studies in which the researcher is attempting to find a relationship between one variable and another. For that purpose, Excel includes several statistical tools to augment scatter charts, such as trendlines that provide the best fitting line or curve to the data. You can add a trendline by right-clicking the data series in the chart, and then clicking Add Trendline on the shortcut menu. From the Format Trendline pane that opens you can select different types of trendlines, including exponential and logarithmic lines as well as linear (straight) lines.

You have created three charts that provide a visual picture of the Levitt Winery business plan. Bob and Carol anticipate lean years as the winery becomes established; but they expect that by the end of 10 years, the winery will be profitable and stable. Next, you'll look at other tools to fine-tune the formatting of these charts. You'll start by looking at the scale applied to the chart values.

Working with Axes and Gridlines

A chart's vertical and horizontal axes are based on the values in the data series and the category values. In many cases, the axes display the data in the most visually effective and informative way. Sometimes, however, you will want to modify the axes' scale, add gridlines, and make other changes to better highlight the chart data.

Editing the Scale of the Vertical Axis

The range of values, or **scale**, of an axis is based on the values in the data source. The default scale usually ranges from 0 (if the data source has no negative values) to the maximum value. If the scale includes negative values, it ranges from the minimum value to the maximum value. The vertical, or value, axis shows the range of values in the data series; the horizontal, or category, axis shows the category values.

Excel divides the scale into regular intervals, which are marked on the axis with **tick marks** and labels. For example, the scale of the vertical axis for the Projected Revenue and Expenses chart ranges from $0 up to $2,000,000 in increments of $200,000. Having more tick marks at smaller intervals could make the chart difficult to read because the tick mark labels might start to overlap. Likewise, having fewer tick marks at larger intervals could make the chart less informative. **Major tick marks** identify the main units on the chart axis while **minor tick marks** identify the smaller intervals between the major tick marks.

Some charts involve multiple data series that have vastly different values. In those instances, you can create dual axis charts. You can plot one data series against a **primary axis**, which usually appears along the left side of the chart, and the other against a **secondary axis**, which is usually placed on the right side of the chart. The two axes can be based on entirely different scales.

By default, no titles appear next to the value and category axes. This is fine when the axis labels are self-explanatory. Otherwise, you can add descriptive axis titles. In general, you should avoid cluttering a chart with extra elements such as axis titles when that information is easily understood from other parts of the chart.

The Levitts think that the value axis scale for the Projected Revenue and Expenses chart is too crowded, and they want tick marks placed at intervals of $250,000 ranging from $0 to $1,750,000. You will modify the scale of the value axis.

To change the scale of the vertical axis:

▶ **1.** Double-click the vertical axis of the Projected Revenue and Expenses chart to open the Format pane.

The Format Axis pane has options to modify the value axis. The Bounds section provides the minimum and maximum boundaries of the axis, which in this case are set from 0.0 to 2.0E6 (which stands for 2,000,000). Note that minimum and maximum values are set to Auto, which means that Excel automatically set these boundaries based on the data values.

▶ **2.** In the Bounds section of the AXIS OPTIONS, click in the **Maximum** box, delete the current value, type **1750000** as the new value, and then press the **Enter** key. Excel changes the maximum value of the vertical axis to $1,750,000.

TIP

To return a scale value to Auto, click the Reset button next to the value in the Format pane.

The Units section provides the intervals between the major tick marks and between minor tick marks. These intervals are also set automatically by Excel.

3. In the Units section, click in the **Major** box, delete the current value, type **250000** as the new interval between major tick marks, and then press the **Enter** key. The scale of the value axis has been changed. See Figure 4-23.

Figure 4-23   **Formatted value axis**

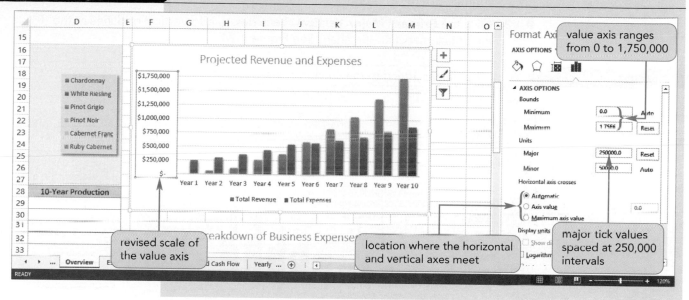

The revised axis scale makes the values easier to read and interpret.

Displaying Unit Labels

When a chart involves large numbers, the axis labels can take up a lot of the available chart area and be difficult to read. You can simplify the chart's appearance by displaying units of measure more appropriate to the data values. For example, you can display the value 20 to represent 20,000 or 20,000,000. This is particularly useful when space is at a premium, such as in an embedded chart confined to a small area of the worksheet.

To display a units label, you double-click the axis to open the Format pane displaying options to format the axis. Select the units type from the Display units box. You can choose unit labels to represent values measured in the hundreds up to the trillions. Excel will modify the numbers on the selected axis and add a label so that readers will know what the axis values represent.

Adding Gridlines

Gridlines are horizontal and vertical lines that help you compare data and category values. Depending on the chart style, gridlines may or may not appear in a chart, though you can add or remove them separately. Gridlines are placed at the major tick marks on the axes, or you can set them to appear at the minor tick marks.

The chart style used for the two column charts and the line chart includes horizontal gridlines. Carol and Bob want you to add vertical gridlines to help further separate one set of year values from another. You'll add major vertical gridlines to the Projected Revenue and Expenses chart.

To add vertical gridlines to the Projected Revenue and Expenses chart:

1. With the Projected Revenue and Expenses chart still selected, click the **Chart Elements** button ＋ next to the selected column chart. The menu of chart elements appears.

2. Point to **Gridlines**, and then click the **right arrow** that appears to open a submenu of gridline options.

3. Click the **Primary Major Vertical** check box to add vertical gridlines at the major tick marks on the chart. See Figure 4-24.

Figure 4-24 **Vertical gridlines added to the column chart**

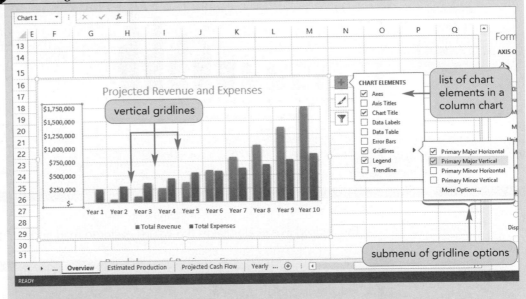

4. Press the **Esc** key to close the Chart Elements menu.

Working with Column Widths

Category values do not have the scale options used with data values. However, you can set the spacing between one column and another in your column charts. You can also define the width of the columns. As with the vertical axis, the default spacing and width are set automatically by Excel. A column chart with several categories will naturally make those columns thinner and more tightly packed.

The Levitts think that the columns in the Projected Revenue and Expenses chart are spaced too closely, making it difficult to distinguish one year's values from another. They want you to increase the gap between the columns.

To format the chart columns:

1. Make sure the Projected Revenue and Expenses chart is still selected and the Format pane is still open.

2. In the Format pane, click the **AXIS OPTIONS arrow**, and then click **Series "Total Revenue"** from the list of chart elements. The Format pane title changes to "Format Data Series" and all of the columns that show total revenue values are selected.

TIP

You can use the up and down spin arrows in the Gap Width box to fine-tune the gap width in 1 percent increments.

3. In the Format pane, click **SERIES OPTIONS** to display the list of options, if necessary. Series Overlap sets the amount of overlap between columns of different data series. Gap Width sets the amount of space between one group of columns and the next.

4. Drag the **Gap Width** slider until **150%** appears in the Gap Width box. The gap between groups of columns increases and the individual column widths decrease to make room for the larger gap. See Figure 4-25.

Figure 4-25   **Gap width between columns**

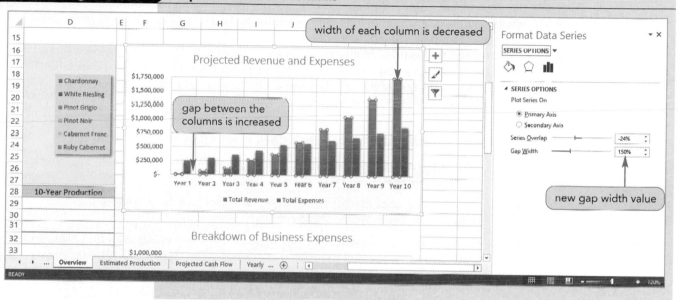

Formatting Data Markers

Each value from a data series is represented by a data marker. In pie charts, the data markers are the individual pie slices. In column charts, the columns are the data markers. In a line chart, the data markers are the points connected by the line. Depending on the line chart style, these data marker points can be displayed or hidden.

In the Cash Flow line chart, the data marker points are hidden and only the line connecting them is visible. Carol wants you to display these data markers and change their fill color to white so that they stand out, making the chart easier to understand.

To display and format the line chart data markers:

1. Scroll down the worksheet to display the Cash Flow line chart, and then double-click the line to change the Format pane to the Format Data Series pane.

2. Click the **Fill & Line** button. You can choose to display the format options for lines or data markers.

3. Click **MARKER**, if necessary, and then click **MARKER OPTIONS** to display a list of options for the line chart data markers. Currently, the None option button is selected to hide the data markers.

4. Click the **Automatic** option button to automatically display the markers. The data markers are now visible in the line chart, but they have a blue fill color. You will change this fill color to white.

▶ **5.** Click **FILL**, if necessary, to expand the fill options.

▶ **6.** Click the **Solid fill** option button, click the **Fill Color** button, and then click the **White, Background 1** theme color. The fill color for the data markers in the line chart changes to white.

▶ **7.** Press the **Esc** key to deselect the data markers in the line chart.

In many charts, you will want to highlight an important data point. Data labels provide a way to identify the different values in a chart. Whether you include data labels depends on the chart, the complexity of the data and presentation, and the chart's purpose. You can include data labels for every data marker, or you can include data labels for individual data points.

Carol and Bob want to highlight that at the end of the tenth year, the winery should have an annual cash flow that exceeds $500,000. They want you to add a data label that displays the value of the last data marker in the chart at that data point.

To add a data label to the last data marker in the line chart:

▶ **1.** Click the line in the line chart to select the entire data series, including all of the data markers.

▶ **2.** Click the last data marker to select it. Selection handles appear around this data marker, but not any of the others.

▶ **3.** Click the **Chart Elements** button [+] next to the line chart, and then click the **Data Labels** check box to insert a checkmark. The data label appears above only the selected data marker.

▶ **4.** Click the **Data Labels arrow** to display a menu of data label positions and options, and then click **Data Callout**. The data label is changed to a data callout box that includes both the category value and the data value, displaying "Year 10, $502,250." You will modify this callout to display only the data value.

▶ **5.** Double-click the data callout to select it. The Format pane is titled "Format Data Labels."

▶ **6.** Click the **Label Options** button [▮▮], and then click **LABEL OPTIONS**, if necessary, to display those options.

▶ **7.** Click the **Category Name** check box to deselect it.

▶ **8.** Press the **Esc** key to deselect the data label. The data callout now displays only $502,250. See Figure 4-26.

Figure 4-26 Formatted data markers and data label

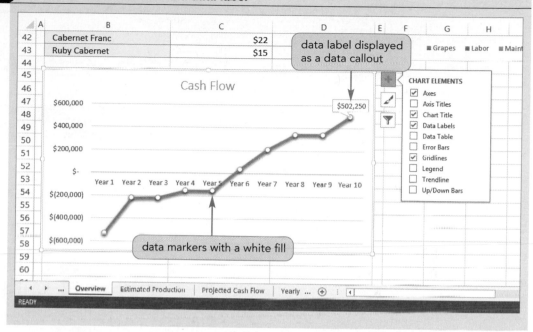

Formatting the Plot Area

The chart area covers the entire background of the chart, whereas the plot area includes only that portion of the chart in which the data markers, such as the columns in a column chart, have been placed or plotted. You can format the plot area by changing its fill and borders, and by adding visual effects. Changes to the plot area are often made in conjunction with the chart area.

Carol and Bob want you to format the chart area and plot area of the Projected Revenue and Expenses chart. You'll set the chart area fill color to a light gold to match the pie chart, and the plot area fill color to white.

To change the fill colors of the chart and plot areas:

1. Scroll the worksheet up and select the Projected Revenue and Expenses chart.

2. On the ribbon, click the **CHART TOOLS FORMAT** tab.

3. In the Current Selection group, click the **Chart Elements** arrow to display a list of chart elements in the current chart, and then click **Chart Area**. The chart area is selected in the chart.

4. In the Shape Styles group, click the **Shape Fill** button, and then click the **Gold, Accent 4, Lighter 80%** theme color in the second row and eighth column. The entire background of the chart changes to light gold.

5. In the Current Selection group, click the **Chart Elements** arrow, and then click **Plot Area** to select that chart element.

6. Change the fill color of the plot area to **white**. See Figure 4-27.

Figure 4-27   **Final Projected Revenue and Expenses chart**

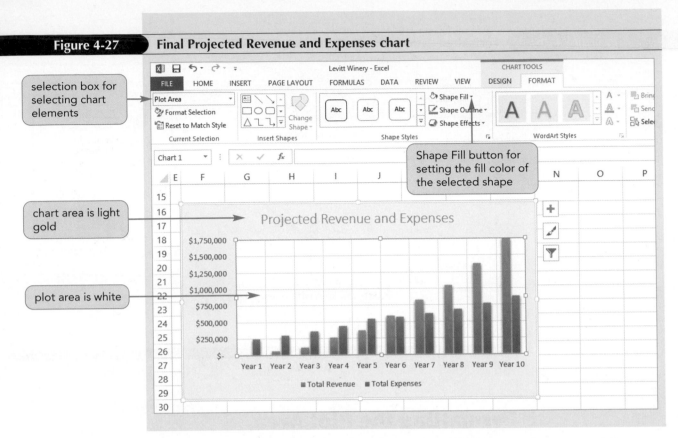

Bob and Carol like the appearance of the Projected Revenue and Expenses chart, and they want the same general design applied to the Breakdown of Business Expenses column chart and the Cash Flow line chart. You will add vertical gridlines to each chart, and then change the chart area fill color to light gold and the plot area fill color to white.

To format the Breakdown of Business Expenses column chart and the Cash Flow line chart:

1. Select the **Breakdown of Business Expenses** column chart.

2. Select the **chart area**, and then set the fill color of the chart area to the **Gold, Accent 4, Lighter 80%** theme color.

3. Select the **plot area**, and then change the fill color to **white**.

   Next, you'll add vertical gridlines to the chart. You can also use the CHART TOOLS DESIGN tab to add chart elements such as gridlines.

4. On the ribbon, click the **CHART TOOLS DESIGN** tab.

5. In the Chart Layouts group, click the **Add Chart Element** button, scroll down the chart elements, point to **Gridlines**, and then click **Primary Major Vertical** on the submenu. Vertical gridlines are added to the chart. See Figure 4-28.

Figure 4-28 **Final Breakdown of Business Expenses chart**

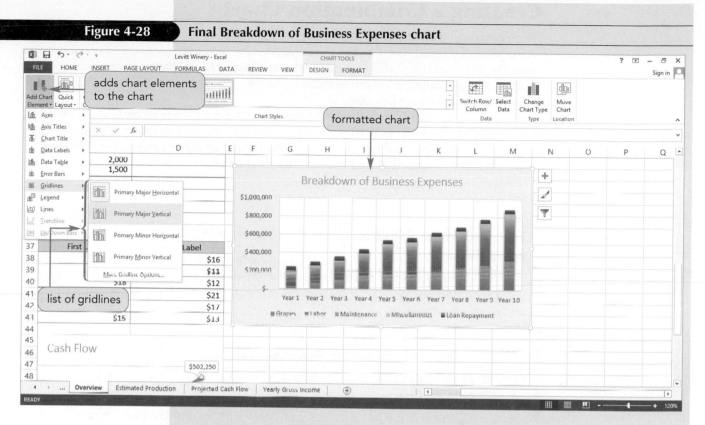

6. Scroll down the worksheet, select the **Cash Flow** line chart, and then repeat Steps 2 through 5 to set the chart area fill color to light gold, set the plot area fill color to white, and add major gridlines to the chart's primary axis.

The Breakdown of Business Expenses column chart and the Cash Flow line chart are now formatted with the same design.

INSIGHT

Overlaying Chart Elements

An embedded chart takes up less space than a chart sheet. However, it can be challenging to fit all of the chart elements into that smaller space. One solution is to overlay one element on top of another. The most commonly overlaid elements are the chart title and the chart legend. To overlay the chart title, click the Chart Title arrow from the list of Chart Elements and select Centered Overlay from the list of position options. Excel will place the chart title on top of the plot area, freeing up more space for other chart elements. Chart legends can also be overlaid by opening the Format pane for the legend and deselecting the Show the legend without overlapping the chart check box in the LEGEND OPTIONS section. Other chart elements can be overlaid by dragging them to new locations in the chart area and then resizing the plot area to recover the empty space.

Don't overuse the technique of overlaying chart elements. Too much overlaying of chart elements can make your chart difficult to read.

Creating a Combination Chart

A combination chart combines two chart types, such as a column chart and a line chart, within a single chart. Combination charts enable you to show two sets of data using the chart type that is best for each data set. Combination charts can have data series with vastly different values. In those instances, you can create dual axis charts, using primary and secondary axes.

Bob and Carol want to include a chart that projects the net income and cases sold by Levitt Winery over the next 10 years. Because these two data series are measuring different things (dollars and wine cases), the chart might be better understood if the Net Income data series was displayed as a column chart and the Cases Produced and Sold data series was displayed as a line chart.

To create a combination chart that shows net income and sales data:

1. Go to the **Projected Cash Flow** worksheet, and then select the nonadjacent range **B4:L5;B23:L23** containing the Year category values, the data series for Cases Produced and Sold, and the data series for Net Income.

2. On the ribbon, click the **INSERT** tab.

3. In the Charts group, click the **Recommended Charts** button. The Insert Chart dialog box opens.

4. Click the **All Charts** tab to view a list of all chart types and subtypes.

5. Click **Combo** in the list of chart types, and then click the **Custom Combination** icon (the fourth subtype). At the bottom of the dialog box, you choose the chart type for each data series and whether that data series is plotted on the primary or secondary axis.

6. For the Cases Produced and Sold data series, click the **Chart Type** arrow, and then click **Line**.

7. Click the **Secondary Axis** check box to display the values for that series on a secondary axis.

8. For the Net Income data series, click the **Chart Type** arrow, and then click **Clustered Column**. See Figure 4-29.

Figure 4-29   Combo chart type

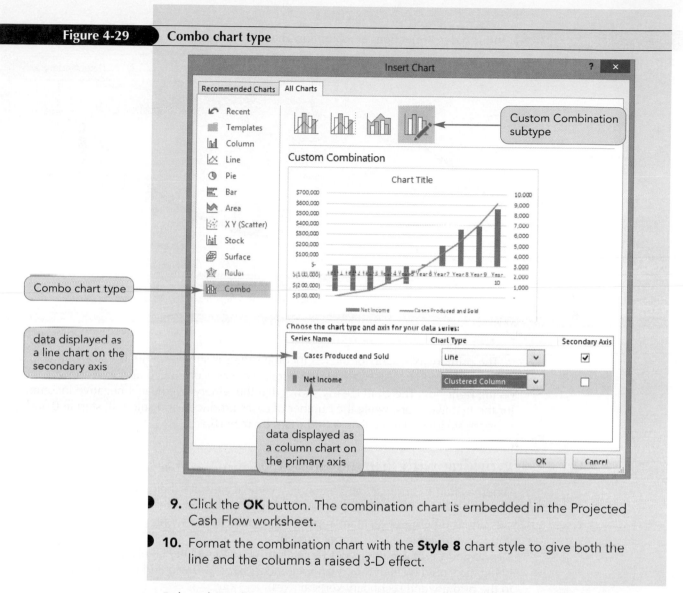

Combo chart type

data displayed as a line chart on the secondary axis

Custom Combination subtype

data displayed as a column chart on the primary axis

> **9.** Click the **OK** button. The combination chart is embedded in the Projected Cash Flow worksheet.

> **10.** Format the combination chart with the **Style 8** chart style to give both the line and the columns a raised 3-D effect.

Bob and Carol want the combination chart to appear in the Overview worksheet and be formatted to resemble the other charts. You will make those changes now.

To move and format the combination chart:

> **1.** Move the combination chart to the **Overview** worksheet.

> **2.** Position and resize the combination chart so that it covers the range **F45:M58**.

> **3.** Change the title of the combination chart to **Sales Projections**, and then format the title in the same **non-bold; Blue, Accent 1; Calibri Light** font you used with the other chart titles.

> **4.** Remove the **Legend** chart element from the combination chart.

> **5.** Add **Primary Major Vertical** gridlines to the combination chart.

> **6.** Change the fill color of the plot area to **white**, and then change the fill color of the chart area to the same light gold (**Gold, Accent 4, Lighter 80%**) as the other charts. See Figure 4-30.

Figure 4-30 **Initial Sales Projections combination chart**

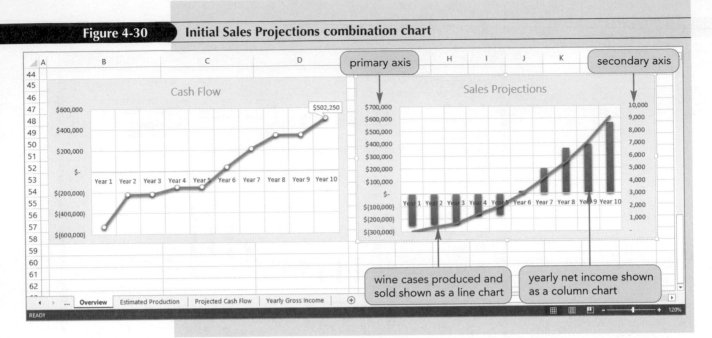

The primary axis scale for the net income values is shown on the left side of the chart; the secondary axis scale for the number of cases produced and sold appears on the right side. The chart clearly shows that the winery will have a negative income for the first five years, while the number of cases produced and sold will start at 0 and increase steadily to more than 9,000 cases by Year 10.

Working with Primary and Secondary Axes

When a chart has primary and secondary vertical axes, it is helpful to identify exactly what each axis is measuring. You can do this by adding an axis title to the chart. An axis title is descriptive text that appears next to the axis. As with other chart elements, you can add, remove, and format axis titles.

Bob and Carol want the Sales Projections chart to include labels describing what is being measured by the primary and secondary axes. You will add descriptive axis titles to the primary and secondary vertical axes.

To add axis titles to the primary and secondary vertical axes:

1. Click the **Chart Elements** button ➕ next to the combination chart, and then click the **Axis Title** check box to select it. Titles with the placeholders "Axis Title" are added to the primary and secondary axes.

2. Click the left axis title to select it, type **Net Income** as the descriptive title, and then press the **Enter** key.

3. With the left axis title selected, change the font color to the **Orange, Accent 2, Darker 25%** theme color to match the color of the columns in the chart.

4. Select the numbers on the left axis scale, and then change the font color to the **Orange, Accent 2, Darker 25%** theme color. The left axis title and scale are now the same color as the columns that reference that axis.

5. Select the right axis title, type **Cases Sold** as the descriptive title, and then press the **Enter** key.

6. With the right axis title still selected, change the font color to the **Blue, Accent 1, Darker 25%** theme color to match the color of the line in the chart.

7. Change the orientation of the right axis title to **Rotate Text Down**. The text is easier to read in this orientation.

8. Select the numbers on the right axis scale, and then change the font color to the **Blue, Accent 1, Darker 25%** theme color. The right axis title and scale are now the same color as the line that references that axis.

Excel added the "Axis Title" placeholder to the horizontal category values axis. You can remove this title, freeing up more space for other chart elements.

9. Click the horizontal axis title to select it, and then press the **Delete** key to remove it from the chart. See Figure 4-31.

Figure 4-31   Combination chart with axis titles

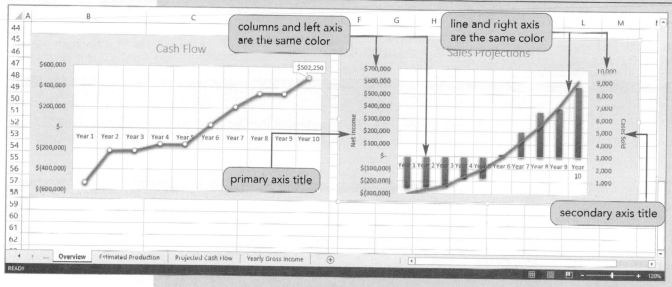

The Levitts are concerned that the line chart portion of the graph makes it look as if the number of cases produced and sold was negative for the first five years. This is because the secondary axis scale, which is automatically generated by Excel, goes from a minimum of 0 to a maximum of 10,000. You will change the scale so that the 0 tick mark for Cases Sold better aligns with the $0 for Net Income.

To modify the secondary axis scale:

1. Double-click the secondary axis scale to select it and open the Format pane.

2. Verify that the **AXIS OPTIONS** list of commands is displayed.

3. Click the **Minimum** box, change the value from 0.0 to **–4000**, and then press the **Enter** key. The secondary axis scale is modified. The Cases Sold scale is now better aligned with the Net Income scale, providing a more realistic picture of the data.

4. Close the Format pane, and then press the **Esc** key to deselect the secondary axis. See Figure 4-32.

Figure 4-32 | **Final combination chart**

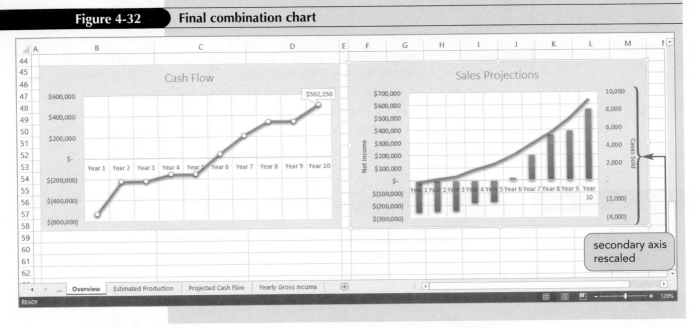

You have completed the charts portion of the Overview worksheet. These charts provide a good overview of the financial picture of the winery that Bob and Carol plan to open.

Copying and Pasting a Chart Format

You will often want to use the same design over and over again for the charts in your worksheet. Rather than repeating the same commands, you can copy the formatting from one chart to another. To copy a chart format, first select the chart with the existing design that you want to replicate, and then click the Copy button in the Clipboard group on the HOME tab (or press the Ctrl+C keys). Next, select the chart that you want to format, click the Paste button arrow in the Clipboard group, and then click Paste Special to open the Paste Special dialog box. In the Paste Special dialog box, select the Formats option button, and then click the OK button. All of the copied formats from the original chart—including fill colors, font styles, axis scales, and chart types—are then pasted into the new chart. Be aware that the pasted formats will overwrite any formats previously used in the new chart.

Editing a Chart Data Source

Excel automates most of the process of creating and formatting a chart. However, sometimes the rendered chart does not appear the way you expected. One situation where this happens is when the selected cells contain numbers you want to treat as categories, but Excel treats them as a data series. When this happens, you can modify the data source to specify exactly which ranges should be treated as category values and which ranges should be treated as data values.

Modifying a Chart's Data Source

- Click the chart to select it.
- On the CHART TOOLS DESIGN tab, in the Data group, click the Select Data button.
- In the Legend Entries (Series) section of the Select Data Source dialog box, click the Add button to add another data series to the chart, or click the Remove button to remove a data series from the chart.
- Click the Edit button in the Horizontal (Category) Axis Labels section to select the category values for the chart.

The Yearly Gross Income worksheet contains a table that projects the winery's gross income for 2015 through 2024. Carol wants to see a simple line chart of this data.

To create the line chart:

1. Go to the **Yearly Gross Income** worksheet, and then select the range **B4:C14**.

2. On the ribbon, click the **INSERT** tab.

3. In the Charts group, click the **Insert Line Chart** button 📉.

4. In the 2-D Line charts section, click the **Line with Markers** subtype (the first subtype in the second row). The 2-D line chart is created. See Figure 4-33.

Figure 4-33 Line chart with Year treated as a data series

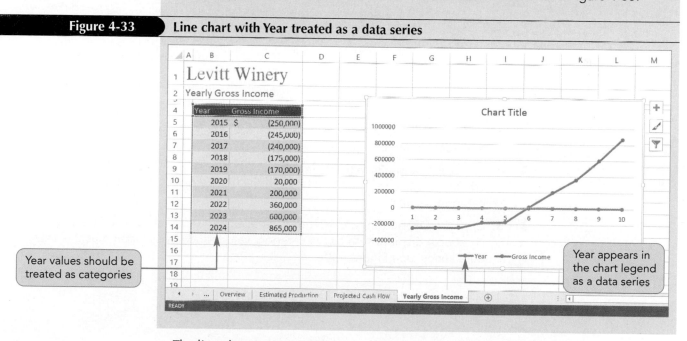

Year values should be treated as categories

Year appears in the chart legend as a data series

The line chart is incorrect because the Year values from the range B5:B14 are treated as another data series rather than category values. The line chart actually doesn't even have category values; the values are charted sequentially from the first value to the tenth. You can correct this problem from the Select Data dialog box by identifying the data series and category values to use in the chart.

To edit the chart's data source:

▶ **1.** On the CHART TOOLS DESIGN tab, in the Data group, click the **Select Data** button. The Select Data Source dialog box opens. Note that Year is selected as a legend entry and the category values are simply the numbers 1 through 10. See Figure 4-34.

Figure 4-34   **Select Data Source dialog box**

▶ **2.** With Year selected (highlighted in gray) in the list of legend entries, click the **Remove** button. Year is removed from the line chart.

▶ **3.** Click the **Edit** button for the Horizontal (Category) Axis Labels. You'll specify that Year should be used as the category values.

▶ **4.** Select the range **B5:B14** containing the Year values, and then click the **OK** button. The values 2015 through 2024 now appear in the list of category values.

▶ **5.** Click the **OK** button to close the Select Data Source dialog box. The line chart now displays Year as the category values and Gross Income as the only data series. See Figure 4-35.

TIP

You can organize your data series in rows rather than columns by clicking the Switch Row/Column button in the Select Data Source dialog box.

Figure 4-35   **Revised Gross Income line chart**

Figure 4-35   **Revised Gross Income line chart**

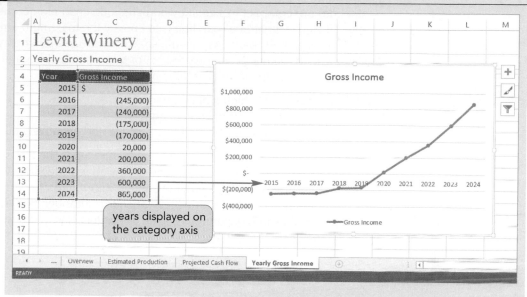

The Select Data Source dialog box is also useful when you want to add more data series to a chart. For example, if Bob and Carol wanted to include other financial estimates in an existing chart, they could add the data series to the existing chart rather than creating a new chart. To add a data series to a chart, select the chart, click the Select Data button in the Data group on the CHART TOOLS DESIGN tab to open the Select Data Source dialog box, click the Add button, and then select the range for the data series.

PROSKILLS

Decision Making: Choosing the Right Chart

Excel supports a wide variety of charts and chart styles. To decide which type of chart to use, you must evaluate your data and determine the ultimate purpose or goal of the chart. Consider how your data will appear in each type of chart before making a final decision.

- In general, pie charts should be used only when the number of categories is small and the relative sizes of the different slices can be easily distinguished. If you have several categories, use a column or bar chart.
- Line charts are best for categories that follow a sequential order. Be aware, however, that the time intervals must be a constant length if used in a line chart. Line charts will distort data that occurs at irregular time intervals, making it appear that the data values occurred at regular intervals when they did not.
- Pie, column, bar, and line charts assume that numbers are plotted against categories. In science and engineering applications, you will often want to plot two numeric values against one another. For that data, use **XY scatter charts**, which show the patterns or relationship between two or more sets of values. XY scatter charts are also useful for data recorded at irregular time intervals.
- If you still can't find the right chart to meet your needs, you can create a custom chart based on the built-in chart types. Third-party vendors also sell software to allow Excel to create chart types that are not built into the software.

Choosing the right chart and chart style can make your presentation more effective and informative.

Creating Sparklines

A sparkline is a chart that is displayed entirely within a worksheet cell. Because sparklines are compact in size, they don't include chart elements such as legends, titles, or gridlines. The goal of a sparkline is to convey the maximum amount of information within a very small space. As a result, sparklines are useful when you don't want charts to overwhelm the rest of your worksheet or take up valuable page space.

You can create the following three types of sparklines:

- A line sparkline for highlighting trends
- A column sparkline for column charts
- A win/loss sparkline for highlighting positive and negative values

Figure 4-36 shows examples of each sparkline type. The line sparklines show the sales history from each department and across all four departments of a computer manufacturer. The sparklines provide enough information for you to examine the sales trend within and across departments. Notice that although total sales rose steadily during the year, some departments, such as Printers, showed a sales decline midway through the year.

Figure 4-36   Types of sparklines

line sparklines

	A	B	C
1	Sales by Department		
2	(sales in millions)		
3	Department	Current	1-Year
4	Tablets	$ 29.40	
5	Printers	13.25	
6	Monitors	13.55	
7	Peripherals	11.75	
8	All Departments	$ 67.95	

column sparklines

	A	B	C
1	Temperature Record		
2	City	Yearly	Monthly
3	Seattle	37.7 °C	
4	Buenos Aires	54.0 °C	
5	Moscow	14.3 °C	
6	Melbourne	47.4 °C	

win/loss sparklines

	A	B	C
1	Team	Record	Season
2	Cutler Tigers	10-2	
3	Apsburg Hawks	8-4	
4	Central City Spartans	6-6	
5	Liddleton Lions	3-9	

The column sparklines present a record of monthly temperature averages for four cities. Temperatures above 0 degrees Celsius are presented in blue columns; temperatures below 0 degrees Celsius are presented in red columns that extend downward. The height of each column is related to the magnitude of the value it represents.

Finally, the win/loss sparklines reveal a snapshot of the season results for four sports teams. Wins are displayed in blue; losses are in red. From the sparklines, you can quickly see that the Cutler Tigers finished their 10–2 season with six straight wins and the Liddleton Lions finished their 3–9 season with four straight losses.

To create a set of sparklines, you first select the data you want to graph, and then select the location range where you want the sparklines to appear. Note that the cells in which you insert the sparklines do not need to be blank. Sparklines are added as part of the cell background and do not replace any cell content.

REFERENCE

Creating and Editing Sparklines

- On the INSERT tab, in the Sparklines group, click the Line, Column, or Win/Loss button.
- In the Data Range box, enter the range for the data source of the sparkline.
- In the Location Range box, enter the range into which to place the sparkline.
- Click the OK button.
- To edit a sparkline's appearance, click the SPARKLINE TOOLS DESIGN tab.
- In the Show group, click the appropriate check boxes to specify which markers to display on the sparkline.
- In the Group group, click the Axis button, and then click Show Axis to add an axis to the sparkline.

The Levitts' business plan involves rolling out the different wine types gradually, starting with Chardonnay and Cabernet Franc and then adding more varietals over the first five years. They won't start producing all six wines until Year 6. They want you to add a column sparkline to the Overview worksheet that displays this 10-year production plan.

To insert column sparklines showing the 10-year production plan in the Overview worksheet:

1. Go to the **Overview** worksheet, and then select the range **D29:D34**. This is the location range into which you will insert the sparklines.

2. On the INSERT tab, in the Sparklines group, click the **Column** button. The Create Sparklines dialog box opens. The location range is already entered because you selected it before opening the dialog box.

3. With the insertion point in the Data Range box, click the **Estimated Production** sheet tab, and then select the data in the range **C6:L11**. This is the range that contains the data you want to chart in the sparklines.

4. Click the **OK** button. The Create Sparklines dialog box closes and the column sparklines are added to the location range in the Overview worksheet. See Figure 4-37.

Figure 4-37   **Column sparklines of annual wine production**

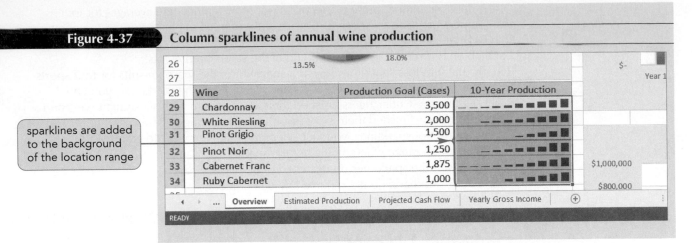

sparklines are added to the background of the location range

The column sparklines make it clear how the wines are placed into production at different times—Chardonnay and Cabernet Franc first, and Pinot Grigio in Year 6. Each wine, once it is introduced, is steadily produced in greater quantities as the decade progresses.

Formatting the Sparkline Axis

Because of their compact size, you have few formatting options with sparklines. One thing you can change is the scale of the vertical axis. The vertical axis will range from the minimum value to the maximum value. By default, this range is defined differently for each cell to maximize the available space. But this can be misleading. For example, the column sparklines in Figure 4-37 seem to show that Levitt Winery will be producing the same amount of each wine by the end of Year 10 because the heights of the last columns are all the same. You can change the vertical axis scale to be the same for the related sparklines.

Carol and Bob want to use the same vertical axis range for each sparkline showing the 10-year production. You will set the scale of the vertical axis to range from 0 cases to 3500 cases.

To set the scale of the vertical axis of the column sparklines:

1. If necessary, select the range **D29:D34**. Because you have selected the sparklines, the SPARKLINE TOOLS DESIGN tab appears on the ribbon.

2. On the SPARKLINE TOOLS DESIGN tab, in the Group group, click the **Axis** button, and then click **Custom Value** in the Vertical Axis Maximum Value Options section. The Sparkline Vertical Axis Setting dialog box opens.

3. Replace the value in the box with **3500**, and then click the **OK** button. You do not have to set the vertical axis minimum value because Excel assumes this to be 0 for all of the column sparklines. The column sparklines are now based on the same vertical scale, and the height of each column is based on the number of cases produced per year.

Working with Sparkline Groups

The sparklines in the location range are part of a single group. Clicking any cell in the location range selects all of the sparklines in the group. Any formatting you apply to one sparkline affects all of the sparklines in the group, as you saw when you set the range of the vertical axis. This ensures that the sparklines for related data are formatted consistently. To format each sparkline differently, you must first ungroup them.

Carol and Bob think that the column sparklines would look better if they used the same colors as the pie chart for the different wines. You will first ungroup the sparklines so you can format them separately, and then you will apply a different fill color to each sparkline.

To ungroup and format the column sparklines:

▶ **1.** Make sure the range **D29:D34** is still selected.

▶ **2.** On the DESIGN tab, in the Group group, click the **Ungroup** button. The sparklines are ungrouped, and selecting any one of the sparklines will no longer select the entire group.

▶ **3.** Click cell **D30** to select it and its sparkline.

▶ **4.** On the DESIGN tab, in the Style group, click the **Sparkline Color** button, and then click the **Orange, Accent 2, Darker 25%** theme color in the sixth row and fifth column. The fill color of the column sparkline changes to a medium orange.

▶ **5.** Click cell **D31**, click the **Sparkline Color** button, and then click the **Gray-50%, Accent 3** theme color.

▶ **6.** Set the color of the sparkline in cell **D32** to **Gold, Accent 4**, set the color of the sparkline in cell **D33** to **Green, Accent 6, Lighter 60%**, and then set the color of the sparkline in cell D34 to **Green, Accent 6**.

▶ **7.** Select cell **B35** to deselect the sparklines. See Figure 4-38.

Figure 4-38   **Formatted sparklines**

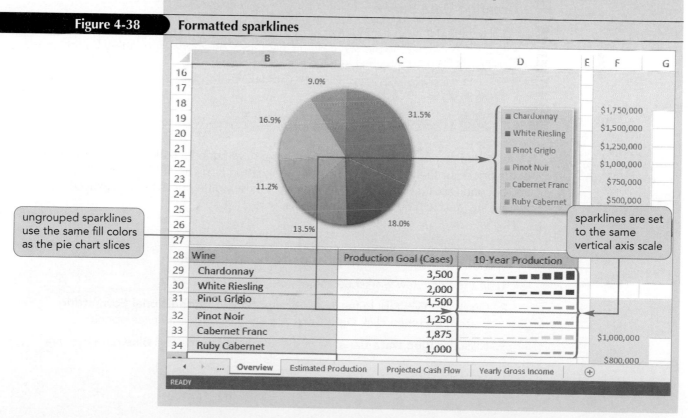

To regroup sparklines, you select all of the cells in the location range containing the sparklines, and then click the Group button in the Group group on the SPARKLINE TOOLS DESIGN tab. Be aware that regrouping sparklines causes them to share a common format, so you will lose any formatting applied to individual sparklines.

The Sparkline Color button applied a single color to the entire sparkline. You can also apply colors to individual markers within a sparkline by clicking the Marker Color button. Using this button, you can set a distinct color for negative values, maximum values, minimum values, first values, and last values. This is useful with line sparklines that track data across a time range in which you might want to identify the maximum value within that range or the minimum value.

Creating Data Bars

A data bar is a conditional format that adds a horizontal bar to the background of a cell containing a number. When applied to a range of cells, the data bars have the same appearance as a bar chart, with each cell containing one bar. The lengths of data bars are based on the value of each cell in the selected range. Cells with larger values have longer bars; cells with smaller values have shorter bars. Data bars are dynamic, which means that if one cell's value changes, the lengths of the data bars in the selected range are automatically updated.

Data bars differ from sparklines in that the bars are always placed in the cells containing the value they represent, and each cell represents only a single bar from the bar chart. By contrast, a column sparkline can be inserted anywhere within the workbook and can represent data from several rows or columns. However, like sparklines, data bars can be used to create compact graphs that can be easily integrated alongside the text and values stored in worksheet cells.

REFERENCE

Creating Data Bars

- Select the range containing the data you want to chart.
- On the HOME tab, in the Styles group, click the Conditional Formatting button, point to Data Bars, and then click the data bar style you want to use.
- To modify the data bar rules, click the Conditional Formatting button, and then click Manage Rules.

As part of their business plan, Bob and Carol have added a table with the proposed bottle prices for their six wines under the designation First Label (highest quality) and Second Label (average quality). They want these bottle prices to be displayed graphically. You will do this using data bars.

To add data bars to the proposed bottle prices:

1. In the Overview worksheet, select the range **C38:D43**.

2. On the HOME tab, in the Styles group, click the **Conditional Formatting** button, and then click **Data Bars**. A gallery of data bar styles opens.

3. Click the **Blue Data Bar** style in the Gradient Fill section. Blue data bars are added to each of the bottle price cells.

4. Select cell **B44** to deselect the range. See Figure 4-39.

Figure 4-39   Data bars added to the Overview worksheet

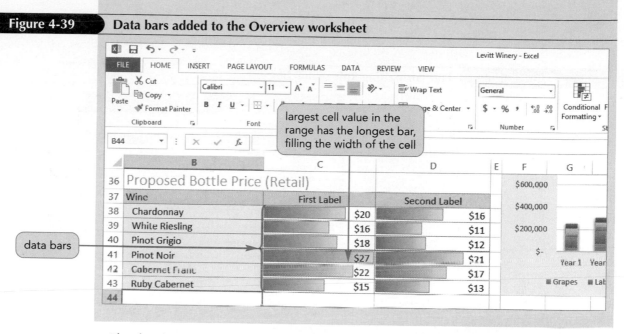

The data bars make it easy to visually compare the proposed prices of the different wines. Pinot Noir will be the most expensive wine sold by the Levitts; White Riesling and Ruby Cabernet will be the least expensive.

Modifying a Data Bar Rule

The lengths of the data bars are determined based on the values in the selected range. The cell with the largest value contains a data bar that extends across the entire width of the cell, and the lengths of the other bars in the selected range are determined relative to that bar. In some cases, this will result in the longest data bar overlapping its cell's data value, making it difficult to read. You can modify the length of the data bars by altering the rules of the conditional format.

The first label price for Pinot Noir in cell C41 contains the largest value ($27) in the range C38:D43 and has the longest data bar. The data bar for the second label price for Ruby Cabernet ($13) fills only half the cell width by comparison. The Levitts don't want data bars to overlap the cell values. You will change the data bar rule that sets the maximum length of the data bars to 35 so that the longest bar no longer fills the entire cell.

To modify the data bar rule:

1. Select the range **C38:D43** containing the data bars.

2. On the HOME tab, in the Styles group, click the **Conditional Formatting** button, and then click **Manage Rules**. The Conditional Formatting Rules Manager dialog box opens, displaying all the rules applied to any conditional format in the workbook.

3. Make sure **Current Selection** appears in the Show formatting rules for box. You'll edit the rule applied to the current selection—the data bars in the Sectors worksheet.

4. Click the **Edit Rule** button. The Edit Formatting Rule dialog box opens. You want to modify this rule so that the maximum value for the data bar is set to 35. All data bar lengths will then be defined relative to this value.

5. In the Type row, click the **Maximum** arrow, and then click **Number**.

6. Press the **Tab** key to move the insertion point to the Maximum box in the Value row, and then type **35**. See Figure 4-40.

Figure 4-40   **Edit Formatting Rule dialog box**

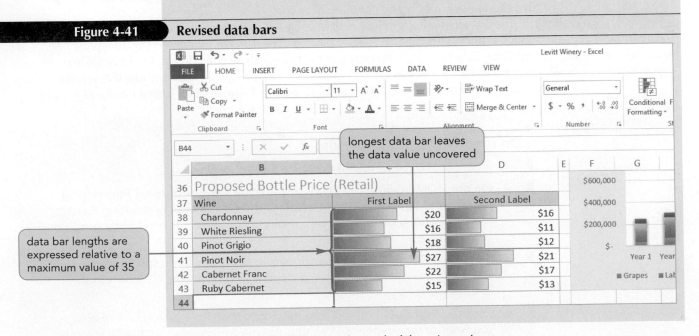

7. Click the **OK** button in each dialog box, and then select cell **B44**. The lengths of the data bars are reduced so that the longest bar covers about three-fourths of the cell width. See Figure 4-41.

Figure 4-41   **Revised data bars**

The data bars provide a good visual of the wine prices.

INSIGHT

Edward Tufte and Chart Design Theory

Any serious study of charts will include the works of Edward Tufte, who pioneered the field of information design. One of Tufte's most important works is *The Visual Display of Quantitative Information*, in which he laid out several principles for the design of charts and graphics.

Tufte was concerned with what he termed as "chart junk," in which a proliferation of chart elements—chosen because they look "nice"—confuse and distract the reader. One measure of chart junk is Tufte's data-ink ratio, which is the amount of "ink" used to display quantitative information compared to the total ink required by the chart. Tufte advocated limiting the use of non-data ink. Non-data ink is any part of the chart that does not convey information about the data. One way of measuring the data-ink ratio is to determine how much of the chart you can erase without affecting the user's ability to interpret the chart. Tufte would argue for high data-ink ratios with a minimum of extraneous elements and graphics.

To this end, Tufte helped develop sparklines, which convey information with a high data-ink ratio within a compact space. Tufte believed that charts that can be viewed and comprehended at a glance have a greater impact on the reader than large and cluttered graphs, no matter how attractive they might be.

Inserting a Watermark

TIP

Fill colors hide a watermark. So if a sheet has a watermark, don't use a fill color for the worksheet background.

Many businesses distinguish works in progress from final versions by including the word "Draft" as a watermark on each page. A **watermark** is text or an image that appears in the background behind other content. You insert a watermark into the header or footer of a worksheet. Even though the watermark is inserted into the header or footer, a large watermark will overflow those sections and appear on the entire sheet. Generally, watermarks are given a "washed-out" appearance and are placed behind text or charts on the sheet so that they don't obscure any of the other content on the sheet. Because the watermark is included in the header/footer section, it is visible in Page Layout view and Page Break Preview but not in Normal view.

Because the current business plan for Levitt Winery will change as Bob and Carol continue to explore their financial options and the status of the wine market, they want to include a watermark with the word "Draft" on the Overview worksheet.

To insert a watermark into the worksheet:

1. On the ribbon, click the **PAGE LAYOUT** tab.

2. In the Page Setup group, click the **Dialog Box Launcher** to open the Page Setup dialog box.

3. Click the **Header/Footer** tab to display options for the header or footer of the current worksheet.

4. Click the **Custom Header** button to open the Header dialog box.

5. Click the **Center section** box. You want to insert the watermark in the center section of the header.

6. Click the **Insert Picture** button 🖻 to open the Insert Pictures dialog box.

7. Click the **From a file**, navigate to the **Excel4 ▸ Tutorial** folder included with your Data Files, click the **Draft.png** file, and then click the **Insert** button. Code for the inserted picture is added to the center section of the header. See Figure 4-42.

Figure 4-42   Inserting a watermark graphic image

Generally, watermarks are lighter or washed out so that they don't obscure or distract from the sheet content. You can format the appearance of the watermark from the Header dialog box.

To format the appearance of the watermark:

1. In the Header dialog box, click the **Format Picture** button 📷 to open the Format Picture dialog box.

2. Click the **Picture** tab, click the **Color** box, and then click **Washout** from the color options.

3. Click the **OK** button in each dialog box to return to the Page Setup dialog box.

4. Click the **Print Preview** button to preview the printed worksheet in Backstage view. As shown in Figure 4-43, the Draft graphic image appears in the background, faded out so as to not obscure the sheet contents.

| Figure 4-43 | Print preview of the worksheet with the watermark |

Watermark courtesy of Patrick Carey

5. Click the **Back** button to return to the workbook.

6. Save and close the workbook.

The Levitts are pleased with the charts and graphics you have created. They provide useful visuals for anyone who is studying the Levitts' proposal.

Session 4.2 Quick Check

1. What is the difference between a line chart and a scatter chart?
2. A researcher wants to plot weight versus blood pressure. Should the researcher use a line chart or a scatter chart? Explain why.
3. What are major tick marks, minor tick marks, and gridlines?
4. How do you change the scale of a chart axis?
5. What is the difference between the chart area and the plot area?
6. What are sparklines? Describe the three types of sparklines.
7. What are data bars? How do data bars differ from sparklines?
8. What is a watermark?

SAM Projects

Put your skills into practice with SAM Projects! SAM Projects for this tutorial can be found online. If you have a SAM account, go to www.cengage.com/sam2013 to download the most recent Project Instructions and Start Files.

Review Assignments

Data Files needed for the Review Assignments: Market.xlsx, Watermark.png

Another part of Carol and Bob Levitt's business plan for the new Levitt Winery is to analyze current market conditions. The Levitts have created a workbook that explores customer preferences and sales of wine in the United States. The workbook also explores the current wineries in Michigan against which the Levitt Winery will be competing. Bob and Carol asked you to complete their workbook by presenting this data in graphic form using Excel charts. Complete the following:

1. Open the **Market** workbook located in the Excel4 ▶ Review folder included with your Data Files, and then save the workbook as **Market Analysis** in the location specified by your instructor.

2. In the Documentation sheet, enter your name in cell B3 and the date in cell B4.

3. In the Loan Analysis sheet, enter the data values and formulas required to calculate the monthly payment on a business loan of **$225,000** at **8.2** percent annual interest to be repaid in **15** years.

4. In the Market Summary worksheet, use the data in the range E21:F27 showing the types of grapes cultivated by Michigan wineries to create a pie chart comparing production rates. Embed the pie chart in the Market Summary worksheet covering the range B5:G18.

5. Format the pie chart by removing the chart title, applying the Style 11 chart style, and aligning the legend with the right edge of the chart area.

6. In the Michigan Wineries worksheet, create a line chart based on the data in the nonadjacent range B4:B16;F4:F16 showing the increase in the number of wineries in Michigan over the past 12 years. Embed the line chart in the Market Summary worksheet covering the range I5:O16.

7. Format the line chart by making the following changes:

    a. Format the chart with the Style 14 chart style.

    b. Change the chart title to **Michigan Wineries**.

    c. Change the fill color of the chart area to light blue and the plot area to white.

    d. Add primary major vertical gridlines to the plot area.

    e. Change the scale of the primary axis to range from **50** to **140** in steps of **10** units.

8. In the Michigan Wineries worksheet, create a clustered column chart using the data in the range B4:E16 showing the growth of Michigan wineries by region. Embed the chart in the Market Summary worksheet over the range I18:O28.

9. Format the column chart by making the following changes:

    a. Format the chart with the Style 13 chart style.

    b. Change the chart title to **Michigan Wineries** and reduce its font size to 14 points.

    c. Set the fill color of the chart area to light blue and the plot area to white.

    d. Add primary major vertical gridlines to the plot area.

10. In the U.S. Wine Sales worksheet, create a stacked column chart using the data in the range B3:E15 showing the breakout of the wine market into table wines, dessert wines, and sparkling wines or champagne. Embed the stacked column chart in the range B30:G43 of the Market Summary worksheet.

11. Format the stacked column chart by making the following changes:
    a. Format the chart with the Style 6 chart style.
    b. Change the chart title to **U.S. Wine Sales** and set its font size to 14 points.
    c. Add a primary vertical axis title with the text **Millions of Cases** and remove the primary horizontal axis title.
    d. Add primary major vertical gridlines.
    e. Set the fill color of the chart area to light blue and the plot area to white.

12. In the U.S. Wine Consumption worksheet, create a combination chart based on the data in the range B3:D15 showing how much wine Americans consume annually. Display the Gallons (millions) data series as a clustered column chart on the primary axis, and then display the Gallons (per Capita) data series as a line chart on the secondary axis.

13. Move the combination chart to the Market Summary worksheet; embed it over the range I30:O43.

14. Format the combination chart by making the following changes:
    a. Format the chart with the Style 4 chart style.
    b. Change the chart title to **U.S. Wine Consumption** and set its font size to 14 points.
    c. Add the primary axis title **Gallons (millions)** and the secondary axis title **Gallons (per Capita)**. Change the font color of the axis titles and scales to match the column and line markers.
    d. Remove the horizontal axis title and chart legend.
    e. Change the rotation of the secondary axis title to Rotate Text Down.
    f. Change the primary axis scale to range from **650** to **950** in intervals of **50**. Change the scale of the secondary axis to range from **2.2** to **3.0** in steps of **0.1** units.
    g. Change the fill color of the chart area to light blue and the plot area to white.
    h. Add primary major vertical gridlines to the chart.

15. Insert column sparklines in the range G21:G27 of the Market Summary worksheet based on the data in the range C5:N11 of the Michigan Grapes worksheet to show whether the number of wineries growing their own grapes has increased over the past 12 years.

16. Set the axis of the sparklines so that the column heights range from **0** to a maximum of **26** for each sparkline. Ungroup the sparklines and set the color of each to match the color of the corresponding grape in the pie chart.

17. Because the Levitts plan to grow their own grapes rather than purchasing them from out-of-state vendors, they are interested in knowing how many wineries in Michigan also grow their own grapes. The results of their survey are shown in the range B20:C22 in the Market Summary worksheet. Add data bars to the values in the range C20:C22 using the blue gradient fill. Define a rule that sets the maximum length of the data bars in those cells to a value of **100**.

18. Insert the **Watermark.png** graphic file located in the Excel4 ▶ Review folder as a washed-out watermark in the center section of the header of the Market Summary worksheet.

19. Save the workbook, and then close it.

Case Problem 1

Data File needed for this Case Problem: Bertrand.xlsx

Bertrand Family Budget   Andrew and Maria Bertrand of Santa Fe, New Mexico, are hoping to purchase their first home and they are using Excel to help manage their family budget. The couple needs to estimate the monthly payments required for a $275,000 mortgage. They want to track their income and expenses using tables, charts, data bars, and sparklines. You will help them do all of these tasks. Complete the following:

1. Open the **Bertrand** workbook located in the Excel4 ▶ Case1 folder included with your Data Files, and then save the workbook as **Bertrand Budget** in the location specified by your instructor.

2. In the Documentation sheet, enter your name in cell B3 and the date in cell B4.

APPLY

3. In the Budget worksheet, in the range O4:O6, enter the parameters of a **$275,000** loan that is repaid at an annual interest rate of **4.35** percent over **30** years.

4. In the range O8:O9, calculate the total number of months to repay the loan and the interest rate per month.

5. In cell O11, use the PMT function to calculate the monthly payment. Multiply the PMT function by –1 so that the result appears as a positive currency value rather than a negative value.

6. In the range D25:O25, enter the value of the monthly mortgage payment by creating an absolute reference to the value in cell O11.

7. In the range D18:O18, calculate the total income per month. In the range D27:O27, calculate the total expenses incurred each month. In the range D28:O28, calculate the couple's net income (total income minus total expenses) each month.

8. In the range C4:C11, calculate the average monthly value of each expense category.

9. Add green gradient data bars to the values in the range C4:C11. Set the maximum length of the data bars to a value of **2500**.

⊕ **Explore** 10. Insert line sparklines in the range D4:D11 using the expense values in the range D19:O26. On the SPARKLINE TOOLS DESIGN tab, in the Show group, click the High Point check box to mark the high point of each sparkline.

11. Create a clustered column chart of the income, expenses, and net income for each month of the year based on the data in the nonadjacent range D15:O15;D18:O18;D27:O28. Place the chart within the range E2:K13.

12. Format the clustered column chart by making the following changes:

   a. Format the chart with the Style 8 chart style.

   b. Change the chart title to **Income and Expenses** and format it in a Calibri, non-bold 12-point font.

   c. Change the vertical scale of the chart to range from **–1000** to **6500** in steps of **1000**.

   d. Change the series overlap of the columns to **0%** and the gap width to **200%**.

13. Save the workbook.

14. Perform a what-if analysis by changing the length of the loan from 30 years to **15** years. Determine the monthly payments under this new mortgage plan, and then analyze its impact on the couple's projected income and expenses.

15. Save the workbook as **Bertrand Budget 2**, and then close it.

Case Problem 2

APPLY

Data File needed for this Case Problem: PetroChart.xlsx

PetroChart Reports   William Rawlings runs a blog called *PetroChart Reports* that deals with the energy market with special emphasis on crude oil production and consumption. William likes to augment his writing with informative charts and graphics. He has an Excel workbook with some historic data on the crude oil market. He has asked you to create charts from that data that he can use in an article that reviews the history of oil production and consumption, and their impact on the size of the proven world oil reserves. Complete the following:

1. Open the **PetroChart** workbook located in the Excel4 ▸ Case2 folder included with your Data Files, and then save the workbook as **PetroChart Reports**.

2. In the Documentation sheet, enter your name in cell B3 and the date in cell B4.

3. In the World Oil Production worksheet, create a line chart of world oil production from 1980 to 2010 using the data from the range A6:G37. Move the chart to the Summary worksheet covering the range B4:H19.

4. Format the chart with the Style 9 chart style, and then change the chart title to **Oil Production Historic Trends**.

5. Change the line color for the North America data series to white, which is easier to read against the black backdrop.

✛ **Explore** 6. Revise the vertical axis scale so that the display unit is expressed in terms of thousands (most oil production reports are quoted in terms of thousands of barrels per day). Change the text of the display unit from Thousands to **Thousands of Barrels per Day**.

7. In the World Oil Production worksheet, create a pie chart that displays the relative size of the oil production values for different regions in 2010 based on the data in the nonadjacent range B6:G6;B37:G37. Move the pie chart to the Summary worksheet covering the range J4:P19.

8. Make the following changes to the pie chart:

   a. Format the chart with the Style 7 chart style.

   b. Change the chart title to **2010 Oil Production** and reduce its font size to 14 points.

   c. Move the chart legend to the left edge of the chart area.

   d. Add data labels outside of the pie slices showing the percentage associated with each region.

   e. Change the color of the pie slice for the North America region to white.

9. In the World Oil Consumption worksheet, create a line chart that shows how oil consumption changed from 1980 to 2010 based on the data in the range A6:G37. Move the chart to the Summary worksheet covering the range B21:H36.

10. Change the chart title to **Oil Consumption Historic Trends**.

✛ **Explore** 11. Copy the Oil Production Historic Trends line chart. Use Paste Special to paste the format of that chart into the Oil Consumption Historic Trends line chart.

12. In the World Oil Consumption worksheet, create a pie chart showing the 2010 regional breakdown of oil consumption based on the data in the range B6:G6;B37:G37. Move the chart to the Summary worksheet covering the range J21:P36.

✛ **Explore** 13. Change the chart title to **2010 Oil Consumption**. Use Paste Special to copy the 2010 Oil Production pie chart and paste its format into the 2010 Oil Consumption pie chart.

14. There was a fear that with increased oil production and consumption from 1980 to 2010, there would be decreasing amounts of proven reserves. Was this the case? In the Proven Reserves worksheet, create a combination chart based on the data in the range A5:D36. Display the Oil Production and Oil Consumption data series as line charts on the primary axis. Display the Proven Reserves data series as an area chart on the secondary axis. Move the chart to the Summary worksheet covering the range F38:M53.

15. Make the following changes to the combination chart:

   a. Format the chart with the Style 6 chart style.

   b. Change the chart title to **Historic Trends in Proven Oil Reserves**; reduce the font size to 12 points.

   c. Change the primary axis scale to range from **50,000** to **90,000** in steps of **5,000**.

   d. Change the line color of the Oil Production data series to white.

16. Save the workbook, and then close it.

Case Problem 3

Data Files needed for this Case Problem: Frame.xlsx, Confidential.png

Frame Financial   Jeri Carbone is the owner of Frame Financial, a small financial consulting firm in Marion, Iowa. Among her many tasks is to maintain Excel workbooks with information on companies and their stock market activity. One of her workbooks contains information on Harriman Scientific, a company traded on the stock exchange. She wants you to complete the workbook by adding charts that describe the company's financial status and stock charts to display recent values of the company's stock. The stock chart should display the stock's daily opening, high, low, and closing values, and the number of shares traded for each day of the past few weeks. The volume of shares traded should be expressed in terms of millions of shares. Complete the following:

1. Open the **Frame** workbook located in the Excel4 ▸ Case3 folder included with your Data Files, and then save the workbook as **Frame Financial** in the location specified by your instructor.

2. In the Documentation sheet, enter your name in cell B3 and the date in cell B4.

CHALLENGE

3. Insert the **Confidential.png** graphics file located in the Excel4 ▶ Case3 folder as a washed-out watermark in the center section of the header of the Documentation worksheet.

4. In the Overview worksheet, create a 3-D pie chart describing the company's shareholders based on the data source values in the range K4:L6.

5. Remove the chart title and chart legend, and then resize the chart so that it is contained within the range M3:O7.

6. Change the fill colors of the ranges K4:L4, K5:L5, and K6:L6 to match their corresponding pie slice colors. Change the font color in those ranges to white.

7. Add pink gradient-colored data bars to the values in the range L10:O14. Edit the data bar rules so that the maximum data bar length corresponds to a value of **15,000**, and the bar direction goes from right to left.

8. In the Income Statement worksheet, create a 3-D clustered column chart of the company's net revenue and operating expenses using the data values in the nonadjacent range B4:F4;B6:F6;B12:F12. Move the chart to the Overview worksheet.

⊕ **Explore** 9. On the CHART TOOLS FORMAT tab, use the Size group to set the height of the chart to 2.44" and the width to 3.51". Move the chart so that its upper-left corner is aligned with the upper-left corner of cell B17.

10. Format the chart with the Style 11 chart style, change the chart title to **Revenue and Expenses**, and then reduce the font size of the chart title to 11 points.

11. In the Balance Sheet worksheet, create a 3-D clustered column chart of the company's assets and liabilities using the data in the range B4:F4;B18:F18;B26:F26. Move the chart to the Overview worksheet. Set its size to 2.44" high by 3.51" wide and place the chart so that it is directly to the right of the Revenue and Expenses chart.

⊕ **Explore** 12. Change the chart title to **Assets and Liabilities**. Copy and paste the format used with the Revenue and Expenses chart into this chart.

13. In the Cash Flow Statement worksheet, create a 2-D line chart of the data in the range C4:F4;C28:F28. Move the chart to the Overview worksheet. Resize the chart to 2.44" high by 3.51" wide and place the chart directly to the right of the Assets and Liabilities chart.

14. In the line chart, apply the Style 15 chart style, change the chart title to **Net Cash Flow**, and then reduce the font size of the chart title to 11 points.

15. In the Income Statement, Balance Sheet, and Cash Flow Statement worksheets, add line sparklines in the Trend column based on the financial values for 2012 through 2015.

⊕ **Explore** 16. In the Stock Values worksheet, select the range A4:F34, and then insert a Volume-Open-High-Low-Close stock chart.

⊕ **Explore** 17. Move the chart to a new chart sheet named **Stock History**.

18. Make the following changes to the stock chart:

   a. Change the chart title to **Recent Stock History** and increase the font size to 24 points.

   b. Set the font size of the horizontal and vertical axes to 12 points.

   c. Add Axis titles to the chart. Set the primary vertical axis title to **Volume of Shares Traded**, the secondary vertical axis title to **Stock Value**, and the horizontal axis title to **Date**.

   d. Set the font size of the axis titles to 16 points and rotate the text of the secondary axis title down.

   e. Remove the chart legend.

   f. Change the scale of the primary vertical axis to range from **200,000** to **2,000,000**, and then change the display unit of the primary vertical axis to Thousands.

   g. Change the scale of the secondary vertical axis to range from **10** to **35**.

   h. Add primary major horizontal and vertical gridlines, and remove any secondary gridlines.

   i. Set the gap width of the columns in the stock chart to **20%**.

19. Save the workbook, and then close it.

TROUBLESHOOT

Case Problem 4

Data File needed for this Case Problem: Mortgage.xlsx

The Mortgage White Paper   Kyle Lewis of Rockford, Illinois, runs a newsletter and blog called *The Mortgage White Paper* containing valuable financial information for investors, entrepreneurs, and homeowners. Kyle's emphasis is on tracking the world of home mortgages and home equity loans. Kyle's assistant has been creating an Excel workbook with an updated listing of the 15-year and 30-year interest rates on home loans. Now, his assistant reports that the formulas and charts in the workbook aren't working correctly. Kyle has asked you to fix the problems and finish the workbook. Complete the following:

1. Open the **Mortgage** workbook located in the Excel4 ▶ Case4 folder included with your Data Files, and then save the workbook as **Mortgage Report**.

2. In the Documentation sheet, enter your name in cell B3 and the date in cell B4.

3. In the Mortgage Calculator worksheet, calculate the monthly payments required to repay loans of different amounts, which are listed in the range A9:A24. The annual interest rate and length of the loan in years are provided in the range B5:C6 for 15-year and 30-year fixed loans.

⚙ **Troubleshoot** 4. The formulas used to calculate the monthly payments are displaying error values. Kyle is sure that the value in cell B9 is correct, but something happened when the formula was copied to the range B9:C24. Make the necessary changes so that the formula results are shown instead of the error values.

⚙ **Troubleshoot** 5. The line chart that displays the monthly payments for the 15-year and 30-year fixed rate loans is showing the loan amounts plotted as a third data series rather than as category values. Find the problem and fix it.

6. Format the line chart with the chart style and design you think is most appropriate for the data. Make sure the finished chart is easy to read and interpret.

⚙ **Troubleshoot** 7. In the Mortgage Trends worksheet, the data bars that were added to the Mortgage Application Index values in the range D7:D56 all have the same length. Fix the data bars so that reasonable bar lengths are displayed in the cells.

8. Create a combination chart that displays the 15-year and 30-year fixed rates in a line chart on the primary axis, and the Mortgage Application Index in an area chart on the secondary axis. Move and resize the chart to cover the range F6:M22.

9. Make the following changes to the chart:

   a. Format the chart with the Style 1 chart style.

   b. Change the chart title to **Interest Rates vs. Mortgage Applications** and reduce the font size of the title text to 14 points.

   c. Move the legend to the bottom of the chart area.

   d. Add the axis title **Interest Rate** to the primary vertical axis, and then add the axis title **Application Index** to the secondary vertical axis.

   e. Rotate the text of the secondary vertical axis title down.

   f. Change the scale of the primary vertical axis to range from 2 percent to 4.5 percent in increments of 0.5 percent, and then change the scale of the secondary vertical axis to range from 500 to 1000 in increments of 50.

   g. Add primary major vertical gridlines to the plot area.

   h. Set the fill color of the plot area to white and the fill color of the chart area to Brown, Accent 3, Lighter 80%.

10. Save the workbook.

11. Return to the Mortgage Calculator worksheet. One of Kyle's clients wants to take out a $200,000 mortgage but can afford only an $850 monthly payment. Use Goal Seek to determine how low the 30-year fixed rate needs to be to meet that goal.

12. Save the workbook as **Mortgage Report 2**, and then close it.

ProSkills

Decision Making

Creating a Budget Worksheet to Make Financial Decisions

Decision making is the process of choosing between alternative courses of action, usually in response to a problem that needs to be solved. Having an understanding of decision-making processes will lead to better decisions and greater confidence in carrying out those decisions. This is especially important when making financial decisions.

Gather Relevant Information

Begin by collecting data and information related to the decision you need to make. This information can include data expressed as currency or numbers, as well as data that cannot be measured numerically. For example, when creating a budget, numerical data includes your income and expenses, current savings, future savings and purchases, and so on. Other data might include the amount of savings you need in order to feel comfortable before making a large purchase, such as buying a car or paying tuition.

Evaluate the Gathered Information and Develop Alternatives

Evaluate the data you collected and determine possible alternatives. Excel workbooks are well suited to evaluating numerical data. You can also use workbooks to evaluate potential outcomes based on other data by assigning numerical weights to them. For example, you can enter your monthly income and fixed expenses into a worksheet along with variable expenses to determine your cash flow. You can then consider this information along with your current savings to determine how much money to contribute to savings or earmark for a purchase. Based on these results, you can develop alternatives for how to distribute your available money among variable expenses (such as entertainment), savings, and a large purchase.

Select the Best Alternative

Carefully evaluate the alternatives you developed based on your analysis. Before making a decision, be sure to take into account all factors. Consider such questions as:

- Does this alternative make sense for the long term? For example, does this budget allow you to achieve all your financial goals?
- Can you realistically carry out this alternative? For example, does this budget provide enough for necessities such as food and housing as well as for luxuries such as entertainment?
- Will this alternative be acceptable even if its outcome is not perfect or some unconsidered factors emerge? For example, will this budget cover unforeseen expenses such as car repairs or an unexpected trip?
- How comfortable are you with this decision? For example, does this budget relieve or add stress about managing your finances?

After analyzing all the factors, one alternative should begin to emerge as the best alternative. If it doesn't, you might need to develop additional alternatives.

Prepare an Action Plan

After making a decision, you need to plan how to implement that decision. Consider what steps you need to take to achieve the final outcome. For example, do you need to open a bank account or change services to reduce expenses (such as switching to a less expensive cell phone plan)? Determine a reasonable time table. When do you want to start? How long will each task take? What tasks must be completed before others start? Can tasks be performed at the same time? Develop milestones to track the success of your plan. For example, one milestone might be to increase your savings by 10 percent in three months. Finally, identify what resources you need to be successful. For example, do you need to talk to a financial advisor at your bank?

Take Action and Monitor the Results

After you develop the action plan, the actual plan begins. For example, you can open bank accounts, change telephone services, and so forth as outlined in your action plan. Be sure to check off completed tasks and assess how well those actions produce the desired outcome. For example, is the budget achieving the financial goals you set? If so, then continue to follow the established plan. If not, you may need to modify the action plan or reevaluate your decision.

PROSKILLS

Develop a Budget Worksheet

Excel is valuable to a wide audience of users: from accountants of Fortune 500 companies to homeowners managing their budgets. An Excel workbook can be a complex document, recording data from thousands of financial transactions, or it can track a few monthly household expenses. Anyone who has to balance a budget, track expenses, or project future income can use the financial tools in Excel to help them make good financial decisions about their financing and future expenditures.

In this exercise, you will use Excel to create a sample budget workbook that will contain information of your choice, using the Excel skills and features presented in Tutorials 1 through 4. Use the following steps as a guide to completing your workbook.

Note: Please be sure *not* to include any personal information of a sensitive nature in any workbooks you create to be submitted to your instructor for this exercise. Later, you can update the workbooks with such information for your personal use.

1. Gather the data related to your monthly cash inflows and outflows. For example, how much do you take home in your paychecks each month? What other sources of income do you have? What expenses do you have—rent, utilities, gas, insurance, groceries, entertainment, car payments, and so on?

2. Create a new workbook for the sample financial data. Use the first worksheet as a documentation sheet that includes your name, the date on which you start creating the workbook, and a brief description of the workbook's purpose.

3. Plan the structure of the second worksheet, which will contain the budget. Include a section to enter values that remain consistent from month to month, such as monthly income and expenses. As you develop the budget worksheet, reference these cells in formulas that require those values. Later, you can update any of these values and see the changes immediately reflected throughout the budget.

4. In the budget worksheet, enter realistic monthly earnings for each month of the year. Use formulas to calculate the total earnings each month, the average monthly earnings, and the total earnings for the entire year.

5. In the budget worksheet, enter realistic personal expenses for each month. Divide the expenses into at least three categories, providing subtotals for each category and a grand total of all the monthly expenses. Calculate the average monthly expenses and total expenses for the year.

6. Calculate the monthly net cash flow (the value of total income minus total expenses).

7. Use the cash flow values to track the savings throughout the year. Use a realistic amount for savings at the beginning of the year. Use the monthly net cash flow values to add or subtract from this value. Project the end-of-year balance in the savings account under your proposed budget.

8. Format the worksheet's contents using appropriate text and number formats. Add colors and borders to make the content easier to read and interpret. Use cell styles and themes to provide your worksheet with a uniform appearance.

9. Use conditional formatting to automatically highlight negative net cash flow months.

10. Insert a pie chart that compares the monthly expenses for the categories.

11. Insert a column chart that charts all of the monthly expenses regardless of the category.

12. Insert a line chart or sparkline that shows the change in the savings balance throughout the 12 months of the year.

13. Insert new rows at the top of the worksheet and enter titles that describe the worksheet's contents.

14. Examine your assumptions. How likely are certain events to occur? Perform several what-if analyses on your budget, providing the impact of (a) reducing income with expenses remaining constant; (b) increasing expenses with income remaining constant; (c) reducing income and expenses; and (d) increasing income and expenses. Discuss the different scenarios you explored. How much cushion does your projected income give you if expenses increase? What are some things you can do in your budget to accommodate this scenario?

15. Think of a major purchase you might want to make—for example, a car or a house. Determine the amount of the purchase and the current annual interest rate charged by your local bank. Provide a reasonable length of time to repay the loan, such as five years for a car loan or 20 to 30 years for a home loan. Use the PMT function to determine how much you would have to spend each month on the payments for your purchase. You can do these calculations in a separate worksheet.

16. Add the loan information to your monthly budget and evaluate the purchase of this item on your budget. Is it affordable? Examine other possible loans you might pursue and evaluate their impact on your budget. Come up with the most realistic way of paying off the loan while still maintaining a reasonable monthly cash flow and a cushion against unexpected expenses. If the payment exceeds your budget, reduce the estimated price of the item you're thinking of purchasing until you determine the monthly payment you can afford under the conditions of the loan.

17. After settling on a budget and the terms of a loan that you can afford, develop an action plan for putting your budget into place. What are some potential pitfalls that will prohibit you from following through on your proposed budget? How can you increase the likelihood that you will follow the budget? Be specific, and write down a list of goals and benchmarks that you'll use to monitor your progress in following your financial plan.

18. With the worksheet set up and your budget in place, you can take action and monitor your results. You will want to update your worksheet each month as income or expense items change to be sure you remain on track to meet your goals. You will also want to confirm that you made a good decision. If not, evaluate your budget and determine what new action you need to take to get yourself back on track.

19. Format the worksheets for your printer. Include headers and footers that display the workbook filename, the workbook's author, and the date on which the report is printed. If the report extends across several pages, repeat appropriate print titles on all of the pages, and include page numbers and the total number of pages on every printed page.

20. Save and close the workbook.

Working with Excel Tables, PivotTables, and PivotCharts

Tracking Cash Receipts

Case | *Laurie's Coffeehouse*

Laurie Kye's dream of opening Laurie's Coffeehouse became a reality three months ago. Laurie's Coffeehouse serves coffee blends and specialty drinks, along with breakfast and lunch items. To keep the shop interesting, Laurie sells unique handcrafted gifts at the counter. The coffeehouse is located in Cave Creek, Arizona, which is a popular tourist attraction and close to a community college campus, so it attracts heavy foot traffic. Recently, the coffeehouse has become a weekend meeting place for many motorcyclists and bikers.

Now that Laurie's Coffeehouse has settled into a smooth routine, Laurie wants to analyze her business operations more carefully. She wants to determine what is working best, and what is selling most each day. In addition, Laurie wants information to help her make ordering and staffing decisions. She has entered the January cash receipts data into an Excel workbook, and has asked you to help her analyze the data. You'll work with the data as an Excel table so you can easily edit, sort, and filter the data. You'll also summarize the data using the Subtotals command, a PivotTable, and a PivotChart.

STARTING DATA FILES

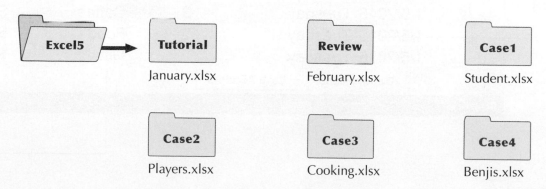

Excel5 →	Tutorial	Review	Case1
	January.xlsx	February.xlsx	Student.xlsx
	Case2	Case3	Case4
	Players.xlsx	Cooking.xlsx	Benjis.xlsx

Session 5.1 Visual Overview:

Every Excel table has a table name, which you can change to a descriptive name.

The filter button changes to a sort icon as a reminder that the data is sorted by that field.

The first row of the range contains field names and is called the **header row**. Although the header row often is row 1, it can begin in any row.

Each row represents a **record**, which is a group of related fields.

You can rearrange, or **sort**, the records in a table or a range based on one or more fields. This table is sorted by the Trn Date field, which is the **sort field**.

You can use a predefined list to sort data in chronological rather than alphabetical order, such as by day of the week.

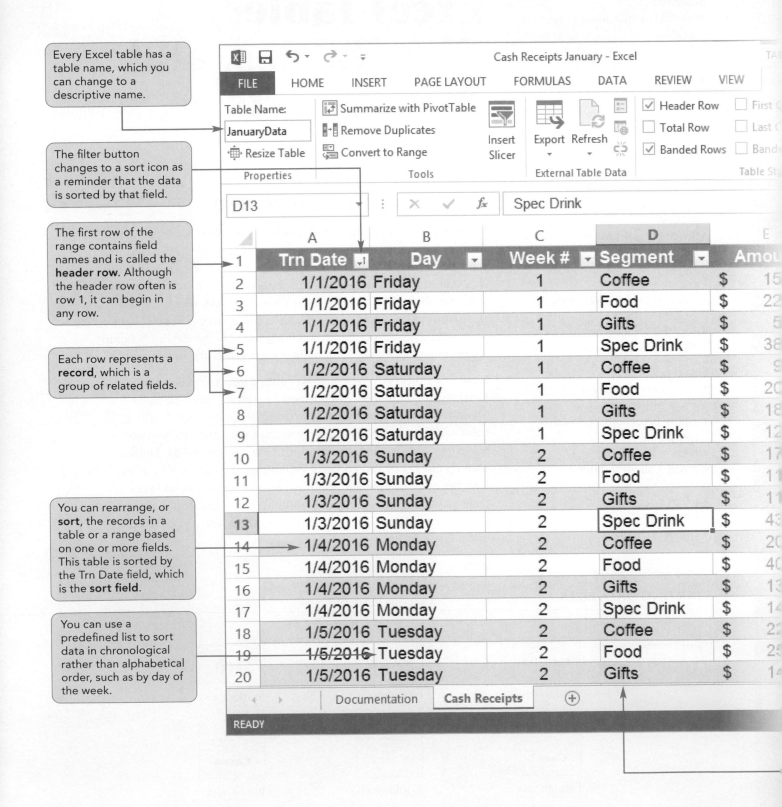

Trn Date	Day	Week #	Segment	Amou
1/1/2016	Friday	1	Coffee	$ 15
1/1/2016	Friday	1	Food	$ 22
1/1/2016	Friday	1	Gifts	$ 5
1/1/2016	Friday	1	Spec Drink	$ 38
1/2/2016	Saturday	1	Coffee	$ 9
1/2/2016	Saturday	1	Food	$ 20
1/2/2016	Saturday	1	Gifts	$ 18
1/2/2016	Saturday	1	Spec Drink	$ 12
1/3/2016	Sunday	2	Coffee	$ 17
1/3/2016	Sunday	2	Food	$ 11
1/3/2016	Sunday	2	Gifts	$ 11
1/3/2016	Sunday	2	Spec Drink	$ 43
1/4/2016	Monday	2	Coffee	$ 20
1/4/2016	Monday	2	Food	$ 40
1/4/2016	Monday	2	Gifts	$ 13
1/4/2016	Monday	2	Spec Drink	$ 14
1/5/2016	Tuesday	2	Coffee	$ 22
1/5/2016	Tuesday	2	Food	$ 28
1/5/2016	Tuesday	2	Gifts	$ 14

Cash Receipts January - Excel

FILE   HOME   INSERT   PAGE LAYOUT   FORMULAS   DATA   REVIEW   VIEW

Table Name:
JanuaryData

Summarize with PivotTable
Remove Duplicates
Resize Table
Convert to Range

Insert Slicer   Export   Refresh

☑ Header Row   ☐ First
☐ Total Row   ☐ Last
☑ Banded Rows   ☐ Band

Properties   Tools   External Table Data   Table St

D13   fx   Spec Drink

Documentation   **Cash Receipts**   ⊕

READY

Elements of an Excel Table

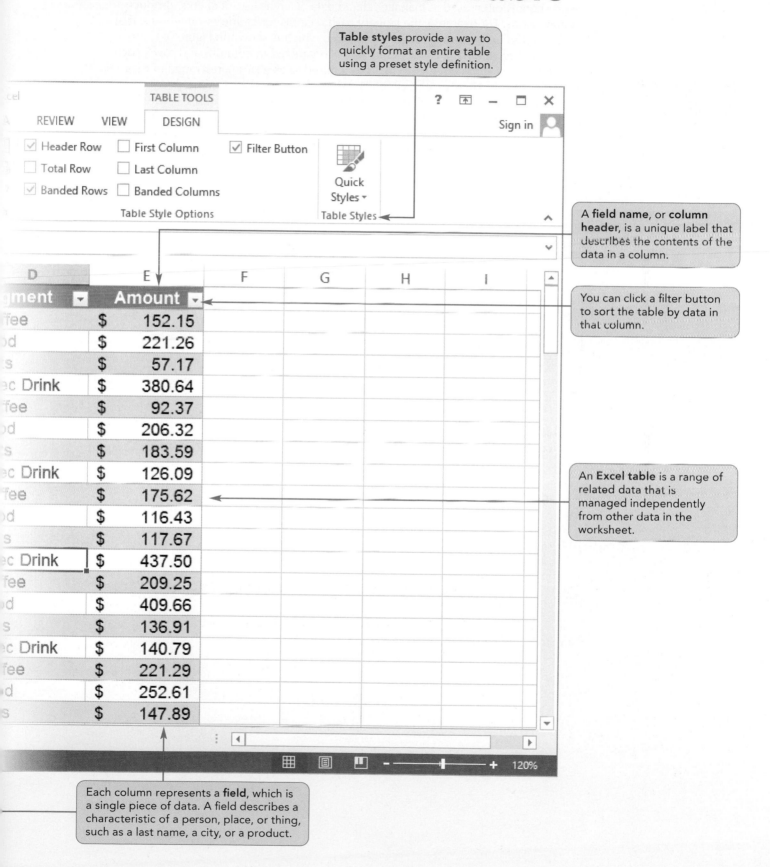

Table styles provide a way to quickly format an entire table using a preset style definition.

A **field name**, or **column header**, is a unique label that describes the contents of the data in a column.

You can click a filter button to sort the table by data in that column.

An **Excel table** is a range of related data that is managed independently from other data in the worksheet.

Each column represents a **field**, which is a single piece of data. A field describes a characteristic of a person, place, or thing, such as a last name, a city, or a product.

Planning a Structured Range of Data

A worksheet is often used to manage related data, such as lists of clients, products, or transactions. For example, the January cash receipts for Laurie's Coffeehouse that Laurie entered in the Cash Receipts worksheet, which is shown in Figure 5-1, are a collection of related data. Related data that is organized in columns and rows, such as the January cash receipts, is sometimes referred to as a structured range of data. Each column represents a field, which is a single piece of data. Each row represents a record, which is a group of related fields. In the Cash Receipts worksheet, the columns labeled Trn Date, Day, Week #, Segment, and Amount are fields that store different pieces of data. Each row in the worksheet is a record that stores one day's cash receipts for a specific segment that includes the Trn Date, Day, Week #, Segment, and Amount fields. All of the cash receipts records make up the structured range of data. A structured range of data is commonly referred to as a list or table.

> **TIP**
>
> In Excel, a range of data is any block of cells, whereas a structured range of data has related records and fields organized in rows and columns.

Figure 5-1 | **January cash receipts data**

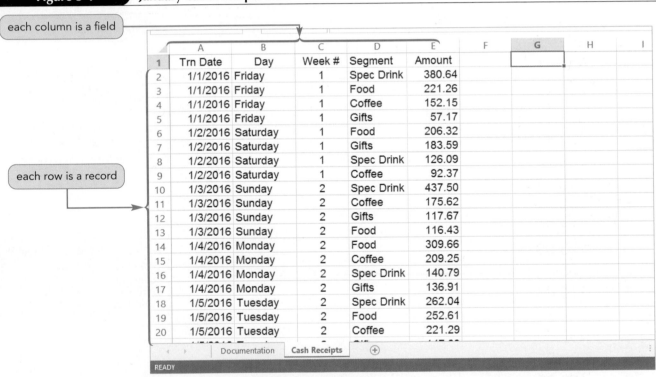

each column is a field

each row is a record

	A	B	C	D	E	F	G	H	I
1	Trn Date	Day	Week #	Segment	Amount				
2	1/1/2016	Friday	1	Spec Drink	380.64				
3	1/1/2016	Friday	1	Food	221.26				
4	1/1/2016	Friday	1	Coffee	152.15				
5	1/1/2016	Friday	1	Gifts	57.17				
6	1/2/2016	Saturday	1	Food	206.32				
7	1/2/2016	Saturday	1	Gifts	183.59				
8	1/2/2016	Saturday	1	Spec Drink	126.09				
9	1/2/2016	Saturday	1	Coffee	92.37				
10	1/3/2016	Sunday	2	Spec Drink	437.50				
11	1/3/2016	Sunday	2	Coffee	175.62				
12	1/3/2016	Sunday	2	Gifts	117.67				
13	1/3/2016	Sunday	2	Food	116.43				
14	1/4/2016	Monday	2	Food	309.66				
15	1/4/2016	Monday	2	Coffee	209.25				
16	1/4/2016	Monday	2	Spec Drink	140.79				
17	1/4/2016	Monday	2	Gifts	136.91				
18	1/5/2016	Tuesday	2	Spec Drink	262.04				
19	1/5/2016	Tuesday	2	Food	252.61				
20	1/5/2016	Tuesday	2	Coffee	221.29				

Documentation   Cash Receipts   (+)

READY

You can easily add and delete data, edit data, sort data, find subsets of data, summarize data, and create reports about related data.

Decision Making: The Importance of Planning

Before you create a structured range of data, you should create a plan. Planning involves gathering relevant information about the data and deciding your goals. The end results you want to achieve will help you determine the kind of data to include in each record and how to divide that data into fields. Specifically, you should do the following to create an effective plan:

• Spend time thinking about how you will use the data.
• Consider what reports you want to create for different audiences (supervisors, customers, directors, and so forth) and the fields needed to produce those reports.
• Think about the various questions, or *queries*, you want answered and the fields needed to create those results.

This information is often documented in a **data definition table**, which lists the fields to be maintained for each record, a description of the information each field will include, and the type of data (such as numbers, text, or dates) stored in each field. Careful and thorough planning will help you avoid having to redesign a structured range of data later.

Before creating the list of cash receipts, Laurie carefully considered what information she needs and how she wants to use it. Laurie plans to use the data to track daily cash receipts for each segment of business activity, which she has identified as coffee, specialty drinks, food, and gifts. She wants to be able to create reports that show specific lists of cash receipts, such as all the cash receipts for a specific date, day of the week, or week of the year. Based on this information, Laurie developed the data definition table shown in Figure 5-2.

Figure 5-2 **Data definition table for the cash receipts**

Data Definition Table			
Field	Description	Data Type	Notes
Trn Date	Date of the cash receipts	Date	Transaction Date (abbreviated to Trn Date) Use the *mm/dd/yyyy* format
Day	Day of the week	Text	Sunday, Monday, Tuesday,
Week #	Week of the year	Number	1–52
Segment	Business category for the cash receipts	Text	Coffee, Spec Drink, Food, Gifts
Amount	Cash receipts total for a specific transaction date and segment	Number	Use the Accounting format and show two decimal places

After you determine the fields and records you need, you can enter the data in a worksheet. You can then work with the data in many ways, including the following common operations:

• Add, edit, and delete data in the range.
• Sort the data range.
• Filter to display only rows that meet specified criteria.
• Insert formulas to calculate subtotals.
• Create summary tables based on the data in the range (usually with PivotTables).

You'll perform many of these operations on the cash receipts data.

INSIGHT

Creating an Effective Structured Range of Data

For a range of data to be used effectively, it must have the same structure throughout. Keep in mind the following guidelines:

- **Enter field names in the top row of the range.** This clearly identifies each field.
- **Use short, descriptive field names.** Shorter field names are easier to remember and enable more fields to appear in the workbook window at once.
- **Format field names.** Use formatting to distinguish the header row from the data. For example, apply bold, color, and a different font size.
- **Enter the same kind of data in a field.** Each field should store the smallest bit of information and be consistent from record to record. For example, enter Los Angeles, Tucson, or Chicago in a City field, but do not include states, such as CA, AZ, or IL, in the same column of data.
- **Separate the data from the rest of the worksheet.** The data, which includes the header row, should be separated from other information in the worksheet by *at least* one blank row and one blank column. The blank row and column enable Excel to accurately determine the range of the data.

Laurie created a workbook and entered the cash receipts data for January based on the plan outlined in the data definition table. You'll open this workbook and review its structure.

To open and review Laurie's workbook:

1. Open the **January** workbook located in the Excel5 ▸ Tutorial folder included with your Data Files, and then save the workbook as **Cash Receipts January** in the location specified by your instructor.

2. In the Documentation sheet, enter your name in cell B3 and the date in cell B4.

3. In the range A7:D13, review the data definition table. This table, which was shown in Figure 5-2, describes the different fields that are used in the Cash Receipts worksheet.

4. Go to the **Cash Receipts** worksheet. This worksheet, which was shown in Figure 5-1, contains data about the coffeehouse's cash receipts. Currently, the worksheet includes 121 cash receipts. Each cash receipt record is a separate row (rows 2 through 122) and contains five fields (columns A through E). Row 1, the header row, contains labels that describe the data in each column.

5. Scroll the worksheet to row **122**, which is the last record. The column headers in row 1 are no longer visible. Without seeing the column headers, it is difficult to know what the data entered in each column represents.

Freezing Rows and Columns

You can select rows and columns to remain visible in the workbook window as you scroll the worksheet. **Freezing** a row or column lets you keep the headers visible as you work with the data in a large worksheet. You can freeze the top row, freeze the first column, or freeze the rows and columns above and to the left of the selected cell. If you freeze the top row, row 1 remains on the screen as you scroll, leaving column headers visible and making it easier to identify the data in each record.

Laurie wants to see the column headers as she scrolls the cash receipts data. You'll freeze row 1, which contains the column headers.

To freeze row 1 of the worksheet:

1. Press the **Ctrl+Home** keys to return to cell A1. You want to freeze row 1.

2. On the ribbon, click the **VIEW** tab.

3. In the Window group, click the **Freeze Panes** button, and then click **Freeze Top Row**. A horizontal line appears below the column labels to indicate which row is frozen.

4. Scroll the worksheet to row **122**. This time, the column headers remain visible as you scroll. See Figure 5-3.

Figure 5-3   Top row of the worksheet is frozen

header row remains visible as you scroll the worksheet

5. Press the **Ctrl+Home** keys. Cell A2, the cell directly below the frozen row, becomes the active cell.

After you freeze panes, the first option on the Freeze Panes button menu changes to Unfreeze Panes. This option releases the frozen panes so that all the columns and rows in the worksheet shift when you scroll. Laurie wants you to use a different method to keep the column headers visible, so you will unfreeze the top row of the worksheet.

To unfreeze the top row of the worksheet:

1. On the VIEW tab, in the Window group, click the **Freeze Panes** button. The first Freeze Panes option is now Unfreeze Panes.

2. Click **Unfreeze Panes**. The headers are no longer frozen, and the dark, horizontal line below the column headers is removed. You can now scroll all the rows and columns in the worksheet.

Creating an Excel Table

You can convert a structured range of data, such as the cash receipts data in the range A1:E122, to an Excel table. An Excel table makes it easier to identify, manage, and analyze the groups of related data. When a structured range of data is converted into an Excel table, you see the following:

- A filter button in each cell of the header row
- The range formatted with a table style
- A sizing handle (a small triangle) in the lower-right corner of the last cell of the table
- The TABLE TOOLS DESIGN tab on the ribbon

You can create more than one Excel table in a worksheet. Although you can leave the cash receipts data as a structured range of data and still perform all of the tasks in this section, creating an Excel table helps you to be more efficient and accurate.

INSIGHT

Saving Time with Excel Tables

Although you can perform the same operations for both a structured range of data and an Excel table, using Excel tables provides many advantages to help you be more productive and reduce the chance of error, such as the following:

- Format the Excel table quickly using a table style.
- Add new rows and columns to the Excel table that automatically expand the range.
- Add a Total row to calculate the summary function you select, such as SUM, AVERAGE, COUNT, MIN, and MAX.
- Enter a formula in one table cell that is automatically copied to all other cells in that table column.
- Create formulas that reference cells in a table by using table and column names instead of cell addresses.

These Excel table features let you focus on analyzing and understanding the data, leaving the more time-consuming tasks for the program to perform.

Laurie wants you to create an Excel table from the cash receipts data in the Cash Receipts worksheet. You'll be able to work with the Excel tables to analyze Laurie's data effectively.

To create an Excel table from the cash receipts data:

1. If necessary, select any cell in the range of cash receipts data to make it the active cell.

2. On the ribbon, click the **INSERT** tab.

3. In the Tables group, click the **Table** button. The Create Table dialog box opens. The range of data you want to use for the table is selected in the worksheet, and a formula with its range reference, =$A$1:$E$122, is entered in the dialog box.

4. Verify that the **My table has headers** check box is selected. The headers are the field names entered in row 1. If the first row did not contain field names, the My table has headers check box would be unchecked and Excel would insert a row of headers with the names Column1, Column2, and so on.

5. Click the **OK** button. The dialog box closes, and the range of data is converted to an Excel table, which is selected. Filter buttons appear in the header row, the sizing handle appears in the lower-right corner of the last cell of the table, the table is formatted with a predefined table style, and the TABLE TOOLS DESIGN tab appears on the ribbon. See Figure 5-4.

Figure 5-4   **Excel table with the cash receipts data**

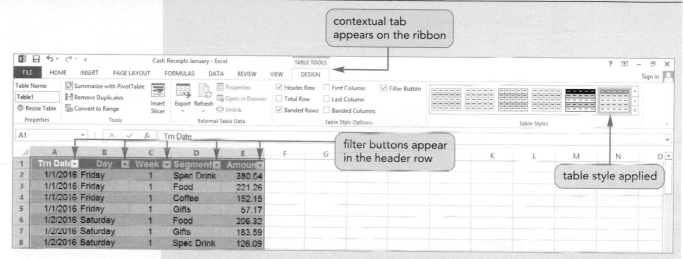

6. Select any cell in the table, and then scroll down the table. The field names in the header row replace the standard lettered column headers (A, B, C, and so on) as you scroll, so you don't need to freeze panes to keep the header row visible. See Figure 5-5.

Figure 5-5   **Cash receipts table scrolled**

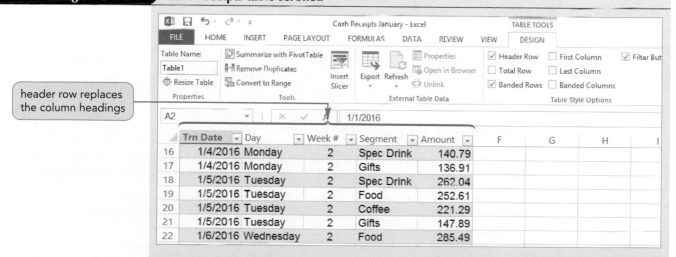

7. Press the **Ctrl+Home** keys to make cell A1 the active cell. The column headers return to the standard display, and the Excel table header row scrolls back into view as row 1.

Renaming an Excel Table

Each Excel table in a workbook must have a unique name. Excel assigns the name Table1 to the first Excel table created in a workbook. Any additional Excel tables you create in the workbook are named consecutively as Table2, Table3, and so forth. You can assign a more descriptive name to a table, making it easier to identify a particular table by its content. Descriptive names are especially useful when you create more than one Excel table in the same workbook because they make it easier to reference the different Excel tables. Table names must start with a letter or an underscore but can use any combination of letters, numbers, and underscores for the rest of the name. Table names cannot include spaces, but you can use an underscore or uppercase letters instead of spaces to separate words in a table name, such as January_Data or JanuaryData.

Laurie wants you to rename the Excel table you just created from the January cash receipts data.

TIP

If you copy a worksheet that contains a table, Excel adds the next consecutive number at the end of the table name to create a unique table name.

To rename the Table1 table:

▶ 1. On the TABLE TOOLS DESIGN tab, in the Properties group, select **Table1** in the Table Name box. See Figure 5-6.

Figure 5-6	Table Name box

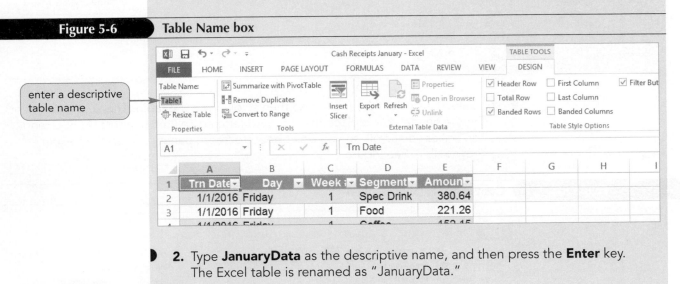

enter a descriptive table name

▶ 2. Type **JanuaryData** as the descriptive name, and then press the **Enter** key. The Excel table is renamed as "JanuaryData."

Modifying an Excel Table

You can modify an Excel table by adding or removing table elements or by changing the table's formatting. For every Excel table, you can display or hide the following elements:

- **Header row**—The first row of the table that includes the field names
- **Total row**—A row at the bottom of the table that applies a function to the column values
- **First column**—Formatting added to the leftmost column of the table
- **Last column**—Formatting added to the rightmost column of the table
- **Banded rows**—Formatting added to alternating rows so that even and odd rows are different colors, making it simpler to distinguish records
- **Banded columns**—Formatting added to alternating columns so they are different colors, making it simpler to distinguish fields
- **Filter buttons**—Buttons that appear in each column of the header row and open a menu with options for sorting and filtering the table data

You can also modify a table by applying a table style. As with other styles, a table style formats all of the selected table elements with a consistent, unified design. You can change the font, fill, alignment, number formats, column widths and row heights, and other formatting of selected cells in the table the same way you would for other cells in the worksheet.

Laurie wants the JanuaryData table to have a format that makes the table easier to read. You will apply a table style and make other formatting changes to the table.

To format the JanuaryData table:

1. On the TABLE TOOLS DESIGN tab, in the Table Styles group, click the **More** button. A gallery of table styles opens.

2. In the Table Styles gallery, in the Medium section, click **Table Style Medium 3**. The table now has an orange style.

TIP

To display or hide alternating column colors, click the Banded Columns check box in the Table Style Options group.

3. In the Table Style Options group, click the **Banded Rows** check box. The alternating row colors disappear. The table is more challenging to read this way, so you will reapply the banded rows formatting.

4. In the Table Style Options group, click the **Banded Rows** check box to select it. The alternating row colors reappear.

5. Change the width of columns A through E to **12** characters. The entire column headers and all values will now be visible.

6. Select the **Amount** column, and then change the values to the **Accounting** format. See Figure 5-7.

| **Figure 5-7** | Modified JanuaryData table |

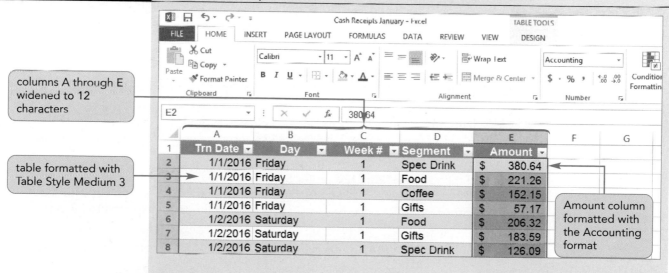

columns A through E widened to 12 characters

table formatted with Table Style Medium 3

Amount column formatted with the Accounting format

7. Select cell **A1** to make it the active cell.

Maintaining Data in an Excel Table

As you develop a worksheet with an Excel table, you may need to add new records to the table, find and edit existing records in the table, and delete records from the table. Laurie wants you to make several changes to the data in the JanuaryData table.

Adding Records

As you maintain data in an Excel table, you often need to add new records. You add a record to an Excel table in a blank row. The simplest and most convenient way to add a record to an Excel table is to enter the data in the first blank row below the last record. You can then sort the data to arrange the table in the order you want. If you want the record in a specific location, you can also insert a row within the table for the new record.

The cash receipts records for January 31 are missing from the JanuaryData table. Laurie asks you to add to the table four new records that contain the missing data.

To add four records to the JanuaryData table:

1. Press the **End** key, and then press the ↓ key to make cell A122 the active cell. This cell is in the last row of the table.

2. Press the ↓ key to move the active cell to cell A123, which is in the first blank row below the table.

TIP

You can drag the sizing handle to add columns or rows to the Excel table or delete them from it.

3. In cell A123, type **1/31/2016**, and then press the **Tab** key. Cell B123 in the Day column becomes the active cell. The table expands to include a new row with the same formatting as the rest of the table. The AutoCorrect Options button appears so you can undo the table formatting if you hadn't intended the new data to be part of the existing table. The sizing handle moves to the lower-right corner of cell E123, which is now the cell in the lower-right corner of the table. See Figure 5-8.

Figure 5-8   New row added to the JanuaryData table

120	1/30/2016	Saturday	5	Food	$	348.08	
121	1/30/2016	Saturday	5	Coffee	$	323.35	sizing handle
122	1/30/2016	Saturday	5	Gifts	$	169.29	
123	1/31/2016						

AutoCorrect Options button

Documentation   Cash Receipts   (+)

READY

Trouble? If cell A124 is the active cell, you probably pressed the Enter key instead of the Tab key. Click cell B123 and then continue entering the data in Step 4.

4. In the range **B123:E123**, enter **Sunday** as the Day, **6** as the Week #, **Food** as the Segment, and **164.50** as the Amount, pressing the **Tab** key after each entry. Cell A124 becomes the active cell and the table expands to include row 124.

5. In the range **A124:E126**, enter the following cash receipts:

1/31/2016	Sunday	6	Coffee	278.98
1/31/2016	Sunday	6	Gifts	178.17
1/31/2016	Sunday	6	Spec Drink	345.88

6. Press the **Enter** key. The records are added to the table. See Figure 5-9.

Figure 5-9   Records added to the JanuaryData table

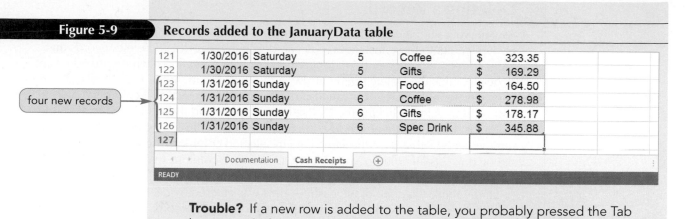

four new records

121	1/30/2016 Saturday	5	Coffee	$	323.35
122	1/30/2016 Saturday	5	Gifts	$	169.29
123	1/31/2016 Sunday	6	Food	$	164.50
124	1/31/2016 Sunday	6	Coffee	$	278.98
125	1/31/2016 Sunday	6	Gifts	$	178.17
126	1/31/2016 Sunday	6	Spec Drink	$	345.88
127					

Documentation   Cash Receipts   ⊕

READY

Trouble? If a new row is added to the table, you probably pressed the Tab key instead of the Enter key after the last entry in the record. On the Quick Access Toolbar, click the Undo button ↰ to remove the extra row.

Finding and Editing Records

Although you can manually scroll through the table to find a specific record, often a quicker way to locate a record is to use the Find command. When using the Find or Replace command, it is best to start at the top of a worksheet to ensure that all cells in the table are searched. You edit the data in a table the same way as you edit data in a worksheet cell.

Laurie wants you to update the January 20 cash receipts for the Gifts segment. You'll use the Find command to locate the record, which is currently blank. Then, you'll edit the record in the table to change the amount to $154.25.

To find and edit the record for Gifts on 1/20/2016:

1. Press the **Ctrl+Home** keys to make cell A1 the active cell so that all cells in the table will be searched.

2. On the HOME tab, in the Editing group, click the **Find & Select** button, and then click **Find** (or press the **Ctrl+F** keys). The Find and Replace dialog box opens.

3. In the Find what box, type **1/20/2016**, and then click the **Find Next** button. Cell A79, which contains the Coffee segment, is selected. This is not the record you want.

4. Click the **Find Next** button three times to display the record for Gifts on 1/20/2016.

5. Click the **Close** button. The Find and Replace dialog box closes.

6. Press the **Tab** key four times to move the active cell to the Amount column, type **154.25**, and then press the **Enter** key. The record is updated.

7. Press the **Ctrl+Home** keys to make cell A1 the active cell.

Deleting a Record

As you work with the data in an Excel table, you might find records that are outdated or duplicated. In these instances, you can delete the records. To delete records that are incorrect, out of date, or no longer needed, select a cell in each record you want to delete, click the Delete button arrow in the Cells group on the HOME tab, and then click Delete Table Rows. You can also delete a field by selecting a cell in the field you want to delete, clicking the Delete button arrow, and then clicking Delete Table Columns. In addition, you can use the Remove Duplicates dialog box to locate and remove records that have the same data in selected columns. The Remove Duplicates dialog box lists all columns in the table. Usually, all columns in a table are selected to identify duplicate records.

Laurie thinks that one of the cash receipts was entered twice. You'll use the Remove Duplicates dialog box to locate and delete the duplicate record from the table.

To find and delete the duplicate record from the JanuaryData table:

1. Scroll to row **64**, and observe that the entries in row 64 and row 65 are exactly the same. One of these records needs to be deleted.

2. On the ribbon, click the **TABLE TOOLS DESIGN** tab.

3. In the Tools group, click the **Remove Duplicates** button. The Remove Duplicates dialog box opens, and all of the columns in the table are selected. Excel looks for repeated data in the selected columns to determine whether any duplicate records exist. If duplicates are found, all but one of the records are deleted. See Figure 5-10.

| Figure 5-10 | Remove Duplicates dialog box |

values in all of the selected columns must be equal for the row to be considered a duplicate

You want to search all columns in the table for duplicated data so that you don't inadvertently delete a record that has duplicate values in all of the selected fields but a unique value in the deselected field.

4. Click the **OK** button. A dialog box opens, reporting "1 duplicate values found and removed; 124 unique values remain."

5. Click the **OK** button.

   Trouble? If you deleted records you did not intend to delete, you can reverse the action. On the Quick Access Toolbar, click the Undo button, and then repeat Steps 3 through 5.

6. Press the **Ctrl+Home** keys to make cell A1 the active cell.

Sorting Data

The records in an Excel table initially appear in the order they were entered. As you work, however, you may want to view the same records in a different order. For example, Laurie might want to view the cash receipts by segment or day of the week. You can sort data in ascending or descending order. **Ascending order** arranges text alphabetically from A to Z, numbers from smallest to largest, and dates from oldest to newest. **Descending order** arranges text in reverse alphabetical order from Z to A, numbers from largest to smallest, and dates from newest to oldest. In both ascending and descending order, blank cells are placed at the end of the table.

Sorting One Column Using the Sort Buttons

You can quickly sort data with one sort field using the Sort A to Z button ▲↓ or the Sort Z to A button ▼↓. Laurie wants you to sort the cash receipts in ascending order by the Segment column. This will rearrange the table data so that the records appear in alphabetical order by Segment.

To sort the JanuaryData table in ascending order by the Segment column:

1. Select any cell in the Segment column. You do not need to select the entire JanuaryData table, which consists of the range A1:E125. Excel determines the table's range when you click any cell in the table.

2. On the ribbon, click the **DATA** tab.

TIP

You can also use the Sort & Filter button in the Editing group on the HOME tab.

3. In the Sort & Filter group, click the **Sort A to Z** button ▲↓. The data is sorted in ascending order by Segment. The Segment filter button changes to show that the data is sorted by that column. See Figure 5-11.

Figure 5-11   **JanuaryData table sorted by the Segment field**

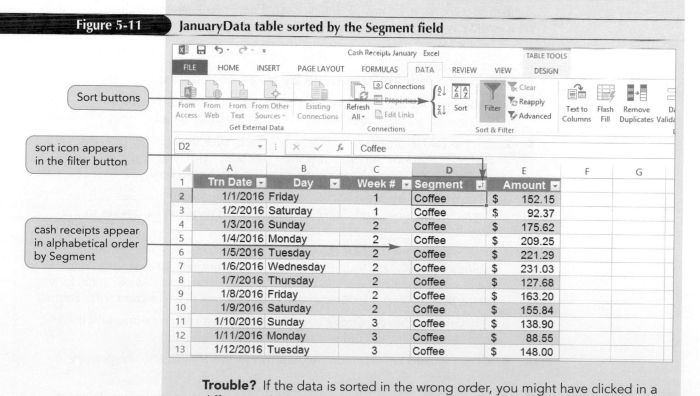

Trouble? If the data is sorted in the wrong order, you might have clicked in a different column than the Segment column. Repeat Steps 1 through 3.

Sorting Multiple Columns Using the Sort Dialog Box

Sometimes one sort field is not adequate for your needs. For example, Laurie wants to arrange the JanuaryData table so that the cash receipts are ordered first by Day (Sunday, Monday, and so forth), then by Segment for each day of the week, and then by Amount (highest to lowest). You must sort by more than one column to accomplish this. The first sort field is called the **primary sort field**, the second sort field is called the **secondary sort field**, and so forth. Although you can include up to 64 sort fields in a single sort, you typically will use one to three sort fields. In this case, the Day field is the primary sort field, the Segment field is the secondary sort field, and the Amount field is the tertiary sort field. When you have more than one sort field, you should use the Sort dialog box to specify the sort criteria.

REFERENCE

Sorting Data Using Multiple Sort Fields

- Select any cell in a table or range.
- On the DATA tab, in the Sort & Filter group, click the Sort button.
- If necessary, click the Add Level button to insert the Sort by row.
- Click the Sort by arrow, select the column heading for the primary sort field, click the Sort On arrow to select the type of data, and then click the Order arrow to select the sort order.
- For each additional column to sort, click the Add Level button, click the Then by arrow, select the column heading for the secondary sort field, click the Sort On arrow to select the type of data, and then click the Order arrow to select the sort order.
- Click the OK button.

Laurie wants to see the cash receipts sorted by day, and then within day by segment, and then within segment by amount, with the highest amounts appearing before the smaller ones for each segment. This will make it easier for Laurie to evaluate business on specific days of the week in each segment.

To sort the JanuaryData table by three sort fields:

1. Select cell **A1** in the JanuaryData table. Cell A1 is the active cell—although you can select any cell in the table to sort the table data.

2. On the DATA tab, in the Sort & Filter group, click the **Sort** button. The Sort dialog box opens. Any sort specifications (sort field, type of data sorted on, and sort order) from the last sort appear in the dialog box.

3. Click the **Sort by** arrow to display the list of the column headers in the JanuaryData table, and then click **Day**. The primary sort field is set to the Day field.

4. If necessary, click the **Sort On** arrow to display the type of sort, and then click **Values**. Typically, you want to sort by the numbers, text, or dates stored in the cells, which are all values. You can also sort by formats such as cell color, font color, and cell icon (a graphic that appears in a cell due to a conditional format).

5. If necessary, click the **Order** arrow to display sort order options, and then click **A to Z**. The sort order is set to ascending.

6. Click the **Add Level** button. A Then by row is added below the primary sort field.

7. Click the **Then by** arrow and click **Segment**, and then verify that **Values** appears in the Sort On box and **A to Z** appears in the Order box.

8. Click the **Add Level** button to add a second Then by row.

9. Click the second **Then by** arrow, click **Amount**, verify that **Values** appears in the Sort On box, click the **Order** arrow, and then click **Largest to smallest** to specify a descending sort order for the Amount values. See Figure 5-12.

| Figure 5-12 | Sort dialog box with three sort fields |

10. Click the **OK** button. Excel sorts the table records first in ascending order by the Day field, then within each Day in ascending order by the Segment field, and then within each Segment in descending order by the Amount field. For example, the first 20 records are Friday cash receipts. Of these records, the first five are Coffee, the next five are Food, and so on. Finally, the Friday Coffee receipts are arranged from highest to lowest in the Amount column. See Figure 5-13.

| Figure 5-13 | Cash receipts sorted by Day, then by Segment, and then by Amount |

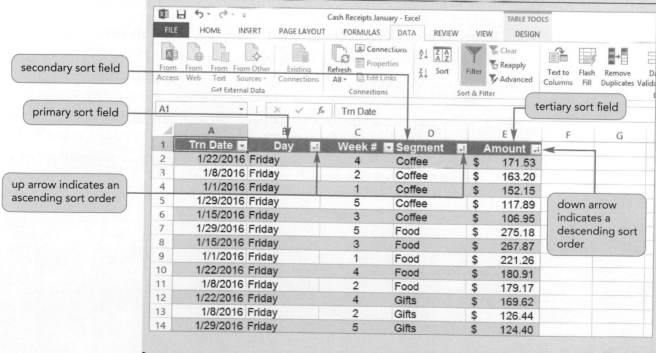

11. Scroll the table to view the sorted table data.

The table data is sorted in alphabetical order by the day of the week: Friday, Monday, Saturday, and so forth. This default sort order for fields with text values is not appropriate for days of the week. Instead, Laurie wants you to base the sort on chronological rather than alphabetical order. You'll use a custom sort list to set up the sort order Laurie wants.

Sorting Using a Custom List

Text is sorted in ascending or descending alphabetical order unless you specify a different order using a custom list. A **custom list** indicates the sequence in which you want data ordered. Excel has two predefined custom lists—day-of-the-week (Sun, Mon, Tues, ... and Sunday, Monday, Tuesday, ...) and month-of-the-year (Jan, Feb, Mar, Apr, ... and January, February, March, April, ...). If a column consists of day or month labels, you can sort them in their correct chronological order using one of these predefined custom lists.

You can also create custom lists to sort records in a sequence you define. For example, you can create a custom list to logically order high-school or college students based on their admittance date (freshman, sophomore, junior, and senior) rather than alphabetical order (freshman, junior, senior, and sophomore).

REFERENCE

Sorting Using a Custom List

- On the DATA tab, in the Sort & Filter group, click the Sort button.
- Click the Order arrow, and then click Custom List.
- If necessary, in the List entries box, type each entry for the custom list (in the desired order) and press the Enter key, and then click the Add button.
- In the Custom lists box, select the predefined custom list.
- Click the OK button.

You'll use a predefined custom list to sort the records by the Day column in chronological order rather than alphabetical order.

To use a predefined custom list to sort the Day column:

1. Make sure the active cell is in the JanuaryData table.

2. On the DATA tab, in the Sort & Filter group, click the **Sort** button. The Sort dialog box opens, showing the sort specifications from the previous sort.

3. In the Sort by Day row, click the **Order** arrow to display the sort order options, and then click **Custom List**. The Custom Lists dialog box opens.

4. In the Custom lists box, click **Sunday, Monday, Tuesday, ...** to place the days in the List entries box. See Figure 5-14.

Figure 5-14   Custom Lists dialog box

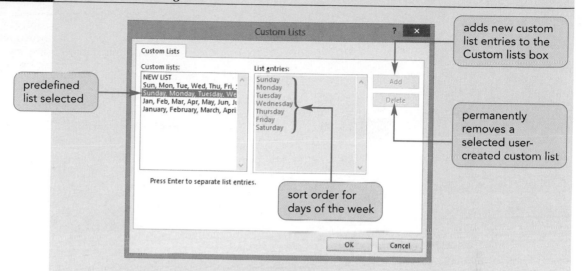

5. Click the **OK** button to return to the Sort dialog box. The custom sort list—Sunday, Monday, Tuesday, …—appears in the Order box.

7. Click the **OK** button. The table is sorted based on the predefined custom list.

8. Scroll the sorted table to verify that the cash receipts are sorted by their chronological day order—Sunday, Monday, Tuesday, Wednesday, Thursday, Friday, Saturday.

So far, you created an Excel table for the cash receipts, and then named and formatted the table. You updated the table by adding, editing, and deleting records. You also sorted the records and used a predefined custom list to sort the Day field by its chronological order. In the next session, you will continue to work with the JanuaryData table.

Session 5.1 Quick Check

REVIEW

1. In Excel, what is the difference between a range of data and a structured range of data?
2. Explain the difference between a field and a record.
3. What is the purpose of the Freeze Panes button in the Window group on the VIEW tab? Why is this feature helpful?
4. What three elements indicate that a range of data is an Excel table?
5. How can you quickly find and delete duplicate records from an Excel table?
6. If you sort table data from the most recent purchase date to the oldest purchase date, in what order have you sorted the data?
7. An Excel table of college students tracks each student's first name, last name, major, and year of graduation. How can you order the table so that students graduating in the same year appear together in alphabetical order by the student's last name?
8. An Excel table of sales data includes the Month field with the values Jan, Feb, Mar, … Dec. How can you sort the data so the sales data is sorted by Month in chronological order (Jan, Feb, Mar, … Dec)?

Session 5.2 Visual Overview:

Filtering is the process of displaying a subset of rows in an Excel table or a structured range of data that meets the criteria you specify. In this case, the table is filtered to show the cash receipts for Week 2.

If you want to change an Excel table back to a structured range of data, you click the Convert to Range button.

The filter button opens the Filter menu, which includes options to sort and filter the table based on the data in that column.

As a reminder that the records are filtered, only the row numbers of the records that match the filter appear (leaving gaps in the consecutive numbering) and are blue. Rows of records that don't match the filter are hidden.

The selection list displays the unique items in the selected column. You can select one or multiple items from the list to filter the table by.

The **Total row** is used to calculate summary statistics (including sum, average, count, maximum, and minimum) for any column in an Excel table.

The status bar indicates that the table is filtered.

Cash Receipts January - Excel

FILE HOME INSERT PAGE LAYOUT FORMULAS DATA REVIEW VIEW

Table Name:
JanuaryData

Resize Table

Properties

Summarize with PivotTable
Remove Duplicates
Convert to Range

Tools

Insert Slicer

Export Refresh

External Table Data

☑ Header Row   ☐ First C
☑ Total Row   ☐ Last C
☑ Banded Rows   ☐ Bande

Table Sty

B126   =SUBTOTAL(103,[Day])

	A	B	C	D	E
1	Trn Date	Day	Week #	Segment	Amou
10	1/3/2016	Sunday			$ 17
11	1/3/2016	Sunday			$ 11
12	1/3/2016	Sunday			$ 11
13	1/3/2016	Sunday			$ 43
14	1/4/2016	Monday			$ 20
15	1/4/2016	Monday			$ 40
16	1/4/2016	Monday			$ 13
17	1/4/2016	Monday			$ 14
18	1/5/2016	Tuesday			$ 22
19	1/5/2016	Tuesday			$ 25
20	1/5/2016	Tuesday			$ 14
21	1/5/2016	Tuesday			$ 26
22	1/6/2016	Wednesday			$ 23
23	1/6/2016	Wednesday			$ 28
24	1/6/2016	Wednesday			$ 14
25	1/6/2016	Wednesday			$ 16
26	1/7/2016	Thursday			$ 12
126	Total		28		$ 5,8
127					

Filter menu:
- A↓ Sort A to Z
- Z↓ Sort Z to A
- Sort by Color ▶
- Clear Filter From "Segment"
- Filter by Color ▶
- Text Filters ▶
- Search
  - ☑ (Select All)
  - ☑ Coffee
  - ☑ Food
  - ☑ Gifts
  - ☑ Spec Drink
- OK   Cancel

◀ ▶ Documentation **Cash Receipts** ⊕

READY   28 OF 124 RECORDS FOUND

Filtering Table Data

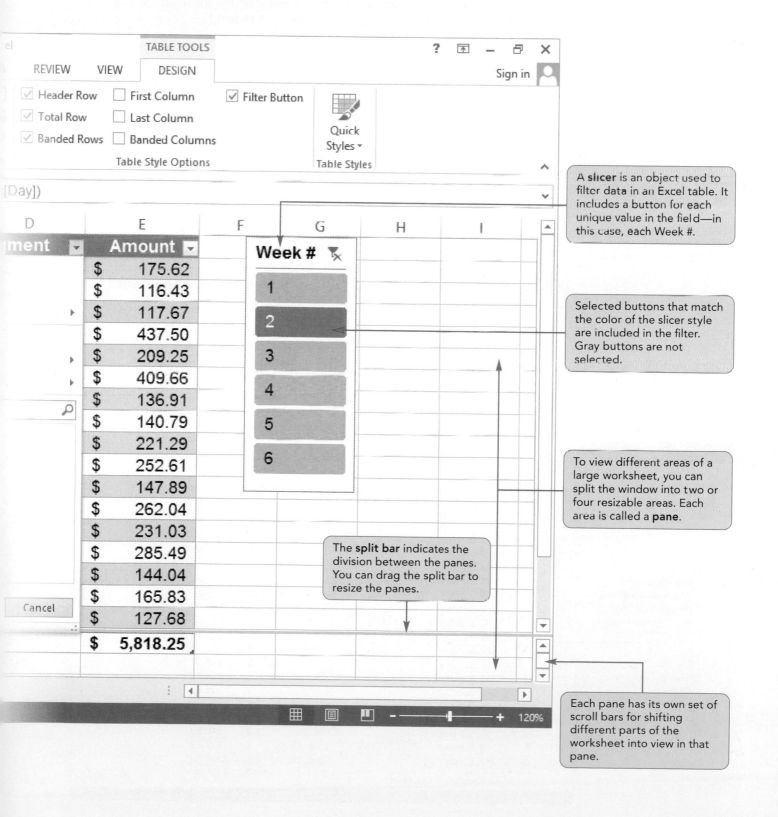

A **slicer** is an object used to filter data in an Excel table. It includes a button for each unique value in the field—in this case, each Week #.

Selected buttons that match the color of the slicer style are included in the filter. Gray buttons are not selected.

To view different areas of a large worksheet, you can split the window into two or four resizable areas. Each area is called a **pane**.

The **split bar** indicates the division between the panes. You can drag the split bar to resize the panes.

Each pane has its own set of scroll bars for shifting different parts of the worksheet into view in that pane.

Filtering Data

Laurie needs to determine if she should increase food orders on Saturdays, her busiest day. She wants to see a list of all Food receipts on Saturdays. Although you could sort the receipts by Segment and Day to group the records of interest to Laurie, the entire table would still be visible. A better solution is to display only the specific records you want. Filtering temporarily hides any records that do not meet the specified criteria. After data is filtered, you can sort, copy, format, chart, and print it.

Filtering Using One Column

When you create an Excel table, a filter button appears in each column header. You click a filter button to open the Filter menu for that field. You can use options on the Filter menu to create three types of filters. You can filter a column of data by its cell colors or font colors. You can filter a column of data by a specific text, number, or date filter, although the choices depend on the type of data in the column. Or, you can filter a column of data by selecting the exact values by which you want to filter in the column. After you filter a column, the Clear Filter command becomes available so you can remove the filter and redisplay all the records.

Laurie wants to see the cash receipts for only Food orders. You'll filter the JanuaryData table to show only those records with the value Food in the Segment column.

To filter the JanuaryData table to show only the Food segment:

▶ **1.** If you took a break after the previous session, make sure the Cash Receipts January workbook is open, the Cash Receipts worksheet is the active sheet, and the JanuaryData table is active.

▶ **2.** Click the **Segment** filter button ⬛. The Filter menu opens, as shown in Figure 5-15, listing the unique entries in the Segment field—Coffee, Food, Gifts, and Spec Drink. All of the items are selected, but you can set which items to use to filter the data. In this case, you want to select Food.

Figure 5-15 ▶ **Filter menu for the Segment column**

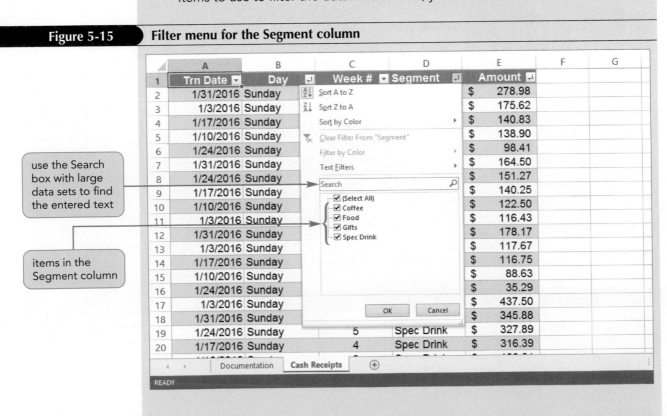

use the Search box with large data sets to find the entered text

items in the Segment column

> **3.** Click the **(Select All)** check box to remove the checkmarks from all of the Segment items.

> **4.** Click the **Food** check box to insert a checkmark. The filter will show only records that match the checked item, and will hide records that contain the unchecked items.

> **5.** Click the **OK** button. The filter is applied. The status bar lists the number of Food rows found in the entire table—in this case, 31 of the 124 records in the table are displayed. See Figure 5-16.

| Figure 5-16 | JanuaryData table filtered to show only Food |

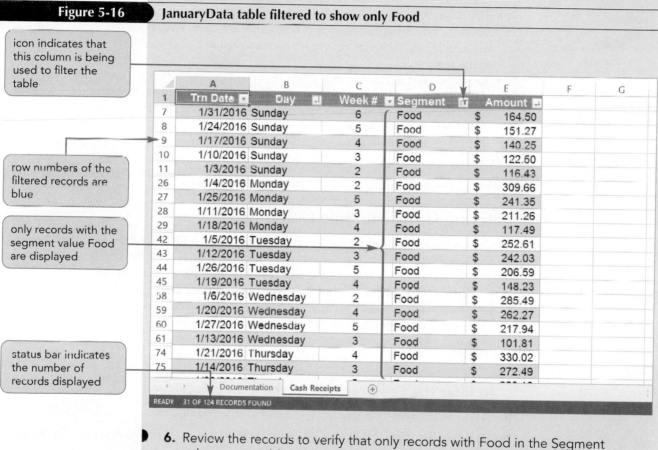

icon indicates that this column is being used to filter the table

row numbers of the filtered records are blue

only records with the segment value Food are displayed

status bar indicates the number of records displayed

> **6.** Review the records to verify that only records with Food in the Segment column are visible. All other records in this column are hidden, leaving gaps in the row numbers.

> **7.** Point to the **Segment** filter button. A ScreenTip—Segment: Equals "Food"—describes the filter applied to the column.

The Filter menu includes options to Sort by Color and Filter by Color. These options enable you to filter and sort data using color, one of many cell attributes. Laurie could use specific cell background colors for certain receipts in the JanuaryData table. For example, she might want to highlight the dates when the coffeehouse could have used an additional employee. So cells in the Trn Date column for busy days would be formatted with yellow as a reminder. You could click the Sort by Color option to display a list of available colors by which to sort, and then click the specific color so that all the records for the days when she needed more help in the store (formatted with yellow) would appear together. Similarly, you could click the Filter by Color option to display a submenu with the available colors by which to filter, and then click a color.

Exploring Text Filters

You can use different text filters to display the records you want. If you know only part of a text value or if you want to match a certain pattern, you can use the Begins With, Ends With, and Contains operators to filter a text field to match the pattern you specify. The following examples are based on a student directory table that includes First Name, Last Name, Address, City, State, and Zip fields:

- To find a student named Smith, Smithe, or Smythe, create a text filter using the Begins With operator. In this example, use "Begins With Sm" to display all records that have "Sm" at the beginning of the text value.
- To Find anyone whose Last Name ends in "son" (such as Robertson, Anderson, Dawson, or Gibson), create a text filter using the Ends With operator. In this example, use "Ends With son" to display all records that have "son" as the last characters in the text value.
- To find anyone whose street address includes "Central" (such as 101 Central Ave., 1024 Central Road, or 457 Avenue De Central), create a text filter using the Contains operator. In this example, use "Contains Central" to display all records that have "Central" anywhere in the text value.

When you create a text filter, determine what results you want. Then, consider what text filter you can use to best achieve those results.

Filtering Using Multiple Columns

If you need to further restrict the records that appear in a filtered table, you can filter by one or more of the other columns. Each additional filter is applied to the currently filtered data and further reduces the number of records that are displayed.

Laurie wants to see only Saturday Food receipts, rather than all of the Food receipts in the JanuaryData table. To do this, you need to filter the Food records to display only those with the value Saturday in the Day column. You'll use the filter button in the Day column to add this second filter criterion to the filtered data.

To filter the Food records to show only Saturday:

1. Click the **Day** filter button ▾↑. The Filter menu opens.

2. Click the **(Select All)** check box to remove the checkmarks from all of the Day check boxes.

3. Click the **Saturday** check box.

4. Click the **OK** button. The JanuaryData table is further filtered and shows the five rows of Saturday Food receipts in January. See Figure 5-17.

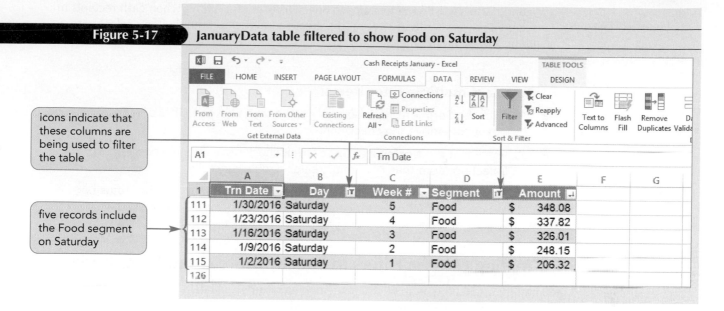

Figure 5-17   **JanuaryData table filtered to show Food on Saturday**

icons indicate that these columns are being used to filter the table

five records include the Food segment on Saturday

Clearing Filters

When you want to redisplay all of the data in a filtered table, you need to **clear** (or remove) the filters. When you clear a filter from a column, any other filters are still applied. For example, in the JanuaryData table, you would see all the food receipts in the table if you cleared the filter from the Day field. Similarly, you would see all the cash receipts on Saturday if you cleared the filter from the Segment field. To redisplay all the cash receipts in the table, you need to clear both the Day filter and the Segment filter. You will do this now to redisplay the entire table of cash receipts.

To clear the filters to show all the records in the JanuaryData table:

1. Click the **Day** filter button 🔽, and then click **Clear Filter From "Day"**. The Day filter is removed from the table. The table shows only Food receipts because the Segment filter is still in effect.

2. Click the **Segment** filter button 🔽, and then click **Clear Filter From "Segment"**. The Segment filter is removed, and all the records in the JanuaryData table are now displayed.

Selecting Multiple Filter Items

You can often find the information you need by selecting a single filter item from a list of filter items. Sometimes, however, you need to specify a more complex set of criteria to find the records you want. Earlier, you selected one filter item for the Segment column and one filter item for the Day column to display the records whose Segment field value equals Food *and* whose Day field value equals Saturday. A record had to contain both values to be displayed. Now you want the Segment column to display records whose Segment field value equals Coffee *or* Spec Drink. The records must have one of these values to be displayed. You do this by selecting two filter items from the list of filter items. For example, checking the Coffee and Spec Drink check boxes in the Segment filter items creates the filter "Segment equals Coffee" *or* "Segment equals Spec Drink."

Laurie wants a list of all Coffee and Spec Drink items on days when cash receipts in a segment are greater than $300. You'll create a filter with multiple items selected to find this information.

To select multiple filter items:

▶ 1. Click the **Segment** filter button ⬇️, and then click the **Gifts** and **Food** check boxes to remove the checkmarks.

▶ 2. Verify that the **Coffee** and **Spec Drink** check boxes remain checked. Selecting more than one item creates a multiselect filter.

▶ 3. Click the **OK** button. The JanuaryData table is filtered, and the status bar indicates that 62 of 124 records are either coffee or a specialty drink.

Creating Criteria Filters to Specify More Complex Criteria

Filter items enable you to filter a range of data or an Excel table based on exact values in a column. However, many times you need broader criteria. With **criteria filters**, you can specify various conditions in addition to those that are based on an equals criterion. For example, you might want to find all cash receipts that are greater than $500 or that occurred after 1/15/2016. You use criteria filters to create these conditions.

The types of criteria filters available change depending on whether the data in a column contains text, numbers, or dates. Figure 5-18 shows some of the options for text, number, and date criteria filters.

Figure 5-18   **Options for text, number, and date criteria filters**

Filter	Criteria	Records Displayed
Text	Equals	Exactly match the specified text
	Does Not Equal	Do not exactly match the specified text
	Begins With	Begin with the specified text
	Ends With	End with the specified text
	Contains	Have the specified text anywhere
	Does Not Contain	Do not have the specified text anywhere
Number	Equals	Exactly match the specified number
	Greater Than or Equal to	Are greater than or equal to the specified number
	Less Than	Are less than the specified number
	Between	Are greater than or equal to *and* less than or equal to the specified numbers
	Top 10	Are the top or bottom 10 (or the specified number)
	Above Average	Are greater than the average
Date	Today	Have the current date
	Last Week	Are in the prior week
	Next Month	Are in the month following the current month
	Last Quarter	Are in the previous quarter of the year (quarters defined as Jan, Feb, Mar; Apr, May, June; and so on)
	Year to Date	Are since January 1 of the current year to the current date
	Last Year	Are in the previous year (based on the current date)

PROSKILLS

Problem Solving: Using Filters to Find Appropriate Data

Problem solving often requires finding information from a set of data to answer specific questions. When you're working with a range of data or an Excel table that contains hundreds or thousands of records, filters help you find that information without having to review each record in the table. For example, a human resources manager can use a filter to narrow the search for a specific employee out of the 2500 working at the company knowing only that the employee's first name is Elliot.

Filtering limits the data to display only the specific records that meet the criteria you set, enabling you to more effectively analyze the data. The following examples further illustrate how filtering can help people to quickly locate the data they need to answer a particular question:

- A customer service representative can use a filter to search a list of 10,000 products to find all products priced between $500 and $1000.
- A donations coordinator can use a filter to prepare a report that shows the donations received during the first quarter of the current year.
- An academic dean can use a filter to retrieve the names of all students with GPAs below 2.0 (probation) or above 3.5 (high honors).
- A professor who has 300 students in a psychology class can use a filter to develop a list of potential student assistants for next semester from the names the professor has highlighted in blue because their work was impressive. Filtering by the blue color generates a list of students to interview.
- The author of a guide to celebrity autographs can use a filter to determine whether an entry for a specific celebrity already exists in an Excel table and, if it does, determine whether the entry needs to be updated. If the entry does not exist, the author will know to add the autograph data to the table.

As these examples show, filtering is a useful tool for locating the answers to a wide variety of questions. You then can use this information to help you resolve problems.

Laurie wants you to display the records for coffee or specialty drinks that were greater than $300. You'll modify the filtered JanuaryData table to add a criteria filter that includes cash receipts with values greater than $300.

To create a number filter that shows cash receipts greater than $300:

1. Click the **Amount** filter button ⏷, and then point to **Number Filters**. A menu opens, displaying the comparison operators available for columns of numbers.

2. Click **Greater Than**. The Custom AutoFilter dialog box opens. The upper-left box displays *is greater than*, which is the comparison operator you want to use to filter the Amount column. You enter the value you want to use for the filter criteria in the upper-right box, which, in this case, is $300.

3. Type **300** in the upper-right box. See Figure 5-19. You use the lower set of boxes if you want the filter to meet a second condition. You click the And option button to display rows that meet both criteria. You click the Or option button to display rows that meet either of the two criteria. You only want to set one criterion for this filter, so you'll leave the lower boxes empty.

Figure 5-19   **Custom AutoFilter dialog box**

4. Click the **OK** button. The status bar indicates that 17 of 124 records were found. The 17 records that appear in the JanuaryData table are either Coffee or Spec Drink, and have an Amount greater than $300.

Next, you'll sort the filtered data to show the largest Amount first. Although you can sort the data using Sort buttons, as you did earlier, these sort options are also available on the Filter menu. If you want to perform a more complex sort, you still need to use the Sort dialog box.

To sort the filtered table data:

1. Click the **Amount** filter button 🔽. The Filter menu opens. The sort options are at the top of the menu.

2. Click **Sort Largest to Smallest**. The filtered table now displays Coffee and Spec Drink categories with daily receipts greater than $300 sorted in descending order. See Figure 5-20.

Figure 5-20   **Filtered and sorted JanuaryData table**

icon shows that this column is filtered

Spec Drink or Coffee with daily amount greater than $300 sorted in descending order by Amount

icon shows that this column is filtered and sorted

	A	B	C	D	E	F	G
1	Trn Date ▼	Day ▼	Week # ▼	Segment 🔽	Amount 🔽		
17	1/23/2016	Saturday	4	Spec Drink	$ 454.14		
18	1/3/2016	Sunday	2	Spec Drink	$ 437.50		
19	1/30/2016	Saturday	5	Spec Drink	$ 425.50		
20	1/1/2016	Friday	1	Spec Drink	$ 380.64		
34	1/9/2016	Saturday	2	Spec Drink	$ 374.25		
50	1/13/2016	Wednesday	3	Spec Drink	$ 360.50		
66	1/22/2016	Friday	4	Spec Drink	$ 353.50		
82	1/31/2016	Sunday	6	Spec Drink	$ 345.88		
101	1/8/2016	Friday	2	Spec Drink	$ 344.79		
102	1/18/2016	Monday	4	Spec Drink	$ 330.99		
103	1/24/2016	Sunday	5	Spec Drink	$ 327.89		
106	1/30/2016	Saturday	5	Coffee	$ 323.35		
107	1/19/2016	Tuesday	4	Spec Drink	$ 322.65		
121	1/17/2016	Sunday	4	Spec Drink	$ 316.39		
122	1/16/2016	Saturday	3	Spec Drink	$ 314.66		
123	1/23/2016	Saturday	4	Coffee	$ 308.43		
124	1/28/2016	Thursday	5	Spec Drink	$ 305.42		
126							
127							

Documentation   **Cash Receipts**   ⊕

READY   17 OF 124 RECORDS FOUND

Laurie will use this data to help her decide on which days she may hire additional workers. You need to restore the entire table of cash receipts, which you can do by clearing all the filters at one time.

To clear all the filters from the JanuaryData table:

1. On the ribbon, click the **DATA** tab, if necessary.

2. In the Sort & Filter group, click the **Clear** button. All of the records are redisplayed in the table.

Creating a Slicer to Filter Data in an Excel Table

Another way to filter an Excel table is with slicers. You can create a slicer for any field in the Excel table. You also can create more than one slicer for a table. Every slicer consists of an object that contains a button for each unique value in that field. For example, a slicer created for the Day field would include seven buttons—one for each day of the week. One advantage of a slicer is that it clearly shows what filters are currently applied—the buttons for selected values are a different color. However, a slicer can take up a lot of space or hide data if there isn't a big enough blank area near the table. You can format the slicer and its buttons, changing its style, height, and width.

Laurie wants to be able to quickly filter the table to show cash receipts for a specific week. You will add a slicer for the Week # field so she can do this.

To add the Week # slicer to the JanuaryData table:

1. On the ribbon, click the **TABLE TOOLS DESIGN** tab.

2. In the Tools group, click the **Insert Slicer** button. The Insert Slicers dialog box opens, listing every available field in all tables in the workbook. You can select any or all of the fields.

3. Click the **Week #** check box to insert a checkmark, and then click the **OK** button. The Week # slicer appears on the worksheet. All of the slicer buttons are selected, indicating that every Week # is included in the table.

4. Drag the **Week #** slicer to the right of the JanuaryData table, placing its upper-left corner in cell G1.

5. If necessary, click the **Week #** slicer to select it. The SLICER TOOLS OPTIONS tab appears on the ribbon and is selected.

6. In the Size group, enter **2.2"** in the Height box and **1"** in the Width box. The slicer is resized, eliminating the extra space below the buttons and to the right of the labels.

7. In the Slicer Styles group, click the **More** button, and then click **Slicer Style Dark 2**. The slicer colors now match the formatting of the Excel table. See Figure 5-21.

Figure 5-21 **JanuaryData table with the Week # slicer**

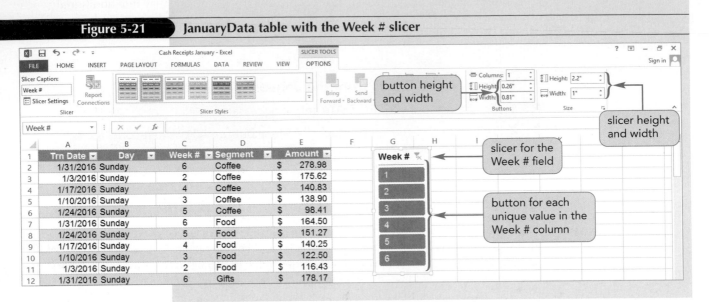

You can use the slicer to quickly filter records in an Excel table. Just click the slicer button corresponding to the data you want to display in the table. If you want to show more than one week, hold down the Ctrl key as you click the buttons that correspond to the additional data you want to show.

Laurie wants you to filter the JanuaryData table to display cash receipts for Week 1 and Week 5. You will use the Week # slicer to do this.

To filter the JanuaryData table using the Week # slicer:

▶ **1.** On the Week # slicer, click the **1** button. Only Week 1 data appears in the JanuaryData table. All of the other buttons are gray, indicating that these weeks are not included in the filtered data.

▶ **2.** Press and hold the **Ctrl** key, click the **5** button, and then release the **Ctrl** key. Cash receipts for Week 5 are now added to the JanuaryData filtered table. See Figure 5-22.

Figure 5-22   JanuaryData table filtered to show Weeks 1 and 5

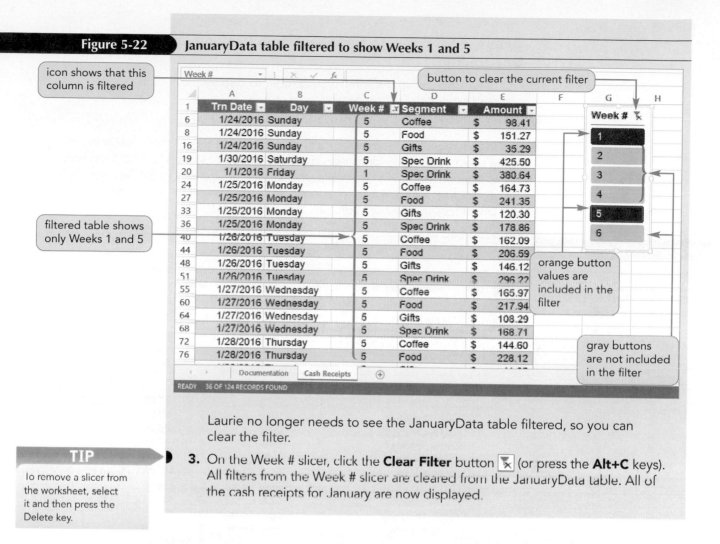

icon shows that this column is filtered

button to clear the current filter

filtered table shows only Weeks 1 and 5

orange button values are included in the filter

gray buttons are not included in the filter

READY   36 OF 124 RECORDS FOUND

Laurie no longer needs to see the JanuaryData table filtered, so you can clear the filter.

TIP

To remove a slicer from the worksheet, select it and then press the Delete key.

3. On the Week # slicer, click the **Clear Filter** button (or press the **Alt+C** keys). All filters from the Week # slicer are cleared from the JanuaryData table. All of the cash receipts for January are now displayed.

Using the Total Row to Calculate Summary Statistics

The Total row is used to calculate summary statistics (including sum, average, count, maximum, and minimum) for any column in an Excel table. The Total row is inserted immediately after the last row of data in the table. A double-line border is inserted to indicate that the following row contains totals, and the label Total is added to the leftmost cell of the row. By default, the Total row adds the numbers in the last column of the Excel table or counts the number of records if the data in the last column contains text. When you click in each cell of the Total row, an arrow appears that you can click to open a list of the most commonly used functions. You can also select other functions by opening the Insert Functions dialog box.

Laurie wants to see the total amount of cash receipts in January and the total number of records being displayed. You will add a Total row to the JanuaryData table, and then use the SUM and COUNT functions to calculate these statistics for Laurie.

To add a Total row to sum the Amount column and count the Day column:

1. Select any cell in the JanuaryData table to display the TABLE TOOLS contextual tab.

2. On the ribbon, click the **TABLE TOOLS DESIGN** tab.

3. In the Table Style Options group, click the **Total Row** check box to insert a checkmark. The worksheet scrolls to the end of the table. The Total row is now the last row in the table, the label Total appears in the leftmost cell of the row, and $24,612.67 appears in the rightmost cell of the row (at the bottom of the Amount column). See Figure 5-23.

| Figure 5-23 | Total row added to the JanuaryData table |

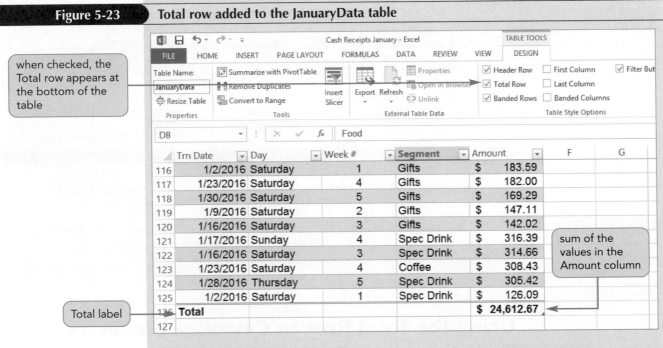

when checked, the Total row appears at the bottom of the table

sum of the values in the Amount column

Total label

Next, you will use the COUNT function to add the number of records displayed.

4. Click cell **B126** (the Day cell in the Total row), and then click the **arrow** button to display a list of functions. None is the default function in all columns except the last column. See Figure 5-24.

Figure 5-24   Total row functions

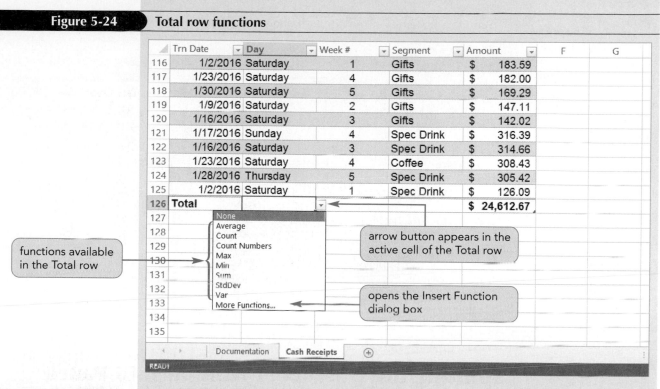

functions available in the Total row

arrow button appears in the active cell of the Total row

opens the Insert Function dialog box

TIP

When you select Sum, Count, or Average, Excel uses the SUBTOTAL function to calculate the summary statistic in the Total row.

5. Click **Count**. The number 124, which is the number of records in the JanuaryData table, appears in the cell.

As you add, edit, or delete data in the table, the Total row values change. This also happens if you filter the table to show only some of the table data. Laurie wants the total cash receipts to include only weeks in January with seven days. You will filter the table to exclude Weeks 1 and 6, displaying the total Amount for Weeks 2 through 5 only. The COUNT function will also change to show only the number of transactions for the filtered data.

To filter cash receipts by excluding receipts from Week 1 and Week 6:

1. Press the **Ctrl+Home** keys to make cell A1 the active cell.

2. On the Week # slicer, click the **2** slicer button, press and hold the **Ctrl** key as you click the **3**, **4**, and **5** slicer buttons, and then release the **Ctrl** key. The JanuaryData table is filtered to display cash receipts for the four full weeks in January.

3. Scroll to the end of the table. The Total row shows that the 112 records contain total cash receipts of $22,225.55. See Figure 5-25.

Figure 5-25 Summary statistics in the filtered table

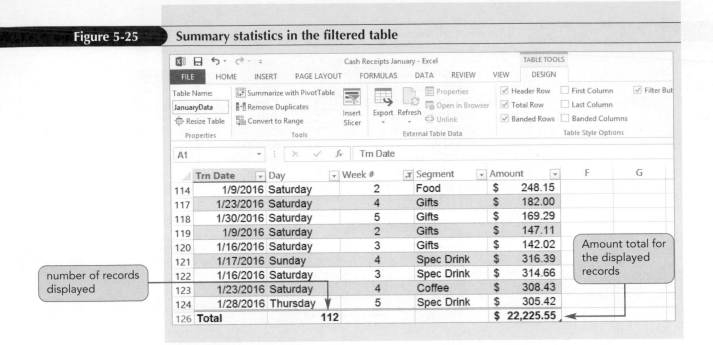

	Trn Date	Day	Week #	Segment	Amount	F	G
114	1/9/2016	Saturday	2	Food	$ 248.15		
117	1/23/2016	Saturday	4	Gifts	$ 182.00		
118	1/30/2016	Saturday	5	Gifts	$ 169.29		
119	1/9/2016	Saturday	2	Gifts	$ 147.11		
120	1/16/2016	Saturday	3	Gifts	$ 142.02		
121	1/17/2016	Sunday	4	Spec Drink	$ 316.39		
122	1/16/2016	Saturday	3	Spec Drink	$ 314.66		
123	1/23/2016	Saturday	4	Coffee	$ 308.43		
124	1/28/2016	Thursday	5	Spec Drink	$ 305.42		
126	**Total**		112		$ 22,225.55		

number of records displayed

Amount total for the displayed records

Splitting the Worksheet Window into Panes

You can split the worksheet window into two or four separate panes. This allows you to easily view data from several areas of the worksheet at the same time. Each pane has its own scroll bars so you can navigate easily within one pane or display different parts of the worksheet. You can move between panes using the mouse. To create two panes, select a cell in row 1 to split the worksheet vertically, or select a cell in column A to split the worksheet horizontally; to create four panes, select any other cell in the worksheet.

Laurie wants to view the JanuaryData summary totals at the same time she views the data on individual cash receipts. You will divide the worksheet into two horizontal panes to view the cash receipt records in the top pane and the totals in the bottom pane.

To split the Cash Receipts worksheet window into panes:

1. Press the **Ctrl+Home** keys to make cell A1 at the top of the table the active cell.

2. Select the cell in column A that is two rows above the last row visible on your screen.

3. On the ribbon, click the **VIEW** tab.

4. In the Window group, click the **Split** button. The worksheet window splits into two panes. Each pane has its own set of scroll bars. The active cell is in the bottom pane below the split bar. See Figure 5-26.

Figure 5-26   Worksheet split into two panes

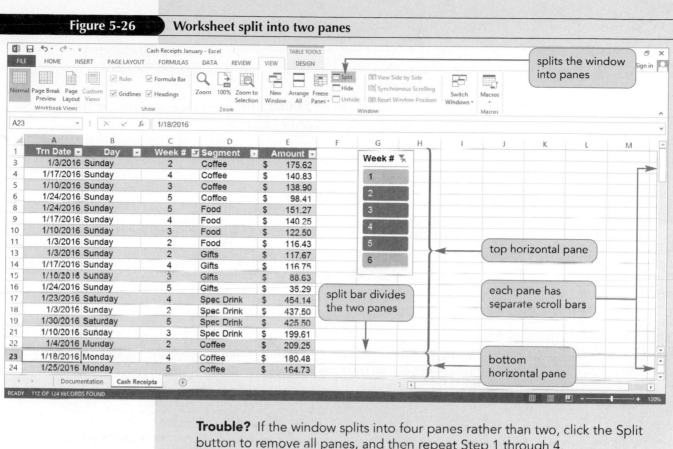

Trouble? If the window splits into four panes rather than two, click the Split button to remove all panes, and then repeat Step 1 through 4.

5. Using the lower scroll bar, scroll down until the Total row appears immediately below the split bar. See Figure 5-27.

Figure 5-27   Total row displayed in the bottom pane

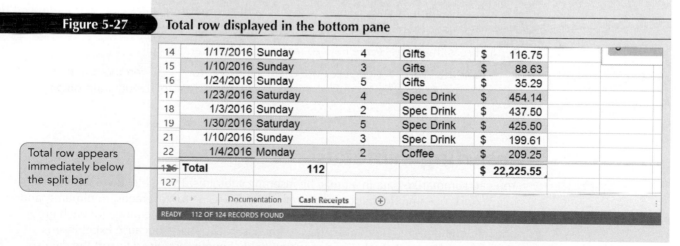

Laurie discovered a data entry error in the receipts amount for Coffee on 1/28/2016. It was entered as 144.60; the correct amount is 244.60. You will change the amount.

To update the amount of the Coffee receipts on 1/28/2016:

▶   **1.** Select any cell in the top pane.

▶   **2.** Use the Find command to locate the 1/28/2016 receipts for Coffee. The amount is 144.60.

▶   **3.** In the Amount column, enter **244.60**. The total receipts amount in the bottom pane changes from $22,225.55 to $22,325.55.

When you want to see a worksheet in a single pane, you remove the split panes from the worksheet window. You will do this now.

To remove the split panes from the Cash Receipts worksheet window:

▶   **1.** On the ribbon, click the **VIEW** tab, if necessary.

▶   **2.** In the Window group, click the **Split** button. The split bar is removed, and the worksheet is again a single window.

TIP

You can also double-click the split bar to remove the panes.

Now, you will hide the Total row and clear the filter. If you later redisplay the Total row, the functions you last used will appear even after you save, close, and then reopen the workbook.

To hide the Total row and clear the filter from the JanuaryData table:

▶   **1.** On the ribbon, click the **TABLE TOOLS DESIGN** tab.

▶   **2.** In the Table Style Options group, click the **Total Row** check box to remove the checkmark. The Total row is no longer visible.

▶   **3.** Press the **Ctrl+Home** keys to make cell A1 the active cell.

▶   **4.** On the Week # slicer, click the **Clear Filter** button ⊠ to remove the filters from the JanuaryData table. All of the cash receipts for January are displayed.

Inserting Subtotals

You can summarize data in a range by inserting subtotals. The Subtotal command offers many kinds of summary information, including counts, sums, averages, minimums, and maximums. The Subtotal command inserts a subtotal row into the range for each group of data and adds a grand total row below the last row of data. Because Excel inserts subtotals whenever the value in a specified field changes, you need to sort the data so that records with the same value in a specified field are grouped together *before* you use the Subtotal command. The Subtotal command cannot be used in an Excel table, so you must first convert the Excel table to a normal range.

REFERENCE

Calculating Subtotals for a Range of Data

- Sort the data by the column for which you want a subtotal.
- If the data is in an Excel table, on the TABLE TOOLS DESIGN tab, in the Tools group, click the Convert to Range button, and then click the Yes button to convert the Excel table to a range.
- On the DATA tab, in the Outline group, click the Subtotal button.
- Click the At each change in arrow, and then click the column that contains the group you want to subtotal.
- Click the Use function arrow, and then click the function you want to use to summarize the data.
- In the Add subtotal to box, click the check box for each column that contains the values you want to summarize.
- To calculate another category of subtotals, click the Replace current subtotals check box to remove the checkmark, and then repeat the previous three steps.
- Click the OK button.

Laurie wants to create a report that shows all the coffeehouse's cash receipts sorted by Trn Date with the total amount of the cash receipts for each date. She also wants to see the total amount for each receipt date after the last item of that date. The Subtotal command is a simple way to provide the information Laurie needs. First, you will sort the cash receipts by Trn Date, then you will convert the Excel table to a normal range, and finally you will calculate subtotals in the Amount column for each Trn Date grouping to produce the results Laurie needs.

To sort the cash receipts and convert the table to a range:

Be sure to sort the table and then convert the table to a range before calculating subtotals.

1. Click the **Trn Date** filter button ▼, and then click **Sort Oldest to Newest** on the Filter menu. The JanuaryData table is sorted in ascending order by the Trn Date field. This ensures one subtotal is created for each date.

2. On the TABLE TOOLS DESIGN tab, in the Tools group, click the **Convert to Range** button. A dialog box opens, asking if you want to convert the table to a normal range.

3. Click the **Yes** button. The Excel table is converted to a range, and the HOME tab is selected on the ribbon. You can tell the table data is now a normal range because the filter buttons, the TABLE TOOLS DESIGN tab, and the slicer disappear.

Next, you'll calculate the subtotals.

To calculate the cash receipts amount subtotals for each date:

1. On the ribbon, click the **DATA** tab.

2. In the Outline group, click the **Subtotal** button. The Subtotal dialog box opens. See Figure 5-28.

Figure 5-28   Subtotal dialog box

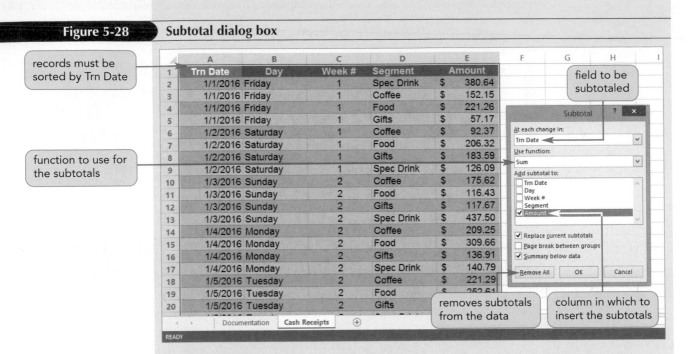

records must be sorted by Trn Date

function to use for the subtotals

field to be subtotaled

removes subtotals from the data

column in which to insert the subtotals

3. If necessary, click the **At each change in** arrow, and then click **Trn Date**. This is the column you want Excel to use to determine where to insert the subtotals; it is the column you sorted. A subtotal will be calculated at every change in the Trn Date value.

4. If necessary, click the **Use function** arrow, and then click **Sum**. The Use function list provides several options for subtotaling data, including counts, averages, minimums, maximums, and products.

5. In the Add subtotal to box, make sure only the **Amount** check box is checked. This specifies the Amount field as the field to be subtotaled.

    If the data already included subtotals, you would check the Replace current subtotals check box to replace the existing subtotals, or uncheck the option to display the new subtotals on separate rows above the existing subtotals. Because the data has no subtotals, it makes no difference whether you select this option.

6. Make sure the **Summary below data** check box is checked. This option places the subtotals below each group of data instead of above the first entry in each group, and places the grand total at the end of the data instead of at the top of the column just below the row of column headings.

7. Click the **OK** button. Excel inserts rows below each Trn Date group and displays the subtotals for the Amount of each Trn Date in the Amount column. A series of Outline buttons appears to the left of the worksheet so you can display or hide the detail rows within each subtotal.

    Trouble? If each item has a subtotal following it, or repeating subtotals appear for the same item, you probably forgot to sort the data by Trn Date. Click the Undo button on the Quick Access Toolbar, sort the data by Trn Date, and then repeat Steps 1 through 7.

8. Scroll through the data to see the subtotals below each category and the grand total at the end of the data. See Figure 5-29.

Figure 5-29   **Subtotals and grand total added to the cash receipts data**

Outline buttons

new rows with the
subtotal added
below each Trn Date

new row with the
grand total added at
the end of the table

Using the Subtotal Outline View

The Subtotal feature "outlines" the worksheet so you can control the level of detail
that is displayed. The three Outline buttons at the top of the outline area, shown in
Figure 5-29, allow you to show or hide different levels of detail in the worksheet.
By default, the highest level is active; in this case, Level 3. Level 3 displays the most
detail—the individual cash receipt records, the subtotals, and the grand total. Level 2
displays the subtotals and the grand total, but not the individual records. Level 1
displays only the grand total.

Laurie wants you to isolate the different subtotal sections so that she can focus on
them individually. You will use the Outline buttons to prepare a report for Laurie that
includes only subtotals and the grand total.

To use the Outline buttons to hide records:

1. Click the **Level 2 Outline** button ⎡2⎤, and then scroll to view the daily subtotals
   and grand total. The individual cash receipt records are hidden; only the
   subtotals for each Trn Date and the grand total are displayed. See Figure 5-30.

Figure 5-30   **Level 2 outline**

TIP

To collapse the outline and hide the rows with details, click the Hide Detail button.

2. Click the **Show Detail** button ⊞ to the left of 1/31/2016 to expand the outline and show the details of daily receipts by unhiding rows for this date. Cash receipts for each segment on 1/31/2016 are now displayed.

3. Click the **Level 1 Outline** button ①. The individual cash receipt records and the subtotals for each Trn Date are hidden. Only the grand total remains visible.

4. Click the **Level 3 Outline** button ③, and then scroll up. All the records along with the subtotals and the grand total are visible.

Laurie has completed her review of the daily cash receipts report for January. She asks you to remove the subtotals from the data.

To remove the subtotals from the cash receipts data:

1. On the DATA tab, in the Outline group, click the **Subtotal** button. The Subtotal dialog box opens.

2. Click the **Remove All** button. The subtotals are removed from the data, and only the records appear in the worksheet.

   You'll reset the cash receipts data as an Excel table.

3. Make sure the active cell is a cell within the normal range of data.

4. On the ribbon, click the **INSERT** tab.

5. In the Tables group, click the **Table** button. The Create Table dialog box opens.

6. Click the **OK** button to create the Excel table, and then click any cell in the table. The table structure is active.

7. On the TABLE TOOLS DESIGN tab, in the Properties group, type **JanuaryData** in the Table Name box, and then press the **Enter** key. The Excel table is again named JanuaryData.

In this session, you filtered the table data, inserted a Total row, and determined totals and subtotals for the data. In the next session, you will work with PivotTables and PivotCharts to gather the information to help Laurie with staffing and ordering decisions.

REVIEW

Session 5.2 Quick Check

1. Explain filtering.
2. What is a slicer and how does it work?
3. How can you display a list of Economics majors with a GPA less than 2.5 from an Excel table with records for 1000 students?
4. An Excel table includes records for 500 employees. What can you use to calculate the average salary of employees in the finance department?
5. If you have a list of employees that includes fields for gender and salary, among others, how can you determine the average salary for females using the Total row feature?
6. Explain the relationship between the Sort and Subtotal commands.
7. After you display subtotals, how can you use the Outline buttons?

Session 5.3 Visual Overview:

This PivotTable uses the data from the Segment field as column labels.

A **PivotTable** is an interactive table used to group and summarize either a range of data or an Excel table into a concise, tabular format for reporting and analysis.

This PivotTable uses the data from the Day field as row labels.

Values fields are the fields that contain summary data in a PivotTable. This PivotTable uses the total of Cash Receipts as the values field.

A **PivotChart** is a graphical representation of the data in a PivotTable.

PivotTable and PivotChart

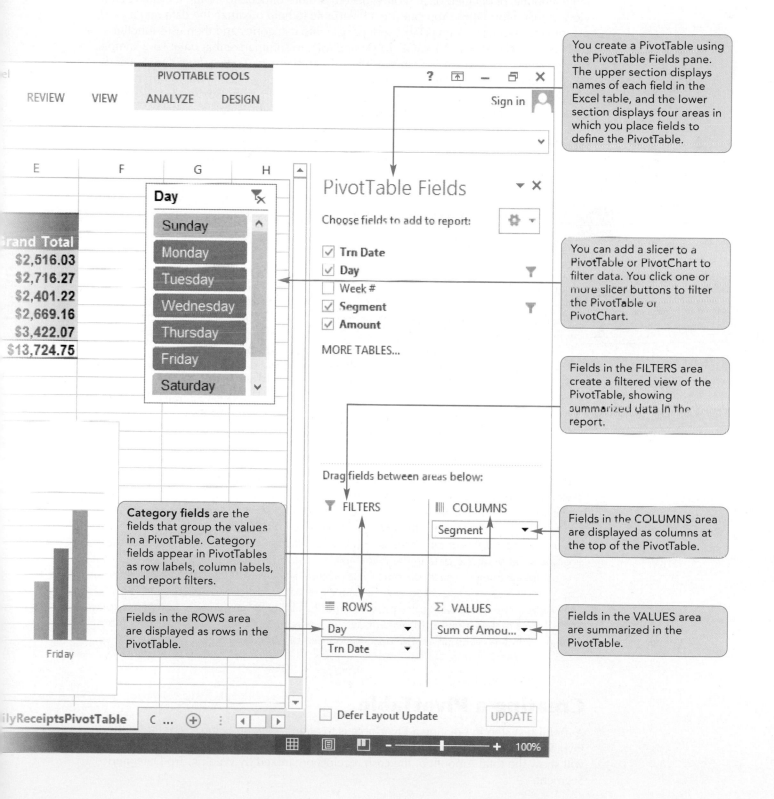

You create a PivotTable using the PivotTable Fields pane. The upper section displays names of each field in the Excel table, and the lower section displays four areas in which you place fields to define the PivotTable.

You can add a slicer to a PivotTable or PivotChart to filter data. You click one or more slicer buttons to filter the PivotTable or PivotChart.

Fields in the FILTERS area create a filtered view of the PivotTable, showing summarized data in the report.

Category fields are the fields that group the values in a PivotTable. Category fields appear in PivotTables as row labels, column labels, and report filters.

Fields in the ROWS area are displayed as rows in the PivotTable.

Fields in the COLUMNS area are displayed as columns at the top of the PivotTable.

Fields in the VALUES area are summarized in the PivotTable.

Analyzing Data with PivotTables

An Excel table can contain a wealth of information. However, when the table contains large amounts of detailed data, it often becomes more difficult to obtain a clear, overall view of that information. You can use a PivotTable to help organize the data into a meaningful summary. A PivotTable groups data into categories and then uses functions such as COUNT, SUM, AVERAGE, MAX, and MIN to summarize that data. For example, Laurie wants to see the daily cash receipts for each segment (Coffee, Spec Drink, Food, Gifts) grouped by week. Although there are several ways to generate the information Laurie needs, you can use a PivotTable like the one shown in the Session 5.3 Visual Overview to generate this information quickly and present it concisely.

You can easily rearrange, hide, and display different category columns in the PivotTable to provide alternative views of the data. This ability to "pivot" the table— for example, change row headings to column positions and vice versa—gives the PivotTable its name and makes it a powerful analytical tool.

PROSKILLS

Written Communication: Summarizing Data with a PivotTable

PivotTables are a great way to summarize data from selected fields of an Excel table or range. The PivotTable omits all the detailed data, enabling readers to focus on the bigger picture. This makes it easier for readers to understand the results and gain insights about the topic. It can also help you back up or support specific points in written documents.

You can show summaries in written documents based on function results in PivotTables. The SUM function is probably the most frequently used function. For example, you might show the total sales for a region. However, you can use many other functions to summarize the data, including COUNT, AVERAGE, MIN, MAX, PRODUCT, COUNT NUMBERS, STDDEV, STDDEVP, VAR, and VARP. Using the functions, you might show the average sales for a region, the minimum price of a product, or a count of the number of students by major.

When you write a report, you want supporting data to be presented in the way that best communicates your points. With PivotTables, you display the values in different views. For example, to compare one item to another item in the PivotTable, you can show the values as a percentage of a total. You can display the data in each row as a percentage of the total for the row. You can also display the data in each column as a percentage of the total for the column, or display the data as a percentage of the grand total of all the data in the PivotTable. Viewing data as a percentage of the total is useful for analyses such as comparing product sales with total sales within a region, or comparing expense categories to total expenses for the year.

As you can see, PivotTables provide great flexibility in how you analyze and display data. This makes it easier to present data in a way that highlights and supports the points you are communicating, making your written documents much more effective.

Creating a PivotTable

A useful first step in creating a PivotTable is to plan its layout. Figure 5-31 shows the PivotTable that Laurie wants you to create. As you can see in the figure, the PivotTable will show the total Amount of the cash receipts organized by Week #, Trn Date, and Segment.

Figure 5-31	PivotTable plan

Week #	xxxx					
Total Cash Receipts						
Trn Date		Coffee	Food	Gifts	Spec Drink	Total
Total						

© 2014 Cengage Learning

You are ready to create the PivotTable summarizing the total cash receipts for Laurie.

Creating a PivotTable

- Click in the Excel table or select the range of data for the PivotTable.
- On the INSERT tab, in the Tables group, click the PivotTable button.
- Click the Select a table or range option button, and then verify the reference in the Table/Range box.
- Click the New Worksheet option button, or click the Existing Worksheet option button and specify a cell.
- Click the OK button.
- Click the check boxes for the fields you want to add to the PivotTable (or drag fields to the appropriate box in the layout section).
- If needed, drag fields to different boxes in the layout section.

When you create a PivotTable, you need to specify where to find the data for the PivotTable. The data can be in an Excel table or range in the current workbook, or an external data source such as an Access database file. You also must specify whether to place the PivotTable in a new or an existing worksheet. If you place the PivotTable in an existing worksheet, you must also specify the cell in which you want the upper-left corner of the PivotTable to appear.

To create the PivotTable that will provide the information Laurie needs, you will use the JanuaryData table and place the PivotTable in a new worksheet.

To create a PivotTable using the JanuaryData table:

1. If you took a break after the previous session, make sure the Cash Receipts January workbook is open, the Cash Receipts worksheet is the active sheet, and the JanuaryData table is active.

2. On the ribbon, click the **INSERT** tab.

3. In the Tables group, click the **PivotTable** button. The Create PivotTable dialog box opens. See Figure 5-32.

TIP

You can also click the Summarize with PivotTable button in the Tools group on the TABLE TOOLS DESIGN tab.

Figure 5-32 **Create PivotTable dialog box**

4. Make sure the **Select a table or range** option button is selected and **JanuaryData** appears in the Table/Range box.

5. Click the **New Worksheet** option button, if necessary. This sets the PivotTable report to be placed in a new worksheet.

6. Click the **OK** button. A new worksheet, Sheet1, is inserted to the left of the Cash Receipts worksheet. On the left is the empty PivotTable report area, where the finished PivotTable will be placed. On the right is the PivotTable Fields pane, which you use to build the PivotTable. The PIVOTTABLE TOOLS tabs appear on the ribbon. See Figure 5-33.

Figure 5-33 **Empty PivotTable report**

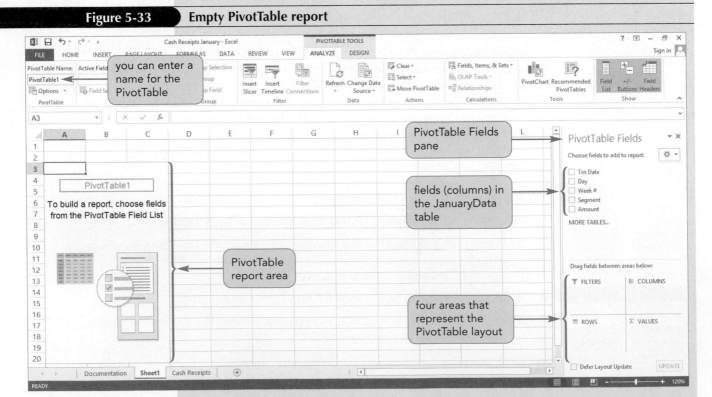

Trouble? If the PivotTable Fields pane is not displayed, you need to display it. On the PIVOTTABLE TOOLS ANALYZE tab, in the Show group, click the Field List button.

Adding Fields to a PivotTable

In order to display data in a PivotTable, you add fields to the PivotTable. In PivotTable terminology, fields that contain summary data are Values fields, and fields that group the values in the PivotTable are Category fields. Category fields appear in PivotTables as row labels, column labels, and filters. You add fields to a PivotTable from the PivotTable Fields pane, which is divided into two sections. The upper section, often referred to as the Fields section, lists the names of each field in the data source, which is the JanuaryData table, in this case. You select a field check box or drag the field into the lower section to add that field to the FILTERS, ROWS, COLUMNS, or VALUES area (described in Figure 5-34). The placement of fields in the area boxes determines the layout of the PivotTable.

| Figure 5-34 | Layout areas for a PivotTable |

Area	Description
ROWS	Fields placed in this area appear as Row Labels on the left side of the PivotTable. Each unique item in this field is displayed in a separate row. Row fields can be nested.
COLUMNS	Fields placed in this area appear as Column Labels at the top of the PivotTable. Each unique item in a field is displayed in a separate column. Column fields can be nested.
FILTERS	Fields placed in this area appear as top-level filters above the PivotTable. These fields are used to select one or more items to display in the PivotTable.
VALUES	Fields placed in this area are the numbers that are summarized in the PivotTable.

© 2014 Cengage Learning

Typically, fields with text or nonnumeric data are placed in the ROWS area. Fields with numeric data are most often placed in the VALUES area and by default are summarized with the SUM function. If you want to use a different function, click the field button in the VALUES area, click Value Field Settings to open the Value Field Settings dialog box, select a different function such as AVERAGE, COUNT, MIN, MAX, etc., and then click the OK button. You can move fields between the areas at any time to change how data is displayed in the PivotTable. You can also add the same field to the VALUES area more than once so you can calculate its sum, average, and count in one PivotTable.

Laurie wants to see the total value of cash receipts first by Week #. Within each Week #, she wants to see total cash receipts for each Day. Finally, she wants each Day further divided to display cash receipts for each Segment. You'll add fields to the PivotTable so that the Week #, Trn Date, and Segment fields are row labels, and the Amount field is the data to be summarized as the Values field.

TIP

By default, Excel uses the COUNT function for nonnumeric fields placed in the VALUES area.

To add fields to the PivotTable:

1. In the PivotTable Fields pane, drag **Week #** from the upper section to the ROWS area in the lower section. The Week # field appears in the ROWS area, and the unique values in the Week # field—1, 2, 3, 4, 5, and 6—appear in the PivotTable report area. See Figure 5-35.

Figure 5-35   **PivotTable with the Week # field values as row labels**

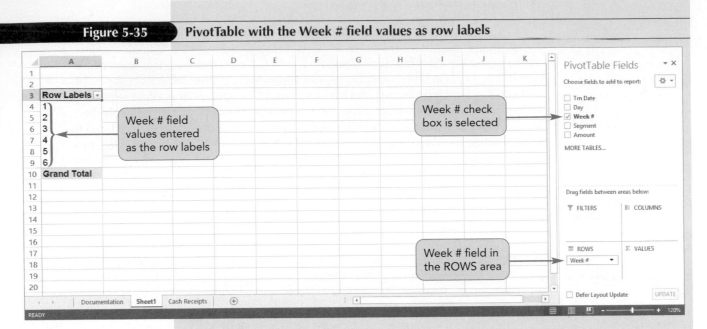

Trouble? If the Week # field appears in the VALUES area, you probably checked the Week # field, which places fields with numeric values in the VALUES area. Drag the Week # field from the VALUES area to the ROWS area.

2. In the PivotTable Fields pane, click the **Amount** check box. The Sum of Amount button is placed in the VALUES box because the field contains numeric values. The PivotTable groups the items from the JanuaryData table by Week # and calculates the total Amount for each week. The grand total appears at the bottom of the PivotTable. See Figure 5-36.

Figure 5-36   **PivotTable shows the sum of the Amounts field for each Week #**

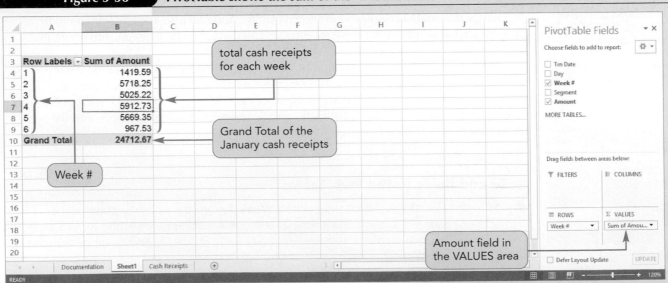

Next, you'll add the Trn Date and Segment fields to the PivotTable.

3. In the PivotTable Fields pane, click the **Trn Date** check box. The Trn Date field appears in the ROWS area box below the Week # field, and the unique items in the Trn Date field are indented below each Week # field item in the PivotTable report.

Trouble? If the PivotTable Fields pane is not visible, the active cell is probably not in the PivotTable. Click any cell within the PivotTable to redisplay the PivotTable Fields pane. If the PivotTable Fields pane is still not visible, click the PIVOTTABLE TOOLS ANALYZE tab, and then click the Field List button in the Show group.

▶ 4. In the PivotTable Fields pane, click the **Segment** check box. The Segment field appears in the ROWS area below the Trn Date field, and its unique items are indented below the Week # and Trn Date fields already in the PivotTable. See Figure 5-37.

Figure 5-37   **PivotTable with Week #, Trn Date, and Segment field items as row labels**

Trouble? If the Segment field button is not visible in the ROWS area, drag the dotted line above the "Drag fields between areas below" label up until the Segment field button is visible.

If a PivotTable becomes too detailed or confusing, you can always remove one of its fields. In the PivotTable Fields pane, click the check box of the field you want to remove. The field is then deleted from the PivotTable and the area box.

Changing the Layout of a PivotTable

You can add, remove, and rearrange fields to change the PivotTable's layout. Recall that the benefit of a PivotTable is that it summarizes large amounts of data into a readable format. After you create a PivotTable, you can view the same data in different ways. Each time you make a change in the areas section of the PivotTable Fields pane, the PivotTable layout is rearranged. This ability to "pivot" the table—for example, change row headings to column positions and vice versa—makes the PivotTable a powerful analytical tool.

Based on Laurie's PivotTable plan that was shown in Figure 5-31, the Segment field items should be positioned as columns instead of rows in the PivotTable. You'll move the Segment field now to produce the layout Laurie wants.

To move the Segment field to the COLUMNS area:

▶ **1.** In the PivotTable Fields pane, locate the **Segment** field button in the ROWS area.

▶ **2.** Drag the **Segment** field button from the ROWS area to the COLUMNS area. The PivotTable is rearranged so that the Segment field is a column label instead of a row label. See Figure 5-38.

| Figure 5-38 | PivotTable rearranged with Segment as a column label |

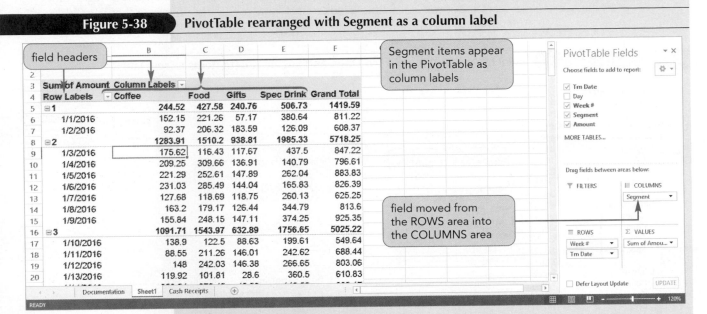

The PivotTable now has the layout that Laurie wants.

Choosing a Report Layout

There are three different report layouts available for PivotTables. The report layout shown in Figure 5-38, which is referred to as the Compact Form, is the default layout. It places all fields from the ROWS area in a single column, and indents the items from each field below the outer fields. In the Outline Form layout, each field in the ROWS area takes a column in the PivotTable. The subtotal for each group appears above every group. The Tabular Form layout displays one column for each field and leaves space for column headers. A total for each group appears below each group. To select a different report layout, click the Report Layout button in the Layout group on the PIVOTTABLE TOOLS DESIGN tab.

Formatting a PivotTable

Like worksheet cells and Excel tables, you can quickly format a PivotTable report using one of the built-in styles available in the PivotTable Styles gallery. As with cell and table styles, you can point to any style in the gallery to see a Live Preview of the PivotTable with that style. You also can modify the appearance of PivotTables by adding or removing banded rows, banded columns, row headers, and column headers.

Laurie wants you to apply the Pivot Style Medium 10 style, which makes each group in the PivotTable stand out and makes subtotals in the report easier to find.

To apply the Pivot Style Medium 10 style to the PivotTable:

▶ **1.** Make sure the active cell is in the PivotTable.

▶ **2.** On the ribbon, click the **PIVOTTABLE TOOLS DESIGN** tab.

▶ **3.** In the PivotTable Styles group, click the **More** button ⤓ to open the PivotTable Styles gallery.

▶ **4.** Move the pointer over each style to see the Live Preview of the PivotTable report with that style.

▶ **5.** Click the **Pivot Style Medium 10** style (the third style in the second row of the Medium section). The style is applied to the PivotTable.

You can format cells in a PivotTable the same way that you format cells in a worksheet. This enables you to further customize the look of the PivotTable by changing the font, color, alignment, and number formats of specific cells in the PivotTable. Laurie wants the numbers in the PivotTable to be quickly recognized as dollars. You'll change the total Amount values in the PivotTable to the Currency style.

To format the Amount field in the PivotTable as currency:

▶ **1.** In the VALUES area of the PivotTable Fields pane, click the **Sum of Amount** button. A shortcut menu opens with options related to that field.

▶ **2.** Click the **Value Field Settings** button on the shortcut menu. The Value Field Settings dialog box opens. See Figure 5-39.

Figure 5-39   **Value Field Settings dialog box**

▶ **3.** In the Custom Name box, type **Total Cash Receipts** as the label for the field. You will leave Sum as the summary function for the field; however, you could select a different function.

▶ **4.** Click the **Number Format** button. The Format Cells dialog box opens. This is the same dialog box you have used before to format numbers in worksheet cells.

5. In the Category box, click **Currency**. You will use the default number of decimal places, currency symbol, and negative number format.

6. Click the **OK** button. The numbers in the PivotTable will be formatted as currency with two decimal places.

7. Click the **OK** button. The Value Field Settings dialog box closes. The PivotTable changes to reflect the label you entered, and the number format for the field changes to currency.

Filtering a PivotTable

As you analyze the data in a PivotTable, you might want to show only a portion of the total data. You can do this by filtering the PivotTable. Filtering a field lets you focus on a subset of items in that field.

Adding a Field to the FILTERS Area

You can drag one or more fields to the FILTERS area of the PivotTable Fields pane to change what values are displayed in the PivotTable. A field placed in the FILTERS area provides a way to filter the PivotTable so that it displays summarized data for one or more items or all items in that field. For example, placing the Week # field in the FILTERS area allows you to view or print the total cash receipts for all weeks, a specific week such as Week 1, or multiple weeks such as Weeks 2 through 5.

Laurie wants you to move the Week # field from the ROWS area to the FILTERS area so that she can focus on specific subsets of the cash receipts.

To add the Week # field to the FILTERS area:

1. In the PivotTable Fields pane, drag the **Week #** button from the ROWS area to the FILTERS area. By default, the Filter field item shows "(All)" to indicate that the PivotTable displays all the summarized data associated with the Week # field. See Figure 5-40.

| Figure 5-40 | PivotTable with the Week # filter |

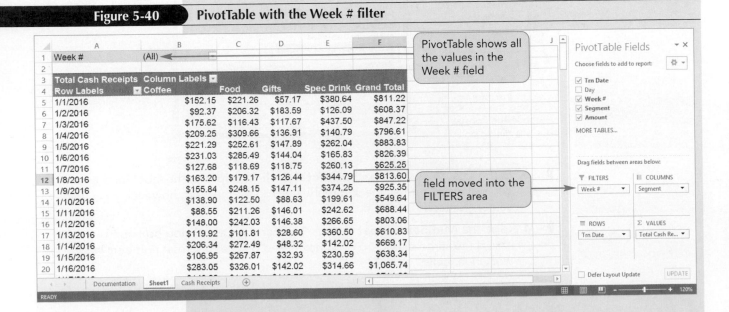

Next, you'll filter the summarized report to show only cash receipts for Week 2.

2. In cell B1, click the **filter** button 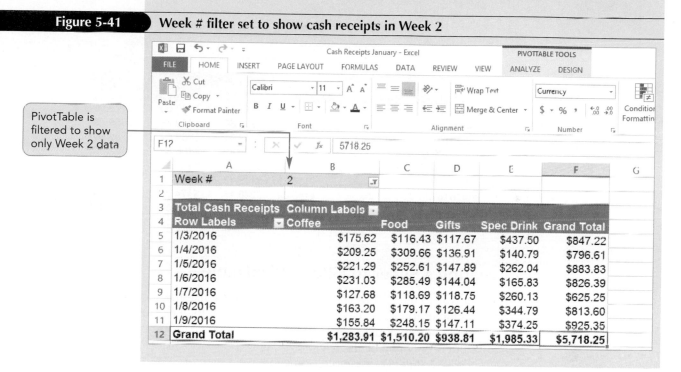. The Filter menu opens, showing the field items displayed.

3. In the Filter menu, click **2**, and then click the **OK** button. The PivotTable displays the total Amount of cash receipts for the dates in Week 2. The filter button changes to indicate the PivotTable is currently filtered. See Figure 5-41.

Figure 5-41   **Week # filter set to show cash receipts in Week 2**

PivotTable is filtered to show only Week 2 data

Row Labels	Coffee	Food	Gifts	Spec Drink	Grand Total
1/3/2016	$175.62	$116.43	$117.67	$437.50	$847.22
1/4/2016	$209.25	$309.66	$136.91	$140.79	$796.61
1/5/2016	$221.29	$252.61	$147.89	$262.04	$883.83
1/6/2016	$231.03	$285.49	$144.04	$165.83	$826.39
1/7/2016	$127.68	$118.69	$118.75	$260.13	$625.25
1/8/2016	$163.20	$179.17	$126.44	$344.79	$813.60
1/9/2016	$155.84	$248.15	$147.11	$374.25	$925.35
Grand Total	$1,283.91	$1,510.20	$938.81	$1,985.33	$5,718.25

Week # = 2   Total Cash Receipts / Column Labels   F12 = 5718.25

Filtering PivotTable Fields

Another way that you can filter field items in the PivotTable is by using the Filter menu, which you open by clicking the Row Labels filter button or the Column Labels filter button. You then check or uncheck items to show or hide them, respectively, in the PivotTable.

Laurie wants to exclude Gifts from her analysis. She asks you to remove the cash receipts for Gifts from the PivotTable.

To filter Gifts from the Segment column labels:

1. In the PivotTable, click the **Column Labels** filter button 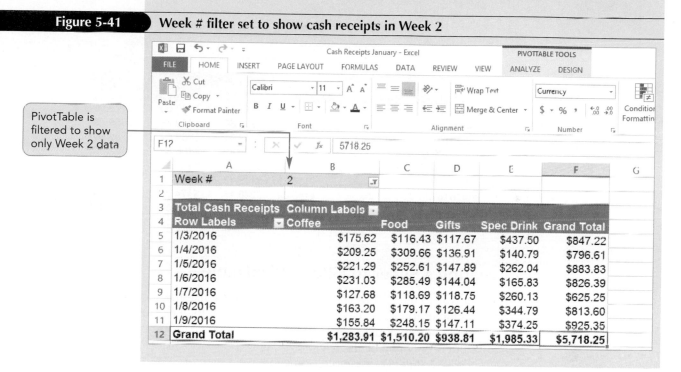. The Filter menu opens, listing the items in the Segment field.

2. Click the **Gifts** check box to remove the checkmark. The Select All check box is filled with black indicating that all items are not selected.

3. Click the **OK** button. The Gifts column is removed from the PivotTable. The PivotTable includes only cash receipts from Coffee, Food, and Spec Drink (specialty drinks). See Figure 5-42. You can show the hidden objects by clicking the Column Labels filter button and checking the Gifts check box.

Figure 5-42 ▶ **PivotTable report filtered by Segment**

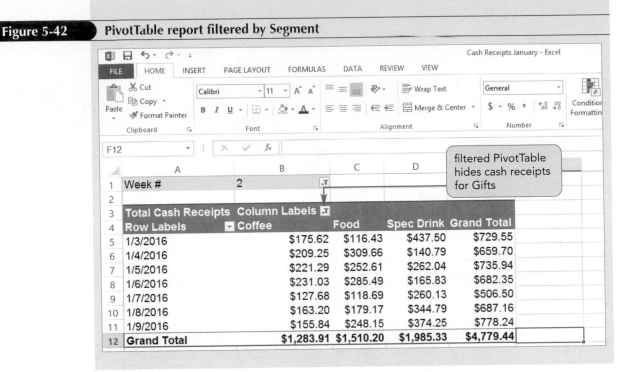

Creating a Slicer to Filter a PivotTable

Another way to filter a PivotTable is with a slicer just like the slicer you created to filter
an Excel table. You can create a slicer for any field in the PivotTable Fields pane. The
slicer contains a button for each unique value in that field. You can format the slicer
and its buttons, changing its style, height, and width. You also can create more than
one slicer at a time. For example, you can have a slicer for Week # that has a button for
each unique Week # value, and a second slicer for Segment. This allows you to filter a
PivotTable report so that it displays the cash receipts for Week 2 sales of coffee, food,
and specialty drinks by clicking the corresponding slicer buttons.

Laurie wants flexibility in how she views the data in the PivotTable, so she asks you
to add a slicer for the Week # field to the current PivotTable.

To add the Week # slicer to the PivotTable:

▶ 1. On the ribbon, click the **PIVOTTABLE TOOLS ANALYZE** tab.

▶ 2. In the Filter group, click the **Insert Slicer** button. The Insert Slicers dialog box
opens, displaying a list of available PivotTable Fields. You can select any or all
of the fields.

▶ 3. Click the **Week #** check box to insert a checkmark, and then click the **OK**
button. The Week # slicer appears on the worksheet. Because the PivotTable
is already filtered to display only the results for Week # 2, the 2 button is
selected. The other slicer buttons are white because those weeks have been
filtered and are not part of the PivotTable.

▶ 4. If necessary, click the **Week #** slicer to select it. The SLICER TOOLS OPTIONS
tab appears on the ribbon.

▶ 5. On the SLICER TOOLS OPTIONS tab, in the Size group, change the height
to **2.2"** and change the width to **1"**. The slicer object is resized, eliminating
the extra space below the buttons and to the right of the labels.

6. In the Slicer Styles group, click the **More** button, and then click **Slicer Style Dark 2**. The slicer colors now match the PivotTable.

7. Drag the **Week #** slicer to the right of the PivotTable, placing its upper-left corner in cell G3. See Figure 5-43.

Figure 5-43 **Week # slicer**

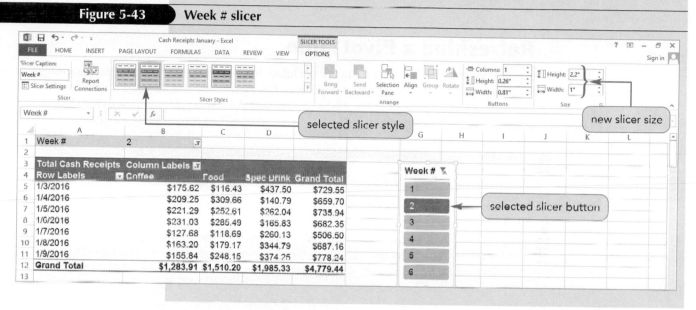

Laurie wants you to display the results of the PivotTable for all the full weeks in January—Weeks 2, 3, 4, and 5. You can do this quickly using the Week # slicer.

To filter the PivotTable using the Week # slicer:

1. Press and hold the **Ctrl** key, click the **3** button, and then release the **Ctrl** key. Week 3 data also appears in the PivotTable.

2. Press and hold the **Ctrl** key, click the **4** button, click the **5** button, and then release the **Ctrl** key. Data for Weeks 4 and 5 is added to the PivotTable.

3. Click the **Week # 2** slicer button. Only the cash receipts for Week 2 are displayed in the PivotTable.

TIP

To remove all filters from the PivotTable, click the Clear Filter button in the upper-right corner of the slicer.

After you have finished creating a PivotTable, you can hide the PivotTable Fields pane so that it won't appear when a cell is selected in the PivotTable. You can also assign more descriptive names to the PivotTable as well as the worksheet that contains the PivotTable.

To hide the PivotTable Fields pane and rename the PivotTable and worksheet:

1. Click in the PivotTable to display the PIVOTTABLE TOOLS contextual tabs on the ribbon.

2. Click the **PIVOTTABLE TOOLS ANALYZE** tab.

3. In the Show group, click the **Field List** button. The PivotTable Fields pane is hidden and won't reappear when a cell in the PivotTable is selected.

▶ **4.** In the PivotTable group, select the default name in the PivotTable Name box, type **WeeklySummary** as the descriptive PivotTable name, and then press the **Enter** key.

▶ **5.** Rename the worksheet as **Weekly Summary PivotTable**.

Refreshing a PivotTable

You cannot change data directly in a PivotTable. Instead, you must edit the data source on which the PivotTable is created. However, PivotTables are not updated automatically when the source data for the PivotTable is updated. After you edit the underlying data, you must **refresh**, or update, the PivotTable report to reflect the revised calculations.

Displaying the Data Source for a PivotTable Cell

As you have seen, PivotTables are a great way to summarize the results of an Excel table. However, at some point, you may question the accuracy of a specific calculation in your PivotTable. In these cases, you can "drill down" to view the source data for a summary cell in a PivotTable. You simply double-click a summary cell, and the corresponding source data of the records for the PivotTable cell is displayed in a new worksheet.

The cash receipts entry for Food on 1/4/2016 should have been $409.66 (not $309.66 as currently listed). You'll edit the record in the JanuaryData table, which is the underlying data source for the PivotTable. This one change will affect the PivotTable in several locations—the Grand Total value of receipts in Week 2 is $1,510.20 for the Food, $659.70 for 1/4/2016, and $4,779.44 overall.

To update the JanuaryData table and refresh the PivotTable:

▶ **1.** Go to the **Cash Receipts** worksheet, and then find the Food cash receipts for 1/4/2016. The amount is $309.66.

▶ **2.** Click the record's **Amount** cell, and then enter **409.66**. The receipt's Amount is updated in the table. You'll return to the PivotTable report to see the effect of this change.

▶ **3.** Go to the **Weekly Summary PivotTable** worksheet. The Amount for Food on 1/4/2016 is still $309.66, the Grand Total for Food is still $1,510.20, the Grand Total for 1/4/2016 is still $659.70, and the overall Grand Total is still $4,779.44. The PivotTable was not automatically updated when the data in its source table changed, so you need to refresh the PivotTable.

▶ **4.** Click any cell in the PivotTable.

▶ **5.** On the ribbon, click the **PIVOTTABLE TOOLS ANALYZE** tab.

▶ **6.** In the Data group, click the **Refresh** button. The PivotTable report is updated. The totals are now $409.66, $1,610.20, $759.70, and $4,879.44. See Figure 5-44.

Figure 5-44   Refreshed PivotTable

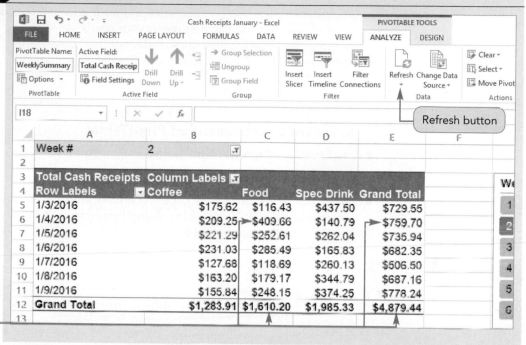

updated cash receipts values

Creating Different Types of PivotTables

This tutorial only scratched the surface of the variety of PivotTables you can create. Here are a few more examples:

- Most PivotTable summaries are based on numeric data; Excel uses SUM as the default calculation. If your analysis requires a different calculation, you can select any of the 11 built-in summary calculations. For example, you could build a report that displays the minimum, maximum, and average receipts for each week in January.
- You can use PivotTables to combine row label and column label items into groups. If items are numbers or dates, they can be grouped automatically using the Grouping dialog box, or they can be grouped manually using the Ctrl key to select items in a group and then clicking Group Selection from the shortcut menu. For example, you can manually combine Saturday and Sunday receipts into a Weekend group, and combine Monday through Friday receipts into a Weekday group, and then display total receipts by these groups within the PivotTable. Over time, you will also be able to group the Trn Date field to summarize daily cash receipts by month, quarter, and year.
- You can develop PivotTables that use the percent of row, percent of column, or percent of total calculation to view each item in the PivotTable as a percent of the total in the current row, current column, or grand total. For example, you can display the total weekly receipts as a percent of the total monthly receipts.
- You can develop PivotTables that display how the current month/quarter/year compares to the previous month/quarter/year. For example, you can compare this month's receipts for each category to the corresponding receipts for the previous month to display the difference between the two months.

Being able to enhance PivotTables by changing summary calculations, consolidating data into larger groups, and creating custom calculations based on other data in the VALUES area gives you flexibility in your analysis.

Creating a Recommended PivotTable

The Recommended PivotTables dialog box shows previews of PivotTables based on the source data. This lets you see different options for how to create the PivotTable, and you can choose the one that best meets your needs.

Laurie wants to summarize sales by days-of-the-week so she can gain insights into staffing and ordering for each day. You will see if a recommended PivotTable meets Laurie's request.

To create a recommended PivotTable:

1. Go to the **Cash Receipts** worksheet, and then select any cell in the Excel table.

2. On the ribbon, click the **INSERT** tab.

3. In the Tables group, click the **Recommended PivotTables** button. The Recommended PivotTables dialog box opens. You can select from several PivotTables. See Figure 5-45.

Figure 5-45 Recommended PivotTable dialog box

The Sum of Amount by Day PivotTable meets Laurie's request.

4. Click **Sum of Amount by Day** (the fourth PivotTable in the left pane). An enlarged version of the selected PivotTable is displayed in the right pane of the dialog box.

5. Click the **OK** button. A PivotTable of the cash receipts by day appears in a new worksheet. See Figure 5-46.

Figure 5-46 | **PivotTable of cash receipts by day**

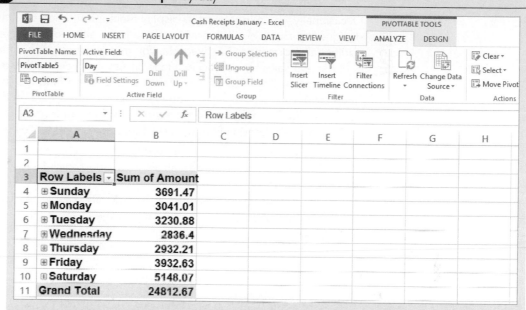

6. In the PivotTable Fields pane, in the VALUES area, click the **Sum of Amount** button, and then click **Value Field Settings** on the shortcut menu. The Value Field Settings dialog box opens.

7. Click the **Number Format** button. The Format Cells dialog box opens.

8. In the Category box, click **Currency**, and then click the **OK** button.

9. Click the **OK** button. The numbers in the PivotTable are formatted as currency with two decimal places.

10. On the ribbon, click the **PIVOTTABLE TOOLS DESIGN** tab.

11. In the PivotTable Styles group, click the **More** button to open the PivotTable Styles gallery, and then click the **Pivot Style Medium 10** style. The style is applied to the PivotTable.

12. Rename the worksheet as **Daily Receipts PivotTable**.

Laurie will use the summary of sales by days-of-the-week in the Daily Receipts PivotTable worksheet to evaluate staffing and ordering for each day.

Adding a Calculated Field to a PivotTable Report

Occasionally, you might need to display more information than a PivotTable is designed to show, but it doesn't make sense to alter your data source to include this additional information. For example, you might want to include a field that shows an 8 percent sales tax on each value in an Amount field. In these instances, you can add a calculated field to the PivotTable. A **calculated field** is a formula you define to generate PivotTable values that otherwise would not appear in the PivotTable. The calculated field formula looks like a regular worksheet formula.

To add a calculated field to a PivotTable, complete the following steps:

1. Select any cell in the PivotTable report.
2. On the ANALYZE tab, in the Calculations group, click Fields, Items & Sets, and then click Calculated Field.
3. In the Name box, type a name for the field, such as Sales Tax.
4. In the Formula box, enter the formula for the field. To use data from another field, click the field in the Fields box, and then click Insert Field. For example, to calculate an 8 percent sales tax on each value in the Amount field, enter =Amount*8%.
5. Click the Add button.
6. Click the OK button. The calculated field is added PivotTable's data area and to the PivotTable Field List

As you can see, you can use calculated fields to include additional information in a PivotTable.

Creating a PivotChart

A PivotChart is a graphical representation of the data in a PivotTable. You can create a PivotChart from a PivotTable. A PivotChart allows you to interactively add, remove, filter, and refresh data fields in the PivotChart similar to working with a PivotTable. PivotCharts can have all the same formatting as other charts, including layouts and styles. You can move and resize chart elements, or change formatting of individual data points.

Laurie wants you to add a PivotChart next to the Sum of Amount by Day PivotTable. You will prepare a clustered column chart next to the PivotTable.

To create and format the PivotChart:

1. Select any cell in the PivotTable.

2. On the ribbon, click the **PIVOTTABLE TOOLS ANALYZE** tab.

3. In the Tools group, click the **PivotChart** button. The Insert Chart dialog box opens.

4. If necessary, click the **Clustered Column** chart (the first chart in the Column charts section), and then click the **OK** button. A PivotChart appears next to the PivotTable along with the PivotChart Fields pane.

   Trouble? If you selected the wrong PivotChart, delete the PivotChart you just created, and then repeat Steps 1 through 4.

5. On the ribbon, click the **PIVOTCHART TOOLS DESIGN** tab.

6. In the Chart Layouts group, click the **Add Chart Element** button, point to **Legend**, and then click **None**. The legend is removed from the PivotChart. You do not need a legend because the PivotChart has only one data series.

7. In the PivotChart, right-click the chart title, and then click **Edit Text** on the shortcut menu. The insertion point appears in the title so you can edit it.

8. Select the title, type **Cash Receipts by Day** as the new title, and then click the chart area to deselect the title.

9. Right-click any column to select the series, and then use the **Fill** button on the Mini toolbar above the shortcut menu to change its fill color to the **Orange, Accent 2** theme color.

10. Drag the PivotChart so its upper-left corner is in cell **D3**. The PivotChart is aligned with the PivotTable. See Figure 5-47.

Figure 5-47 **PivotChart added to the PivotTable report**

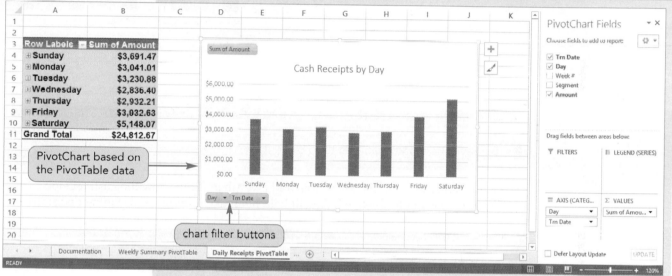

The PIVOTCHART TOOLS contextual tabs enable you to work with and format the selected PivotChart the same way as an ordinary chart. A PivotChart and its associated PivotTable are linked. When you modify one, the other also changes. You can quickly display different views of the PivotChart by using the chart filter buttons on the PivotChart to filter the data.

Laurie wants you to display cash receipts for only Monday through Friday. You will filter the PivotChart to display only those items.

To filter the PivotChart to display cash receipts for Monday through Friday:

1. Make sure the PivotChart is selected, and then click the **Day** axis field button in the PivotChart. The Filter menu opens.

2. Click the **Sunday** and **Saturday** check boxes to remove their checkmarks.

3. Click the **OK** button. The PivotChart displays only cash receipts for the weekdays. The PivotTable is automatically filtered to display the same results.

4. Select cell **A1**. See Figure 5-48.

Figure 5-48 | **Filtered PivotChart**

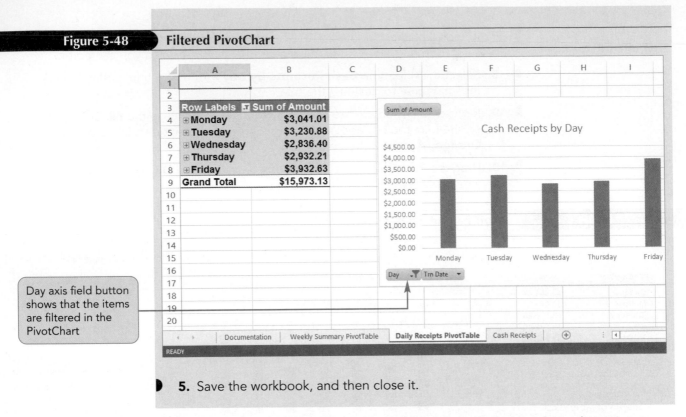

Day axis field button shows that the items are filtered in the PivotChart

5. Save the workbook, and then close it.

Laurie is pleased with the PivotTable and PivotChart. Both show the cash receipts arranged by day of the week, which will help her make ordering and staffing decisions.

Session 5.3 Quick Check

REVIEW

1. What is a PivotTable?
2. How do you add fields to a PivotTable?
3. How are fields such as region, state, and country most likely to appear in a PivotTable?
4. How are fields such as revenue, costs, and profits most likely to appear in a PivotTable?
5. A list of college students includes a code to indicate the student's gender (male or female) and a field to identify the student's major. Would you use a filter or a PivotTable to (a) create a list of all females majoring in history, and (b) count the number of males and females in each major?
6. An Excel table of professional baseball player data consists of team name, player name, position, and salary. What area of a PivotTable report would be used for the Team name field if you wanted to display the average salaries by position for all teams or an individual team?
7. After you update data in an Excel table, what must you do to a PivotTable based on that Excel table?
8. What is a PivotChart?

Review Assignments

Data File needed for the Review Assignments: February.xlsx

Laurie wants to analyze the cash receipts data for February. She entered this data into a new workbook and wants you to sort and filter the data, as well as create summary reports using the Subtotal command, PivotTables, and PivotCharts. Complete the following:

1. Open the **February** workbook located in the Excel5 ▸ Review folder included with your Data Files, and then save the workbook as **Cash Receipts February**.

2. In the Documentation worksheet, enter your name and the date.

3. In the Cash Receipts worksheet, freeze the top row so the headers remain on the screen as you scroll.

4. Make a copy of the Cash Receipts worksheet, and then rename the copied worksheet as **Feb Data**. (*Hint*: To make a copy of the worksheet, press and hold the Ctrl key as you drag the sheet tab to the right of the Cash Receipts sheet tab.)

5. In the Feb Data worksheet, unfreeze the top row.

6. Create an Excel table for the cash receipts data.

7. Format the Excel table with Table Style Medium 25, and then change the Amount field to the Accounting format with two decimal places.

8. Rename the Excel table as **FebruaryData**.

9. Make the following changes to the FebruaryData table:
   a. Add a record for **2/29/2016**, **Monday**, **10**, **Spec Drink**, **353.11**.
   b. Edit the record for Coffee on 2/27/2016 by changing the Amount from 219.71 to **269.71**.
   c. Delete any duplicate records.

10. Make a copy of the Feb Data worksheet, and then rename the copied worksheet as **Sort Trn Date**. In the Sort Trn Date worksheet, sort the cash receipts by Trn Date, displaying the newest receipts first, and then by Amount displaying the largest amounts first.

11. Make a copy of the Feb Data worksheet, and then rename the copied worksheet as **Sort By Day**. In the Sort By Day worksheet, sort the cash receipts by Day (use the custom list order of Sunday, Monday, …), then by Segment (A to Z), and then by Amount (smallest to largest).

12. Make a copy of the Feb Data worksheet, and then rename the copied worksheet as **Filter Omit Gifts**. In the Filter Omit Gifts worksheet, filter the FebruaryData table to display the cash receipts for all items except Gifts.

13. In the Filter Omit Gifts worksheet, insert the Total row to calculate the average amount of the cash receipts for the filtered data. Change the label in the Total row to **Average**. Sort the filtered data by descending order by Amount.

14. Split the Filter Omit Gifts worksheet into two panes above the last row of the table. Display the cash receipt records in the top pane, and display only the Total row in the bottom pane.

15. Make a copy of the Feb Data worksheet, and then rename the copied worksheet as **Filter By Day**. In the Filter By Day worksheet, insert a slicer for the Day column. Move the slicer to row 1. Format the slicer with Slicer Style Light 3. Change the slicer's width to 1.2" and its height to 2.5". Use the slicer to display cash receipts for Saturday and Sunday.

16. Make a copy of the Feb Data worksheet, and then rename the copied worksheet as **Subtotals**. In the Subtotals worksheet, convert the FebruaryData table to a range, and then sort the range by the Segment column.

17. In the Subtotals worksheet, use the Subtotal command to calculate the total cash receipts for each segment in the Amount column. Display only the subtotal results.

18. Based on the data in the Feb Data worksheet, create a PivotTable in a new worksheet that shows the total receipts by Day. Format the data area with the Currency format. Rename the worksheet with the PivotTable as **PivotTable By Day**.

19. In the PivotTable By Day worksheet, insert a Clustered Column PivotChart based on the PivotTable you created. Move the PivotChart to row 3. Remove the legend, and then change the PivotChart title to **Receipts by Day of Week**.

20. Based on the data in the Feb Data worksheet, create a PivotTable in a new worksheet that shows cash receipts by Trn Date. Add the Segment field to the FILTERS area. Format the PivotTable with Pivot Style Medium 4. Format the Amount field with the Accounting format with two decimal places. Rename the worksheet as **PivotTable By Trn Date**.

21. In the PivotTable By Trn Date worksheet, insert a slicer for the Segment field of the PivotTable. Change the slicer height to 1.6" and the width to 1.2". Format the slicer with Slicer Style Dark 3.

22. Use the slicer to filter the PivotTable by Trn Date to display only the Coffee and Spec Drink amounts.

23. Based on the data in the Feb Data worksheet, insert the Recommended PivotTable Sum of Amount By Week # and Segment PivotTable. Rename the worksheet as **Recommended PivotTable**.

24. Save the workbook, and then close it.

Case Problem 1

Data File needed for this Case Problem: Student.xlsx

College of Business Administration   Peg Henderson is an assistant dean at the College of Business Administration (CBA). She uses Excel daily for a variety of tasks, including tracking student internships and alumni. For this project, Peg wants you to create an Excel table from information about current students and then analyze this data. Complete the following.

1. Open the **Student** workbook located in the Excel5 ► Case1 folder included with your Data Files, and then save the workbook as **Student Data**.

2. In the Documentation worksheet, enter your name and the date.

3. In the CBA Data worksheet, create an Excel table. Format the table with Table Style Medium 7, change the GPA data to the Number format showing two decimal places, and then change the Scholarships data to the Accounting format showing no decimal places. Rename the table as **StuData**.

4. Make a copy of the CBA Data worksheet, and then rename the copied worksheet as **Sort by Major**. (*Hint:* Press the Ctrl key as you drag and drop the sheet tab to the right of the CBA Data sheet tab to make a copy of the worksheet.)

5. Sort the data in the StuData table in ascending order by Major, and then in descending order by GPA.

6. Filter the StuData table to remove all undecided majors.

7. Insert a Total row in the StuData table that shows the number of students in the Last Name column, and the average GPA in the GPA column. Change the Total row label to **Average** and remove the entry in the Class column of the Total row.

8. Split the Sort by Major worksheet into two horizontal panes. Place the split bar two rows above the bottom row of the worksheet. In the top pane, display the student data. In the bottom pane, display only the Total row.

9. Make a copy of the CBA Data worksheet, and then rename the copied worksheet as **Filter by Class**. Filter the StuData table to display only those students who have a GPA greater than 3.00.

10. Insert a Class slicer to the right of the StuData table. Resize the slicer's height to 1.7" and its width to 1.2", and then format the slicer with the style that best matches the style of the Excel table.

11. Use the Class slicer to further filter the StuData table to display only Juniors and Seniors. Sort the filtered data in ascending order by Class and then in descending order by GPA.

12. Make a copy of the CBA Data worksheet, and then rename the copied worksheet as **Subtotals**. Convert the table to a normal range because the Subtotal command cannot be used with an Excel table. Use the Subtotal command to display the Average **GPA** for each Major in the GPA column.

13. Based on the data in the CBA Data worksheet, create a PivotTable in a new worksheet that counts the number of students in each class and major. In the Value Settings dialog box, change the Custom Name to Number. Apply Pivot Style Medium 14. Rename the worksheet as **PivotTable by Class and Major**.

14. In the PivotTable by Class and Major worksheet, insert a PivotChart with the Clustered Column chart type. Place the PivotChart to the right of the PivotTable. Filter the PivotChart to exclude the Freshman field. Insert a descriptive title. Remove the legend. Change the fill colors of the bars to match the PivotTable style.

15. Based on the data in the CBA Data worksheet, create a PivotTable that displays the average of GPA and number of students by Residence and Major in a new worksheet. Place Residence in the FILTERS area, and place Major in the ROWS area. Apply the Pivot Style Dark 7 to the PivotTable. Rename the worksheet as **PivotTable by Major**.

16. In the PivotTable, change the Residence filter to show In state students.

17. Save the workbook, and then close it.

APPLY

Case Problem 2

Data File needed for this Case Problem: Players.xlsx

NBA Hoops Blog   Jeff DeMarco is a sports enthusiast. Several years ago, he began writing a basketball blog called *NBA Hoops* that provides information, opinions, and analysis related to teams, players, and games in the National Basketball Association (NBA). To help him more easily respond to comments from his readers, he created an Excel table that tracks teams, positions, and salaries for each player in the league. He asks you to analyze this data. Complete the following:

1. Open the **Players** workbook located in the Excel5 ▸ Case2 folder included with your Data Files, and then save the workbook as **NBA Player Data**.

2. In the Documentation worksheet, enter your name and the date.

3. In the Players worksheet, create an Excel table named **NBAPlayers**. Format the Salary column with the Accounting format and no decimal places. Format the NBAPlayers table with the table style of your choice.

4. Make a copy of the Players worksheet, and then rename the copied worksheet as **Sort Position**. (*Hint*: Press the Ctrl key and drag the Players sheet tab to the right of the Players sheet tab to make a copy of the worksheet.) Sort the NBAPlayers table in ascending order by position, then in descending order by salary.

5. Use conditional formatting to apply a yellow fill with dark yellow text to highlight all players with a salary greater than $10,000,000.

6. Make a copy of the Players worksheet, and then rename the copied worksheet as **Filter Team**. Insert a slicer to filter by Team. Place the slicer to the right of the NBAPlayers table. Select a slicer style that matches the style you used to format the NBAPlayers table. Resize the slicer's height and width to improve its appearance.

7. Use the slicer to filter the NBAPlayers table to display all players on the NY Knicks and Miami Heat teams.

8. Expand the filter to display NY Knicks and Miami Heat players earning more than $5,000,000. Sort the filtered table in ascending order by salary.

9. Make a copy of the Players worksheet, and then rename the copied worksheet as **Filter Top 15%**. Filter the NBAPlayers table to display players whose salaries are in the top 15 percent. Sort the data by Salary in descending order.

10. Use the Total row to include the average salary at the bottom of the table, and then change the Total row label to **Average**. Add the Count of the Team column to the Total row. Remove the entry in the Division column of the Total row.

11. Make a copy of the Players worksheet, and then rename the copied worksheet as **Subtotals**. Use the Subtotal command to display the total salary for each team in the Salary column.

12. Based on the data in the Players worksheet, create a PivotTable in a new worksheet that totals salaries by team and position. Place the Position field in the COLUMNS area. Rename the worksheet as **PivotTable Team Position**. Format the salaries in the PivotTable with the Accounting format and no decimal places. Resize the columns as needed to display all the salaries.

13. Create a Division slicer for the PivotTable. Resize the slicer object and buttons as needed, and then select a slicer style that matches the PivotTable. Use the slicer to filter the PivotTable to display teams from the Atlantic, Central, and Southeast divisions.

14. Based on the data in the Player Salary worksheet, create a PivotTable that calculates the number and average salaries by position in a new worksheet. Format the average salaries, change the label above the average salaries to **Avg Salary**, and then change the label above the count to **Number**. Resize columns as needed to display all cell contents. Rename the worksheet as **PivotTable Avg Sal**.

15. Save the workbook, and then close it.

Case Problem 3

TROUBLESHOOT

Data File needed for this Case Problem: Cooking.xlsx

Healthy Cooking   Lian Michim started Healthy Cooking two years ago to provide prepared gourmet meals to retail food stores, living facilities for seniors, and businesses. Lian tracks orders using Excel. She has entered customer order data for the first half of the year in a worksheet, and wants to analyze the data in several ways. Complete the following:

1. Open the **Cooking** workbook located in the Excel5 ▶ Case3 folder included with your Data Files, and then save the workbook as **Healthy Cooking**.

2. In the Documentation sheet, enter your name and the date.

⚙ **Troubleshoot** 3. Lian wants to view invoices with order amounts that are either less than $100 or greater than $5000. She tried filtering the orders in the Order Amount Filter worksheet, but it's not working as expected. Review the Order Amount Filter worksheet and fix the problem.

4. In the Orders worksheet, create an Excel table, and then rename the table as **CustOrders.**

5. In the CustOrders table, format the Order Amount, Discount, and Net Amount columns so that it is clear that these fields contain dollars.

6. Format the CustOrders table using the table style of your choice.

7. Make a copy of the Orders worksheet, and then rename the copied worksheet as **Sort**. (*Hint*: Press the Ctrl key and drag the sheet tab to the right of the current sheet tab to make a copy of the worksheet.) On the Sort worksheet, sort the data in ascending order by Customer Type, then in ascending order by Delivered To, and then in ascending order by Customer.

8. Using conditional formatting, highlight all orders in the sorted table that have a Net Amount greater than $4000 in the format of your choice.

9. Make a copy of the Orders worksheet, and then rename the copied worksheet as **Filter with Total Row**. Filter the CustOrders table to display all orders with an order date in June 2016 that included a discount.

10. Insert a Total row that calculates the totals for the Order Amount, Discount, and Net Amount columns for the filtered data.

⚙ **Troubleshoot** 11. In the Customer Type Subtotal worksheet, Lian is trying to include the sum of the order amount for each Customer Type and the subtotals in the Order Amount field. However, the subtotal for each customer type appears more than once. Fix this report so it shows only one subtotal for each customer type.

12. In the Order Date column, insert a count of the number of orders for each customer type. This is in addition to the totals already in the worksheet. (*Hint*: Use the options at the bottom of the Subtotals dialog box.)

13. Based on the data in the Orders worksheet, create a PivotTable in a new worksheet that displays the number (Count) and average Order amount by Customer Type and Delivered To. Place the Customer Type and Delivered To fields in the ROWS area of the PivotTable. Apply the PivotTable style that matches the CustOrder table. Format the Average Order values using the Accounting format. Change the labels above the average orders to **Average Order**, and change the label above the count of orders to **Number**.

14. Use a slicer to filter the PivotTable to remove the Seniors customer type from the PivotTable. Format the slicer to match the PivotTable style. Rename the worksheet as **PivotTable**.

15. Based on the data in the Orders worksheet, create a PivotTable that shows the Total Order Amount by Customer in a new worksheet. Apply a PivotTable style to match the style of the CustOrder table. Format the Total Order Amount. Rename the worksheet as **Order Amount by Customers**.

16. Based on the PivotTable in the Order Amount by Customers worksheet, create a PivotChart using the Bar chart type. Move the PivotChart to row 3. Change the chart title to **Orders by Customers**. Change the axis to display units in thousands. Change the fill color of the bars to a color that matches the style in the PivotTable. Remove the legend.

17. Filter the PivotChart to remove the Corner Store and Drac Deli.

18. Save the workbook, and then close it.

Case Problem 4

Data File needed for this Case Problem: Benjis.xlsx

CREATE

Benji's Department Stores   Benji's Department Stores, with corporate headquarters in Colorado Springs, Colorado, operates department stores in midsize towns in selected areas of the West. The organization maintains a large database for its accounting operations; other departments often download data to complete additional analysis. Eve Darden, analyst for the corporate sales department, regularly creates reports based on her analysis of sales by product areas and regions. Right now, Eve is compiling and summarizing data about the best- and worst-performing product group and time period for certain regions and product groups. Complete the following:

1. Open the **Benjis** workbook located in the Excel5 ► Case4 folder included with your Data Files, and then save the workbook as **Benjis Stores**.

2. In the Documentation sheet, enter your name and the date.

3. In the Sales Data worksheet, create an Excel table. Rename the table as **ProductSales**. Format the Sales column in the Accounting format with no decimal places. Apply a table style of your choice.

4. Make a copy of the Sales Data worksheet, and then rename the copied worksheet as **Sort**. (*Hint*: Press the Ctrl key and drag the sheet tab to the right of the Sales Data sheet tab to make a copy of the worksheet.) Sort the table in ascending order by Product group, then in ascending order by Region, then in ascending order by Year, and then in chronological order by Month (Jan, Feb, Mar, ...).

5. Make a copy of the Sales Data worksheet, and then rename the copied worksheet as **Filter with Total Row**. Insert a slicer for the Product Group field. Move the slicer to row 1. Match the slicer style with the style you selected for the ProductSales table. Resize the slicer height and width to eliminate any excess space.

6. Display the records for Gardening and Sporting products in 2016, excluding sales in Utah. Sort this data in descending order of sales.

7. Add a Total row and calculate the average sales for the filtered data. Change the label in the Total row to **Average**.

8. Split the worksheet into two panes. In the top pane, display the table data. In the bottom pane, display the Total row. In the top pane, select cell A1.

9. Make a copy of the Sales Data worksheet, and then rename the copied worksheet as **Subtotals 2016**. Filter the list to display only data for 2016, and then include subtotals that calculate the total Sales by Region and Month. (*Hint*: You need two sets of subtotals.)

10. Make a copy of the Sales Data worksheet, and then rename the copied worksheet as **Bottom 15**. Display the 15 lowest periods based on sales (each row represents a period). Sort the sales so that the lowest sales appear first.

11. Based on the data in the Sales Data worksheet, create the PivotTable and PivotChart shown in Figure 5-49, summarizing sales by year and month. Rename the worksheet as **PivotChart**.

Figure 5-49   **PivotTable and PivotChart summarizing sales by year and month**

12. Based on the data in the Sales Data worksheet, create the PivotTable shown in Figure 5-50 to calculate the sum, average, minimum, and maximum sales categorized by region and product group. Insert a Year slicer and use it to show sales in 2016. Rename the worksheet as **Region Statistics**.

Figure 5-50   PivotTable displaying sales categorized by region and product group

	A	B	C	D	E	F	G
2							
3	Row Labels	Sum of Sales	Average Sales	Minimum Sales	Maximum Sales		Year
4	⊟ Colorado	$ 3,330,178	$ 55,503	$ 7	$ 167,539		
5	Automotive	$ 564,908	$ 47,076	$ 7	$ 130,405		2015
6	Electronics	$ 499,670	$ 41,639	$ 1,738	$ 147,135		
7	Gardening	$ 782,519	$ 65,210	$ 5,607	$ 167,539		2016
8	Housewares	$ 788,597	$ 65,716	$ 21,017	$ 147,298		
9	Sporting	$ 694,484	$ 57,874	$ 2,522	$ 135,193		
10	⊟ Oklahoma	$ 2,636,197	$ 43,937	$ 175	$ 176,220		
11	Automotive	$ 916,489	$ 76,374	$ 969	$ 170,688		
12	Electronics	$ 452,901	$ 37,742	$ 1,154	$ 176,220		
13	Gardening	$ 405,111	$ 33,759	$ 175	$ 119,667		
14	Housewares	$ 333,699	$ 27,808	$ 1,176	$ 107,097		
15	Sporting	$ 527,997	$ 44,000	$ 5,441	$ 105,933		
16	⊟ Utah	$ 2,520,053	$ 42,001	$ 684	$ 168,339		
17	Automotive	$ 499,020	$ 41,585	$ 684	$ 168,220		
18	Electronics	$ 520,268	$ 43,356	$ 7,544	$ 145,865		
19	Gardening	$ 358,252	$ 29,854	$ 2,148	$ 78,942		
20	Housewares	$ 469,331	$ 39,111	$ 1,770	$ 127,490		
21	Sporting	$ 673,182	$ 56,099	$ 3,089	$ 168,339		

13. Based on the data in the Sales Data worksheet, create the PivotTable and slicers shown in Figure 5-51 displaying total sales by Year, Product Group, and Region. Include a second value calculation that displays each Product Group and Region as a percentage of the total company sales. (*Hint:* In Excel Help, read about how to calculate a percentage for subtotals in a PivotTable.) Rename the worksheet as **Percent of Company Sales**.

Figure 5-51   PivotTable displaying sales by Year, Product Group, and Region

	A	B	C	D	E	F	G	H
1	Year	(All)						
2								
3	Row Labels	Sales Total	% of Column Total		Year		Product Group	
4	⊟ Automotive	$ 3,678,817	21.7%					
5	Colorado	$ 950,869	5.6%		2015			
6	Oklahoma	$ 1,496,198	8.8%				Automotive	
7	Utah	$ 1,231,750	7.3%		2016			R
8	⊟ Electronics	$ 3,245,846	19.2%				Electronics	
9	Colorado	$ 1,123,439	6.6%					
10	Oklahoma	$ 1,057,029	6.2%				Gardening	
11	Utah	$ 1,065,378	6.3%					
12	⊟ Gardening	$ 3,174,345	18.7%				Housewares	
13	Colorado	$ 1,437,752	8.5%					
14	Oklahoma	$ 911,470	5.4%				Sporting	
15	Utah	$ 825,123	4.9%					
16	⊟ Housewares	$ 3,109,955	18.3%					
17	Colorado	$ 1,430,658	8.4%					
18	Oklahoma	$ 867,120	5.1%					
19	Utah	$ 812,177	4.8%					
20	⊟ Sporting	$ 3,740,501	22.1%					
21	Colorado	$ 1,314,995	7.8%					

14. Format the PivotTable and slicers with matching styles, and adjust the height and width of the slicers as needed to improve their appearance.

15. Filter the Product Group to display sales in 2016 for the Automotive and Electronics product groups in all Regions except Utah.

16. Save the workbook, and then close it.

OBJECTIVES

Session 6.1
- Create a worksheet group
- Format and edit multiple worksheets at once
- Create cell references to other worksheets
- Consolidate information from multiple worksheets using 3-D references
- Create and print a worksheet group

Session 6.2
- Create a link to data in another workbook
- Create a workbook reference
- Learn how to edit links

Session 6.3
- Insert a hyperlink in a cell
- Create a workbook based on an existing template
- Create a custom workbook template

Managing Multiple Worksheets and Workbooks

Summarizing Recycling Data

Case | *Better World Recycling*

In 2010, Maria Guzman and Edward McKay, a couple of college friends, opened Better World Recycling, a collection site for recyclable plastics. Since then, they have expanded the business to accept other types of recyclable items, including paper, glass, metal, Styrofoam, and plastic. The company also expanded from the original location in Columbia, Kansas, to two additional locations—Richmond, Indiana, and Marion, Iowa. With the expansion, Maria assumed the duties and title of COO (Chief Operating Officer) and Edward became the CEO (Chief Executive Officer).

Maria, working in Columbia, is responsible for analyzing collections at all locations. Each recycling site tracks the amount of each material it collects during each quarter. Each site enters this information in a workbook, which is sent to Maria to consolidate and analyze. Maria has received the workbooks with the quarterly collections data for the past year from all three locations—Columbia, Richmond, and Marion. She wants you to create a worksheet in each workbook that summarizes the collection totals.

STARTING DATA FILES

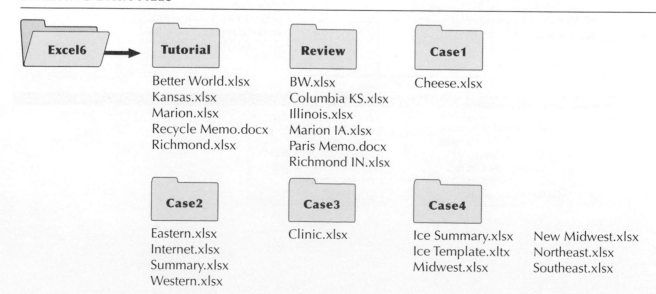

Excel6 →	Tutorial	Review	Case1
	Better World.xlsx	BW.xlsx	Cheese.xlsx
	Kansas.xlsx	Columbia KS.xlsx	
	Marion.xlsx	Illinois.xlsx	
	Recycle Memo.docx	Marion IA.xlsx	
	Richmond.xlsx	Paris Memo.docx	
		Richmond IN.xlsx	

Case2	Case3	Case4	
Eastern.xlsx	Clinic.xlsx	Ice Summary.xlsx	New Midwest.xlsx
Internet.xlsx		Ice Template.xltx	Northeast.xlsx
Summary.xlsx		Midwest.xlsx	Southeast.xlsx
Western.xlsx			

Session 6.1 Visual Overview:

Anything you do in the active sheet—such as entering formulas, adding labels, and formatting—is automatically done to all sheets in the worksheet group, saving you time and ensuring consistency.

When worksheets are grouped, the workbook is in group-editing mode and "[Group]" appears in the title bar.

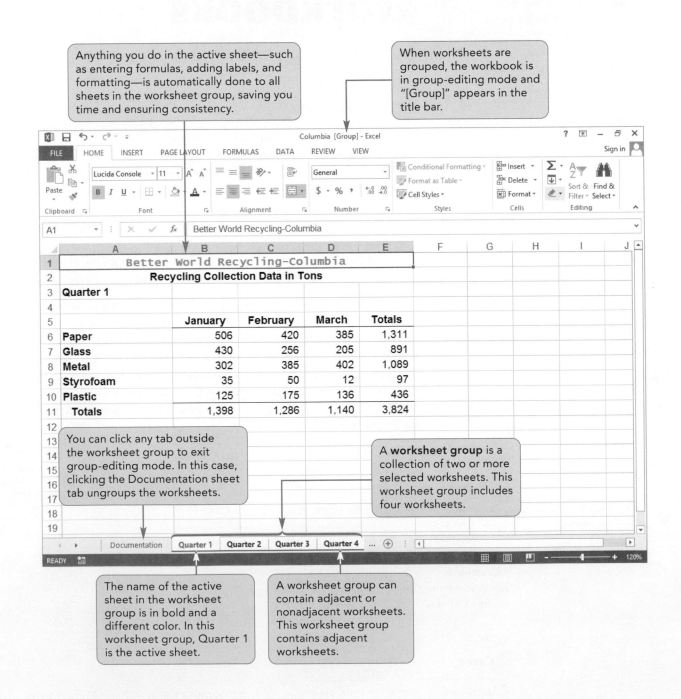

You can click any tab outside the worksheet group to exit group-editing mode. In this case, clicking the Documentation sheet tab ungroups the worksheets.

A **worksheet group** is a collection of two or more selected worksheets. This worksheet group includes four worksheets.

The name of the active sheet in the worksheet group is in bold and a different color. In this worksheet group, Quarter 1 is the active sheet.

A worksheet group can contain adjacent or nonadjacent worksheets. This worksheet group contains adjacent worksheets.

Worksheet Groups and 3-D References

A **3-D reference** is a reference to the same cell or range in multiple worksheets in the same workbook. This 3-D reference refers to cell E10 in the Quarter 1, Quarter 2, Quarter 3, and Quarter 4 worksheets.

When two or more worksheets have identical row and column layouts, as the quarterly worksheets in this workbook do, you can enter formulas with 3-D references to summarize those worksheets in another worksheet.

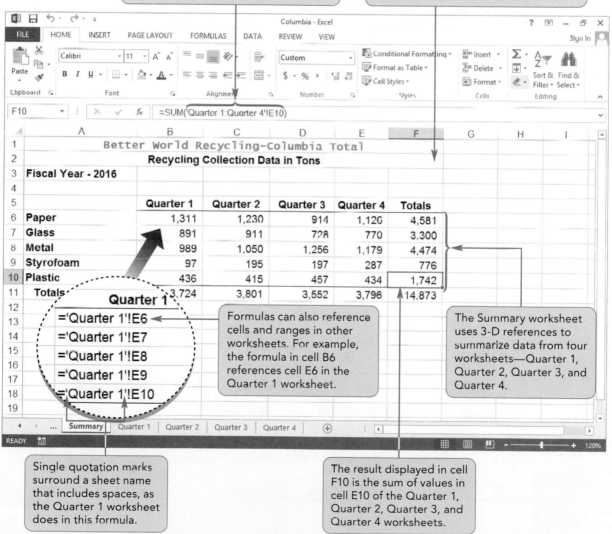

Formulas can also reference cells and ranges in other worksheets. For example, the formula in cell B6 references cell E6 in the Quarter 1 worksheet.

The Summary worksheet uses 3-D references to summarize data from four worksheets—Quarter 1, Quarter 2, Quarter 3, and Quarter 4.

Single quotation marks surround a sheet name that includes spaces, as the Quarter 1 worksheet does in this formula.

The result displayed in cell F10 is the sum of values in cell E10 of the Quarter 1, Quarter 2, Quarter 3, and Quarter 4 worksheets.

Grouping Worksheets

Workbook data is often placed in several worksheets. Using multiple worksheets makes it easier to group and summarize data. For example, a company such as Better World Recycling with branches in different geographic regions can place collection information for each region in separate worksheets. Rather than scrolling through one large and complex worksheet that contains data for all regions, users can access collection information for a specific region simply by clicking a sheet tab in the workbook.

Using multiple worksheets enables you to place summarized data first. Managers interested only in an overall picture can view the first worksheet of summary data without looking at the details available in the other worksheets. Others, of course, might want to view the supporting data in the individual worksheets that follow the summary worksheet. In the case of Better World Recycling, Maria used separate worksheets to summarize the amount of each item collected at the Columbia location for each quarter of the 2016 fiscal year.

You will open Maria's workbook and review the current information.

To open and review the Better World Recycling workbook:

▶ 1. Open the **Kansas** workbook located in the Excel6 ▸ Tutorial folder included with your Data Files, and then save the document as **Columbia** in the location specified by your instructor.

▶ 2. In the Documentation worksheet, enter your name and the date.

▶ 3. Go to the **Quarter 1** worksheet, and then view the recycling data for the first quarter of the year. See Figure 6-1.

| Figure 6-1 | Quarter 1 worksheet for Better World Recycling-Columbia |

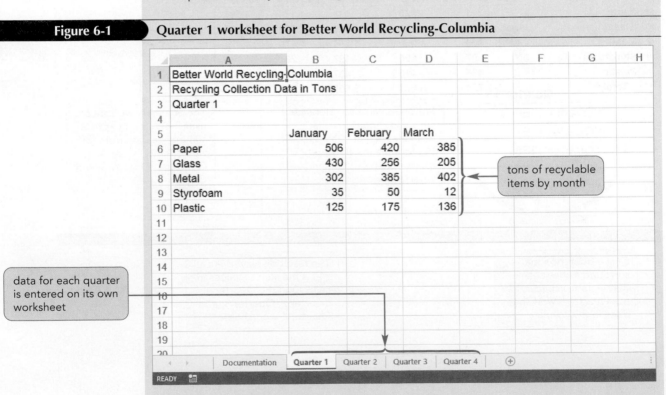

data for each quarter is entered on its own worksheet

tons of recyclable items by month

▶ 4. Review the **Quarter 2**, **Quarter 3**, and **Quarter 4** worksheets. The layout for all four worksheets is identical.

Maria didn't enter any formulas in the workbook. You need to enter formulas to calculate the total number of tons of collected recyclables for each column (columns B through D) in all four worksheets. Rather than retyping the formulas in each worksheet, you can enter them all at once by creating a worksheet group. A worksheet group, like a range, can contain adjacent or nonadjacent worksheets. In group-editing mode, most editing tasks that you complete in the active worksheet also affect the other worksheets in the group. By forming a worksheet group, you can:

- **Enter or edit data and formulas.** Changes made to content in the active worksheet are also made in the same cells in all the worksheets in the group. You can also use the Find and Replace commands with a worksheet group.
- **Apply formatting.** Changes made to formatting in the active worksheet are also made to all the worksheets in the group, including changing row heights or column widths and applying conditional formatting.
- **Insert or delete rows and columns.** Changes made to the worksheet structure in the active worksheet are also made to all the worksheets in the group.
- **Set the page layout options.** Changes made to the page layout settings in one worksheet also apply to all the worksheets in the group, such as changing the orientation, scaling to fit, and inserting headers and footers.
- **Apply view options.** Changes made to the worksheet view such as zooming, showing and hiding worksheets, and so forth are also made to all the worksheets in the group.
- **Print all the worksheets.** You can print all of the worksheets in the worksheet group at the same time.

Worksheet groups save you time and help improve consistency among the worksheets because you can perform an action once, yet affect multiple worksheets.

REFERENCE

Grouping and Ungrouping Worksheets

- To select an adjacent group, click the sheet tab of the first worksheet in the group, press and hold the Shift key, click the sheet tab of the last worksheet in the group, and then release the Shift key.
- To select a nonadjacent group, click the sheet tab of one worksheet in the group, press and hold the Ctrl key, click the sheet tabs of the remaining worksheets in the group, and then release the Ctrl key.
- To ungroup the worksheets, click the sheet tab of a worksheet that is not in the group (or right-click the sheet tab of one worksheet in the group, and then click Ungroup Sheets on the shortcut menu).

In the Columbia workbook, you'll group an adjacent range of worksheets—the Quarter 1 worksheet through the Quarter 4 worksheet.

To group the quarterly worksheets:

1. Click the **Quarter 1** sheet tab to make the worksheet active. This is the first worksheet you want to include in the group.

2. Press and hold the **Shift** key, and then click the **Quarter 4** sheet tab. This is the last worksheet you want to include in the group.

3. Release the **Shift** key. The sheet tabs are white, the green border at the bottom of the sheet tab extends across all the tabs, and the sheet tab labels, Quarter 1 through Quarter 4, are in bold, indicating they are all selected. The text "[Group]" appears in the title bar to remind you that a worksheet group is selected in the workbook. See Figure 6-2.

TIP

If you cannot see the sheet tab of a worksheet you want to include in a group, use the sheet tab scroll buttons to display it.

Figure 6-2 **Grouped worksheets**

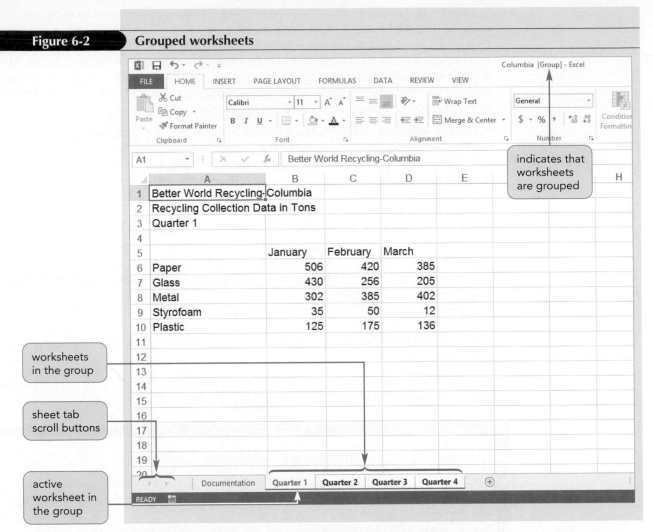

You can change which worksheet in a worksheet group is active. Just click the sheet tab of the worksheet you want to make active. If a worksheet group includes all the worksheets in a workbook, you cannot change which worksheet is the active sheet because clicking a sheet tab ungroups the worksheets.

To change the active sheet in the grouped quarterly worksheets:

1. Click the **Quarter 2** sheet tab to make the worksheet active. The Quarter 2 worksheet is now the active worksheet in the group.

2. Click the **Quarter 4** sheet tab. The Quarter 4 worksheet is now the active worksheet in the group.

Entering Headings and Formulas in a Worksheet Group

When you enter a formula in the active worksheet (in this case, the Quarter 1 worksheet), the formula is entered in the same cells in all the worksheets in the group. The grouped worksheets must have the exact same organization and layout (rows and columns) in order for this to work. Otherwise, any formulas you enter in the active worksheet will be incorrect in the other worksheets in the group and could overwrite existing data.

With the quarterly worksheets grouped, you will enter the formulas to calculate the collection totals for each month.

To enter formulas to calculate the collection totals in the worksheet group:

1. Select cell **B11**. You want to enter the formula in cell B11 in each of the four worksheets in the group.

2. On the HOME tab, in the Editing group, click the **AutoSum** button, and then press the **Enter** key. The formula =SUM(B6:B10) is entered in cell B11 in each worksheet, adding the total tons of recyclable items collected at the Columbia site for the first month of the quarter. For Quarter 4, the October total of collected items shown in cell B11 is 1194.

3. Copy the formula in cell B11 to the range **C11:D11**. The formula calculates the total tons of recyclable items collected for the other months in the quarter. For Quarter 4, the other collection totals are 1209 tons in November and 1413 tons in December.

4. In cell **E6**, enter a formula with the SUM function to add the total tons of paper collected for each quarter at the Columbia site. The formula =SUM(B6:D6) adds the monthly totals of the tons of paper collected. In Quarter 4, 1126 tons of paper were collected.

5. Copy the formula in cell E6 to the range **E7:E11** to calculate the total tons of glass, metal, Styrofoam, and plastic, as well as the total tons of all recyclable items, collected at the Columbia site for each quarter. For Quarter 4, the Columbia site collected 770 tons of glass, 1179 tons of metal, 287 tons of Styrofoam, 454 tons of plastic, and 3816 tons of recyclables overall.

6. In cell **A11** and in cell **E5**, enter the label **Totals**.

7. Select cell **B11**. The formula =SUM(B6:B10) appears in the formula bar, and the formula result 1194 appears in the cell. See Figure 6-3.

| Figure 6-3 | Formulas entered in all of the worksheets in the group |

Quarter 4 worksheet has the same layout as the Quarter 1, 2, and 3 worksheets

formula in cell B11 is the same in all of the grouped worksheets

formula result in cell B11 differs in each of the grouped worksheets

active worksheet in the group

B11   =SUM(B6:B10)

	A	B	C	D	E	F	G	H
1	Better World Recycling-Columbia							
2	Recycling Collection Data in Tons							
3	Quarter 4							
4								
5		October	November	December	Totals			
6	Paper	305	415	406	1126			
7	Glass	215	225	330	770			
8	Metal	452	325	402	1179			
9	Styrofoam	120	42	125	287			
10	Plastic	102	202	160	454			
11	Totals	1194	1209	1413	3816			
12								
13								
14								
15								
16								
17								
18								
19								
20								

Documentation   Quarter 1   Quarter 2   Quarter 3   Quarter 4

READY

The formulas and labels you entered in the Quarter 4 worksheet were entered in the Quarter 1, 2, and 3 worksheets at the same time.

8. Click the **Quarter 3** sheet tab, and then make sure that cell **B11** is the active cell. The formula =SUM(B6:B10), which adds the number of tons collected in Quarter 3, appears in the formula bar, and the formula result 1111 appears in the cell.

9. Click the **Quarter 2** sheet tab, and then make sure cell **B11** is the active cell. The formula =SUM(B6:B10), which adds the number of tons collected in Quarter 2, appears in the formula bar, and the formula result 1395 appears in the cell.

10. Click the **Quarter 1** sheet tab, and then make sure cell **B11** is the active cell. The formula =SUM(B6:B10), which adds the number of tons collected in Quarter 1, appears in the formula bar, and the formula result 1398 appears in the cell.

The grouped worksheets made it quick to enter the formulas needed to calculate the monthly and recyclable item totals for each quarter.

INSIGHT

Editing Grouped Worksheets

When you enter, edit, or format cells in a worksheet group, the changes you make to one worksheet are automatically applied to the other worksheets in the group. For example, if you delete a value from one cell, the content is also deleted from the same cell in all the worksheets in the group. Be cautious when editing a worksheet that is part of a group. If the layout and structure of the other grouped worksheets are not exactly the same, you might inadvertently overwrite data in some of the worksheets. Also, remember to ungroup the worksheet group after you finish entering data, formulas, and formatting. Otherwise, changes you intend to make in one worksheet will be made to all the worksheets in the group, potentially producing incorrect results.

Formatting a Worksheet Group

As when inserting formulas and text, any formatting changes you make to the active worksheet are applied to all worksheets in the group. You will format the quarterly worksheets, which are still grouped.

To apply formatting to the worksheet group:

1. Select cell **A1**, and then format the cell with the **Lucida Console** font, **bold**, and the **Olive Green, Accent 3, Darker 25%** font color. The company name is formatted to match the company name on the Documentation worksheet.

2. Increase the indent of cell **A11** by one. The label shifts to the right.

3. In the nonadjacent range **A2:A3;A6:A11;B5:E5**, bold the text in the headings.

4. Merge and center the range **A1:E1** and the range **A2:E2**.

5. In the range **B5:E5**, center the text.

6. In the range **B6:E11**, apply the **Comma Style** number format with no decimal places. No change is visible in any number that is less than 1000.

7. In the range **B5:E5** and the range **B10:E10**, add a bottom border.

8. Select cell **A1**. All the worksheets in the group are formatted.

9. Go to each worksheet in the group and review the formatting changes, and then go to the **Quarter 1** worksheet. See Figure 6-4.

Figure 6-4   **Formatting applied to the worksheet group**

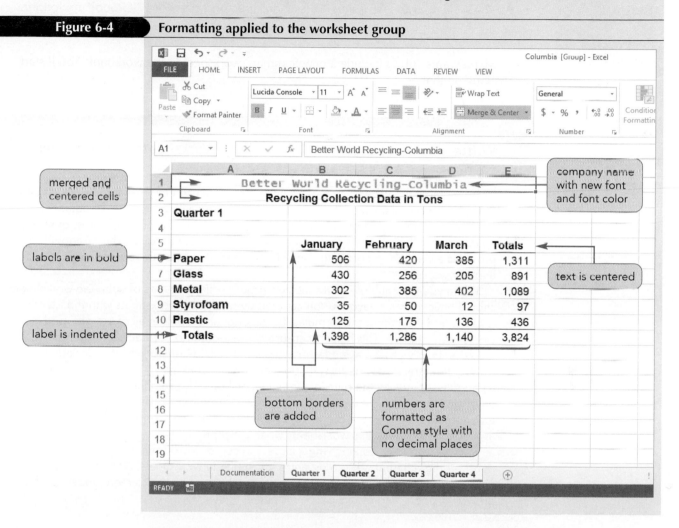

Ungrouping Worksheets

When you ungroup the worksheets, each worksheet functions independently again. If you forget to ungroup the worksheets, any changes you make in one worksheet will be applied to all the worksheets in the group. So be sure to ungroup worksheets when you are finished making changes that apply to multiple worksheets. To ungroup worksheets, click the sheet tab of a worksheet that is not part of the group. If a worksheet group includes all of the sheets in a workbook, click any of the sheet tabs to ungroup the worksheets.

You will ungroup the quarterly worksheets so you can work in each worksheet separately.

To ungroup the quarterly worksheets:

1. Click the **Documentation** sheet tab. The worksheets are ungrouped because the Documentation worksheet was not part of the worksheet group. The text "[Group]" no longer appears in the Excel title bar.

2. Verify that the worksheets are ungrouped and the word "[Group]" no longer appears in the title bar.

Maria wants you to include a new Summary worksheet in the workbook. You'll start working on that next.

PROSKILLS

Written Communication: Using Multiple Worksheets with Identical Layouts

Using multiple worksheets to organize complex data can help make that data simpler to understand and analyze. It also makes it easier to navigate to specific data. For example, a workbook that contains data about a variety of products, stores, or regions could use a different worksheet for each product, store, or region. This arrangement provides a way to view discrete units of data that can be combined and summarized in another worksheet.

When you use multiple worksheets to organize similar types of data, the worksheets should have identical layouts. You can quickly group the worksheets with the identical layouts, and then enter the formulas, formatting, and labels in all of the grouped worksheets at once. This helps to ensure consistency and accuracy among the worksheets as well as make it faster to create the different worksheets needed.

Using multiple worksheets with identical layouts enables you to use 3-D references to quickly summarize the data in another worksheet. The summary worksheet provides an overall picture of the data that is detailed in the other worksheets. Often, managers are more interested in this big picture view. However, the supporting data is still available in the individual worksheets when a deeper analysis is needed.

So, when you are working with a large and complex worksheet filled with data, consider the different ways to organize it in multiple worksheets. Not only will you save time when entering and finding data, but also the data becomes more understandable, and connections and results become clearer.

Working with Multiple Worksheets

As you develop a workbook, you might need to add a worksheet that has the same setup as an existing worksheet. Rather than starting from scratch, you can copy that worksheet as a starting point. For example, Maria wants the workbook to include a Summary worksheet that adds the annual totals of tons of recyclable materials collected from quarterly worksheets. The formulas you create in the Summary worksheet will reference cells in each quarterly worksheet using 3-D references. You can then group the completed worksheets to develop a consistent page setup in all worksheets and then print them all at once.

Copying Worksheets

Often, after spending time developing a worksheet, you can use it as a starting point for creating another, saving you time and energy compared to developing a new worksheet from scratch. Copying a worksheet duplicates all the values, formulas, and formats into the new worksheet, leaving the original worksheet intact. You can then edit, reformat, and enter new content as needed to create the exact worksheet you need.

REFERENCE

Copying Worksheets

- Select the sheet tabs of the worksheets you want to copy.
- Right-click the sheet tabs, and then click Move or Copy on the shortcut menu.
- Click the To book arrow, and then click the name of an existing workbook or click (new book) to create a new workbook for the worksheets.
- In the Before sheet box, click the worksheet before which you want to insert the new worksheet.
- Click the Create a copy check box to insert a checkmark to copy the worksheets.
- Click the OK button.

or

- Select the sheet tabs of the worksheets you want to copy.
- Press and hold the Ctrl key as you drag the selected sheet tabs to a new location in the sheet tabs, and then release the Ctrl key.

Maria wants you to create the Summary worksheet to provide an overall picture of the data in the detailed quarterly worksheets. The Summary worksheet needs the same formatting and structure as the quarterly worksheets. To ensure consistency among worksheets, you will copy the Quarter 1 worksheet to the beginning of the workbook, and then modify its contents.

To copy the Quarter 1 worksheet and create the Summary worksheet:

1. Click the **Quarter 1** sheet tab, and then press and hold the **Ctrl** key as you drag the worksheet to the left of the Documentation worksheet. The pointer changes to ▷ and a triangle indicates the drop location.

2. Release the mouse button, and then release the **Ctrl** key. An identical copy of the Quarter 1 worksheet appears in the new location. The sheet tab shows "Quarter 1 (2)" to indicate that this is the copied sheet.

3. Rename the Quarter 1 (2) worksheet as **Summary**.

4. Move the **Summary** worksheet between the Documentation worksheet and the Quarter 1 worksheet.

> **TIP**
>
> To move a worksheet or a worksheet group to another location in the same workbook, drag its sheet tab and drop it in its new location.

Maria wants the Summary worksheet to show the collection data for each product by quarter, and the total collections for each product and quarter. You will modify the Summary worksheet to do this now.

To modify the Summary worksheet:

1. Make sure the **Summary** worksheet is the active sheet.

2. In cell **A3**, enter **2016**. This is the year to which the summary refers.

3. In cell **A1**, enter **Better World Recycling–Columbia Total**. The new title reflects this worksheet's content. The formatting should remain intact.

4. Delete the collection data from the range **B6:E10**. The formatting remains intact. See Figure 6-5.

Figure 6-5   Summary worksheet created from the Quarter 1 worksheet

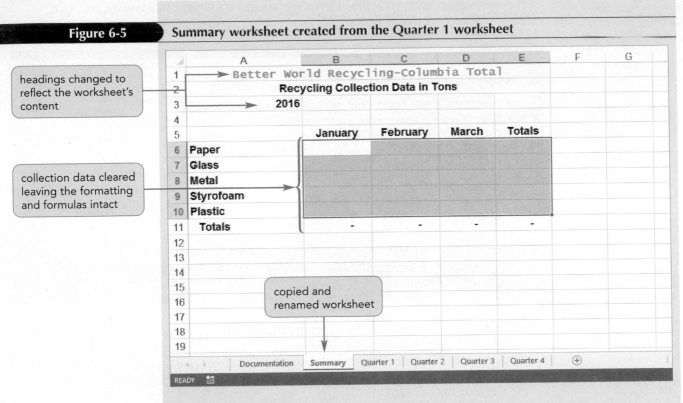

5. Insert a new **column C** into the worksheet. The column appears between the January and February labels with the same formatting as January.

6. In the range **B5:E5**, enter **Quarter 1**, **Quarter 2**, **Quarter 3**, and **Quarter 4** in each respective cell.

7. Copy the formula in cell B11 to cell **C11**. See Figure 6-6.

Figure 6-6   Summary worksheet modified

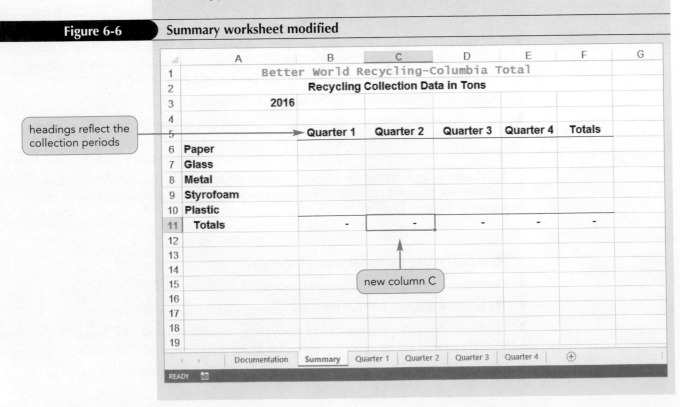

Referencing Cells and Ranges in Other Worksheets

When you use multiple worksheets to organize related data, you can reference a cell or a range in another worksheet in the same workbook. For example, the Summary worksheet references cells in the four quarterly worksheets to calculate the total collections for the entire year. The syntax to reference a cell or a range in a different worksheet is

```
=SheetName!CellRange
```

where `SheetName` is the worksheet's name as listed on the sheet tab and `CellRange` is the reference for the cell or range in that worksheet. An exclamation mark (!) separates the worksheet reference from the cell or range reference. For example, you could enter the following formula in the Summary worksheet to reference cell D10 in the Quarter1 worksheet:

```
=Quarter1!D10
```

If the worksheet name contains spaces, you must enclose the name in single quotation marks. For example, the following formula references cell D10 in the Quarter 1 worksheet:

```
='Quarter 1'!D10
```

You can use these references to create formulas that reference cells in different locations in different worksheets. For example, to add collections from two worksheets—cell C9 in the Quarter 1 worksheet and cell C9 in the Quarter 2 worksheet—you would enter the following formula:

```
='Quarter 1'!C9+'Quarter 2'!C9
```

You could type the formula directly in the cell, but it is faster and more accurate to use your mouse to select cells to enter their references to other worksheets.

REFERENCE

Entering a Formula with References to Another Worksheet

- Select the cell where you want to enter the formula.
- Type = and begin entering the formula.
- To insert a reference from another worksheet, click the sheet tab for the worksheet, and then click the cell or select the range you want to reference.
- When the formula is complete, press the Enter key.

Maria wants you to enter a formula in cell A4 in each quarterly worksheet that displays the fiscal year entered in cell A3 in the Summary worksheet. All four quarterly worksheets will use the formula =Summary!A3 to reference the fiscal year in cell A3 of the Summary worksheet.

To enter the formula that references the Summary worksheet:

1. Click the **Quarter 1** sheet tab, press and hold the **Shift** key, and then click the **Quarter 4** worksheet. The Quarter 1 through Quarter 4 worksheets are grouped.

2. Select cell **A4**. This is the cell in which you want to enter the formula to display the fiscal year.

3. Type **=** to begin the formula, click the **Summary** sheet tab, and then click cell **A3**. The reference to cell A3 in the Summary worksheet is added to the formula in cell A4 in the grouped worksheets.

4. On the formula bar, click the **Enter** button ✓. The formula =Summary!A3 is entered in cell A4 in all the worksheets in the group. The formula appears in the formula bar and 2016 appears in cell A4. See Figure 6-7.

Figure 6-7   **Formula with a worksheet reference**

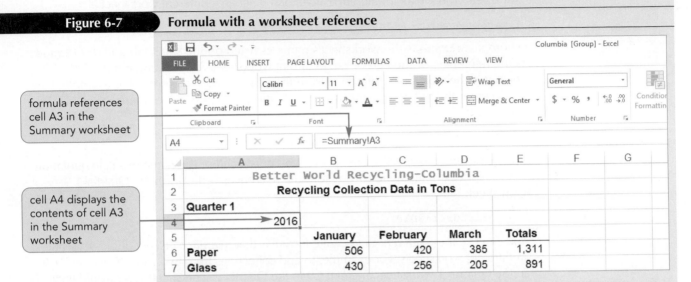

formula references cell A3 in the Summary worksheet

cell A4 displays the contents of cell A3 in the Summary worksheet

5. Go to each worksheet in the group and verify that the formula =Summary!A3 appears in the formula bar, and 2016 appears in cell A4.

6. Go to the **Summary** worksheet. The quarterly worksheets are ungrouped.

7. In cell **A3**, enter **Fiscal Year - 2016**. The descriptive label in cell A3 is entered in the Summary worksheet and is also displayed in the quarterly worksheets because of the formula you entered.

8. Go to the **Quarter 1** through **Quarter 4** worksheets and verify that the label "Fiscal Year - 2016" appears in cell A4 in each worksheet. See Figure 6-8.

Figure 6-8   **Edited content displayed in the cell with the worksheet reference**

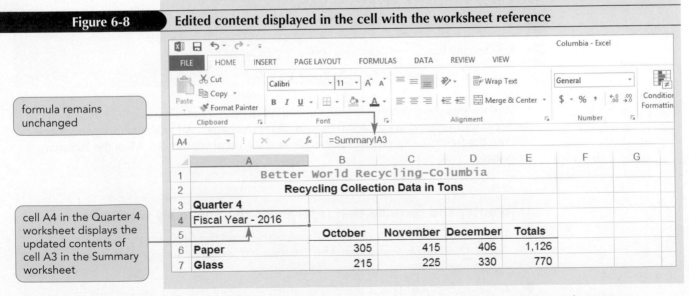

formula remains unchanged

cell A4 in the Quarter 4 worksheet displays the updated contents of cell A3 in the Summary worksheet

The Summary worksheet needs to include the quarterly totals for each category.

To enter worksheet references for the quarterly totals:

1. In the Summary worksheet, select cell **B6**.

2. Type **=** to begin the formula.

3. Click the **Quarter 1** sheet tab, and then click cell **E6**. The cell is selected and added to the formula.

4. Click the **Enter** button ✓ on the formula bar to complete the formula and return to the Summary worksheet. Cell B6 remains selected, and the formula ='Quarter 1'!E6 appears in the formula bar. The formula result showing the total tons of paper collected in the first quarter of 2016—1,311—appears in cell B6.

5. Repeat Steps 2 through 4 to enter formulas with worksheet references in cells **C6**, **D6**, and **E6** that add the total tons of paper collected in Quarter 2 (=**'Quarter 2'!E6**), Quarter 3 (=**'Quarter 3'!E6**), and Quarter 4 (=**'Quarter 4'!E6**). The quarterly totals are 1,230, 914, and 1,126 tons of paper, respectively.

6. Select the range **B6:E6**, and then drag the fill handle over the range **B7:E10**. The formulas with the worksheet references are copied to the rest of the item rows. The Auto Fill Options button appears below the copied range.

7. Click the **Auto Fill Options** button 🖳, and then click the **Fill Without Formatting** option button. You didn't copy the formatting in this case because you want to keep the bottom border formatting in the range B10:E10. The total values for the year appear in the range.

8. Click cell **B6** to deselect the range. The Summary worksheet now shows the 2016 total of each recyclable item collected in Columbia. The formula in cell F11 that was copied with the worksheet shows the total for all items collected in 2016. See Figure 6-9.

Figure 6-9   Recycling collection totals for Columbia in 2016

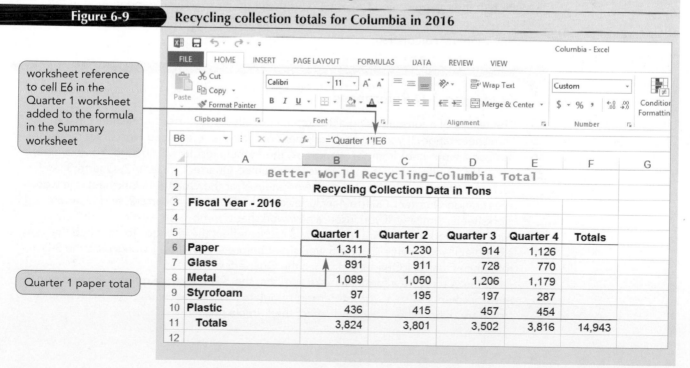

worksheet reference to cell E6 in the Quarter 1 worksheet added to the formula in the Summary worksheet

Quarter 1 paper total

Using 3-D References to Add Values Across Worksheets

Maria wants you to calculate the total tons of each material collected for the year and display the totals for the fiscal year in the Summary worksheet. To calculate the totals for the year, you can add the results from each quarterly worksheet and place the sum in the Summary worksheet. For example, in cell B6 of the Summary worksheet, you can enter the following formula:

```
='Quarter 1'!E6+'Quarter 2'!E6+'Quarter 3'!E6+'Quarter 4'!E6
```

This formula calculates the total amount of paper collected by adding the values in cell E6 in each of the quarterly worksheets. Continuing this approach for the entire worksheet would be time consuming and error prone.

Instead, when two or more worksheets have *identical* row and column layouts, as the quarterly worksheets in the Columbia workbook do, you can enter formulas with 3-D references to summarize those worksheets in another worksheet. The 3-D reference specifies not only the range of rows and columns, but also the range of worksheet names in which the cells appear. The general syntax of a 3-D reference is

WorksheetRange!*CellRange*

where *WorksheetRange* is the range of worksheets you want to reference and is entered as *FirstSheetName*:*LastSheetName* with a colon separating the first and last worksheets in the worksheet range. If the sheet names include spaces, they are surrounded by ' ' (single quotation marks). *CellRange* is the same cell or range in each of those worksheets that you want to reference. An exclamation mark (!) separates the worksheet range from the cell or range. For example, the following formula adds the values in cell D11 in the worksheets between Quarter1 and Quarter4, including Quarter1 and Quarter4:

```
=SUM(Quarter1:Quarter4!D11)
```

If worksheets named Quarter1, Quarter2, Quarter3, and Quarter4 are included in the workbook, the worksheet range Quarter1:Quarter4 references all four worksheets. Although the Quarter2 and Quarter3 worksheets aren't specifically mentioned in this 3-D reference, all worksheets positioned within the starting and ending names are included in the calculation.

INSIGHT

Managing 3-D References

The results of a formula using a 3-D reference reflect the current worksheets in the worksheet range. If you move a worksheet outside the referenced worksheet range or remove a worksheet from the workbook, the formula results will change. For example, consider a workbook with four worksheets named Quarter1, Quarter2, Quarter3, and Quarter4. If you move the Quarter3 worksheet after the Quarter4 worksheet, the worksheet range Quarter1:Quarter4 includes only the Quarter1, Quarter2, and Quarter4 worksheets. Similarly, if you insert a new worksheet or move an existing worksheet within the worksheet range, the formula results reflect the change. To continue the example, if you insert a Quarter5 worksheet before the Quarter4 worksheet, the 3-D reference Quarter1:Quarter4 includes the Quarter5 worksheet.

When you create a formula, make sure that the 3-D reference reflects the appropriate worksheets. Also, if you later insert or delete a worksheet within the 3-D reference, be aware of how the change will affect the formula results.

3-D references are often used in formulas that contain Excel functions, including SUM, AVERAGE, COUNT, MAX, and MIN.

Entering a Function That Contains a 3-D Reference

- Select the cell where you want to enter the formula.
- Type = to begin the formula, type the name of the function, and then type (to indicate the beginning of the argument.
- Click the sheet tab for the first worksheet in the worksheet range, press and hold the Shift key, and then click the tab for the last worksheet in the worksheet range.
- Select the cell or range to reference, and then press the Enter key.

In the Columbia workbook, Maria wants to use 3-D references in the Summary worksheet to add the total tons of each material collected for the year. You will begin by entering a formula to add the total tons collected for paper and glass in the first quarter. Then, you'll copy this formula to calculate the total tons of metal, Styrofoam, and plastic in the first quarter.

To use a 3-D reference to enter the total amount of paper collected:

1. In the Summary worksheet, select cell **F6**, and then type **=SUM(** to begin the formula.

2. Click the **Quarter 1** sheet tab, press and hold the **Shift** key, click the **Quarter 4** sheet tab, and then release the **Shift** key. The quarterly worksheets are grouped to create the worksheet range.

3. In the Quarter 1 worksheet, click cell **E6**. Cell E6 is selected in each quarterly worksheet and added to the function. Notice that the worksheet names are enclosed in single quotation marks because the worksheet names include spaces. See Figure 6-10.

Figure 6-10 | **3-D reference added to the SUM function**

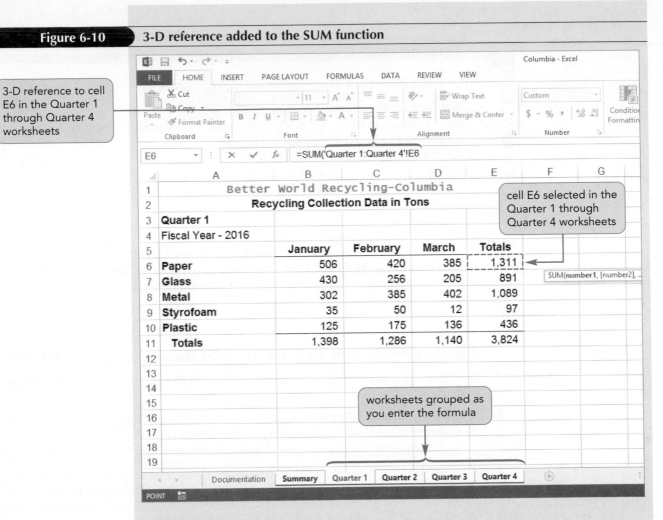

3-D reference to cell E6 in the Quarter 1 through Quarter 4 worksheets

cell E6 selected in the Quarter 1 through Quarter 4 worksheets

worksheets grouped as you enter the formula

4. Press the **Enter** key. The completed formula adds the total tons of paper collected in 2016.

5. In the Summary worksheet, select cell **F6**. The formula with the 3-D reference, =SUM('Quarter 1:Quarter 4'!E6), appears in the formula bar. The formula result—4,581—appears in the cell. See Figure 6-11.

| Figure 6-11 | 3-D reference used in the SUM function |

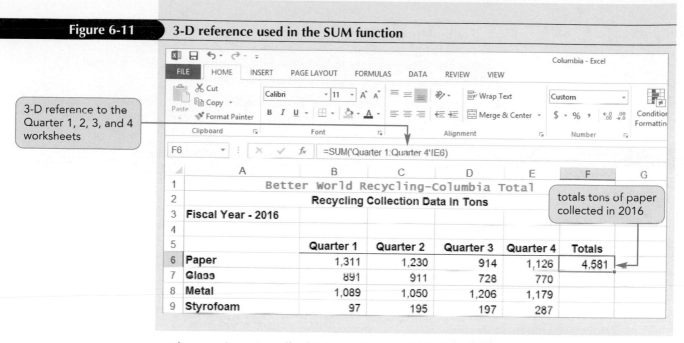

3-D reference to the Quarter 1, 2, 3, and 4 worksheets

F6   =SUM('Quarter 1:Quarter 4'!E6)

totals tons of paper collected in 2016

Better World Recycling–Columbia Total
Recycling Collection Data in Tons
Fiscal Year - 2016

	Quarter 1	Quarter 2	Quarter 3	Quarter 4	Totals
Paper	1,311	1,230	914	1,126	4,581
Glass	891	911	728	770	
Metal	1,089	1,050	1,206	1,179	
Styrofoam	97	195	197	287	

The next formula will add the total tons of glass collected in the first quarter. It will also use a 3-D reference.

To use a 3-D reference to calculate the total glass collected:

1. In the Summary worksheet, click cell **F7**, and then type **=SUM(** to begin the formula.

2. Click the **Quarter 1** sheet tab, press and hold the **Shift** key, click the **Quarter 4** sheet tab, and then release the **Shift** key. The quarterly worksheets are grouped to create the worksheet range.

3. In the Quarter 1 worksheet, click cell **E7**. Cell E7 is selected in each quarterly worksheet and added to the function.

4. Press the **Enter** key to complete the formula that adds the total tons of glass collected in 2016.

5. In the Summary worksheet, click cell **F7**. The formula with the 3-D reference, =SUM('Quarter 1:Quarter 4'!E7), appears in the formula bar, and the formula result 3,300 appears in cell F7.

Instead of entering formulas with 3-D references to create the totals for the remaining recyclable materials, you can copy the formulas to the rest of the range. You copy formulas with 3-D references the same way you copy other formulas—using copy and paste or AutoFill.

Maria wants you to calculate the total tons of recyclable materials collected in 2016.

To copy the formulas with 3-D references:

1. In the Summary worksheet, make sure cell **F7** is selected. This cell contains the formula with the 3-D reference you already entered.

2. Drag the fill handle over the range **F8:F10**. The formulas are copied for the rest of the recyclable totals. The Auto Fill Options button appears below the copied range.

3. Click the **Auto Fill Options** button , and then click the **Fill Without Formatting** option button. You don't want to copy the formatting in this case because you want to keep the bottom border formatting in cell F10. The total values for the year appear in the range.

4. Select cell **B6** to deselect the range. The Summary worksheet now shows the totals for 2016 in Columbia for each recyclable material. See Figure 6-12.

Figure 6-12 **Summary worksheet with the Columbia recycling collection totals**

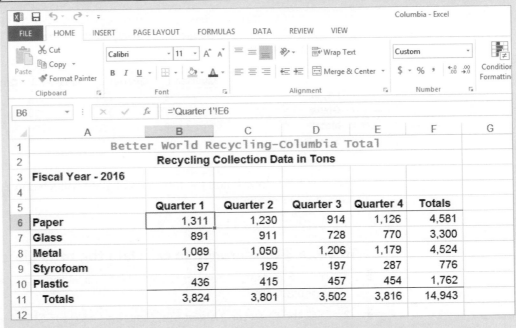

One benefit of summarizing data using formulas with 3-D references, like any other formula, is that if you change the value in one worksheet, the results of formulas that reference that cell reflect the change.

Maria has discovered an error in the collection data. The Columbia site collected 525 tons of metal in September (which is in Quarter 3), not 475. You will correct the tons of metal collected in September.

To change the tons of metal collected in the Quarter 3 worksheet:

1. In the Summary worksheet, note that 1,206 tons of metal were collected in Quarter 3.

2. Go to the **Quarter 3** worksheet.

3. In cell **D8**, enter **525**. The total tons collected for Quarter 3 is now 1,256.

    The results in the Summary worksheet are also updated because of the 3-D references in the formulas.

4. Go to the **Summary** worksheet. The total number of tons of metal collected in Quarter 3 is now 1,256. The Quarter 3 total is now 3,552, and the 2016 total is now 4,574. See Figure 6-13.

Figure 6-13 Summary worksheet with updated Quarter 3 metal data

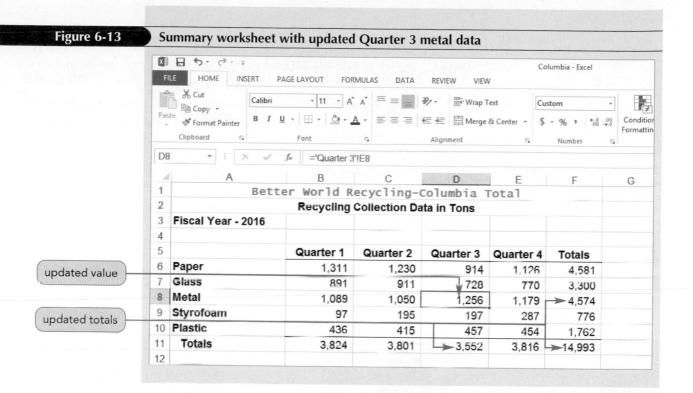

Printing a Worksheet Group

When you create a worksheet group, you apply the same page layout settings to all of the worksheets in the group at the same time. You can also print all of the worksheets in the group at once. The process for printing a worksheet group is the same as for printing a single worksheet, except that you must first group the worksheets you want to print.

Maria wants a printed copy of the five collection data worksheets to include in her report. Each page should have the same setup. Because the layout will be the same for all the quarterly worksheets in the Columbia workbook, you can speed the page layout setup by creating a worksheet group before selecting settings.

To preview the Summary and quarterly worksheets with a custom header and footer:

> Be sure to include all five worksheets in the group so you can apply page layout settings and print the worksheets at once.

1. Group the **Summary**, **Quarter 1**, **Quarter 2**, **Quarter 3**, and **Quarter 4** worksheets. The five worksheets are grouped.

2. On the ribbon, click the **PAGE LAYOUT** tab.

3. In the Page Setup group, click the **Dialog Box Launcher**. The Page Setup dialog box opens with the Page tab active.

4. Click the **Margins** tab, and then click the **Horizontally** check box in the Center on page section to insert a checkmark. The printed content will be centered horizontally on the page.

5. Click the **Header/Footer** tab, click the **Custom Header** button to open the Header dialog box, click in the **Center section** box, click the **Insert Sheet Name** button to add the &[Tab] code in the section box (which inserts the sheet tab name in the center section of the header), and then click the **OK** button. A preview of the header appears in the upper portion of the dialog box.

6. Click the **Custom Footer** button to open the Footer dialog box, type your name in the Left section box, click in the Right section box, click the **Insert Date** button to add the &[Date] code in the section box (which inserts the current date in the right section of the footer), and then click the **OK** button.

7. Click the **Print Preview** button. The preview of the Summary worksheet, the first worksheet in the group, appears on the Print screen in Backstage view. See Figure 6-14.

Figure 6-14 ▸ **Preview of the worksheet group**

8. Below the preview, click the **Next Page** button ▶ four times to view the other worksheets in the group. Each page has the same page layout but the header shows the sheet tab names.

Trouble? If only one page appears in the preview, the worksheets are not grouped. Click the Back button to exit Backstage view, and then repeat Steps 1 through 8.

9. Click the **Back** button ⊙ to exit Backstage view without printing the worksheet group.

10. Go to the **Documentation** worksheet to ungroup the worksheets, and then go to the **Summary** worksheet.

In this session, you consolidated the data in Better World Recycling's Columbia workbook into a Summary worksheet so that Maria can quickly see the collection totals for the recyclable items. In the next session, you will help Maria determine the annual totals for the other Better World Recycling collection sites—Richmond and Marion.

Session 6.1 Quick Check

1. What is a worksheet group?
2. How do you select an adjacent worksheet group? How do you select a nonadjacent worksheet group? How do you deselect a worksheet group?
3. What formula would you enter in the Summary worksheet to reference cell C8 in the Quarter 2 worksheet?
4. What is the 3-D reference to cell E6 in the adjacent Summary 1, Summary 2, and Summary 3 worksheets?
5. Explain what the formula =AVERAGE(Sheet1:Sheet4!B1) calculates.
6. If you insert a new worksheet named Sheet5 after Sheet4, how would you change the formula =MIN(Sheet1:Sheet4!B1) to include Sheet5 in the calculation?
7. If you insert a new worksheet named Sheet5 before Sheet4, how would you change the formula =SUM(Sheet1:Sheet4!B1) to include Sheet5 in the calculation?
8. How do you apply the same page layout to all of the worksheets in a workbook at one time?

Session 6.2 Visual Overview:

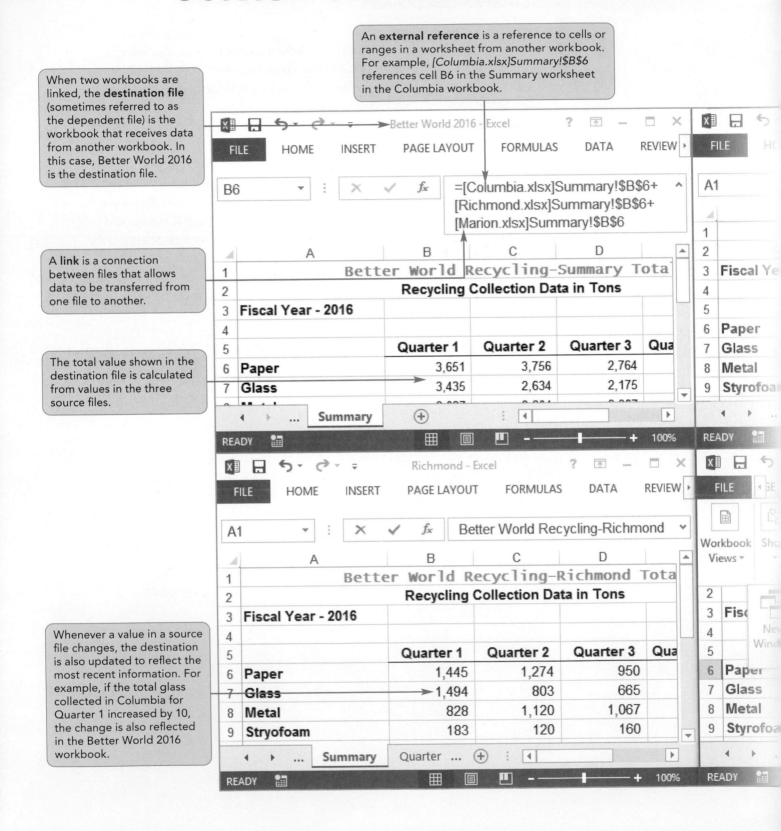

When two workbooks are linked, the **destination file** (sometimes referred to as the dependent file) is the workbook that receives data from another workbook. In this case, Better World 2016 is the destination file.

An **external reference** is a reference to cells or ranges in a worksheet from another workbook. For example, *[Columbia.xlsx]Summary!$B$6* references cell B6 in the Summary worksheet in the Columbia workbook.

A **link** is a connection between files that allows data to be transferred from one file to another.

The total value shown in the destination file is calculated from values in the three source files.

Whenever a value in a source file changes, the destination is also updated to reflect the most recent information. For example, if the total glass collected in Columbia for Quarter 1 increased by 10, the change is also reflected in the Better World 2016 workbook.

Links and External References

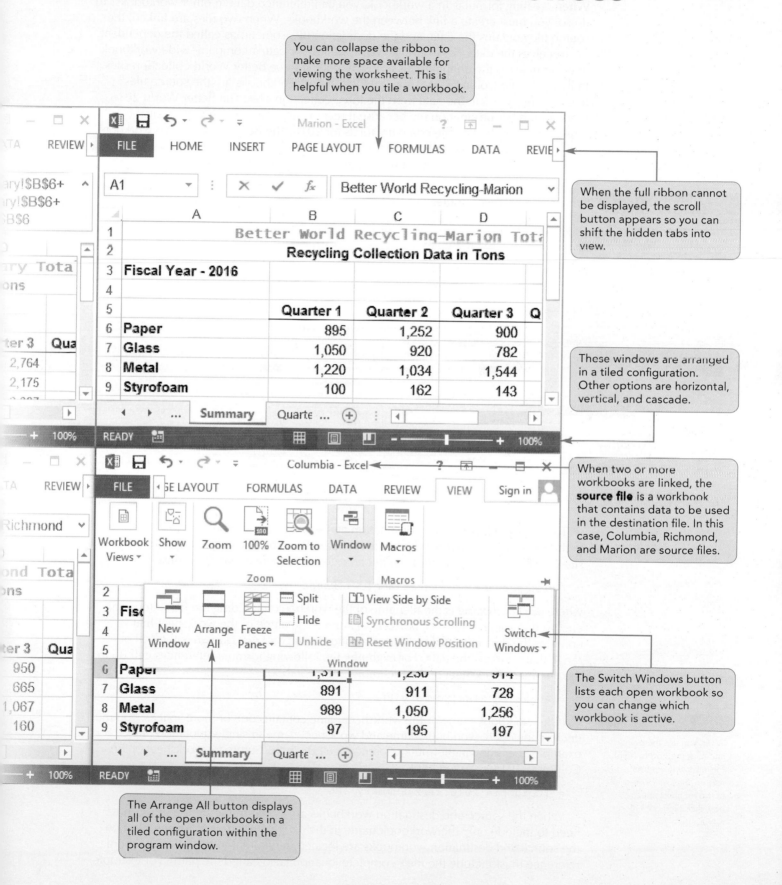

You can collapse the ribbon to make more space available for viewing the worksheet. This is helpful when you tile a workbook.

When the full ribbon cannot be displayed, the scroll button appears so you can shift the hidden tabs into view.

These windows are arranged in a tiled configuration. Other options are horizontal, vertical, and cascade.

When two or more workbooks are linked, the **source file** is a workbook that contains data to be used in the destination file. In this case, Columbia, Richmond, and Marion are source files.

The Switch Windows button lists each open workbook so you can change which workbook is active.

The Arrange All button displays all of the open workbooks in a tiled configuration within the program window.

Linking Workbooks

When creating formulas in a workbook, you can reference data in other workbooks. To do so, you must create a link between the workbooks. When two files are linked, the source file contains the data, and the destination file (sometimes called the dependent file) receives the data. For example, Maria wants to create a company-wide workbook that summarizes the annual totals from each of the three Better World collection sites. In this case, the Columbia, Marion, and Richmond workbooks are the source files because they contain the data from the three collection sites. The Better World 2016 workbook is the destination file because it receives the data from the three site workbooks to calculate the company totals for 2016. The Better World 2016 workbook will always have access to the most recent information in the site workbooks because it can be updated whenever any of the linked values change. See Figure 6-15.

Figure 6-15   **Source and destination files**

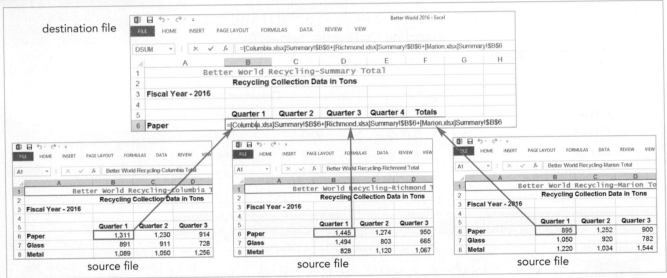

© 2014 Cengage Learning

To create the link between destination and source files, you need to insert a formula in the Better World 2016 workbook that references a specific cell or range in the three site workbooks. That reference, called an external reference, has the syntax

`[WorkbookName]WorksheetName!CellRange`

where `WorkbookName` is the filename of the workbook (including the file extension) enclosed in square brackets; `WorksheetName` is the name of the worksheet that contains the data followed by an exclamation mark; and `CellRange` is the cell or range that contains the data. For example, the following formula references cell B6 in the Summary worksheet of the Richmond.xlsx workbook:

`=[Richmond.xlsx]Summary!B6`

If the workbook name or the worksheet name contains one or more spaces, you must enclose the entire workbook name and worksheet name in single quotation marks. For example, the following formula references cell B6 in the Summary worksheet of the Columbia 2016.xlsx workbook:

`='[Columbia 2016.xlsx]Summary'!B6`

When the source and destination workbooks are stored in the same folder, you need to include only the workbook name in the external reference. However, when the source and destination workbooks are located in different folders, the workbook reference must include the file's complete location (also called the path). For example,

TIP

When you use the point-and-click method to build formulas with external references, Excel enters all of the required punctuation, including quotation marks.

if the destination file is stored in C:\Recycle Data and the source file is stored in C:\Recycle Data\Local Data, the complete reference in the destination file would be:

```
='C:\Recycle Data\Local Data\[Columbia.xlsx]Summary'!B6
```

The single quotation marks start at the beginning of the path and end immediately before the exclamation mark.

PROSKILLS

Decision Making: Understanding When to Link Workbooks

More than one person is usually involved in developing information that will be used in an organization's decision-making process. If each person has access to only part of the data, everyone's ability to see the whole picture and make good decisions is limited. Linking workbooks provides one way to pull together all of the data being compiled by different people or departments to support the decision-making process.

When deciding whether to link workbooks, consider the following questions:

- **Can separate workbooks have the same purpose and structure?** With linked workbooks, each workbook can focus on a different store, branch office, or department with the same products or expenditure types and reporting periods (such as weekly, monthly, and quarterly).
- **Is a large workbook too unwieldy to use?** A large workbook can be divided into smaller workbooks for each quarter, division, or product and then linked to provide the summary information.
- **Can information from different workbooks be summarized?** Linked workbooks provide a way to quickly and accurately consolidate information from multiple source workbooks, and the summary worksheet will always contain the most current information even when information is later updated.
- **Are source workbooks continually updated?** With linked workbooks, an outdated source workbook can be replaced and the destination workbook will then reflect the latest information.
- **Will the source workbooks be available to the destination workbook?** If the person who is working with the destination workbook cannot access the source workbooks, then the destination workbook cannot be updated.

If you can answer yes to these questions, then linked workbooks are the way to go. Creating linked workbooks can help you analyze data better, leading to better decision making. It also provides greater flexibility as data becomes more expansive and complex. However, keep in mind that workbooks with many links can take a long time to open and update.

Navigating Multiple Workbooks

When you create external reference formulas, you'll need to move between open workbooks. The Switch Windows button in the Window group on the VIEW tab lists each open workbook so you can change which workbook is active. Another method is to click the Excel button on the taskbar and then click the thumbnail of the workbook you want to make active.

Maria received workbooks from the Richmond and Marion managers that are similar to the one you helped prepare. These three collection data workbooks (named Columbia, Richmond, and Marion) contain the tons of recyclable materials collected in 2016. Maria wants to create a company-wide workbook that summarizes the annual totals from each site workbook. You'll combine the three site workbooks into one regional summary workbook. First you need to open the workbooks that you want to reference. Then you'll switch between them to make each Summary worksheet the active sheet in preparation for creating the external references.

To open the regional workbooks and switch between them:

1. If you took a break after the previous session, make sure the Columbia workbook is open and the Summary worksheet is active.

2. Open the **Better World** workbook located in the Excel6 ▶ Tutorial folder included with your Data Files, and then save the workbook as **Better World 2016** in the location specified by your instructor.

3. In the Documentation worksheet of the Better World 2016 workbook, enter your name and the date, and then make the **Summary** worksheet active.

4. Open the **Marion** and **Richmond** workbooks located in the Excel6 ▶ Tutorial folder included with your Data Files.

5. On the ribbon, click the **VIEW** tab.

6. In the Window group, click the **Switch Windows** button to display a list of all the workbooks that are currently open.

7. Click **Marion** to make it the active workbook, and then go to the **Summary** worksheet.

8. On the ribbon, click the **VIEW** tab.

9. In the Window group, click the **Switch Windows** button, click **Richmond** to make the Richmond workbook active, and then go to the **Summary** worksheet.

10. Make the **Better World 2016** workbook the active workbook. The Summary worksheet is the active sheet in each workbook.

Arranging Multiple Workbooks

Rather than continually switching between open workbooks, you can display all the open workbooks on your screen at the same time. This way, you can easily click among the open workbooks to create links as well as quickly compare the contents of worksheets in different workbooks. You can arrange workbooks in the following layouts:

- **Tiled**—divides the open workbooks evenly on the screen
- **Horizontal**—divides the open workbooks into horizontal bands
- **Vertical**—divides the open workbooks into vertical bands
- **Cascade**—layers the open workbooks on the screen

The layout you select will depend on the contents being displayed and your purpose.

REFERENCE

Arranging Workbooks

- On the VIEW tab, in the Window group, click the Arrange All button.
- Select the layout in which you want to arrange the open workbooks.
- When arranging multiple workbooks, uncheck the Windows of active workbook option. When arranging multiple worksheets within one workbook, check this option.
- Click the OK button.

Currently, the four workbooks are open but only one is visible. You'll arrange the workbooks using the tiled arrangement.

To tile the open workbooks:

1. On the VIEW tab, in the Window group, click the **Arrange All** button. The Arrange Windows dialog box opens so you can select the layout arrangement you want.

2. Click the **Tiled** option button, if necessary. The Tiled option arranges the four Better World Recycling workbooks evenly on the screen.

3. Click the **OK** button. The four open workbooks appear in a tiled layout.

4. Click in the **Better World 2016** workbook to make it the active workbook, if necessary. In the tiled layout, the active workbook contains the active cell.

   The ribbon appears in each window, taking up a lot of the workbook space. To see more of the worksheets, you will collapse the ribbon in each window to show only the ribbon tabs.

5. In each window, click the **Collapse the Ribbon** button ⌃ in the lower-right corner of the ribbon (or press the **Ctrl+F1** keys). Only the ribbon tabs are visible in each window. If the ribbon includes more tabs than can be displayed, a ribbon scroll button ▶ appears to the right of the last visible tab, which you can click to display the other tabs. See Figure 6-16.

TIP

You can click the Windows of active workbook check box to tile the sheets in the current workbook on the screen.

Figure 6-16   **Four workbooks arranged in a tiled layout**

Creating Formulas with External References

A formula can include a reference to another workbook (called an external reference), which creates a set of linked workbooks. The process for entering a formula with an external reference is the same as for entering any other formula using references within the same worksheet or workbook. You can enter the formulas by typing them or using the point-and-click method. In most situations, you will use the point-and-click method to switch between the source files and the destination files so that Excel enters the references to the workbook, worksheet, and cell using the correct syntax.

You need to enter the external reference formulas in the Better World 2016 workbook to summarize the recycling center totals into one workbook for Maria. You'll start by creating the formula that adds the total tons of paper collected in Columbia, Marion, and Richmond for Quarter 1 of 2016. You cannot use the SUM function with 3-D references here because you are referencing multiple workbooks, and 3-D references can only be used to reference multiple worksheets in the same workbook.

To create the formula with external references to add the total tons of paper collected:

1. In the Better World 2016 workbook, in the Summary worksheet, select cell **B6**, and then type **=** to begin the formula.

As you create the formula, be sure to verify each external reference before going to the next step.

2. Click anywhere in the **Columbia** workbook to make the Columbia workbook active and place the formula in its formula bar, and then click cell **B6** in the Summary worksheet. The external reference to cell B6 in the Summary worksheet of the Columbia workbook—'[Columbia.xlsx]Summary'!$B$6—is added to the formula in the Better World 2016 workbook. See Figure 6-17.

Figure 6-17 | **Formula with an external cell reference**

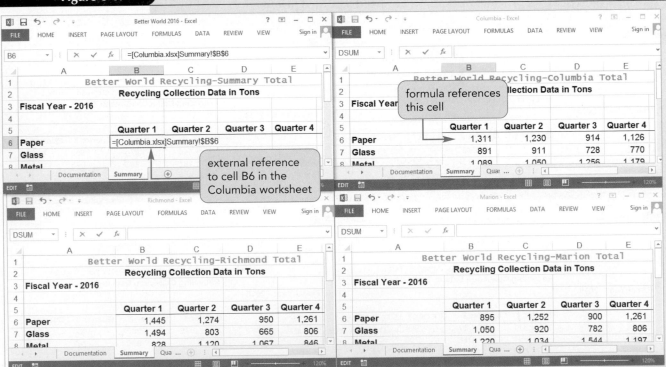

The reference created in a 3-D reference is an absolute cell reference, which does not change when the formula is copied. The formula remains in the formula bar of both the Better World 2016 and Columbia workbooks until you make another workbook active. At that time, the formula will appear in the Better World 2016 workbook and the active worksheet.

3. Type **+**. The Better World 2016 workbook becomes active and you can continue entering the formula. You need to create an external reference to the Richmond workbook.

4. Click anywhere in the **Richmond** workbook, click cell **B6** in the Summary worksheet, and then type **+**. The formula in the Better World 2016 workbook includes the external reference to the cell that contains the total tons of paper collected in Richmond during Quarter 1.

5. Click anywhere in the **Marion** workbook, click cell **B6** in the Summary worksheet, and then press the **Enter** key. The formula with three external references is entered in the Summary worksheet in the Better World 2016 workbook.

6. In the Better World 2016 workbook, in the Summary worksheet, click cell **B6**. The complete formula is too long to appear in the formula bar of the tiled window. You will expand the formula bar so that it can display the full formula.

7. At the right edge of the formula bar, click the **Expand Formula Bar** button (or press the **Ctrl+Shift+U** keys). The complete formula now is visible in the formula bar, and the Collapse Formula Bar button appears at the right edge of the formula bar, which you can click to return the formula bar to a single line. The formula results in cell B6 show that 3651 tons of paper were collected during Quarter 1 in the three recycling sites—1,311 in Columbia, 895 in Marion, and 1,445 in Richmond. See Figure 6-18.

| Figure 6-18 | Total paper collections from Columbia, Richmond, and Marion in Quarter 1 |

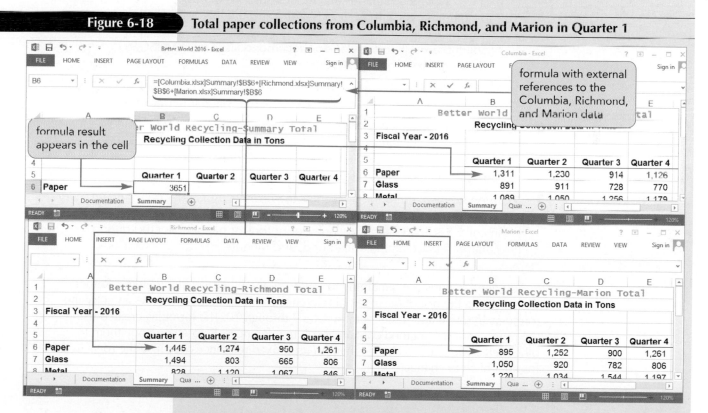

Trouble? If 3651 doesn't appear in cell B6 in the Summary worksheet in the Better World 2016 workbook, you might have clicked an incorrect cell for an external reference in the formula. Repeat Steps 1 through 6 to correct the formula.

You'll use the same process to enter the external reference formula for cells C6, D6, and E6, which contain the total tons of paper collected in Quarter 2, Quarter 3, and Quarter 4, respectively. These formulas will calculate the total collection amounts from all three locations.

To create the remaining external reference formulas:

1. In the Better World 2016 workbook, in the Summary worksheet, select cell **C6**, and then type **=** to begin the formula.

2. Click the **Columbia** workbook, click cell **C6** in the Summary worksheet, and then type **+**. The formula in the Better World 2016 workbook includes the external reference to cell C6 in the Summary worksheet in the Columbia workbook.

3. Click the **Richmond** workbook, click cell **C6** in the Summary worksheet, and then type **+**. The formula includes an external reference to cell C6 in the Summary worksheet in the Richmond workbook.

4. Click the **Marion** workbook, click cell **C6** in the Summary worksheet, and then press the **Enter** key. The external reference formula is complete.

5. In the Better World 2016 workbook, in the Summary worksheet, click cell **C6**. Cell C6 displays 3756, the total number of tons of paper collected in Quarter 2 in Columbia, Richmond, and Marion, and the following formula appears in the formula bar:
   =[Columbia.xlsx]Summary!$C$6+[Richmond.xlsx]Summary!$C$6
   +[Marion.xlsx]Summary!$C$6.

   Next, you'll enter the external reference formulas in cells D6 and E6 to add the total number of tons collected in Quarter 3 and Quarter 4.

6. Repeat Steps 1 through 4 to enter the formula from cell **D6** in the Summary worksheet in the Better World 2016 workbook. The formula result displayed in cell D6 is 2764—the total number of tons of paper collected during Quarter 3 in Columbia, Richmond, and Marion.

7. Repeat Steps 1 through 4 to enter the formula from cell **E6** in the Summary worksheet in the Better World 2016 workbook. The formula result displayed in cell E6 is 3648—the total number of tons of paper collected during Quarter 4 in Columbia, Richmond, and Marion.

You need to enter the remaining formulas for the other recyclable items. Rather than creating the rest of the external reference formulas manually, you can copy the formulas in row 6 and paste them in rows 7 through 10. The formulas created using the point-and-click method contain absolute references. Before you copy them to other cells, you need to change them to use mixed references because the rows in the formula need to change.

To edit the external reference formulas to use mixed references:

1. Maximize the Better World 2016 workbook, click the **Ribbon Display Options** button 🔼 in the title bar, and then click **Show Tabs and Commands** (or press the **Ctrl+F1** keys) to pin the ribbon to show both the tabs and the commands. The other workbooks are still open but are not visible.

2. At the right edge of the formula bar, click the **Collapse Formula Bar** button 🔼 (or press the **Ctrl+Shift+U** keys) to reduce the formula bar to one line.

3. In the Summary worksheet, double-click cell **B6** to enter Edit mode and display the formula in the cell.

TIP

You can also create the mixed reference by deleting the $ symbol from the row references in the formula.

4. Click in the first absolute reference in the formula, and then press the **F4** key twice to change the absolute reference $B$6 to the mixed reference $B6.

5. Edit the other two absolute references in the formula to be mixed references with absolute column references and relative row references.

6. Press the **Enter** key, and then select cell **B6**. The formula is updated to include mixed references, but the formula results aren't affected. Cell B6 still displays 3,651, which is correct. See Figure 6-19.

Figure 6-19   **External reference formula with mixed references**

7. Edit the formulas in cells **C6**, **D6**, and **E6** to change the absolute references to the mixed references **$C6**, **$D6**, and **$E6**, respectively. The formulas are updated, but the cells in the range C6:E6 still correctly display 3,756, 2,764, and 3,648, respectively.

With the formulas corrected to include mixed references, you can now copy the external reference formulas in the range B6:E6 to the other rows. Then you'll enter the SUM function to total the values in each row and column.

To copy and paste the external reference formulas:

1. Select the range **B6:E6**, and then drag the fill handle to select the range **B7:E10**. The formulas are copied to the range B7:E10 and the formula results appear in the cells. The Auto Fill Options button appears in the lower-right corner of the selected range, but you do not need to use it.

Trouble? If all of the values in the range B7:E10 are the same as those in the range B6:E6, you didn't change the absolute cell references to mixed cell references in the formulas in the range B6:E6. Repeat Steps 3 through 7 in the previous set of steps, and then repeat Step 1 in this set of steps.

2. In cell **B11**, enter the SUM function to add the range **B6:B10**. A total of 12,439 tons of recyclable materials were collected in Quarter 1.

3. Copy the formula in cell B11 to the range **C11:E11**. The total recyclable materials collected were 11,401 tons in Quarter 2, 10,713 tons in Quarter 3, and 11,434 tons in Quarter 4.

▶ **4.** In cell **F6**, enter the SUM function to add the range B6:F6. A total of 13,819 tons of paper were collected at all sites in 2016.

▶ **5.** Copy the formula in cell F6 to the range **F7:F11**. The total recyclable materials collected in 2016 were 10,626 tons of glass, 13,430 tons of metal, 2,043 tons of Styrofoam, and 6,069 tons of plastic, with a grand total of 45,987 tons collected for the year.

▶ **6.** Format the range B6:F11 with the **Comma style** and no decimal places.

▶ **7.** Format the range B10:F10 with a **bottom border**, and then select cell **A1** to deselect the range. See Figure 6-20.

| Figure 6-20 | Completed summary of collection data |

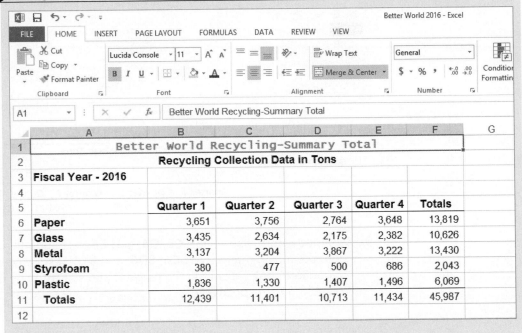

Maria is pleased; the regional summary results match her expectations.

INSIGHT

Managing Linked Workbooks

As you work with a linked workbook, you might need to replace a source file or change where you stored the source and destination files. However, replacing or moving a file can affect the linked workbook. Keep in mind the following guidelines to manage your linked workbooks:

- If you rename a source file, the destination workbook won't be able to find it. A dialog box opens, indicating "This workbook contains one or more links that cannot be updated." Click the Continue button to open the workbook with the most recent values, or click the Change Source button in the Edit Links dialog box to specify the new name of that linked source file.
- If you move a source file to a different folder, the link breaks between the destination and source files. Click the Change Source button in the Edit Links dialog box to specify the new location of the linked workbook.
- If you receive a replacement source file, you can swap the original source file with the replacement file. No additional changes are needed.
- If you receive a destination workbook but the source files are not included, Excel will not be able to find the source files, and a dialog box opens with the message "This workbook contains one or more links that cannot be updated." Click the Continue button to open the workbook with the most recent values, or click the Break Link button in the Edit Links dialog box to replace the external references with the existing values.
- If you change the name of a destination file, you can open that renamed version destination file without affecting the source files or the original destination file.

Updating Linked Workbooks

When workbooks are linked, it is important that the data in the destination file accurately reflects the contents of the source file. When data in a source file changes, you want the destination file to reflect those changes. If both the source and destination files are open when you make a change, the destination file is updated automatically. If the destination file is closed when you make a change in a source file, you choose whether to update the link to display the current values, or continue to display the older values from the destination file when you open the destination file.

Updating a Destination Workbook with Source Workbooks Open

When both the destination and source workbooks are open, any changes you make in a source workbook automatically appear in the destination workbook. Maria tells you that Columbia actually collected 100 fewer tons of metal in March than was recorded. After you correct the March value in the Quarter 1 worksheet, the amount in the Summary worksheet of the Columbia workbook and the regional total in the Better World 2016 workbook will also change if both the source and destination files are open.

To update the source workbook with the destination file open:

1. Make the **Columbia** workbook active, and then go to the **Quarter 1** worksheet. You'll update the total for metal collected in March.

2. If the ribbon is still collapsed, pin the ribbon so you can see both the tabs and the groups.

3. In cell **D8**, enter **302**. Columbia's collection data is updated.

4. Go to the **Summary** worksheet in the Columbia workbook, and then verify that the total of metal collected in Quarter 1 (cell B8) is 989 tons, the total of recyclable materials collected in Quarter 1 (cell B11) is 3,724 tons, and the total of recyclable materials collected in 2016 (cell F11) is 14,893 tons. See Figure 6-21.

Figure 6-21   **Summary worksheet in the Columbia workbook with the revised Quarter 1 data**

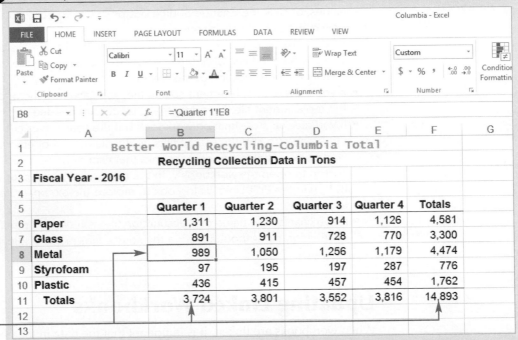

5. Make the **Better World 2016** workbook active, and then verify in the Summary worksheet that the total of metal collected in Quarter 1 (cell B8) is 3,037 tons, the total of recyclable materials collected in Quarter 1 (cell B11) is 12,339 tons, and the total of recyclable materials collected in 2016 (cell F11) is 45,887 tons, reflecting the new value you entered in the Columbia workbook. Because both the destination and source files are open, Excel updated the destination file automatically. See Figure 6-22.

Figure 6-22   Summary worksheet in the Better World 2016 workbook with the revised Quarter 1 data

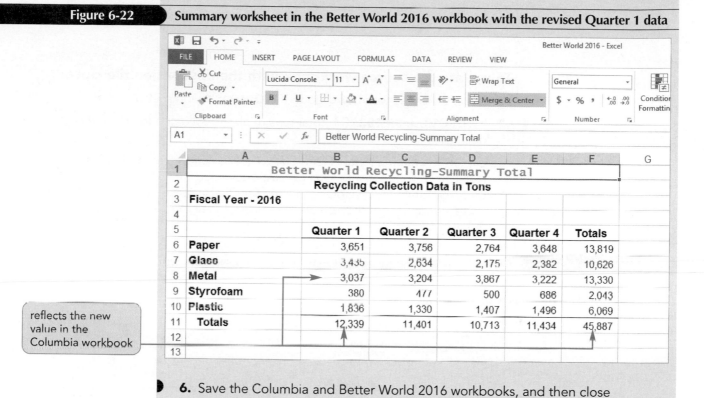

6. Save the Columbia and Better World 2016 workbooks, and then close the Marion, Richmond, and Better World 2016 workbooks. The Columbia workbook remains open.

Updating a Destination Workbook with Source Workbooks Closed

When you save a workbook that contains external reference formulas, such as the Better World 2016 workbook, Excel stores the most recent results of those formulas in the destination file. Source files, such as the Columbia, Richmond, and Marion workbooks, are often updated while the destination file is closed. In that case, the values in the destination file are not updated at the same time the source files are updated. The next time you open the destination file, the cells containing external reference formulas still display the old values. Therefore, some of the values in the edited source workbooks are different from the values in the destination workbook.

To update the destination workbook with the current data, you must specify that you want the update to occur. As part of the Excel security system that attempts to protect against malicious software, links to other workbooks are not updated without your permission. When you open a workbook with external reference formulas (the destination file), a dialog box appears, notifying you that the workbook contains links to an external source that could be unsafe. You then can choose to update the content, which allows the external reference formulas to function and updates the links in the destination workbook; or, you can choose not to update the links, which lets you continue working with the data you have. The old values in the destination workbook are displayed and the links to the source files have an unknown status.

Maria realizes that the Columbia workbook needs a second correction. In Quarter 4, the total plastic recycled in November was 182 tons, not 202 tons as currently entered in the Columbia workbook. She asks you to decrease the total tons of plastic collected in November by 20. As a result, the totals in the Summary worksheet of the Columbia workbook and the regional total in the Better World 2016 workbook will both decrease by 20. You'll edit the source file, the Columbia workbook, while the destination file is closed.

To update the source workbook with the destination file closed:

1. In the Columbia workbook, go to the **Quarter 4** worksheet.

2. In cell **C10**, enter **182**. The total tons of plastic collected in Quarter 4 decreases to 1,189.

3. Go to the **Summary** worksheet. The total of plastic collected for Quarter 4 (cell E10) is 434 tons, the total of plastic collected for 2016 (cell F10) is 1,742 tons, the total of recyclables collected for Quarter 4 (cell E11) is 3,796 tons, and the total of recyclables collected in 2016 (cell F11) is 14,873 tons. See Figure 6-23.

| Figure 6-23 | Revised plastic collections for Quarter 4 in the Columbia workbook |

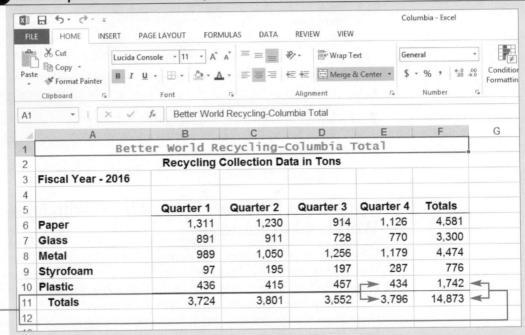

reflects changes to plastic collected in Quarter 4

4. Save the Columbia workbook, and then close it.

Now you'll open the destination file (the Better World 2016 workbook). The total tons of recycling from the source workbooks won't be updated until you specify that they should. When the destination file is open and the source files are closed, the complete file path is included as part of the external reference formula that appears in the formula bar.

To open and update the destination workbook:

1. Open the **Better World 2016** workbook, and then go to the **Summary** worksheet, if necessary. The value in cell E10 has *not* changed; it is still 1,496. A dialog box appears, indicating that the workbook contains links to one or more external sources that could be unsafe. See Figure 6-24.

| Figure 6-24 | Dialog box warning of possible unsafe links |

Trouble? If the Message Bar appears below the ribbon with the SECURITY WARNING Automatic update of links has been disabled, click the Enable Content button. The values in the destination workbook are updated. Continue with Step 3.

You want the current values in the source files to appear in the destination workbook.

2. In the dialog box, click the **Update** button. The values in the destination file are updated. The total amount of plastic collected in Quarter 4, shown in cell E10 of the Better World 2016 workbook, has decreased to 1,476 tons, the total plastic collected for 2016 (cell F10) is 6,049 tons, the total Quarter 4 recyclables (cell E11) is 11,414 tons, and the grand total of all recyclables collected by the company in 2016 (cell F11) decreased to 45,867 tons.

3. Select cell **E10**, and then look at the complete file path for each external reference in the formula. The full path appears because the source workbooks are closed. Note that the path you see will match the location where you save your workbooks.

4. Save the workbook.

Managing Links

When workbooks are linked, the Edit Links dialog box provides ways to manage the links. You can review the status of the links and update the data in the files. You can repair **broken links**, which are references to files that have been moved since the link was created. Broken links appear in the dialog box as having an unknown status. You can also open the source file and break the links, which converts all external reference formulas to their most recent values.

After the fiscal year audit is completed and the source workbooks are final, Maria will archive the summary workbook and move the files to an off-site storage location as part of her year-end backup process. You will save a copy of the Better World 2016 workbook and then break the links to the source files in the copy.

To save a copy of the Better World 2016 workbook and open the Edit Links dialog box:

1. Save the Better World 2016 workbook as **Better World 2016 Audited** in the location specified by your instructor. The Better World 2016 workbook closes, and the Better World 2016 Audited workbook remains open.

2. On the ribbon, click the **DATA** tab.

3. In the Connections group, click the **Edit Links** button. The Edit Links dialog box opens. Note that the path you see for source files will match the location where you save your workbooks. See Figure 6-25.

Figure 6-25	Edit Links dialog box

your paths will match the location where you save your workbooks

replaces the links to source files with the current values of the linked cells

updates the destination file with data from the latest saved version of the selected course file

The Edit Links dialog box lists all of the files to which the destination workbook is linked so that you can update, change, open, or remove the links. You can see that the destination workbook—Better World 2016 Audited—has links to the Richmond, Columbia, and Marion workbooks. The dialog box shows the following information about each link:

- **Source**—indicates the file to which the link points. The Better World 2016 Audited workbook contains three links pointing to the Columbia.xlsx, Richmond.xlsx, and Marion.xlsx workbooks.
- **Type**—identifies the type of each source file. In this case, the type is an Excel worksheet, but it could also be a Word document, a PowerPoint presentation, or some other type of file.
- **Update**—specifies the way values are updated from the source file. The letter *A* indicates the link is updated automatically when you open the workbook, or when both the source and destination files are open simultaneously. The letter *M* indicates the link must be updated manually by the user, which is useful when you want to see the older data values before updating to the new data. To manually update the link and see the new data values, click the Update Values button.
- **Status**—shows whether Excel successfully accessed the link and updated the values from the source document (status is OK), or Excel has not attempted to update the links in this session (status is Unknown). The status of the three links in the Better World 2016 Audited workbook is Unknown.

Maria wants you to break the links so that the Better World 2016 Audited workbook contains only the updated values (and is no longer affected by changes in the source files). Then she wants you to save the Better World 2016 Audited workbook for her to archive. This allows Maria to store a "snapshot" of the data at the end of the fiscal year.

To convert all external reference formulas to their current values:

1. In the Edit Links dialog box, click the **Break Link** button. A dialog box opens, alerting you that breaking links in the workbook permanently converts formulas and external references to their existing values.

2. Click the **Break Links** button. No links appear in the Edit Links dialog box.

3. Click the **Close** button. The Better World 2016 Audited workbook now contains values instead of formulas with external references.

4. Select cell **B6**. The value 3,651 appears in the cell and the formula bar; the link (the external reference formula) was replaced with the data value. All of the cells in the range B6:E10 contain values rather than external reference formulas.

5. Save the Better World 2016 Audited workbook, and then close it. The Better World 2016 workbook contains external reference formulas, and the Better World 2016 Audited workbook contains current values.

In this session, you worked with multiple worksheets and workbooks, summarizing data and linking workbooks. This ensures that the data in the summary workbook is accurate and remains updated with the latest data in the source files. In the next session, you will create templates and hyperlinks.

Session 6.2 Quick Check

REVIEW

1. What is the external reference to the range B6:F6 in the Grades worksheet in the Grade Book workbook located in the Course folder on drive D?
2. What is a source file?
3. What is a destination file?
4. How are linked workbooks updated when both the destination and source files are open?
5. How are linked workbooks updated when the source file is changed and the destination file is closed?
6. How would you determine to what workbooks a destination file is linked?
7. What are the layouts that you can use to arrange multiple workbooks?
8. When you have broken the links for a cell, what appears in the formula bar when you select that cell?

Session 6.3 Visual Overview:

This Weekly time sheet workbook was created from one of the templates available from Office.com. Microsoft provides many templates that you can download.

A template is a workbook with labels, formats, and formulas already built into it with data removed. In other words, a template includes everything but the variable data.

A template can use any Excel feature, including formatting, formulas, and charts. The template used to create this workbook includes labels, formatting, and formulas.

Variable data is entered in the workbook created from the template. In this workbook, employee data was entered to fill out the weekly time record.

These formulas to calculate the total hours worked were included in the template.

Templates and Hyperlinks

The Hyperlink button opens the Insert Hyperlink dialog box, which is used to create a hyperlink.

A **hyperlink** is a link in a file, such as a workbook, to information within that file or another file. In this case, the link opens a memo created in Word, which is supporting information for the workbook.

The Insert Hyperlink dialog box provides options to enter the hyperlink text, specify what the hyperlink links to, and set a custom ScreenTip.

This text appears in the cell that has the hyperlink.

Document that will open when the hyperlink is clicked.

Creating a Hyperlink

A hyperlink is a link in a file, such as a workbook, to information within that file or another file. Although hyperlinks are most often found on webpages, they can also be placed in a worksheet and used to quickly jump to a specific cell or range within the active worksheet, another worksheet, or another workbook. Hyperlinks can also be used to jump to other files, such as a Word document or a PowerPoint presentation, or sites on the web.

Inserting a Hyperlink

You can insert a hyperlink directly in a workbook file to link to information in that workbook, another workbook, or a file associated with another application on your computer, a shared file on a network, or a website. Hyperlinks are usually represented by words with colored letters and underlines or images. When you click a hyperlink, the computer switches to the file or portion of the file referenced by the hyperlink.

REFERENCE

Inserting a Hyperlink

- Select the text, graphic, or cell in which you want to insert the hyperlink.
- On the INSERT tab, in the Links group, click the Hyperlink button.
- To link to a file or webpage, click Existing File or Web Page in the Link to list, and then select the file or webpage from the Look in box.
- To link to a location in the current workbook, click Place in This Document in the Link to list, and then select the worksheet, cell, or range in the current workbook.
- To link to a new document, click Create New Document in the Link to list, and then specify the filename and path of the new document.
- To link to an email address, click E-mail Address in the Link to list, and then enter the email address of the recipient (such as name@example.com) and a subject line for the message.
- Click the OK button.

Maria wrote a memo summarizing the collection results for Columbia, Marion, and Richmond in 2016. She wants the Better World 2016 workbook to include a link that points to the Recycle Memo Word document. You'll insert the hyperlink to the memo now.

To insert a hyperlink in the Better World 2016 workbook:

1. Open the **Better World 2016** workbook, but don't update the links.

2. Maximize the Better World 2016 worksheet window.

3. Go to the **Documentation** worksheet, and then select cell **A8**. You want to create the hyperlink in this cell.

4. On the ribbon, click the **INSERT** tab.

5. In the Links group, click the **Hyperlink** button. The Insert Hyperlink dialog box opens. You use this dialog box to define the hyperlink.

6. If necessary, click the **Existing File or Web Page** button in the Link to bar, and then click the **Current Folder** button in the Look in area. All the existing files and folders in the current folder are displayed. See Figure 6-26, which shows the Excel6 ▸ Tutorial folder included with your Data Files.

Figure 6-26 Insert Hyperlink dialog box

Word document to use as the file to link to (you may see additional files)

7. Click the **Text to display** box, and then type **Click here to read the Executive Memo**. This is the hyperlink text that will appear in cell A8 in the Documentation worksheet.

8. Click the **Recycle Memo** Word document in the list of files. This is the file you want to open when the hyperlink is clicked.

9. Click the **OK** button. The hyperlink text entered in cell A8 is underlined and in a blue font, indicating that the text within the cell is a hyperlink. See Figure 6-27.

Figure 6-27 Hyperlink to the Recycle Memo Word document

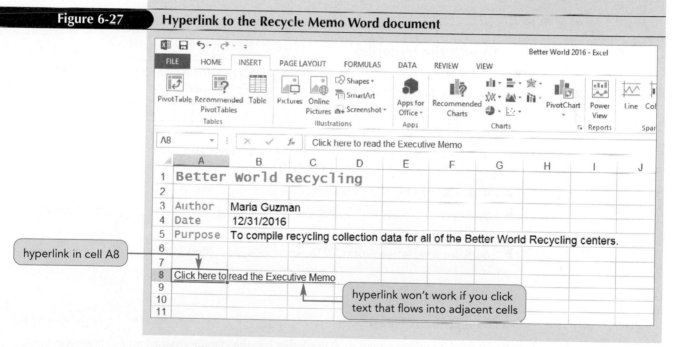

hyperlink in cell A8

hyperlink won't work if you click text that flows into adjacent cells

You will test the hyperlink that you just created to ensure it works correctly. To use a hyperlink in a worksheet, you must click the text inside the cell that contains the link. If you click white space in the cell or any text that flows into an adjacent cell, the hyperlink does not work.

To test the hyperlink to the Recycle Memo:

1. Point to the text in cell **A8** so that the pointer changes to 🖑, and then click the **Click here to read the Executive Memo** hyperlink. The Recycle Memo document opens in Word.

   Trouble? If the hyperlink doesn't work, you might have clicked the text that overflows cell A8. Point to the text within cell A8, and then click the hyperlink.

2. Close the Word document and Word. The Documentation worksheet in the Better World 2016 workbook is active. The hyperlink in cell A8 changed color to indicate that you used the link.

Editing a Hyperlink

TIP

To delete a hyperlink, right-click the hyperlink cell and then click Clear Contents. To delete the hyperlink but keep the text, right-click the hyperlink cell, and then click Remove Hyperlink.

You can modify an existing hyperlink by changing its target file or webpage, modifying the text that is displayed, or changing the ScreenTip for the hyperlink. ScreenTips, which appear whenever you place the pointer over a hyperlink, provide additional information about the target of the link. The default ScreenTip is the folder location and filename of the file you will link to, which isn't very helpful. You can insert a more descriptive ScreenTip when you create a hyperlink or edit an existing hyperlink.

Maria wants you to edit the hyperlink to the memo so that it has a more descriptive ScreenTip.

To edit the hyperlink:

1. In the Documentation worksheet, right-click cell **A8**, and then click **Edit Hyperlink** on the shortcut menu. The Edit Hyperlink dialog box opens; it has the same layout and information as the Insert Hyperlink dialog box.

2. Click the **ScreenTip** button. The Set Hyperlink ScreenTip dialog box opens.

3. In the ScreenTip text box, type **Click to view the Executive Summary for 2016**, and then click the **OK** button.

4. Click the **OK** button to close the Edit Hyperlink dialog box.

5. Point to the text in cell **A8** and confirm that the ScreenTip "Click to view the Executive Summary for 2016" appears just below the cell.

6. Save the Better World 2016 workbook, and then close it.

Using Templates

If you want to create a new workbook that has the same format as an existing workbook, you could save the existing workbook with a new name and replace the values with new data or blank cells. The potential drawback to this method is that you might forget to rename the original file and overwrite data you intended to keep. A better method is to create a template workbook that includes all the text (row and column labels), formatting, and formulas but does not contain any data. The template workbook is a model from which you create new workbooks. When you create a new workbook from a template, an unnamed copy of the template opens. You can then enter data as well as modify the existing content or structure as needed. Any changes or additions you make to the new workbook do not affect the template file; the next time you create a workbook based on the template, the original text, formatting, and formulas will be present.

PROSKILLS

Teamwork: Using Excel Templates

A team working together will often need to create the same types of workbooks. Rather than each person or group designing a different workbook, each team member should create a workbook from the same template. The completed workbooks will then all have the same structure with identical formatting and formulas. Not only does this ensure consistency and accuracy, it also makes it easier to compile and summarize the results. Templates help teams work better together and avoid misunderstandings.

For example, a large organization may need to collect the same information from several regions. By creating and distributing a workbook template, each region knows what data to track and where to enter it. The template already includes the formulas, so the results are calculated consistently. If you want to review the formulas that are in the worksheet, you can display them using the Show Formula command in the Formula Auditing group on the FORMULAS tab or by pressing the Ctrl+` keys.

The following are just some of the advantages of using a template to create multiple workbooks with the same features:

- Templates save time and ensure consistency in the design and content of workbooks because all labels, formatting, and formulas are entered once.
- Templates ensure accuracy because formulas can be entered and verified once, and then used with confidence in all workbooks.
- Templates standardize the appearance and content of workbooks.
- Templates prevent data from being overwritten when an existing workbook is inadvertently saved with new data rather than saved as a new workbook.

If you are part of a team that needs to create the same type of workbook repeatedly, it's a good idea to use a template to both save time and ensure consistency in the design and content of the workbooks.

Creating a Workbook Based on an Existing Template

The Blank workbook template that you have used to create new, blank workbooks contains no text or formulas, but it includes formatting—General format applied to numbers, Calibri 11-point font, text left-aligned in cells, numbers and formula results right-aligned in cells, column widths set to 8.38 characters, one worksheet inserted in the workbook, and so forth.

Excel has many other templates available. Some are automatically installed on your hard drive when you install Excel. Other templates are available to download from the Office.com site or other sites that you can find by searching the web. These templates provide commonly used worksheet formats, saving you from "reinventing the wheel." Some of the task-specific templates available from the Office.com site include:

- **Family Monthly Budget Planner**—builds projections and actual expenditures for items such as housing, transportation, and insurance
- **Inventory List**—tracks the cost and quantity reorder levels of inventory
- **Team Roster**—organizes a list with each player's name, phone number, email address, and so forth
- **Time sheets**—creates an online time card to track employees' work hours
- **Expense Report**—creates an expense report to track employee expenses for reimbursement

Using a template to create a new workbook lets you focus on the unique content for that workbook.

Creating a Workbook Based on a Template

- Click the FILE tab, and then click New in the navigation bar.
- On the New screen, click a template category for the type of workbook you want to create (or type a keyword in the Search for online template box, and then press the Enter key).
- Click the template you want to create.
- Save the workbook based on the template with a new filename.

Deborah Tibbs works for Maria as the office receptionist. She uses the Weekly time sheet template to submit her work hours to Maria. You'll download the Weekly time sheet template and enter Deborah's most recent hours.

Note that you need an Internet connection to complete the following set of steps. If you don't have an Internet connection, you should read but not complete the steps involving creating and using the online template.

To create a workbook based on the Weekly time sheet template:

1. On the ribbon, click the **FILE** tab.

2. Click **New** in the navigation bar. The New screen in Backstage view shows the available templates on your computer and template categories on Office.com.

3. Click in the **Search for online templates** box, type **time sheets**, and then press the **Enter** key. All of the available time sheet templates are displayed. See Figure 6-28.

Figure 6-28 **New screen with available time sheet templates**

4. Click **Weekly time sheet (8 1/2 x 11, portrait)**. A preview of a worksheet based on the selected template appears in the center of the screen. If this is not the template you need, you can scroll through the time sheets by clicking the left or right arrow button. See Figure 6-29.

Figure 6-29 Weekly time record preview

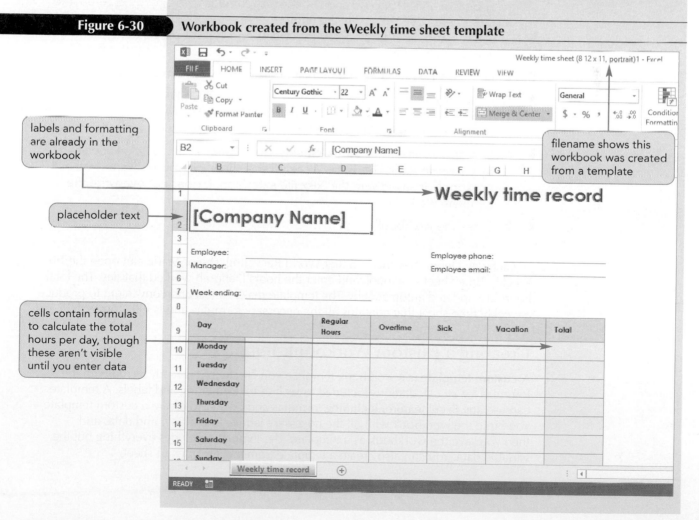

Back and Forward buttons appear so you can scroll through the available templates

preview of the selected template

Weekly time sheet (8 1/2 x 11, portrait)

Provided by: Microsoft Corporation

This time sheet can be filled out by employees each week to document their regular time worked, overtime, and sick and vacation hours used. Totals are calculated automatically.

Rating: ★ ★ ☆ ☆ ☆ (6 Votes)

button to create a workbook based on this template

Create

5. Click the **Create** button. A new workbook based on the selected template opens. See Figure 6-30.

Figure 6-30 Workbook created from the Weekly time sheet template

labels and formatting are already in the workbook

filename shows this workbook was created from a template

placeholder text

Weekly time record

[Company Name]

Employee:

Manager:

Week ending:

Employee phone:

Employee email:

cells contain formulas to calculate the total hours per day, though these aren't visible until you enter data

Day	Regular Hours	Overtime	Sick	Vacation	Total
Monday					
Tuesday					
Wednesday					
Thursday					
Friday					
Saturday					
Sunday					

Weekly time record

A workbook based on a specific template always displays the name of the template followed by a sequential number. Just as a blank workbook that you open is named Book1, Book2, and so forth, the workbook based on the Weekly time sheet template is named "Weekly time sheet1" in the title bar, not "Weekly time sheet." Any changes or additions to data, formatting, or formulas that you make affect only this workbook and not the template (in this case, the Weekly time sheet template). When you save the workbook, the Save As screen opens so you can save the workbook with a new name and to the location you specify.

Look at the labels and formatting already included in the Weekly time sheet workbook. Some cells have descriptive labels, others are blank so you can enter data in them, and still other cells contain formulas where calculations for total hours worked each day and pay category will be automatically displayed as data is entered. The formulas aren't apparent unless you click in the cell and look at the cell contents in the formula bar, or you enter data and a calculation occurs.

Maria asks you to enter Deborah's data for the previous week in the Weekly time record worksheet based on the Weekly time sheet template.

To enter Deborah's data in the Weekly time sheet1 workbook:

▶ 1. In cell **B2**, enter **Better World Recycling** as the company name, and then format the text in **20** point font size.

▶ 2. In cell **C4**, enter **Deborah Tibbs** as the employee.

▶ 3. In cell **D10**, enter **8** for the regular hours Deborah worked on Monday. Totals appear in cells I10, D17, and I17 because formulas are already entered into these cells. Cell I10 shows the number of hours worked on Monday, cell D17 shows 8 regular hours worked that week, and cell I17 shows the total hours worked that week.

▶ 4. In cell **D11**, enter **8** for the regular hours Deborah worked on Tuesday.

▶ 5. In cell **E11**, enter **2** for the overtime hours Deborah worked on Tuesday. The totals are updated to 10 hours worked on Tuesday, 16 regular hours worked that week, 2 overtime hours worked that week, and 18 total hours worked that week.

▶ 6. Save the workbook as **Tibbs Weekly Time Sheet** in the location specified by your instructor. The Tibbs Weekly Time Sheet workbook, like any other workbook, is saved with the .xlsx file extension. It does not overwrite the template file.

▶ 7. Close the workbook.

Each day Deborah works at Better World Recycling, she or Maria can open the Tibbs Weekly Time Sheet workbook and enter the hours Deborah worked that day. The total hours are updated automatically. The template makes it fast and convenient to produce a weekly time sheet that contains all the necessary formulas and is fully formatted.

Creating a Custom Workbook Template

A **custom template** is a workbook template you create that is ready to run with the formulas for all calculations included as well as all formatting and labels. A template can use any Excel feature, including formulas and charts. To create a custom template, you build the workbook with all the necessary labels, formatting, and data, and then you save the workbook as a template. The template includes everything but the variable data. You can also create a template from a chart or chart sheet.

TIP

You can apply a fill color to cells in which users enter data to differentiate them from other cells in the worksheet.

Before you create a template from an existing workbook, you should make sure that all of the formulas work as intended, the numbers and text are entered correctly, and the worksheet is formatted appropriately. You should also remove any values and text that will change in each workbook created from the custom template. Be careful not to delete the formulas. When you are sure the workbook is complete and accurate, you save it as an Excel template file. You can store template files in any folder, but custom template files stored in the Templates folder are available on the New screen in Backstage view.

REFERENCE

Creating a Custom Template

- Prepare the workbook—enter values, text, and formulas as needed; apply formatting; and replace data values with zeros or blank cells.
- On the ribbon, click the FILE tab, and then click Save As in the navigation bar.
- Click the Browse button to open the Save As dialog box.
- In the File name box, enter the template name.
- Click the Save as type button, and then click Excel Template.
- If you don't want to save the template in the Custom Office Templates folder, select another folder in which to save the template file.
- Click the Save button.

or

- Create the chart you want to use for the template.
- Right-click the chart, and then click Save as Template.
- In the Save Chart Template dialog box, enter a filename, then select a folder in which to save the template file if you don't want to store it in the Charts subfolder of the Templates folder.
- Click the Save button.

The three collection workbooks for 2016 have the same format. Maria wants to use this workbook format for data collection and analysis for next year. She asks you to create a template from one of the recycling center workbooks. You'll use the Columbia workbook to build the custom template.

To prepare a custom template from the Columbia workbook:

1. Make sure that the latest version of the **Columbia** workbook is open.

2. Group the **Quarter 1** through **Quarter 4** worksheets. The worksheet group includes the four quarterly worksheets but not the Summary and Documentation worksheets.

3. Select the range **B6:D10**. This range includes the specific recycling data for each recycling site. You want to delete these values.

4. Right-click the selected range, and then click **Clear Contents** on the shortcut menu. The data values are cleared from the selected range in each of the quarterly worksheets, but the formulas and formatting remain intact. The cleared cells are blank. The ranges E6:E11 and B11:D11 display dashes, representing zeros, where there are formulas.

5. Change the fill color of the selected range to the standard **Orange** color. The orange fill color indicates where users should enter data for the tons of material collected in the quarterly worksheets.

6. In cell **A1**, enter **Better World Recycling**.

7. In cell **B3**, enter **[Site Name Here]**, and then merge and center the range **B3:C3**.

8. Go to the **Summary** worksheet. The quarterly worksheets are ungrouped, and dashes, representing zeros, appear in the cells in the ranges B6:F11, which contain formulas.

9. In cell **A1**, enter **Better World Recycling**. This text will remind users to enter the correct site name.

10. In cell **B3**, enter **[Site Name Here]**, and then merge and center **B3:C3**.

11. In cell **A3**, enter **[Enter Fiscal Year - yyyy]**. This text will remind users to enter the year.

12. Group the **Summary** through **Quarter 4** worksheets, and then increase the width of column A so you can see the entire contents of cell A3. See Figure 6-31.

Figure 6-31   **Worksheet modified to be used as the basis of a custom template**

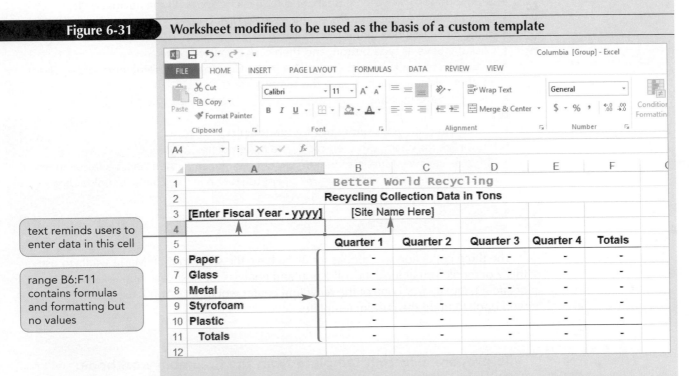

13. Go to the **Documentation** worksheet, and then delete your name and the date from the range B3:B4.

14. In cell **A6**, enter **To compile the recycling collection data for:**.

15. In cell **B6**, enter **[Site Name Here]**, and then select cell **A1**. The Documentation worksheet is updated to reflect the purpose of the workbook.

By default, Excel looks for template files in the Templates folder. This location opens when you save a workbook as a template and is where custom templates are often stored. However, you can change in which folder a template is saved. All template files have the .xltx file extension. This extension differentiates template files from workbook files, which have the .xlsx file extension. After you have saved a workbook in a template format, you can make the template accessible to other users.

The Columbia workbook no longer contains any specific data, but the formulas and formatting will still be in effect when new data is entered. Maria asks you to save this workbook as a template.

To save the Columbia workbook as a template:

1. On the ribbon, click the **FILE** tab to open Backstage view, and then in the navigation bar, click **Save As**. The Save As screen appears.

2. Select the location where you are saving the files for this tutorial. If you are saving files to your hard drive, select **Computer**, and then click the **Browse** button. The Save As dialog box opens.

   Trouble? If you are saving your files in your SkyDrive, select **SkyDrive**, click **Sign In** to sign in to your account if necessary, and then follow the instructions for saving a document in SkyDrive.

3. In the File name box, type **Better World Recycling Template** as the template name.

4. Click the **Save as type** button, and then click **Excel Template**. The save location changes to the Custom Office Templates folder on your computer. You want to save the template in the same location as the other files you created in this tutorial.

   Make sure you change the save location so you can easily find and use the template file later in the next set of steps.

5. Navigate to the location where you are storing the files you create in this tutorial.

6. Click the **Save** button. The Better World Recycling Template is saved in the location you specified.

7. Close the Better World Recycling Template workbook template.

Maria will use the Better World Recycling Template file to create the workbooks to track next year's collections for each site, and then distribute the workbooks to each site manager. By basing these new workbooks on the template file, Maria has a standard workbook with identical formatting and formulas for each manager to use. She also avoids the risk of accidentally changing the workbook containing the 2016 data when preparing for 2017.

INSIGHT

Copying Styles from One Template to Another

Consistency is a hallmark of professional documents. If you have already created a template with a particular look, you can easily copy the styles from that template into a new template. This is much faster and more accurate than trying to recreate the same look by performing all of the steps you used originally. Copying styles from template to template guarantees uniformity. To copy styles from one template to another:

1. Open the template with the styles you want to copy.
2. Open the workbook or template in which you want to place the copied styles.
3. On the HOME tab, in the Styles group, click the Cell Styles button, and then click Merge Styles. The Merge Styles dialog box opens, listing the currently open workbooks and templates.
4. Select the workbook or template with the styles you want to copy, and then click the OK button to copy those styles into the current workbook or template.
5. If a dialog box opens, asking if you want to "Merge Styles that have the same names?", click the YES button.
6. Save the workbook with the new styles as the Excel Template file type.

Creating a New Workbook from a Template

A template file has special properties that allow you to open it, make changes, and save it in a new location. Only the data must be entered because the formulas are already in the template file. The original template file is not changed by this process. After you have saved a template, you can access the template from the New screen in Backstage view or in the location you saved it.

Maria wants all Better World Recycling locations to collect data in the same format and submit the workbooks to the central office for analysis. She wants you to create a workbook for fiscal year 2017 based on the Better World Recycling Template file. You will enter Columbia as the site name where indicated on all of the worksheets, and then enter test data for January.

To create a new workbook based on the Better World Recycling Template file:

> **TIP**
>
> To create a copy of workbook based on a template stored in the Custom Office Templates folder, click the FILE tab, click New in the navigation bar, click PERSONAL below the Search for online templates box, and then click the template.

1. On the taskbar, click the **File Explorer** button 📁. The Libraries window opens.

2. Navigate to the location where you stored the template file.

3. Double-click the **Better World Recycling Template** file. A new workbook opens named "Better World Recycling Template1" to indicate this is the first copy of the Better World Recycling workbook created during the current Excel session.

4. Go to the **Summary** worksheet, enter **Columbia Total** in cell B3, and then enter **Fiscal Year - 2017** in cell A3.

5. Group the **Quarter 1** through **Quarter 4** worksheets, and then in cell **B3**, enter **Columbia** as the site name in the Site Name Here box.

6. Go to the **Documentation** worksheet to ungroup the worksheets.

7. In cell **B6**, enter **Columbia**.

8. Go to the **Quarter 1** worksheet. The text "Fiscal Year - 2017" appears in cell A4.

9. Enter the following test data in the range **B6:B10**, which has the orange fill color:

    cell B6: **150**

    cell B7: **50**

    cell B8: **123**

    cell B9: **45**

    cell B10: **23**

10. Review the totals in the range **E6:E11** (the cells that contain formulas to sum each column). See Figure 6-32.

Figure 6-32   New workbook based on the Better World Recycling Template file

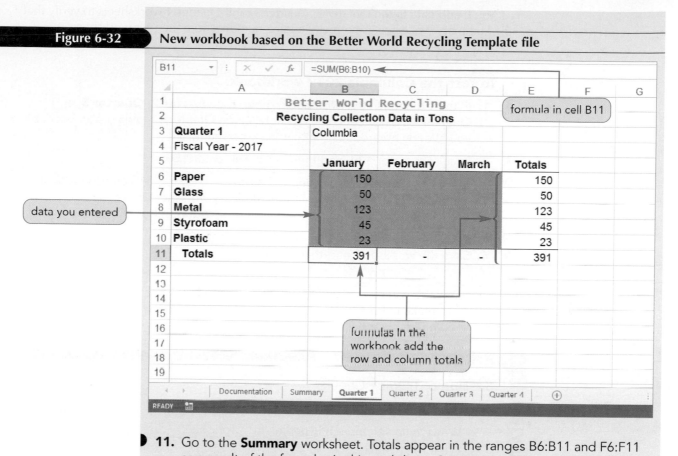

11. Go to the **Summary** worksheet. Totals appear in the ranges B6:B11 and F6:F11 as a result of the formulas in this worksheet. See Figure 6-33.

Figure 6-33   Summary worksheet with test data

12. Save the workbook as **Columbia 2017** in the location specified by your instructor. The copy of the template is saved as a workbook with the .xlsx file extension. The original template file is not changed.

You'll add data to the Quarter 2, Quarter 3, and Quarter 4 worksheets to verify that the Summary worksheet is correctly adding numbers from the four worksheets.

To test the Columbia 2017 workbook:

▷ 1. In the Columbia 2017 workbook, group the **Quarter 2**, **Quarter 3**, and **Quarter 4** worksheets. You did not include Quarter 1 in this group because you already entered test data in this worksheet.

▷ 2. In cell **C6**, enter **120**, and then in cell **D8**, enter **150**.

▷ 3. Go to the **Summary** worksheet. The total in cell F6 is 510 and the total in cell F8 is 573. The formulas in the Summary worksheet correctly add values from all the quarterly worksheets. The template workbook is functioning as intended.

▷ 4. Save the workbook, and then close it.

The templates you created will ensure that all recycling centers enter data consistently, making it simpler for Maria to add the total number of tons recycled by item and time period for Better World Recycling.

Session 6.3 Quick Check

REVIEW

1. How do you insert a hyperlink into a worksheet cell?
2. Why would you insert a hyperlink in a worksheet?
3. What is a template?
4. What is a custom template?
5. What is one advantage of using a custom template rather than simply using the original workbook file to create a new workbook?
6. What are some examples of task-specific templates available from the Office.com site?
7. How do you save a workbook as a template?
8. How do you create a workbook based on a template that is not saved in the Custom Office Templates folder?

Review Assignments

Data Files needed for the Review Assignments: Illinois.xlsx, Paris Memo.docx, BW.xlsx, Columbia KS.xlsx, Marion IA.xlsx, Richmond IN.xlsx

Based on its success in Columbia, Richmond, and Marion, Better World Recycling expanded to Paris, Illinois. The new site opened on January 1, 2016. Willa Jaworska, the manager of the Paris site, collected the center's recycling data in a workbook provided by Maria Guzman at the central office. Before Willa can send the completed workbook to Maria for the year-end reporting, she needs to summarize the results and format the worksheets. Complete the following:

1. Open the **Illinois** workbook located in the Excel6 ▸ Review folder included with your Data Files. Save the workbook as **Paris IL** in the location specified by your instructor.

2. In the Documentation worksheet, enter your name and the date, and then review the worksheets in the workbook.

3. Create a worksheet group that contains the Quarter 1 through Quarter 4 worksheets.

4. In the worksheet group, enter formulas in the range B11:D11 to total each column, and then enter formulas in the range E6:F11 to total each row.

5. Format the quarterly worksheets as specified below:
   a. In cell E5 and cell A11, enter **Totals**.
   b. In the range A2:A3;A6:A11;B5:E5, bold the text.
   c. Merge and center the range A1:E1 and the range A2:E2.
   d. In the range B5:E5, center the text.
   e. Add a bottom border to the range B5:E5 and the range B10:E10.
   f. Format the range B6:E11 with the Comma style and no decimal places.

6. Ungroup the worksheets, make a copy of the Quarter 1 worksheet, rename it as **Summary**, and then place it after the Documentation worksheet.

7. In the Summary worksheet, make the following changes:
   a. In cell A1, change the heading to **Better World Recycling - Paris Total**.
   b. Change cell A3 to **Fiscal Year - 2016**.
   c. Insert a column between columns B and C.
   d. In the range B5:E5, change the headings to **Quarter 1**, **Quarter 2**, **Quarter 3**, and **Quarter 4**, respectively.
   e. In the range B5:F5, center the text.
   f. Clear the data from the range B6:F11.

8. Complete the formulas in the Summary worksheet using the following steps. Remember to use the Fill Without Formatting so that you can keep the bottom border on the range B10:F10.
   a. Create formulas referencing cells in other worksheets to collect the quarterly totals for the recyclable products in the range B6:E10 in your Summary worksheet.
   b. Create 3-D cell references in the range F6:F10 to calculate totals for each type of recyclable product.
   c. Total the data in columns B through F using the SUM function.

9. The March collection total for metal should have been **164**. Make that correction, and then verify that the total metal collected in Quarter 1 in the Summary worksheet has changed to 384 tons, the total recyclables collected in Quarter 1 has changed to 2,065 tons, and the total metal collected in 2016 has changed to 2,111 tons.

10. Group the Quarter 1 through Quarter 4 worksheets, and then enter a formula in cell A4 to reference cell A3 in the Summary worksheet.

11. In cell A8 of the Documentation worksheet, insert a hyperlink pointing to the **Paris Memo** located in the Tutorial6 ▸ Review folder included with your Data Files. Make sure the text to display is **Click here to read Paris Executive Memo**.

12. Edit the hyperlink to use the ScreenTip **Paris Site Summary for 2016**.

13. Save the Paris IL workbook.

14. Open the **BW** workbook located in the Excel6 ▸ Review folder included with your Data Files. Save the workbook as **BW Totals** in the location specified by your instructor. In the Documentation worksheet enter your name and the date. Open the **Columbia KS**, **Marion IA**, and **Richmond IN** workbooks located in the Excel6 ▸ Review folder included with your Data Files.

15. In each workbook, make the maximum amount of data from the Summary worksheet viewable, make the BW Totals the active worksheet, and then tile the workbooks.

16. In the Summary worksheet, enter external reference formulas to create a set of linked workbooks to summarize the totals for Columbia KS, Marion IA, Paris IL, and Richmond IN, in the BW Totals workbook. Format the Summary worksheet in the BW Totals workbook making sure that the numbers are readable and the range B10:F10 has a bottom border. Save the BW totals workbook. Close the Columbia KS, Marion IA, and Richmond IN workbooks.

17. In the BW Totals workbook, break the links. Select some cells and notice that the formulas have been replaced with the values. Save the workbook as **BW Totals Audited**.

18. Prepare the Summary worksheet for printing. Display the name of the workbook and the name of the worksheet on separate lines in the right section of the header. Display your name and the date on separate lines in the right section of the footer. Save and close the BW Totals Audited workbook.

19. Save the Paris IL workbook as an Excel template with the filename **Paris IL Template** in the location specified by your instructor.

20. Create a new workbook based on the Paris IL Template. Save the workbook as **Paris IL 2017** in the location specified by your instructor. In the Documentation worksheet, enter your name and the date.

21. In the Summary worksheet, enter **2017** in cell A3. In the Quarter 1 worksheet, enter **1000** in each cell in the range B6:D10. In the Quarter 2 worksheet, enter **2000** in each cell in the range B6:D10. Confirm that the values entered in this step are correctly totaled in the Summary worksheet.

22. Save the Paris IL 2017 workbook, and then close it.

Case Problem 1

Data File needed for this Case Problem: Cheese.xlsx

Cheese Plus Pizzeria   Cheese Plus Pizzeria has three locations in Great Bend, Kansas—Downtown, East Side, and West Side. Mitch Samuels manages the three pizzerias. He uses Excel to summarize sales data from each location. He has compiled the year's data for each location in a workbook. He asks you to total the sales by type of service and location for each quarter, and then format each worksheet. Mitch also needs you to calculate sales for all of the locations and types of service. Complete the following:

1. Open the **Cheese** workbook located in the Excel6 ▸ Case1 folder included with your Data Files. Save the document as **Cheese Plus** in the location specified by your instructor.

2. In the Documentation worksheet, enter your name and the date.

3. Group the Downtown, East Side, and West Side worksheets.

4. In the grouped worksheets, calculate the quarterly totals in the range B7:E7 and the types of service totals in the range F4:F7.

5. Improve the look of the quarterly worksheets using the formatting of your choice. Ungroup the worksheets.

6. Place a copy of one of the location worksheets between the Documentation and Downtown worksheets, and then rename the new worksheet as **Summary Sales**.

7. Delete the values in the range B4:E6, and then change the label in cell A2 to **Summary Sales**.

8. In the range B4:E6, enter formulas that add the sales in the corresponding cells of the four quarterly worksheets. Use 3-D references to calculate the totals for each product group and location.

9. Set up the Summary Sales and the three location worksheets for printing. Each worksheet should be centered horizontally, fit on one page, display the name of the worksheet centered in the header, and display your name and the date on separate lines in the right section of the footer.

10. Save the Cheese Plus workbook, and then remove the sales data, but not the formulas, from each of the location worksheets.

11. Go to the Documentation worksheet, and then save the workbook as an Excel template with the name **Cheese Plus Template** in the location specified by your instructor.

12. Create a new workbook based on the Cheese Plus Template file. Save the workbook as **Cheese Plus 2016** in the location specified by your instructor.

13. In all three location worksheets, in the range B4:E6, enter **10**. Verify that the formulas in each worksheet summarize the data accurately.

14. Save and close the workbook.

Case Problem 2

TROUBLESHOOT

Data Files needed for this Case Problem: Eastern.xlsx, Internet.xlsx, Western.xlsx, Summary.xlsx

Sweet Dreams Bakery   Sweet Dreams Bakery opened its first retail location on June 1, 2000 in Jerome, Idaho, on the eastern side of town, with a dream and some great family dessert recipes. It opened a location on the western side of town three years later. In the past year, the bakery has developed a presence on the Internet. Each location tracks its sales by major categories—cupcakes, tarts, cookies, and pies. James Ray, the bakery manager, has asked the three locations to provide sales data for the past year. That data will be used at the next meeting of the senior managers to determine whether the bakery should expand to a fourth location. To analyze sales and service at each division, James wants you to prepare a report showing the sales of bakery items by quarter and location. Complete the following:

1. Open the **Eastern** workbook located in the Excel6 ▶ Case2 folder included with your Data Files, and then save the document as **Sweet Dreams Eastern** in the location specified by your instructor.

2. In the Documentation worksheet, enter your name and the date.

3. In the Eastern Sales worksheet, calculate the totals for each type of product in the range B8:E8, and the total for each quarter in the range F4:F8. Improve the look of the worksheet by using the formatting of your choice including a bottom underline in the range A7:F7.

4. Repeat Steps 1 through 3 for the **Internet** and **Western** workbooks, naming them **Sweet Dreams Internet** and **Sweet Dreams Western**, respectively.

5. Open the **Summary** workbook located in the Excel6 ▶ Case2 folder included with your Data Files, and then save the workbook as **Sweet Dreams Summary** in the location specified by your instructor.

6. In the Documentation worksheet, enter your name and the date.

7. Rename Sheet1 as **Summary**. In cell A2, enter **Summary Sales** as the new label.

⚙ **Troubleshoot** 8. The quarterly totals in the Sweet Dreams Summary worksheet are not displaying the correct results. Make any necessary corrections to the formulas so that they add the correct cells from the Sweet Dreams Eastern, Sweet Dreams Western, and Sweet Dreams Internet workbooks.

9. Insert formulas to calculate the totals for the range B4:E7.

⚙ **Troubleshoot** 10. The Documentation worksheet in the Sweet Dreams Summary workbook includes hyperlinks in the range A10:A12 for each region's corresponding workbook (Sweet Dreams Eastern, Sweet Dreams Internet, and Sweet Dreams Western located in the Excel6 ▶ Case2 folder). The hyperlink descriptions and source files are inconsistent. Check the hyperlinks and correct any links that have different descriptions and source files.

11. Add appropriate text for the ScreenTip to each hyperlink. Test each hyperlink.

12. Prepare each workbook for printing. For all worksheets except the Documentation worksheet, display the name of the workbook and the name of the worksheet on separate lines in the right section of the header and display your name and the date on separate lines in the right section of the footer.

13. Save and close all of the workbooks.

Case Problem 3

Data File needed for this Case Problem: Clinic.xlsx

C & M Veterinary Clinic   C & M Veterinary Clinic has been treating small and medium-sized animals in the Marlow, Oklahoma, area for more than 10 years. The staff veterinarians perform all checkups and surgeries, and the staff technician handles all other visits. With the population explosion in the area, the clinic's patient list has increased beyond the current staff's capabilities. Bessie Neal, the manager of the clinic, has been tracking the clinic's activity by month for the past year. Before meeting with the clinic's veterinarians to discuss adding staff or facilities, she wants you to compile the data she has collected and create some preliminary charts. Complete the following:

1. Open the **Clinic** workbook located in the Excel6 ▸ Case3 folder included with your Data Files, and then save the workbook as **Vet Clinic** in the location specified by your instructor.

2. In the Documentation worksheet, enter your name and the date.

3. Group the 12 monthly worksheets to ensure consistency in headings and for ease in entering formulas. Enter the heading **Totals** in cells A11 and E4. For each month (January through December), enter formulas to calculate the total for each type of visit (the range B11:D11) and the total for each type of animal (the range E5:E11).

4. Improve the formatting of the monthly worksheets using the formatting of your choice. Make sure that you have included a lower border in the ranges A4:E4 and A10:E10. Ungroup the worksheets.

5. In the Service Analysis by Month worksheet, enter formulas with worksheet references in the range B5:B16. (=January!B11 through =December!B11) for the total checkup appointments for each month. Copy these formulas to the range C5:C16 (Surgery) and the range D5:D16 (Technician).

6. In cells A17 and E4, enter the label **Total**. Enter formulas to add the total by type of appointment (the range B17:E17) and total appointments each month (the range E5:E17). Bold the ranges A4:A17 and B4:E4. Center the range A4:E4. Place a bottom border in the ranges A4:E4 and A16:E16.

7. Create a bar or column chart to compare the type of service by month (the range A4:D16). Include an appropriate chart title and a legend. Make any formatting changes to the chart that you feel necessary to develop an attractive and effective chart. Position the chart below the data.

8. In the Service Analysis by Animal worksheet, create 3-D cell references to total the appointment type for each animal for each month of the year. Formulas for Small Dog would be Checkup =SUM(January:December!B5), Surgery =SUM(January:December!C5), and Technician =SUM(January:December!D5). These formulas can be copied down through all animal types (the range B5:D10).

9. In cells A11 and E4, enter the label **Total**. Enter formulas to add the total by type of appointment (the range B11:D11) and the total by type of animal (the range E5:E11). Bold the ranges A4:A11 and B4:E4. Center the range A4:E4. Place a bottom border in the ranges A4:E4 and A10:E10.

10. Create a pie chart based on the annual total for each type of animal. Include an appropriate chart title and a legend. Make any formatting changes to the chart that you feel necessary. Position the pie chart below the data in the Service Analysis by Animal worksheet.

11. Group all worksheets except Documentation. Prepare the workbook for printing with the name of the workbook and the name of the worksheet on separate lines in the right section of the header. Display your name and the date on separate lines in the right section of the footer.

12. Save and close the workbook.

CHALLENGE

Case Problem 4

Data Files needed for this Case Problem: Midwest.xlsx, Northeast.xlsx, Southeast.xlsx, Ice Summary.xlsx, New Midwest.xlsx, Ice Template.xltx

Cubed Ice Sales   Cubed Ice Sales manufactures and distributes ice products east of the Mississippi River. Located in Lancaster, Pennsylvania, it claims to make "everything ice," including ice cubes, ice blocks, and dry ice to name a few of its products. The chief financial analyst, Joni Snapp, asks you to prepare the annual sales and bonus summary based on workbooks from the Midwest, Northeast, and Southeast regions. In December, each salesperson establishes his or her monthly target sales and negotiates a bonus percentage for any sales over that amount. Each region submits a workbook that contains a worksheet for each salesperson in that region. The salesperson's worksheet contains his or her sales by month, monthly target sales, and bonus by percentage. Joni wants you to calculate the bonus for each month for each salesperson using the data he or she provided. She also wants you to summarize each workbook, reporting the quarterly gross sales, bonus sales, and bonus amount. After you have added this information to each workbook, Joni wants you to consolidate the information from the three regional workbooks into a single workbook. Complete the following:

1. Open the **Midwest** workbook located in the Excel6 ▶ Case4 folder included with your Data Files, and then save the workbook as **Cubed Ice Midwest** in the location specified by your instructor.

2. In the Documentation worksheet, enter your name and the date.

3. Repeat Steps 1 and 2, opening the **Northeast** and **Southeast** workbooks, and saving them as **Cubed Ice Northeast** and **Cubed Ice Southeast**, respectively.

4. Complete the salesperson worksheets in each region's workbook by doing the following:

   a. Group the Salesperson worksheets.

   b. Calculate the Bonus Sales for each month using the formula Gross Sales – Target. (A bonus will be paid only on sales over this amount.) If the salesperson did not sell more than the target, he or she receives no bonus. (*Hint*: Use an IF statement and absolute cell references.)

   c. Calculate the Bonus Amount using the formula Bonus Sales * Bonus Rate. (*Hint*: Remember to use absolute cell references.)

   d. Enter **Total** in cell A16. Total the Gross Sales, Bonus Sales, and Bonus Amount.

   e. Bold the ranges A4:A16 and B3:D3. Wrap the text and center the range B3:D3. Display all numbers with a comma and no decimal places. Display the total row values (the range B16:D16) with a dollar sign.

   f. Ungroup the worksheets.

5. In each of the regional workbooks, do the following:

   a. Make a copy of the first salesperson's worksheet. Rename it **Summary**, and then place it after the Documentation worksheet.

   b. Change the subheading (Salesperson name) to indicate that this is a summary worksheet. Clear the Gross Sales, Bonus Sales, and Bonus amounts, leaving the formulas for the totals.

   c. Clear the headings and data in the range A19:B20.

   d. Create 3-D reference formulas to calculate the totals by month for Gross Sales, Bonus Sales, and Bonus.

   e. Group all worksheets except the Documentation worksheet. Prepare the workbook for printing with the name of the workbook and the name of the worksheet on separate lines in the right section of the header. Display your name and the date on separate lines in the right section of the footer.

   f. Ungroup the worksheets and save the workbook.

6. Open the **Ice Summary** workbook located in the Excel6 ▶ Case4 folder included with your Data Files, and then save the workbook as **Cubed Ice Summary** in the location specified by your instructor.

7. Make sure all four of the Cubed Ice Workbooks are open and have the Summary worksheet as the active sheet.

8. Enter external reference formulas to create a set of linked workbooks to summarize Gross Sales, Bonus Sales, and Bonus Amount.

9. Enter **Total** in cell A16. Total the Gross Sales, Bonus Sales, and Bonus Amount. Bold the ranges A4:A16 and B3:D3. Wrap the text and center the range B3:D3. Display all numbers with a comma and no decimal places. Display the total row values (the range B16:D16) with a dollar sign.

10. Prepare the Summary worksheet for printing with the name of the workbook and the name of the worksheet on separate lines in the right section of the header. Display your name and the date on separate lines in the right section of the footer.

11. Save the Summary workbook.

⊕ **Explore** 12. The office manager for the Midwest Cubed Ice location found a newer workbook for that location's sales and commissions, and has submitted it to you. Close the Cubed Ice Midwest workbook that you have been working with, open the **New Midwest** workbook located in the Excel6 ▸ Case4 folder included with your Data Files, and then save the workbook as **New Midwest 2016** in the location specified by your instructor. Use Update Links to update the totals on the Summary worksheet in the Cubed Ice Summary workbook. The Totals before the update are Gross Sales $5,155,415; Bonus Sales $2,502,265; and Bonus Amount $125,133. The totals after the update are Gross Sales $5,155,415; Bonus Sales $2,502,265; and Bonus Amount $209,478.

13. Save and close all of the open workbooks for Cubed Ice.

⊕ **Explore** 14. Modify the template named **Ice Template** located in the Excel6 ▸ Case4 folder included with your Data Files. Make the following changes to the template, and then save the modified template as **Ice Template Revised**:

    a. Change the company name to **Ice Cubed**.

    b. Change the color of the company name to Dark Green.

15. Create a new workbook from the Ice Template Revised template. In the Documentation worksheet, enter your name and date.

16. Enter **10,000** for each month's sales, **1** for Bonus Rate, and **5000** for Target Sales. Verify that the formulas are working correctly.

17. Save the workbook as **Cubed Ice Test** in a location specified by your instructor, and then close it.

Developing an Excel Application

Creating a Receipt

OBJECTIVES

Session 7.1
- Create an application
- Create, edit, and delete defined names for cells and ranges
- Paste a list of defined names as documentation
- Use defined names in formulas
- Add defined names to existing formulas

Session 7.2
- Create validation rules for data entry
- Protect the contents of worksheets and workbooks
- Add, edit, and delete comments

Session 7.3
- Learn about macro viruses and Excel security features
- Add the DEVELOPER tab to the ribbon
- Create and run a macro
- Edit a macro using the Visual Basic Editor
- Assign a macro to a keyboard shortcut and a button
- Save and open a workbook in macro-enabled format

Case | *Youth Soccer League*

Sharon Hale, business manager for the Youth Soccer League in Oak Hill, West Virginia, is automating several processes for the league's business office. Each spring, the league mails a brochure to parents in the elementary schools in the area with information about the soccer league and a registration form. Then, parents complete the registration form and mail it in with their payment. Sharon wants to automate the process of creating the receipt, which will include capturing the data, calculating the charges, and printing a receipt. She also wants the process to collect the data for soccer clothing that registered students will require (soccer shirts and socks).

Many of these tasks can be accomplished in Excel. But without validating data entry, protecting cells with formulas from accidental deletion, and reducing repetitive keystrokes and mouse clicks, Sharon realizes too many opportunities for errors exist. In addition, as a nonprofit organization, the league relies on numerous volunteers who have varying degrees of computer experience and skill. To accommodate these varying skill levels and reduce potential errors, Sharon wants to create a custom interface for this project that does not rely exclusively on the ribbon, galleries, and so forth. You will help Sharon create a unique Excel application that can resolve these issues and help ensure accurate data entry.

STARTING DATA FILES

Excel7 → Tutorial
Soccer.xlsx

Review
TBall.xlsx

Case1
Study.xlsx

Case2
Cloggers.xlsm

Case3
Music.xlsx

Case4
(none)

Session 7.1 Visual Overview:

The Name box displays the cell reference or the defined name of the selected cell.

You can make the Name box longer so you can see the complete defined names by dragging its sizing handle.

An **Excel application** is a spreadsheet written or tailored to meet specific needs. It typically includes reports and charts, a data entry area, a custom interface, as well as instructions and documentation.

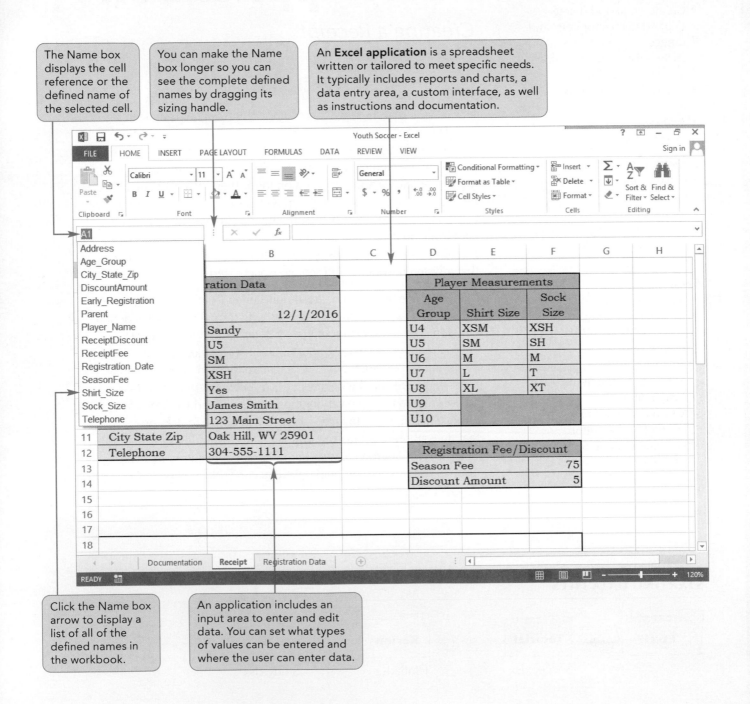

Click the Name box arrow to display a list of all of the defined names in the workbook.

An application includes an input area to enter and edit data. You can set what types of values can be entered and where the user can enter data.

Excel Application and Defined Names

A **defined name** (often called a **range name** is a word or string of characters assigned to a cell or range. The defined name Parent is assigned to cell B27.

The Defined Names group on the FORMULAS tab contains buttons to create, edit, delete, and manage defined names.

If a formula is too long to display in the formula bar, you can expand the formula bar so that the entire formula is visible.

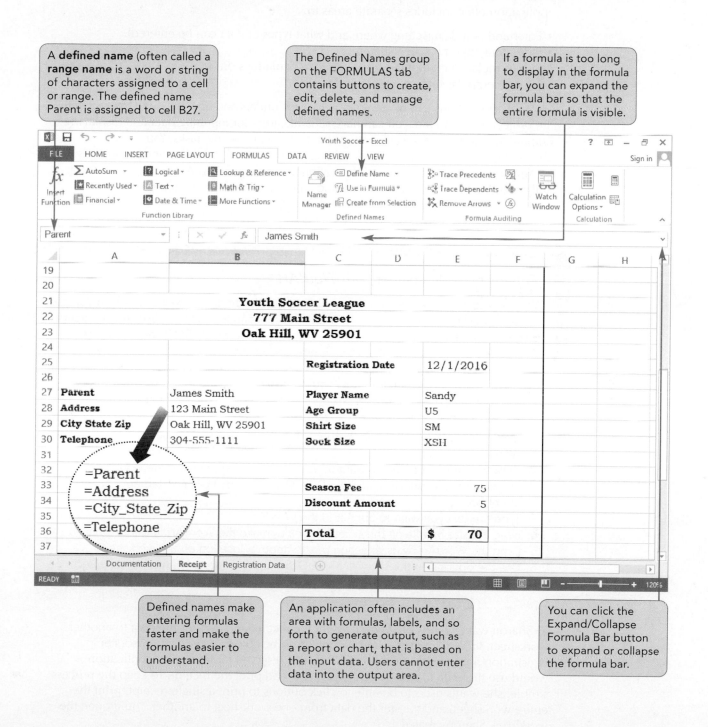

Defined names make entering formulas faster and make the formulas easier to understand.

An application often includes an area with formulas, labels, and so forth to generate output, such as a report or chart, that is based on the input data. Users cannot enter data into the output area.

You can click the Expand/Collapse Formula Bar button to expand or collapse the formula bar.

Planning an Excel Application

An Excel application is a spreadsheet written or tailored to meet specific needs, such as creating a receipt for Youth Soccer League registrations. Planning an Excel application includes designing how the worksheet(s) will be organized. You can include different areas for each function, depending on the complexity of the project. For example, an application often includes separate areas to:

- Enter and edit data (setting where and what types of data can be entered).
- Store data after it has been entered.
- Use formulas to manipulate and perform calculations on data.
- Display outputs, such as reports and charts.

Excel applications can be set up to help users understand how they will interact with the project. For example, you can have separate areas for inputting data and displaying outputs. You can create special buttons for performing specific tasks. You can also change the entire Excel interface by adding custom menus, toolbars, and commands.

An application often includes information about the workbook, such as its purpose, author, and date developed, in a Documentation worksheet as well as comments to explain cell contents and provide instructions. It can also include a set of clearly written instructions. All of these help you and others use the workbook correctly and accurately.

INSIGHT

Enhancing a Worksheet with WordArt

You can use WordArt to enhance any worksheet. **WordArt** is a text box in which you can enter stylized text. For example, the Youth Soccer League might use WordArt to create a special look for the organization's name or to add the word "PAID" angled across the receipt. WordArt is an object that is embedded in the worksheet the same way a chart is; it appears over the cells, covering any content they contain. After you insert the WordArt text box, you enter the text you want to display, and then you can format it by changing its font, color, size, and position—creating the exact look you want.

To add WordArt to a worksheet:

1. On the INSERT tab, in the Text group, click the Insert WordArt button. A gallery of WordArt styles opens.
2. Click the WordArt style you want to use. A text box appears on the worksheet with placeholder text selected, and the DRAWING TOOLS FORMAT tab appears on the ribbon.
3. Type the text you want to appear in the WordArt.
4. Drag a resize handle on the selection box to make the WordArt larger or smaller.
5. Drag the WordArt by its selection box to another location on the worksheet.
6. Use the options on the DRAWING TOOLS FORMAT tab to change the selected WordArt's shape, style, text, fill, size, and position.

Sharon wants to be able to easily print the receipt and transfer the data to another worksheet. In addition, she wants volunteers to be able to enter data for soccer registration in a specific area of the worksheet reserved for input. The application would use this data to automatically generate and print the receipt. To keep the process simple, she wants users to be able to click buttons to print a single receipt, print the entire worksheet, and transfer the data from one worksheet to another. You'll open the workbook Sharon created.

To open and review the Soccer workbook:

▶ **1.** Open the **Soccer** workbook located in the Excel7 ▶ Tutorial folder included with your Data Files, and then save the workbook as **Youth Soccer** in the location specified by your instructor.

▶ **2.** In the Documentation worksheet, enter your name and the date.

▶ **3.** Review the contents of each worksheet, and then go to the **Receipt** worksheet. See Figure 7-1.

Figure 7-1 Youth Soccer initial receipt worksheet – input area

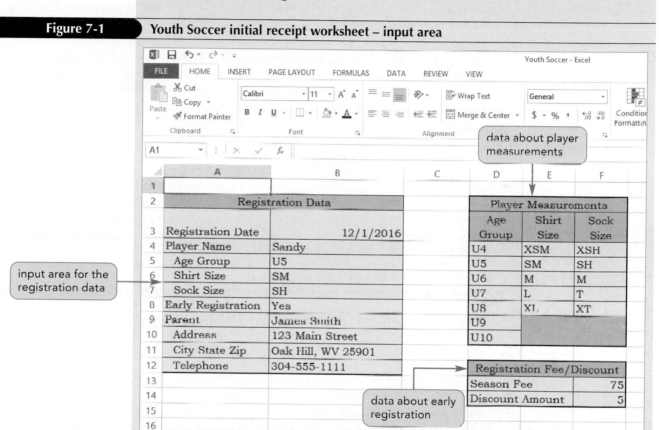

In addition to the Documentation worksheet, the Youth Soccer workbook includes two other worksheets—Receipt and Registration Data. The Receipt worksheet contains input, output, and transfer areas. The input area is divided into the following three parts:

- Registration Data includes items that change for each registration, such as parent name, address, telephone, player name, age group, shirt size, sock size, and early registration discount.
- Player Measurements is the list of codes for the different age groups, shirt sizes, and sock sizes.
- Registration Fee/Discount includes costs that will not change during the upcoming season, such as season fee ($75/player) and early registration discount ($5/player).

The output section contains formulas and labels used to generate the receipt based on data in the input section. The receipt in the output section will be printed. The transfer section gathers selected data from the receipt in one area before the data is transferred to the Registration Data worksheet for storage. The transfer section makes it simpler and easier to identify the data to be moved to the Registration Data worksheet for storage and future analysis.

Naming Cells and Ranges

So far, you have referred to a cell or range by its address except when you entered formulas within an Excel table. Cell and range references do not indicate what data is stored in those cells. Instead, you can use a defined name to assign a meaningful, descriptive name to a cell or range. For example, if the range D1:D100 contains sales data for 100 transactions, you can use the defined name Sales to refer to the range of sales data.

A defined name enables you to quickly navigate within a workbook to the cell or range with the defined name. You can also use defined names to create more descriptive formulas. However, keep in mind that the defined name includes only the specified range. Any cells you insert within that range are then included with the defined name, but any cells you insert outside the range with the defined name are not included in the defined name.

In the Receipt worksheet, the range B3:B12 contains the data values for each soccer registration. As you can see, this range includes many variables. It will be simpler to remember where different data is stored by assigning a descriptive name to each cell or range rather than using its cell address. For example, the name PlayerName better identifies what is stored in the cell than cell B4.

PROSKILLS

Written Communication: Saving Time with Defined Names

Words can be more descriptive than numbers. This is especially true in cell references. Instead of using the letter and number references for cells, you can create defined names to provide more intuitive references. Defined names have several advantages over cell references, especially as a worksheet becomes longer and more complex. Some advantages include:

- Names, such as TaxRate and TotalSales, are more descriptive than cell references, making it easier to remember what a cell or range contains.
- Names can be used in formulas, making it easier for users to understand the calculations being performed. For example, =GrossPay–Deductions is more understandable than =C15–C16.
- When you move a named cell or range within a worksheet, its name moves with it. Any formulas that contain the name automatically reference the new location.
- In a formula, referencing a named cell or range is the same as referencing the cell or range's absolute reference. So, if you move a formula that includes a defined name, the reference remains pointed to the correct cell or range.

By using defined names, you'll often save time and everyone reviewing the worksheet will have a clearer understanding of what a formula is calculating.

Creating defined names for cells or ranges makes it easier to create and understand the formulas in a workbook. When you define a name for a cell or range, keep in mind the following rules:

- The name must begin with a letter or _ (an underscore).
- The name can include letters and numbers as well as periods and underscores, but not other symbols or spaces. To distinguish multiword names, use an underscore between the words or capitalize the first letter of each word. For example, the names Net_Income and NetIncome are valid, but Net Income and Net-Income are not.
- The name cannot be a valid cell address (such as FY2016), function name (such as Average), or reserved word (such as Print_Area).
- The name can include as many as 255 characters, although short, meaningful names of 5 to 15 characters are more practical.
- The name is not case sensitive. For example, both Sales and SALES refer to the same cell or range.

REFERENCE

Creating a Defined Name for a Cell or Range

- Select the cell or range to which you want to assign a name.
- Click in the Name box, type the name, and then press the Enter key (or on the FORMULAS tab, in the Defined Names group, click the Define Name button, type a name in the Name box, and then click the OK button).

or

- Select the range with labels to which you want to assign a name.
- On the FORMULAS tab, in the Defined Names group, click the Create from Selection button.
- Specify whether to create the ranges based on the top row, bottom row, left column, or right column in the list.
- Click the OK button.

Using the Name Box to Create Defined Names

The Name box is a quick way to create a defined name for a selected cell or range. Sharon wants you to create defined names for cells and ranges in the Receipt worksheet. You'll start by using the Name box to define some of these names.

To create defined names for the input area using the Name box:

1. Select cell **F13**, and then click the **Name box** to the left of the formula bar. The cell reference for the active cell, F13, is selected in the Name box.

2. Type **SeasonFee**, and then press the **Enter** key. Cell F13 remains active, and SeasonFee appears in the Name box instead of the cell reference. See Figure 7-2.

| Figure 7-2 | Defined name for cell F13 |

defined name
for cell F13

Trouble? If SeasonFee appears in cell F13, you did not click the Name box before typing the name. On the Quick Access Toolbar, click the Undo button ↶, and then repeat Steps 1 and 2.

3. Select cell **F14**, click the **Name box** to select the cell reference, type **DiscountAmount**, and then press the **Enter** key. Cell F14 remains active, and DiscountAmount appears in the Name box instead of the cell reference.

4. Select the range **D2:F10**. The cell reference for the active cell in the range appears in the Name box.

5. Click the **Name box**, type **PlayerMeasurements**, and then press the **Enter** key. The name PlayerMeasurements is assigned to the range D2:F10.

6. Select the range **A40:F40**, click the **Name box**, type **TransferArea**, and then press the **Enter** key. The name TransferArea is assigned to the range A40:F40.

7. Select cell **E33**, click the **Name box** to select the cell reference, type **ReceiptSeasonFee**, and then press the **Enter** key. Cell E33 remains active, and ReceiptSeasonFee appears in the Name box instead of the cell reference.

8. Select cell **E34**, click the **Name box** to select the cell reference, type **ReceiptDiscountAmount**, and then press the **Enter** key. Cell E34 remains active, and ReceiptDiscountAmount appears in the Name box instead of the cell reference.

Selecting Cells and Ranges by Their Defined Names

The Name box displays all of the defined names in a workbook. You can click a name in the Name box list to quickly select the cell or range referenced by that name. Sharon wants you to verify that defined names are associated with the correct cell or range. You'll view the defined names you added to the workbook, and then use them to select cells and ranges.

To select cells and ranges with the Name box:

1. Click the **Name box arrow** to open a list of defined names in the workbook. Six names appear in the list. The names are longer than the Name box. You can make the Name box wider so that the full names are visible.

2. Press the **Esc** key to close the Name box.

3. On the right side of the Name box, drag the sizing handle (the three vertical dots) to the right until you can see the full names.

4. Click the **Name box arrow** to display the list of defined names. See Figure 7-3.

Figure 7-3   Name box with the defined names in the workbook

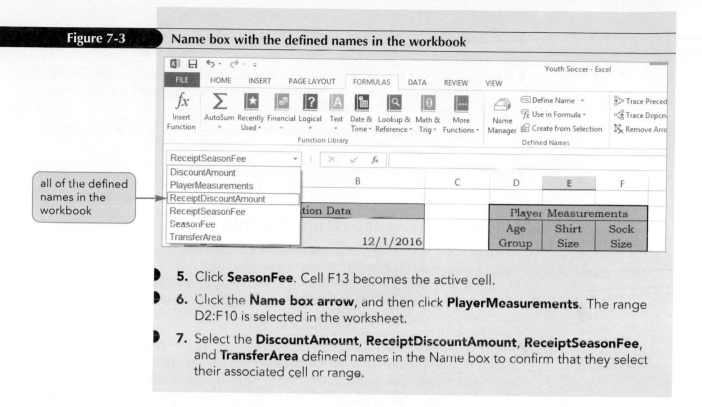

all of the defined
names in the
workbook

5. Click **SeasonFee**. Cell F13 becomes the active cell.

6. Click the **Name box arrow**, and then click **PlayerMeasurements**. The range
   D2:F10 is selected in the worksheet.

7. Select the **DiscountAmount**, **ReceiptDiscountAmount**, **ReceiptSeasonFee**,
   and **TransferArea** defined names in the Name box to confirm that they select
   their associated cell or range.

Creating Defined Names by Selection

You can quickly define names without typing them if the data is organized as a
structured range of data with labels in the first or last column, or in the top or bottom
row. The defined names are based on the row or column labels. For example, the
Registration Data area contains labels in column A that can be used as the defined
names for the corresponding cells in column B. Any blank space or parenthesis in a
label is changed to an underscore (_) in the defined name.

Sharon wants you to create names for each cell in the Registration Data area using
the labels in the range A3:B12.

To create defined names by selection for the registration data:

Select only the range
A3:B12; otherwise,
formulas you create later in
this tutorial will not work.

1. Select the range **A3:B12**. Column A contains the labels you want to use as
   the defined names, and column B contains the cells you want to name.

2. On the ribbon, click the **FORMULAS** tab.

3. In the Defined Names group, click the **Create from Selection** button.
   The Create Names from Selection dialog box opens. See Figure 7-4.

Figure 7-4   Create Names from Selection dialog box

left column of the
selected range has
the labels for the
defined names of
the adjacent cells

▶ **4.** Make sure only the **Left column** check box contains a checkmark. The labels in the left column will be used to create the defined names.

▶ **5.** Click the **OK** button. Each cell in the range B3:B12 is named based on its label in column A. For example, cell B3 is named Registration_Date based on the Registration Date label in cell A3.

▶ **6.** Click the **Name box arrow** to see the 16 defined names in the list. Notice that underscores have replaced spaces in the names.

▶ **7.** Press the **Esc** key to close the list of defined names.

Editing and Deleting Defined Names

Although you can use the Name box to verify that the names were created, the Name Manager dialog box lists all of the names currently defined in the workbook, including Excel table names. In addition to the name, it identifies the current value for that name as well as the worksheet and cell or range it references. You can use the Name Manager dialog box to create a new name, edit or delete existing names, and filter the list of names.

The names ReceiptSeasonFee and ReceiptDiscountAmount define the location of these two cells on the worksheet. Although the names are descriptive, they are also fairly long. Sharon wants you to use the shorter names ReceiptFee and ReceiptDiscount, respectively, which still reflect the stored data in each cell. Sharon also decides that the TransferArea and PlayerMeasurements defined names are not needed, so you will delete them.

To edit and delete defined names with the Name Manager dialog box:

▶ **1.** On the FORMULAS tab, in the Defined Names group, click the **Name Manager** button (or press the **Ctrl+F3** keys). The Name Manager dialog box opens, listing the 16 defined names in the workbook. See Figure 7-5.

Figure 7-5   Name Manager dialog box

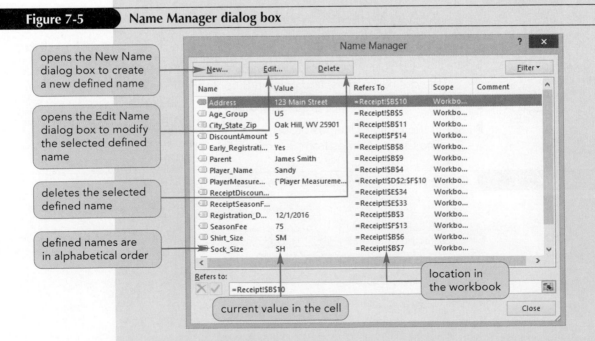

opens the New Name dialog box to create a new defined name

opens the Edit Name dialog box to modify the selected defined name

deletes the selected defined name

defined names are in alphabetical order

location in the workbook

current value in the cell

2. Click **ReceiptSeasonFee** in the Name list, and then click the **Edit** button. The Edit Name dialog box opens. You can change the name and its referenced cell or range in this dialog box. See Figure 7-6.

Figure 7-6   **Edit Name dialog box**

3. In the Name box, type **ReceiptFee** to create a shorter defined name, and then click the **OK** button. The edited name appears in the list in the Name Manager dialog box.

4. Repeat Steps 2 and 3 to rename the ReceiptDiscountAmount defined name as **ReceiptDiscount**.

5. Scroll down to find the TransferArea name, click **TransferArea**, and then click the **Delete** button. A dialog box opens to confirm that you want to delete the selected name.

6. Click the **OK** button. The name is removed from the list.

7. Repeat Steps 5 and 6 to delete the **PlayerMeasurements** name.

8. Click the **Close** button. The Name Manager dialog box closes.

Using the Paste Names Command

When a workbook contains many defined names, it can be helpful to list all of the defined names and their corresponding cell addresses in the workbook's documentation. You can generate a list of names using the Paste Names command.

To create a list of the defined names in the Documentation worksheet:

1. Go to the **Documentation** worksheet.

2. In cell **B10**, enter **Defined Names**, and then format the label with bold.

3. Select cell **B11**. This is the upper-left cell of the range where you want to paste the list of defined names.

4. On the ribbon, click the **FORMULAS** tab, if necessary.

5. In the Defined Names group, click the **Use in Formula** button (or press the **F3** key). The list includes all of the defined names in the workbook followed by the Paste Names command.

6. Click **Paste Names**. The Paste Name dialog box opens. You can paste any selected name, or you can paste the entire list of names.

7. Click the **Paste List** button. The defined names and their associated cell references are pasted into the range B11:C24.

8. Deselect the range. See Figure 7-7. Only some names in the pasted list of defined names include underscores in place of spaces. The names with underscores were created using the Create from Selection button; you entered the names without underscores in the Name box.

| Figure 7-7 | Defined names in the Youth Soccer workbook |

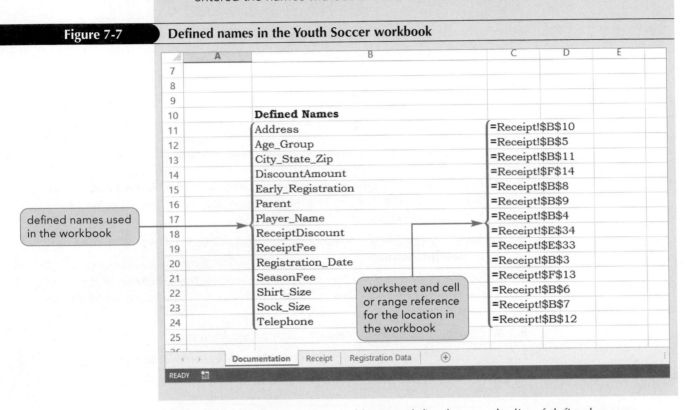

If you edit a defined name or add a new defined name, the list of defined names and their addresses in the Documentation worksheet is not updated. You must paste the list again to update the names and locations. Usually, it is a good idea to wait until the workbook is complete before pasting defined names in the Documentation worksheet.

Using Defined Names in Formulas

You can create more descriptive formulas by using defined names instead of cell or range references in formulas. For example, in the following formulas, the defined name Sales replaces the range reference D1:D100 in a formula to calculate average sales:

Range reference   =AVERAGE(D1:D100)
Defined name   =AVERAGE(Sales)

Keep in mind that range references in formulas are not updated with their defined names. So, if you enter a range reference in a formula, its corresponding defined name does *not* automatically replace the range reference in the formula.

Sharon wants you to enter the formulas required to generate the receipt. You'll start by entering formulas to display the registration date, the parent's name, and the parent's address entered in the Registration Data area in the receipt.

To enter formulas to display the parent's name and address on the receipt:

▶ **1.** Go to the **Receipt** worksheet.

▶ **2.** In cell **B27**, enter **=B9**. James Smith, the parent's name, appears in the cell.

▶ **3.** In cell **B28**, enter **=B10**. 123 Main Street, the parent's street address, appears in the cell.

▶ **4.** In cell **B29**, enter **=B11**. The parent's city, state, and zip code—Oak Hill, WV 25901—appears in the cell.

▶ **5.** Select cell **B29**. The formula =B11 appears in the formula bar. See Figure 7-8.

Figure 7-8   **Formula to display the City, State, and Zip data**

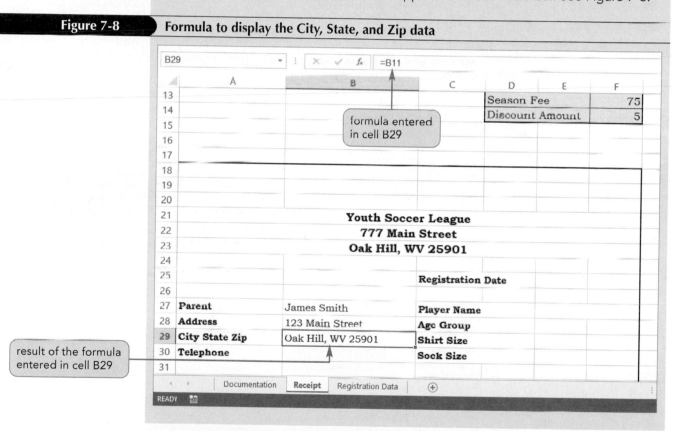

result of the formula entered in cell B29

You entered these formulas using cell addresses rather than defined names. Although you defined names for cells B9, B10, and B11, the names do not automatically replace the cell addresses in the formula when you type the cell addresses.

Using Defined Names in Formulas

Defined names make formulas simpler to enter and understand. To use a defined name in a formula, you enter the formula as usual. As you type a defined name in a formula, the Formula AutoComplete box appears, listing functions and defined names that begin with the letters you typed. As you type additional letters, the list narrows. You can double-click the name you want in the Formula AutoComplete box or press the Tab key to enter the selected name. You can also just continue to type the rest of the name.

Sharon wants you to use named cells and ranges in the remaining formulas. You'll enter these now.

To type defined names in formulas:

▶ **1.** In cell **B30**, type **=T** to display a list of functions and defined names that begin with the letter *T*.

▶ **2.** Type **el** to narrow the list to the defined name =Telephone.

▶ **3.** Press the **Tab** key to enter the defined name in the formula, and then press the **Enter** key. The parent's telephone number appears in the cell.

▶ **4.** Select cell **B30**. The data from cell B12 appears in the cell, and the formula with the defined name =Telephone appears in the formula bar.

▶ **5.** In cell **E25**, enter **=Reg** to list the defined name =Registration_Date, press the **Tab** key to insert the defined name in the formula, and then press the **Enter** key.

▶ **6.** Select cell **E25**. The data from cell B3 appears in the cell, and the formula with the defined name =Registration_Date appears in the formula bar. See Figure 7-9.

Figure 7-9   **Formula with a defined name**

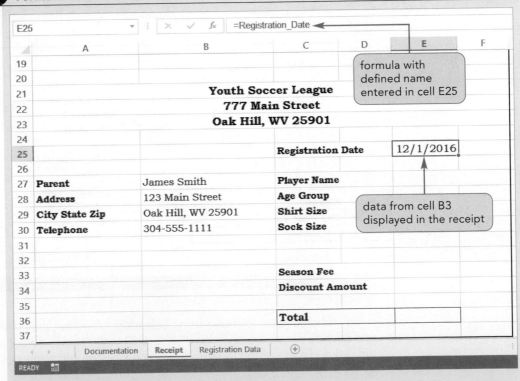

Trouble? If the date is displayed as an integer, you need to reformat the cell as a date. Format cell E25 in the Short Date format (*mm/dd/yyyy*) and then AutoFit column E so that the date is displayed.

You can also use the point-and-click method to create a formula with defined names. When you click a cell or select a range, Excel substitutes the defined name for the cell reference in the formula. You'll use this method to enter formulas that display the Player Name, Age Group, Shirt Size, and Sock Size from the Registration Data area in the Registration Receipt.

To enter formulas with defined names using the point-and-click method:

1. Select cell **E27**, type **=**, and then click cell **B4**. The formula uses the defined name Player_Name rather than the cell reference B4.

2. Press the **Enter** key. Sandy, which is the name of the player, appears in cell E27.

3. In cell **E28**, type **=**, and then click cell **B5**. The formula uses the defined name Age_Group rather than the cell reference B5.

4. Press the **Enter** key. The value is U5, indicating the age group U5, appears in cell E28.

5. In cell **E29**, type **=**, click cell **B6**, and then press the **Enter** key. The player's shirt size, SM, appears in cell E29, and the formula with the defined name =Shirt_Size appears in the formula bar.

6. In cell **E30**, type **=**, click cell **B7**, and then press the **Enter** key. The player's sock size, SH, appears in cell E30, and the formula with the defined name =Sock_Size appears in the formula bar.

7. In cell **E33**, type **=**, click cell **F13**, and then click the **Enter** button ✓ on the formula bar. The season fee, 75, appears in cell E33 and the formula with the defined name =SeasonFee appears in the formula bar. See Figure 7-10.

Figure 7-10 ▶ **SeasonFee formula**

Next, Sharon wants you to enter the formula to calculate the total registration paid based on the data in the Registration Fee/Discount area. All players pay the season fee ($75). Anyone who registers at least four weeks before the season starts receives a $5 discount. Because the formula results are based on the registration date, you need to use an IF function to determine whether the player will receive the $5 discount.

To enter the IF function to calculate the registration total:

1. Select cell **E34**. The defined name ReceiptDiscount appears in the Name box.

2. On the FORMULAS tab, in the Function Library group, click the **Logical** button, and then click **IF**. The Function Arguments dialog box opens.

3. In the Logical_test box, type **Early_Registration="Yes"**. This logical test evaluates whether the player qualifies for the early registration discount. If the value in cell B8 equals Yes, then the condition is true. TRUE appears to the right of the Logical_test box, indicating that this player qualifies for the early registration discount of $5.00.

   Trouble? If an error value appears to the right of the Logical_test box, you probably mistyped the formula. If the error value is #NAME?, you mistyped the defined name or didn't include quotation marks around the word "Yes." If the error value is Invalid, you used single quotation marks ('') around the word "Yes." Edit the content in the Logical_test box as needed.

4. In the Value_if_true box, type **DiscountAmount**—the defined name for cell F14, which has the value 5. This discount amount will be added to the receipt if the logical test is true.

5. In the Value_if_false box, type **0** to indicate no discount will be applied if the value in cell B8 does not equal Yes. See Figure 7-11.

Figure 7-11	Completed IF Function Arguments dialog box

6. Click the **OK** button to enter the IF function in cell E34, which displays 5.

7. Select cell **E36**.

8. Enter the formula **=ReceiptFee-ReceiptDiscount** to calculate the registration total, which is $70. See Figure 7-12.

Figure 7-12 Receipt with all formulas entered

formula subtracts the discount amount from the season fee

IF function displays discount for early registrations

total registration fee

Adding Defined Names to Existing Formulas

Sometimes you might name cells after creating formulas in the worksheet. Other times you might not use the defined names when you create formulas (as with the first three formulas you created in the receipt for the parent; parent address; and city, state, and zip). Because defined names are not automatically substituted for the cell addresses in a formula, you can replace cell addresses in existing formulas in the worksheet with their defined names to make the formulas more understandable.

REFERENCE

Adding Defined Names to Existing Formulas

- On the FORMULAS tab, in the Defined Names group, click the Define Name button arrow, and then click Apply Names (if the cell reference and defined name are in the same worksheet).
- In the Apply Names dialog box, select the names you want to apply.
- Click the OK button.

or

- Edit the formula by selecting the cell reference and typing the defined name or clicking the appropriate cell.

In the two formulas you created to display the parent's name and address in the receipt, Sharon wants you to use defined names instead of cell references. This will make the formulas much clearer to anyone who looks at the worksheet.

To add defined names to existing formulas in the receipt:

▶ 1. On the FORMULAS tab, in the Defined Names group, click the **Define Name button arrow**, and then click **Apply Names**. The Apply Names dialog box opens. See Figure 7-13.

| **Figure 7-13** | Apply Names dialog box |

defined names in the workbook →

You want to select only the names you need for the existing formulas with cell references.

| **TIP** |
| You can also select a cell that contains a formula, click the Use in Formula button in the Defined Names group, click the name to replace the cell reference, and then press the Enter key. |

▶ 2. If any name is selected in the Apply names list, click that name to deselect it.

▶ 3. In the Apply names list, click **Address**, **City_State_Zip**, and **Parent**. The three names you want to apply to the formulas are selected.

▶ 4. Make sure that the **Use row and column names** check box is unchecked. If you leave this checked, the formula will contain too many characters and return an error.

▶ 5. Click the **OK** button. The three selected names are applied to the formulas.

▶ 6. Click cell **B27** and verify that the formula changed to =Parent.

▶ 7. Click cell **B28** and verify that the formula changed to =Address.

▶ 8. Click cell **B29** and verify that the formula changed to =City_State_Zip. The formulas now use the defined names in the files.

Sharon wants to store the following items in the Registration Data worksheet—parent, telephone, player name, age group, shirt size, and sock size. Displaying this data in the Transfer Area enables you to copy and paste all of the items to the Registration Data worksheet at once. You'll enter formulas to display the appropriate items in this section of the worksheet.

To enter formulas to display data in the Transfer Area:

▶ 1. In cell **A40**, enter **=Parent**. The formula displays the parent name (James Smith).

▶ 2. In cell **B40**, enter **=Telephone**. The formula displays the telephone number (304-555-1111).

   3. In cell **C40**, enter **=Player_Name**. The formula displays the name of the player (Sandy).

   4. In cell **D40**, enter **=Age_Group**. The formula displays the age group of the player (U5).

   5. In cell **E40**, enter **=Shirt_Size**. The formula displays the player shirt size (SM).

   6. In cell **F40**, enter **=Sock_Size**. The formula displays the sock size (SH). See Figure 7-14.

Figure 7-14   **Formulas entered in the Transfer Area**

The worksheet contains all of the formulas required to create the receipt based on the registration data. Because Sharon relies on volunteers to enter registration data into the worksheet and print receipts, she wants to be sure the values entered are correct. You will continue to work on Sharon's application by creating validation checks, which are designed to prevent users from inserting incorrect data values. You will also protect cells so that volunteers cannot accidentally overwrite or delete the formulas. You'll complete both of these tasks in the next session.

REVIEW

Session 7.1 Quick Check

1. What is an Excel application?
2. What areas of a worksheet should you consider including in an Excel application?
3. What are two advantages of using defined names in workbooks?
4. What are three ways to create a defined name?
5. Is Annual Sales a valid defined name? Explain why or why not.
6. How do you select a cell or range using its defined name?
7. In the Report workbook, the defined name "Expenses" refers to a list of expenses in the range D2:D100. Currently, the total expenses are calculated by the formula =SUM(D2:D100). Change this formula to use the defined name.
8. How do you add defined names to existing formulas?

Session 7.2 Visual Overview:

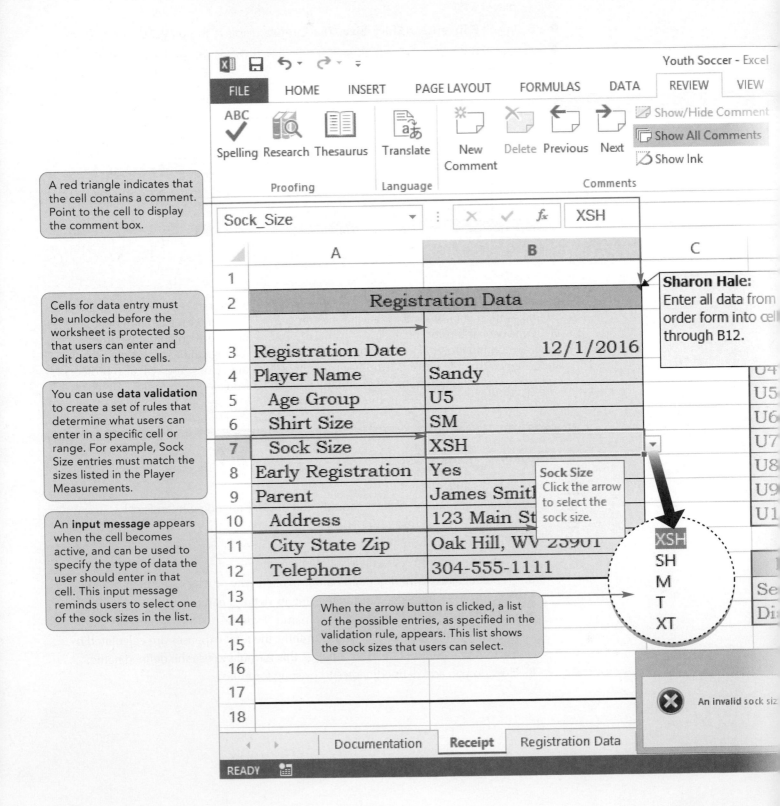

A red triangle indicates that the cell contains a comment. Point to the cell to display the comment box.

Cells for data entry must be unlocked before the worksheet is protected so that users can enter and edit data in these cells.

You can use **data validation** to create a set of rules that determine what users can enter in a specific cell or range. For example, Sock Size entries must match the sizes listed in the Player Measurements.

An **input message** appears when the cell becomes active, and can be used to specify the type of data the user should enter in that cell. This input message reminds users to select one of the sock sizes in the list.

When the arrow button is clicked, a list of the possible entries, as specified in the validation rule, appears. This list shows the sock sizes that users can select.

Sharon Hale: Enter all data from order form into cell through B12.

Sock Size — Click the arrow to select the sock size.

An invalid sock siz

Data Validation and Protection

Worksheet protection limits users' ability to modify the worksheet's contents, structure, or formatting.

Workbook protection limits users' ability to make changes to the workbook's structure and windows.

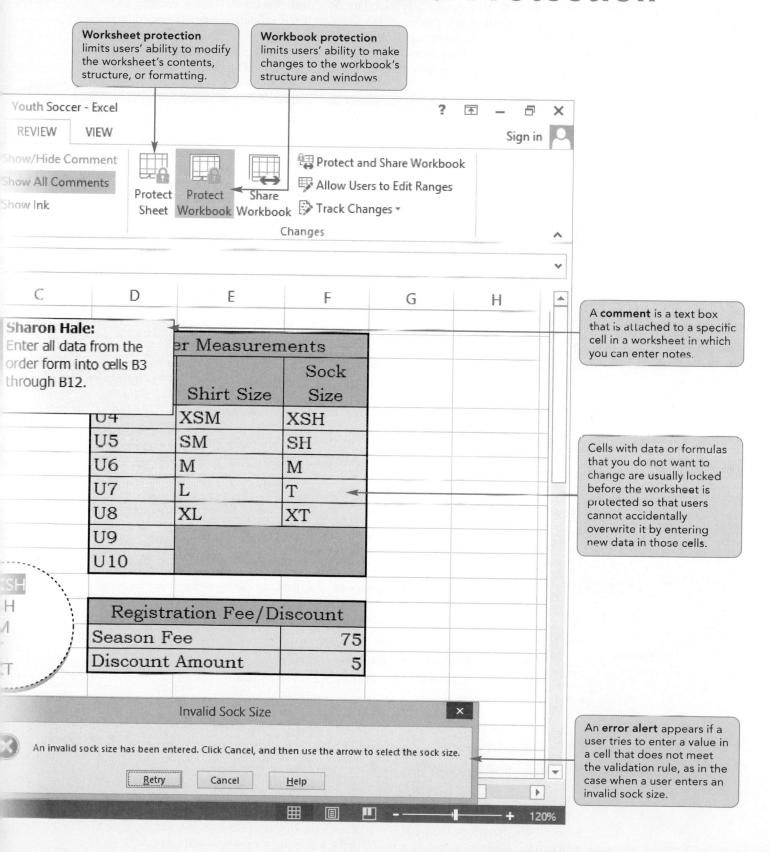

Youth Soccer - Excel

REVIEW   VIEW   Sign in

Show/Hide Comment
Show All Comments
Show Ink

Protect Sheet   Protect Workbook   Share Workbook
Protect and Share Workbook
Allow Users to Edit Ranges
Track Changes

Changes

Sharon Hale:
Enter all data from the order form into cells B3 through B12.

A **comment** is a text box that is attached to a specific cell in a worksheet in which you can enter notes.

er Measurements

	Shirt Size	Sock Size
U4	XSM	XSH
U5	SM	SH
U6	M	M
U7	L	T
U8	XL	XT
U9		
U10		

Cells with data or formulas that you do not want to change are usually locked before the worksheet is protected so that users cannot accidentally overwrite it by entering new data in those cells.

Registration Fee/Discount	
Season Fee	75
Discount Amount	5

Invalid Sock Size

An invalid sock size has been entered. Click Cancel, and then use the arrow to select the sock size.

Retry   Cancel   Help

An **error alert** appears if a user tries to enter a value in a cell that does not meet the validation rule, as in the case when a user enters an invalid sock size.

120%

Validating Data Entry

When collecting data, accuracy is important. To ensure that correct data is entered and stored in a worksheet, you can use data validation. Each **validation rule** defines criteria for the data that can be entered and stored in a cell or range. You can also add input and error alert messages for the user to that cell or range. You specify the validation criteria, the input message, and the error alert for the active cell in the Data Validation dialog box.

REFERENCE

Validating Data

- On the DATA tab, in the Data Tools group, click the Data Validation button.
- Click the Settings tab.
- Click the Allow arrow, click the type of data allowed in the cell, and then enter the validation criteria for that data.
- Click the Input Message tab, and then enter a title and text for the input message.
- Click the Error Alert tab, and then, if necessary, click the Show error alert after invalid data is entered check box to insert a checkmark.
- Select an alert style, and then enter the title and text for the error alert message.
- Click the OK button.

Specifying Validation Criteria

When you create a validation rule, you specify the type of data that is allowed as well as a list or range of acceptable values (called **validation criteria**). For example, you might specify integers between 1 and 100, or a list of codes such as Excellent, Good, Fair, and Poor. Figure 7-15 describes the types of data you can allow and the acceptable values for each type.

Figure 7-15 ▶ **Allow options for validation**

Type	Acceptable Values
Any value	Any number, text, or date; removes any existing data validation
Whole Number	Integers only; you can specify the range of acceptable integers
Decimal	Any type of number; you can specify the range of acceptable numbers
List	Any value in a range or entered in the Data validation dialog box separated by commas
Date	Dates only; you can specify the range of acceptable dates
Time	Times only; you can specify the range of acceptable times
Text Length	Text limited to a specified number of characters
Custom	Values based on the results of a logical formula

© 2014 Cengage Learning

Sharon wants you to add the following six validation rules to the workbook to help ensure that volunteers enter valid data in the Receipt worksheet:

- In cell B3, make sure a valid date is entered.
- In cell B4, specify an input message.
- In cell B5, make sure the value is one of the following age groups—U4, U5, U6, U7, U8, U9, or U10.
- In cell B6, make sure the value is one of the following shirt sizes—XSM, SM, M, L, or XL.
- In cell B7, make sure the value is one of the following sock sizes—XSH, SH, M, T, or XT.
- In cell B8, make sure the value is Yes or No.

Cell B3, which contains the Registration Date, requires the current date. Sharon wants to be sure everyone enters a valid date in this cell. You will define the validation rule for the Registration Date.

To create the validation rule for the Registration Date cell:

▶ **1.** If you took a break after the previous session, make sure the Youth Soccer workbook is open and the Receipt worksheet is active.

▶ **2.** Select cell **B3**. You will enter a date validation rule to ensure that a valid date is entered in this cell.

▶ **3.** On the ribbon, click the **DATA** tab.

TIP

To apply a validation rule to all cells in an Excel table column, select the column of data, and then create the validation rule.

▶ **4.** In the Data Tools group, click the **Data Validation** button. The Data Validation dialog box opens with the Settings tab displayed. You use the Settings tab to enter the validation rule for the active cell.

▶ **5.** On the Settings tab, click the **Allow** arrow, and then click **Date**. The Data Validation dialog box expands to display the options specific to dates.

▶ **6.** Click the **Ignore blank** check box to deselect it. You want to ensure that cell B3 is not left blank, and require users to enter a date value in the cell.

▶ **7.** If necessary, click the **Data** arrow, and then click **greater than or equal to**. The dialog box reflects the selected criteria.

▶ **8.** Enter **1/1/2010** in the Start date box to provide an example of what to look for when checking the cell. You cannot use data validation to simply check for the presence of data. You must provide an example for checking. See Figure 7-16.

Figure 7-16   Settings tab in the Data Validation dialog box

type of value to allow in the cell

these options change to reflect the allowed value

uncheck to apply the validation rule to empty cells (which means that the cell cannot be blank)

If you wanted to create a validation rule that checks if the date is the current date, you would select "equal to" in the Data list and then enter =TODAY() in the Date box. Then, a user cannot enter any date other than the current date. Sharon wants to check only for the presence of a date because sometimes the registration form is completed on a different day than the data was received.

Validating Existing Data

Validation rules come into play only during data entry. If you add validation rules to a workbook that already contains data with erroneous values, Excel does not determine if any existing data is invalid. Instead, you can use the Circle Invalid Data command to help identify invalid data that is already in the workbook. (You'll learn about the Circle Invalid Data command in the Circle Invalid Data Command InSight box later in the tutorial.)

Creating an Error Alert Style and Message

An error alert determines what happens after a user tries to make an invalid entry in a cell that has a validation rule defined. The three error alert styles are Stop, Warning, and Information. The Stop alert prevents the entry from being stored in the cell. The Warning alert prevents the entry from being stored in the cell unless the user overrides the rejection and decides to continue using the data. The Information alert accepts the data value entered, but allows the user to choose to cancel the data entry.

Sharon wants to display an error alert if a volunteer enters data that violates the validation rule. Although the registration date is usually equal to the current date, a user might forget to enter the date. To account for this possibility, Sharon wants you to create a Warning error alert that appears when a user does not enter a registration date or enters a date prior to 1/1/2010. The user can then verify the date entered. If the entry is correct, the user can accept the entry. If the entry is incorrect, the user can reenter the correct date.

You'll create the Warning error alert for the Registration Date cell.

To create the Warning error alert for the Registration Date cell:

1. Make sure cell **B3** is still the active cell and the Data Validation dialog box is open.

2. In the Data Validation dialog box, click the **Error Alert** tab. You use this tab to select the type of error alert and enter the message you want to appear.

3. Make sure that the **Show error alert after invalid data is entered** check box is selected. If unchecked, the error alert won't appear when an invalid value is entered in the cell.

4. Click the **Style** arrow, and then click **Warning**. This style allows the user to accept the invalid value, return to the cell and reenter a valid value, or cancel the data entry and restore the previous value to the cell.

5. Click in the **Title** box, and then type **Invalid Registration Date**. This text will appear as the title of the error alert box.

6. Press the **Tab** key to move the insertion point to the Error message box, and then type **Invalid Registration Date. Enter a Registration Date after 1/1/2010. If the date you entered is correct, click Yes. If it is incorrect, click No. If you are not sure, click Cancel.** See Figure 7-17.

Figure 7-17   **Error Alert tab in the Data Validation dialog box**

> **7.** Click the **OK** button. The Data Validation dialog box closes.

Creating an Input Message

One way to reduce the chance of a data-entry error is to display an input message when a user makes the cell active. An input message provides additional information about the type of data allowed for that cell. Input messages appear as ScreenTips next to the cell when the cell is selected. You can add an input message to a cell even if you don't set up a rule to validate the data in that cell.

Sharon wants volunteers to see that they must enter a value for the player name in cell B4. An input message will minimize the chance of a volunteer skipping this cell, so you will create an input message for cell B4.

To create an input message for the Player Name cell:

> **1.** Select cell **B4**. You will create an input message for this cell.

> **2.** On the DATA tab, in the Data Tools group, click the **Data Validation** button. The Data Validation dialog box opens.

> **3.** Click the **Input Message** tab. You enter the input message title and text on this tab.

> **4.** Verify that the **Show input message when cell is selected** check box contains a checkmark. If you uncheck this option, you cannot enter a new input message and any existing input message will not be displayed when the selected cell becomes active.

> **5.** Click in the **Title** box, and then type **Player Name**. This title will appear in bold at the top of the ScreenTip above the text of the input message.

> **6.** Press the **Tab** key to move the insertion point to the Input message box, and then type **Enter the Player's first name**. See Figure 7-18.

Figure 7-18   **Input Message tab in the Data Validation dialog box**

7. Click the **OK** button. The Data Validation dialog box closes. The input message appears in a ScreenTip because the cell is active. See Figure 7-19.

Figure 7-19   **Input message for the Player Name cell**

Creating a List Validation Rule

You can use the data validation feature to restrict a cell to accept only entries that are on a list you create. You can create the list of valid entries in the Data Validation dialog box, or you can use a list of valid entries in a single column or row. Once you create a list validation rule for a cell, a list box with the possible values appears when the user selects the cell.

Sharon wants you to use list validation rules for the Age Group, Shirt Size, and Sock Size cells to ensure that users enter one of the correct values. The Age Group has seven possible values—U4, U5, U6, U7, U8, U9, and U10. You will create a validation rule so that users can enter only one of the seven possible values. You will also create an input message for the cell.

To create a validation rule and an input message for the Age Group cell:

1. Select cell **B5**. You will create a list validation rule for this cell.

2. On the DATA tab, in the Data Tools group, click the **Data Validation** button to open the Data Validation dialog box, and then click the **Settings** tab.

3. Click the **Allow** arrow, and then click **List**. The dialog box expands to display the Source box. You can enter values separated by commas directly in the Source box, or you can select a range of valid entries in the worksheet.

4. Next to the Source box, click the **Collapse** button 🔢 so you can see the entire worksheet.

5. Select the range **D4:D10**, which contains the seven valid entry values, and then click the **Expand** button 🔢. The Data Validation dialog box returns to its full size and =$D$4:$D$10 appears in the Source box. See Figure 7-20.

Figure 7-20 Settings tab in the Data Validation dialog box

type of data validation

range that contains the entry values

Next, you'll create an input message and an error alert.

6. Click the **Input Message** tab, click in the **Title** box, and then type **Age Group** to enter the title of the input message.

7. Click in the **Input message** box, and then type **Click the arrow to select the player's age group.** to enter the text of the input message.

8. Click the **Error Alert** tab, and then make sure that **Stop** appears in the Style box. You want to prevent a user from entering a value that is not included in the list of values you specified.

9. In the Title text box, type **Invalid Age Group** to enter the title of the error alert.

10. In the Error message box, type **An invalid age group has been entered. Click Cancel, and then use the arrow to select a valid age group.** as the error message. See Figure 7-21.

Figure 7-21 Stop error alert for the Age Group cell

Stop error alert prevents user from entering invalid values

title of the error alert

text of the error message

▶ **11.** Click the **OK** button. The Data Validation dialog box closes, an arrow appears to the right of cell B5, and the input message appears in a ScreenTip.

▶ **12.** Click the **arrow** button ▼ to the right of cell B5 to view the list of valid age group entries. See Figure 7-22.

Figure 7-22 List of valid age group entries

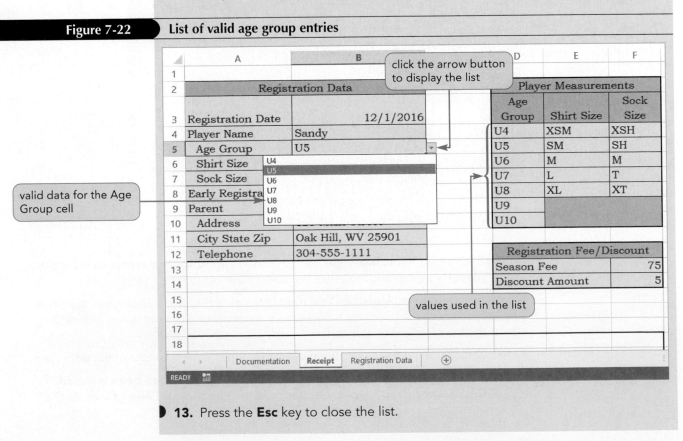

click the arrow button to display the list

valid data for the Age Group cell

values used in the list

▶ **13.** Press the **Esc** key to close the list.

Next, Sharon wants you to enter a list validation rule for cells B6 and B7, which specify the player's shirt size (XSM, SM, M, L, or XL) and sock size (XSH, SH, M, T, or XT), respectively. Both rules will include an error alert.

To create list validation rules for the Shirt Size and Sock Size cells:

1. Select cell **B6**. You will create a list validation rule for the Shirt Size cell.

2. On the DATA tab, in the Data Tools group, click the **Data Validation** button. The Data Validation dialog box opens.

3. Click the **Settings** tab, select **List** in the Allow box, click the **Source** box, and then select the range **E4:E8**. This range contains the five values you want to allow users to select for the shirt size.

4. Click the **Input Message** tab, type **Shirt Size** in the Title box, and then type **Click the arrow to select the shirt size.** in the Input message box.

5. Click the **Error Alert** tab, verify that **Stop** appears in the Style box, type **Invalid Shirt Size** in the Title box, and then type **An invalid shirt size has been entered. Click Cancel, and then use the arrow to select the shirt size.** in the Error message box.

6. Click the **OK** button. The dialog box closes, an arrow button appears to the right of cell B6, and the input message appears in a ScreenTip.

7. Select cell **B7** so you can create the validation rule for the Sock Size cell.

8. In the Data Tools group, click the **Data Validation** button to open the Data Validation dialog box, and then click the **Settings** tab.

9. Select **List** in the Allow box, click the **Source** box, and then select the range **F4:F8**. This range contains the five values you want to allow users to select for the sock size.

10. Click the **Input Message** tab, type **Sock Size** in the Title box, and then type **Click the arrow to select the sock size.** in the Input message box.

11. Click the **Error Alert** tab, make sure that **Stop** appears in the Style box, type **Invalid Sock Size** in the Title box, and then type **An invalid sock size has been entered. Click Cancel, and then use the arrow to select the sock size.** in the Error message box.

12. Click the **OK** button. An arrow button appears to the right of cell B7, and the input message appears in a ScreenTip.

Sharon also wants you to enter a validation rule for cell B8 to limit the Early Registration cell to either Yes or No. This rule will also include an input message and an error alert. To specify the entries that the list includes, you will type each entry separated by commas in the Source box on the Settings tab in the Data Validation dialog box.

To create a list validation rule for the Early Registration cell:

1. Select cell **B8** so you can create a validation rule for the Early Registration cell.

2. On the DATA tab, in the Data Tools group, click the **Data Validation** button. The Data Validation dialog box opens.

3. Click the **Settings** tab, select **List** in the Allow box, click the **Source** box, and then type **Yes, No** in the Source box. You typed the items for the list because they are not already contained in any range of the worksheet. See Figure 7-23.

Figure 7-23   Validation rule for the Early Registration cell

entries for the list are separated by commas

4. Click the **Input Message** tab, type **Early Registration** in the Title box, and then type **Click the arrow to select the correct response.** in the Input message box.

5. Click the **Error Alert** tab, make sure that **Stop** appears in the Style box, type **Invalid Early Registration** in the Title box, and then type **An invalid response for Early Registration has been entered. Click Cancel, and then use the arrow to the right of cell B8 to select the response.** in the Error message box.

6. Click the **OK** button. An arrow button appears to the right of cell B8, and the input message appears in a ScreenTip.

You can edit an existing validation rule, input message, or error alert at any time by selecting the cell with the current validation rule and then opening the Data Validation dialog box. You can also add or remove an input message or error alert to an existing validation rule. Sharon notices that the Registration Date cell does not have an input message. For consistency, she wants you to add one now.

To create an input message for the Registration Date cell:

1. Select cell **B3**.

2. On the DATA tab, in the Data Tools group, click the **Data Validation** button.

3. Click the **Settings** tab. The validation rule you created earlier is displayed.

4. Click the **Input Message** tab, type **Registration Date** in the Title box, and then type **Enter the registration date.** in the Input message box.

5. Click the **OK** button. The input message is added to the Registration Date cell.

Testing Data Validation Rules

After you create validation rules, you should test them. You do this by entering incorrect values that violate the validation rules. Keep in mind that the only way an error occurs in cells that have a list validation is if an incorrect entry is typed or pasted in the cell. Entering invalid data will ensure that validation rules work as expected. Sharon asks you to test the validation rules you just created.

To test the data validation rules:

1. Select cell **B3**, type **01/30/2004**, and then press the **Tab** key. The Invalid Registration Date message box opens, informing you that the value you entered might be incorrect. You'll enter a valid date.

2. Click the **No** button to return to cell B3, type the current date, and then press the **Enter** key. The date is entered in cell B3. Cell B4 is the active cell, and the input message for the Player Name cell appears.

3. In cell **B4**, type your name, and then press the **Enter** key. The value is accepted.

4. Select cell **B5** if necessary to display the list arrow, click the **arrow** to the right of cell B5, and then click **U6**. The value is accepted. The only way an error occurs in cells that have a list validation is if an incorrect entry is typed or copied in the cell. You'll try typing in cell B6.

5. In cell **B6**, enter **LG**. The Invalid Shirt Size message box opens.

6. Click the **Cancel** button to close the message box and return to the original value in the cell.

7. Click the **arrow** button ▼ to the right of cell B6, and then click **SM**.

8. In cell B7, enter **XSH**. An error alert does not appear because this is a valid entry. You could also have selected XSH from the validation list.

9. Select cell **B8**, click the **arrow** button ▼ to the right of cell B8, and then click **Yes** for Early Registration.

TIP

If you press the Retry button in the error alert dialog box, you must press the Esc key to return to the original cell value; otherwise, the error alert reappears when you click the arrow button.

The validation rules that you entered for cells B3 through B8 work as intended.

INSIGHT

Using the Circle Invalid Data Command

Validation rules come into play only during data entry. If you add validation rules to a workbook that already contains data with erroneous values, Excel does not determine if any existing data is invalid.

To ensure the entire workbook contains valid data, you need to also verify any data previously entered in the workbook. You can use the Circle Invalid Data command to find and mark cells that contain invalid data. Red circles appear around any data that does not meet the validation criteria, making it simple to scan a worksheet for errors. After you correct the data in a cell, the circle disappears.

To display circles around invalid data, perform the following steps:

1. Apply validation rules to an existing cell range.
2. On the DATA tab, in the Data Tools group, click the Data Validation button arrow, and then click Circle Invalid Data. Red circles appear around cells that contain invalid data.
3. To remove the circle from a single cell, enter valid data in the cell.
4. To hide all circles, on the DATA tab, in the Data Tools group, click the Data Validation button arrow, and then click Clear Validation Circles.

To ensure an error-free workbook, you should use the Circle Invalid Data command to verify data entered before you set up the validation criteria, or to verify data in a workbook you inherited from someone else, such as a coworker.

Protecting a Worksheet and a Workbook

Another way to minimize data-entry errors is to limit access to certain parts of the workbook. Worksheet protection prevents users from changing cell contents, such as editing formulas in a worksheet. Workbook protection also prevents users from changing the workbook's organization, such as inserting or deleting worksheets in the workbook. You can even keep users from viewing the formulas used in the workbook.

Sharon wants to protect the contents of the Receipt and Registration Data worksheets. She wants volunteers to have access only to the range B3:B12 in the Receipt worksheet, where new receipt data is entered. She also wants to prevent volunteers from editing the contents of any cells in the Registration Data worksheet.

Locking and Unlocking Cells

Every cell in a workbook has a **locked property** that determines whether changes can be made to that cell. The locked property has no impact as long as the worksheet is unprotected. However, after you protect a worksheet, the locked property controls whether the cell can be edited. You unlock a cell by turning off the locked property. By default, the locked property is turned on for each cell, and worksheet protection is turned off.

So, unless you unlock cells in a worksheet *before* protecting the worksheet, all of the cells in the worksheet will be locked, and you won't be able to make any changes in the worksheet. Usually, you will want to protect the worksheet but leave some cells unlocked. For example, you might want to lock cells that contain formulas and formatting so they cannot be changed, but unlock cells in which you want to enter data.

To protect some—but not all—cells in a worksheet, you first turn off the locked property of cells in which data can be entered. Then, you protect the worksheet to activate the locked property for the remaining cells.

In the Receipt worksheet, Sharon wants users to be able to enter data in the range B3:B12, but not in any other cell. To do this, you must unlock the cells in the range B3:B12.

To unlock the cells in the range B3:B12:

▶ 1. In the Receipt worksheet, select the range **B3:B12**. You want to unlock the cells in this range before you protect the worksheet.

▶ 2. On the ribbon, click the **HOME** tab.

> **TIP**
>
> You can also click the Format button in the Cells group and then click Lock Cell to add or remove the locked property for the selected cells.

▶ 3. In the Cells group, click the **Format** button, and then click **Format Cells** (or press the **Ctrl+1** keys). The Format Cells dialog box opens. The locked property is on the Protection tab.

▶ 4. Click the **Protection** tab, and then click the **Locked** check box to remove the checkmark. See Figure 7-24.

Figure 7-24   **Protection tab in the Format Cells dialog box**

Locked property is turned off for the selected cells

Format Cells

Number | Alignment | Font | Border | Fill | Protection

☐ Locked
☐ Hidden

Locking cells or hiding formulas has no effect until you protect the worksheet (Review tab, Changes group, Protect Sheet button).

OK   Cancel

▶ **5.** Click the **OK** button. The cells in the range B3:B12 are unlocked.

▶ **6.** Select cell **A1** to deselect the range.

Protecting a Worksheet

When you set up worksheet protection, you specify which actions are still available to users in the protected worksheet. For example, you can choose to allow users to insert new rows or columns, or to delete rows and columns. You can limit the user to selecting only unlocked cells, or allow the user to select any cell in the worksheet. These choices remain active as long as the worksheet is protected.

A protected worksheet can always be unprotected. You can also add a password to the protected worksheet that users must enter in order to turn off the protection. Passwords are case sensitive, which means the uppercase and lowercase letters are considered different letters. If you are concerned that users will turn off protection and make changes to formulas, you should use a password; otherwise, it is probably best to not specify a password. Keep in mind that if you forget the password, it is very difficult to remove the worksheet protection.

Protecting a Worksheet

- Select the cells and ranges to unlock so that users can enter data in them.
- On the HOME tab, in the Cells group, click the Format button, and then click Format Cells (or press the Ctrl+1 keys).
- In the Format Cells dialog box, click the Protection tab.
- Click the Locked check box to remove the checkmark, and then click the OK button.
- On the REVIEW tab, in the Changes group, click the Protect Sheet button.
- Enter a password (optional).
- Select all of the actions you want to allow users to take when the worksheet is protected.
- Click the OK button.

Sharon wants to protect the Receipt and Registration Data worksheets, but she doesn't want a password specified. You will enable worksheet protection that will allow users to select any cell in the worksheets, but enter data only in the unlocked cells.

To protect the Receipt worksheet:

1. On the ribbon, click the **REVIEW** tab.

2. In the Changes group, click the **Protect Sheet** button. The Protect Sheet dialog box opens. See Figure 7-25.

Figure 7-25   Protect Sheet dialog box

users will able to perform checked actions in the protected worksheet

TIP

Keep passwords in a safe place. Remember, passwords are case sensitive. If you forget the password, it is very difficult to remove the worksheet protection.

You will leave the Password to unprotect sheet box blank because you do not want to use a password. By default, users can select both locked and unlocked cells, which constitute all of the cells in the worksheet, but they can enter or edit values only in unlocked cells.

3. Click the **OK** button. The Protect Sheet dialog box closes, and the Protect Sheet button changes to the Unprotect Sheet button.

Any time you modify a worksheet, you should test the worksheet to ensure that changes work as intended. You'll test the protection you added to the Receipt worksheet by trying to edit a locked cell, and then trying to edit an unlocked cell.

To test the Receipt worksheet protection:

1. Select cell **F13**, and then type **1**. As soon as you press any key, a dialog box opens, indicating that the cell is protected and cannot be modified. See Figure 7-26.

Figure 7-26   **Cell protection error message**

2. Click the **OK** button.

3. Click cell **B8**, type **No**, and then press the **Enter** key. The Early Registration cell is updated because you allowed editing in the range B3:B12. A user can enter and edit values in these cells. Although users can select any cell in the worksheet, they cannot make an entry in any other cell outside of that range.

4. On the Quick Access Toolbar, click the **Undo** button to return the Early Registration cell to Yes.

You will repeat this process to protect all of the cells in the Registration Data worksheet. Then you will test to see what would happen if someone tried to edit one of the cells. Because you did not unlock any cells in the Registration Data worksheet, no cells may be edited.

To protect and test the Registration Data worksheet:

1. Go to the **Registration Data** worksheet.

2. On the REVIEW tab, in the Changes group, click the **Protect Sheet** button. The Protect Sheet dialog box opens.

3. Click the **OK** button to accept the default set of user actions.

4. Select cell **A2**, and then type **B**. A dialog box opens, indicating that the cell is protected and cannot be modified. All of the cells in this worksheet are protected because no cells have been unlocked.

5. Click the **OK** button to close the dialog box.

Protecting a Workbook

Worksheet protection applies only to the contents of a worksheet, not to the worksheet itself. To keep a worksheet from being modified, you need to protect the workbook. You can protect both the structure and the windows of a workbook. Protecting the structure prevents users from renaming, deleting, hiding, or inserting worksheets. Protecting the windows prevents users from moving, resizing, closing, or hiding parts of the Excel window. The default is to protect only the structure of the workbook, not the windows used to display it.

You can also add a password to the workbook protection. However, the same guidelines apply as for protecting worksheets. Add a password only if you are concerned that others might unprotect the workbook and modify it. If you add a password, keep in mind that it is case sensitive and you cannot unprotect the workbook without it.

Protecting a Workbook

- On the REVIEW tab, in the Changes group, click the Protect Workbook button.
- Click the check boxes to indicate whether you want to protect the workbook's structure, windows, or both.
- Enter a password (optional).
- Click the OK button.

The contents of the Receipt and Registration Data worksheets, with the exception of the range B3:B12 in the Receipt worksheet, cannot be changed. However, a volunteer could inadvertently rename or delete the protected worksheet. To keep the worksheets themselves from being modified, you will protect the workbook. Sharon doesn't want users to be able to change the structure of the workbook, so you will set workbook protection for the structure, but not the window.

To protect the Youth Soccer workbook:

▶ **1.** On the REVIEW tab, in the Changes group, click the **Protect Workbook** button. The Protect Structure and Windows dialog box opens. See Figure 7-27.

| Figure 7-27 | Protect Structure and Windows dialog box |

▶ **2.** Make sure the **Structure** check box is checked and the **Password** box is blank. The Windows check box is unavailable and unchecked.

▶ **3.** Click the **OK** button to protect the workbook without specifying a password.

▶ **4.** Right-click the **Registration Data** sheet tab. On the shortcut menu, notice that the Insert, Delete, Rename, Move or Copy, Tab Color, Hide, and Unhide commands are gray. This indicates that the options for modifying the worksheets are no longer available for the Registration Data worksheet.

▶ **5.** Press the **Esc** key to close the shortcut menu.

Unprotecting a Worksheet and a Workbook

You can turn off worksheet protection at any time. This is often referred to as *unprotecting* the worksheet. You must unprotect a worksheet to edit its contents. If you assigned a password when you protected the worksheet, you would need to enter the password to remove worksheet protection. Likewise, you can unprotect the workbook. If you need to insert a new worksheet or rename an existing worksheet, you can unprotect the protected workbook, make the changes to the structure, and then reapply workbook protection.

At this point, Sharon wants you to make additional changes to the Receipt worksheet, so you'll turn off worksheet protection in that worksheet. Later, when you've completed your modifications, Sharon can turn worksheet protection back on.

To turn off worksheet protection for the Receipt worksheet:

1. Go to the **Receipt** worksheet.

2. On the REVIEW tab, in the Changes group, click the **Unprotect Sheet** button. Worksheet protection is removed from the Receipt worksheet. The button changes back to the Protect Sheet button.

TIP

To remove workbook protection, click the Protect Workbook button in the Changes group on the REVIEW tab.

Inserting Comments

Comments are often used in workbooks to: (a) explain the contents of a particular cell, such as a complex formula; (b) provide instructions to users; and (c) share ideas and notes from several users collaborating on a project. The username for your installation of Excel appears in bold at the top of the comments box. If you collaborate on a workbook, the top of the comment boxes would show the name of each user who created that comment. A small red triangle appears in the upper-right corner of a cell with a comment. The comment box appears when you point to a cell with a comment.

REFERENCE

Inserting a Comment

- Select the cell to which you want to attach a comment.
- Right-click the selected cell, and then click Insert Comment on the shortcut menu (or press the Shift+F2 keys; or on the REVIEW tab, in the Comments group, click the New Comment button).
- Type the comment into the box.
- Click a cell to hide the comment.

Sharon wants you to insert a note in cell A2 about entering data from the order form into the input section, and a note in cell E34 explaining how the IF functions are used to determine whether to give the discount for early registration.

To insert comments in cells A2 and E34:

1. In the Receipt worksheet, select cell **A2**.

2. On the REVIEW tab, in the Comments group, click the **New Comment** button (or press the **Shift+F2** keys). A comment box opens to the right of cell A2. The username for your installation of Excel appears in bold at the top of the box. An arrow points from the box to the small red triangle that appears in the upper-right corner of the cell.

3. Type **Enter all data from the order form into cells B3 through B11.** in the box. A selection box with sizing handles appears around the comment box. If the box is too small or too large for the comment, you can drag a sizing handle to increase or decrease the size of the box. See Figure 7-28.

TIP

You can also add a comment by right-clicking the cell, and then clicking Insert Comment on the shortcut menu.

Figure 7-28   Comment added to cell A2

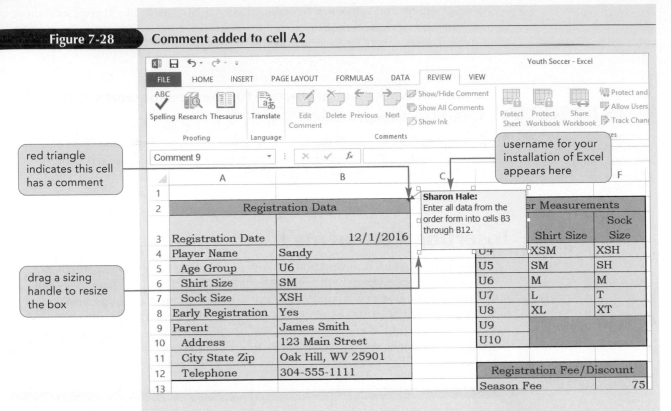

4. Click cell **B12** to hide the comment. The comment disappears. A small red triangle remains in the upper-right corner of cell A2 to indicate this cell contains a comment.

   Trouble? If the comment box did not disappear, comments are set to be displayed in the worksheet. On the REVIEW tab, in the Comments group, click the Show All Comments button to deselect it.

5. Move the pointer over cell **A2**. The comment appears.

6. Click cell **A2**.

7. In the Comments group, click the **Edit Comment** button. The comment appears with the insertion point at the end of the comment text, so you can edit the incorrect cell reference.

8. Select **B11** in the comment box, and then type **B12**. The comment in cell A2 now correctly references the range B3:B12.

9. Select any other cell to hide the comment, and then point to cell **A2** to view the edited comment.

10. Click cell **E34**, and then on the REVIEW tab, in the Comments group, click the **New Comment** button. A comment box opens to the right of cell E34.

11. In the comment box, type **This IF function determines whether to allow the early registration discount.**

12. Select cell **E35** to hide the comment. A small red triangle remains in the upper-right corner of cell E34 to indicate it contains a comment.

13. Point to cell **E34** to see the comment.

   Sharon decides that the volunteers don't need to know how the early registration discount is calculated. You'll delete the comment in cell E34.

TIP

To keep an active cell's comment displayed, click the Show/Hide Comment button in the Comments group on the REVIEW tab. Click the button again to hide the active cell's comment.

14. Select cell **E34**.

15. In the Comments group, click the **Delete** button. The comment is deleted, and the red triangle in the upper-right corner of cell E34 is removed.

The comments provide helpful information for anyone using the Receipt worksheet.

PROSKILLS

Written Communication: Documenting a Spreadsheet

Providing documentation for a spreadsheet is important because it provides instructions on the spreadsheet's use, defines technical terms, explains complex formulas, and identifies assumptions. By documenting a spreadsheet, you help users work more effectively. In addition, documentation helps you recall what is in the spreadsheet that might otherwise be forgotten months or years from now. Furthermore, when someone else becomes responsible for modifying the spreadsheet in the future, the documentation will help that person get up to speed quickly.

You can create a Documentation worksheet to provide an overview, definitions, assumptions, and instructions on how to use various parts of a workbook. Excel also offers a variety of tools to help you document spreadsheets, including:

- Defined names and structured references to make formulas easier to create and understand
- Data validation including input messages specifying what to enter in a cell, and error messages providing instructions on what to do if the data entered is incorrect
- Cell comments to explain complex formulas, give reminders, and so on
- Formula mode to view all formulas in a worksheet at one time

Providing documentation will help users better understand the application, which will save time and minimize frustration.

In this session, you used data validation to help ensure that all values entered in the Receipt worksheet are valid. You created validation rules that included input messages and error alert messages. You learned how to protect and unprotect both the worksheet and the workbook. In addition, you used comments to add notes to specific cells. In the next session, you'll automate some of the steps in the application by recording macros.

REVIEW

Session 7.2 Quick Check

1. Why would you want to validate data?
2. What is the purpose of the input message in the Data Validation command?
3. Describe the three types of error alert messages Excel can display when a user violates a validation rule.
4. What is a locked cell? What are unlocked cells?
5. What is the difference between worksheet protection and workbook protection?
6. Can you rename a protected worksheet? Explain why or why not.
7. Give two reasons for adding a comment to a worksheet cell.

Session 7.3 Visual Overview:

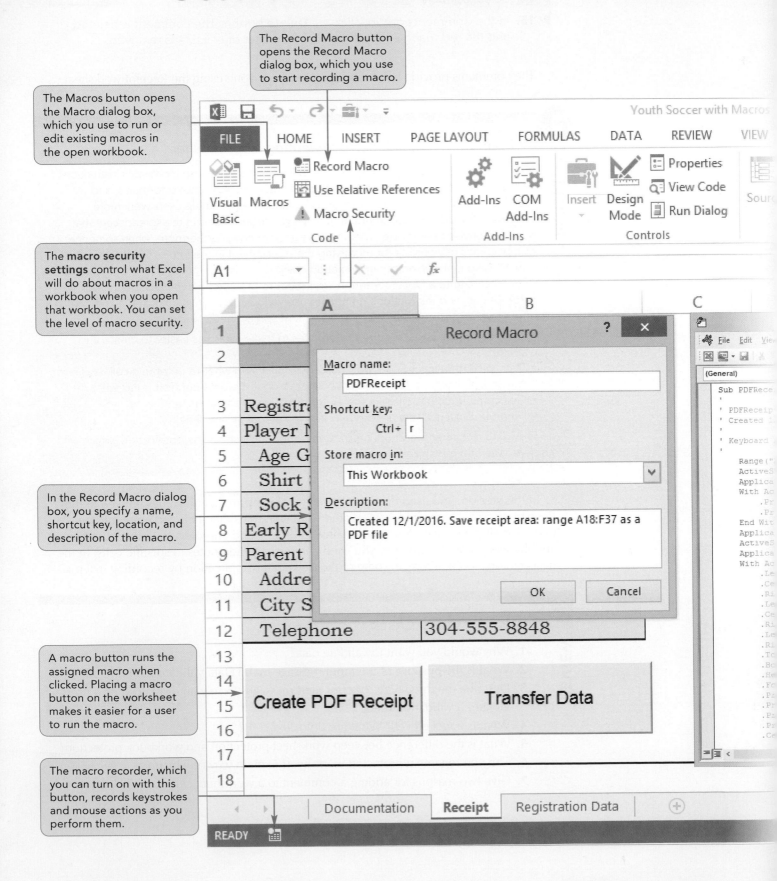

The Macros button opens the Macro dialog box, which you use to run or edit existing macros in the open workbook.

The Record Macro button opens the Record Macro dialog box, which you use to start recording a macro.

The **macro security settings** control what Excel will do about macros in a workbook when you open that workbook. You can set the level of macro security.

In the Record Macro dialog box, you specify a name, shortcut key, location, and description of the macro.

A macro button runs the assigned macro when clicked. Placing a macro button on the worksheet makes it easier for a user to run the macro.

The macro recorder, which you can turn on with this button, records keystrokes and mouse actions as you perform them.

Record Macro

Macro name:
PDFReceipt

Shortcut key:
Ctrl+ r

Store macro in:
This Workbook

Description:
Created 12/1/2016. Save receipt area: range A18:F37 as a PDF file

OK   Cancel

Create PDF Receipt   Transfer Data

Working with Macros

You can customize the ribbon by showing or hiding tabs. You need to show the DEVELOPER tab to create macros.

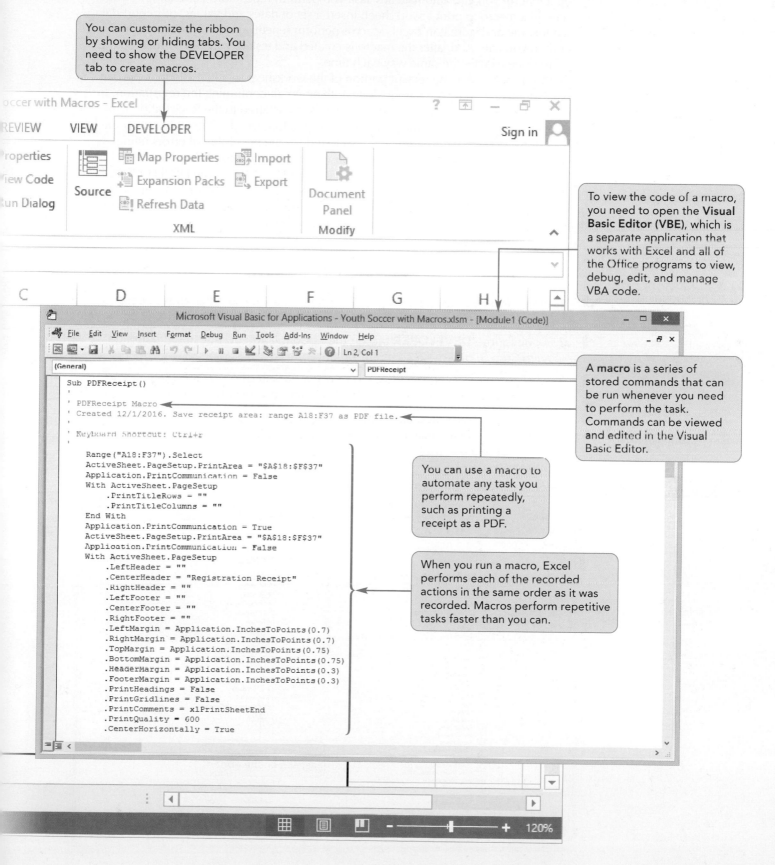

To view the code of a macro, you need to open the **Visual Basic Editor (VBE)**, which is a separate application that works with Excel and all of the Office programs to view, debug, edit, and manage VBA code.

A **macro** is a series of stored commands that can be run whenever you need to perform the task. Commands can be viewed and edited in the Visual Basic Editor.

You can use a macro to automate any task you perform repeatedly, such as printing a receipt as a PDF.

When you run a macro, Excel performs each of the recorded actions in the same order as it was recorded. Macros perform repetitive tasks faster than you can.

```
Sub PDFReceipt()
'
' PDFReceipt Macro
' Created 12/1/2016. Save receipt area: range A18:F37 as PDF file.
'
' Keyboard Shortcut: Ctrl+r
'
    Range("A18:F37").Select
    ActiveSheet.PageSetup.PrintArea = "$A$18:$F$37"
    Application.PrintCommunication = False
    With ActiveSheet.PageSetup
        .PrintTitleRows = ""
        .PrintTitleColumns = ""
    End With
    Application.PrintCommunication = True
    ActiveSheet.PageSetup.PrintArea = "$A$18:$F$37"
    Application.PrintCommunication = False
    With ActiveSheet.PageSetup
        .LeftHeader = ""
        .CenterHeader = "Registration Receipt"
        .RightHeader = ""
        .LeftFooter = ""
        .CenterFooter = ""
        .RightFooter = ""
        .LeftMargin = Application.InchesToPoints(0.7)
        .RightMargin = Application.InchesToPoints(0.7)
        .TopMargin = Application.InchesToPoints(0.75)
        .BottomMargin = Application.InchesToPoints(0.75)
        .HeaderMargin = Application.InchesToPoints(0.3)
        .FooterMargin = Application.InchesToPoints(0.3)
        .PrintHeadings = False
        .PrintGridlines = False
        .PrintComments = xlPrintSheetEnd
        .PrintQuality = 600
        .CenterHorizontally = True
```

Automating Tasks with Macros

Using a macro, you can automate any task you perform repeatedly. For example, you can create a macro to print a worksheet, insert a set of dates and values, or import data from a text file and store it in Excel. Macros perform repetitive tasks consistently and faster than you can. And, after the macro is created and tested, you can be assured the tasks are done exactly the same way each time.

Sharon wants to save the receipt portion of the worksheet as a PDF file that she can send as an attachment to the parent along with an email confirming the registration. In addition, Sharon wants data from the receipt to be transferred to the Registration Data worksheet. Sharon wants to simplify these tasks so volunteers don't need to repeat the same actions for each registration, and also to reduce the possibility of errors being introduced during the repetitive process. You will create a macro for each action.

To create and run macros, you need to use the DEVELOPER tab. The DEVELOPER tab has five groups—one for code, one for add-ins, one for controls, one for XML, and one to modify document controls. You'll use the Code group when working with macros. By default, the DEVELOPER tab is not displayed on the ribbon, so you'll display it.

To display the DEVELOPER tab on the ribbon:

1. If you took a break after the previous session, make sure the Youth Soccer workbook is open and the Receipt worksheet is active.

2. Look for the **DEVELOPER** tab on the ribbon. If you do not see it, continue with Step 3; otherwise continue with Step 7.

TIP

You can also right-click the ribbon and click Customize the Ribbon on the shortcut menu to add a ribbon tab.

3. On the ribbon, click the **FILE** tab to open Backstage view, and then click **Options** in the navigation bar. The Excel Options dialog box opens.

4. In the left pane, click **Customize Ribbon**. The different commands and tabs you can add and remove from the ribbon are displayed. See Figure 7-29.

Figure 7-29 | **Customize the Ribbon options in the Excel Options dialog box**

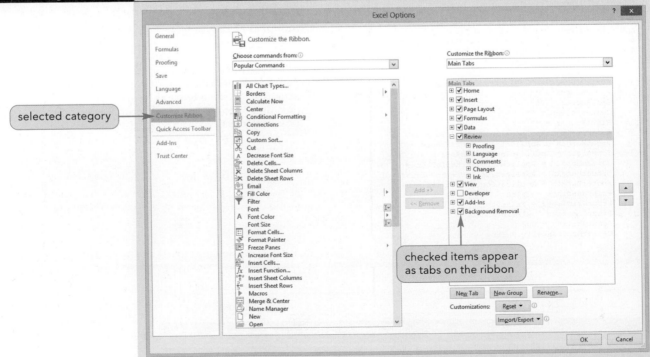

5. In the right pane, click the **Developer** check box to insert a checkmark.

6. Click the **OK** button. The DEVELOPER tab appears on the ribbon.

7. On the ribbon, click the **DEVELOPER** tab. See Figure 7-30.

Figure 7-30   DEVELOPER tab on the ribbon

tab added to the ribbon

Protecting Against Macro Viruses

Viruses can be and have been attached as macros to files created in Excel and other Office programs. A **virus** is a computer program designed to copy itself into other programs with the intention of causing mischief or harm. When unsuspecting users open these infected workbooks, Excel automatically runs the attached virus-infected macro. **Macro viruses** are a type of virus that uses a program's own macro programming language to distribute the virus. Macro viruses can be destructive and can modify or delete files that may not be recoverable. Because it is possible for a macro to contain a virus, Microsoft Office 2013 provides several options from which you can choose to set a security level you feel comfortable with.

Macro Security Settings

The macro security settings control what Excel will do about macros in a workbook when you open that workbook. For example, one user may choose to run macros only if they are "digitally signed" by a developer who is on a list of trusted sources. Another user might want to disable all macros in workbooks and see a notification when a workbook contains macros. The user can then elect to enable the macros. Excel has four macro security settings, which are described in Figure 7-31.

Figure 7-31   Macro security settings

Setting	Description
Disable all macros without notification	All macros in all workbooks are disabled and no security alerts about macros are displayed. Use this setting if you don't want macros to run.
Disable all macros with notification	All macros in all workbooks are disabled, but security alerts appear when the workbook contains a macro. Use this default setting to choose on a case-by-case basis whether to run a macro.
Disable all macros except digitally signed macros	The same as the "Disable all macros with notification" setting except any macro signed by a trusted publisher runs if you have already trusted the publisher. Otherwise, security alerts appear when a workbook contains a macro.
Enable all macros	All macros in all workbooks run. Use this setting temporarily in such cases as when developing an application that contains macros. This setting is not recommended for regular use.

You set macro security in the Trust Center. The **Trust Center** is a central location for all of the security settings in Office. By default, all potentially dangerous content, such as macros and workbooks with external links, is blocked without warning. If content is blocked, the Message Bar (also called the trust bar) opens below the ribbon, notifying you that some content was disabled. You can click the Message Bar to enable that content.

You can place files you consider trustworthy in locations you specify; the file paths of these locations are stored as Trusted Locations in the Trust Center. Any workbook opened from a trusted location is considered safe, and content such as macros will work without the user having to respond to additional security questions in order to use the workbook.

Setting Macro Security in Excel

- On the DEVELOPER tab, in the Code group, click the Macro Security button.
- Click the option button for the macro setting you want.
- Click the OK button.

or

- Click the FILE tab, and then click Options in the navigation bar (or right-click the ribbon, and then click Customize the Ribbon on the shortcut menu).
- Click the Trust Center category, and then click the Trust Center Settings button.
- Click the Macro Settings category, and then click the option button for a macro setting.
- Click the OK button.

Sharon wants the workbook to have some protection against macro viruses, so she asks you to set the security level to "Disable all macros with notification." When you open a file with macros, this macro security level disables the macros and displays a security alert, allowing you to enable the macros if you believe the workbook comes from a trusted source. After the macros are enabled, you can run them.

To set the macro security level:

1. On the DEVELOPER tab, in the Code group, click the **Macro Security** button. The Trust Center dialog box opens with the Macro Settings category displayed.

2. In the Macro Settings section, click the **Disable all macros with notification** option button if it is not already selected. See Figure 7-32.

Figure 7-32   **Macro Settings in the Trust Center dialog box**

selected macro security level

Macro Settings selected

3. Click the **OK** button.

Each time you open a workbook that contains a macro detected by the Trust Center, the macro is disabled and a Message Bar containing the Security Warning that macros have been disabled appears below the ribbon. If you developed the workbook or trust the person who sent you the workbook, click the Enable Content button to run the macros in the workbook. If you do not click the Enable Content button, you cannot run the macros in the workbook, but you can use the rest of the workbook.

INSIGHT

Using Digital Signatures with Macros

A **digital signature** is like a seal of approval. It is often used to identify the author of a workbook that contains macros. You add a digital signature as the last step before you distribute a file. Before you can add a digital signature to a workbook, you need to obtain a digital ID (also called a digital certificate) that proves your identity. Digital certificates are typically issued by a certificate authority. After you have a digital certificate, do the following to digitally sign a workbook:

- On the ribbon, click the FILE tab, and then, in the navigation bar, click Info.
- On the Info screen, click the Protect Workbook button, and then click Add a Digital Signature.
- If a dialog box opens asking if you would like to get a digital ID from a Microsoft Partner, click the Yes button. Your browser opens to a website with information about digital signature providers and available digital IDs.
- Read the information.
- Select a provider and follow the steps to obtain a digital ID from that provider.

By digitally signing a workbook that contains a macro you intend to publicly distribute, you assure others (1) of the identity of the creator of the macro; and (2) that the macro has not been altered since the digital signature was created. When you open a digitally signed file, you can see who the author is, and decide whether the information in the file is authentic and whether you trust that the macros in the workbook are safe to run.

The digital signature is removed any time a file with a digital signature is saved. This ensures that no one (including the original workbook author) can open a digitally signed file, make changes to the workbook, save the workbook, and then send the file to another user with the digital signature intact.

Recording a Macro

You can create an Excel macro in one of two ways: You can use the macro recorder to record keystrokes and mouse actions as you perform them, or you can enter a series of commands in the **Visual Basic for Applications (VBA)** programming language. The macro recorder can record only those actions you perform with the keyboard or mouse. The macro recorder is a good choice for creating simple macros. For more sophisticated macros, you might need to write VBA code directly in the Visual Basic Editor (VBE).

For Sharon's application, the actions you need to perform can all be done with the keyboard and the mouse, so you will use the macro recorder to record the two macros. One macro will save the receipt as a PDF file, which is a file format created by Adobe Systems for document exchange. The second macro will transfer data from the Receipt worksheet to the Registration Data worksheet.

PROSKILLS

Decision Making: Planning and Recording a Macro

Advance planning and practice help to ensure you create an error-free macro. First, decide what you want to accomplish. Then, consider the best way to achieve those results. Next, practice the keystrokes and mouse actions before you actually record the macro. This may seem like extra work, but it reduces the chance of error when you actually record the macro. As you set up the macro, consider the following:

- Choose a descriptive name that helps you recognize the macro's purpose.
- Weigh the benefits of selecting a shortcut key against its drawbacks. Although a shortcut key is an easy way to run a macro, you are limited to one-letter shortcuts, which can make it difficult to remember the purpose of each shortcut key. In addition, the macro shortcut keys will override the standard Office shortcuts for the workbook.
- Store the macro with the current workbook unless the macro can be used with other workbooks.
- Include a description that provides an overview of the macro and perhaps your name and contact information.

Good decision making includes thinking about what to do and what not to do as you progress to your goals. This is true when developing a macro as well.

Each macro must have a unique name that begins with a letter. The macro name can contain up to 255 characters, including letters, numbers, and the underscore symbol. The macro name cannot include spaces or special characters. It is helpful to use a descriptive name that describes the macro's purpose.

Macro shortcut keys are used to run a macro directly from the keyboard. You can assign a shortcut key to run the macro by selecting the Ctrl key plus a letter or the Ctrl+Shift keys plus a letter. If you use the same set of shortcut keys that are already assigned to a default Excel shortcut, the new shortcut you create overrides the default Excel shortcut for the open workbook. For example, using the Ctrl+p keys to run a macro overrides the default Excel 2013 shortcut for opening the Print screen while the workbook containing the macro is open. Some people find macro shortcut keys a quick way to run a macro; others dislike them because they override the original function of the shortcut key. It's a personal preference.

A macro needs to be stored somewhere. By default, the macro is stored in the current workbook, making the macro available in only that workbook when it is open. Another option is to store the macro in the **Personal Macro workbook**, a hidden workbook named PERSONAL.xlsb that opens whenever you start Excel, making the macro available any time you use Excel. The Personal Macro workbook stores commonly used macros that apply to many workbooks. It is most convenient for users on stand-alone computers. Finally, you can store the macro in a new workbook. Keep in mind that the new workbook must be open in order to use the macro. For example, an accountant might store a set of macros that help with end-of-the-month tasks in a separate workbook.

You can also add a description of the macro to briefly explain what it does. The description can also include the name of the person to contact and the date it was created.

REFERENCE

Recording a Macro

- On the DEVELOPER tab, in the Code group, click the Record Macro button.
- Enter a name for the macro.
- Specify a shortcut key (optional).
- Specify the location to store the macro.
- Enter a description of the macro (optional).
- Click the OK button to start the macro recorder.
- Perform the tasks you want to automate.
- Click the Stop Recording button.

Sharon provided you with the following outline of the actions needed for the macro to save the receipt as a PDF file:

1. Set the range A18:F37 as the print area for the Registration Receipt.
2. Create the custom header "Registration Receipt" centered horizontally on the page.
3. Create the PDF file and name it "Receipt."
4. Remove the custom header and horizontal centering from the page.
5. Remove the print area.
6. Make cell A1 the active cell.

You'll record the steps for this macro using a macro named PDFReceipt that is assigned a keyboard shortcut, has a description, and is stored in the Youth Soccer workbook. Practice these steps before recording the macro. Once you feel comfortable with the steps, you can start the macro recorder.

To start the macro recorder:

Save the workbook before recording a macro in case you make a mistake and need to restart.

1. Save the Youth Soccer workbook. If you make a mistake when recording the macro, you can close the workbook without saving, reopen the workbook, and then record the macro again.

2. On the DEVELOPER tab, in the Code group, click the **Record Macro** button. The Record Macro dialog box opens. The Macro name box displays a default name for the macro that consists of the word "Macro" followed by a number that is one greater than the number of macros already recorded in the workbook during the current Excel session. See Figure 7-33.

Figure 7-33   Record Macro dialog box

enter a descriptive macro name

select the location to store the macro

enter a description of the macro (optional)

enter a shortcut key (optional)

3. In the Macro name box, type **PDFReceipt** to change the selected default name to a more descriptive one, and then press the **Tab** key.

4. In the Shortcut key box, type **r** to set the Ctrl+r keys as the shortcut to run the macro from the keyboard, and then press the **Tab** key.

5. Verify that the Store macro in box is set to **This Workbook** to store the macro in the Youth Soccer workbook, and then press the **Tab** key.

6. In the Description box, type **Created 12/1/2016. Save receipt area, range A18:F37, as PDF file.** to enter notes about the macro.

7. Click the **OK** button. The workbook enters macro record mode. The Record Macro button changes to the Stop Recording button, which also appears on the status bar.

From this point on, *every* mouse click and keystroke you perform will be recorded and stored as part of the PDFReceipt macro. For that reason, it is very important to follow the instructions in the next steps precisely. Take your time as you perform each step, reading the entire step carefully first. After you finish recording the keystrokes, click the Stop Recording button to turn off the macro recorder.

To record the PDFReceipt macro:

1. Select the range **A18:F37**. This range contains the receipt that you want to print.

2. On the ribbon, click the **PAGE LAYOUT** tab.

3. In the Page Setup group, click the **Print Area** button, and then click **Set Print Area**. The receipt is set as the print area. Next, you'll insert a custom header.

4. In the Page Setup group, click the **Dialog Box Launcher** to open the Page Setup dialog box.

5. Click the **Header/Footer** tab, and then click the **Custom Header** button to open the Header dialog box.

6. Click in the **Center section** box, type **Registration Receipt**, and then click the **OK** button to close the Header dialog box.

7. In the Page Setup dialog box, click the **Margins** tab, click the **Horizontally** check box to select it, and then click the **OK** button. The receipt is centered on the page.

8. On the ribbon, click the **FILE** tab to open Backstage view, and then click **Export** in the navigation bar.

9. On the Export screen, make sure **Create PDF/XPS Document** is selected in the left pane, and then click the **Create PDF/XPS** button in the right pane. The Publish as PDF or XPS dialog box opens, which is similar to the Save As dialog box.

10. In the File name box, type **Receipt** to replace the suggested filename.

11. Make sure the folder is set to the location specified by your instructor.

12. Click the **Publish** button. The receipt is saved as a PDF file, and automatically opens in Adobe Reader or Adobe Acrobat, depending on which program is installed on your computer.

   Trouble? If the receipt doesn't open, you probably don't have Adobe Reader or Adobe Acrobat installed on your computer. Continue with Step 14.

▶ **13.** Close the PDF file. You should now see the Receipt worksheet in the Youth Soccer workbook.

▶ **14.** On the PAGE LAYOUT tab, in the Page Setup group, click the **Print Area** button, and then click **Clear Print Area**.

▶ **15.** In the Page Setup group, click the **Dialog Box Launcher** to open the Page Setup dialog box, click the **Header/Footer** tab, and then click the **Custom Header** button to open the Header dialog box.

▶ **16.** Click in the **Center section** box, delete the custom header, and then click the **OK** button to close the Header dialog box.

▶ **17.** In the Page Setup dialog box, click the **Margins** tab, click the **Horizontally** check box so that the printout is no longer centered on the page, and then click the **OK** button.

▶ **18.** In the Receipt worksheet, click cell **A1**.

You have completed all of the steps in the PDFReceipt macro. You'll turn off the macro recorder.

Be sure to turn off the macro recorder; otherwise, you'll continue to record your keystrokes and mouse clicks, leading to unintended consequences.

▶ **19.** Click the **Stop Recording** button ☐ on the status bar. The macro recorder turns off, and the button changes to the Record Macro button.

Trouble? If you made a mistake while recording the macro, close the Youth Soccer workbook without saving. If you got past the creation of the Registration Receipt, you will need to delete the Receipt file that you created.

Reopen the workbook, and then repeat all of the steps beginning with the "To start the macro recorder" steps.

Be aware that the process for saving a workbook that contains a macro is different from saving one that does not contain a macro. If you need to save the workbook before you complete this session, refer to the "Saving a Workbook with Macros" section later in this session.

Running a Macro

After you record a macro, you should run it to test whether it works as intended. Running a macro means Excel performs each of the steps in the same order as when it was recorded. To run the macro you created, you can either use the shortcut key you specified or select the macro in the Macro dialog box. The Macro dialog box lists all of the macros in the open workbooks. From this dialog box, you can select and run a macro, edit the macro with VBA, run the macro one step at a time so you can determine in which step an error occurs, or delete it.

REFERENCE

Running a Macro

• Press the shortcut key assigned to the macro.

or

• On the DEVELOPER tab, in the Code group, click the Macros button.
• Select the macro from the list of macros.
• Click the Run button.

You will test the PDFReceipt macro by running it.

To run the PDFReceipt macro:

▶ **1.** On the ribbon, click the **DEVELOPER** tab.

▶ **2.** In the Code group, click the **Macros** button. The Macro dialog box opens, listing all of the macros in the open workbooks. See Figure 7-34.

Figure 7-34 ▶ **Macro dialog box**

all macros in the workbooks open on your computer are listed

runs the selected macro

opens VBE so you can edit the selected macro

deletes the selected macro

▶ **3.** Verify that **PDFReceipt** is selected in the Macro name box, and then click the **Run** button. The PDFReceipt macro runs. The receipt is saved as a PDF file and the file is opened in Adobe Reader or Adobe Acrobat.

▶ **4.** Close Adobe Reader or Adobe Acrobat. No print area is selected, and cell A1 is the active cell in the Receipt worksheet.

Trouble? If the PDFReceipt macro did not run properly, you might have made a mistake in the steps while recording the macro. On the DEVELOPER tab, in the Code group, click the Macros button. Select the PDFReceipt macro, and then click the Delete button. Click the OK button to confirm the deletion, and then repeat all of the steps beginning with the "To start the macro recorder" steps.

Next, you will test the shortcut keys you used for the PDFReceipt macro.

▶ **5.** Press the **Ctrl+r** keys. The PDFReceipt macro runs. The receipt is saved as a PDF file. No print area is selected, and cell A1 in the Receipt worksheet is the active cell.

▶ **6.** Close Adobe Reader or Adobe Acrobat.

Trouble? If your macro doesn't end on its own, you need to end it. Press the Ctrl+Break keys to stop the macro from running.

The macro works as expected, printing the receipt as a PDF file.

How Edits Can Affect Macros

Be careful when making seemingly small changes to a workbook, as these can have a great impact on macros. If a run-time error (an error that occurs while running a macro) appears when you run a macro that has worked in the past, some part of the macro code no longer makes sense to Excel. For example, simply adding a space to a worksheet name can affect a macro that references the worksheet. If you recorded a macro that referenced a worksheet named RegistrationData (no spaces in the name) that you later changed to Registration Data (space added to the name), the macro no longer works because the RegistrationData worksheet no longer exists. You could record the macro again, or you could edit the macro in VBA by changing RegistrationData to Registration Data.

Creating the TransferData Macro

You need to record one more macro. The data you entered earlier in the input section of the Receipt worksheet was never added to the Registration Data worksheet. Sharon wants to add this data to the next available blank row in the Registration Data worksheet. You'll record another macro to do this. You may want to practice the following steps before recording the macro:

1. Go to the Registration Data worksheet.
2. Turn off worksheet protection in the Registration Data worksheet.
3. Switch to the Receipt worksheet.
4. Select and copy the Transfer Area to the Clipboard.
5. Go to the Registration Data worksheet.
6. Go to cell A1, and then go to the last row in the Registration Data area.
7. Turn on Use Relative References. The Use Relative Reference button controls how Excel records the act of selecting a range in the worksheet. By default, the macro will select the same cells regardless of which cell is first selected because the macro records a selection using absolute cell references. If you want a macro to select cells regardless of the position of the active cell when you run the macro, set the macro recorder to record relative cell references.
8. Move down one row.
9. Turn off Use Relative References.
10. Paste values to the Registration Data worksheet.
11. Go to cell A1.
12. Turn on worksheet protection.
13. Switch to the Receipt worksheet, and then make cell B3 the active cell.

You may want to practice these steps before recording the macro. Sharon wants you to name this new macro "TransferData" and assign the Ctrl+t keys as the shortcut.

To record the TransferData macro:

1. Click the **Record Macro** button 🔲 on the status bar to open the Record Macro dialog box, type **TransferData** in the Macro name box, type **t** in the Shortcut key box, type **Created 12/1/2016. Copy values in the transfer area in the Receipt worksheet to the Registration Data worksheet.** in the Description box, and then click the **OK** button. The macro recorder is on.

2. Go to the **Registration Data** worksheet.

3. Click the **REVIEW** tab on the ribbon, and then click the **Unprotect Sheet** button in the Changes group to turn off protection.

4. Go to the **Receipt** worksheet, and then select the range **A40:F40** in the Transfer Area.

5. Click the **HOME** tab on the ribbon, and then click the **Copy** button in the Clipboard group.

6. Click the **Registration Data** sheet tab, click cell **A1**, and then press the **Ctrl+↓** keys to go to the last row with values.

7. Click the **DEVELOPER** tab on the ribbon.

8. In the Code group, click the **Use Relative References** button. Relative references ensure that the receipt data being transferred is inserted in the next blank row (in this case, row 3) and not always in row 3 in the Registration Data worksheet.

9. Press the **↓** key to move to the first blank cell in the worksheet.

10. On the DEVELOPER tab, in the Code group, click the **Use Relative References** button. The Use Relative References button is toggled off.

11. On the ribbon, click the **HOME** tab.

12. In the Clipboard group, click the **Paste button arrow**, and then click the **Values** button 🗋 in the Paste Values section. This option pastes the values rather than the formulas from the Transfer Area.

   Trouble? If #REF! appears in row 3 of the Registration Data worksheet, you clicked the Paste button instead of the Paste Values button. Stop the macro recorder. Delete the macro and begin recording the macro again.

13. Click cell **A1**, and then click the **REVIEW** tab on the ribbon.

14. In the Changes group, click the **Protect Sheet** button. The Protect Sheet dialog box opens.

15. In the Protect Sheet dialog box, click the **OK** button.

16. Click the **Receipt** sheet tab, and then click cell **B3**.

TIP
You can also turn off the macro recorder by clicking the Stop Recording button in the Code group on the DEVELOPER tab.

17. Click the **Stop Recording** button ☐ on the status bar. The macro recorder turns off, and the button changes to the Record Macro button.

You have completed recording the TransferData macro. Next, you'll test whether it works. Sharon has a new registration to add to the worksheet. You'll enter this data as you test the TransferData macro.

To test the TransferData macro:

1. Enter the following data into the range B3:B12, pressing the **Enter** key after each entry:

   12/01/2016

   Jason

   U10

   XL

   XT

   No

   Sofia Kilmer

   294 Hott Street

> **Moorefield, WV 26836**
>
> **304-555-3444**
>
> ▶ **2.** Press the **Ctrl+t** keys. The TransferData macro runs, and the data transfers to the Registration Data worksheet.
>
> ▶ **3.** Go to the **Registration Data** worksheet, and then verify that the data for Sofia Kilmer appears in row 4.
>
> ▶ **4.** Go to the **Receipt** worksheet.

The TransferData macro makes it easy for the entered data to be transferred to the Registration Data worksheet.

Fixing Macro Errors

If a macro does not work correctly, you can fix it. Sometimes you'll find a mistake when you test a macro you just created. Other times you might not discover that error until later. No matter when you find an error in a macro, you have the following options:

- Rerecord the macro using the same macro name.
- Delete the recorded macro, and then record the macro again.
- Run the macro one step at a time to locate the problem, and then use one of the previous methods to correct the problem.

You can delete or edit a macro by opening the Macro dialog box (shown earlier in Figure 7-34), selecting the macro from the list, and then clicking the appropriate button. To rerecord the macro, simply restart the macro recorder and enter the same macro name you used earlier. Excel overwrites the previous version of the macro.

Working with the Visual Basic Editor

To view the code of a macro, you need to open the Visual Basic Editor, which is a separate application that works with Excel and all of the Office programs to view, debug, edit, and manage VBA code. The VBE consists of several components, including the Code window that contains the VBA code, the Project Explorer window that displays a tree-like diagram consisting of every open workbook, and a menu bar with menus of commands you use to edit, debug, and run VBA statements. You can access the Visual Basic Editor through the Macro dialog box or the Visual Basic button in the Code group on the DEVELOPER tab.

REFERENCE

Editing a Macro

- On the DEVELOPER tab, in the Code group, click the Macros button, select the macro in the Macro name list, and then click the Edit button (or on the DEVELOPER tab, in the Code group, click the Visual Basic button).
- Use the Visual Basic Editor to edit the macro code.
- Click File on the menu bar, and then click Close and Return to Microsoft Excel.

Sharon wants the PDFReceipt macro to stop in cell B3 of the Receipt worksheet. Right now, the macro stops with cell A1 selected. Although you can delete the PDFReceipt macro and record it again, it is simpler to edit the existing macro. You will edit the VBA command in the macro.

To view the code for the PDFReceipt macro:

1. On the ribbon, click the **DEVELOPER** tab.

2. In the Code group, click the **Macros** button. The Macro dialog box opens.

3. Click **PDFReceipt** in the Macro name list, and then click the **Edit** button. The Visual Basic Editor opens as a separate program, consisting of two windows—the Project Explorer and the Code window.

4. If the Code window is not maximized, click the **Maximize** button ☐ on the Code window title bar. The Code window contains the VBA code generated by the macro recorder. You will see the beginning of the PDFReceipt sub. See Figure 7-35 (your window may differ).

Figure 7-35   **Visual Basic for Applications Editor window**

Code window for Module1

Sub and the macro name indicate the first line of a macro

command to select the range A18:F37

command to set the center section of the header

command to make cell A1 the active cell

comments appear in green

End of sub

Trouble? If you see a different number of windows in the Visual Basic Editor, your computer is configured differently. You will be working with the Code window, so you can ignore any other windows.

Understanding the Structure of Macros

The VBA code in the Code window lists all of the actions you performed when recording the PDFReceipt macro. In VBA, macros are called **sub procedures**. Each sub procedure begins with the keyword *Sub* followed by the name of the sub procedure and a set of parentheses. In the example in Figure 7-35, the code begins with

```
Sub PDFReceipt()
```

which provides the name of this sub procedure—PDFReceipt—the name you gave the macro. The parentheses are used to include any arguments in the procedure. These arguments pass information to the sub procedure and have roughly the same purpose as the arguments in an Excel function. If you write your own VBA code, sub procedure arguments are an important part of the programming process. However, they are not used when you create macros with the macro recorder.

Following the `Sub PDFReceipt()` statement are comments about the macro taken from the macro name, shortcut key, and description you entered in the Record Macro dialog box. Each line appears in green and is preceded by an apostrophe ('). The apostrophe indicates that the line is a comment and does not include any actions Excel needs to perform.

After the comments is the body of the macro, a listing of all of the commands performed by the PDFReceipt macro as written in the VBA language. Your list of commands might look slightly different, depending on the exact actions you performed when recording the macro. Even though you might not know VBA, some of the commands are easy to interpret. For example, near the top of the PDFReceipt macro, you should see the command:

```
Range("A18:F37").Select
```

which tells Excel to select the range A18:F37. Several lines below this command you see the following command, which sets the words "Registration Receipt" at the top of the print page in the center of the custom header:

```
.CenterHeader = "Registration Receipt"
```

At the bottom of the macro is the following statement, which indicates the end of the PDFReceipt sub procedure:

```
End Sub
```

A Code window can contain several sub procedures, with each procedure separated from the others by the `SubProcedureName()` statement at the beginning, and the End Sub statement at the end. Sub procedures are organized into **modules**. As was shown in Figure 7-35, all of the macros that have been recorded are stored in the Module1 module (your window may differ).

Editing a Macro Using the Visual Basic Editor

The Visual Basic Editor provides tools to assist you in writing error-free code. As you type a command, the editor will provide pop-up windows and text to help you insert the correct code.

Sharon wants you to edit the following command in the PDFReceipt sub procedure, which sets the active cell to cell A1:

```
Range("A1").Select
```

You'll change the command to

```
Range("B3").Select
```

to change the active cell from cell A1 to cell B3.

To edit a command in the macro:

1. Scroll down the Code window to the line immediately before End Sub in the PDFReceipt macro.

2. In the line with the command Range("A1"), select **A1**, and then type **B3**. The command in the macro is edited to select a different cell. See Figure 7-36.

Figure 7-36　　Edited Macro

```
            .FirstPage.RightHeader.Text = ""
            .FirstPage.LeftFooter.Text = ""
            .FirstPage.CenterFooter.Text = ""
            .FirstPage.RightFooter.Text = ""
        End With
        Application.PrintCommunication = True
        ActiveWindow.SmallScroll Down:=-18
        Range("B3").Select
    End Sub
    Sub TransferData()
    '
    ' TransferData Macro
    ' Recorded 12/1/2016. Copy values in the transfer area in the Receipt worksheet to the Registration
    '
    ' Keyboard Shortcut: Ctrl+t
    '
        Sheets("Registration Data").Select
        ActiveSheet.Unprotect
        Sheets("Receipt").Select
        ActiveWindow.SmallScroll Down:=24
        Range("A40:F40").Select
        Selection.Copy
```

cell reference changed from A1 to B3

---

3. On the menu bar, click **File**, and then click **Close and Return to Microsoft Excel**. The Visual Basic Editor closes, and the Youth Soccer workbook is displayed.

Sharon wants you to test the macro. You'll check to see whether cell B3 is the active cell once the macro has run.

To test the edited PDFReceipt macro:

1. Press the **Ctrl+r** keys. The PDFReceipt macro runs.

   Trouble? If a Microsoft Visual Basic message box appears with a run-time error, click the End button, click the Macros button, click PDFReceipt in the Macro name box, and then click the Edit button. In the Code window, find the line you edited (one line above End Sub), and then change it to Range("B3").Select. On the menu bar, click File, and then click Close and Return to Microsoft Excel.

2. Close Adobe Reader. Cell B3 is the active cell.

Creating Macro Buttons

Another way to run a macro is to assign it to a button placed directly in the worksheet. Macro buttons are often a better way to run macros than shortcut keys. Clicking a button (with a descriptive label) is often more intuitive and simpler for users than trying to remember different combinations of keystrokes.

REFERENCE

Creating a Macro Button

- On the DEVELOPER tab, in the Controls group, click the Insert button.
- In the Form Controls section, click the Button (Form Control) button.
- Click the worksheet where you want the macro button to be located, drag the pointer until the button is the size and shape you want, and then release the mouse button.
- In the Assign Macro dialog box, select the macro you want to assign to the button.
- With the button still selected, type a new label.

Sharon wants you to add two macro buttons to the Receipt worksheet—one for each of the macros you've created. You will create the macro buttons in the blank range A14:B16 so they don't obscure any existing data.

To insert a macro button in the worksheet:

1. Scroll so that the range **A14:B16** of the Receipt worksheet is completely visible.

2. On the DEVELOPER tab, in the Controls group, click the **Insert** button. The Form Controls appear, with a variety of objects that can be placed in the worksheet. You'll insert the Button form control. See Figure 7-37.

Figure 7-37   **Form Controls**

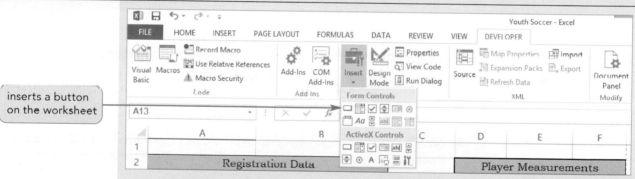

inserts a button on the worksheet

Trouble? If the Insert button is unavailable, the worksheet is protected. Click the REVIEW tab. In the Changes group, click the Unprotect Sheet button to unprotect the Receipt worksheet, and then repeat Step 2.

3. In the Form Controls section, click the **Button (Form Control)** button □, and then point to cell **A14**. The pointer changes to **+**.

4. Click and drag the pointer over the range **A14:A16**, and then release the mouse button. A button appears on the worksheet. The Assign Macro dialog box opens with the button's default name in the Macro name box. See Figure 7-38.

Figure 7-38   Assign Macro dialog box

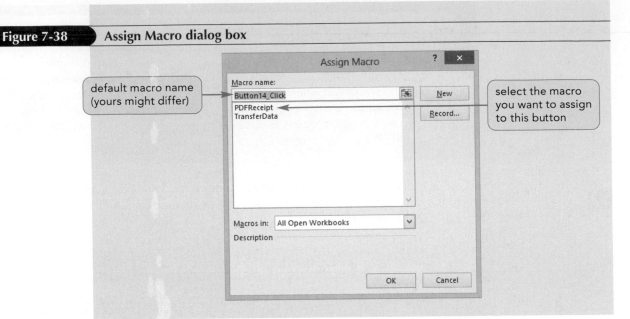

From the Assign Macro dialog box, you can assign a macro to the button. After you assign a macro to the button, the button appears with a default label. You can change the default label to a descriptive one that will indicate which macro will run when the button is clicked.

Sharon wants you to assign the PDFReceipt macro to this new button, and then rename the button with a label that reflects the PDFReceipt macro.

To assign the PDFReceipt macro to the new button:

1. In the Macro name box, click **PDFReceipt**.

2. Click the **OK** button. The PDFReceipt macro is assigned to the selected button.

3. With the sizing handles still displayed around the button, type **Create PDF Receipt** (do not press the Enter key). The new label replaces the default label.

   Trouble? If no sizing handles appear around the button, the button is not selected. Right-click the button, click Edit Text to place the insertion point within the button, and then repeat Step 3.

   Trouble? If a new line appeared in the button, you pressed the Enter key after entering the label. Press the Backspace key to delete the line, and then continue with Step 4.

4. Click any cell in the worksheet to deselect the macro button.

At this point, if you click the Create PDF Receipt button, the PDFReceipt macro will run. Before you test the Create PDF Receipt button, you will add the other button.

To add another macro button to the Receipt worksheet:

1. On the DEVELOPER tab, in the Controls group, click the **Insert** button, and then click the **Button (Form Control)** button ▭.

2. Drag the pointer over the range **B14:B16**.

3. In the Assign Macro dialog box, click **TransferData** in the Macro name box, and then click the **OK** button.

4. Type **Transfer Data** as the button label, and then click any cell in the worksheet to deselect the button. See Figure 7-39.

TIP

To move or resize a macro button, right-click it, press the Esc key, and then drag a sizing handle or the selection box.

Figure 7-39   Macro buttons on Receipt worksheet

				Age Group	Shirt Size	Sock Size
3	Registration Date	12/1/2016		U4	XSM	XSH
4	Player Name	Jason		U5	SM	SH
5	Age Group	U10		U6	M	M
6	Shirt Size	XL		U7	L	T
7	Sock Size	XT		U8	XL	XT
8	Early Registration	No		U9		
9	Parent	Sofia Kilmer		U10		
10	Address	294 Hott Street				
11	City State Zip	Moorefield, WV 26836		Registration Fee/Discount		
12	Telephone	304-555-3444				
13				Season Fee		75
14				Discount Amount		5
15	Create PDF Receipt	Transfer Data				
16						
17						
10						

Documentation   Receipt   Registration Data   ⊕

READY

macro buttons added to the worksheet

Trouble? If the macro buttons on your screen do not match the size and location of the buttons shown in the figure, right-click a button to select it, press the Esc key to close the shortcut menu, and then resize or reposition the button on the worksheet as needed.

You have completed the application, so you will reset worksheet protection.

5. On the ribbon, click the **REVIEW** tab.

6. In the Changes group, click the **Protect Sheet** button. The Protect Sheet dialog box opens.

7. Click the **OK** button to turn on worksheet protection.

You have completed the Create PDF Receipt and TransferData macro buttons.

Creating a Macro Button with Pictures or Shapes

You are not restricted to using the control buttons on the DEVELOPER tab for macro buttons. A macro can also be assigned to a picture or shape. For example, sometimes you might want to assign to an arrow a macro that takes you to another worksheet.

1. On the INSERT tab, in the Illustrations group, click the button for the picture, online picture, or shape you want to use for a macro button.
2. Drag the pointer over the range where you want to insert the picture or shape on the worksheet.
3. Resize and position the picture or shape as needed.
4. Right-click the picture or shape, and then click Edit Text on the shortcut menu to add a name to the button.
5. Change the style, fill, and outline of the picture or shape as needed.
6. Right-click the picture or shape, and then click Assign Macro on the shortcut menu. The Assign Macro dialog box opens.
7. In the Macro name box, select the macro you want to assign to the button, and then click the OK button.

No matter what picture or shape you use for the macro button, the macro runs when the button is clicked.

Sharon has a new season registration to add to the worksheet. You'll enter this data and then test the Create PDF Receipt and TransferData macro buttons.

To test the macro buttons:

1. In the range **B3:B12**, enter the following subscriber order:

   12/2/2016

   Noah

   U8

   M

   M

   Yes

   Christopher Miller

   1231 Viking Avenue

   Wheeling, WV 26003

   304-555-8848

2. Click the **Create PDF Receipt** button to save the current receipt as a PDF file. See Figure 7-40.

Figure 7-40   PDF file created from the PDFReceipt macro

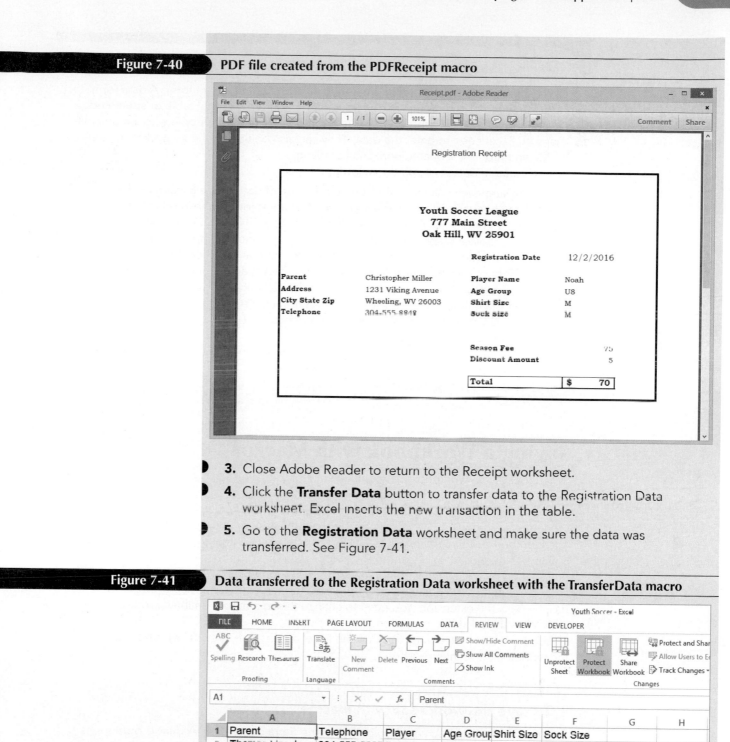

3. Close Adobe Reader to return to the Receipt worksheet.

4. Click the **Transfer Data** button to transfer data to the Registration Data worksheet. Excel inserts the new transaction in the table.

5. Go to the **Registration Data** worksheet and make sure the data was transferred. See Figure 7-41.

Figure 7-41   Data transferred to the Registration Data worksheet with the TransferData macro

new record inserted

The macro buttons make it simpler to create the receipt and transfer the data from the Receipt worksheet into the Registration Data worksheet.

Making Data Entry Easier with a Data Form

When a lot of data needs to be entered, consider creating a data form. A data form is a dialog box that lists the labels and entry boxes from an Excel table or structured range of data in a worksheet. Data forms can be helpful when people who are unfamiliar with Excel need to enter the data. They can also be useful when a worksheet is very wide and requires repeated horizontal scrolling.

To create a data form, do the following:

1. Make sure each column in the structured range of data or the Excel table has column headers. These headers become the labels for each field on the form.
2. Add the Form button to the Quick Access Toolbar. Click the Customize Quick Access Toolbar button, and then click More Commands. In the Quick Access Toolbars options, click the Choose commands from arrow, click Commands Not in the Ribbon, click the Form button in the box, click the Add button, and then click the OK button. The Form button appears on the Quick Access Toolbar.
3. Select the range or table for which you want to create the data form.
4. On the Quick Access Toolbar, click the Form button. The data form opens with the selected fields ready for data entry.
5. Enter data in each box, and then click the New button to add the complete record to end of the range or table and create a new record.
6. Click the Close button to close the data form.

Saving a Workbook with Macros

When you save a workbook that contains macros, a dialog box opens indicating that the workbook you are trying to save contains features that cannot be saved in a macro-free workbook. The default Excel workbook does not allow macros to be stored as part of the file. If you want to save the workbook without the macros, click the Yes button. The workbook will be saved as a macro-free workbook, which means the macros you created will be lost. If you want to save the workbook with the macros, click the No button, and then save the workbook as a new file—one that allows macros to be saved as part of the file. The default Excel Workbook format, which is a macro-free workbook, has the .xlsx file extension. You need to change this to a macro-enabled workbook, which has the .xlsm file extension.

You have completed your work on the Excel application, so you will save and close the workbook and then exit Excel.

To save the workbook with macros:

▶ **1.** On the Quick Access Toolbar, click the **Save** button 🔚. A dialog box opens indicating that the workbook you are trying to save contains features that cannot be saved in a macro-free workbook. See Figure 7-42.

Figure 7-42 Macro warning dialog box

2. Click the **No** button. The Save As dialog box opens so you can save the workbook as a macro-enabled workbook.

3. In the File name box, type **Youth Soccer with Macros** so you can easily determine which workbook contains macros.

4. Click the **Save as type** button, and then click **Excel Macro-Enabled Workbook**.

5. Navigate to the location where you saved the files you created in this tutorial.

6. Click the **Save** button. The workbook is saved with the macros.

7. Close the workbook.

Opening a Workbook with Macros

TIP

After you enable the content, the filename is added to a list of trusted files and the Security Warning will not reappear as long as the workbook name or location is not changed.

When you open a file with macros, Excel checks the opening workbook to see if it contains any macros. The response you see is based on the security level set on the computer. Earlier, you disabled all macros with notification. Therefore, all of the macros will be disabled when the workbook opens. When the workbook opens the first time, a SECURITY WARNING appears in the Message Bar providing the option to enable the macros so they can be run, or to open the workbook with the macros disabled. If you know a workbook contains macros that you or a coworker created, you can enable them, which adds the filename to a list of trusted files so that you won't see the SECURITY WARNING when you open this file again. If you do not click the Enable Content button, the macros remain disabled and unavailable during the current session, but the other features of the workbook are still available.

You'll open the Youth Soccer with Macros workbook and enable the macros.

To open the Youth Soccer with Macros workbook and enable the macros:

1. Open the **Youth Soccer with Macros** workbook. The workbook opens, and "SECURITY WARNING Macros have been disabled." appears in the Message Bar below the ribbon. See Figure 7-43.

Figure 7-43 **SECURITY WARNING in the Message Bar**

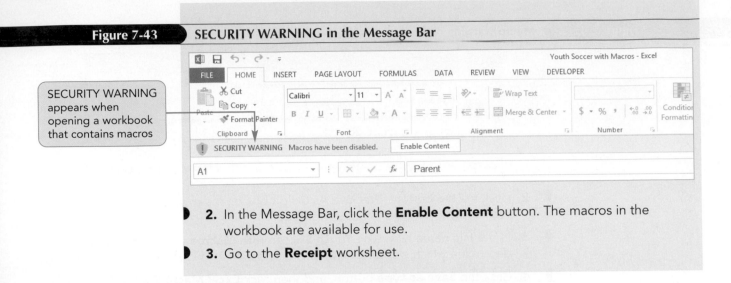

SECURITY WARNING appears when opening a workbook that contains macros

2. In the Message Bar, click the **Enable Content** button. The macros in the workbook are available for use.

3. Go to the **Receipt** worksheet.

Removing a Tab from the Ribbon

If you decide you don't want a tab displayed on the ribbon, you can remove it. Now that the macros are completed, Sharon doesn't need the DEVELOPER tab to appear on the ribbon. You will remove it.

To remove the DEVELOPER tab from the ribbon:

1. Right-click any tab on the ribbon, and then click **Customize the Ribbon** on the shortcut menu. The Excel Options dialog box opens with the Customize Ribbon options displayed.

2. In the right box listing the Main Tabs, click the **Developer** check box to remove the checkmark.

3. Click the **OK** button. The DEVELOPER tab is removed from the ribbon.

4. Save the workbook, and then close it.

Sharon is pleased with your work on the Youth Soccer workbook. The workbook protection and macros will streamline the data entry process for volunteers.

Session 7.3 Quick Check

REVIEW

1. Which tab must be displayed on the ribbon in order to record a macro?
2. What types of actions should you record as a macro?
3. Describe two ways of creating a macro.
4. What are the three places in which you can store a macro?
5. Identify two ways to run a macro.
6. What are the steps to edit a macro?
7. How do you insert a macro button into a worksheet?
8. What happens when you save a workbook with the .xlsx extension and it contains a macro?

Review Assignments

Data File needed for the Review Assignments: TBall.xlsx

You did such a good job helping Sharon with the Youth Soccer application that she recommended you to a friend, Terry Winkel, who has a similar project within the youth sports community. Terry wants to create a receipt system for the Youth T-Ball league. Complete the following:

1. Open the **TBall** workbook located in the Excel7 ▸ Review folder included with your Data Files, and then save the workbook as **Youth TBall** in the location specified by your instructor.
2. In the Documentation worksheet, enter your name and the date.
3. In the Receipt worksheet, do the following:
    a. Create defined names from selection using the range A3:B11 to name all of the input cells.
    b. Change the defined name Address to **Street Address**.
    c. Use the Name box to create the defined name **Player_Sizes** for the range D2:E8.
    d. Paste the list of defined names in the Documentation worksheet.
4. Create the validation rules shown in Figure 7-44 for the range B5:B7.

Figure 7-44   Validation rules for cells B5, B6, and B7

Cell	Settings	Input Message	Error Alert
B5	List Source (4YO, 5-6YO)	Title: Age Group Message: Click arrow to select the player's age group.	Style: Stop Title: Invalid Age Group Message: Invalid Age Group. Use arrow to select Age Group.
B6	List Source (D4:D8)	Title: Shirt Size Message: Click arrow to select shirt size.	Style: Stop Title: Invalid Shirt Size Message: Invalid Shirt Size. Use arrow to select Shirt Size.
B7	List Source (D4:D7)	Title: Hat Size Message: Click arrow to select hat size.	Style: Stop Title: Invalid Hat Size Message: Invalid Hat Size. Use arrow to select Hat Size.

© 2014 Cengage Learning

5. In the range B3:B11, enter the data shown in Figure 7-45.

Figure 7-45   Registration Data

Registration Date	12/1/2016
Player Name	Nicole
Age Group	5-6YO
Shirt Size	SM
Hat Size	SM
Parent	Jason Headley
Address	1154 Wallenberg Place
City State Zip	Oak Hill, WV 25901
Telephone	304-555-3456

© 2014 Cengage Learning

6. Enter the following formulas for the transfer area in the specified cells using the defined names you created earlier:

Cell A37: **=Parent**

Cell B37: **=Telephone**

Cell C37: **=Player_Name**

Cell D37: **=Age_Group**

Cell E27: **=Shirt_Size**

Cell F27: **=Hat_Size**

7. Unlock the input cells on the Receipt worksheet so that the user can enter data only in the range B3:B11.

8. Enter the following formulas in the specified cells to add information to the registration receipt:

Cell B26: **=Parent**

Cell B27: **=Street_Address**

Cell B28: **=City_State_Zip**

Cell B29: **=Telephone**

Cell E24: **=Registration_Date**

Cell E26: **=Player_Name**

Cell E27: **=Age_Group**

Cell E28: **=Shirt_Size**

Cell E29: **=Hat_Size**

9. In cell E33, enter a formula with an IF function. If the player is in the 4YO age group, the fee will be the value in cell E11; otherwise, it will be the value in cell E12.

10. Protect the Documentation and Registration Data worksheets so that the user cannot enter data. Do not use a password.

11. Add the DEVELOPER tab to the ribbon.

12. Save the workbook. If you have any trouble as you record the macros, you can close the workbook without saving, open the workbook that you saved, and start with Step 13.

13. Create a macro named **PDF_TBReceipt** with **Ctrl+r** as the shortcut key. Store the macro in the current workbook. Type **Created 12/1/2016. Save receipt area: range A17:F34 as PDF file.** as the description. Record the following steps to create the PDF_TBReceipt macro:

a. Make the Receipt worksheet the active sheet.

b. Select the range A17:F34 and set the range as the print area.

c. Open the Page Setup dialog box.

d. Type **T-Ball Registration Receipt** in the center pane of the custom header.

e. Export the worksheet to create a PDF/XPS document with the filename **Receipt** saved to the location specified by your instructor.

f. Close the PDF file.

g. Clear the print area.

h. In the Receipt worksheet, make cell B3 the active cell.

14. Remove worksheet protection from the Registration Data worksheet.

15. Create a macro named **TransferData** with **Ctrl+t** as the shortcut key. Store the macro in the current workbook. Type **Created 12/1/2016. Copy values in the transfer area of the Receipt worksheet to the Registration Data worksheet.** in the macro description. Record the following steps to create the TransferData macro:

a. Make the Receipt worksheet the active worksheet.

b. Select the transfer area and copy it to the Clipboard.

c. Go to the Registration Data worksheet.

d. Click cell A1, and then go to the last row with values. (Hint: Press the Ctrl+↓ keys.)

e. On the DEVELOPER tab, turn on Use Relative References located on the DEVELOPER tab.

f. Move down one row.

g. Turn off Use Relative References.

h. Paste values in the Registration Data worksheet.

i. Click cell A1.

j. Turn on Use worksheet protection.

k. Go to the Receipt worksheet, and then make cell B3 the active cell.

16. Create a macro named **ClearInput** with **Ctrl+i** as the shortcut key. Store the macro in the current workbook. Type **Created 12/1/2016. Clear the values in the input area, range B3:B11.** as the description. Record the following steps to create the ClearInput macro:

a. In the Receipt worksheet, select the range B3:B11, and then delete the data from those cells.

b. Make cell B3 the active cell.

17. Test each macro using the shortcut keys you assigned to it.

18. Create a macro button for each of the three macros, and place them between the Registration Data and the Receipt form on the Receipt worksheet. Assign the following labels to the macro buttons:

a. **Print PDF Receipt** for the PDF_TBReceipt macro button

b. **Transfer Data** for the TransferData macro button

c. **Clear Input** for the ClearInput macro button

(*Hint*: You may need to remove cell protection to create the buttons and then reset it.)

19. Remove the DEVELOPER tab from the ribbon.

20. Test the macro buttons. Save the workbook as **Youth TBall with Macros**, a macro-enabled workbook, and then close the workbook.

Case Problem 1

APPLY

Data File needed for this Case Problem: Study.xlsx

Greater Southern University   The administration and faculty of Greater Southern University in Harrodsburg, Kentucky, have started a study abroad program and want to collect data from students who have completed this study. A group of volunteers will contact the students who participated in the program to get their information and impressions of the program. Adam Anderson, the dean of instruction, has started to design a form to enter this information, but he needs your help. He wants you to set up data validation rules and table lookups, and record macros to enter the data. Complete the following:

1. Open the **Study** workbook located in the Excel7 ▶ Case1 folder included with your Data Files, and then save the workbook as **Study Abroad** in the location specified by your instructor.

2. In the Documentation worksheet, enter your name and the date.

3. In the Input worksheet, create defined names from selection using the range A2:B9 to name all of the input cells.

4. On the Data Tables worksheet, paste the list of defined names.

5. Create the validation rules shown in Figure 7-46 for the range B4:B9.

Figure 7-46   Validation rules for the range B4:B9

Cell	Validation	Input Message	Error Alert
B4	List Source (A2:A10 on Data Tables worksheet)	Title: Major Message: Click arrow to select major.	Type: Stop Title: Invalid Major Message: Invalid Major. Use arrow to select Major.
B5	Must be greater than or equal to 2012	Title: Year of Study Message: Enter a year of study greater than or equal to 2012 (the starting year of the program).	Type: Stop Title: Invalid Year of Study Message: Invalid Year of Study. Enter a year of study greater than or equal to 2012 (the starting year of the program).
B6	List Source (FA, SP, SU)	Title: Semester of Study Message: Click arrow to select semester of study.	Type: Stop Title: Invalid Semester of Study Message: Invalid Semester of Study. Use arrow to select Semester of Study.
B7	List Source (C2:C11 on Data Tables worksheet)	Title: Country Message: Click arrow to select country.	Type: Stop Title: Invalid Country Message: Invalid Country. Use arrow to select Country.
B8	List Source (Yes, No)	Title: Completed Message: Click arrow to select response.	Type: Stop Title: Invalid Response Message: Invalid response. Use arrow to select response.
B9	Text input. Minimum of 0 characters, maximum of 1500 characters.	Title: Comments Message: Enter your comments. You will be limited to 1500 characters.	Type: Warning Title: Invalid Comments Message: Invalid comments. You have exceeded the limit of characters for comment. Those characters above the limit will be dropped.

© 2014 Cengage Learning

6. In the range B2:B8, enter the following data:
    Cell B2: **=12/1/2016**
    Cell B3: **=Otis Davidson**
    Cell B4: **=International Relations**
    Cell B5: **=2012**
    Cell B6: **=SP**
    Cell B7: **=Switzerland**
    Cell B8: **=Yes**
    Cell B9: **=I would LOVE to go back!**
7. Enter the following formulas for the specified cells in the transfer area:
    Cell A12: **=B2**
    Cell B12: **=B3**
    Cell C12: **=B4**
    Cell D12: **=B5**
    Cell E12: **=B6**
    Cell F12: **=B7**
    Cell G12: **=B8**
    Cell H12: **=B9**
8. Unlock the Input cells in the Input worksheet so that the user can enter data only in the range B2:B9.

9. Protect the Documentation, Data, and Data Tables worksheets so that the user cannot enter data. Do not use a password.

10. Add the DEVELOPER tab to the ribbon.

11. Save the workbook so that you can return to Step 12 and rerecord the macros if you have trouble.

12. Create a macro named **TransferData** with **Ctrl+t** as the shortcut key. Store the macro in the current workbook. Type **Created 12/1/2016. Copy values in the transfer area of the Input worksheet to the Data worksheet** as the description. Record the following steps to create the TransferData macro:

   a. Make the Input worksheet the active worksheet.

   b. Select the transfer area and then copy it to the Clipboard.

   c. Go to the Data worksheet and turn off the worksheet protection.

   d. Go to cell A1, and then go to the last row with values. (*Hint*: Press the Ctrl+↓ keys.)

   e. On the DEVELOPER tab, turn on Use Relative References.

   f. Move down one row.

   g. Turn off Use Relative References.

   h. Paste values to the Data worksheet.

   i. Go to cell A1.

   j. Turn on the worksheet protection.

   k. Go to the Input worksheet, and then make cell B2 the active cell.

13. Create a macro named **ClearInput** with **Ctrl+i** as the shortcut key. Store the macro in the current workbook. Type **Created 12/1/2016. Clear the values in the input area, range B2:B9.** in the macro description. Record the following steps to create the ClearInput macro:

   a. Select the range B2:B9 in the Input worksheet, and then delete the data from those cells.

   b. Make cell B3 the active cell.

14. Test the macros using the shortcut keys you assigned to each of them.

15. Create macro buttons for both macros to the right of the Study Abroad Input form. Enter labels that describe the corresponding macro. You will need to remove protection while creating the buttons. Be sure to reapply the cell protection once you have created the buttons.

16. Remove the DEVELOPER tab from the ribbon.

17. Test the macro buttons. Save your workbook as **Study Abroad with Macros**, a macro-enabled workbook, and then close the workbook.

TROUBLESHOOT

Case Problem 2

Data File needed for this Case Problem: Cloggers.xlsm

OMG Cloggers   OMG Cloggers is a group of traveling dancers based in Avon, Connecticut. The group goes from event to event demonstrating the techniques of clogging. It has been able to support its travels with a series of fundraisers. The most popular and profitable has been an annual fruit sale. The group sells cartons of various fresh fruits during the winter holidays. Armen Maslov, the director of the group, has started developing a workbook that will allow him to analyze the sales from the fruit fundraiser. He asks you to finish creating the application that would allow volunteers to enter order and sales data for any year and chart the profit. Complete the following:

1. Open the macro-enabled **Cloggers** workbook located in the Excel7 ▸ Case2 folder included with your Data Files, and then save the macro-enabled workbook as **OMG Fundraiser** in the location specified by your instructor.

2. In the Documentation worksheet, enter your name and the date. Review the formulas, defined names, and data validation information in the Fundraiser Data worksheet and the Fundraiser Chart worksheet.

⚙ **Troubleshoot** 3. The profit calculation is not returning the correct results. Identify the error in the calculation and correct it.

⚙ **Troubleshoot** 4. In the Documentation worksheet, Armen pasted a list of defined names used in the workbook; but then he continued to modify the worksheet. Make sure all of the defined names are included in the list and are accurate. Fix any errors you find or replace the list.

5. Unlock the ranges B5:B9 and E5:E9 in the Fundraiser Data worksheet so that the user can enter data only in those cells.

6. Protect the Fundraiser Data worksheet. Do not use a password.

7. Make sure that the DEVELOPER tab is on the ribbon.

8. Save the workbook to back it up in case you have problems with your macros.

⚙ **Troubleshoot** 9. The macro ClearInput has already been recorded and saved with the Ctrl+i shortcut key. The macro should perform the following tasks, but is not working correctly. Edit the macro as needed to make it work as intended.

a. Select the range B5:B9 and clear the contents.

b. Select the range E5:E9 and clear the contents.

c. Make cell A1 the active cell.

Run the macro using the shortcut key. It does not perform all of the steps correctly. Locate the problem and correct it using the Visual Basic for Applications editor. If the macro still does not run correctly, close the workbook without saving your changes, reopen the workbook, and then edit the macro again.

10. Create a macro named **PrintChart** with the **Ctrl+c** shortcut key and an appropriate macro description that performs the following actions:

a. Select the Fundraiser Chart worksheet.

b. Export the Fundraiser Chart worksheet to a PDF named **Chart** in the location specified by your instructor.

c. In the Fundraiser Data worksheet, make cell A1 the active cell.

11. Test the PrintChart macro. If the macro doesn't work, close the workbook without saving your changes, reopen the workbook, and record the macro again.

12. Create a button below the totals on the Fundraiser Data worksheet, and then assign the PrintChart macro to the button. Change the default label to a more descriptive one. Remember to remove cell protection while creating buttons. Make sure you reapply cell protection once you have finished creating your buttons.

⚙ **Troubleshoot** 13. The label is missing from the second button. Determine the name of the macro that is assigned to the button and correct the descriptive label. Remember to remove cell protection while modifying buttons. Make sure you reapply cell protection after you have finished editing the button.

14. Run the PrintChart and ClearInput macros to test the buttons and revise the macros if necessary.

15. Remove the DEVELOPER tab from the ribbon.

16. Save the workbook as **OMG Fundraiser with Macros**, a macro-enabled workbook, and then close the workbook.

Case Problem 3

Data File needed for this Case Problem: Music.xlsx

Music Inventory   Christian Wirth has an extensive collection of music CDs. He wants to create a better way to organize the inventory of what he owns. Christian has started a workbook that he can use to enter each artist, CD, genre, and song in his collection. He asks you to finish it by incorporating input validation, cell protection, and macros to help ensure that the collected information is accurate. Complete the following:

1. Open the **Music** workbook located in the Excel7 c Case3 folder included with your Data Files, and then save the workbook as **Music Inventory** in the location specified by your instructor.

2. In the Documentation sheet, enter your name and the date, and then review all of the worksheets in the workbook.

3. In the Music Entry worksheet, create appropriate defined names for each cell in the ranges A2:B4 and A12:B14.

4. Create the following validation rules:

   a. Genre (cell B4): The list of genres is in the range D2:D11. Enter an appropriate input message and error alert.

   b. Artist (cell B12): The list of artists are in the range A2:A3 on the CDs worksheet. Enter an appropriate input message and error alert.

   c. CD (cell B13): The list of CDs is in the range B2:B3 on the CDs worksheet. Enter an appropriate input message and error alert.

5. Test the validation rules for cells B4, B12, and B13 to ensure that the correct data appears in the validation lists.

⊕ **Explore**   6. Insert a WordArt text box, and then enter **Music Inventory** as the text. Rotate the WordArt so that it is vertical in column E. Change the text fill to a color complementing the shade of green in the headings. (*Hint*: On the INSERT tab, click the Insert WordArt button. Then use the DRAWING TOOLS FORMAT tab to format the WordArt.)

7. Create the following formulas for the specified cells in the CD Transfer Area:

   Cell A22: **=Artist_Name**

   Cell B22: **=CD_Name**

   Cell C22: **=Genre**

8. Create the following formulas for the specified cells in the Song Transfer Area:

   Cell A25: **=Artist**

   Cell B5: **=CD**

   Cell C25: **=Song**

9. In the Music Entry worksheet, unlock the input cells, which are in the ranges B2:B4 and B12:B14.

10. Protect the Documentation, Music Entry, CDs, and Songs worksheets.

11. Enter the following data as a new CD:

    Artist_Name: **Sam Jones**

    CD Name: **Live Like You Were Having Fun**

    Genre: **Jazz**

12. Enter the following data as a new Song:

    Artist: **Josh Green**

    CD: **Darkness**

    Song: **Clouds of New York City**

    (*Hint*: The CD Darkness by Josh Green was entered earlier. In order to enter a new Song, the CD must have been already added.)

13. Save the workbook to back it up before recording macros.

14. Make sure that the DEVELOPER tab is displayed on the ribbon.

15. Create a macro named **AddCD** with the shortcut key **Ctrl+c** that performs the following actions:

    a. Go to the CDs worksheet, and then remove the cell protection.

    b. Insert a blank line above row 3, and then make the blank cell A3 the active cell.

    c. Make the Music Entry worksheet the active sheet.

    d. Select the CD Transfer Area and copy it to the Clipboard.

    e. Return to the CDs worksheet.

    f. In row 3, paste the values from the Clipboard.

    g. Select cell A1, and then turn on cell protection.

    h. Go to the Music Entry worksheet, and then make cell B2 the active cell.

16. Create a macro named **AddSong** with the shortcut key **Ctrl+s** that performs the following actions:

    a. Go to the Songs worksheet and remove the cell protection.

    b. Insert a blank line above row 3.

    c. Make the blank cell A3 the active cell.

    d. Make the Music Entry worksheet the active sheet.

    e. Select the Song Transfer Area and copy it to the Clipboard.

    f. Return to the Songs worksheet.

    g. In row 3, paste the values from the Clipboard.

    h. Select cell A1, and then turn on cell protection.

    i. Go to the Music Entry worksheet, and then make cell B2 the active cell.

17. Record a macro named **ClearCDInput** with no shortcut key to clear the range B2:B4 of the New CD input area. The last step should make cell B2 the active cell.

18. Record a macro named **ClearSongInput** with no shortcut key to clear the range B12:B14 of the New Song input area. The last step should make cell B2 the active cell.

19. Test all of the macros by selecting and running the macros on the DEVELOPER tab.

Explore 20. Remove the cell protection on the Music Entry worksheet. Create macro buttons for all four macros using either clip art or shapes. Make sure that you have used descriptive labels for each macro button. Set cell protection again for the Music Entry worksheet.

21. Test all of the macro buttons. Check the CDs and Songs worksheets to see how and where new records were added.

22. Remove the DEVELOPER tab from the ribbon.

23. Save the workbook as **Music Inventory with Macros**, a macro-enabled workbook, and then close the workbook.

Case Problem 4

There are no Data Files needed for this Case Problem.

Trinette's Trilbies & Fedoras   Several years ago, Trinette Jalbert started making trilby hats (commonly called trilbies), which are narrow-brimmed fedora hats, for male family friends. As the requests started pouring in, she turned her hobby into a business. Her customers now include men and women, and she makes fedoras in addition to trilbies. Trinette wants a billing/invoicing system to expedite her work. You will create the finished application for her. Complete the following:

1. Open a new, blank workbook, and then save it as **Hats** in the location specified by your instructor.

2. Rename the sheet as **Documentation**, and then enter the company name, your name, the date, and a purpose statement. Insert two additional sheets, and then rename them as **Invoice** and **Product Information**.

3. In the Product Information worksheet, enter the data for the available colors, fabrics, sizes, hat types, standard hat price, surcharge, and shipping fee shown in Figure 7-47.

Figure 7-47   **Input data for Trinette's Trilbies & Fedoras**

	A	B	C	D	E	F	G	H
1	Color		Size		Hat Type		Shipping	
2	Dark Brown		XS		Trilby		15	
3	Navy Blue		S		Fedora			
4	Black		M					
5			L		Standard			
6	Fabric		XL		75			
7	Tweed		XXL					
8	Wool		XXXL		Surcharge			
9	Felt				15			
10								
11								

4. In the Invoice worksheet, create the invoice shown in Figure 7-48. Use defined names and structured references to assist in creating formulas. (*Hint*: Review the steps below before you begin to create the invoice.)

   a. Enter the labels as shown in Figure 7-48.

   b. Change the column widths and format the labels appropriately.

   c. Use a function to insert the current date.

   d. Insert a comment in the Sold To: cell with a reminder about what data should be entered in cells B10, B11, and B12.

   e. Use data validation rules to create lists of the different hat types, fabrics, colors, and sizes you entered on the Product Information worksheet. Use appropriate input messages and error alerts.

   f. Create defined names for the data on the invoice.

   g. For the unit price, enter a formula to display the standard price listed on the Product Information worksheet.

   h. Enter a formula to display for the fabric surcharge listed on the Product Information worksheet only when a customer purchases a hat with felt fabric. (*Hint*: You will need to use an IF function.)

   i. In the Subtotal cell, enter a formula that uses defined names to add the unit price and the surcharge.

   j. In the Sales Tax cell, enter a formula that uses a defined name to calculate 6.5% of the subtotal.

   k. In the Shipping cell, enter a formula to display the shipping fee listed on the Product Information worksheet.

   l. In the Total Due cell, enter a formula that sums the Subtotal, Sales Tax, and Shipping cells.

   m. Format the cells and add borders and shading where you feel they will make the invoice clearer to read.

Figure 7-48   **Finished invoice for Trinette's Trilbies & Fedoras**

	A	B	C	D	E	F	G	H	I
1									
2				Trinette's Trilbies & Fedoras					
3				56745 North Street					
4				Fredericktown, OH 43019					
5				740-555-6565					
6							Date		
7							7/19/2016		
8									
9		Sold To:							
10		Sam Smith							
11		123 Main Street							
12		Zanesville, OH 43701							
13									
14				Hat Information			Unit Price		
15		Hat Type	Trilby				$ 75.00		
16		Fabric	Tweed			Fabric Surcharge*	$ -		
17		Color	Navy Blue						
18		Size	M						
19									
20						Subtotal	$ 75.00		
21						Sales Tax	$ 4.88		
22						Shipping	$ 15.00		
23						Total Due	$ 94.88		
24		* Fabric Surcharge is on Felt only							
25									
26									

5. Protect the worksheet so a user can enter the Sold To: (cells B10, B11, and B12) and Hat Information (cells C15, C16, C17, and C18) data, but cannot enter data in any other cells. Do not use a password. Protect the entire Documentation and Product Information worksheets. Do not use a password.

6. Save the workbook.

7. Create a macro named **PrintInvoice** that prints the invoice. Assign a shortcut key and type an appropriate macro description as you begin recording this macro. Set the print area to the range A1:H25 and center the worksheet horizontally. The heading has the label **I N V O I C E** in the center of the page heading. Create a macro button on the Invoice worksheet, assign the PrintInvoice macro to the button, and then enter a descriptive label for the button.

8. Create a macro named **ClearInputs** that deletes the values from cells B10, B11, B12, C15, C16, C17, and C18. Assign a shortcut key and type an appropriate macro description as you begin recording this macro. Create a macro button on the Invoice worksheet, assign the ClearInputs macro to the button, and then enter a descriptive label for the button. (*Hint*: Use the Delete key to clear a value from a cell.)

9. Remove the cell protection from the Documentation worksheet. In the Documentation worksheet, paste a list of the defined names with their locations. Below this entry, type a list of the macro names and their shortcut keys. Reapply cell protection to the Documentation worksheet.

10. Test the worksheet by entering the data shown in Figure 7-47.

11. Use the PrintInvoice macro button to print the invoice for the data you entered in Step 10, and then use the ClearInputs macro button to remove the input data.

12. Remove the DEVELOPER tab from the ribbon.

13. Save the workbook as **Hats with Macros**, and then close the workbook.

Working with Advanced Functions

Calculating Employee Compensation and Benefits

OBJECTIVES

Session 8.1
- Use the IF function
- Use the AND function
- Use the OR function
- Use structured references in formulas

Session 8.2
- Nest the IF function
- Use the VLOOKUP function
- Use the HLOOKUP function
- Use the IFERROR function

Session 8.3
- Use conditional formatting to highlight duplicate values
- Summarize data using the COUNTIF, SUMIF, and AVERAGEIF functions

Case | *Educational Video Games*

Educational Video Games (EVG) is a software development company that develops and markets educational games for children in pre-school through second grade. The business has expanded rapidly in the five years since it was founded and now has nearly 100 employees in four locations within the United States.

Patrick Yang, director of compensation and benefits, uses Excel to track basic employee information such as each employee's name, gender, birth date, hire date, medical and dental plans, job status, and current salary. Now he needs to track employee enrollment in and costs related to the compensation and benefit programs offered by the company, such as how much the company contributes to each employee's 401(k) retirement account and medical and dental plans. He also needs to calculate the amount EVG will spend on bonuses and salary increases for the next fiscal year. In addition, the human resources staff wants to send cards to each employee during her/his birthday month.

To provide Patrick with all this information, you'll use a variety of logical and lookup functions. After you calculate those values, you'll summarize information in the Employee Summary worksheet so Patrick can quickly see the impact of the compensation and benefits package on the company.

STARTING DATA FILES

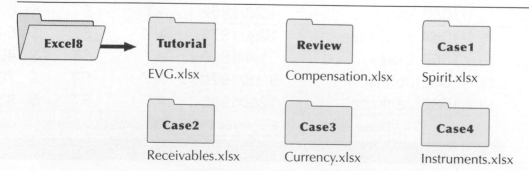

Excel8 → Tutorial	Review	Case1
EVG.xlsx	Compensation.xlsx	Spirit.xlsx

Case2	Case3	Case4
Receivables.xlsx	Currency.xlsx	Instruments.xlsx

Microsoft product screenshots used with permission from Microsoft Corporation.

Session 8.1 Visual Overview:

When you create a formula that references all or parts of an Excel table, you can replace a specific cell or range address with a **structured reference**, which is the actual table name or column header.

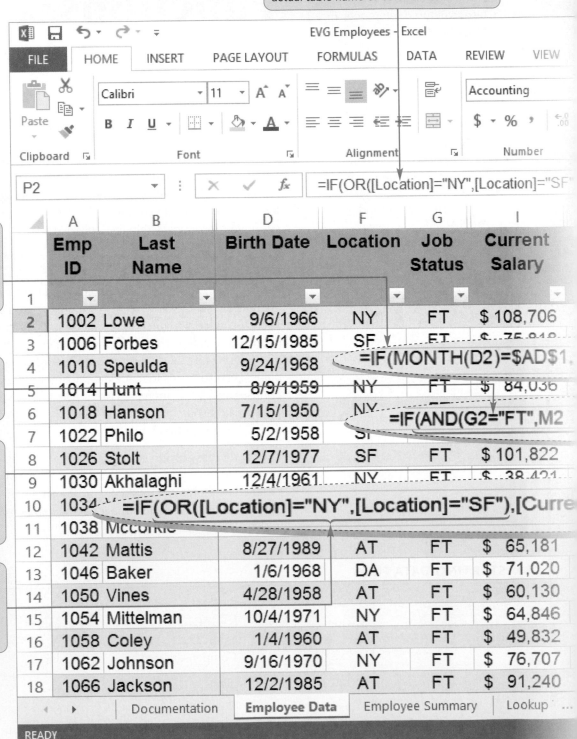

The IF function is a logical function that evaluates a condition, and then returns one value if the condition is true and a different value if the condition is false.

A **logical condition** is an expression such as G2="FT" that returns either a TRUE value or a FALSE value.

The **AND function** is a logical function that returns a TRUE value if all of the logical conditions are true, and a FALSE value if any of the logical conditions are false.

The **OR function** is a logical function that returns a TRUE value if any of the logical conditions are true, and a FALSE value if none of the logical conditions are true.

P2   =IF(OR([Location]="NY",[Location]="SF"

Emp ID	Last Name	Birth Date	Location	Job Status	Current Salary
1002	Lowe	9/6/1966	NY	FT	$ 108,706
1006	Forbes	12/15/1985	SF	FT	$ 75,818
1010	Speulda	9/24/1968		=IF(MONTH(D2)=$AD$1.	
1014	Hunt	8/9/1959	NY	FT	$ 84,036
1018	Hanson	7/15/1950	NY		
1022	Philo	5/2/1958	SF	=IF(AND(G2="FT",M2	
1026	Stolt	12/7/1977	SF	FT	$ 101,822
1030	Akhalaghi	12/4/1961	NY	FT	$ 38,421
1034		=IF(OR([Location]="NY",[Location]="SF"),[Curre			
1038	McCorkle				
1042	Mattis	8/27/1989	AT	FT	$ 65,181
1046	Baker	1/6/1968	DA	FT	$ 71,020
1050	Vines	4/28/1958	AT	FT	$ 60,130
1054	Mittelman	10/4/1971	NY	FT	$ 64,846
1058	Coley	1/4/1960	AT	FT	$ 49,832
1062	Johnson	9/16/1970	NY	FT	$ 76,707
1066	Jackson	12/2/1985	AT	FT	$ 91,240

Documentation   **Employee Data**   Employee Summary   Lookup

READY

Logical Functions

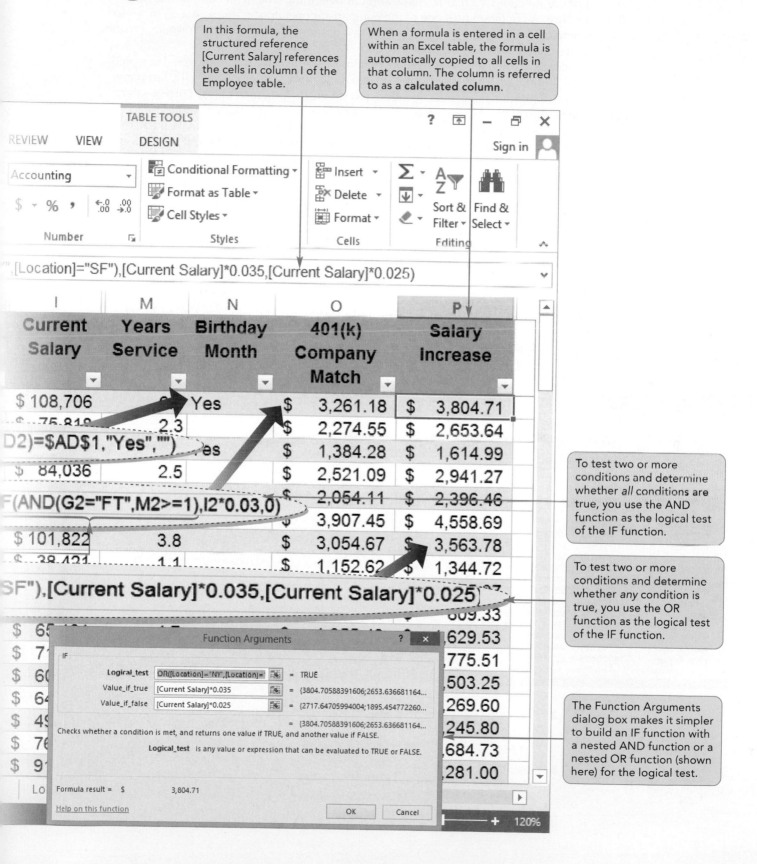

In this formula, the structured reference [Current Salary] references the cells in column I of the Employee table.

When a formula is entered in a cell within an Excel table, the formula is automatically copied to all cells in that column. The column is referred to as a **calculated column**.

To test two or more conditions and determine whether *all* conditions are true, you use the AND function as the logical test of the IF function.

To test two or more conditions and determine whether *any* condition is true, you use the OR function as the logical test of the IF function.

The Function Arguments dialog box makes it simpler to build an IF function with a nested AND function or a nested OR function (shown here) for the logical test.

Working with Logical Functions

Logical functions such as IF, AND, and OR determine whether a condition is true or false. A condition uses one of the comparison operators <, <=, =, <>, >, or >= to compare two values. You can combine two or more functions in one formula, creating more complex conditions.

Patrick created a workbook that contains data for each EVG employee. He stored this information in an Excel table. The table includes each employee's ID, last name, hire date, birth date, gender, location, job status, performance rating, current salary, medical plan, dental plan, age, and years of service at EVG. Patrick wants you to determine if an employee birthday occurs in a specified month, calculate the 401(k) company cost, and calculate a proposed salary increase. You will use IF, AND, and OR functions to do this after you open Patrick's workbook and review the employee data.

To open and review the EVG workbook:

▶ **1.** Open the **EVG** workbook located in the Excel8 ▶ Tutorial folder included with your Data Files, and then save the workbook as **EVG Employees** in the location specified by your instructor.

▶ **2.** In the Documentation worksheet, enter your name and the date.

▶ **3.** Go to the **Employee Data** worksheet. The worksheet contains an Excel table named Employee, which includes each employee's ID, last name, hire date, birth date, gender, location, job status, performance rating, current salary, medical plan, dental plan, age, and years of service at EVG. See Figure 8-1.

Figure 8-1	Employee Data worksheet

	Emp ID	Last Name	Hire Date	Birth Date	Gender	Location	Job Status	Perf Rating	Current Salary	Medical Plan	Dental Plan	Age	Years Service	N
2	1002	Lowe	5/24/2010	9/6/1966	F	NY	FT	3	$ 108,706	SPOUSE2500	EMP+SPOUSE	49	6.6	
3	1006	Forbes	8/28/2014	12/15/1985	F	SF	FT	2	$ 75,818	NONE	NONE	30	2.3	
4	1010	Speulda	4/24/2015	9/24/1968	M	SF	FT	2	$ 46,143	FAMILY1000	EMP+FAMILY	47	1.7	
5	1014	Hunt	7/18/2014	8/9/1959	M	NY	FT	3	$ 84,036	SPOUSE1000	NONE	56	2.5	
6	1018	Hanson	8/21/2015	7/15/1950	F	NY	FT	1	$ 68,470	FAMILY1000	EMP+FAMILY	65	1.4	
7	1022	Philo	3/5/2015	5/2/1958	F	SF	FT	2	$ 130,248	FAMILY1000	EMP+FAMILY	57	1.8	
8	1026	Stolt	3/1/2013	12/7/1977	M	SF	FT	3	$ 101,822	FAMILY2500	NONE	38	3.8	
9	1030	Akhalaghi	12/8/2015	12/4/1961	F	NY	FT	2	$ 38,421	SPOUSE1000	EMP+SPOUSE	54	1.1	
10	1034	Vankeuren	8/11/2011	1/10/1959	F	NY	PT	3	$ 53,582	FAMILY1000	EMP+FAMILY	56	5.4	
11	1038	Mccorkle	6/12/2009	1/30/1942	F	AT	FT	2	$ 24,373	FAMILY2500	EMP+FAMILY	73	7.6	
12	1042	Mattis	5/4/2012	8/27/1989	M	AT	FT	2	$ 65,181	SINGLE1000	EMP	26	4.7	
13	1046	Baker	12/18/2015	1/6/1968	F	DA	FT	3	$ 71,020	FAMILY2500	EMP+FAMILY	47	1.0	
14	1050	Vines	5/4/2011	4/28/1958	M	AT	FT	2	$ 60,130	SINGLE1000	EMP	57	5.7	
15	1054	Mittelman	11/26/2004	10/4/1971	M	NY	FT	2	$ 64,846	SPOUSE2500	EMP+SPOUSE	44	12.1	
16	1058	Coley	2/22/2008	1/4/1960	F	AT	FT	1	$ 49,832	SINGLE1000	EMP	55	8.9	
17	1062	Johnson	12/4/2015	9/16/1970	F	NY	FT	2	$ 76,707	FAMILY1000	EMP+FAMILY	45	1.1	
18	1066	Jackson	10/12/2015	12/2/1985	F	AT	FT	3	$ 91,240	SINGLE2500	EMP	30	1.2	

Documentation   Employee Data   Employee Summary   Lookup Tables   ⊕

READY

▶ **4.** Scroll down and to the right. Although the column headers remain visible as you scroll down, the employee ID and name disappear as you scroll to the right.

▶ **5.** Select cell **C2**, and then freeze the panes so columns A and B remain on the screen as you scroll across the screen.

Inserting Calculated Columns in an Excel Table

TIP

Calculated columns work only in Excel tables. In a range of data, you must copy and paste the formula or use the AutoFill feature.

An Excel table does not have a fixed structure. When you add a column to an Excel table, the table expands and the new column has the same table formatting style as the other columns. If you enter a formula in one cell of a column, the formula is automatically copied to all cells in that column. These calculated columns are helpful as you add formulas to an Excel table.

If you need to modify the formula in a calculated column, you edit the formula in any cell in the column and the formulas in all of the cells in that table column are also modified. If you want to edit only one cell in a calculated column, you need to enter a value or a formula that is different from all the others in that column. A green triangle appears in the upper-left corner of the cell with the custom formula in the calculated column, making the inconsistency easy to find. After a calculated column contains one inconsistent formula or value, any other edits you make to that column are no longer automatically copied to the rest of the cells in that column. Excel does not overwrite custom values.

PROSKILLS

Written Communication: Creating Excel Table Fields

Excel tables should be easy to use as well as understand. This requires labeling and entering data in a way that effectively communicates a table's content or purpose. If a field is entered in a way that is difficult to use and understand, it becomes more difficult to find and present data in a meaningful way.

To effectively communicate a table's function, keep the following guidelines in mind when creating fields in an Excel table:

- **Create fields that require the least maintenance.** For example, hire date and birth date require no maintenance after they are entered, unlike age and years of service, whose values change each year. If you need to know the specific age or years of service, use calculations to determine them based on values in the Hire Date and Birth Date columns.
- **Store the smallest unit of data possible in a field.** For example, use three separate fields for City, State, and Zip code rather than one field. Using separate fields for each unit of data enables you to sort or filter each field. If you want to display data from two or more fields in one column, you can use a formula to reference the City, State, and Zip code columns. For example, you can use the & operator to combine the city, state, and zip code in one cell as follows: `=C2&D2&E2`
- **Apply a text format to fields with numerical text data.** For example, formatting fields such as zip codes and Social Security numbers as text ensures that leading zeros are stored as part of the data. Otherwise, the zip code 02892 is stored as a number and displayed as 2892.

Using these guidelines means that you and others will spend less time interpreting data and more time analyzing results. This lets you more effectively communicate the data in an Excel table.

Using the IF Function

In many situations, the value you store in a cell depends on certain conditions. Consider the following examples:

- An employee's gross pay depends on whether that employee worked overtime.
- An income tax rate depends on the taxpayer's adjusted taxable income.
- A shipping charge depends on the dollar amount of an order.

To evaluate these types of conditions, you use the IF function. Recall that the IF function is a logical function that evaluates a condition, and then returns one value if the condition is true and another value if the condition is false. The value can be text, numbers, cell references, formulas, or functions. The IF function has the syntax

```
IF(logical_test, value_if_true, value_if_false)
```

where *logical_test* is a condition that is either true or false, *value_if_true* is the value returned by the function if the condition is true, and *value_if_false* is the value returned by the function if the condition is false. The IF function results in only one value—either the *value_if_true* or the *value_if_false*.

You will use an IF function to alert Patrick that an employee has a birthday during a specified month. EVG employees who have an upcoming birthday receive a birthday card. A Yes value in the Birthday Month column will indicate that an employee has a birthday during the specified month, and a blank cell will indicate that an employee does not have a birthday during the specified month.

The flowchart shown in Figure 8-2 illustrates Patrick's logic for determining whether a birthday occurs in a specified month. The flowchart shows that if an employee's birth month occurs in the specified month (*birth month = specified month* is True), "Yes" is entered in the cell. If the employee does not have a birthday in the specified month, the cell is left blank.

| Figure 8-2 | **Flowchart with logic to determine if an employee's birthday is in the specified month** |

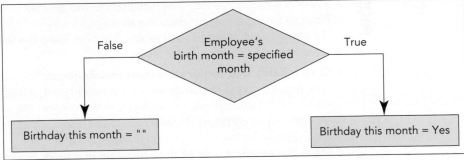

© 2014 Cengage Learning

The Employee table doesn't include a column that lists only the birth month; this information is included as part of the employee's complete birth date, which is stored in column D. To extract the month portion of the employee's birth date, you will use the MONTH function. This function is a Date function that returns the month as a number from 1 (January) to 12 (December). The MONTH function has the syntax

```
MONTH(date)
```

where *date* is a date that includes the month you want to extract. Recall that Excel stores dates as a number equal to the number of days between January 1, 1900 and the specified date so they can be used in calculations. For example, January 1, 2016 is stored as the serial number 42370 because it occurs 42370 days since the start of Excel's calendar. The MONTH function determines the month number from the stored serial number. For example, the birth date of the employee in row 2 of the Employee table is 9/6/1966, which is stored in cell D2. The following MONTH function extracts the month portion of this stored date, which is 9:

```
=MONTH(D2)
```

You'll use the MONTH function in the logical test of the IF function, which will check whether the employee's birth month matches the month number entered in cell AD1 of the Employee Data worksheet. Patrick wants to know which employees have birthdays in September, so he entered 9 as the month number in cell AD1. The following formula includes the complete IF function to determine if an employee has a birthday in September:

```
=IF(MONTH(D2)=$AD$1,"Yes","")
```

The logical test MONTH(D2)=$AD$1 determines if the employee's birth month is equal to the birth month stored in cell AD1. If the condition is TRUE, Yes is displayed in the Birthday Month column; otherwise, the cell is left blank.

You'll add a column to the Employee table to display the results of the IF function that determines if an employee's birthday occurs in the specified month.

To determine which employees have birthdays in the specified month:

1. In cell **N1**, enter **Birthday Month**. The Excel table expands to include this column and applies the table formatting to all the rows in the new column.

2. Make sure cell **N2** is the active cell, and then click the **Insert Function** button f_x next to the formula bar. The Insert Function dialog box opens.

3. Click **Logical** in the Or select a category list, click **IF** in the Select a function box, and then click the **OK** button. The Function Arguments dialog box for the IF function opens.

4. In the Logical_test box, type **MONTH(D2)=$AD$1** and then press the **Tab** key. This condition tests whether the employee's birth month is equal to the month specified in cell AD1. The function MONTH returns the month number of the date specified in cell D2. TRUE appears to the right of the Logical_test argument box, indicating this employee has a birthday in the specified month.

5. In the Value_if_true box, type **Yes** and then press the **Tab** key. This argument specifies that if the condition is true (the employee's birth month matches the value in cell AD1), display Yes as the formula result. The value to the right of the Value_if_true argument box is Yes because the condition is true. Notice Excel inserts quotation marks around the text value because you did not include them.

6. In the Value_if_false box, type **""**. This argument specifies that if the condition is false (the employee's birth month does not match the value in cell AD1), display nothing in cell N2. The value to the right of the Value_if_false argument box is "", which indicates that cell N2 appears blank if the condition is false. See Figure 8-3.

Figure 8-3   Function Arguments dialog box for the IF function

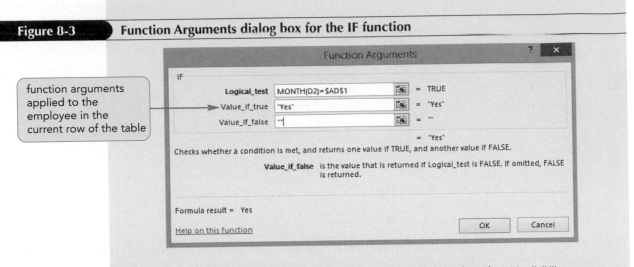

function arguments applied to the employee in the current row of the table

7. Click the **OK** button. The formula =IF(MONTH(D2)=$AD$1,"Yes","") appears in the formula bar, and Yes appears in cell N2 because the condition is true. The formula is automatically copied to all cells in column N of the table. See Figure 8-4.

Figure 8-4   Birthday Month column added to the Employee table

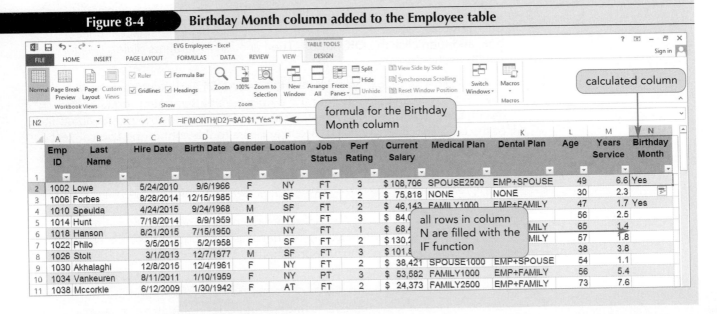

calculated column

formula for the Birthday Month column

all rows in column N are filled with the IF function

Using the AND Function

The IF function evaluates a single condition. However, you often need to test two or more conditions and determine whether *all* conditions are true. You can do this with the AND function. The AND function is a logical function that returns the value TRUE if all of the logical conditions are true, and returns the value FALSE if any or all of the logical conditions are false. The syntax of the AND function is

```
AND(logical1[,logical2]...)
```

where *logical1* and *logical2* are conditions that can be either true or false. If all of the logical conditions are true, the AND function returns the logical value TRUE; otherwise, the function returns the logical value FALSE. You can include up to 255 logical conditions in an AND function. However, keep in mind that *all* of the logical conditions listed in the AND function must be true for the AND function to return a TRUE value.

Figure 8-5 illustrates how the AND function is used to determine student eligibility for the dean's list. In this scenario, when students have 12 or more credits (stored in cell B1) *and* their GPA is greater than 3.5 (stored in cell B2), they are placed on the dean's list. Both conditions must be true for the AND function to return the logical value TRUE.

Figure 8-5   **AND function example**

Purpose:	To determine dean's list requirements
Logic Scenario:	12 or more semester credits and GPA above 3.5
Formula:	AND function with two conditions `=AND(B1>=12,B2>3.5)`
Data:	cell B1 stores number of credits cell B2 stores student's GPA

Example:

Data		Condition1	Condition2	Results
Cell B1	**Cell B2**	**B1>=12**	**B2>3.5**	**(Dean's List?)**
15	3.6	True	True	True
12	3.25	True	False	False
6	3.8	False	True	False
10	3.0	False	False	False

© 2014 Cengage Learning

Patrick wants you to use an AND function to determine employee eligibility for the company's 401(k) plan. EVG employees are eligible for the 401(k) benefit if they are full-time employees (FT in Job Status) *and* have worked for the company for one or more years (1 or greater in Years Service). As long as *both* conditions are true, the company contributes an amount equal to 3 percent of the employee's salary to the employee's 401(k). If neither condition is true or if only one condition is true, the employee is not eligible for the 401(k) benefit and the company's contribution is 0. Patrick outlined these eligibility conditions in the flowchart shown in Figure 8-6.

Figure 8-6   **Flowchart illustrating AND logic for the 401(k) benefit**

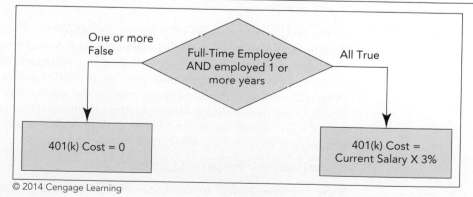

© 2014 Cengage Learning

To calculate the cost of the 401(k) plan for each employee, you need to use the AND function with the IF function. You use the AND function shown in the following formula as the logical test to evaluate whether each employee in the Employee table fulfills the eligibility requirements:

```
=AND(G2="FT",M2>=1)
```

This formula tests whether the value in cell G2 (the job status for the first employee) is equal to FT (an abbreviation for full time), and whether the value in cell M2 (the years of service for the first employee) is greater than or equal to 1 (indicating one or more years of employment at EVG). When an employee is a full-time employee (G2="FT") *and* has worked one or more years at EVG (M2>=1), the AND function returns the value TRUE; otherwise, the AND function returns the value FALSE. Figure 8-7 shows the result returned by the AND function for four different sets of employee values for job status and years of service.

Figure 8-7   **AND function results for 401(k) plan eligibility**

Purpose:	To determine employee eligibility for the company's 401(k) plan		
Logic Scenario:	An employee is eligible for the 401(k) plan if the employee's status is full time (FT) AND the employee's years of service total one or more years.		
Formula:	AND function with two conditions =AND(G2="FT",M2>=1)		
Data:	cell G2 stores Job Status cell M2 stores Years Service		

Example:

Data		Condition1	Condition2	Results
Cell G2	**Cell M2**	**G2="FT"**	**M2>=1**	**(Eligible?)**
FT	1	True	True	True
FT	0	True	False	False
PT	5	False	True	False
PT	0	False	False	False

© 2014 Cengage Learning

The AND function shows only whether an employee is eligible for the 401(k) plan. It does not calculate how much EVG will contribute to that employee's 401(k) plan if the employee is eligible. To determine whether an employee is eligible *and* to calculate the amount of the 401(k) contribution, you use this AND function within an IF function. When the results of one function are used as the argument of another function, the functions are *nested*. In the following formula, the AND function (shown in red) is nested within the IF function and is used as the logical test that determines whether the employee is eligible for a 401(k) contribution:

```
=IF(AND(G2="FT",M2>=1),I2*0.03,0)
```

If the employee is eligible, the AND function returns the logical value TRUE and the IF function multiplies the employee's current salary by 3 percent. If the AND function returns the logical value FALSE, the IF function displays the value 0.

You'll insert a new column in the Employee table, and then enter the formula to calculate the 401(k) company match.

To calculate the 401(k) company match using the IF and AND functions:

1. In cell **O1**, enter **401(k) Company Match** as the column header. The Excel table expands to include the new column, and cell O2 is the active cell.

2. Make sure cell **O2** is the active cell, and then click the **Insert Function** button f_x next to the formula bar. The Insert Function dialog box opens.

3. Click **IF** in the Select a function box, and then click the **OK** button. The Function Arguments dialog box opens.

4. In the Logical_test box, type **AND(G2="FT",M2>=1)** and then press the **Tab** key. This logical test evaluates whether the employee is full time, indicated by FT in cell G2, *and* has worked at EVG for one year or more. TRUE appears to the right of the Logical_test box, indicating that the condition for the employee in row 2 is true. This employee is eligible for the 401(k) plan.

5. In the Value_if_true box, type **I2*0.03** and then press the **Tab** key. This argument specifies that if the condition is true (the employee is eligible for the 401(k) plan as determined by the AND function), the amount in the employee's salary cell is multiplied by 3 percent. The amount of the employer's 401(k) matching contribution, 3261.18, appears to the right of the Value_if_true box.

6. In the Value_if_false box, type **0**. This argument specifies that if the condition is false (the employee is not eligible for the 401(k) plan as determined by the AND function), the amount displayed in cell O2 is 0, which appears to the right of the Value_if_false box. See Figure 8-8.

Figure 8-8   Function Arguments dialog box for the IF function with the AND function

7. Click the **OK** button. The formula with the IF function that you just created is entered in cell O2 and copied to all rows in column O of the table.

8. Position the pointer at the top of cell **O1** until the pointer changes to ⬇, click to select the 401(k) data values, format the range using the **Accounting** format, and then widen the column to display all values.

TIP

Double-click above the header row to select the column header and data.

▶ **9.** Select cell **O2**. The formula =IF(AND(G2="FT",M2>=1),I2*0.03,0) appears in the formula bar and $3,261.18 appears in cell O2 because the condition is true. See Figure 8-9.

| Figure 8-9 | IF function with the AND function to calculate EVG's 401(k) contribution |

The company match values are calculated for all employees.

Using the DATEDIF Function to Calculate Employee Age

In the Employee table, the Age column was calculated using the DATEDIF function. The **DATEDIF function** calculates the difference between two dates and shows the result in months, days, or years. The syntax for the DATEDIF function is

    DATEDIF(Date1,Date2,Interval)

where *Date1* is the earliest date, *Date2* is the latest date, and *Interval* is the unit of time the DATEDIF function will use in the result. You specify the *Interval* with one of the following interval codes:

Interval Code	Meaning	Description
"m"	Months	The number of complete months between *Date1* and *Date2*
"d"	Days	The number of complete days between *Date1* and *Date2*
"y"	Years	The number of complete years between *Date1* and *Date2*

For example, the following formula calculates an employee's age in complete years:

    =DATEDIF(D2,$AF$1,"y")

The earliest date is located in cell D2, the birth date. The latest date is in cell $AF$1, which shows the date used to compare against the birth date—as of a cut-off date. The interval "y" indicates that you want to display the number of complete years between these two dates.

The DATEDIF function is undocumented in Excel, but it has been available since Excel 97. To learn more about this function, search the web using "DATEDIF function in Excel" as the search text in your favorite search engine.

Using the OR Function

The OR function is a logical function that returns a TRUE value if any of the logical conditions are true, and returns a FALSE value if all of the logical conditions are false. The syntax of the OR function is

```
OR(logical1[,logical2]...)
```

where `logical1` and `logical2` are conditions that can be either true or false. If any of the logical conditions are true, the OR function returns the logical value TRUE; otherwise, the function returns the logical value FALSE. You can include up to 255 logical conditions in the OR function. However, keep in mind that if *any* logical condition listed in the OR function is true, the OR function returns a TRUE value.

Figure 8-10 illustrates how the OR function is used to determine eligibility for a 10 percent discount. In this scenario, anyone who is 65 years or older (stored in cell B1) *or* anyone who is a college student (stored in cell B2) receives a 10 percent discount. At least one condition must be true for the OR function to return the logical value TRUE.

Figure 8-10	Example of the OR function

Purpose:	To determine who is eligible for a discount
Logic Scenario:	Discount is 10 percent for seniors (65 or older) or college students (Status =STU)
Formula:	OR function with two conditions =OR(B1>=65,B2="STU")
Data:	cell B1 stores Age cell B2 stores Status (STU, FAC, STF)

Example:

Data		Condition1	Condition2	Results
Cell B1	Cell B2	B1>=65	B2="STU"	(Discount?)
22	STU	False	True	True
67	FAC	True	False	True
65	STU	True	True	True
45	STF	False	False	False

© 2014 Cengage Learning

EVG is considering awarding a 3.5 percent raise to employees working in areas with a high cost of living, and a 2.5 percent raise for all other employees. The criteria for awarding a salary increase are based on location. If the employee is working in either New York (NY) or San Francisco (SF), the employee will receive the 3.5 percent raise. In other words, if either Location equals NY or Location equals SF is True, the condition is true and the employee will receive the 3.5 percent raise. If the condition is false—meaning the employee is located in a city other than New York or San Francisco—the employee receives a 2.5 percent raise. Patrick outlined the salary increase criteria in the flowchart shown in Figure 8-11.

Figure 8-11 Flowchart of the OR function to calculate salary increase

© 2014 Cengage Learning

You need to use the OR function to test whether an employee meets the criteria for the 3.5 percent or 2.5 percent salary increase. The following formula uses the OR function to test whether the value in cell F2 (the work location for the first employee) is equal to NY *or* whether the value in cell F2 is equal to SF:

`=OR(F2="NY",F2="SF")`

If the employee works in New York (NY) *or* the employee works in San Francisco (SF), the OR function returns the value TRUE; otherwise, the OR function returns the value FALSE.

Figure 8-12 shows the results returned using the OR function for four different employee work locations—New York (NY), San Francisco (SF), Dallas (DA), and Atlanta (AT).

Figure 8-12 OR function results for four employee work locations

Purpose:	To determine an employee's salary increase percentage
Logic Scenario:	Proposed 3.5 percent salary increase to full-time (FT) employees located in NY or SF
Formula:	OR function with two conditions `=OR(F2="NY",F2="SF")`
Data:	cell F2 stores Location

Example:

Data	Condition1	Condition1	Results
Cell F2	**F2="NY"**	**F2="NY"**	**(OR function)**
NY	True	True	True
SF	False	False	True
DA	False	False	False
AT	False	False	False

© 2014 Cengage Learning

The OR function only determines which raise an employee is eligible for. It does not calculate the amount of the salary increase. To determine the amount of the salary increase, the OR function must be nested within an IF function. In the formula

```
=IF(OR(F2="NY",F2="SF"),I2*0.035,I2*0.025)
```

the logical test of the IF function uses the OR function (shown in red) to determine whether an employee is either working in New York *or* working in San Francisco. If the OR function returns a TRUE value, the IF function multiplies the Current Salary by 3.5 percent. If the OR function returns a FALSE value, the IF function multiplies the Current Salary by 2.5 percent.

Using Structured References to Create Formulas in Excel Tables

When you create a formula that references all or parts of an Excel table, you can replace the specific cell or range address with a structured reference, the actual table name, or a column header. This makes the formula easier to create and understand. The default Excel table name is Table1, Table2, and so forth unless you entered a more descriptive table name, as Patrick did for the Employee table. Column headers provide a description of the data entered in each column. Structured references make it easier to create formulas that use portions or all of an Excel table because the names or headers are usually simpler to identify than cell addresses. For example, in the Employee table, the table name Employee refers to the range A2:O101, which is the range of data in the table excluding the header row and the Total row. When you want to reference an entire column of data in a table, you create a column qualifier, which has the syntax

```
Tablename[qualifier]
```

where `Tablename` is the name entered in the Table Name box in the Properties group on the TABLE TOOLS DESIGN tab, and `qualifier` is the column header enclosed in square brackets. For example, the following structured reference references the Current Salary data in the range I2:I101 of the Employee table (excluding the column header and total row, if any):

```
Employee[Current Salary]
```

You can use structured references in formulas. The following formula adds the Current Salary data in the range I2:I101 of the Employee table; in this case, [Current Salary] is the column qualifier:

```
=SUM(Employee[Current Salary])
```

When you create a calculated column, as you did to calculate the 401(k) contributions in the Employee table, you can use structured references in the formula. A formula that includes a structured reference can be fully qualified or unqualified. In a fully qualified structured reference, the table name precedes the column qualifier. In an unqualified structured reference, only the column qualifier (column header enclosed in square brackets) appears in the reference. For example, you could have used either of the following formulas with structured references to calculate the 401(k) company match in the calculated column you added to the Employee table:

Fully qualified

```
=IF(AND(Employee[Job Status]="FT",Employee[Years Service]>=1),
[Current Salary]*0.035,0)
```

Unqualified
```
=IF(AND([Job Status]="FT",[Years Service]>=1),
[Current Salary]*0.035,0)
```

If you are creating a calculated column or formula within an Excel table, you can use either the fully qualified structured reference or the unqualified structured reference in the formula. If you use a structured reference outside the table or in another worksheet to reference an Excel table or portion of the table, you must use a fully qualified reference.

You'll use structured references to calculate the salary increases for EVG employees.

To calculate the salary increase using the IF and OR functions:

1. In cell **P1**, enter **Salary Increase** as the column header. The Excel table expands to include the new column, and cell P2 is the active cell.

2. Make sure cell **P2** is the active cell, and then click the **Insert Function** button f_x next to the formula bar. The Insert Function dialog box opens.

3. Click **IF** in the Select a function box, and then click the **OK** button. The Function Arguments dialog box opens.

> Be sure to type square brackets and use the exact spelling and location shown. Otherwise, the formula will return an error.

4. In the Logical_test box, type **OR([Location]="NY",[Location]="SF")** to enter the OR function with structured references. This logical test evaluates whether the employee works in New York or works in San Francisco.

5. Click the **Collapse dialog box** button [icon] to so you can see the entire function in the Logical_test box. See Figure 8-13.

Figure 8-13   **Logical_test argument for the OR function**

6. Click the **Expand dialog box** button [icon], and then press the **Tab** key. TRUE appears to the right of the Logical_test box because the employee in the active row, row 2, is eligible for the 3.5 percent salary increase.

   Trouble? If Invalid appears instead of TRUE as the logical test results, you probably mistyped the logical test. Compare the function in your Logical_test box to the one shown in Figure 8-13, confirming that you used square brackets around the structured reference [Location] and typed all the text correctly.

7. In the Value_if_true box, type **[Current Salary]*0.035** and then press the **Tab** key. This argument specifies that if the logical test is true (the employee is eligible for the 3.5 percent increase), the amount in the employee's salary cell is multiplied by 3.5 percent. The salary increases for all employees, beginning in row 2, whose logical test is true appear to the right of the Value_if_true box.

8. In the Value_if_false box, type **[Current Salary]*0.025**. This argument specifies that if the logical test is false (the employee is not eligible for the 3.5 percent salary increase), the amount in the employee's salary cell is multiplied by 2.5 percent. The salary increases for all employees, beginning in row 2, whose logical test is false appear to the right of the Value_if_false box. See Figure 8-14.

| Figure 8-14 | Function Arguments dialog box for the IF function with an OR function |

9. Click the **OK** button. The formula =IF(OR([Location]="NY",[Location]="SF"), [Current Salary]*0.035,[Current Salary]*0.025) appears in the formula bar, and the value 3804.705884 appears in cell P2 because the condition is true. The formula is automatically copied to all rows in column P of the table.

10. Position the pointer at the top of cell **P1** until the pointer changes to ↓, and then click the left mouse button to select the Salary Increase data values.

11. Format the range with the **Accounting** format, and then increase the column width to display all values.

▶ **12.** Select cell **P2** to deselect the column. See Figure 8-15.

Figure 8-15   IF function with the OR function calculates salary increase

formula uses structured references to calculate the salary increases

salary increase for employees

P2   fx   =IF(OR([Location]="NY",[Location]="SF"),[Current Salary]*0.035,[Current Salary]*0.025)

Emp ID	Last Name	Location	Job Status	Perf Rating	Current Salary	Medical Plan	Dental Plan	Age	Years Service	Birthday Month	401(k) Company Match	Salary Increase
1002	Lowe	NY	FT	3	$ 108,706	SPOUSE2500	EMP+SPOUSE	49	6.6	Yes	$ 3,261.18	$ 3,804.71
1006	Forbes	SF	FT	2	$ 75,818	NONE	NONE	30	2.3		$ 2,274.55	$ 2,653.64
1010	Speulda	SF	FT	2	$ 46,143	FAMILY1000	EMP+FAMILY	47	1.7	Yes	$ 1,384.28	$ 1,614.99
1014	Hunt	NY	FT	3	$ 84,036	SPOUSE1000	NONE	56	2.5		$ 2,521.09	$ 2,941.27
1018	Hanson	NY	FT	1	$ 68,470	FAMILY1000	EMP+FAMILY	65	1.4		$ 2,054.11	$ 2,396.46
1022	Philo	SF	FT	2	$ 130,248	FAMILY1000	EMP+FAMILY	57	1.8		$ 3,907.45	$ 4,558.69
1026	Stolt	SF	FT	3	$ 101,822	FAMILY2500	NONE	38	3.8		$ 3,054.67	$ 3,563.78
1030	Akhalaghi	NY	FT	2	$ 38,421	SPOUSE1000	EMP+SPOUSE	54	1.1		$ 1,152.62	$ 1,344.72
1034	Vankeuren	NY	PT	3	$ 53,582	FAMILY1000	EMP+FAMILY	56	5.4		$ -	$ 1,875.37
1038	Mccorkle	AT	FT	2	$ 24,373	FAMILY2500	EMP+FAMILY	73	7.6		$ 731.20	$ 609.33
1042	Mattis	AT	FT	2	$ 65,181	SINGLE1000	EMP	26	4.7		$ 1,955.43	$ 1,629.53
1046	Baker	DA	FT	3	$ 71,020	FAMILY2500	EMP+FAMILY	47	1.0		$ 2,130.61	$ 1,775.51
1050	Vines	AT	FT	2	$ 60,130	SINGLE1000	EMP	57	5.7		$ 1,803.90	$ 1,503.25
1054	Mittelman	NY	FT	2	$ 64,846	SPOUSE2500	EMP+SPOUSE	44	12.1		$ 1,945.37	$ 2,269.60
1058	Coley	AT	FT	1	$ 49,832	SINGLE1000	EMP	55	8.9		$ 1,494.96	$ 1,245.80
1062	Johnson	NY	FT	2	$ 76,707	FAMILY1000	EMP+FAMILY	45	1.1	Yes	$ 2,301.20	$ 2,684.73
1066	Jackson	AT	FT	3	$ 91,240	SINGLE2500	EMP	30	1.2		$ 2,737.20	$ 2,281.00

Documentation   **Employee Data**   Employee Summary   Lookup Tables

In this session, you used the IF, AND, and OR functions to determine if an employee's birth date occurs in a specified month, calculate 401(k) costs, and calculate next year's salary increases for EVG employees. Patrick still needs to calculate the employee bonuses, medical plan costs, dental plan costs, and the employee service award for each employee. In the next session, you will create formulas with functions to perform these calculations.

Session 8.1 Quick Check

REVIEW

1. What changes occur in the appearance and size of an Excel table after you enter a new column header named "Phone"?

2. Whenever you enter a formula in an empty column of an Excel table, Excel automatically fills the column with the same formula. What is this called?

3. If an Excel worksheet stores the cost per meal in cell Q5, the number of attendees in cell Q6, and the total cost of meals in cell Q7, what IF function would you enter in cell Q7 to calculate the total cost of meals (cost per meal times the number of attendees) with a minimum cost of $10,000?

4. When does the AND function return a TRUE value?

5. Write the formula that displays the label "Outstanding" in cell Y5 if the amount owed (cell X5) is greater than 0 and the transaction date (cell R5) is after 3/1/2016 (stored in cell R1), but otherwise leaves the cell blank.

6. When you create a formula that references all or parts of an Excel table, what can you use to replace the specific cell or range addresses with the actual table or column header names?

7. If the formula =IF(OR(B25="NY",B25="CA",B25="TX"),"Select","Ignore") is entered in cell B26, and "PA" is entered in cell B25, what is displayed in cell B26?

8. Write the OR function that represents the following rule—"A potential enlistee in the Army is not eligible to enlist if younger than 17 or older than 42." The age is stored in cell B25. Display "Eligible" if the potential enlistee can enlist, and display "Not Eligible" if the potential enlistee cannot enlist.

Session 8.2 Visual Overview:

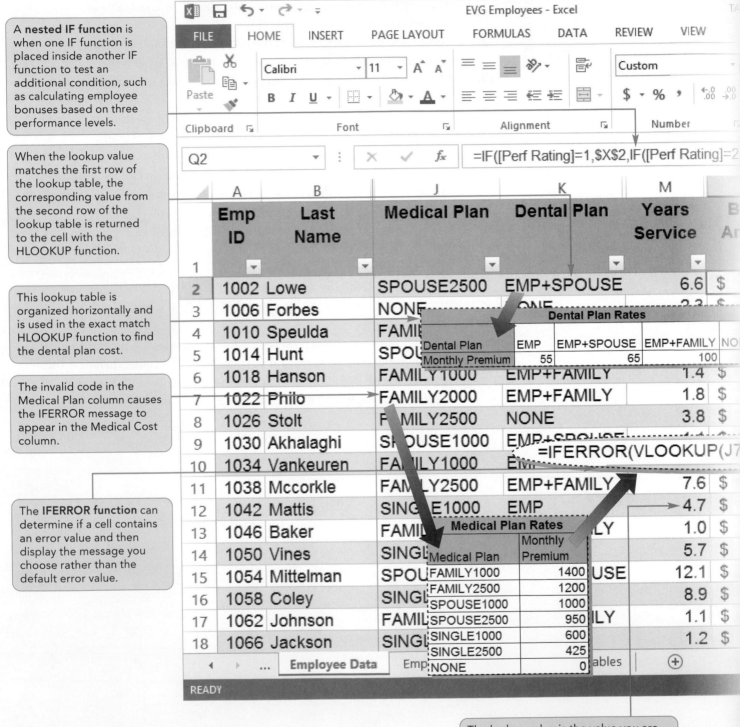

A **nested IF function** is when one IF function is placed inside another IF function to test an additional condition, such as calculating employee bonuses based on three performance levels.

When the lookup value matches the first row of the lookup table, the corresponding value from the second row of the lookup table is returned to the cell with the HLOOKUP function.

This lookup table is organized horizontally and is used in the exact match HLOOKUP function to find the dental plan cost.

The invalid code in the Medical Plan column causes the IFERROR message to appear in the Medical Cost column.

The **IFERROR function** can determine if a cell contains an error value and then display the message you choose rather than the default error value.

The lookup value is the value you are trying to find. In this case, the lookup value is the employee's years of service in the Years Service column, which is used to find the return value in the Service Award Payout table.

EVG Employees - Excel

FILE　HOME　INSERT　PAGE LAYOUT　FORMULAS　DATA　REVIEW　VIEW

Q2　=IF([Perf Rating]=1,$X$2,IF([Perf Rating]=2

	A	B	J	K	M
1	Emp ID	Last Name	Medical Plan	Dental Plan	Years Service
2	1002	Lowe	SPOUSE2500	EMP+SPOUSE	6.6
3	1006	Forbes	NONE	NONE	2.3
4	1010	Speulda	FAMI		
5	1014	Hunt	SPOU		
6	1018	Hanson	FAMILY1000	EMP+FAMILY	1.4
7	1022	Philo	FAMILY2000	EMP+FAMILY	1.8
8	1026	Stolt	FAMILY2500	NONE	3.8
9	1030	Akhalaghi	SPOUSE1000	EMP+SPOUSE	
10	1034	Vankeuren	FAMILY1000	EMP	
11	1038	Mccorkle	FAMILY2500	EMP+FAMILY	7.6
12	1042	Mattis	SINGLE1000	EMP	4.7
13	1046	Baker	FAMIL	LY	1.0
14	1050	Vines	SINGL		5.7
15	1054	Mittelman	SPOU	USE	12.1
16	1058	Coley	SINGL		8.9
17	1062	Johnson	FAMIL	ILY	1.1
18	1066	Jackson	SINGL		1.2

Dental Plan Rates

Dental Plan	EMP	EMP+SPOUSE	EMP+FAMILY	NO
Monthly Premium	55	65	100	

=IFERROR(VLOOKUP(J7

Medical Plan Rates

Medical Plan	Monthly Premium
FAMILY1000	1400
FAMILY2500	1200
SPOUSE1000	1000
SPOUSE2500	950
SINGLE1000	600
SINGLE2500	425
NONE	0

... Employee Data　Emp ... ables

READY

Nested IFs and Lookup Tables

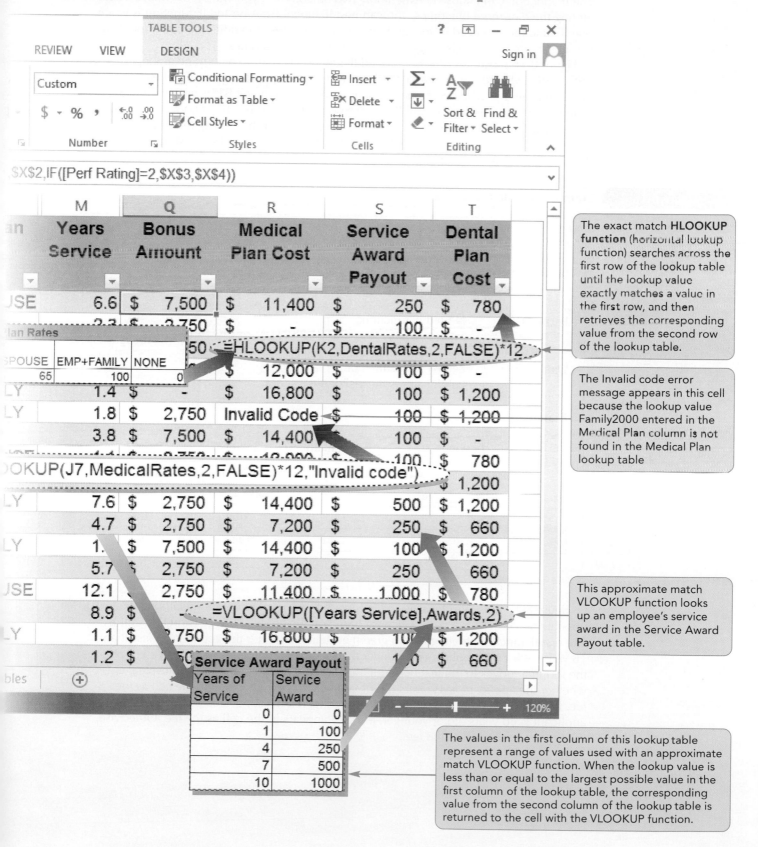

The exact match **HLOOKUP function** (horizontal lookup function) searches across the first row of the lookup table until the lookup value exactly matches a value in the first row, and then retrieves the corresponding value from the second row of the lookup table.

The Invalid code error message appears in this cell because the lookup value Family2000 entered in the Medical Plan column is not found in the Medical Plan lookup table

This approximate match VLOOKUP function looks up an employee's service award in the Service Award Payout table.

The values in the first column of this lookup table represent a range of values used with an approximate match VLOOKUP function. When the lookup value is less than or equal to the largest possible value in the first column of the lookup table, the corresponding value from the second column of the lookup table is returned to the cell with the VLOOKUP function.

Creating Nested IFs

The IF function can choose between only two outcomes. If you want it to choose from among three or more outcomes, you can nest IF functions. A nested IF function is when one IF function is placed inside another IF function to test an additional condition. You can nest more than one IF function to test for multiple outcomes.

Figure 8-16 illustrates how one nested IF function is used to determine among three outcomes—whether the home football team won, lost, or tied a game. The first IF function evaluates whether the home team score (stored in cell B1) is greater than the visiting team score (stored in cell B2). If the home team score is higher, Won appears in the cell. If not, the nested IF function evaluates whether the visiting team score is greater than the home team score. If the visiting team score is higher, Lost appears in the cell. Otherwise, Tie appears in the cell.

Figure 8-16	Example of nested IF functions

Purpose: To determine the outcome of football games for the home team

Logic Scenario: Display Won, Lost, or Tie based on home team and visitor team scores

Formula: Nested IF functions
=IF(B1>B2,"Won",IF(B2>B1,"Lost","Tie"))

Data: cell B1 stores the home team score
cell B2 stores the visitor team score

Example:

Data		Condition1	Condition2	Results
Cell B1	Cell B2	B1>B2	B2>B1	(Outcome)
21	18	True	Not evaluated	Won
17	24	False	True	Lost
9	9	False	False	Tie

© 2014 Cengage Learning

Figure 8-17 illustrates how nested IF functions are used to determine among four possible outcomes for a driver's license based on the applicant's age (stored in cell B1). The first IF function (highlighted in green) evaluates whether the applicant is less than 16 years old. If the applicant is younger than 16, Too Young appears in the cell. If not, the formula moves to the first nested IF function (highlighted in blue) and evaluates whether the applicant is 45 years old or younger. If so, 30 appears in the cell as the fee. If not, the second nested IF function (highlighted in red) evaluates whether the applicant is 60 years old or younger. If so, 25 appears in the cell as the fee. Otherwise, 20 appears in the cell as the fee.

Figure 8-17	Additional example of nested IF functions

Purpose: To determine the fee for a driver's license

Logic Scenario: Driver's license fee varies by age

    Below 16   "Too Young"
    16–45 $30
    46–60 $25
    61 and older $20

Formula: Nested IF functions
`=IF(B1<16,"Too Young",IF(B1<=45,30,IF(B1<=60,25,20)))`

Data: cell B1 stores the driver's age

Example:

Data	Condition1	Condition2	Condition3	Results
Cell B1	**B1<16**	**B1<=45**	**B1<=60**	**(Fee)**
15	True	Not evaluated	Not evaluated	Too Young
25	False	True	Not evaluated	30
55	False	False	True	25
65	False	False	False	20

© 2014 Cengage Learning

You need to use nested IF functions to determine employee bonus amounts. EVG pays three levels of employee bonuses based on an employee's performance evaluation. EVG has three performance ratings (1=below average, 2=average, and 3=above average). Performance rating 1 has a bonus of $0, performance rating 2 has a bonus of $2,500, and performance rating 3 has a bonus of $7,500. In this case, you need to nest IF functions to calculate the different series of outcomes for the employee bonuses.

Patrick created the flowchart shown in Figure 8-18 to illustrate the logic for determining bonus awards. He used different colors to identify each IF function. The flowchart shows that if an employee's pay performance rating equals 1, the bonus amount equals 0 and the IF function (shown in green) is finished. If the employee's performance rating does not equal 1, then the second IF function (shown in blue) is evaluated. If the employee's performance rating equals 2, then the bonus amount equals 2500 and the IF function is finished. If the employee's performance rating does not equal 2, then the bonus amount equals 7500.

Figure 8-18   **Flowchart of nested IF functions to determine the bonus amount**

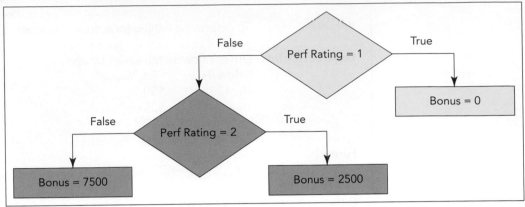

© 2014 Cengage Learning

The following formula converts Patrick's flowchart into a formula with nested IF functions:

```
=IF([Perf Rating]=1,0,IF([Perf Rating]=2,2500,7500))
```

The first IF function (shown in green) tests whether the value in the Perf Rating (performance rating) cell of the Employee table is equal to 1. If this condition ([Perf Rating]=1) is true, the formula returns 0 in the Bonus cell. If this condition is false (the performance rating cell is not equal to 1), the second IF function (shown in blue) is evaluated. The second IF function tests whether the value in the performance rating cell is equal to 2. If this condition ([Perf Rating]=2) is true, the formula returns 2500 in the Bonus cell. If this condition is false (the value in the current performance rating cell is not equal to 2), the formula returns 7500 in the Bonus cell.

PROSKILLS

Problem Solving: Finding and Fixing Errors in Formulas

If formulas in a worksheet are returning errors or not working as expected, you need to find and fix the problems. Two common categories of formula errors in Excel are syntax errors and logic errors. A syntax error is an error in a statement that violates the rules of Excel. A syntax error might occur due to unmatched parentheses or a required argument that is omitted in a function. Logic errors occur in formulas that work but return an incorrect result. Logic errors are often detected by the user because the results seem out of line. A logic error could occur because the formula uses the wrong calculation, the formula references the wrong cell, or the formula uses faulty reasoning, leading to incorrect results.

Some problem-solving approaches can help resolve these types of errors. First, examine the formulas in worksheet cells instead of the results by pressing the Ctrl+~ keys to display the formulas in each cell. Next, troubleshoot problem areas in the worksheet by pressing the F9 key to highlight part of a formula and temporarily display the actual value in the cell so you can check intermediate results. Press the Esc key to return the cell references. Finally, you can use the Formula Auditing tools on the FORMULAS tab to visually identify and trace cells used in a formula. This can help you locate and fix inaccurate cell references and faulty logic.

By carefully evaluating formulas and fixing any problems, you help to ensure that a worksheet is error-free and returns accurate results.

Patrick wants the Employee table to include a column that contains a formula to calculate the bonus amount. Patrick stored the three bonus amounts (0, 2500, and 7500) in the Employee worksheet. You will reference these cells in the formula to calculate the employee bonus. This approach enables you to quickly update the calculated bonus amounts in the Employee worksheet without having to edit the bonus formula.

To enter nested IFs to calculate employee bonuses:

1. If you took a break at the end of the previous session, make sure the EVG Employees workbook is open and the Employee Data worksheet is active.

2. In cell **Q1**, enter **Bonus Amount** as the column header. The Excel table expands to include the new column, and cell Q2 is the active cell.

3. Make sure cell **Q2** is the active cell, and then click the **Insert Function** button [fx] next to the formula bar. The Insert Function dialog box opens.

4. Click **IF** in the Select a function box, and then click the **OK** button. The Function Arguments dialog box opens.

5. In the Logical_test box, type **[Perf Rating]=1** and then press the **Tab** key to enter the logical test using a structured reference. This logical test evaluates whether the employee has a performance rating equal to 1. The values to the right of the Logical_test box are {False; False;... indicating that the performance ratings for the first few employees are false.

   Trouble? If the value to the right of the Logical_test box is Invalid, you probably mistyped the logical test. Select the text in the Logical_test box, and then repeat Step 5, typing the logical test exactly as shown, being sure to use square brackets around the structured reference.

6. In the Value_if_true box, type **$X$2** and then press the **Tab** key. The value to the right of the Value_if_true argument box is 0, which is the value in cell X2. This argument specifies that if the logical test is true (the performance rating cell is equal to 1), the value stored in cell X2 (the 0 bonus amount) is displayed. You used an absolute reference because you want the formula in each row to refer to cell X2, which contains the bonus amount. Note that a separate worksheet is often used to store values that change, such as the Bonus Amount values.

7. In the Value_if_false box, type **IF([Perf Rating]=2,$X$3,$X$4)** and then press the **Tab** key. This argument is a nested IF function that specifies if the logical condition is true (the performance rating cell is equal to 2), the value stored in cell X3 (the 2500 bonus amount) is displayed; otherwise, the value stored in cell X4 (the 7500 bonus amount) is displayed. Again, you used absolute references to ensure that the formula will always refer to cell X3 and cell X4, respectively. The values to the right of the Value_if_false box are {7500;2500;2500;... indicating the bonus amounts for the employees in the first few rows. See Figure 8-19.

TIP

If you type a formula directly in a cell, the available structured references appear when you type the opening bracket. Double-click the structured reference to add it to the formula, and then type the closing bracket.

Figure 8-19   **Function Arguments dialog box with a nested IF**

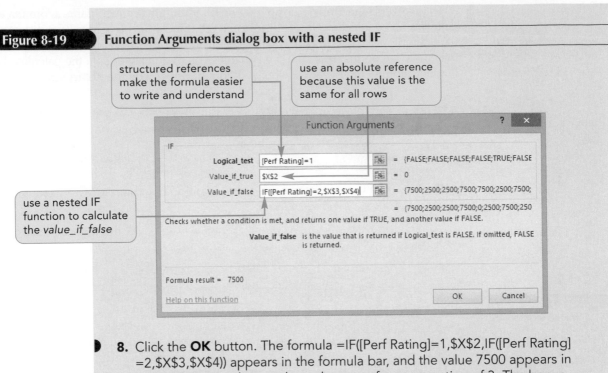

structured references make the formula easier to write and understand

use an absolute reference because this value is the same for all rows

use a nested IF function to calculate the *value_if_false*

Function Arguments

IF

Logical_test   [Perf Rating]=1   = {FALSE;FALSE;FALSE;FALSE;TRUE;FALSE

Value_if_true $X$2   = 0

Value_if_false   IF([Perf Rating]=2,$X$3,$X$4)   = {7500;2500;2500;7500;7500;2500;7500;

= {7500;2500;2500;7500;0;2500;7500;250

Checks whether a condition is met, and returns one value if TRUE, and another value if FALSE.

Value_if_false   is the value that is returned if Logical_test is FALSE. If omitted, FALSE is returned.

Formula result =   7500

Help on this function   OK   Cancel

8. Click the **OK** button. The formula =IF([Perf Rating]=1,$X$2,IF([Perf Rating] =2,$X$3,$X$4)) appears in the formula bar, and the value 7500 appears in cell Q2 because this employee has a performance rating of 3. The bonus formula is automatically copied to all other rows in the Bonus Amount column. The references to cells X2, X3, and X4 are absolute references and do not change from cell to cell in the Bonus Amount column.

9. Select the Bonus values, and then format the selected range using the **Accounting** format with no decimal places.

10. Select cell **Q2** to deselect the column. See Figure 8-20.

Figure 8-20   **Nested IF function calculating the employee bonus amounts**

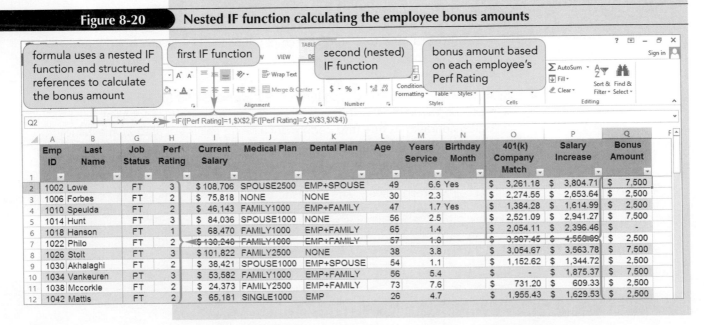

formula uses a nested IF function and structured references to calculate the bonus amount

first IF function

second (nested) IF function

bonus amount based on each employee's Perf Rating

Q2   =IF([Perf Rating]=1,$X$2,IF([Perf Rating]=2,$X$3,$X$4))

Emp ID	Last Name	Job Status	Perf Rating	Current Salary	Medical Plan	Dental Plan	Age	Years Service	Birthday Month	401(k) Company Match	Salary Increase	Bonus Amount
1002 Lowe		FT	3	$ 108,706	SPOUSE2500	EMP+SPOUSE	49	6.6	Yes	$ 3,261.18	$ 3,804.71	$ 7,500
1006 Forbes		FT	2	$ 75,818	NONE	NONE	30	2.3		$ 2,274.55	$ 2,653.64	$ 2,500
1010 Speulda		FT	2	$ 46,143	FAMILY1000	EMP+FAMILY	47	1.7	Yes	$ 1,384.28	$ 1,614.99	$ 2,500
1014 Hunt		FT	3	$ 84,036	SPOUSE1000	NONE	56	2.5		$ 2,521.09	$ 2,941.27	$ 7,500
1018 Hanson		FT	1	$ 68,470	FAMILY1000	EMP+FAMILY	65	1.4		$ 2,054.11	$ 2,396.46	$ -
1022 Philo		FT	2	$ 130,248	FAMILY1000	EMP+FAMILY	57	1.8		$ 3,907.45	$ 4,558.69	$ 2,500
1026 Stolt		FT	3	$ 101,822	FAMILY2500	NONE	38	3.8		$ 3,054.67	$ 3,563.78	$ 7,500
1030 Akhalaghi		FT	2	$ 38,421	SPOUSE1000	EMP+SPOUSE	54	1.1		$ 1,152.62	$ 1,344.72	$ 2,500
1034 Vankeuren		PT	3	$ 53,582	FAMILY1000	EMP+FAMILY	56	5.4		$ -	$ 1,875.37	$ 7,500
1038 Mccorkle		FT	2	$ 24,373	FAMILY2500	EMP+FAMILY	73	7.6		$ 731.20	$ 609.33	$ 2,500
1042 Mattis		FT	2	$ 65,181	SINGLE1000	EMP	26	4.7		$ 1,955.43	$ 1,629.53	$ 2,500

The Bonus Amount column shows the bonuses for each employee.

Checking Formulas for Matching Parentheses

A common problem when creating formulas is mismatched parentheses. As you write a formula, you should verify that you enclosed the correct argument, function, or term within the parentheses of the formula you are creating. This is especially important when you develop a complex formula that includes many parentheses, such as a nested IF function. Excel color-codes the parentheses as you build a formula so you can quickly determine whether the formula includes complete pairs of them. You can also verify that the formula includes matching pairs of parentheses by selecting the cell with the formula and then clicking in the formula bar. Press the → key to move the insertion point through the formula one character at a time. When the insertion point moves across one parenthesis, its matching parenthesis is also highlighted briefly. This color-coding helps you ensure that all parentheses in a formula are paired (opening and closing parentheses).

By using cell references to Input values rather than including constants in formulas, you make a worksheet more flexible and easier to update. The executive team has increased the bonus for employees in performance rating 2 from $2,500 to $2,750. Patrick asks you to update this bonus amount so the employee bonuses will be current.

To update the bonus amount for performance rating 2:

1. In cell **X3**, enter **2750**.

2. Scroll to the **Bonus Amount** column and observe that all employees with a performance rating equal to 2 now have a bonus amount of $2,750.

Using LOOKUP Functions

Recall that lookup functions allow you to find values in a table of data and insert them in another worksheet location. For example, you might enter a product table in a worksheet that includes the product ID, product name, and price of all products a company sells. You could then use this product table to build an invoice in another worksheet by entering a product ID and having Excel look up the product name and price, and insert these values in the invoice. The table that stores the data you want to retrieve is called a lookup table.

Both the VLOOKUP and HLOOKUP functions are used to return a value from a lookup table. The VLOOKUP function always searches for a value in the first column of the lookup table. The HLOOKUP function always searches for a value in the first row of the lookup table. Both these functions can retrieve a value from lookup tables designed for *exact match* or *approximate match* lookups. Recall that an exact match lookup occurs when the lookup value must match one of the values in the first column (or row) of the lookup table. An approximate match lookup occurs when the lookup value is found within a range of numbers in the first column (or row) of the lookup table. Which function you use depends on how the data in the lookup table has been arranged. If the first column of the lookup table is searched, then use VLOOKUP; if the first row of the lookup table is searched, then use HLOOKUP.

At EVG, all employees are eligible for the company's medical plan. Employees can choose one of six plans—a family plan with either a $1000 or $2500 deductible (FAMILY1000 or FAMILY2500); an employee and spouse plan with either a $1000 or $2500 deductible (SPOUSE1000 or SPOUSE2500); and an employee plan with either a $1000 or $2500 deductible (SINGLE1000 or SINGLE2500). Each plan has a different cost, and EVG pays the entire amount. If an employee provides evidence of health coverage elsewhere, there is no medical plan cost (NONE). You could calculate the medical plan costs for each employee using several nested IF functions. However, a simpler approach is to use a lookup function.

You can use the Medical Plan Rates data shown in Figure 8-21 as an exact match lookup table. The lookup table includes the available plans and their corresponding monthly premiums. The medical plan cost for each eligible employee is based on the plan the employee selected. To retrieve the monthly cost for an employee, Excel moves down the first column in the Medical Plan Rates lookup table until it finds the medical plan code that matches the employee's medical plan. Then it moves to the second column in the lookup table to locate the monthly premium, which is then displayed in the cell where the lookup formula is entered or used as part of a calculation. If the employee's Medical Plan code doesn't match one of the values in the first column of the MedicalRates table (spelling or spaces are different), the #N/A error value is displayed. For example, to find the return value for the SPOUSE2500 lookup value, Excel searches the first column of the lookup table until the SPOUSE2500 entry is found. Then, Excel moves to the second column of the lookup table to locate the corresponding return value, which is 950, in this case.

Figure 8-21   **MedicalRates lookup table used for an exact match lookup**

Lookup Value = "SPOUSE2500"

search down the first column until the lookup value exactly matches the value in the first column

Medical Plan Rates	
Medical Plan	Monthly Premium
FAMILY1000	1400
FAMILY2500	1200
SPOUSE1000	1000
SPOUSE2500	950
SINGLE1000	600
SINGLE2500	425
NONE	0

return the corresponding value from the second column of the lookup table

Return Value = 950

© 2014 Cengage Learning

Lookup tables can also be constructed as approximate match lookups. A discount based on the quantity of items purchased where each discount covers a range of units purchased is an example of an approximate match lookup. Figure 8-22 shows the approximate match lookup table for these quantity discounts. In this example, purchases of fewer than 25 units receive no discount, purchases of between 25 and 99 units receive a 2 percent discount, purchases of between 100 and 499 units receive a 3 percent discount, and purchases of 500 or more units receive a 4 percent discount. For example, to find the quantity discount for a purchase of 55 units, Excel searches the first column of the lookup table until the largest value that is less than or equal to 55 (the lookup value) is found, which is 25 in this example. Then, Excel moves to the second column of the lookup table and returns 2 percent as the quantity discount.

Figure 8-22 | Approximate match lookup table

© 2014 Cengage Learning

Using the VLOOKUP Function to Find an Exact Match

To retrieve the correct value from the lookup table, you use the VLOOKUP function. Recall that the VLOOKUP function searches vertically down the first column of the lookup table for the value you entered, and then retrieves the corresponding value from another column of the table. The VLOOKUP function has the syntax

VLOOKUP(*lookup_value*,*table_array*,*col_index_num*[,*range_lookup*])

where *lookup_value* is the value, cell reference, a defined name, or a structured reference you want to search for in the first column of the lookup table; *table_array* is a range reference, a defined name, or the name of an Excel table that is the lookup table; *col_index_num* is the number of the column in the lookup table that contains the value you want to return; and *range_lookup* indicates whether the lookup table is an exact match (FALSE) or an approximate match (TRUE). The *range_lookup* argument is optional; if you don't include a *range_lookup* value, the value is considered TRUE (an approximate match).

You'll use the VLOOKUP function to calculate the annual medical plan cost for FVG because you want to search the values in the first column of the lookup table. You can use the range reference (the range A5:B11 on the Lookup Tables worksheet) or the defined name MedicalRates when you reference the lookup table in the VLOOKUP formula to determine the annual medical plan cost for an employee:

Range reference   =VLOOKUP(J2,'Lookup Tables'!$A$5:$B$11,2,FALSE)*12

Defined name   =VLOOKUP(J2,MedicalRates,2,FALSE)*12

Both of these formulas use the VLOOKUP function to search for the employee's Medical Plan code (column J) in the Employee table, in the first column of the Medical Rates lookup table (the range A5:B11 in the Lookup Tables worksheet), and then return the corresponding value from the second column of the lookup table, which shows the monthly cost. The formulas use FALSE as the *range_lookup* argument because you want the lookup value to exactly match a value in the first column of the lookup table.

Patrick wants you to enter the VLOOKUP function using the defined name to reference the lookup table in the VLOOKUP function so he can easily determine what's included in the function. This is also simpler than entering range references, and you don't need to change the reference to an absolute reference.

To find an exact match in the MedicalRates table using the VLOOKUP function:

1. In cell **R1**, enter **Medical Plan Cost**. The table expands to include the new column.

2. Make sure cell **R2** is the active cell, and then click the **Insert Function** button ƒₓ next to the formula bar. The Insert Function dialog box opens.

3. Click the **Or select a category** arrow, click **Lookup & Reference**, and then double-click **VLOOKUP** in the Select a function box. The Function Arguments dialog box opens.

4. Drag the Function Arguments dialog box below row 2 so you can see the column headers.

5. In the Lookup_value box, enter **J2** and then press the **Tab** key. The lookup value is the employee's medical plan code, which is located in column J.

6. In the Table_array box, type **MedicalRates** and then press the **Tab** key. MedicalRates is the defined name assigned to the range A5:B11 in the Lookup Tables worksheet. If the MedicalRates data was entered as a range rather than a defined name, the *table_array* argument would be entered as 'Lookup Tables'!A5:B11, and you would need to change the range to absolute references ('Lookup Tables'!$A$5:$B$11) so the formula would copy correctly to other cells.

For the *col_index_num* value, be sure to enter the number of the column's position in the table, not its column letter, to avoid receiving #NAME? or #VALUE! as the result.

7. In the Col_index_num box, type **2** and then press the **Tab** key. The number 2 indicates the monthly cost is stored in the second column of the MedicalRates lookup table.

8. In the Range_lookup box, type **FALSE**. This sets the function to find an exact match in the lookup table. See Figure 8-23.

Figure 8-23   **Function Arguments dialog box for the VLOOKUP function**

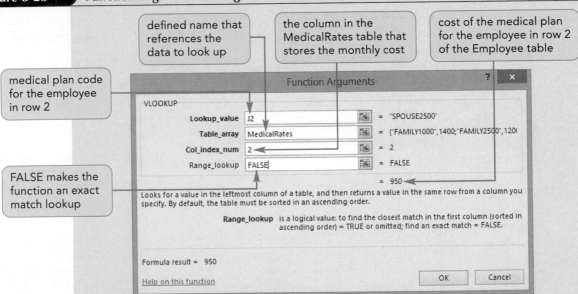

9. Click the **OK** button. The dialog box closes, 950 appears in cell R2, and the formula =VLOOKUP(J2,MedicalRates,2,FALSE) appears in the formula bar. The remaining rows in the Medical Plan Cost column are filled with the VLOOKUP function. If the value in column J does not match a value in the first column of the MedicalRates table, an exact match does not exist and the function returns #N/A in the cell.

10. Select the Medical Plan Cost values, and then format the range using the **Accounting** format with no decimal places.

11. Select cell **R2** to deselect the column. See Figure 8-24.

Figure 8-24   **Exact match VLOOKUP function calculating employee medical plan costs**

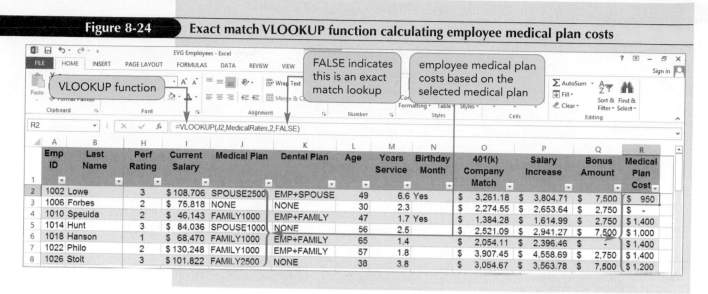

The medical plan costs in the Employee table are monthly amounts rather than annual amounts. Patrick wants you to modify the formula in the Medical Plan Cost column to reflect the annual amounts. Because the formula in the Excel table is a calculated column, you need to make the change in only one cell and the change will automatically be copied to all the cells in the column.

To modify the formula in the Medical Plan Cost column:

1. Double-click cell **R2** to enter Edit mode and display the formula in the cell.

2. Click at the end of the formula, type ***12** to multiply the monthly amount by 12, and then press the **Enter** key.

3. If necessary, increase the width of column R to display all the values in the Medical Plan Cost column.

The amount in cell R2 changes to $11,400, and all the other cells in the column are updated with the revised formula and display the annual cost.

Using the VLOOKUP Function to Find an Approximate Match

You can also use a VLOOKUP function to return a value from a lookup table that is based on an approximate match lookup. The previous lookup used the MedicalRates table to return a value only if Excel found an exact match in the first column of the lookup table. The values in the first column or row of a lookup table can also represent a range of values. Quantity discounts, shipping charges, and income tax rates are a few examples of approximate match lookups.

As part of EVG's 10-year anniversary, management plans to give employee-service awards based on the number of years employees have worked for EVG. Patrick developed the criteria shown in Figure 8-25 to summarize how the company plans to distribute the service awards.

Figure 8-25   **Criteria for the Service Award Payout lookup table**

Years of Service	Service Award
>=0 and <1	0
>=1 and <4	100
>=4 and <7	250
>=7 and <10	500
>=10	1000

© 2014 Cengage Learning

In the Service Award Payout table, you are not looking for an exact match for the lookup value. Instead, you need to use an approximate match lookup to determine which range of values the lookup value falls within. You want to use the lookup table to determine what years of service range an employee falls into, and then return the service award payout based on the appropriate row. To accomplish this, you must rearrange the first column of the lookup table so that each row in the table represents the *low end* of the years of service range, as shown in Figure 8-26.

Figure 8-26   **Service Award Payout lookup table for an approximate match lookup**

Lookup Value = 6

search down the first column until the largest value less than or equal to the lookup value is found

Service Award Payout	
Years of Service	Service Award
0	0
1	100
4	250
7	500
10	1000

return the corresponding value from the second column of the lookup

Return Value = 250

© 2014 Cengage Learning

To determine whether a lookup value falls within a range of values in the lookup table, Excel searches the first column of the table until it locates the largest value that is less than or equal to the lookup value. Then Excel moves across the row in the table to retrieve the corresponding value. For example, for an employee working at EVG for six years, Excel would search the lookup table until the value in the first column is 4 (the largest value in the lookup table that is less than or equal to the lookup value) and retrieve 250 from column 2 of the corresponding row.

When a lookup table is used with a range of values (approximate match), the values in the first column must be sorted in low-to-high order. When the first column's values are arranged in a different order, Excel may not retrieve the correct value, leading to incorrect results. The setup of the lookup table in an approximate match is critical for a VLOOKUP formula to work properly.

Setting Up an Approximate Match Lookup Table

Approximate lookup tables are commonly used to find a taxpayer's tax rate in a tax table, find a shipping charge based on the weight of a package in a shipping charges table, or determine a student's letter grade from a table of grading criteria. Setting up the lookup tables for an approximate match lookup can be tricky. Consider the following example, in which an instructor uses Excel to calculate grades. The instructor assigns final grades based on the following grading policy table:

Score	Grade
90–100	A
80–89	B
70–79	C
60–69	D
0–59	F

To set up the lookup table so it works in Excel, the leftmost column in the lookup table must (1) represent the lower end of the range for each category; and (2) be sorted in ascending order based on the value in the first column. Otherwise, Excel cannot retrieve the correct result. Following this structure, the lookup table for the instructor's grading policy would be arranged as follows:

Score	Grade
0	F
60	D
70	C
80	B
90	A

In the Employee table, you will create the formula

```
=VLOOKUP([Years Service],Awards,2)
```

to determine the recognition award for each employee, where [Years Service] is the structured reference for the employee's years of service (the lookup value), Awards is the defined name that references the lookup table, and 2 specifies the column in the lookup table in which to find the service awards payout. The fourth argument is not needed because this is an approximate match lookup. You will use an approximate match VLOOKUP formula because each cell in the Years of Service column in the lookup table represents a range of values.

To insert the approximate match VLOOKUP formula:

1. In cell **S1**, enter **Service Award Payout**. A new column is added to the table, and cell S2 is the active cell.

2. Click the **Insert Function** button f_x next to the formula bar. The Insert Function dialog box opens with the Lookup & Reference category active.

3. In the Select a function box, double-click **VLOOKUP**. The Function Arguments dialog box opens.

4. In the Lookup_value box, type **[Years Service]** and then press the **Tab** key. The lookup value is entered using the column header (structured reference) for the employee's years of service, which is located in column M. You can also enter the lookup value as M2. The number 6.6 appears as the lookup value for the current row.

5. In the Table_array box, type **Awards** and then press the **Tab** key. Awards is the defined name assigned to the range D5:E9 in the Lookup Tables worksheet. If the Awards data was entered as a range reference, the *table_array* argument would be entered as 'Lookup Tables'!D5:E9, and you would need to change the range to absolute references ('Lookup Tables'!$D$5:$E$9) so that the formula would copy correctly to other cells.

6. In the Col_index_num box, type **2**. The number 2 indicates the column where the amount of the award is stored—the second column of the Awards table. See Figure 8-27. You do not need to enter the optional fourth argument in the VLOOKUP formula because Excel assumes the value to be TRUE and will use an approximate match table lookup.

Figure 8-27   **Function Arguments dialog box for the VLOOKUP function**

Function Arguments

VLOOKUP

Lookup_value	[Years Service]	= 6.610958904
Table_array	Awards	= {0,0;1,100;4,250;7,500;10,1000}
Col_index_num	2	= 2
Range_lookup		= logical

= 250

Looks for a value in the leftmost column of a table, and then returns a value in the same row from a column you specify. By default, the table must be sorted in an ascending order.

Col_index_num   is the column number in table_array from which the matching value should be returned. The first column of values in the table is column 1.

Formula result =   250

Help on this function   OK   Cancel

omitting the range_lookup entry is the same as entering TRUE and creates an approximate match lookup

7. Click the **OK** button. All the cells in the Service Award Payout calculated column are filled with the VLOOKUP formula and display the award amounts. The employee in row 2 has 6.6 years of service and will receive a service award of $250. This is a good illustration of the approximate match lookup because 6.6 does not equal a value in the first column of the lookup table. Instead, it falls between two values in the table.

8. Make sure that the values in the Service Award Payout column are formatted with the **Accounting** format and no decimal places.

9. Select cell **S2** to deselect the column. See Figure 8-28.

Figure 8-28   **Approximate match VLOOKUP function for calculating the service award payout**

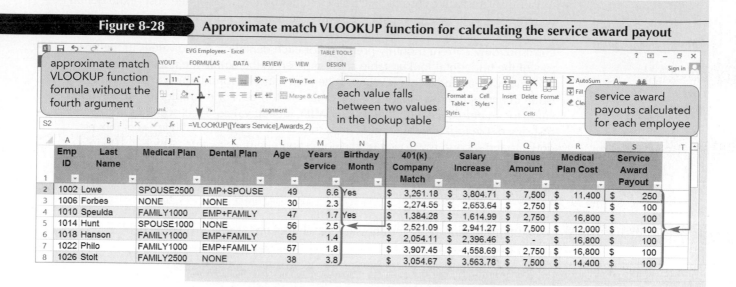

Using the HLOOKUP Function to Find an Exact Match

The HLOOKUP function is very similar to the VLOOKUP function. The HLOOKUP function (horizontal lookup function) searches across the top row of the lookup table until the lookup value is found, and then retrieves the value from the same column in the lookup table. The HLOOKUP function has the syntax

```
HLOOKUP(lookup_value,table_array,row_index_num[,range_lookup])
```

where *lookup_value* is the value, cell reference, defined name, or structured reference you want to search for in the first row of the lookup table; *table_array* is the range reference, defined name, or Excel table name of the lookup table; *row_index_num* is the number of the row in the lookup table that contains the value you want to return; and *range_lookup* indicates whether the lookup table is an exact match (FALSE) or an approximate match (TRUE). The *range_lookup* argument is optional; if you don't include a *range_lookup* value, the value is considered TRUE (an approximate match).

The major difference between the HLOOKUP and VLOOKUP functions is the way the lookup tables are organized. Figure 8-29 shows how the MedicalRates and Awards tables would be arranged for a lookup using the HLOOKUP function.

Figure 8-29   **Lookup tables for the HLOOKUP function**

	B	C	D	E	F	G	H	I	J
4	Medical Plan	FAMILY1000	FAMILY2500	SPOUSE1000	SPOUSE2500	SINGLE1000	SINGLE2500	NONE	
5	Monthly Premium	1400	1200	1000	950	600	425	0	
6									
7									
8	Years of Service	0	1	4	7	10			
9	Service Award Payout	0	100	250	500	1000			

With the lookup tables arranged as shown in Figure 8-29, the exact match formula to calculate the annual medical plan cost is

```
=HLOOKUP(J2,MedicalRates,2,FALSE)*12
```

and the approximate match formula to calculate the service award payout is

```
=HLOOKUP(M2,Awards,2)
```

Patrick wants you to use the HLOOKUP function to calculate the cost of the dental plan for each employee. Figure 8-30 shows the DentalRates table in the Lookup Tables worksheet, which includes the different options available to EVG employees and the corresponding current monthly premium for each dental plan. The values in the first row of the horizontal lookup table are compared to the employee's dental plan code that you want to find (lookup value). When the match is found, the corresponding value in one of the rows in the lookup table is returned. For example, to find the return value for an employee with the EMP+FAMILY lookup value, Excel searches across the first row of the lookup table until it finds the EMP+FAMILY entry. Then Excel moves down to the second row to locate the corresponding return value, which is 100 in this case. The table in Figure 8-30 is an exact match lookup because if the employee's dental plan code does not match one of the values in the first row of the lookup table, the #N/A error value is returned.

Figure 8-30 **DentalRates lookup table for an exact match lookup**

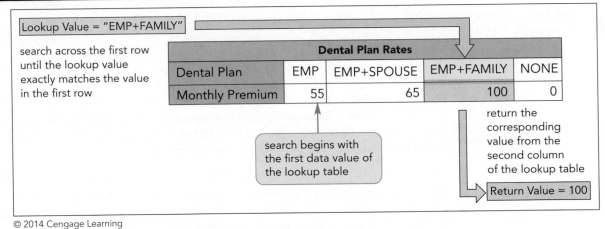

© 2014 Cengage Learning

The following formula uses the employee's dental plan code and the DentalRates table to calculate the annual cost of the dental plan for each employee:

```
=HLOOKUP(K2,DentalRates,2,FALSE)*12
```

In this formula, K2 is the cell that stores the employee's dental plan in the Employee table, DentalRates is the defined name that references the lookup table, 2 specifies the row to find the monthly premium, and FALSE indicates that this is an exact match lookup. You will enter this formula to calculate the annual cost of the dental plan for each employee into the Employee table.

To find an exact match in the DentalRates table using the HLOOKUP function:

1. In cell **T1**, enter **Dental Plan Cost**. The table expands to include the new column.

2. Make sure cell **T2** is the active cell, and then click the **Insert Function** button f_x in the formula bar. The Insert Function dialog box opens.

3. Click the **Or select a category** arrow and click **Lookup & Reference**, if necessary, and then double-click **HLOOKUP** in the Select a function box. The Function Arguments dialog box opens.

4. If necessary, drag the Function Arguments dialog box below row 2 so you can see the column headers.

5. In the Lookup_value box, enter **K2** and then press the **Tab** key. The lookup value is the employee's dental plan code, which is located in column K.

6. In the Table_array box, type the defined name **DentalRates** and then press the **Tab** key. DentalRates references the range H4:K5 in the Lookup Tables worksheet. If the defined name DentalRates was not defined, the table_array argument would be entered as 'Lookup Tables'!H4:K5, and you would need to change the range to absolute references ('Lookup Tables'!$H$4:$K$5) so the formula would copy correctly to other cells.

7. In the Row_index_num box, type **2** and then press the **Tab** key. The number 2 indicates the monthly cost is stored in the second row of the DentalRates lookup table.

8. In the Range_lookup box, type **FALSE**. This sets the function to find an exact match in the lookup table. See Figure 8-31.

Figure 8-31	Function Arguments dialog box for the HLOOKUP function

9. Click the **OK** button. The dialog box closes, 65 appears in cell T2, and the formula =HLOOKUP(K2,DentalRates,2,FALSE) appears in the formula bar. The remaining rows in the Dental Plan Cost column are filled with the HLOOKUP function.

   Trouble? If #N/A appears in the Dental Plan Cost column, you may have used a VLOOKUP function. If necessary, edit the formula in cell T2 to use HLOOKUP instead of VLOOKUP.

10. Click at the end of the formula, type ***12** to multiply the monthly amount by 12, and then press the **Enter** key. The amount in cell T2 changes to $780, the annual amount, and all the other cells in the Dental Plan Cost column are updated.

11. Select the values in the Dental Plan Cost column, format the range in the **Accounting** format with no decimal places, and then widen the column width as needed to display all of the values.

12. Select cell **T2** to deselect the column. See Figure 8-32.

Figure 8-32 **Exact match HLOOKUP function for calculating the dental plan cost**

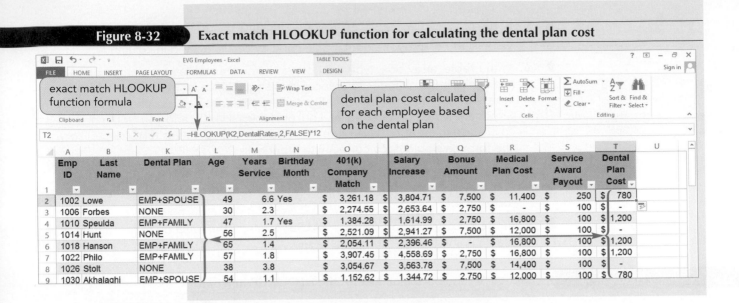

Using the IFERROR Function

Error values indicate that some element in a formula or a cell referenced in a formula is preventing Excel from returning a calculated value. Recall that an error value begins with a number sign (#) followed by an error name that indicates the type of error. For instance, the error value #N/A appears in a Medical Plan Cost cell when the VLOOKUP function cannot find the medical plan code in the MedicalRates lookup table. This error value message is not particularly descriptive or helpful.

You can use the IFERROR function to display a more descriptive message that helps users fix the problem. The IFERROR function can determine if a cell contains an error value and then display the message you choose rather than the default error value; or if no error value exists in the formula, display the result of the formula. The IFERROR function has the syntax

```
IFERROR(expression,valueIfError)
```

where *expression* is the formula you want to check for an error, and *valueIfError* is the message you want displayed if Excel detects an error in the formula you are checking. If Excel does not detect an error, the result of the *expression* is displayed.

You can use the IFERROR function to find and handle formula errors. For example, you can enter the following formula to determine whether an invalid code was entered in the Medical Plan Cost column of the Employee table, and then display a more descriptive message if Excel detects an error:

```
=IFERROR(VLOOKUP(J2,MedicalRates,2,FALSE)*12,"Invalid code")
```

Based on this formula, if the value in cell J2 is SPOUSE2500, the result of the VLOOKUP formula is $950 (the corresponding value from the MedicalRates table), the first argument in the IFERROR function (shown in red) is executed, and the medical plan cost is displayed. On the other hand, if cell J2 has an invalid medical plan code, such as FAMILY1500, the VLOOKUP function returns the error value #N/A, the second argument in the IFERROR function (shown in blue) is executed, and Invalid code is displayed.

Patrick wants to verify that all employees have an amount assigned in the Medical Plan Cost column. You will check whether any cell in the Medical Plan Cost column contains an error value.

To check for an error value in the Medical Plan Cost column:

1. Scroll to row **54** in the Medical Plan Cost column, and notice the error value #N/A in cell R54.

2. Select cell **R54**. See Figure 8-33.

Figure 8-33   **Error value in the Medical Plan Cost column**

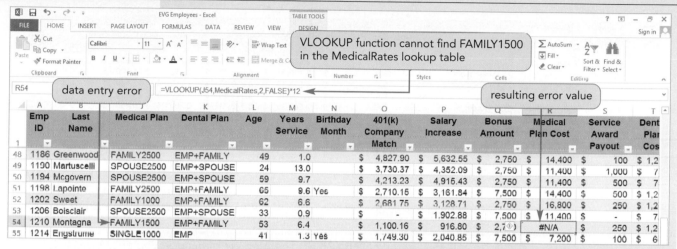

3. In row 54, in the Medical Plan column, observe that the medical plan code is FAMILY1500, which is an invalid code.

Patrick asks you to modify the formulas in the Medical Plan Cost column so that the descriptive error message "Invalid code" appears rather than the error value. The IFERROR function will check for errors in the formula and display the error message you create rather than the error value if it finds an error.

You'll nest the VLOOKUP function within the IFERROR function to display "Invalid code" in the Medical Plan Cost column if Excel detects an error value.

To nest the VLOOKUP function within the IFERROR function:

1. Double-click cell **R54** to enter Edit mode. The formula =VLOOKUP(J54,MedicalRates,2,FALSE)*12 appears in the cell and the formula bar. You'll nest this formula within the IFERROR function.

2. Click to the right of **=** (the equal sign), and then type **IFERROR(** to begin entering the IFERROR function. The first argument in the IFERROR function is the formula you want to use if no error value is found; this is the VLOOKUP function already entered in the cell.

> Be sure to type a comma before the error message.

3. Move the insertion point to the right of the entire formula, and then type **,"Invalid code")** to add the text you want to display if an error is found.

4. Press the **Enter** key. The error message "Invalid code" appears in cell R54, and the revised formula is automatically copied to all cells in the column. See Figure 8-34.

Figure 8-34   **Invalid code message in the Medical Plan Cost column**

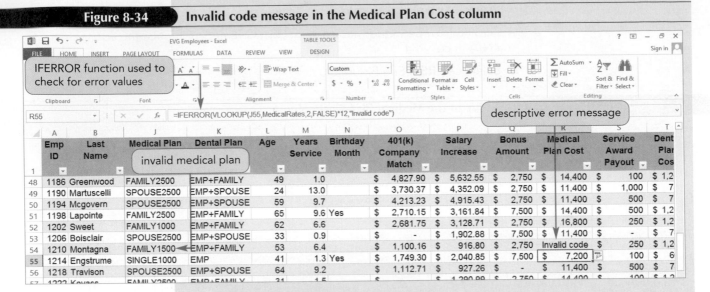

Trouble? If the error #NAME? appears in cell R54, you may have omitted quotation marks around the "Invalid code" error message. Correct the formula, and then continue with Step 5.

5. In cell **J54**, enter **FAMILY2500**. The medical plan code you entered is valid, so the medical cost value $14,400 appears in cell R54.

6. Scroll to the top of the table, select cell **R2**, and then observe in the formula bar that the IFERROR formula was copied to this cell.

In this session, you used nested IF functions to determine employee bonuses, you used the VLOOKUP function to calculate the medical plan cost, and you used the HLOOKUP function to calculate the dental plan cost and service award payouts. You also used the IFERROR function to display a descriptive message if invalid medical plan codes are entered in the Employee table. In the next session, you will use conditional formatting to identify duplicate records, and use the COUNTIF, SUMIF, and AVERAGEIF functions to report on employee salaries.

Session 8.2 Quick Check

REVIEW

1. What is a nested IF function?
2. If cell Y5 displays the value 35, cell Y6 displays the value 42, and cell Y7 contains the following formula, what is displayed in cell Y7?

   `=IF(Y5>Y6,"Older",IF(Y5<Y6,"Younger","Same Age"))`
3. Explain the difference between an exact match and an approximate match lookup.
4. A customer table includes columns for name, street address, city, state abbreviation, and zip code. A second table includes state abbreviations and state names from all 50 states (one state per row). You need to add a new column to the customer table with the state name. What is the most appropriate function to use to display the state name in this new column?
5. Convert the following criteria used to determine a student's level to a table that can be used in a VLOOKUP function to display the level of each student:

Earned Credits	Level
>=0 and <=30	Freshman
>=31 and <=60	Sophomore
>=61 and <=90	Junior
>=91	Senior

6. In cell X5, the error value #DIV/0! appears when you divide by 0. What IFERROR function can you use with the formula =W5/W25 so that instead of the error value #DIV/0! being displayed, the message "Dividing by zero" appears in the cell?
7. In cell X5, the formula =W5/W25 results in the error value #DIV/0! when W25 stores the value 0. Use the IF function to modify the formula =W5/W25 so that instead of the error value #DIV/0! being displayed when W25 stores 0, the message "Dividing by zero" appears in the cell.
8. Which function could be used with the following Sales Tax Rate table to display the sales tax rate for a customer in one of these four states?

State	CO	NM	OK	TX
Sales Tax Rate	10%	7%	9%	9.5%

Session 8.3 Visual Overview:

Highlighting duplicate values adds formatting to cells that have the same entry. In this instance, a gold fill highlights cells with the same employee ID.

The Conditional Formatting button provides access to the Duplicate Values conditional format and the Manage Rules option, which opens the Conditional Formatting Rules Manager dialog box.

You can edit existing conditional formatting rules from the Conditional Formatting Rules Manager dialog box. Click the Edit Rule button and make the appropriate changes.

Each time you apply a conditional format, you are defining a conditional formatting rule. You can also create a new rule from this dialog box by clicking the New Rule button.

A **conditional formatting rule** specifies the condition, the formatting, and the cell or range to apply the rule to. This rule highlights duplicate values with a gold fill in the range A1:A102.

Conditional Formatting and Functions

These formulas use fully qualified structured references to make them easier to create and understand.

The **AVERAGEIF** function calculates the average of values in a range that match criteria you specify, such as calculating the average salary paid to employees in NY and SF.

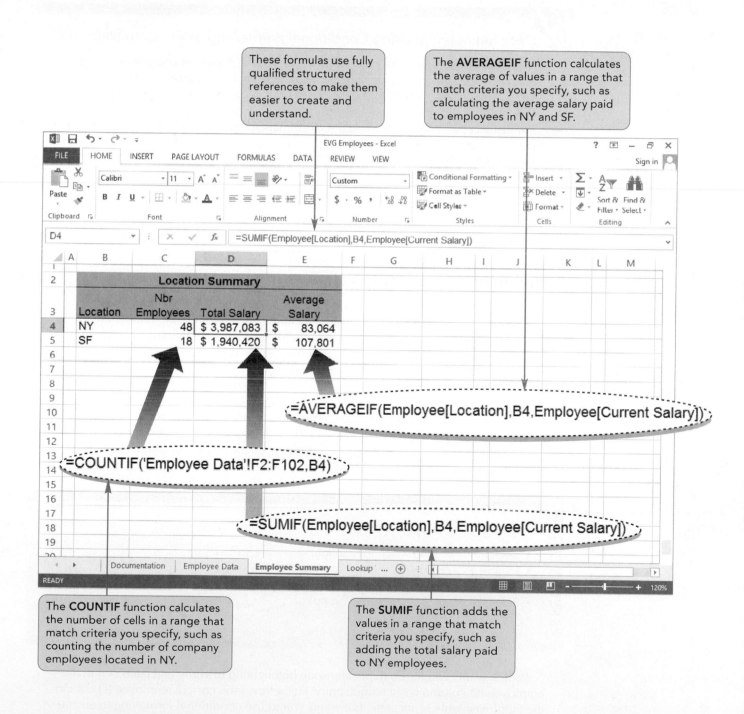

=AVERAGEIF(Employee[Location],B4,Employee[Current Salary])

=COUNTIF('Employee Data'!F2:F102,B4)

=SUMIF(Employee[Location],B4,Employee[Current Salary])

The **COUNTIF** function calculates the number of cells in a range that match criteria you specify, such as counting the number of company employees located in NY.

The **SUMIF** function adds the values in a range that match criteria you specify, such as adding the total salary paid to NY employees.

Applying Conditional Formatting

Conditional formatting changes a cell's formatting when its contents match a specified condition. You have already used conditional formatting to highlight cells based on their values, and to add data bars that graph the relative values in a range. You can also use conditional formatting to highlight duplicate values in a column of data.

PROSKILLS

Decision Making: Using Conditional Formatting to Evaluate Data

Decisions are made by evaluating data. However, this becomes complex when large quantities of data or dynamic data are involved. In these instances, conditional formatting can be a useful tool to help with your decision making. Conditional formatting is designed to make searching a data range both simple and efficient. For instance, you can quickly find the latest market prices in a real-time stock quote spreadsheet by using conditional formatting to highlight them. You can use conditional formatting to find stocks whose price drops below the target buy price by highlighting the row of any stock that meets the buy criteria. You can use conditional formatting to quickly identify bank accounts with a bank balance that is overdrawn by highlighting accounts with a negative balance. Mastering the art of conditional formatting will help you make better decisions.

Highlighting Duplicate Values

Excel is often used to manage lists of data, such as employee information, inventory, or phone numbers. These types of lists often include data that repeats in different records, such as the employee's state in his or her mailing address, a warehouse location for inventory, or an area code for phone numbers. On the other hand, some of the data is usually unique for each record, such as an employee ID or a product number. As the list of data becomes more extensive, duplicate entries may inadvertently occur. One way to identify unintended duplicate entries is to use conditional formatting to highlight duplicate values in a range with a font and/or fill color. This color coding makes it easier to identify the duplicates so you can then determine whether an entry needs to be corrected. In addition to the colors provided, you can create a custom format for the highlighting.

REFERENCE

Highlighting Duplicate Values

- Select the range in which to highlight duplicate values.
- On the HOME tab, in the Styles group, click the Conditional Formatting button, point to Highlight Cells Rules, and then click Duplicate Values.
- Select the appropriate formatting option.
- Click the OK button.

Patrick wants you to use duplicate value highlighting to verify that each cell in the employee ID column has a unique entry. He believes the current employee ID data in the Employee table is accurate, but wants you to use conditional formatting to ensure that there are no duplicate entries.

To highlight duplicate employee IDs using conditional formatting:

1. If you took a break at the end of the previous session, make sure the EVG Employees workbook is open and the Employee Data worksheet is active.

2. Select the data in column A. Rows 2 through 101 in the Emp ID column are selected.

3. On the ribbon, click the **HOME** tab, if necessary.

4. In the Styles group, click the **Conditional Formatting** button, point to **Highlight Cells Rules**, and then click **Duplicate Values**. The Duplicate Values dialog box opens.

5. Click the **values with** arrow to display a list of formatting options, and then click **Custom Format** to create a format that is not in the list. The Format Cells dialog box opens. You'll change the background fill color to red.

6. Click the **Fill** tab, and then, in the Background Color palette, click **red** (the second color in the last row).

7. Click the **OK** button in the Format Cells dialog box, and then click the **OK** button in the Duplicate Values dialog box. Any duplicate values in the ID column appear in a red cell.

8. Scroll the table to ensure that no duplicate values are found, then select cell **A2**.

After you enter a formula, you should test all situations to verify how the formula performs in each case. In this case, you should test the column both with duplicate values and without duplicate values. No duplicate records appear in the Employee table, so you'll change the ID of the last record from 1398 to 1002, which is the ID of the first employee. The backgrounds of the cells with the duplicate IDs should turn red, which will confirm that the conditional formatting is working as intended. Then, you will return the ID to its original value and confirm that the duplicate value highlighting disappears.

To test the duplicate value conditional formatting:

1. Click in the **Name** box, and then enter **A101**. The active cell moves to the last row in the Employee table.

2. In cell **A101**, enter **1002**. The ID changes from 1398 to 1002, and cell A101 is filled with red because it contains a duplicate ID. See Figure 8-35.

Figure 8-35 | Duplicate record highlighted

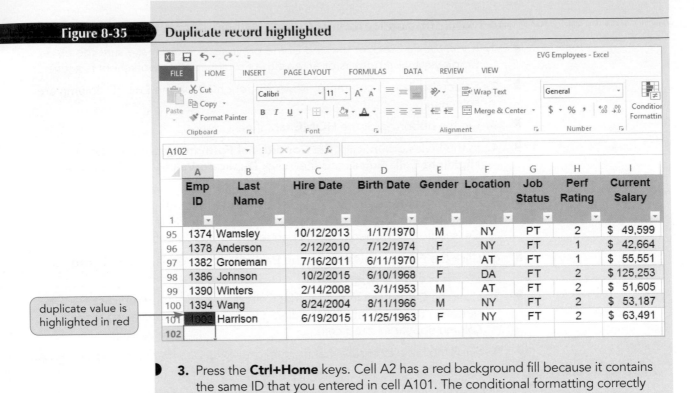

duplicate value is
highlighted in red

> 3. Press the **Ctrl+Home** keys. Cell A2 has a red background fill because it contains the same ID that you entered in cell A101. The conditional formatting correctly identified the duplicate values.

Using the Conditional Formatting Rules Manager

Each time you apply a conditional format, you are defining a conditional formatting rule. A rule specifies the type of condition (such as formatting cells greater than a specified value), the type of formatting when that condition occurs (such as light red fill with dark red text), and the cell or range the formatting is applied to. You can edit existing conditional formatting rules from the Conditional Formatting Rules Manager dialog box.

REFERENCE

Editing a Conditional Formatting Rule

- Select the range with the conditional formatting you want to edit.
- On the HOME tab, in the Styles group, click the Conditional Formatting button, and then click Manage Rules.
- Select the rule you want to edit, and then click the Edit Rule button.
- In the Select a Rule Type box, click a rule type, and then make the appropriate changes in the Edit the Rule Description section.
- Click the OK button in each dialog box.

The red background fill makes the cell content difficult to read. Patrick asks you to use a gold fill color to better contrast with the black text. You'll use the Conditional Formatting Rules Manager dialog box to edit the rule that specifies the formatting applied to duplicate values in the ID column.

To change the duplicate values fill color using the Conditional Formatting Rules Manager:

1. On the HOME tab, in the Styles group, click the **Conditional Formatting** button, and then click **Manage Rules**. The Conditional Formatting Rules Manager dialog box opens, listing all the formatting rules for the current selection, which, in this case, is the Employee table.

2. Verify that the Show formatting rules for box shows **This Table**. All the rules currently in effect in the Employee table are displayed. You can add new rules and edit or delete existing rules. You also can control which formatting rules are displayed in the dialog box, such as all rules in a specific worksheet or table. See Figure 8-36.

Figure 8-36   **Conditional Formatting Rules Manager dialog box**

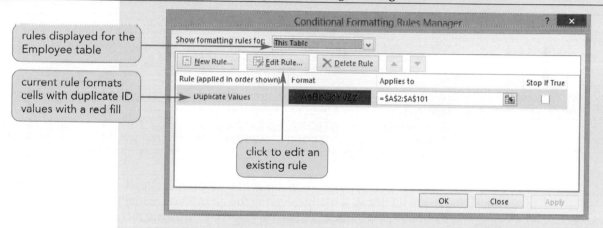

rules displayed for the Employee table

current rule formats cells with duplicate ID values with a red fill

click to edit an existing rule

3. Click the **Edit Rule** button. The Edit Formatting Rule dialog box opens. See Figure 8-37.

Figure 8-37   **Edit Formatting Rule dialog box**

selected rule type

preview of the formatting for the selected rule type

click to open the Format Cells dialog box

TIP

You can click a filter arrow, point to Filter by Color, and click a color to display only cells with that fill or click No Fill to display only cells without a fill.

▶ **4.** Click the **Format** button. The Format Cells dialog box opens.

▶ **5.** Click the **Fill** tab, if necessary, and then, in the Background Color palette, click **gold** (the third color in the last row).

▶ **6.** Click the **OK** button in each dialog box. The duplicate records in the table are formatted with a gold background color. See Figure 8-38.

Figure 8-38 | **Edited conditional formatting for duplicate records**

background color of duplicate value is gold

The cell text is easier to read on the gold background. Patrick wants you to correct the duplicate ID in cell A101 by entering the employee's actual ID number. The conditional format will remain active and apply to any new records that Patrick adds to the Employee table.

To correct the duplicate ID:

▶ **1.** Make cell **A101** the active cell, and then enter **1398**. The employee's ID is updated and the conditional formatting disappears because the value in the ID column is no longer a duplicate.

▶ **2.** Scroll to the top of the Employee table, and verify that the conditional formatting no longer appears in cell A2.

Keep in mind that the Duplicate Values rule enables you to verify that each entry in the ID column is unique, but it does not ensure that each unique value is accurate.

INSIGHT

Creating a Formula to Conditionally Format Cells

Sometimes the built-in conditional formatting rules do not apply the formatting you need. In these instances, you may be able to create a conditional formatting rule based on a formula that uses a logical expression to describe the condition you want. For example, you can create a formula that uses conditional formatting to compare cells in different columns or to highlight an entire row.

When you create the formula, keep in mind the following guidelines:

- The formula must start with an equal sign.
- The formula must be in the form of a logical test that results in a True or False value.
- In most cases, the formula should use relative references and point to the first row of data in the table. If the formula references a cell or range outside the table, use an absolute reference.
- After you create the formula, enter test values to ensure the conditional formatting works in all situations that you intended.

For example, to use conditional formatting to highlight whether the hire date entered in column C is less than the birth date entered in column D, you need to enter a formula that applies conditional formatting and compares cells in different columns of a table. The following steps describe how to create this formula:

1. Select the range you want to format (in this case, the Hire Date column).
2. On the HOME tab, in the Styles group, click the Conditional Formatting button, and then click New Rule.
3. In the Select a Rule Type box, click the "Use a formula to determine which cells to format" rule.
4. In the "Format values where this formula is true" box, enter the appropriate formula (in this case, =C2<D2).
5. Click the Format button to open the Format Cells dialog box, and then select the formatting you want to apply.
6. Click the OK button in each dialog box.

Another example is to highlight the entire row if an employee has 10 or more years of service. In this case, you would select the range of data, such as A2:T101, and then enter =M$2>=10 in the "Format values where this formula is true" box. The other steps remain the same.

Using Functions to Summarize Data Conditionally

The COUNT function tallies the number of data values in a range, the SUM function adds the values in a range, and the AVERAGE function calculates the average of the values in a range. However, sometimes you need to calculate a conditional count, sum, or average using only those cells that meet a particular condition. In those cases, you need to use the COUNTIF, SUMIF, and AVERAGEIF functions. For example, Patrick wants to create a report that shows the number, total, and average salaries for employees in New York and San Francisco. You will use the COUNTIF, SUMIF, and AVERAGEIF functions to do this.

Using the COUNTIF Function

You can calculate the number of cells in a range that match criteria you specify by using the COUNTIF function, which is sometimes referred to as a **conditional count**. The COUNTIF function has the syntax

COUNTIF(*range*, *criteria*)

where *range* is the range of cells you want to count, and *criteria* is a number, an expression, a cell reference, or text that defines which cells to count.

There are many ways to express the criteria in a COUNTIF function, as shown in Figure 8-39.

Figure 8-39   Examples of COUNTIF function criteria

Formula	Explanation of Formula	Result
=COUNTIF(F2:F101,"DA")	Number of employee in DA (Dallas)	13
=COUNTIF(F2:F101,F2)	Number of employees in cell F2 (NY)	48
=COUNTIF(I2:I101,"<50000")	Number of employees with salary <50000	22
=COUNTIF(I2:I101,">=" &I2)	Number of employees with salary >= value in cell I2 (108706)	24

© 2014 Cengage Learning

TIP

You can use structured references or cell and range addresses to reference cells within an Excel table.

Patrick wants to know how many employees are located in New York. You can use the COUNTIF function to find this answer because you want a conditional count (a count of employees who meet a specified criterion; in this case, employees located in New York). The location information is stored in column F of the Employee table. To count the number of employees in New York, you can use either one of the following formulas:

Range reference =COUNTIF('Employee Data'!F2:F101,"=NY")

Fully qualified structured reference =COUNTIF(Employee[Location],"=NY")

With either formula, Excel counts all of the cells in the Location column of the Employee table that contain the text equal to NY. Because NY is text, you must enclose it within quotation marks. It is not necessary to enclose numbers in quotation marks.

You will enter this formula using the COUNTIF function in the Employee Summary worksheet. You will use the Insert Function dialog box to help you build the formula using worksheet and range references to calculate the number of employees who work in New York.

To count employees located in New York using the COUNTIF function:

▶ **1.** Go to the **Employee Summary** worksheet.

▶ **2.** Select cell **C4**, and then click the **Insert Function** button f_x next to the formula bar. The Insert Function dialog box opens.

▶ **3.** Click the **Or select a category** arrow, and then click **Statistical**.

▶ **4.** In the Select a function box, double-click **COUNTIF**. The Function Arguments dialog box opens.

▶ **5.** In the Range box, type **'Employee Data'!F2:F101** to enter the range to search, and then press the **Tab** key. The range 'Employee Data'!F2:F101 refers to all data values in the range F2:F101 (Location column) in the Employee Data worksheet.

6. In the Criteria box, type **B4**. Cell B4 contains NY, which is the criterion you want Excel to use to determine which employee records to count. See Figure 8-40. You could also have typed "=NY" or "NY" in the criteria box.

Function Arguments dialog box for the COUNTIF function

reference to values in the Location column

criterion to determine which employee records to count

number of cells in the range that contain the criterion "NY"

7. Click the **OK** button. Cell C4 remains active. The formula =COUNTIF('Employee Data'!F2:F101,B4) appears in the formula bar, and 48 appears in cell C4, indicating that the company has 48 employees in New York. See Figure 8-41.

Location Summary for NY employees

completed COUNTIF function

number of employees located in NY

You will enter a similar formula to calculate the number of employees who work in San Francisco. This time, however, you will use structured references to specify the range to search.

To count the number of employees who work in San Francisco:

1. Select cell **C5**, and then click the **Insert Function** button next to the formula bar. The Insert Function dialog box opens with the Statistical category still selected.

2. In the Select a function box, double-click **COUNTIF**. The Function Arguments dialog box opens.

3. In the Range box, type **Employee[Location]** to enter the range to search, and then press the **Tab** key. The range Employee[Location] is a structured reference that refers to all data values in the Location column in the Employee table (the range F2:F101). The beginning values in the Location column appear to the right of the Range box.

4. In the Criteria box, type **B5**. Cell B5 contains SF (the value shown to the right of the Criteria box), which is the criterion Excel will use to determine which employee records to count.

5. Click the **OK** button. Cell C5 remains active. The formula =COUNTIF(Employee[Location],B5) appears in the formula bar and 17 appears in cell C5, indicating 17 employees work in San Francisco.

Using the SUMIF Function

The SUMIF function adds the values in a range that meet criteria you specify. The SUMIF function is also called a **conditional sum**. The syntax of the SUMIF function is

```
SUMIF(range, criteria[, sum_range])
```

where *range* is the range of cells you want to filter before calculating a sum; *criteria* is a number, an expression, a cell reference, or text that defines which cells to count; and *sum_range* is the range of cells to total. The *sum_range* is optional; if you omit it, Excel will total the values specified in the *range* argument. For example, if you want to total the salaries for all employees with salaries greater than $50,000 (">50000"), you do not use the optional third argument.

Patrick wants to compare the total salaries paid to employees in New York and San Francisco. You can use the SUMIF function to do this because Patrick wants to conditionally add salaries of employees at a specified location. Location is recorded in column F of the Employee Data worksheet, and the salary data is stored in column K. You can use either of the following formulas to calculate this value:

Range references
```
=SUMIF('Employee Data'!F2:F101,"NY",'Employee Data'!I2:I101)
```

Fully qualified structured references
```
=SUMIF(Employee[Location],"NY",Employee[Current Salary])
```

Both of these formulas state that the salary of any employee whose location is New York will be added to the total. Using the SUMIF function, you will insert the formula with structured references into the Employee Summary worksheet.

To sum employee salaries in the New York and San Francisco locations using the SUMIF function:

1. Select cell **D4**, and then click the **Insert Function** button f_x next to the formula bar. The Insert Function dialog box opens.

2. Click the **Or select a category** arrow, and then click **Math & Trig**.

3. In the Select a function box, double-click **SUMIF**. The Function Arguments dialog box opens.

4. In the Range box, type **Employee[Location]** to specify the range of data to filter, and then press the **Tab** key. The range Employee[Location] is a structured reference that refers to all data values in the Location column in the Employee table (the range F2:F101).

5. In the Criteria box, type **B4** and then press the **Tab** key. Cell B4 contains "NY" (shown to the right of the Criteria box), which is the criterion Excel will use to determine which employee records to sum.

6. In the Sum_range box, type **Employee[Current Salary]** to indicate that the Current Salary column in the Employee table contains the data to sum in the filtered rows. The values to the right of the Sum_range box are the amounts in the filtered Current Salary column. See Figure 8-42.

Figure 8-42   Function Arguments dialog box for the SUMIF function

reference to values in the Location column using a structured reference

criterion to determine how to filter the employee records

total annual salary for NY employees

data to sum in the filtered records

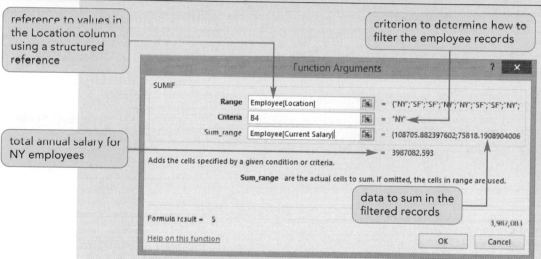

7. Click the **OK** button. Cell D4 is active. The formula =SUMIF(Employee[Location],B4,Employee[Current Salary]) appears in the formula bar and $3,987,083 appears in cell D4, indicating the total annual salaries paid to New York employees.

   Trouble? If Invalid appears in the cell or an error message appears, you probably mistyped some part of the formula. Review the SUMIF formula you entered and make sure it matches the formula =SUMIF(Employee[Location],B4, Employee[Current Salary]).

8. Copy the SUMIF formula in cell D4 to **D5**. The total Current Salary for employees working in San Francisco is $1,917,420.

Using the AVERAGEIF Function

The AVERAGEIF function is similar to the SUMIF function. You use the AVERAGEIF function to calculate the average of values in a range that meet criteria you specify. The syntax of the AVERAGEIF function is

```
AVERAGEIF(range, criteria[, average_range])
```

where *range* is the range of cells you want to filter before calculating the average, *criteria* is the condition used to filter the range, and *average_range* is the range of cells to average. The *average_range* is optional; if you omit it, Excel will average the values specified in the *range* argument.

Patrick also wants to compare the average salaries paid to employees in New York and San Francisco. Location is recorded in column F of the Employee Data worksheet, and the current salary data is stored in column I. The formulas to calculate this value are:

Range references

```
=AVERAGEIF('Employee Data'!F2:F101,"NY",'Employee Data'!I2:I101)
```

Fully qualified structured references

```
=AVERAGEIF(Employee[Location],"NY",Employee[Current Salary])
```

Both of these formulas state that the current salary of any employee whose location is New York will be included in the average. You will enter the formula into the Employee Summary worksheet using the AVERAGEIF function with structured references.

> **To average employee salaries in New York and San Francisco using the AVERAGEIF function:**
>
> **1.** Select cell **E4**, and then click the **Insert Function** button f_x next to the formula bar. The Insert Function dialog box opens.
>
> **2.** Click the **Or select a category** arrow, and then click **Statistical**.
>
> **3.** In the Select a function box, double-click **AVERAGEIF**. The Function Arguments dialog box opens.
>
> **4.** In the Range box, type the structured reference **Employee[Location]** to specify the range of data to filter, and then press the **Tab** key. The range Employee[Location] is a structured reference that refers to all data values in the Location column in the Employee table (the range F2:F101).
>
> **5.** In the Criteria box, type **B4** and then press the **Tab** key. Cell B4 contains "NY" (shown to the right of the Criteria box), which is the criterion Excel will use to determine which employee records to average.
>
> **6.** In the Average_range box, type **Employee[Current Salary]** to indicate that the Current Salary column in the Employee table contains the data to average in the filtered rows. See Figure 8-43.

Figure 8-43	Function Arguments dialog box for the AVERAGEIF function

7. Click the **OK** button. Cell E4 remains active. The formula =AVERAGEIF(Employee[Location],B4,Employee[Current Salary]) appears in the formula bar and $83,064 appears in cell E4, indicating the average salary paid to New York employees.

8. Copy the formula in cell E4 to cell **E5**. EVG pays an average of $112,789 to employees working in San Francisco. See Figure 8-44.

Figure 8-44 **Completed Location Analysis report**

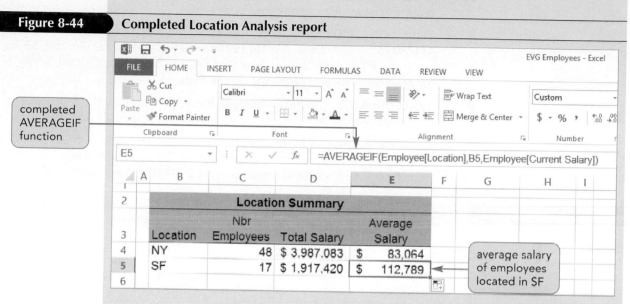

completed AVERAGEIF function

E5 =AVERAGEIF(Employee[Location],B5,Employee[Current Salary])

	Location Summary		
Location	Nbr Employees	Total Salary	Average Salary
NY	48	$ 3,987,083	$ 83,064
SF	17	$ 1,917,420	$ 112,789

average salary of employees located in SF

As Patrick enters new employees or edits the location or current salary values of current employees, the values in the Employee Summary worksheet will be automatically updated because the formulas reference the Employee table.

INSIGHT

Using the TRANSPOSE Function

The **TRANSPOSE function** is used to change the orientation of a range—that is, return a vertical range of cells as a horizontal range, or vice versa. The TRANSPOSE function has the syntax

TRANSPOSE(array)

where *array* is the range you want to convert from row data to column data (or vice versa). To use the TRANSPOSE function, complete the following steps:

1. Select the range where you want to place the transposed data. Be sure to select the opposite number of rows and columns as the original data. For example, if the range has five rows and three columns you would select a range that has three rows and five columns.
2. In the first cell of the selected range, type =TRANSPOSE(to begin the function.
3. Type the range reference of the original range of data.
4. Type) to complete the function.
5. Press the Ctrl+Shift+Enter keys to enter the function. (Note that pressing only the Enter key would create incorrect formula results.) Excel places curly brackets {} around the array formula and enters the formula in every cell of the selected range.

Keep in mind that the TRANSPOSE function only copies the data from the cells in the initial range. Any formatting applied to the original range must be reapplied to the new range. However, any changes made to the data in the original range are automatically made to the data in the transposed range. To delete the transposed range, select the entire range, and then press the Delete key.

Patrick has recently hired a new employee and he asks you to add the new record to the Excel table.

To add a record to the Employee table:

1. Go to the **Employee Data** worksheet, and then select cell **A102**. You will enter the new employee record in this row.

2. In the range **A102:K102**, enter **1402** for Emp ID, **Joplin** for Last Name, **4/1/2016** for Hire Date, **11/15/1970** for Birth Date, **M** for Gender, **SF** for Location, **PT** for Job Status, **3** for Perf Rating, **23000** for Current Salary, **None** for Medical Plan, and **None** for Dental Plan.

3. Select cell **A103**. The new employee record is added to the Employee table, and all values in the calculated columns are automatically updated.

4. Go to the **Employee Summary** worksheet. The Location Analysis report has been updated to reflect the new employee. The number of employees in San Francisco is 18 and the average salary is $107,801. See Figure 8-45.

Figure 8-45   **Updated Location Analysis report**

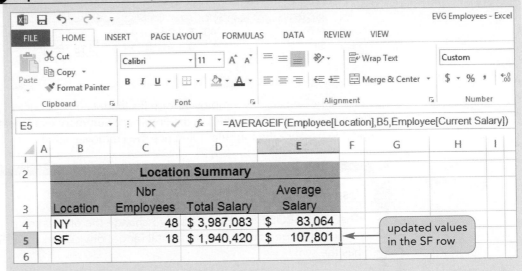

5. Save the workbook, and then close it.

If the employee data had been stored as a range of data instead of an Excel table, the Location Analysis report would not have automatically updated. Instead, you would have had to modify all the formulas in the report to reflect the expanded range of employee data. Patrick is pleased with the formulas you added to the Employee Data and Employee Summary worksheets.

REVIEW

Session 8.3 Quick Check

1. Would you apply the duplicate value conditional formatting rule to a table column of last names? Why or why not?

2. If you receive a worksheet that includes conditional formatting, which dialog box would you use to find out what criteria were used for the formatting?

3. Explain what the following formula calculates:
   =COUNTIF(Employee[Gender],"=F")

4. Explain what the following formula calculates:
   =AVERAGEIF(Employee[Age],">50",Employee[Current Salary]) calculates.

5. Explain what the following formula calculates:
   =SUMIF(Employee[Job Status],"=FT",Employee[Current Salary])

6. Explain what the following formula calculates:
   =COUNTIF(Employee[Current Salary],">100000")

7. To display the number of employees working in Dallas (DA), which function would you use—the VLOOKUP, COUNTIF, IF, or COUNT function?

8. To identify duplicate values in a column of an Excel table, what Excel feature would you use?

Review Assignments

Data File needed for the Review Assignments: Compensation.xlsx

Patrick wants you to try using some alternative calculations for bonuses and benefits for EVG employees. Complete the following:

1. Open the **Compensation** workbook located in the Excel8 ▸ Review folder included with your Data Files, and then save the workbook as **Bonus and Benefits**.

2. In the Documentation worksheet, enter your name and the date.

3. In the Employee Data worksheet, rename the Excel table as **EmpData**.

4. Employees who are age 50 or older are allowed to contribute up to $22,000 during the year to their 401(k) plan; all employees under age 50 can contribute a maximum of $17,000 during the year. In the 401(k) Max Contrib column, use an IF function to determine the maximum 401(k) contribution for each employee.

5. Only full-time (Job Status) employees over the age of 30 (Age) with more than one year of service are eligible for the 401(k) benefit. In the 401(k) Company Match column, enter the IF and AND functions to calculate the 401(k) company match as a percentage of the employee's current salary; use a reference to cell X1 to obtain the 401(k) matching percent rate (3 percent). If the employee is not eligible, enter **0**.

6. All full-time (FT) employees are eligible for a bonus. Pay Grade A employees receive $3,000 (cell X2), Pay Grade B employees receive $6,000 (cell X3), and Pay Grade C employees receive $8,000 (cell X4). In the Bonus Amount column, enter nested IF functions to calculate the bonus. For employees not eligible for a bonus, display the text **NE**.

7. In the Eligible Salary Increase column, enter IF and OR functions to insert the text **Not Eligible** if the employee's pay grade is C or the employee's job status is a consultant (CN). Leave the cell blank if the individual is eligible for a salary increase.

8. In the Vision Plan Cost column, enter the HLOOKUP function to do an exact match lookup to calculate the annual vision plan cost. Use the VisionRates data (the range $H$3:$K$4 in the Lookup Tables worksheet), which contains the monthly vision rates. (*Hint*: The HLOOKUP function provides the monthly rate, which you will need to multiply by 12 to determine the annual rate.)

9. In the Years Service column, modify the formula to incorporate the IFERROR function and display the message **Invalid hire date** if an error value occurs. Test the modified formula by changing the date in cell C2 from 8/28/2014 to **18/28/2014**. Increase the column width as needed to display the entire message.

10. Edit the Duplicate Values conditional formatting rule applied to the Emp ID column so that the fill color of the duplicate value is formatted as light blue (the seventh color in the bottom row of the Background Color palette). Test this change by typing **1002** in cell A101.

11. In the Employee Summary worksheet, enter the COUNTIF function in cells C3 and C4 to count the number of female and male employees, respectively.

12. In cells D3 and D4, enter the AVERAGEIF function to calculate the average salary of female employees and the average salary of male employees, respectively. Format the average salary column using the Accounting format with two decimal places.

13. Save the workbook, and then close it.

Case Problem 1

Data File needed for this Case Problem: Spirit.xlsx

The Spirit Store   Alice Meachen established The Spirit Store, which sells products to loyal alums of Central State College. Products offered by Alice on her website range from tee shirts and backpacks to mugs and blankets—and all feature the school's logo. Alice has a large, steady base of clients who find these uniquely designed products a great reminder of their college days. To ensure the timely receipt of payments, Alice wants you to use Excel to create an invoice she can use for each customer transaction. Complete the following:

1. Open the **Sprit** workbook located in the Excel8 ▸ Case1 folder included with your Data Files, and then save the workbook as **Spirit Store**.

2. In the Documentation worksheet, enter your name and the date.

3. In the Product Pricing and Shipping worksheet, assign the defined name **ShippingCost** to the data stored in the range D2:E7, which can be used for an approximate match lookup. (*Hint*: The lookup table includes only the values, not the descriptive labels.)

4. In the Invoice worksheet, use data validation to make it easier to enter ordered items in the range C16:C36 by creating a list of the different items in the Product Pricing table in the Product Pricing and Shipping worksheet. (*Hint*: Select the entire range before setting the validation rule.)

5. In the Per Unit column (the range G16:G36), use a VLOOKUP function to retrieve the per-unit price of each ordered product from the Product Pricing data in the range A3:B28 in the Product and Shipping worksheet. (*Hint*: Use the defined name ProductPrice that was assigned to the Product Pricing data.)

6. Modify the formula in the Per Unit column by combining the IFERROR function with the VLOOKUP function to display either the per-unit price or a blank cell if an error value occurs.

7. In the Total column (the range H16:H36), enter a formula to calculate the total charge for that row (Qty × Per Unit). Use the IFERROR function to display either the total charge or a blank cell if an error value occurs. Format the column appropriately.

8. In the Subtotal cell (cell H37), add a formula to sum the Total column. Use the IFERROR function to display either the subtotal or a blank cell if an error value occurs. Format this cell appropriately.

9. In the Sales Tax cell (cell H38), enter a formula with nested IF functions to calculate 8.25 percent of the subtotal (cell H37) if the customer's state (cell D12) is OH, or 8.75 percent if the state is MI; otherwise, use 0 percent for the sales tax. Format this cell appropriately. (*Hint*: The defined name Subtotl is assigned to cell H37. Note that the defined name "Subtotl" is intentionally not spelled as "Subtotal," which is the name of an Excel function. The defined name State is assigned to cell D12.)

10. In the Shipping cell (cell H39), enter a formula that looks up the shipping cost from the Shipping Cost table in the Product Pricing and Shipping worksheet based on the subtotal in cell H37. If the subtotal is 0, the shipping cost should display 0. Format this cell appropriately. (*Hint*: Use the defined name you created for the Shipping Cost table data.)

11. In the Total Due cell (cell H40), calculate the invoice total by entering a formula that adds the values in the Subtotal, Sales Tax, and Shipping cells. Format this cell appropriately.

12. Test the worksheet using the following data:

Sold to:	**Ellen Farmer**
	222 Central Avenue
	Arlington, MI 60005
Date:	**6/15/2016**
Items ordered:	**Blanket**, 2
	Duffle Bag - Large, 1
	Scarf, 2

13. Save the workbook, and then close it.

TROUBLESHOOT

Case Problem 2

Data File needed for this Case Problem: Receivables.xlsx

Ward Consulting   Doug Gold is an accountant for Ward Consulting, a firm that provides research services for various corporate and government agencies. Each month, Doug provides the controller with an analysis of the outstanding accounts. Doug uses Excel to track these accounts. He asks you to enter formulas to allow him to analyze the data. Complete the following:

1. Open the **Receivables** workbook located in the Excel8 ▸ Case2 folder included with your Data Files, and then save the workbook as **Receivables Overdue**.

2. In the Documentation worksheet, enter your name and the date.

3. In the Invoices worksheet, in cell B1, enter **7/1/2016** as the current date. Note the defined name CurrentDate has been assigned to cell B1.

⚙ **Troubleshoot** 4. The sales rep commission rate varies for each sales rep. In column D, Doug used a VLOOKUP function to look up the commission rate for each sales rep, and then multiplied the commission rate by the invoice amount to calculate the commission. Although the first two rows in column D of the Excel table named Aging display the correct commission, all the other cells display #N/A. Find the problem with the formulas in the Commission column and fix it.

5. In column G, calculate the days past due. If the number of days since the invoice was sent (CurrentDate – Invoice Date) is greater than 30, calculate the days past due (Current Date – Invoice Date – 30); otherwise, enter 0.

6. Create the following formulas to assign the value in the Invoice Amount column to one of five columns—Current, 1–30 days, 31–60 days, 61–90 days, and Over 90 days:

   a. In the Current column, create a formula to display the invoice amount (column F) in the Current column if the number of days past due is 0.

   b. In the 1–30 days column, create a formula to display the invoice amount if the number of days past due is greater than or equal to 1 and less than or equal to 30.

   c. In the 31–60 days column, create a formula to display the invoice amount if the number of days past due is greater than or equal to 31 and less than or equal to 60.

   d. In the 61–90 days column, create a formula to display the invoice amount if the number of days past due is greater than or equal to 61 and less than or equal to 90.

   e. In the Over 90 days column, create a formula to display the invoice amount if the number of days past due is greater than or equal to 91 days.

   f. Format columns H through L in the Accounting format with two decimal places.

7. The invoice amount (column F) for each invoice can only appear once in columns H through L. In column N, do the following to create a formula to verify this rule.

   a. In cell N3, enter the label **Error Check**.

   b. In the range N4:N105, enter a formula using the IF and COUNT functions. The logical test of the IF function counts the number of cells that have an entry in columns H through L for each invoice. If the count is greater than one, the formula displays **Error**; otherwise, it leaves the cell blank.

8. Copy the Invoices worksheet to a new sheet and name it **Overdue Accts**. In the Overdue Accts worksheet, do the following:

   a. Filter the records so only invoices whose balance is past due are displayed.

   b. Sort the filtered data by invoice date (oldest first).

   c. Include a Total row in this table and display sums for columns I through L.

   d. Hide columns C, D, F, H, and N.

   e. Remove the filter buttons and gridlines from the table. (*Hint*: Use options on VIEW tab and the TABLE TOOLS DESIGN tab.)

Troubleshoot 9. In the Invoice Reports worksheet, Doug used the COUNTIF function to count the number of invoices for each sales rep. The formulas he created display only zeros. Fix the formulas in the range B3:B7 so that they display the number of invoices processed by each sales rep.

10. In the Invoice Reports worksheet, complete the Sales Rep Analysis report. In the Commission and Total Amount columns (columns C and D), use the SUMIF function to summarize commissions (column D in the Aging table in the Invoice worksheet) and the invoice amount (column F in the Aging table) for each sales rep. In row 7 of the report, calculate the totals. Format these columns appropriately.

11. In the Invoice Reports worksheet, complete the Accounts Receivable Aging report in the range F1:H8 by creating formulas that count the number of invoices for each group in the Invoices worksheet and sum the total amounts for those invoices.

12. In the Invoice Reports worksheet, in the range A12:B17, use the COUNTIF, SUMIF, and AVERAGEIF functions to complete the report. (*Hint*: The formulas will reference the Invoice Amount (column F) in the Invoices worksheet. Review Figure 8-39 to see various ways to enter criteria in the COUNTIF, SUMIF and AVERAGEIF functions.)

    a. In cell B15, use the COUNTIF function to count the number of invoices greater than the amount in cell B13.

    b. In cell B16, use the SUMIF function to add the total value of invoices greater than the amount in cell B13.

    c. In cell B17, use the AVERAGEIF function to calculate the average value of these invoices.

13. In cell B13, enter **1000** as the invoice amount above which invoices are included in the report.

14. Save the workbook, and then close it.

Case Problem 3

CREATE

Data File needed for this Case Problem: Currency.xlsx

Convenient Currency Exchange   Tourists about to travel from the United States to another country often need to obtain funds in the local currency of the country to which they are traveling. To satisfy this need, the Convenient Currency Exchange (CCE) set up kiosks at international airports around the country to provide currency exchange for a small fee. CCE's owner has asked you to complete the Excel workbook to simplify the calculation process. Complete the following:

1. Open the **Currency** workbook located in the Excel8 ▸ Case3 folder included with your Data Files, and then save the workbook as **Currency Calculator** in the location specified by your instructor.

2. In the Documentation worksheet, enter your name and the date.

3. In the Currency Calculator worksheet, in the range A3:D14, complete the Currency Conversion Table. Search the web to find the name of each country's currency (column B), its three-character currency code (column D), and what $1 (U.S.) equals in each country's currency (column C). As an example, the first row in the table has been completed for Australia. Be sure to update the $1 U.S. Equals cell for Australia to the current exchange rate.

4. In cell H4, create a data validation to create a list of countries in column A that users can select from to avoid data entry errors when entering the country name. (*Hint*: Use the defined name CountryList to reference countries.) Select Australia from the list.

5. In cell H5, enter **1000** as the U.S. dollars received.

6. In cell H6, enter a formula to calculate the conversion fee. If cell H5 is blank, cell H6 should also be blank. Otherwise, CCE charges a conversion fee of 3 percent (cell B17) of the total U.S. dollars received with a minimum charge of $5 (cell B18).

7. In cell H7, subtract the conversion fee (entered in cell H6) from the dollars received (in cell H5) to obtain the amount to be converted to the foreign currency.

8. In cell H9, use a VLOOKUP function to calculate the amount of foreign currency the traveler will receive. Multiply the amount being converted (in cell H7) by the correct exchange rate.

9. In cell G10, display the appropriate currency name of the country being visited. (*Hint*: Use a VLOOKUP function to retrieve the currency name. If cell H4 is blank, cell G10 should also be blank.)

10. In cell G12, look up and display the exchange rate for this transaction from the Currency Conversion Table.

11. In cell H12, lookup and display the currency code for this transaction from the Currency conversion table. If cell H4 is blank, cell G12 should also be blank.

12. In cell I12, enter the function that displays today's date.

13. Test the Currency Converter by deleting the country visiting (cell H4) and amount (cell H5) entries, and then modifying the formulas in any cell that displays an error value so that a blank cell is displayed instead of the error value.

14. Protect all cells except the cells into which you enter data (cells H4 and H5). Do not use a password.

15. Test the calculator by converting **500** U.S. dollars to Japanese yen.

16. Save the workbook, and then close it.

Case Problem 4

CHALLENGE

Data File needed for this Case Problem: Instruments.xlsx

Anthony's Music Store Anthony Malone sells and rents musical instruments. One part of his business involves renting instruments to K–12 students who participate in school bands and orchestras. Instruments available for rent include flutes, clarinets, trombones, oboes, piccolos, saxophones, accordions, bassoons, and French horns. Anthony maintains an Excel worksheet to track instrument rentals that includes the following information:

- **Renter**—the name of the renter
- **Instrument**—the type of instrument rented
- **Rental Date**—the date the instrument was rented
- **Rental Period**—either 3 or 9 months, as shown in the Rental Period column; no other rental periods are allowed
- **Ins Cov**—indicates whether renters elected to purchase instrument insurance; if elected, Yes appears in the Ins Cov column; otherwise, No is entered
- **Shipping Code**—indicates whether the renter wants the instrument delivered directly to the school (either Ground or Rush), or the renter will pick up the instrument at the store (Pickup).

Anthony wants you to expand the information that is tracked. Complete the following:

1. Open the **Instruments** workbook located in the Excel8 ▸ Tutorial folder included with your Data Files, and then save the workbook as **Instrument Rentals** in the location specified by your instructor.

2. In the Documentation worksheet, enter your name and the date.

3. In the Rental Data worksheet, in column G, create a formula that uses the HLOOKUP function to assign a group code (A, B, C, D, or E) from the InstrumentGroups range in the Rental Information worksheet to the instrument listed in column B.

✛ **Explore** 4. In column H, create a formula to determine the return date. Add the 3 or 9 month rental period (column D) to the rental date (column C) to calculate the return date. For example, if the rental date is 9/10/2016 and the rental period is 3 months, the return date is 12/10/2016. If the rental period is 9 months, then the return date is 6/10/2017. (*Hint*: Use the DATE function to calculate the return date. Use MONTH([Rental Date]), DAY([Rental Date]), and YEAR([Rental Date]) functions as arguments of the DATE function. Finally, add the rental period to the month argument.)

5. In column I, create a formula using the IF and VLOOKUP functions to calculate the rental charges for each instrument based on the instrument's group code, the rental period, and the Instrument Rental Charges table. (*Hint*: For the IF function arguments, use one VLOOKUP function for 3 months and another for 9 months. The defined name RentalCharges has been assigned to the Instrument Rental Charges table.)

6. In column J, enter a formula to calculate the insurance cost if the renter has elected insurance coverage (Yes in column E). Use the instrument's group code and the Monthly Insurance column in the RentalCharges table to look up the insurance cost. Remember to multiply the monthly insurance charge by the rental period. If the renter has not elected insurance, the cost is 0.

7. In column K, create a nested IF function to determine the shipping cost for each instrument. Use the shipping code (column F) and the shipping charge options Pickup (0), Ground ($25), and Rush ($50) to assign shipping costs to each rental instrument.

8. In column L, calculate the total cost, which is the sum of the rental charges, the insurance cost, and the shipping cost.

9. Format columns I through L with the Accounting format with no decimal places.

10. In the Rental Report worksheet, complete the Rental Summary report by creating formulas in the range C4:D5 using the COUNTIF and SUMIF functions.

11. In the Rental Data worksheet, enter the following new record:

Renter:	**Allen**
Instrument:	**Flute**
Rental Date:	**9/15/2016**
Rental Period:	**9**
Ins Cov:	**Yes**
Shipping Code:	**Rush**

⊕ **Explore** 12. Create the PivotTable shown in Figure 8-46 to display the number of rentals and rental $ by rental month. Rename the worksheet as **Monthly Rentals**. (*Hint*: Select any Rental Date in the PivotTable, and then on the PIVOTTABLE TOOLS ANALYZE tab, in the Group group, click the Group Field button to open the Grouping dialog box. Use Months as the grouping field.)

Figure 8-46	Monthly Rental Summary PivotTable

	# of Renters	Total Rental $
Jul	14	$ 2,262
Aug	16	$ 1,322
Sep	11	$ 1,494
Grand Total	**41**	**$ 5,078**

⊕ **Explore** 13. In the PivotTable, drill down to display the renters (all fields) in the source data that represent the 11 rentals in September. Rename the worksheet that is created as **SeptDetail**. (*Hint*: Double-click the appropriate cell in PivotTable to open a new worksheet with the supporting data.)

14. Save the workbook, and then close it.

Problem Solving

Solving a Problem Using an Excel Table

Problem solving is the ability to identify a gap between an existing state and a desired state of being. A problem can be a one-time issue such as which car to purchase, or a process-oriented dilemma such as how to track orders. The process of solving a problem follows a logical progression that consists of (1) recognizing and defining the problem; (2) determining feasible courses of action; (3) collecting information about those actions; and (4) evaluating the merits and drawbacks of each one in order to make a choice. Problem solving leads to decision making, and enables you to evaluate different courses of action and make an informed decision or select a good solution.

Recognize and Define the Problem

A problem is the gap between a desired state and reality. In order to recognize and define a problem, ask questions to determine the real issue and identify your ultimate goal. For example, ask such questions as: Why do I think there is a problem? Where is it occurring? When and how frequently is it occurring? What is causing the problem? Who is involved? Why is it occurring? The answers to these questions help you define the problem and determine what information you need in order to solve the problem. For instance, a company might want to make sure that employee benefits and overtime payments don't exceed a certain amount; therefore, it needs to track the cost of each employee's benefit package, salary, and overtime as well as determine that the total costs fall within the intended levels.

Determine Feasible Alternatives

With the problem defined, you can brainstorm possible solutions by collecting as many ideas as possible about how to correct the problem or achieve your goal. Write them all down. Don't discount any ideas as too radical, expensive, or impossible to achieve. Think creatively. Ask what-if questions, such as the following: What if we had unlimited resources? What if we had new skills? What if our competitors, suppliers, or customers acted in a certain way? What if I do nothing? For instance, a company might want to create a consistent way to track employee data—collecting the same data each time, categorizing the data by department or employee type, and then ensuring that paid benefits and overtime don't exceed a certain amount.

Collect Information Needed to Evaluate the Alternatives

Data is crucial to problem solving. Collect data and information related to each possible solution or alternative. This information can include data expressed as currency or numbers, as well as data that cannot be measured numerically. All collected data should be organized in a way that provides information for effective decision making and follow-up. For example, a business needs to collect data that enables it to write checks to employees, prepare reports about overtime, report payroll taxes to government agencies, provide premiums to health insurance companies, track Social Security payments, and so on. This requires an organized system to capture the appropriate data such as employee IDs, employee names, hours worked each day, salary or hourly rate, and insurance premium. You'll likely start to see relationships between the collected information that can provide insights into the feasibility of the possible solutions.

Evaluate and Choose an Alternative

Document both the benefits and costs of all alternatives, whether numerical (cost savings) or other (employee morale). Spreadsheet software often helps problem solvers track and quantify merits and drawbacks. Consider the resources required—financial, human, equipment, and so on. Are they affordable? Is there enough time to implement the different solutions? What risks are associated with an alternative? What consequences would result if the solution didn't work? The best choice is to go with the solution that offers the greatest reward for the least amount of risk. In some cases, the solution may require developing a "Plan B" to fall back on in case the chosen solution fails to solve the problem. For instance, when collecting payroll data, it may become apparent that insurance premiums constitute a higher percentage of payroll than previously thought, which requires further investigation and an alternative solution.

Don't try to select a solution that addresses every aspect of a problem, especially if it is complex. Solutions are rarely perfect. Instead, consider the overall effect each alternative may have. Will the resulting change generate positive results while solving the problem? Will the chosen alternative resolve the problem in the long term? Given the merits and drawbacks identified, what is realistic?

PROSKILLS

Develop an Excel Table

In daily life, you solve all sorts of problems, such as which car purchase makes the most economic sense when comparing purchase price, mileage, and maintenance, or which software package will help your biking club manage its funds, plan road trips, and keep memberships up to date. To solve these and other problems, you need to collect data that tracks the current situation, determine your ultimate goal, and then follow a logical progression to the best solution. Developing an Excel table can help you track the data you need to solve such problems.

In this exercise, you need to select an activity in which you participate or an organization to which you belong, and identify a one-time or process-oriented problem that needs to be solved. Then, create a worksheet and develop an Excel table to track relevant data and create a solution to the problem, using the Excel skills and features presented in Tutorials 5 through 8.

Note: Please be sure *not* to include any personal information of a sensitive nature in any worksheets you create to submit to your instructor. Later, you can update the worksheets with such information for your own personal use.

1. Identify a problem to solve. This can be a one-time problem, such as a car purchase, or a process-oriented problem, such as tracking membership data for a club to which you belong. Determine feasible alternatives to solve the problem, and then collect the data you need to evaluate these alternatives.

2. Plan the organization of your workbook and the Excel table you will develop based on how you will use the data. Consider the outputs you want to create, and the fields needed to produce those outputs. Decide what each record represents (such as data on a participant), and then identify the fields and field names (such as last name, first name, birth date, and so on) within each record. What calculations will you need to perform? How do you want to format the information?

3. Create a Documentation worksheet that includes your name, the date, and the purpose of your workbook. Include a data definition table to document the fields in each record. Format the worksheet appropriately.

4. Create an Excel table to track the data needed to solve the problem you identified. Enter an appropriate table name and column headers. Add one or more calculated columns to the table to perform calculations on the data that you will use to solve the problem.

5. Improve the appearance of the table by using appropriate formatting.

6. Apply validity checks to improve the accuracy of data entry.

7. Add records to the table.

8. Apply conditional formatting to at least one column in the table to visually highlight some aspect of the data that will help you evaluate and solve the problem.

9. Add a comment to the column with the conditional formatting to explain what the conditional formatting shows, and how it will help you to evaluate and solve the problem.

10. Insert a Total row in the table, and then make appropriate summary calculations that you can use to evaluate and solve the problem.

11. Divide the table into two horizontal panes—one for the data, and one for the Total row.

12. Sort the data in a logical way.

13. Use a filter to answer a question about the data to help you evaluate and solve the problem.

14. Create a PivotTable and a PivotChart to analyze the data. Format, filter, and sort the PivotTable appropriately.

15. In a Word document, explain the problem you solved, identify the alternatives you considered, document the data you collected to evaluate the alternatives, and then describe the results of your analysis. Include the PivotChart in the Word document.

16. In an appropriate worksheet, insert a hyperlink that links to the Word document you created.

17. Create at least one macro to automate a repetitive task you need to perform in the workbook, such as printing or saving a worksheet as a PDF file.

18. Prepare your workbook for printing. Include headers and footers that indicate the filename of your workbook, the workbook's author, and the date on which the report is printed. If a printed worksheet will extend across several pages, repeat appropriate print titles across all of the pages, and include page numbers and the total number of pages on each printed page.

19. Save the workbook.

OBJECTIVES

- Open a workbook in Compatibility Mode
- Use the LEN function
- Use the LEFT function
- Apply the Paste Values command
- Use the PROPER function
- Use the CONCATENATE function
- Apply the Text to Columns command
- Use the UPPER function
- Use the SUBSTITUTE function
- Apply a special format to phone numbers
- Create custom formats for numbers and dates
- Use the Compatibility Checker

Working with Text Functions and Creating Custom Formats

Cleaning Data in a Spreadsheet

Case | *Sharp Blades Hockey Club*

The town of Drumright, Oklahoma, started the Sharp Blades Hockey Club in 2010. The adult division of the club has members from the towns in the area, and the average age of the members is 42. They have elected officers for president, secretary, and treasurer. James Perez has been elected secretary, and part of his job is to keep the records for the club. The officers of the club would like to know more about the players and the prospects for the growth of the club.

The club has a spreadsheet containing data about the current players, but the data was compiled by volunteers and is not organized for any kind of analysis. Before James begins his analysis, he needs to "clean" the data, and he has asked for your help.

STARTING DATA FILES

ExcelA →	Tutorial	Review	Case1	Case2
	Hockey.xls	Early.xlxs	Golf.xlxs	Lawn.xlxs

Opening and Saving Workbooks Created in Earlier Versions of Excel

When you open a workbook that was created in Excel 2003 or earlier, it opens in Compatibility Mode. **Compatibility Mode** keeps the workbook in the older file format with the .xls file extension, making the workbook accessible for users who do not have the current version of Excel installed. The words "[Compatibility Mode]" appear in the title bar, indicating the file is not in the latest Excel format. You can work in Compatibility Mode. However, to have access to all the latest features and tools in Excel 2013, you must convert the workbook to the current file format, which has the .xlsx file extension. This is the file format you have used to save workbooks in the tutorials.

The workbook James received from the previous secretary was created in Excel 2003. James wants you to convert the workbook to the current format.

To save the workbook in the current Excel file format:

▶ **1.** Open the **Hockey** workbook located in the ExcelA ▶ Tutorial folder included with your Data Files. The workbook opens in Compatibility Mode because the workbook was created in an earlier version of Excel. See Figure A-1.

Figure A-1	Workbook in Compatibility Mode

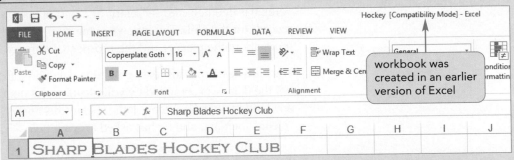

▶ **2.** On the ribbon, click the **FILE** tab to open Backstage view, and then click the **Save As** command in the navigation bar.

▶ **3.** Click the **Browse** button to open the Save As dialog box.

▶ **4.** In the File name box, type **Sharp Blades**. The Save as type box shows that the current file format is Excel 97-2003 Workbook, which is the earlier file format. You'll change this to the latest file format.

▶ **5.** Click the **Save as type** button, and then click **Excel Workbook**. This is the file format for Excel 2007, 2010, and 2013.

▶ **6.** Click the **Save** button. The workbook is saved with the new name and file type.

As you can see from the title bar, the workbook remains in Compatibility Mode. You can continue to work in Compatibility Mode, or you can close the workbook and then reopen it in the new file format. You will open the workbook in the current file format.

To open the Sharp Blades workbook in the current file format:

1. Close the Sharp Blades workbook.

2. Open the **Sharp Blades** workbook. The text "[Compatibility Mode]" no longer appears in the title bar, indicating that the workbook is in the current version file format of Excel.

3. In the Documentation worksheet, enter your name and the date.

The Players worksheet contains data about the club members. Before working with this data, James wants you to convert it to an Excel table.

To create an Excel table from the list of player information:

1. Go to the **Players** worksheet.

2. On the ribbon, click the **INSERT** tab.

3. In the Tables group, click the **Table** button. The Create Table dialog box opens with the range $A$1:$G$45 selected, and the My table has headers box is checked.

4. Click the **OK** button to create the Excel table. Note that filter arrows appear in the column heading cells.

5. On the TABLE TOOLS DESIGN tab, in the Properties group, enter **Player** in the Table Name box to rename the table.

6. On the ribbon, click the **DATA** tab.

7. Select any cell in the Excel table.

Using Text Functions

If you receive a workbook from a coworker or obtain data from other software packages, you often have to edit (sometimes referred to as *clean* or *scrub*) and manipulate the data before it is ready to use. To help users edit and correct the text values in their workbooks, Excel provides Text functions. Text, also referred to as a *text string* or *string*, contains one or more characters and can include spaces, symbols, and numbers as well as uppercase and lowercase letters. You can use Text functions to return the number of characters in a string, remove extra spaces, and change the case of text strings. Figure A-2 reviews some of the common Text functions available in Excel.

Figure A-2   **Text functions**

Function	Syntax	Description	Example
LEFT	=LEFT(*text, nbr chars*)	Returns a specified number of characters at the left of the string	=LEFT("Michael",3) returns Mic
RIGHT	=RIGHT(*text, nbr chars*)	Returns a specified number of characters at the right of the string	=RIGHT("Michael",3) returns ael
MID	=MID(*text, start nbr, nbr chars*)	Returns a specified number of characters from a string, starting at a position you specify	=MID("Net Income",5,3) returns Inc
UPPER	=UPPER(*text*)	Converts all lowercase characters in a string to uppercase	=UPPER("kim") returns KIM
LOWER	=LOWER(*text*)	Converts all uppercase characters in a string to lowercase	=LOWER("KIM") returns kim
PROPER	=PROPER(*text*)	Capitalizes the first letter of each word in a string	=PROPER("JASON BAKER") returns Jason Baker
LEN	=LEN(*text*)	Returns the number of characters in a string	=LEN("Judith Tinker") returns 13
SEARCH	=SEARCH(*find_text, within_text, start_nbr*)	Returns the number of the character at which the find_text is first found reading from left to right	=SEARCH("Main","1234 Main St.",1) returns 6
TEXT	=TEXT(*value, format_text_code*)	Formats numbers within text using a specific number format	=TEXT(SUM(D5:D75), "$#,0.00") returns $1,052.00
TRIM	=TRIM(*text*)	Removes all spaces from a string except for single spaces between words	=TRIM(" Mariah Ells") returns Mariah Ells

© 2014 Cengage Learning

Using the LEN and LEFT Functions

The Zip column in the Players worksheet includes zip codes in both five-digit and 10-digit formats. James wants only the five-digit component of the zip code. You can use the LEN and LEFT functions nested in an IF function to convert all of the zip codes to the shorter form. The IF function uses the LEN function to test whether the zip code has 10 digits. If true (the zip code is 10 digits), the LEFT function displays the first five digits in the cell. If false (the code is not 10 digits), all the digits in the cell are displayed.

The **LEN function** returns the number of characters (length) of the specified string. Cell C6 stores the text "Cushing, ok" so the formula =LEN(C6) returns 11, which is the number of characters, including spaces, in "Cushing, ok." You will use the LEN function to determine how many characters are in each cell of the Zip column.

The **LEFT function** returns a specified number of characters from the beginning of the string. To extract the five-digit zip code from the zip code 74079-1236 stored in cell D3, you use the formula =LEFT(D3,5) to return 74079.

The following formula shows the LEN and LEFT functions nested in an IF function to display a five-digit zip code—=IF(LEN([Zip])=10,LEFT([Zip],5),[Zip]).

Before you enter the IF function to extract the five-digit zip code, you need to prepare the worksheet. First, you need to insert a new column to the left of the Phone # column. Then, you will copy the zip code data into the new column, pasting the data as values so you can use the data in a formula. The results of the formula will appear in the new column as well.

To extract the five-digit zip code from the Zip column:

1. Select cell **E2**. You'll insert the table column to the left of this column.

2. On the ribbon, click the **HOME** tab.

3. In the Cells group, click the **Insert button arrow**, and then click **Insert Table Columns to the Left**. A new column named Column1 is inserted with the Text number format, which is the same format as the Zip column (column D). The columns in the worksheet automatically adjust as you add new columns. For example, the phone number in cell F2 changed to 9.186E+09. You will adjust column widths later, so you don't need to be concerned about these automatic adjustments.

4. Select the range **E2:E45**. Because the range is formatted as Text, you cannot enter a formula in a cell. You need to change the formatting of the selected range.

5. On the HOME tab, in the Number group, click the **Dialog Box Launcher**. The Format Cells dialog box opens with the Number tab displayed.

6. In the Category box, click **General**, then click the **OK** button. Now, you can enter the formula in cell E2.

7. Select cell **E2**, and then click the **Insert Function** button f_x next to the formula bar. The Insert Function dialog box opens.

8. Click **Logical** in the Or select a category list, click **IF** in the Select a function box, and then click the **OK** button. The Function Arguments dialog box opens.

9. In the Logical_test box, type **LEN([Zip])=10**. The logical test tests whether the number of characters in the current cell of the Zip column equals 10.

10. In the Value_if_true box, type **LEFT([Zip],5)**. This argument specifies that if the condition is true, the first five characters from the cell are displayed.

11. In the Value_if_false box, type **[Zip]**. This argument specifies that if the condition is false, all the characters from the cell are displayed. See Figure A-3.

| Figure A-3 | IF function with LEN and LEFT functions |

12. Click the **OK** button. The formula =IF(LEN([Zip])=10,LEFT([Zip],5),[Zip]) appears in the formula bar, and the value 74079 appears in cell E2 because the condition is false. The results are automatically copied to all rows in column E of the table. Each cell in column E displays the five-digit zip code. See Figure A-4.

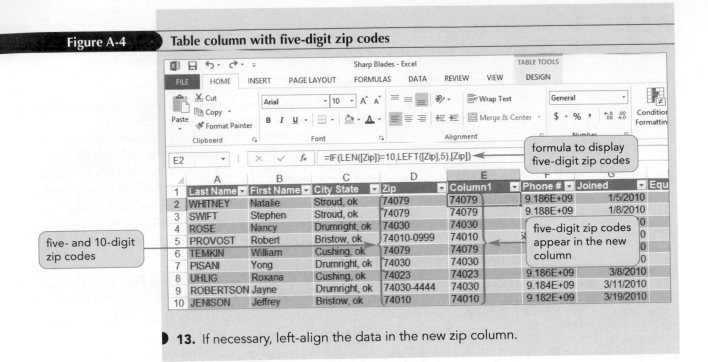

Figure A-4   Table column with five-digit zip codes

13. If necessary, left-align the data in the new zip column.

Using the Paste Values Command

You now have two columns with zip codes (columns D and E). You need to keep only the column that displays the five-digit zip code. However, the data in column E is dependent on column D. If you delete column D, column E will display the #REF! error value. Therefore, before you delete column D, you need to convert the data in column E, which is based on a formula, to values. The easiest way to do that is to copy and paste the formula results, but not the actual formula, in the same column using the Paste Values command. Then, you can delete column D.

To convert the five-digit zip code formula results to values:

1. Select the range **E2:E45**, which contains the formula results you want to convert to values.

2. On the HOME tab, in the Clipboard group, click the **Copy** button 📋, and then select cell **E2**.

3. In the Clipboard group, click the **Paste button arrow**, and then click the **Values** button 🔢. The values are pasted over the original formulas, replacing them.

4. Select the range **E2:E45**. You need to format these values as text, in case any zip codes start with zeros.

5. In the Number group, click the **Number Format box arrow**, and then click **Text**.

6. Select column **D**, right-click the selected column, and then click **Delete** on the shortcut menu. The column is removed.

> **7.** In cell **D1**, enter **Zip**. Column D, which stores the five-digit zip code values, now has a descriptive column header.

> **8.** Autofit the Zip column to fit the five-digit zip codes.

Using the PROPER Function and the CONCATENATE Function

The **PROPER function** converts the first letter of each word to uppercase, capitalizes any letter that does not follow another letter, and changes all other letters to lowercase. The formula =PROPER("WHITNEY") changes the word "WHITNEY" to "Whitney." You will first use the PROPER function to convert the last name so that the first letter is capitalized.

The **CONCATENATE function** joins, or concatenates, two or more text values. The syntax of the CONCATENATE function is

=CONCATENATE(*text1*,*text2*,...)

where *text1*, *text2*, etc., are constants or cells storing text or numbers. The CONCATENATE function joins these values to produce a single string. For example, if the last name "WHITNEY" is in cell A2 and the first name "Natalie" is in cell B2, you can use the formula =CONCATENATE(A2,B2) to join the contents of the two cells (last name and first name) to display the full name in cell C2. However, this formula returns "WHITNEYNatalie" in cell C2. To include a comma and a space between the two names, you must change the formula to =CONCATENATE(PROPER(A2),", ",B2), which uses a function, two values, and a string constant (a comma and a space enclosed in quotation marks) to display "Whitney, Natalie" in the cell.

James wants to combine the Last Name and First Name columns into one column and use standard capitalization for the names. You will use a formula that includes the PROPER function and the CONCATENATION function to do this.

To combine the names in one column with standard capitalization:

> **1.** Select cell **C2**, and then insert a table column to the left. A new column named Column1 is inserted to the left of the City State column.

> **2.** In cell **C2**, type **=CONCATENATE(PROPER([Last Name]),", ",[First Name])** and then press the **Enter** key. The formula is entered for every record in column C, and displays the player's last name and first name with standard capitalization separated by a comma.

> **3.** AutoFit column C to accommodate the longest entry. Each cell in column C displays the player's name in the form *Last name, First name* with the first letter of each name capitalized. Notice that the Joined column is no longer wide enough to display some of the entries; you will resize the column later. See Figure A-5.

Figure A-5   **Player's name displayed in one column**

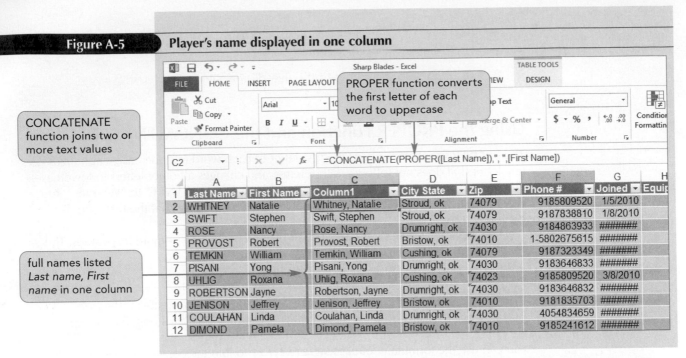

CONCATENATE function joins two or more text values

PROPER function converts the first letter of each word to uppercase

full names listed *Last name, First name* in one column

Now that the players' name data is stored in column C, you no longer need the data in column A (Last Name) and column B (First Name). Because the results in column C are based on a formula, you need to convert the formula in column C to values before you delete the other columns.

To paste the formula results as values and delete the original data:

1. Select the range **C2:C45**, and then copy the range to the Clipboard.

2. Select cell **C2**, and then paste the values from the Clipboard to column C.

3. Press the **Esc** key, and then AutoFit column C so you can see the players' full names.

4. In cell **C1**, enter **Player** as the column header.

5. Delete columns **A** and **B**. The Player column remains in the Excel table.

Applying the Text to Columns Command

When multiple pieces of data are stored in one cell, you can separate each piece of data into a different column by using the Text to Columns command. This command starts the Convert Text to Column Wizard. You specify how to split the data based on how the data is stored. You can select what **delimits**, or separates, the data, such as a tab, a semicolon, a comma, or a space. For fixed-width data, you specify break locations. For example, you might need to specify a break location in a string where the first character identifies the warehouse location, characters 2 through 4 identify the aisle, and characters 5 through 8 identify the actual location on the shelf. Each entry in a fixed-width field is the same length no matter how many characters are entered in the field.

The Players worksheet has the city and state separated by a comma delimiter. James wants you to split the city and state data into different columns.

To split the city and state data into separate columns:

1. Select cell **C2**, and then insert a table column to the left. A new column named Column1 is inserted to the left of the Zip column.

2. Select the range **B2:B45**. These cells contain the values you want to split.

3. On the ribbon, click the **DATA** tab.

4. In the Data Tools group, click the **Text to Columns** button. The Convert Text to Columns Wizard - Step 1 of 3 dialog box opens. You select how the data is organized in this step—delimited or a fixed width.

5. In the Original data type area, verify that the **Delimited** option button is selected, and then click the **Next** button. The Convert Text to Columns Wizard - Step 2 of 3 dialog box opens. You select the delimiter character in this step. The data in the City State column is separated by a comma.

6. Click any check box with a checkmark in the Delimiters section to remove the checkmark, and then click the **Comma** check box to insert a checkmark. The Data preview box shows the City and State data in separate columns. See Figure A-6.

Figure A-6 **Convert Text to Columns Wizard - Step 2 of 3 dialog box**

check to separate data at the comma

data split into two columns

7. Click the **Next** button. The Convert Text to Columns Wizard - Step 3 of 3 dialog box opens so you can set the data format for each column. The Data preview box shows that each column is set to the General number format, which is what you want.

8. Click the **Finish** button. Cities remain in column B; states move to column C.

9. In cell **B1**, enter **City** and then in cell **C1**, enter **State**.

10. AutoFit the widths of columns B and C. See Figure A-7.

Figure A-7	City and State displayed in separate columns

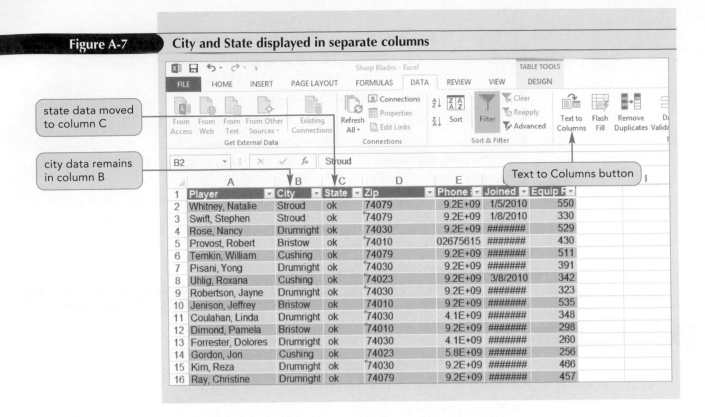

state data moved to column C

city data remains in column B

Text to Columns button

Using the UPPER Function to Convert Case

The **UPPER function** converts all letters of each word in a text string to uppercase. For example, the formula =UPPER("ri") returns RI. James wants you to change state abbreviations in column D from lowercase to uppercase. You'll use the UPPER function to do this.

To use the UPPER function to capitalize the state abbreviations:

1. Select cell **D2**, and then insert a table column to the left. A new column named Column1 is inserted to the left of the Zip column.

2. In cell **D2**, type **=U** and then double-click the **UPPER** function in the list. The beginning of the formula =UPPER(is in the cell and the formula bar.

3. Type **[** to begin the column specifier, double-click **State** in the list of column qualifiers, type **]** to end the column specifier, and then type **)**. The formula =UPPER([State]) appears in the formula bar.

4. Press the **Enter** key. The state abbreviation appears in all uppercase letters in column E. See Figure A-8.

Figure A-8	UPPER function converted state abbreviations to uppercase

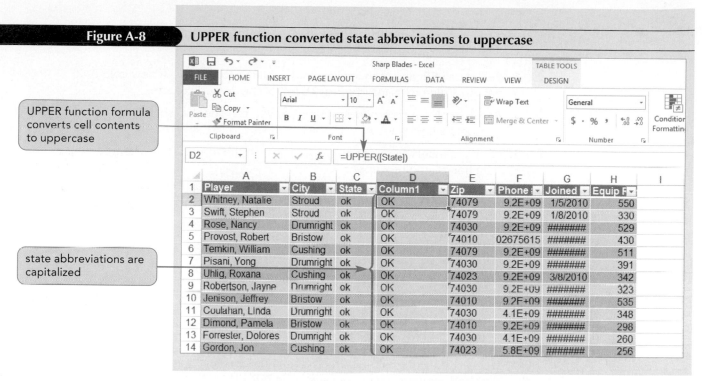

UPPER function formula converts cell contents to uppercase

state abbreviations are capitalized

You want to keep only the data in column D. Because the results of column D are based on a formula, you again will convert the formula in column D to values before you delete column C.

To paste the state abbreviations as values:

1. Select the range **D2:D45**, and then copy the range to the Clipboard.

2. Select cell **D2**, and then paste the values from the Clipboard. Verify that the formula bar displays a value and not a formula.

3. Press the **Esc** key.

4. Delete column **C**.

5. In cell **C1**, enter **State**. The column is renamed with a more descriptive header.

Using the SUBSTITUTE Function

The **SUBSTITUTE function** replaces existing text with new text. The SUBSTITUTE function has the syntax

    SUBSTITUTE(text,old_text,new_text,instance_num)

where *text* is a string constant or reference to a cell containing text you want to replace, *old_text* is the existing text you want to replace, *new_text* is the text you want to replace *old_text* with, and *instance_num* specifies which occurrence of *old_text* you want to replace. If you omit *instance_num*, every instance of *old_text* is replaced. The formula

    =SUBSTITUTE("164-45-890","-","")

returns 16445890.

The entries for the phone numbers in column E are inconsistent. Sometimes they are an eight-digit value, and other times they are preceded with 1- (which James wants you to remove from the Phone # column). You'll enter a formula with the SUBSTITUTE function to remove the preceding 1- from this data.

To remove the preceding 1- from the phone number data and paste the values:

1. Select cell **F2**, and then insert a table column to the left. A new column named Column1 is inserted to the left of the Joined column.

2. AutoFit column E (Phone # column) so you can see that some phone numbers are preceded by 1-.

3. Click the **Insert Function** button 𝑓ₓ next to the formula bar. The Insert Function dialog box opens.

4. Click the **Or select a category** arrow, click **Text** to display the Text functions, and then scroll down to and double-click **SUBSTITUTE** in the Select a function box. The Function Arguments dialog box opens.

5. In the Text box, type **E2**. The text in cell E2 is displayed.

6. In the Old_text box, type **"1-"**. The text you want to remove is enclosed in quotation marks.

7. In the New_text box, type **""**. You want to replace the old text with nothing. You do not need to enter anything in the Instance_num box because you want to replace every instance of 1-.

8. Click the **OK** button. All of the phone numbers are changed to 10-digit numbers, and wherever necessary, the preceding 1- is replaced with an empty string (a blank, or nothing).

9. AutoFit column F, and then select cell **F2**. See Figure A-9.

| Figure A-9 | SUBSTITUTE function removed 1- from the phone numbers |

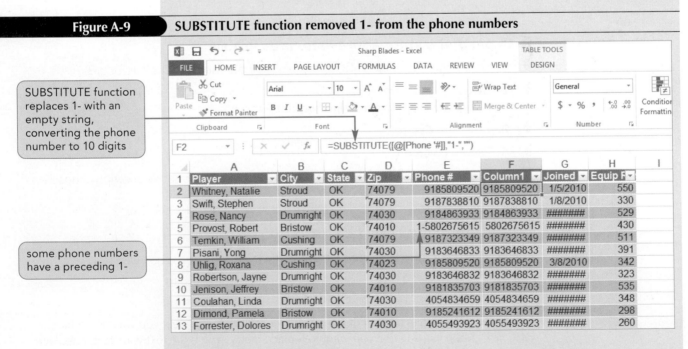

SUBSTITUTE function replaces 1- with an empty string, converting the phone number to 10 digits

some phone numbers have a preceding 1-

10. Select the range **F2:F45**, and then copy this range to the Clipboard.

11. Select cell **F2**, paste the values from the Clipboard, and then press the **Esc** key.

12. Delete column **E**.

13. In cell **E1**, enter **Phone #** to identify the data in the column.

14. AutoFit the columns as needed to display their entire contents.

Using Special Formats

Four commonly used formats, referred to as special formats, are available—two zip code formats (five-digit and 10-digit), a phone number format (with the area code in parentheses and a hyphen between the prefix and the last four digits), and a Social Security number format (a nine-digit number with hyphens after the third and fifth digits). Using these special formats allows you to type a number without punctuation, yet still display that number in its common format.

James wants you to display the phone number using the common format of area code in parentheses and a hyphen between the prefix and the last four digits.

To format the phone numbers with the Phone Number format:

1. Select the range **E2:E45**. Notice the green triangle in the upper-left corner for the cells in this range.

2. Point to any triangle to display the Error Alert button, click the **Error Alert button arrow**, and then click **Convert to Number** in the list of options.

3. With the range E2:E45 still selected, on the HOME tab, in the Number group, click the **Dialog Box Launcher**. The Format Cells dialog box opens with the Number tab active.

4. In the Category box, click **Special**. Four special formats appear in the Type list—Zip Code, Zip Code + 4, Phone Number, and Social Security Number.

5. In the Type box, click **Phone Number**. See Figure A-10.

Figure A-10 **Special category on the Number tab**

special format for phone numbers

6. Click the **OK** button. The phone numbers are formatted in a standard telephone format.

Creating Custom Formats

TIP

Any custom format you create is stored only in the workbook in which it was created. To use it in another workbook, you must reenter it.

Excel supplies a generous collection of formats and styles to improve the appearance and readability of worksheets. However, sometimes you will need a format and style to accommodate a specific requirement. In these cases, you can create your own formats, called **custom formats**. Custom formats use **format codes**, a series of symbols, to describe exactly how Excel should display a number, date, time, or text string. You can use format codes to display text strings and spaces, and determine how many decimal places to display in a cell.

Creating a Custom Number Format

Each number is composed of digits. In displaying these digits, Excel makes special note of **insignificant zeros**, which are zeros whose omission from the number does not change the number's value. For example, the number 0.1 is displayed in the General number format, but changes to 0.10 when the cell is formatted as a number. To format a value, Excel uses the **placeholders** shown in Figure A-11 to represent individual digits.

Figure A-11 Description of digit placeholders

Placeholder	Description
#	Displays only significant digits; insignificant zeros are omitted
0 (zero)	Displays significant digits as well as insignificant zeros
?	Replaces insignificant zeros with spaces on either side of the decimal point so that decimal points align when formatted with a fixed-width font, such as Courier

© 2014 Cengage Learning

A custom format can use combinations of these placeholders. For example, the custom format #.00 displays the value 8.9 as 8.90. If a value has more digits than placeholders in the custom format, Excel rounds the value to match the number of placeholders. Thus, the value 8.938 formatted with the custom format #.## is displayed as 8.94. Figure A-12 shows how the same series of numbers appears with different custom number formats.

Figure A-12 Examples of digit placeholders

	Custom Formats			
Cell Value	**#.##**	**0**	**?.??**	**#.#0**
0.57	0.57	0.57	0.57	0.57
123.4	123.4	123.4	123.4	123.4
3.45	3.45	3.45	3.45	3.45

© 2014 Cengage Learning

Number formats also include the decimal point separator (.), the thousands separator (,), and the fraction separator (/). You can use the thousands separator to separate a number in groups of 1,000 or to scale a number by a multiple of 1,000.

The fraction separator displays decimal values as fractions. The general syntax is *placeholder/placeholder*, where *placeholder* is one or more of the custom format placeholders. Excel displays the fraction that best approximates the decimal value. You can also specify the denominator for the fraction to convert the decimals to halves, quarters, and so forth. Figure A-13 provides examples of the thousands and fraction separators.

| **Figure A-13** | **Examples of thousands and fraction separators** |

Value	Custom Format	Appearance
12000	#,###	12,000
12000	#,	12
12200000	0.0,,	12.2
5.4	# #/#	5 2/5

© 2014 Cengage Learning

You can combine all of the numeric format codes in a single custom format. If you don't specify a numeric code for data values, Excel uses the General format code, which hides all insignificant zeros.

James wants equipment rentals displayed as a number with two decimal positions followed by the letter "p" to indicate paid. You'll create a custom format for the equipment rental.

To create a custom format for the equipment rentals:

1. Select the range **G2:G45**.

2. On the HOME tab, in the Number group, click the **Dialog Box Launcher**. The Format Cells dialog box opens with the Number tab displayed.

3. In the Category box, click **Custom**. You will enter a custom format to display the numbers to the nearest thousand.

4. In the Type box, double-click **General** to select it, and then type **.00?p?** as the custom format code. See Figure A-14.

| **Figure A-14** | **Custom category on the Number tab** |

Trouble? If you return to the worksheet, you double-clicked General in the list of custom formats. Repeat Step 4, making sure you double-click General in the Type box.

> 5. Click the **OK** button. The equipment rentals are displayed as a number with two decimal positions followed by the letter "p" to indicate paid. Because you used the custom format, this text is treated as a number even though it has a letter character (the character is ignored).

Creating a Custom Date Format

When you have dates, times, or both in a workbook, you can use a predefined date and time format to display this information in a readable format. Although the predefined time and date formats are usually fine, you can also create your own custom date formats. Figure A-15 describes the format codes used for dates and times.

Figure A-15   Date and Time format codes

Code	Displays
m	Months as 1 through 12
mm	Months as 01 through 12
mmm	Months as Jan through Dec
mmmm	Months as January through December
d	Days as 1 through 31
dd	Days as 01 through 31
ddd	Days as Sun through Sat
dddd	Days as Sunday through Saturday
yy	Years as 00 through 99
yyyy	Years as 1900 through 9999
h	Hours as 1 through 24
mm	Minutes as 01 through 60 (when immediately following h, mm signifies minutes; otherwise, months)
ss	Seconds as 01 through 60

© 2014 Cengage Learning

James wants the date values in the Joined column to show the name of the month followed by the year (for example, 7/22/2016 should be displayed as July 2016). You need to apply the custom format code *mmmm yyyy* to do this.

To apply a custom date format to the Joined dates:

> 1. Select the range **F2:F45**.

> 2. On the HOME tab, in the Number group, click the **Dialog Box Launcher**. The Format Cells dialog box opens with the Number tab active.

> 3. In the Category box, click **Custom**.

> 4. In the Type box, select the current format, and then type **mmmm yyyy**. The Sample box shows an example of the custom format you entered.

> 5. Click the **OK** button, and then click cell **A1** to deselect the range. See Figure A-16.

| Figure A-16 | **Final formatted workbook** |

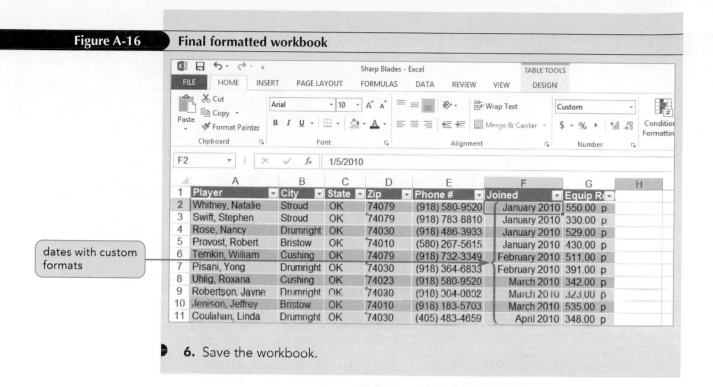

dates with custom formats

6. Save the workbook.

Using the Compatibility Checker

When you save an Excel 2007, 2010, or 2013 workbook in an earlier format, the **Compatibility Checker** alerts you to any features that are not supported by earlier versions of Excel. You can click the Cancel button and redo the worksheet using a different approach, or you can click the Continue button to save the workbook in the earlier format. If you save the workbook in an earlier format, unsupported features will be lost.

You'll save a copy of the workbook in the Excel 2003 format.

To convert the workbook to the Excel 2003 file format:

1. On the ribbon, click the **FILE** tab to open Backstage view, and then click **Save As** in the navigation bar. The Save As screen appears.

2. Click the **Browse** button to open the Save As dialog box, navigate to the location specified by your instructor, and then change the filename to **Sharp Blades 2003**.

3. Click the **Save as type** button, and then click **Excel 97-2003 Workbook**. This is the earlier Excel file format you want to use.

4. Click the **Save** button. The Compatibility Checker dialog box opens, alerting you to features not supported by earlier versions of Excel. See Figure A-17.

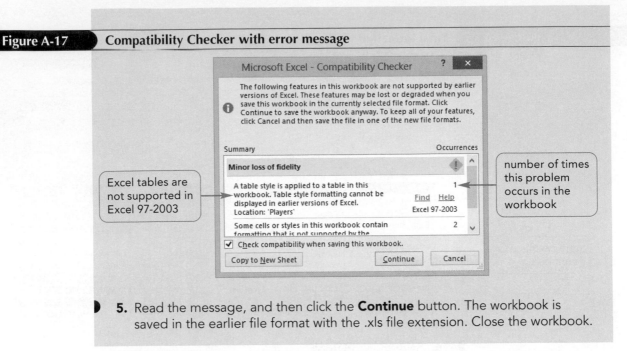

Excel tables are not supported in Excel 97-2003

number of times this problem occurs in the workbook

5. Read the message, and then click the **Continue** button. The workbook is saved in the earlier file format with the .xls file extension. Close the workbook.

The workbook data is clean and the workbook is formatted as James requested. He'll be able to analyze this data for the club.

Review Assignments

PRACTICE

Data File needed for the Review Assignments: Early.xlsx

The Sharp Blades Hockey Club also has a youth division for players from 6 to 18 years of age. James has a second workbook to store the information that has been collected for these players. James asks you to clean and format the data. Complete the following:

1. Open the **Early** workbook located in the ExcelA ► Review folder included with your Data Files, and then save the workbook in Excel Workbook format as **Sharp Youth** in the location specified by your instructor.

2. In the Documentation worksheet, enter your name and the date.

3. In the Youth Players worksheet, create an Excel table for the data in the range A1:F40. Name the table **Youth**. (*Hint*: Remember to remove the filter arrows.)

4. Insert a blank column to the left of column B to store the first name, and leave the last name in column A.

5. Use the Text to Columns command to split the Player column into two columns named **Last Name** and **First Name**.

6. In cell H1, enter **Status** as the column header. In cell H2, use the IF and LEFT functions to display the word **Discard** if the address begins with PO; otherwise, leave the cell blank.

7. In cell I1, enter **Addr** as the column header. In cell I2, enter a formula to trim the extra spaces from the address.

8. In cell J1, enter **Twn** as the column header. In cell J2, enter a formula to convert the data in the Town column to proper case.

9. In cell K1, enter **St** as the column header. In column K, enter a formula to convert the data in the State column to uppercase.

10. In cell L1, enter **Town State** as the column header. In column L, combine the town and state data from columns J and K into one column using the format *town, state*.

11. Format the data in the Phone column (column F) with the Phone Number format.

12. Save the workbook, and then close it.

Case Problem 1

APPLY

Data File needed for this Case Problem: Golf.xlsx

Early Bird Golf Group Camilla Cortez, organizer of the Early Bird Golf Group, has begun compiling a list of the group's members. She has asked you to clean and format the data in the worksheet before she continues working on the project. Complete the following:

1. Open the **Golf** workbook located in the ExcelA ► Case1 folder and save the workbook in the Excel Workbook format as **Early Bird** in the location specified by your instructor.

2. In the Documentation worksheet, enter your name and the date.

3. In the Members worksheet, create an Excel table for the data. Name the table **Golf**.

4. Apply the Phone Number format to the data in the Telephone column.

5. Split the data in the Name column into two columns. Store the first names in column B and the last names in column C. Change the column headers to **First Name** and **Last Name**, respectively.

6. In the Member Since column, apply a custom format that displays only the year.

7. Split the City, State Zip column into three columns named **City**, **State**, and **Zip**, respectively. (*Hint*: Repeat the split twice. The second split is a fixed width.)

8. The locker numbers were entered from an old system. The only characters that are important are the three numbers after the letter. Use the MID function in column I (name it **L Number**) to separate those numbers.

9. The last number in the locker number is the actual row that the locker is in. Use the RIGHT function in column J (name it **L Row**) to separate that value.

10. Save the workbook, and then close it.

Case Problem 2

Data File needed for this Case Problem: Lawn.xlsx

Dianna's Lawncare   Every two weeks, Dianna Turley collects payroll information for the employees who work for her at her lawncare business. The worksheet with the information is sent to a payroll service that generates the paychecks. Dianna has started to collect the information, but she needs you to clean up the data before it is sent. Complete the following:

1. Open the **Lawn** workbook located in the ExcelA ► Case2 folder included with your Data Files, and then save the workbook in the Excel Workbook format as **Lawncare** in the location specified by your instructor.

2. In the Documentation worksheet, enter your name and the date.

3. In the Employee Hours worksheet, create an Excel table named **Hours** with a blue table style.

4. Split the data in the Name column into two columns. Store the first name data in column A and the last name data in column B. Change the column headers to **First Name** and **Last Name**, respectively.

5. Split the data in the City, State Zip column into three columns. Store the city data in column D, the state data in column E, and the zip codes in column F. (*Hint*: Repeat the split twice.) Change the column headers to **City**, **State**, and **Zip**, respectively.

6. Use functions as needed to change the data in the City and State columns to use standard capitalization. (*Hint*: Remember to copy the data as values and remove any unnecessary columns.)

7. Apply the Social Security Number format to the data in the SS Number column.

8. Use a function to change the data in the Type of Work column so that it is all lowercase. (*Hint*: Remember to copy the data as values and remove any unnecessary columns.)

9. Apply a custom format to the data in the Hourly Rate column that shows two decimal places.

10. Apply a custom format to the data in the Overtime Hours column so that full hours display only significant digits and partial hours display two digits whether significant or insignificant. (*Hint*: Refer to Figure A-11 to see a description of the digit placeholders used in custom formats for values.)

11. Save the workbook, and then close it.

OBJECTIVES

- Use advanced filters
- Create a criteria range
- Use Database functions
- Summarize data using the COUNTIFS, SUMIFS, and AVERAGEIFS functions

Advanced Filters, Database Functions, and Summary IFS Functions

Filtering and Summarizing Database Information

Case | *E-Quip Tools*

E-Quip Tools, a tool supplier in Bethel, Alaska, has been tracking the computer equipment at its main location on Tundra Way and its secondary location at Chief Eddie Hoffman Highway. Recognizing the need to keep current with ever-changing technology, Patricia Koon, the IT manager for both locations, has developed a replacement plan for the company's technology equipment. She has established the following criteria to plan the technology-related equipment replacement:

- Equipment with no service agreement should be replaced at "end of life," which is today, 12/31/2016.
- Equipment under service agreement with a value less than $600 and with an "end-of-life" date one year after today's date (12/31/2017). This would allow enough time to acquire budget to replace the equipment before "end-of-life" is reached.

In addition to identifying equipment eligible for replacement, Patricia wants to know the average value of the company's inventory, and to review a summary of the equipment's lifetime as well as its total and average values. She asks you to use advanced filters to generate the list of equipment that is eligible for replacement, and then to use Database functions and other Excel functions to calculate the summary information.

STARTING DATA FILES

ExcelB	→	Tutorial	Review	Case1	Case2
		Tools.xlsx	Tools Review.xlsx	Donations.xlsx	House.xlsx

Using Advanced Filters

Advanced filtering displays a subset of the rows in an Excel table or a range of data that match the criteria you specify. With advanced filtering, you specify the filter criteria in a separate range. Advanced filtering enables you to perform Or conditions across multiple fields, such as the criteria Patricia wants you to use to find eligible equipment for replacement within E-Quip Tools. You can also use advanced filtering to create complex criteria using functions and formulas. For example, Patricia could use advanced filtering to find all equipment with no service agreement at the end of life.

Patricia created a workbook that contains an Excel table named Equipment to store the data for all of the equipment. For each piece of equipment, Patricia has listed the Date Acquired, Life (Years), and End of Life, which is calculated using the Date Acquired and Life data. You will open Patricia's workbook and filter the inventory data to identify equipment eligible for replacement.

To open and review Patricia's workbook:

1. Open the **Tools** workbook located in the ExcelB ▸ Tutorial folder included with your Data Files, and then save the workbook as **E-Quip** in the location specified by your instructor.

2. In the Documentation worksheet, enter your name and the date.

3. Go to the **Equipment Inventory** worksheet, and then review the Equipment table. See Figure B-1.

Figure B-1	Equipment table in the Equipment Inventory worksheet

ID	Description	Date Acquired	Life	End of Life	Location	Status	Service	Value
1064	Tower	1/8/2014	5	1/7/2019	Tundra	R	Y	$ 350
1025	Server	5/24/2009	8	5/22/2017	Hoffman	A	Y	$12,000
1026	Keyboard	11/26/2014	2	11/25/2016	Hoffman	A	N	$ 60
1024	Tower	11/26/2014	5	11/25/2019	Tundra	A	Y	$ 475
1027	Tower	11/26/2014	5	11/25/2019	Tundra	A	Y	$ 475
1029	Keyboard	11/26/2014	2	11/25/2016	Hoffman	A	N	$ 60
1028	Tower	11/26/2014	5	11/25/2019	Tundra	A	Y	$ 475
1030	Tower	11/26/2014	5	11/25/2019	Hoffman	A	Y	$ 500
1032	Keyboard	8/28/2016	2	8/28/2018	Hoffman	R	N	$ 55
1033	Monitor	11/26/2014	5	11/25/2019	Hoffman	A	N	$ 150
1034	Monitor	11/26/2014	5	11/25/2019	Tundra	A	N	$ 120
1031	Tower	11/26/2014	5	11/25/2019	Hoffman	A	Y	$ 500
1036	Monitor	5/4/2016	5	5/3/2021	Tundra	R	N	$ 495
1042	Tower	11/26/2014	5	11/25/2019	Tundra	A	Y	$ 475
1038	Monitor	11/26/2016	5	11/25/2021	Hoffman	A	N	$ 150
1043	Tower	11/26/2014	5	11/25/2019	Hoffman	A	Y	$ 500
1040	Keyboard	11/26/2014	2	11/25/2016	Tundra	A	N	$ 90

Documentation Equipment Inventory Inventory Summary ⊕

READY

Understanding the Criteria Range

The **criteria range** is an area in a worksheet, separate from a range of data or an Excel table, used to specify the criteria for the data to be displayed after the filter is applied to the range or Excel table. The criteria range consists of a header row that lists field names from the table's header row, and at least one row with the specific filtering criteria for each field. The criteria range specifies which records from the data range will be included in the filtered data.

Criteria placed on the same row are considered to be connected with the logical operator And. That means all criteria in the same row must be met before a record is included in the filtered data. Figure B-2 shows an And criteria range filter to retrieve all equipment not under service agreements at end of life on or before December 31, 2016.

Figure B-2	And filter specified in a criteria range

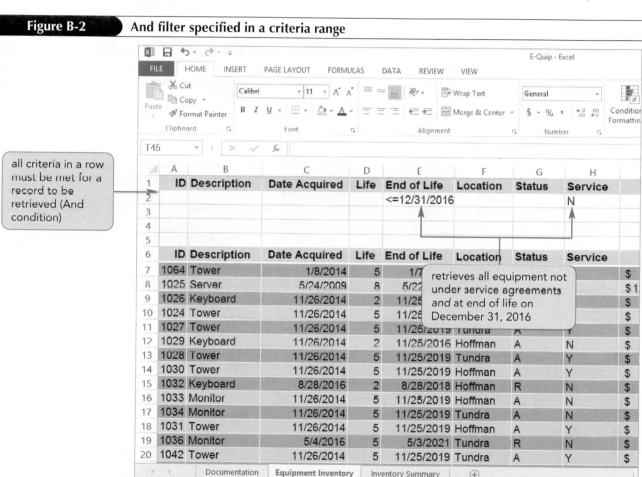

Criteria placed on separate rows of the criteria range are treated as being connected by the logical operator Or. That means records that meet all the criteria on either row in the criteria range will be displayed. Figure B-3 shows an example of the Or filter to retrieve all equipment not under service agreements at end of life on December 31, 2016 or equipment in the Hoffman location.

Figure B-3   **Or filter specified in a criteria range**

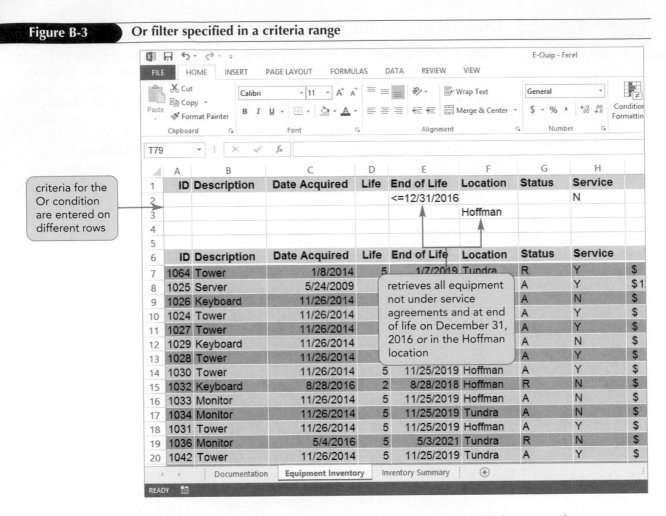

criteria for the Or condition are entered on different rows

retrieves all equipment not under service agreements and at end of life on December 31, 2016 or in the Hoffman location

To specify criteria between a range of values in the same field, you use the same field name repeated in separate cells within the same row to match a range of values (Between criteria). Figure B-4 shows a criteria range to retrieve all equipment at end of life between January 1, 2016 and December 31, 2016.

Between filter specified in a criteria range

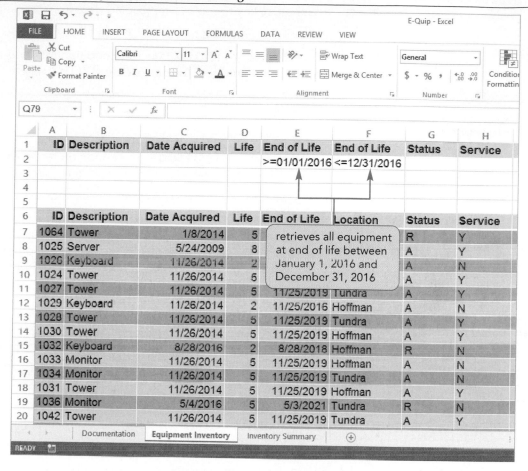

Creating a Criteria Range

Typically, you place a criteria range above the data range to keep it separate from the data. If you place a criteria range next to the data range, the criteria might be hidden when the advanced filtering causes rows to be hidden. You can also place a criteria range in a separate worksheet, particularly if you need to use several criteria ranges in different cells to perform calculations based on various sets of filtered records.

You will place the criteria range in rows 1 through 4 of the Equipment Inventory worksheet to make it easier to locate. Because the field names in the criteria range must exactly match the field names in the Excel table or range except for capitalization, you should copy and paste the field names instead of retyping them. In row 2, you will enter an And criteria range with the criteria for equipment with no service agreement at end of life. In row 3, you will enter the criteria for equipment under service agreement with a value of less than $600 and an end of life one year before today's date.

To create the criteria range to find equipment with or without service agreements:

1. Point to the left side of cell **A6** until the pointer changes to ➡, and then click the mouse button. The column headers in row 6 are selected.

2. Copy the field names to the Clipboard.

3. Select cell **A1**, and then paste the field names. The field names for the criteria range appear in row 1.

4. Press the **Esc** key to remove the copied data from the Clipboard.

Now, you will enter the first set of criteria.

5. In cell **E2**, enter **<=12/31/2016**. This condition retrieves all equipment with an end of life equivalent to today's date (12/31/2016).

TIP

Text entered in the criteria range is not case sensitive.

6. In cell **H2**, enter **N**. This condition retrieves equipment with no service agreement.

Next, you will enter the second set of criteria.

7. In cell **E3**, enter **<=12/31/2017**. The condition retrieves all equipment with an end of life that is one year after today's date (12/31/2016).

8. In cell **H3**, enter **Y**. This condition retrieves all equipment with a service agreement.

9. In cell **I3**, enter **<600**. This condition retrieves all equipment with a value of less than $600. The criteria in row 3 retrieve equipment with a service agreement that has a value of less than $600 and is within a year of its end of life. See Figure B-5.

Figure B-5	Criteria range to filter records

all criteria in a row must be met for a record to be retrieved (And condition)

Or condition represented by two rows

Now that the criteria range is established, you can use the Advanced Filter command to filter the Equipment table. You can filter the records in their current location by hiding rows that don't match your criteria, as you have done with the Filter command. Or, you can copy the records that match your criteria to another location in the worksheet. Patricia wants you to filter the records in their current location.

To filter the Equipment table in its current location:

1. Select any cell in the Equipment table to make the table active.

2. On the ribbon, click the **DATA** tab.

3. In the Sort & Filter group, click the **Advanced** button. The Advanced Filter dialog box opens.

4. Make sure the **Filter the list, in-place** option button is selected and the range **$A$6:$I$79** appears in the List range box. The range $A$6:$I$79 is the current location of the Equipment table, which is the table you want to filter.

5. Make sure the Criteria range box displays **$A$1:$I$3**. This range references the criteria range, which includes the field names.

6. Make sure the **Unique records only** option box is unchecked. Every record in the Equipment table is unique. You would check this option if the table contained duplicate records that you did not want to display. See Figure B-6.

Figure B-6   Advanced Filter dialog box

filters the table in its current location

copies filtered records to a different range

location of the Equipment table

location of the criteria range

range where the filtered records are copied to if filtering to another location

7. Click the **OK** button, and then scroll through the worksheet. The list is filtered in its current location, and 15 equipment records (as shown in the status bar) match the criteria. See Figure B-7.

Figure B-7   **Filtered equipment inventory data**

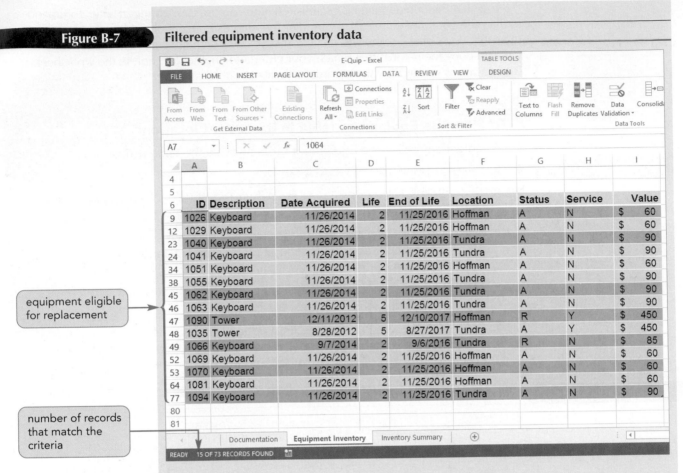

equipment eligible for replacement

number of records that match the criteria

Trouble? If all of the data in the table is filtered, the list range or criteria range might be incorrect. Click the Clear button in the Sort & Filter group on the DATA tab, and then repeat Steps 1 through 6, making sure the list range is $A$6:$I$79 and the criteria range is $A$1:$I$3 in the Advanced Filter dialog box.

After providing the list of eligible equipment to Patricia, she asks you to remove the filter to display all of the records in the Equipment table.

To show all of the records in the table:

▶ 1. On the DATA tab, in the Sort & Filter group, click the **Clear** button. All of the records in the Equipment table are redisplayed.

Using Database Functions to Summarize Data

Database functions (or **Dfunctions**) perform summary data analysis, such as sum, average, and count, on an Excel table or data range based on criteria specified in a criteria range. Figure B-8 lists the Database functions. Although you can often use the SUMIF, AVERAGEIF, and COUNTIF functions; the Total row of an Excel table; and PivotTables to achieve the same results as Database functions, some situations require Database functions. For example, the type of summary analysis, the placement of the summary results, or the complexity of the criteria might require using Database functions.

| Figure B-8 | Database functions |

Function	Description
DAVERAGE	Returns the average of the values that meet specified criteria
DCOUNT	Returns the number of cells containing numbers that meet specified criteria
DCOUNTA	Returns the number of nonblank cells that meet specified criteria
DMAX	Returns the maximum value in the search column that meets specified criteria
DMIN	Returns the minimum value in the search column that meets specified criteria
DSTDEV	Returns the estimate of standard deviation based on a sample of entries that meet the specified criteria
DSUM	Returns the sum of the values in the summary column that meet specified criteria

© 2014 Cengage Learning

Patricia needs to know the average value of the equipment by location and by status. The status of the equipment indicates whether or not it is in use (active), or whether it is not in use but available if needed (reserve). To generate this information, you must set up a criteria range to retrieve the appropriate records for each calculation. Consequently, a Database function is a good approach.

Database functions use a criteria range to specify the records to summarize. In a Database function, the criteria range is used as one of the arguments of the function. The general syntax for any Database function is

```
DatabaseFunctionName(table range, column to summarize,
criteria range)
```

where *table range* refers to the cells where the data to summarize is located, including the column header; *column to summarize* is the column name of the field to summarize entered within quotation marks; and *criteria range* is the range where the criteria that determine which records are used in the calculation are specified.

You will use Database functions to summarize the average inventory for each location by status. First, you will set up a criteria range. Although the criteria range often includes all fields from the table, even those not needed to select records, you do not have to include all field names from the table when setting up a criteria range. In this case, you will use only the fields needed to specify the criteria.

You will create two criteria ranges to complete the Average Inventory section in the Inventory Summary sheet.

To create criteria ranges for the active and reserve equipment for the Tundra and Hoffman locations:

1. Go to the **Inventory Summary** worksheet. The column headers for the criteria range have already been copied from the Equipment Inventory worksheet.

2. In cell **G6**, enter **Tundra** and then in cell **H6**, enter **A**. These are the criteria to find all active equipment at the Tundra location.

3. In cell **J6**, enter **Tundra** and then in cell **K6**, enter **R**. These are the criteria to find all reserve equipment at the Tundra location.

4. In cell **G10**, enter **Hoffman** and then in cell **H10**, enter **A**. These are the criteria to find all active equipment at the Hoffman location.

5. In cell **J10**, enter **Hoffman** and then in cell **K10**, enter **R**. These are the criteria to find all reserve equipment at the Hoffman location. See Figure B-9.

| Figure B-9 | Criteria ranges for the active and reserve equipment in both locations |

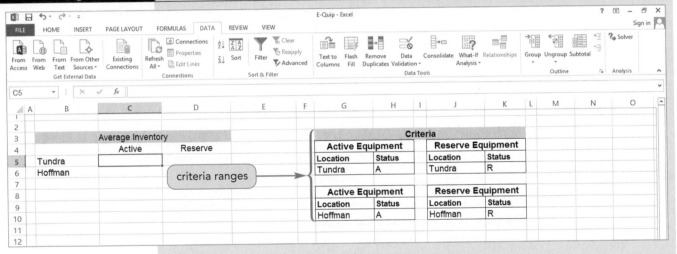

The criteria ranges are complete, so you can use the DAVERAGE function to calculate the average value of active equipment by location. The first two arguments are the same for each location. The third argument, the criteria range, is different for each location so you can average a different subset of each location inventory.

To find the average value of the active equipment for the Tundra and Hoffman locations:

1. Select cell **C5**, and then click the **Insert Function** button f_x next to the formula bar. The Insert Function dialog box opens.

2. Click the **Or select a category** arrow, and then click **Database** in the list of functions.

3. In the Select a function box, select **DAVERAGE**, if necessary, and then click the **OK** button. The Function Arguments dialog box opens.

TIP

You could use the Equipment table reference in the Database box named Equipment to reference all of the equipment.

4. In the Database box, type **'Equipment Inventory'!$A$6:$I$79** to enter the range to search, and then press the **Tab** key. In this case, 'Equipment Inventory'!$A$6:$I$79 refers to all data values in the range A6:I79 of the Equipment Inventory worksheet.

   Trouble? If the error "Invalid" appears to the right of the Database box, you probably mistyped the range to search. Make sure you typed apostrophes (') and not quotation marks (") around the Equipment Inventory worksheet name, included a space in the Equipment Inventory worksheet name, and typed ! (an exclamation mark) before the criteria range.

5. In the Field box, type **"Value"** and then press the **Tab** key. The field specifies the table column that contains the data to be averaged.

6. In the Criteria box, type **G5:H6** to specify the criteria for active equipment in the Tundra location. See Figure B-10.

Figure B-10   DAVERAGE Function Arguments dialog box

7. Click the **OK** button. The formula =DAVERAGE('Equipment Inventory'!$A$6:$I$79,"Value",G5:H6) appears in the formula bar, and $1,065 appears in cell C5, indicating the average value of the active equipment in the Tundra location. See Figure B-11.

Figure B-11   Average value of the active equipment in the Tundra location

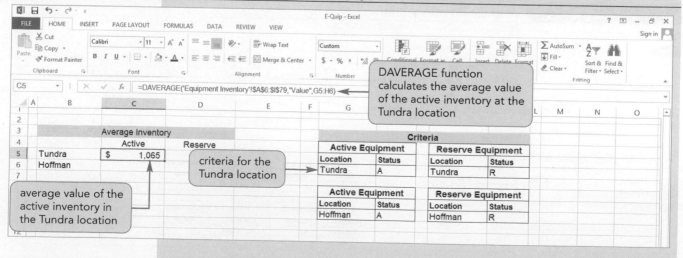

8. Select cell **C6**, and then click the **Insert Function** button f_x next to the formula bar.

9. Repeat Step 3 to open the DAVERAGE Function Arguments dialog box, and then repeat Steps 4 and 5 to enter the first two arguments for the DAVERAGE function, specifying all data values in the Equipment table and the field name.

10. In the Criteria box, type **G9:H10** to specify the active equipment in the Hoffman location.

11. Click the **OK** button. The formula =DAVERAGE ('Equipment Inventory' !$A$6:$I$79,"Value",G9:H10) appears in the formula bar, and $827 appears in cell C6, indicating the average value of the active equipment in the Hoffman location.

To calculate the average inventory value for the reserve equipment in the Tundra and Hoffman locations, you will copy the formulas in the range C5:C6 to cells D5 and D6, and then edit the third argument.

To find the average inventory value for reserve equipment for the Tundra and Hoffman locations:

1. Copy the formula in cell **C5** to cell **D5**.

2. Select cell **D5**, and then change the criteria range (the third argument) from H5:I6 to **J5:K6**. The formula =DAVERAGE('Equipment Inventory'!$A$6:$I$79,"Value",J5:K6) appears in the formula bar, and $2,816 appears in cell D5, indicating the average value of the reserve equipment in the Tundra location.

3. Copy the formula from cell **C6** to cell **D6**.

4. Select cell **D6**, and then change the criteria range (the third argument) from K5:L6 to **J9:K10**. The formula =DAVERAGE('Equipment Inventory'!$A$6:$I$79, "Value",J9:K10) appears in the formula bar, and $2,151 appears in cell D6, indicating the average value of the reserve equipment in the Hoffman location. See Figure B-12.

Figure B-12   Average inventory values

Summarizing Data Using the COUNTIFS, SUMIFS, and AVERAGEIFS Functions

Patricia wants you to summarize the years of service for the company's inventory. She needs to know the total and average values of the active equipment based on the life of the equipment.

The COUNTIFS, SUMIFS, and AVERAGEIFS functions are similar to the COUNTIF, SUMIF, and AVERAGEIF functions except the latter functions enable you to specify only one condition to summarize the data, whereas the former functions enable you to summarize the data using several conditions.

The **COUNTIFS function** counts the number of cells within a range that meet multiple criteria. Its syntax is

```
COUNTIFS(criteria_range1,criteria1[,criteria_range2,criteria2,…])
```

where *criteria_range1*, *criteria_range2*, and so on represent up to 127 ranges (columns of data) in which to evaluate the associated criteria; and *criteria1*, *criteria2*, and so on represent up to 127 criteria in the form of a number, an expression, a cell reference, or text that define which cells will be counted. Criteria can be expressed as a number such as 50 to find a number equal to 50; an expression such as ">10000" to find an amount greater than 10,000; text such as "A" to find a text value equal to A; or a cell reference such as B4 to find the value equal to the value stored in cell B4. Each cell in a range is counted only if all of the corresponding criteria specified in the COUNTIFS function are true.

To count the number of pieces of Active (A) equipment in the Tundra location (Tundra) and with a value more than $500, you can use the COUNTIFS function.

```
=COUNTIFS(Equipment[Status],"A",Equipment[Location],"Tundra",
Equipment[Value],">500")
```

The criteria are treated as if they are connected by an AND function, so all conditions must be true for a record to be counted.

The SUMIFS and AVERAGEIFS functions have a slightly different syntax. The **SUMIFS function** adds values in a range that meet multiple criteria using the syntax

```
SUMIFS(sum_range,criteria_range1,criteria1[,criteria_range2,
criteria2,…])
```

where *sum_range* is the range you want to add; *criteria_range1*, *criteria_range2*, and so on represent up to 127 ranges (columns of data) in which to evaluate the associated criteria; and *criteria1*, *criteria2*, and so on represent up to 127 criteria in the form of a number, an expression, a cell reference, or text that define which cells will be added.

To calculate the total value of active equipment acquired after 2016 in the Tundra location, you can use the following SUMIFS function to add the values (Equipment[Value]) of the equipment located in Tundra (Equipment[Location],"Tundra") that was acquired on or later than 1/1/2016 (Equipment[Date Acquired],">=1/1/2016") and has an active status (Equipment[Status],"A"):

```
=SUMIFS(Equipment[Value],Equipment[Location],"Tundra",
Equipment[Date Acquired],">=1/1/2016",Equipment[Status],"A")
```

The **AVERAGEIFS function** calculates the average of values within a range of cells that meet multiple conditions. Its syntax is

```
AVERAGEIFS(average_range,criteria_range1,criteria1
[,criteria_range2, criteria2,…])
```

where *average_range* is the range to average; *criteria_range1*, *criteria_range2*, and so on represent up to 127 ranges in which to evaluate the associated criteria; and *criteria1*, *criteria2*, and so on represent up to 127 criteria in the form of a number, an expression, a cell reference, or text that define which cells will be averaged.

To calculate the value of active equipment that has a two-year lifetime, you can use the following AVERAGEIFS function to average the values (Equipment[Value]) of active equipment (Equipment[Status],"A") having two years of life (Equipment[Life],"2"):

```
=AVERAGEIFS(Equipment[Value],Equipment[Status],"A",
Equipment[Life],"2")
```

One of the first items you need for the Years' Service Summary report is a count of equipment with a two-year lifetime. You will use the COUNTIFS function to compute statistical information for the active equipment in both locations.

To calculate the total amount of active equipment with lifetimes of two, five, and greater than five years:

1. Select cell **C16**, and then click the **Insert Function** button 𝑓ₓ next to the formula bar. The Insert Function dialog box opens.

2. Click the **Or select a category** arrow, and then click **Statistical**.

3. In the Select a function box, click **COUNTIFS**, and then click the **OK** button. The Function Arguments dialog box opens.

TIP

You could also use the worksheet reference 'Equipment Inventory'!G7:G79 to reference all of the equipment.

4. In the Criteria_range1 box, enter **Equipment[Status]** and then press the **Tab** key. This criterion selects all of the equipment in the Equipment table that is in active use.

5. In the Criteria1 box, type **"A"** to specify active equipment, and then press the **Tab** key. The first condition is complete, and 60 appears as the total count in the middle of the Function Arguments dialog box.

6. In the Criteria_range2 box, enter **Equipment[Life]** and then press the **Tab** key. This criterion selects equipment that will have a lifetime of two years.

7. In the Criteria2 box, type **"2"** to select equipment with a lifetime of two years, and then press the **Tab** key. The second condition is complete, and 17 appears as the total count. See Figure B-13.

Figure B-13   **COUNTIFS Function Arguments box**

value updates as each criterion is entered

8. Click the **OK** button. The formula =COUNTIFS(Equipment[Status],"A", Equipment[Life],"2") appears in the formula bar, and the value 17 appears in cell C16. See Figure B-14.

| Figure B-14 | Summary of the equipment with a two-year lifetime |

COUNTIFS function calculates the number of items that have a life of two years

9. Copy the formula from cell **C16** to the range **C17:C18**.

10. In cell **C17**, change the second criteria argument from "2" to **"5"**. The criteria specify a lifetime of five years. The formula =COUNTIFS(Equipment[Status], "A",Equipment[Life],"5") appears in the formula bar, and 40 appears in cell C17.

11. In cell **C18**, change the second criteria argument from 2 to **">5"**. The criteria specify a lifetime of greater than five years. The formula =COUNTIFS(Equipment[Status],"A",Equipment[Life],">5") appears in the formula bar, and 3 appears in cell C18.

Next, you will calculate the total value of the active equipment based on the life of the equipment. To do this, you will use the SUMIFS function.

To calculate the total value of active equipment based on the life of the equipment:

1. Select cell **D16**, and then click the **Insert Function** button f_x next to the formula bar. The Insert Function dialog box opens.

2. Click the **Or select a category** arrow, and then click **Math & Trig**.

3. In the Select a function box, click **SUMIFS**, and then click the **OK** button. The Function Arguments dialog box opens.

4. In the Sum_range box, type **Equipment[Value]** to enter the range of data to sum, and then press the **Tab** key.

5. In the Criteria_range1 box, enter **Equipment[Status]** and then press the **Tab** key.

6. In the Criteria1 box, type **"A"** to specify active equipment, and then press the **Tab** key. The first condition is complete. See Figure B-15.

| Figure B-15 | **SUMIFS Function Arguments dialog box** |

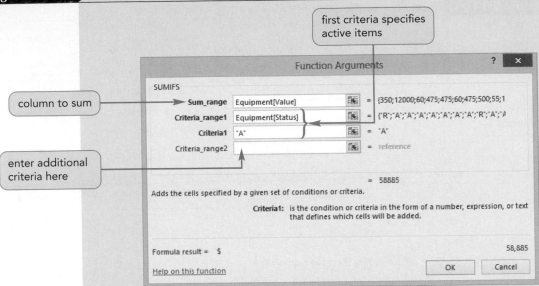

7. In the Criteria_range2 box, enter **Equipment[Life]** for the range referencing the life of the equipment, and then press the **Tab** key.

8. In the Criteria2 box, type **"2"** to specify the lifetime of the equipment, and then press the **Tab** key.

9. Click the **OK** button. The formula =SUMIFS(Equipment[Value], Equipment[Status],"A",Equipment[Life],"2") appears in the formula bar, and $1,325 appears in cell D16.

10. Copy the formula from cell **D16** to the range **D17:D18**.

11. In cell **D17**, change the second criteria argument from "2" to **"5"**. The formula =SUMIFS(Equipment[Value],Equipment[Status],"A", Equipment[Life],"5") appears in the formula bar, and $25,560 appears in cell D17.

12. In cell **D18**, change the second criteria argument to **">5"**. The formula =SUMIFS(Equipment[Value],Equipment[Status],"A",Equipment[Life],">5") appears in the formula bar, and $32,000 appears in cell D18.

Next, you will calculate the average value of active equipment based on the life of the equipment. You will use the AVERAGEIFS function to do this.

To calculate the average value of active equipment based on the life of the equipment:

1. Select cell **E16**, and then click the **Insert Function** button f_x next to the formula bar. The Insert Function dialog box opens.

2. Click the **Or select a category** arrow, and then click **Statistical**.

3. In the Select a function box, click **AVERAGEIFS**, and then click the **OK** button. The Function Arguments dialog box opens.

4. In the Average_range box, type **Equipment[Value]** to enter the range to be averaged, and then press the **Tab** key.

5. In the Criteria_range1 box, enter **Equipment[Status]** and then press the **Tab** key.

6. In the Criteria1 box, type **"A"** to specify active equipment, and then press the **Tab** key. The first condition is complete.

7. In the Criteria_range2 box, enter **Equipment[Life]** for the range referencing the life of the equipment, and then press the **Tab** key.

8. In the Criteria2 box, type **"2"** to specify a lifetime of two years for the equipment, and then press the **Tab** key.

9. Click the **OK** button. The formula =AVERAGEIFS(Equipment[Value], Equipment[Status],"A",Equipment[Life],"2") appears in the formula bar, and $78 appears in cell E16.

10. Copy the formula from cell E16 to the range **E17:E18**.

11. In cell **E17**, change the second criteria argument from "2" to **"5"**. The formula =AVERAGEIFS(Equipment[Value],Equipment[Status],"A", Equipment[Life],"5") appears in the formula bar, and $639 appears in cell E17.

12. In cell **E18**, change the second criteria argument to **">5"**. The formula =AVERAGEIFS(Equipment[Value],Equipment[Status],"A", Equipment[Life],">5" appears in the formula bar, and $10,667 appears in cell E18.

13. Select cell **E18**. See Figure B-16.

Figure B-16   Equipment Life Summary report

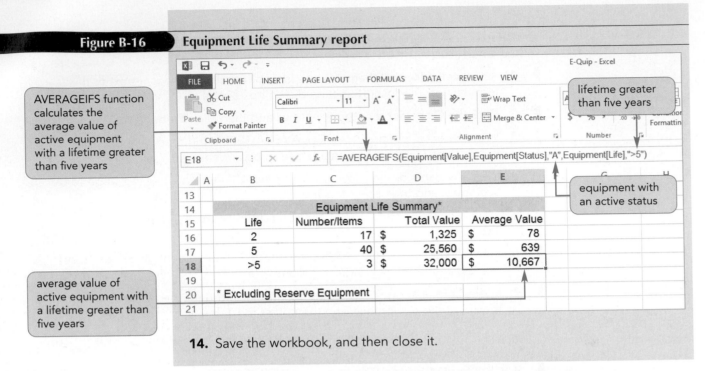

AVERAGEIFS function calculates the average value of active equipment with a lifetime greater than five years

lifetime greater than five years

=AVERAGEIFS(Equipment[Value],Equipment[Status],"A",Equipment[Life],">5")

equipment with an active status

	Life	Number/Items	Total Value	Average Value
		Equipment Life Summary*		
	2	17	$ 1,325	$ 78
	5	40	$ 25,560	$ 639
	>5	3	$ 32,000	$ 10,667
	* Excluding Reserve Equipment			

average value of active equipment with a lifetime greater than five years

14. Save the workbook, and then close it.

The Inventory Summary worksheet is complete. In this appendix, you used advanced filtering techniques to evaluate the equipment inventory. You also used the DAVERAGE and AVERAGEIFS functions to calculate the average value of inventory broken down by location and status.

Review Assignments

PRACTICE

Data File needed for the Review Assignments: Tools Review.xlsx

Patricia wants you to perform advanced filtering tasks that focus on items with service contracts in the Hoffman location. Complete the following:

1. Open the **Tools Review** workbook located in the ExcelB ► Review folder included in your Data Files, and then save the workbook as **Tools Update** in the location specified by your instructor.

2. In the Documentation worksheet, enter your name and the date.

3. Place the criteria range in rows 1 to 4 of the Equipment Inventory worksheet. Enter the And criteria to select items at the Hoffman location with a service contract (Y in column H). Then, enter the Or criteria to select items with a value of >1000. Filter the data. (*Hint*: Watch the criteria range to make sure that the proper range is selected.)

4. Use the DAVERAGE function on the Inventory Summary worksheet to calculate the average value of equipment with and without service agreements at the Tundra and Hoffman locations:
   a. Enter criteria in the criteria ranges G5:H6, G9:H10, J5:K6, and J9:K10.
   b. Enter the DAVERAGE formulas in the range C5:D6 using the criteria you entered in the criteria ranges.

5. Complete the Equipment Summary for each type of item (Description). The summary should only include active items. Complete the summary using the following:
   a. Use COUNTIFS for the range C16:C18.
   b. Use SUMIFS for the range D16:D18.
   c. Use AVERAGEIFS for the range E16:E18.

6. Save the workbook, and then close it.

Case Problem 1

APPLY

Data File needed for this Case Problem: Donations.xlsx

Personal Donations   Bradley Cassidy wants to analyze the donations and monetary gifts he has made over the past few years. Complete the following:

1. Open the **Donations** workbook located in the ExcelB ► Case1 folder included with your Data Files, and then save the workbook as **Bradley Gifts** in the location specified by your instructor.

2. In the Documentation worksheet, enter your name and the date.

3. Make a copy of the Gifts worksheet and rename the copied sheet as **Q4**. Format the data on each sheet as a table; name the table on the Gifts worksheet **Gifts** and name the table on the Q4 sheet **Gifts4**.

4. In the Q4 worksheet, use advanced filtering to display donations in 2016 that were greater than $25. Sort the filtered data in the Amount column from highest to lowest, and format the Amount column appropriately.

5. In the Summary worksheet, complete the following gift analysis:
   a. Total tax deductions and non-tax deductions by year
   b. Total count by gift type by year

6. Save the workbook, and then close it.

Case Problem 2

Data File needed for this Case Problem: House.xlsx

Tea House   Linda Hill is analyzing sales orders from salespeople in several European countries. Complete the following:

1. Open the **House** workbook located in the ExcelB ▸ Case2 folder included with your Data Files, and then save the workbook as **Tea House** in the location specified by your instructor.

2. In the Documentation worksheet, enter your name and the date.

3. Make a copy of the Orders worksheet, and then rename the copied worksheet as **March**. In the March worksheet, use advanced filtering to display all sales in Sweden and all sales for Janet Leverling.

4. Make a copy of the Orders worksheet, and then rename the copied worksheet as **Sept**. In the Sept worksheet, use advanced filtering to display all records for Laura Callahan with sales greater than $1,500 in September.

5. In the Summary worksheet, complete the summary analysis for France. Use the DAVERAGE and DSUM functions to enter formulas in row 11 to average and sum the orders in March for France. Format the range B11:C11 with the Accounting format and no decimal places. Set up an appropriate criteria range in rows 1 and 2.

6. In the Summary worksheet, complete the summary analysis for the United Kingdom (UK). Use the AVERAGEIFS and SUMIFS functions to enter formulas in row 12 to average and sum the orders in March in the U.K. Format the range B12:C12 with the Accounting format and no decimal places.

7. Save the workbook, and then close it.

GLOSSARY/INDEX

TASK REFERENCE

TASK	PAGE #	RECOMMENDED METHOD
3-D reference, use	EX 343	*See* Reference box: Entering a Function That Contains a 3-D Reference
Absolute reference, create	EX 154	Type a $ before both the row and column references
Action, undo or redo	EX 19	Click ↶ or ↷ on the Quick Access Toolbar
Advanced filter, clear	EX B8	On the DATA tab, in the Sort & Filter group, click the Clear button
Advanced filter, create	EX B5	On the DATA tab, in the Sort & Filter group, click the Advanced button, set filter options, data, and criteria ranges, click OK
AutoSum feature, enter function with	EX 37	Click a cell, click ∑ AutoSum ⏷ in the Editing group on the HOME tab, click a function, verify the range, press Enter
Border, add to cells	EX 50	Select a range, click ⊞ ⏷ in the Font group on the HOME tab, click a border
Cell, change fill color	EX 76	Click 🪣 ⏷ in the Font group on the HOME tab, click a color
Cell, clear contents of	EX 58	Select a cell, press Delete
Cell, delete	EX 46	Select a cell, range, column, or row; click Delete button in the Cells group on the HOME tab
Cell, edit	EX 19	Double-click a cell, enter changes
Cell, go to	EX 10	Click Find & Select button in the Editing group on the HOME tab, click Go To
Cell contents, align within a cell	EX 87	Click ☰, ☰, or ☰ in the Alignment group on the HOME tab
Cell contents, change indent of	EX 88	Click 🡢☰ or ☰🡠 in the Alignment group on the HOME tab
Cell contents, rotate	EX 91	Click ⤢ ⏷ in the Alignment group on the HOME tab, click angle
Cell or range, select by their defined name	EX 396	Click the Name box arrow, click a defined name
Cells, lock or unlock	EX 420	Select a cell or range, on the HOME tab, in the Cells group, click the Format button, click Format Cells (or press Ctrl+1), click then Protection tab, check or uncheck the Locked check box, click OK
Cells, merge and center	EX 90	Select adjacent cells, click ▦ in the Alignment group on the HOME tab
Cells, reference in other worksheets	EX 339	Enter a reference in the format =*SheetName!CellRange*
Chart, choose style	EX 204	Select the chart, click ✐, select a chart style
Chart, create	EX 197	*See* Reference box: Creating a Chart
Chart, resize	EX 202	Select the chart, drag the sizing handle
Chart element, format	EX 205	Double-click the chart element, make changes in the Format pane
Chart type, change	EX 214	Select the chart, click the Change Chart Type button in the Type group on the CHART TOOLS DESIGN tab, click a new chart type
Column, change width	EX 25	Drag the right border of the column heading left or right
Column, select	EX 26	Click the column heading

TASK	PAGE #	RECOMMENDED METHOD
Compressed folder, extract all files and folders from	FM 27	Click the compressed folder, click the Compressed Folder Tools Extract tab, click the Extract all button
Compressed folder, open	FM 27	Double-click the compressed folder
Comment, delete	EX 427	Click a cell with a comment, on the REVIEW tab, in the Comments group, click the Delete button
Comment, edit	EX 426	Click a cell with a comment, on the REVIEW tab, in the Comments group, click the Edit Comment button, edit comment text as needed
Comment, insert	EX 425	See Reference box: Inserting a Comment
Comment, show or hide	EX 426	Click a cell with a comment, the Show/Hide Comment button
Conditional format, apply	EX 108	See Reference box: Highlighting a Cell with a Conditional Format
Conditional formatting rule, edit	EX 508	See Reference box: Editing a Conditional Formatting Rule
Custom format, create	EX A15	Select a range, on the Home tab, in the Number group, click the Dialog Box Launcher, click Number tab, click Custom in the Category box, enter the format codes in the Type box, click OK
Data, split from one column into separate columns	EX A9	Select the range, on the DATA tab, in the Data Tools group, click the Text to Columns button, complete the wizard
Data bars, create	EX 242	See Reference Box: Creating Data Bars
Date, enter into a cell	EX 23	Click a cell, type the date, press Enter or Tab
Date, insert the current	EX 167	Enter TODAY() or NOW() function in cell
Defined name, create	EX 395	See Reference box: Creating a Defined Name for a Cell or Range
Defined name, edit or delete	EX 398	On the FORMULAS tab, in the Defined Names group, click the Name Manager button (or press Ctrl+F3), select a name, click Edit and modify or click Delete, click OK, click Close
Defined names, add to existing formulas	EX 405	See Reference Window: Adding Defined Names to Existing Formulas
Defined names, paste list in worksheet	EX 399	Click the upper-left cell of the range for the list, on the FORMULAS tab, in the Defined Names group, click the Use in Formula button (or press F3), click Paste Names, click the Paste List button
Developer tab, display or hide on the ribbon	EX 430	Click the FILE tab, click Options in the navigation pane, click Customize Ribbon, check or uncheck Developer check box, click OK
Documents library, open	FM 10	In File Explorer, click ▷ next to Libraries, click ▷ next to Documents
Duplicate values, highlight	EX 506	See Reference box: Highlighting Duplicate Values
Error alert message, create	EX 410	See Reference box: Validating Data
Excel, start	EX 4	Click the Excel 2013 title on the Start screen
Excel table, add a record	EX 268	Click the row below the Excel table, type values for the new record, pressing Tab to move from field to field
Excel table, apply a style	EX 267	On the TABLE TOOLS DESIGN tab, in the Table Styles group, click the More button, click a table style
Excel table, create	EX 264	On the INSERT tab, in the Tables group, click the Table button, verify the range of data, click OK
Excel table, delete a record	EX 270	Select a record, on the HOME tab, in the Cells group, click the Delete button arrow, click Delete Table Rows
Excel table, filter using a slicer	EX 286	Click a slicer button on the slicer

TASK	PAGE #	RECOMMENDED METHOD
Excel table, find and replace a record	FX 269	Click in the Excel table, on the HOME tab, in the Editing group, click the Find & Select button, use the Find and Replace dialog box
Excel table, modify	EX 267	On TABLE TOOLS DESIGN tab, in the Table Style Options group, check or uncheck options
Excel table, remove duplicate records	EX 270	Click in the Excel table, on the TABLE TOOLS DESIGN tab, in the Tools group, click Remove Duplicates button, use Remove Duplicates dialog box to select columns to find duplicate records, click OK
Excel table, rename	EX 266	Click in the Excel table, on the TABLE TOOLS DESIGN tab, in the Properties group, select the name in the Table Name box, type a name, press Enter
File, copy	FM 24	Right-click the file, click Copy, right-click destination, click Paste
File, delete	FM 25	Right-click the file, click Delete
File, move	FM 21	Drag the file to the folder
File, open from File Explorer	FM 15	Right-click the file, point to Open with, click an application
File, rename	FM 26	Right-click the file, click Rename, type the new filename, press Enter
File, save with new name in WordPad	FM 18	Click the File tab, click Save as, enter the filename, click Save
File Explorer, open	FM 10	Click [icon] on the taskbar
File Explorer, return to a previous location	FM 22	Click [icon]
File list, sort	FM 14	Click the column heading button
Files, select multiple	FM 24	Press and hold the Ctrl key and click the files
Files, view in Large Icons view	FM 13	Click the View tab, click [icon] in the Layout group
Files and folders, compress	FM 27	Select the files to compress, click the Share tab, click the Zip button in the Send group
Fill handle, use	EX 162	See Reference box: Copying Formulas and Formats with AutoFill
Filter, clear from a column	EX 281	Click the filter button, click Clear Filter From "column"
Filter, clear from an Excel table	EX 285	On the DATA tab, in the Sort & Filter group, click the Clear button
Filter, select multiple items	EX 282	Click the filter button, check two or more items, click OK
Filter, specify complex criteria	EX 283	Click the filter button, point to Number Filters, Text Filters, or Date Filters, specify the filter criteria, click OK
Filter, use multiple columns	EX 280	Filter for one column, repeat to filter for additional columns
Filter, use one column	EX 278	Click a filter button, deselect the (Select All) check box, click the item to filter by, click OK
Filter buttons, display or hide	EX 278	On the DATA tab, in the Sort & Filter group, click the Filter button
Find and replace, text or format	EX 104	Click Find & Select in the Editing group on the HOME tab, click Replace
Flash Fill, apply	EX 49	Type a few entries in a column to establish a pattern, Flash Fill adds the remaining entries
Folder, create	FM 19	Click the New folder button in the New group on the Home tab
Font, change color	EX 73	Click [A] in the Font group on the HOME tab, click a color
Font, change size	EX 71	Click the Font Size arrow in the Font group on the HOME tab, click a point size
Font, change style	EX 71	Click [B], [I], or [U] in the Font group on the HOME tab

TASK	PAGE #	RECOMMENDED METHOD
Font, change typeface	EX 71	Click the Font arrow in the Font group on the HOME tab, click a font
Formula, enter	EX 32	Click the cell, type = and then a formula, press Enter or Tab
Formula, reference another worksheet	EX 339	*See* Reference box: Entering a Formula with References to Another Worksheet
Formula results, copy and paste as values	EX A6	Copy the range with formula results, click the first cell in the paste location, on the HOME tab, in the Clipboard group, click the Paste button arrow, click the Values button
Formula with an external reference, create	EX 356	Click a cell in the destination file, type =, click a cell in the source file, complete the formula as usual
Formulas, display in a worksheet	EX 56	Press Ctrl+`
Function, insert	EX 145	Click a function category in the Function Library group on the FORMULAS tab, click a function, enter arguments, click OK
Goal seek, perform	EX 180	*See* Reference box: Performing What-if Analysis and Goal Seek
Hyperlink, create	EX 370	*See* Reference box: Inserting a Hyperlink
Hyperlink, edit	EX 372	Right-click the cell with the hyperlink, click Edit Hyperlink, make edits in the Edit Hyperlink dialog box, click OK
Input message, create	EX 410	*See* Reference box: Validating Data
Invalid data, circle	EX 419	On the DATA tab, in the Data Tools group, click the Data Validation button arrow, click Circle Invalid Data
Linked workbooks, update	EX 361	Click in the source file, edit as usual
Links, manage	EX 365	On the DATA tab, in the Connections group, click the Edit Links button, select an option, click OK
Macro, edit	EX 441	*See* Reference box: Editing a Macro
Macro, record	EX 435	*See* Reference box: Recording a Macro
Macro, run	EX 437	*See* Reference box: Running a Macro
Macro, set security level for	EX 432	*See* Reference box: Setting Macro Security in Excel
Macro, view code	EX 441	*See* Reference box: Editing a Macro
Macro button, create	EX 445	*See* Reference box: Creating a Macro Button
Macro button, move or resize	EX 447	Right-click the macro button, press Esc, drag the button by its selection box to new location or drag a sizing handle
Margins, set	EX 121	Click the Margins button in the Page Setup group on the PAGE LAYOUT tab, select a margin size
Mixed reference, create	EX 154	Type $ before either the row or column reference
My Documents folder, open	FM 10	In File Explorer, click ▷ next to Libraries, click ▷ next to Documents, click My Documents
Number, enter as text	EX 21	Type ' and then type the number
Number format, apply	EX 82	Click $, %, ', or the Number Format arrow in the Number group on the HOME tab
Page break, insert or remove	EX 116	*See* Reference box: Inserting and Removing Page Breaks
PivotChart, create	EX 316	On the PIVOTTABLE TOOLS ANALYZE tab, in the Tools group, click the PivotChart button, select a chart, click OK
PivotTable, create	EX 301	*See* Reference box: Creating a PivotTable
PivotTable, create recommended	EX 314	Click in an Excel table, on the INSERT tab, in the Tables group, click the Recommended PivotTables button, select a PivotTable, click OK

TASK	PAGE #	RECOMMENDED METHOD
PivotTable, filter using slicer	EX 311	Click a slicer button
PivotTable, rearrange	EX 306	In the PivotTable Fields pane, drag field buttons between the ROWS, COLUMNS and FILTERS areas
PivotTable, refresh	EX 312	On the PIVOTTABLE TOOLS ANALYZE tab, in the Data group, click the Refresh button
PivotTable field, filter	EX 309	Click a filter arrow, click a filter item, click OK
PivotTable Fields pane, show or hide	EX 311	Click in the PivotTable, on the PIVOTTABLE TOOLS ANALYZE tab, in the Show group, click the Field List button
PivotTable report, filter	EX 308	Drag a field button from PivotTable Fields pane to FILTERS area or drag a field button from ROWS or COLUMNS area to FILTERS area
PivotTable Row and Column field items, filter	EX 309	In the PivotTable, click the Column Labels or Row Labels filter button, check or uncheck items, click OK
PivotTable style, apply	EX 307	On the PIVOTTABLE TOOLS DESIGN tab, in the PivotTable Styles group, click the More button, click a style
PivotTable value fields, format	EX 307	In the VALUES area of the PivotTable Fields pane, click the button, click the Value Field Settings button, click the Number Format button, select a format, click OK
Print area, set	EX 115	Select range, click the Print Area button in the Page Setup group on PAGE LAYOUT tab, click Set Print Area
Print titles, add	EX 117	Click the Print Titles button in the Page Setup group on the PAGE LAYOUT tab, click Rows to repeat at top, select a range, click OK
Range, select adjacent	EX 11	Click a cell, drag the pointer from the selected cell to the cell in the lower-right corner of the range
Range, select nonadjacent	EX 12	Select a cell or an adjacent range, press the Ctrl key as you select additional cells or adjacent ranges
Relative reference, create	EX 150	Type the cell reference as it appears in the worksheet
Ribbon, expand in File Explorer	FM 13	Click ⌄
Row, change height	EX 29	Drag the bottom border of the row heading up or down
Row, select	EX 44	Click the row heading
Row(s) and column(s), freeze	EX 263	Click the cell below and to the right of row(s) and column(s) to freeze, on the VIEW tab, in the Window group, click the Freeze Panes button, click an option
Row(s) and column(s), unfreeze	EX 263	On the VIEW tab, in the Window group, click the Freeze Panes button, click Unfreeze Panes
Rows, repeat in printout	EX 118	Click the Print Titles button in the Page Setup group on the PAGE LAYOUT tab, click Rows to repeat at top, select range, click OK
Series, create with AutoFill	EX 164	Enter the first few entries in a series, drag the fill handle over the adjacent range
Slicer, create for a PivotTable	EX 310	On the PIVOTTABLE TOOLS ANALYZE tab, in the Filter group, click the Click Insert Slicer button, click a field check box, click OK
Slicer, create for an Excel table	EX 285	On the TABLE TOOLS DESIGN tab, in the Tools group, click the Insert Slicer button, select one or more field check boxes, click OK
Slicer, format	EX 285	On the SLICER TOOLS OPTONS tab, set the slicer's size and style
Sort, multiple columns	EX 272	See Reference box: Sorting Data Using Multiple Sort Fields
Sort, one column	EX 271	Click in the column to sort, on the DATA tab, in the Sort & Filter group, click ↓ or ↓

TASK	PAGE #	RECOMMENDED METHOD
Sort, with a custom list	EX 274	*See* Reference box: Sorting Using a Custom List
Sparklines, create	EX 239	*See* Reference box: Creating and Editing Sparklines
Special format, apply to data	EX A13	Select a range, on the HOME tab, in the Number group, click the Dialog Box Launcher, click Number tab, click Special in the Category box, click a format, click OK
Structured reference, create for Excel table	EX 477	Use the format *Tablename[qualifier]*
Subtotal Outline view, use	EX 295	Click an outline button to show or hide the selected outline level
Subtotals, insert	EX 293	*See* Reference box: Calculating Subtotals for a Range of Data
Subtotals, remove	EX 296	On the DATA tab, in the Outline group, click the Subtotal button, click the Remove All button
Template, create a custom	EX 377	*See* Reference box: Creating a Custom Template
Total row, add or remove from an Excel table	EX 288	On the TABLE TOOLS DESIGN tab, in the Table Style Options group, click the Total Row check box
Total row, select a summary statistics	EX 288	In the Total row cell, click the arrow button, click a summary function
Text, enter into a cell	EX 18	Click cell, type entry, press Enter or Tab
Text, enter multiple lines in a cell	EX 28	Type the first line of the entry, press Alt+Enter, type the next line
Text, wrap within a cell	EX 28	Select the cell, click 📑 in the Alignment group on the HOME tab
Theme, change for workbook	EX 107	Click the Themes button in the Themes group on the PAGE LAYOUT tab, click a theme
Validation circle, clear from a cell	EX 419	Enter valid data in the circled cell
Validation circles, clear all	EX 419	On the DATA tab, in the Data Tools group, click the Data Validation button arrow, click Clear Validation Circles
Validation rule, create	EX 410	*See* Reference box: Validating Data
VBA code, view	EX 441	*See* Reference box: Editing a Macro
View, change in File Explorer	FM 12	*See* Reference box: Changing the View in File Explorer
Visual Basic Editor, open or close	EX 441	*See* Reference box: Editing a Macro
Workbook, close	EX 13	Click the FILE tab, click Close
Workbook, create a new	EX 15	Click the FILE tab, click New
Workbook, create from an existing template	EX 374	*See* Reference box: Creating a Workbook Based on a Template
Workbook, open an existing	EX 4	Click Open Other Workbooks link on the Recent screen (or click the FILE tab, click Open), select the workbook file
Workbook, preview and print	EX 55	Click the FILE tab, click Print
Workbook, protect	EX 424	*See* Reference box: Protecting a Workbook
Workbook, save	EX 17	Click 💾 on the Quick Access Toolbar
Workbook, save earlier Excel file format in current format	EX A2	Click the FILE tab, click the Save As in the navigation bar, click Browse button, type filename, click the Save as type button, click Excel Workbook, click Save
Workbook, save in the Excel 2003 file format	EX A17	Click the FILE tab, click the Save As command, click the Browse button, click the Save as type button, click Excel 97-2003 Workbook, click Save, click Continue
Workbook, save with macros	EX 450	On the Quick Access Toolbar, click the Save button, click No, select the save location, enter the filename, click the Save as type button, click Excel Macro-Enabled Workbook, click Save

TASK	PAGE #	RECOMMENDED METHOD
Workbooks, arrange	EX 354	*See* Reference box: Arranging Workbooks
Workbooks, link	EX 352	Enter a formula in the format =[*WorkbookName*]*WorksheetName*!*CellRange*
Workbooks, switch between	EX 354	On the VIEW tab, in the Window group, click the Switch Windows button, click the workbook to make active
Worksheet, change orientation	EX 53	Click the Orientation button in the Page Setup group on the PAGE LAYOUT tab, click Landscape or Portrait
Worksheet, change view	EX 52	Click ▦, ▤, or ⬛ on the status bar
Worksheet, copy	EX 16	Hold down Ctrl and drag a sheet tab to a new location
Worksheet, delete	EX 17	Right-click a sheet tab, click Delete
Worksheet, insert	EX 16	Click ⊕
Worksheet, move	EX 16	Drag the sheet tab to a new location
Worksheet, protect	EX 422	*See* Reference box: Protecting a Worksheet
Worksheet, rename	EX 16	Double-click the sheet tab, type a new name, press Enter
Worksheet, scale for printing	EX 54	Set the width and height in the Scale to Fit group on the PAGE LAYOUT tab
Worksheet, unprotect	EX 425	Go to the worksheet, on the REVIEW tab, in the Changes group, click the Unprotect Sheet button
Worksheet group, print	EX 347	Create a worksheet group, apply page layout settings, print as usual
Worksheet window, split into panes or remove split	EX 290	On the VIEW tab, in the Window group, click the Split button
Worksheets, copy to another workbook	EX 337	*See* Reference box: Copying Worksheets
Worksheets, group or ungroup	EX 331	*See* Reference box: Grouping and Ungrouping Worksheets
Worksheets, move between	EX 8	Click a sheet tab or click a tab scrolling button and then click a sheet tab